Race Critical Theories

Race Critical Theories

Text and Context

Edited by

Philomena Essed
and
David Theo Goldberg

BLACKWELL PUBLISHING
350 Main Street, Malden, MA 02148-5020, USA
9600 Garsington Road, Oxford OX4 2DQ, UK
550 Swanston Street, Carlton, Victoria 3053, Australia

First published 2002

4   2007

Library of Congress Cataloging-in-Publication Data

Race critical theories: text and context / edited by Philomena Essed and
    David Theo Goldberg.
        p. cm.
    Includes bibliographical references and index.
    ISBN 0-631-21437-2 (alk. paper) – ISBN 0-631-21438-0 (pbk: alk.
paper) 1. Race. 2. Racism. I. Essed, Philomena, 1955-
II. Goldberg, David Theo.
HT1521.R235227 2001
305.8 – dc21

                                        2001018135

ISBN-13: 978-0-631-21437-3 (alk. paper) – ISBN-13: 978-0-631-21438-0 (pbk: alk. paper)

A catalogue record for this title is available from the British Library.

Set in 10/12 on 13pt Photina
by Best-set Typesetter Ltd, Hong Kong
Printed and bound in India by
Replika Press Pvt. Ltd

The publisher's policy is to use permanent paper from mills that operate a sustainable
forestry policy, and which has been manufactured from pulp processed using acid-free
and elementary chlorine-free practices. Furthermore, the publisher ensures that the text
paper and cover board used have met acceptable environmental accreditation standards.

For further information on
Blackwell Publishing, visit our website:
www.blackwellpublishing.com

Contents

Contributors

Etienne Balibar is Professeur de philosophie politique et morale, Université de Paris X Nanterre, France, and Professor of Critical Theory at the University of California, Irvine.

Martin Barker is Reader in Media Studies, Sussex University.

Vikki Bell is Senior Lecturer in the Sociology department at Goldsmiths College, University of London.

Homi Bhabha is Chester D. Tripp Distinguished Service Professor in the Humanities, Department of English, University of Chicago.

Patricia Hill Collins is Charles Phelps Taft Professor of Sociology in the Department of African-American Studies at the University of Cincinnati.

Angela Y. Davis is University Professor, History of Consciousness at the University of California, Santa Cruz.

Teun A. van Dijk is Professor of Discourse Studies at the University of Amsterdam, and Visiting Professor at the Universitat Pompeu Fabra, Barcelona.

Philomena Essed is Senior Researcher at the Amsterdam Research Institute for Global Issues and Development Studies, University of Amsterdam, and Visiting Professor at the University of California, Irvine.

Johanna Fernandez is a graduate student in History at Columbia University.

Kim Benita Furumoto is a student in the College of Law and the Ph.D. program in the School of Justice Studies at Arizona State University.

Paul Gilroy is Professor of Sociology and African-American Studies at Yale University.

David Theo Goldberg is Director, University of California Humanities Research Institute, and Professor of African-American Studies and Criminology, Law, and Society, University of California, Irvine.

Ranajit Guha has been a Visiting Fellow with the Department of Anthropology, Research School of Pacific and Asian Studies, The Australian National University.

Stuart Hall is Emeritus Professor of Sociology, Goldsmiths College, University of London.

Sue Kim is a graduate student in English at Cornell University.

Kelli M. Kobor received her Ph.D. in History from Duke University. She teaches currently at George Mason University in Fairfax, VA.

Saree Makdisi is Associate Professor of English and Comparative Literature at the University of Chicago.

Manning Marable is Professor of History and Director of the Institute for Research in African-American Studies at Columbia University.

Maria R. Markus is Senior Lecturer in Sociology at the University of New South Wales, Sydney, Australia.

Howard McGary is Professor of Philosophy at Rutgers, The State University of New Jersey.

Chandra Talpade Mohanty is Professor of Women's Studies at Hamilton College, and Core Faculty at the Union Institute Graduate School, Cincinnati.

Toni Morrison is Robert F. Goheen Professor in the Humanities at Princeton University.

Michael Omi is a Professor of Ethnic Studies at the University of California, Berkeley.

David Roediger is Professor of History at the University of Minnesota.

Maria P. P. Root, Vice-President Washington State Psychological Association, is a psychologist and independent scholar.

Edward Said is University Professor of English and Comparative Literature at Columbia University.

Suzette Spencer is a graduate student in the African Diaspora Studies Program at the University of California, Berkeley.

Ann Laura Stoler is Professor of Anthropology and History at the University of Michigan-Ann Arbor.

Cornel West is Professor of Afro-American Studies and Philosophy of Religion at Harvard University.

Howard Winant is Professor of Sociology at Temple University.

Ruth Wodak is Professor of Applied Linguistics, University of Vienna, and Director of the Research Center for "Discourse, Politics and Identity" at the Austrian Academy of Sciences.

Preface

The idea for this book grew out of a series of rich discussions with Andrew McNeillie, editor extraordinaire, in restaurants and pubs, between riffs of Ahmad Jamal and Eric Dolphy, in Oxford and Tempe, San Francisco and London. The shape of the book inevitably transformed in our conversations about the state and styles of race critical scholarship as we walked through Amsterdam and Berkeley, Cape Town and Jerusalem. Initially the idea had been to collect in a single volume the principal contemporary contributors to race theorizing over the past two decades, to offer in a readily available teaching text the representative work in critical theorizing about race. But along the way we thought of soliciting brief reflections on the writing and reception of the articles and extracts we were looking to anthologize. We thus approached a mix of principal authors and engaged commentators, well-established and younger emergent scholars. We have been inspired by the insightful responses. The book is the result of these multiple collaborations.

Andrew McNeillie and Jayne Fargnoli, our editors at Blackwell, as always, have made this book a delight to complete. Kay Korman, David's office manager in the School of Justice Studies at Arizona State University, once again, cared so much that the manuscript would look as complete at the time of submission as it would upon publication. The colleagues we approached to contribute, often at short notice and under enormous time pressure, responded more graciously than we could have hoped or certainly expected. Friendships were made or deepened in the process, theoretical positions illuminated, political commitments revealed. Barbara Christian provided us with a wonderfully supportive environment in which to work and think about this book during a stay in Berkeley in 1998–9. The book could not have been conceivable in this way without her. We had invited her to contribute, but due to a tragically unforeseen twist of events she was unable to do so. The book was completed as she passed away in June.

We hope the pedagogy of the reflective texts – the critical dimensions of race theorizing, the racial dimensions of critical theory – have enhanced the product.

Tempe and Amsterdam and Irvine

Acknowledgments

We are grateful to the publishers for allowing us to reprint sections of the following original material:

Etienne Balibar, "The Nation Form: History and Ideology." In E. Balibar and I. Wallerstein, *Race, Nation and Class: Ambiguous Identities* (London: Verso, 1991), pp. 87–106; "Reflections on 'The Nation Form: History and Ideology,'" reprinted by permission of the author.

Martin Barker, "The Problems with Racism." In M. Barker, *The New Racism: Conservatives and the Ideology of the Tribe* (London: Junction Books, 1981/1982), pp. 1–11; "Reflections on 'The Problems with Racism,'" reprinted by permission of the author.

Vikki Bell, "Reflections on 'The End of Antiracism' (P. Gilroy)," reprinted by permission of the author.

Homi Bhabha, "Of Mimicry and Man: The Ambivalence of Colonial Discourse." In H. Bhabha, *The Location of Culture* (London and New York: Routledge, 1984/1994), pp. 85–92. Copyright © 1984 and 1994, reprinted by permission of Taylor & Francis, Inc.

Barbara Christian, "The Race for Theory." *Feminist Studies*, 14, 1 (Spring 1988), pp. 67–79; p. 75.

Angela Y. Davis, "Education and Liberation: Black Women's Perspective." In A. Y. Davis, *Women, Race and Class* (New York: Random House, 1981), pp. 99–109. Copyright © 1981 by Angela Davis. Used by permission of Random House, Inc.; "Reflections on 'Education and Liberation: Black Women's Perspective,'" reprinted by permission of the author.

Philomena Essed, "A New Approach to the Study of Racism" and "Macro and Micro Dimensions of Racism." In Philomena Essed, *Understanding Everyday Racism: An Interdisciplinary Theory* (Thousand Oaks, CA: Sage, 1991), pp. 1–53; "Reflections on 'Everyday Racism,'" reprinted by permission of the author.

Johanna Fernandez, "Reflections on 'Affirmative Action and the Politics of Race' (M. Marable)," reprinted by permission of the author.

Kim Benita Furumoto, "Reflections on 'Of Mimicry and Man: The Ambivalence of Colonial Discourse' (H. Bhabha)," reprinted by permission of the author.

Paul Gilroy, "The End of Antiracism." In J. Donald and A. Rattansi (eds.), *"Race," Culture and Difference* (London: Sage, in association with the Open University, 1992), pp. 49–61. Reprinted by permission of Sage Publications Ltd.

David Theo Goldberg, "Modernity, Race, and Morality." In D. T. Goldberg, *Racist Culture: Philosophy and the Politics of Meaning* (Oxford: Blackwell, 1993), pp. 14–40; "Reflections on 'Modernity, Race, and Morality,'" reprinted by permission of the author.

Ranajit Guha, "Preface." In R. Guha, *Dominance Without Hegemony: History and Power in Colonial India* (Cambridge, MA: Harvard University Press, 1987), pp. ix–xv.

Stuart Hall, "Race, Articulation, and Societies Structured in Dominance." In UNESCO (ed.), *Sociological Theories: Race and Colonialism* (Paris: UNESCO, 1980), pp. 305–45; "Reflections on 'Race, Articulation, and Societies Structured in Dominance,'" reprinted by permission of the author.

Patricia Hill Collins, "Defining Black Feminist Thought." In P. H. Collins, *Black Feminist Thought: Knowledge, Consciousness, and the Politics of Empowerment* (Boston: Unwin Hyman, 1990), pp. 19–40; "Reflections on 'Defining Black Feminist Thought,'" reprinted by permission of the author.

Sue Kim, "Reflections on 'Cartographies of Struggle: Third World Women and the Politics of Feminism' (C. T. Mohanty)," reprinted by permission of the author.

Kelli M. Kobor, "Reflections on the 'Preface' to *Dominance Without Hegemony* (R. Guha)," reprinted by permission of the author.

Howard McGary, "Reflections on 'A Genealogy of Modern Racism' (C. West)," reprinted by permission of the author.

Saree Makdisi, "Reflections on 'Imaginative Geography and Its Representations: *Orientalizing the Oriental*' (E. Said)," reprinted by permission of the author.

Manning Marable, "Affirmative Action and the Politics of Race." In M. Marable, *Beyond Black and White: Transforming African American Politics* (London: Verso, 1995), pp. 81–90.

Maria R. Markus, "Cultural Pluralism and the Subversion of the 'Taken-for-Granted' World." In R. Bauböck and J. Rundell (eds.), *Blurred Boundaries: Migration, Ethnicity, Citizenship* (Aldershot: Ashgate, 1998), pp. 245–58; "Reflections on 'Cultural Pluralism and the Subversion of the "Taken-for-Granted" World,'" reprinted by permission of the author.

Chandra T. Mohanty, "Cartographies of Struggle: Third World Women and the Politics of Feminism." In C. T. Mohanty, A. Russo, and L. Torres (eds.), *Third World Women and the Politics of Feminism* (Bloomington: Indiana Univerrsity Press, 1991), pp. 1–47.

Toni Morrison, "Black Matters." In T. Morrison, *Playing in the Dark: Whiteness and the Literary Imagination* (Cambridge, MA: Harvard University Press, 1992), pp. 3–27.

Michael Omi and Howard Winant, "Racial Formation." In M. Omi and H. Winant, *Racial Formation in the United States: From the Sixties to the Nineties* (New York: Routledge and Kegan Paul, 1986/1999), pp. 53–76. Copyright © 1986 and 1999, reprinted by permission of Taylor & Francis, Inc.; "Reflections on 'Racial Formation,'" reprinted by permission of the authors.

David Roediger, "Whiteness and Ethnicity in the History of 'White Ethnics' in the United States." In D. roediger, *Towards the Abolition of Whiteness: Essays on Race, Politics, and Working Class History* (London: Verso, 1994), pp. 181–98; "Reflections on 'Whiteness and Ethnicity in the History of "White Ethnics" in the United States,'" reprinted by permission of the author.

Maria P. P. Root, "A Bill of Rights for Racially Mixed People." In M. P. P. Root (ed.), *The Multicultural Experience: Racial Borders as the New Frontier* (Thousand Oaks, CA: Sage, 1996), pp. 3–14; "Reflections on 'A Bill of Rights for Racially Mixed People,'" reprinted by permission of the author.

Edward Said, "Imaginative Geography and Its Representations: *Orientalizing the Oriental.*" In E. Said, *Orientalism* (New York: Vintage, 1978), pp. 49–73. Used by permission of Random House, Inc.

Suzette Spencer, "Reflections on 'Black Matters' (T. Morrison)," reprinted by permission of the author.

Ann Laura Stoler, "Racial Histories and Their Regimes of Truth." In D. Davies (ed.), *Political Power and Social Theory* (Westport, CT: Jai Press, 1997), pp. 183–206; "Reflections on 'Racial Histories and Their Regimes of Truth,'" reprinted by permission of the author.

Teun A. van Dijk, "Denying Racism: Elite Discourse and Racism." In J. Wrench and J. Solomos (eds.), *Race and Migration in Western Europe* (Oxford: Berg, 1993), pp. 179–93; "Reflections on 'Denying Racism: Elite Discourse and Racism,'" reprinted by permission of the author.

Cornel West, "A Genealogy of Modern Racism." Adapted from C. West, *Prophesy Deliverance! Towards an Afro-American Revolutionary*

Christianity (Philadelphia: Westminster Press, 1982), pp. 47–65. Copyright © 1982 by Cornel West. Used by permission of Westminster John Knox Press.

Ruth Wodak, "Turning the Tables: Antisemitic Discourse in Post-war Austria." *Discourse and Society*, 2, 1 (1991), pp. 65–83. Reprinted by permission of Sage Publications Ltd; "Reflections on 'Turning the Tables: Antisemitic Discourse in Post-war Austria,'" reprinted by permission of the author.

It is this tendency toward the monolithic, monotheistic, and so on, that worries me about the race for theory

Barbara Christian, "The Race for Theory" (1987/8)

Introduction: From Racial Demarcations to Multiple Identifications

David Theo Goldberg and Philomena Essed

There has been an explosion in writing on race and racism since the mid-1970s. Contributions have originated from every corner of the world and spanned a vast variety of intellectual, political, and ideological gamuts.

The dramatically critical work of the 1980s and 1990s has not been matched more recently. Instead we have come to see reproductions of the central lines of thought from that pathbreaking work, as reflected in numerous edited collections. We are trying modestly with this book to look back reflectively as a way forward. *Race Critical Theories* brings together a range of influential theorists of race and racism in the critical tradition over the past twenty years. The volume includes some of the seminal work of these contributors, and more. We accompany these contributions with newly written essays revealing how authors or expert readers excavate the critical past and what we can learn as a consequence.

We have chosen analysts and texts in a broadly transnational frame, seeking out contrasting though complementary works to weave a rich tapestry of the scope and depth of critical theorizing about race and racism. Of course, we are not suggesting that those we have included are the only interesting or significant contributors or that one could not argue for different representative samples of their work.

We are concerned, in the organization of the volume, accordingly to clarify conceptual influences and links, to reveal the play of concepts and the intersection of arguments, to identify contrasting assumptions and frames of analysis and to show their implications. To this end, we have pared down many of the original articles from which we have drawn to their central and most pressing lines of argument. This makes for pedagogical clarity, even as we realize, and regret, that it leads in some cases to loss of nuance and scope. We should point out also that this concern with lines of argumentation had led us to ordering the volume according to a double axis.

Part I of the volume is chronologically driven. It reveals something of the temporal development and influences within the field. Thus we have included a table of contents indicating the history of appearance of the articles, so exhibiting the lines of conceptual influence across time: what came first, what concepts were already in circulation when a later article was written, what sorts of theoretical and conceptual influences prevailed in the field at varying moments in its development. Part II is conceptually driven. We have divided the reflections on the twenty-two primary texts under five headings: "Histories and Values"; "Knowledge and Representation"; "Systems and Experiences"; "Elites and Politics"; and "Dominance and Struggles." We were curious about a range of issues: How does one think back upon texts written five, ten, fifteen, or twenty years ago? What sorts of contemporary assumptions, mediated by the influence of intervening work and conditions, does one bring to understanding how these texts were written, what they were written to address, theoretically and politically, conceptually and practically; what sorts of impact have they had on understanding and on transforming conditions? And where conditions have transformed, perhaps partly in response to the changed understandings and interventions of these works, what new conceptual apparatus has come to be elaborated to address these changed circumstances?

The thematic order of reflections best captures, in our view, the relations between texts and originals. But we can imagine that teachers may find it useful to structure the originals differently in order to fulfill different pedagogical purposes. Taken as a whole, the categories of composition do strike us as offering the prevailing themes engaged in critical analysis of race, racism, and their related categories of domination and exclusion over the past two decades. We have located each essay based on the fact that the principal focus of the article upon which it reflects captures the concepts and categories under which we have placed them.

Alternatively, Part II may be useful in itself as a body of work initiating students to methodologies of developing race critical theories. The reflections are a mix of the autobiography of writing as opposed to autobiographical writing, of the personal and political, of the new and the more established. Some young scholars have reflected on esteemed scholars' work while bringing fresh insights to that work. The gender shift – from a higher representation of men in Part I to a higher proportion of women in Part II – shows also that with the closing of the past century the number of women engaged in race critical theory has increased along with more women entering the universities.

Our intentions are multifold. *First*, we seek to introduce to the uninitiated, and to collect conveniently for the initiated, central lines of critical theorizing about race and racism over the past two decades. The *second* purpose of this volume is to demonstrate that there is no singular national space that does or should dominate thinking about race and racism. Multiple theories have generated from multiple sites. Concepts that are articulated resonate beyond the sites in which they were created. Contributors originate from the Americas and Asia, Europe and Africa, the Middle East and the Caribbean. They look variously for their objects of analysis to the US and Britain, the Netherlands and France, Austria and Australia, South Africa and Palestine, the "Third World" and the "First," the "Orient" and the "Occident," the "West and the Rest." In a sense, they reveal that one can no longer – if one ever could – think about race and racism simply within a local national frame, that the particularities of racial configurations and racist manifestations anywhere are linked to their expression in some more or less direct and complex way everywhere. Thus, while a significant number of the contributors reside in the United States, there is no simple way in which it could be said that the US context does or should dominate our understanding of the processes of racial formation and racist structure and expression. Thinking through the structure of this volume, as thinking seriously about "race," about "racism" and about all their ramifications, has been an interactive process, a dialogue across continents and contexts. These contexts drive home the fact that race is formed and fashioned and racism operates in relation to and through other systems of exclusion, marginalization, abuse, and repression.

Third, there has been a tendency recently in thinking about racial concerns to suggest at least that racism matters less than it once did, or at most that it is largely a thing of the past. The articles collected here, by contrast, show that the manifestations of racism remain complexly articulated, deeply embedded, and subtly intertwined with seemingly neutral or innocent social phenomena. Even contemporary calls for colorblindness, race neutrality, and tolerance towards those different from oneself often cover over hidden, invisible, forms of racist expression and well-established patterns of racist exclusion that remain, unaddressed and uncompensated, structurally marking opportunities and access, patterns of income and wealth, privilege and relative power.

The title of the book, then, is designed to capture the interweaving of these commitments. We are suggesting that we are trying to capture something central to the social and political theory of modernity, something very basic especially about late modern social and political life, in refusing to ignore racial conditions and racist expressions. These cannot be taken for granted or assumed away, because they reference so much else in social life. All variations on and through "race" serve as codes and manifestations of power more generally, and they so often factor more or less quietly or more or less explicitly into a complex of causes for political, economic, and social conditions. So critical theory necessarily requires a focus, among others, on race; and racial theory cannot help but be, in a normative sense, critical. Race, critique, and theory, we want to insist, are constitutive of the possibilities of thinking each other in any satisfactory way. We insist, thus, on taking race critically and theory race-critically. Hence our title *Race Critical Theories*. We do not intend this as a play of words, but as an indication of a specific theoretical disposition.

As a popularized frame of analysis "critical race theory" foremostly has been a theoretical exercise identified strongly with the one discipline of law in the United States of America. It is important to emphasize that its contributions have been crucial in reinvigorating the issues of race in the legal sense. At the same time, critical legal race theory is unfortunately marked by an American parochialism, with being caught up with the more or less restricted considerations of legal structures, conditions, and rationalities in the US context. Scant attention is paid either to the applicability and implications of its key concepts outside of that context, or perhaps more importantly (because more constitutively) to thinking its central concepts through their globalizing significance and circulation. Thus, we are inviting critical race theory (in its American legal formation) to face outwards in its conceptual disposition. Finally, we also would like to see critical race theory more generous in acknowledging its conceptual debt to the wider history of racial theorizing in the critical tradition.

This principal and principled concern with identifying the critical historical tradition of theorizing about race and racism suggests a set of historical texts that serve as the influential background for race critical theorizing. These seminal texts reveal as much as anything else the interface of race and racism with other modes and structures, cultures and representations of social inequalities and exclusions. They signal the major markers in the pre- and post-war conceptual history of race critical thought. They have revealed concepts and issues, frameworks and paradigms from which have flowed much of the more recent work in the race critical tradition. W. E. B. Du Bois's *Souls of Black Folk* first formulated the notion of "double consciousness" within the context of predicting at the outset that the twentieth century would be concerned above all with "the color line." Many have since struggled over spelling out what "double consciousness" might signify in respect of race. The work collected In *Race Critical Theories* reveals a concern central to Du Bois's account though often overlooked. "Double consciousness" is a complex and constant play between the exclusionary conditions of social structure marked by race and the psychological and cultural strategies employed by the racially excluded and marginalized to accommodate themselves to everyday indignities as well as to resist them. At mid-century, Oliver Cromwell Cox expanded this focus on the interplay between racism and other structural systems and conditions of domination, most notably class, in his justifiably classic text, *Race, Caste, and Class*. Cox was responding to the prevailing social science at the time that conceived of racism strictly in terms of race prejudice, thus ignoring social conditions and reducing the determinants of racism to wayward irrational individual psychologies and dispositions. Cox, by contrast, undertakes to account for what he calls "racial antagonism" by showing individual racist expressions to be embedded in and reflective of material social conditions at different historical moments.

The importance of sociohistorical embeddedness, and the mutually constitutive interplay of social structure and culture, material conditions and psychological dispositions, is further elaborated in the work of the great theorist of colonialism and the voice of anticolonial struggles,

Frantz Fanon. In his trilogy of works – *Black Skin, White Masks, A Dying Colonialism,* and *Wretched of the Earth* – Fanon relates the internalized self-degradations of racism to the structural and cultural impositions of colonial domination. Fanon thus offers an analytic language and logic that continues to resonate deeply in postcolonial writing today. In particular, Fanon first fashioned the now overused notion of "racializing" conditions and expressions, contrasting them significantly with "humanizing" ones to suggest the ways in which racial conceptions and structural conditions order lives and delimit human possibilities. This concern with more or less silent structural embeddedness is furthered by Stokely Carmichael and Charles Hamilton's important formulation in 1968 of a notion of "institutional racism." Carmichael and Hamilton call our attention to the hidden ways in which racism is extended into every facet of life by virtue of the fact that it informs the institutional rules and regulations, the ordering conceptions, of work and play, economic and political arrangements and cultural conceptions. What they reveal, accordingly, is that eroding individual prejudice would no longer be sufficient to counter the racial ordering of social formation in historically racist societies. Also at the end of the 1960s, an especially rich period for thinking critically about the ways in which race was fashioned in social life and conditions, Winthrop Jordan was the first to offer a comprehensive reading of racial intellectual history. He thus paved the way for more detailed studies of how race has pervaded even the most cherished scientific, philosophical, and literary contributions of European and European-derivative peoples over the past 500 years.

These texts accordingly offered the conceptual apparatus for thinking critically about race and racism, their social and intellectual conditions and manifestations, their causes and effects, as well as their interplay with other socially significant expressions like class and gender. It is notable that all the influential figures we cite were men of color, men of course dominating intellectual and institutional life across this period, while whites overwhelmingly considered racism a matter of individual prejudice and false belief. There were indeed black women intellectual activists, most notably in the United States, whose work was of enormous importance in more local anti-abolition and antilynching campaigns – Harriet Tubman and Sojourner Truth in the former instances, Ida B. Wells in the latter, for example. And their examples have served as defining influences also in the work of critical race theorizing, especially regarding the intersections of race, gender, and class.

Feminist theorizing about questions of race and gender began to flourish in the wake of the extraordinary developments in feminist thinking
generally in the 1960s, 1970s, and 1980s. Thus Audre Lorde, Gloria
Anzaldúa, Gerda Lerner, Angela Davis, Adrienne Rich, Joyce Ladner,
Gloria Joseph and Jill Lewis, Colette Guillaumin, Michele Wallace, Julia
Kristeva, bell hooks and Hazel Carby, among others, set the stage for a
younger generation of incisive race critical scholarship in the late 1980s
and 1990s. Finally, contemporary racial analysis in the critical tradition
represented here owes a considerable conceptual debt to the Italian
social theorist, Antonio Gramsci. While Gramsci himself barely turned
his attention explicitly to racial questions, he did fashion a conceptual
vocabulary illuminating for thinking about the social conditions of race
and racism. Thus, notions of "articulation," "social formation," "hegemony," social forces" have been widely taken up in the work of which
the texts collected here are representative.

We hope that readers feel inspired, and that teachers encourage their
students, to go back to the original articles. Because of space we have
had to edit contributions down to their central lines of argument, but
in developing this volume we also wanted to offer more than texts only.
The text has a life of its own but remains part of the ongoing experiences of authors in relation to their social and political environments.
The text's production is contextualized in a certain historical-political
mode, and so are responses to it. Race critical research demands
courage, rigor, and honesty, as it is neither an innocent nor a safe
venture. Going against the grain means by definition accepting extreme
responses and insecurities. What do we know, apart from our immediate colleagues or friends, about the tensions, risks, and, no doubt,
rewards scholars experience in doing critical research? We thought it
would be enlightening to engage the students in some of the issues
involved in the production of the books and articles they read. In
particular, what has the text meant over the years, for the authors
themselves, and for others?

Reluctant indeed to offer students texts about and from the past
without a contemporary context, we thought of an unconventional way
of introducing the articles, a way that at the same time could serve as
an insightful pedagogical tool. We have solicited additional contributions to contextualize each article, in short essays, in terms of current
views on the text in question. The results are a mix of authors' own
reflections and reflections by others, mostly younger scholars, who

have seen themselves influenced by the particular text in question. In certain ways the essays bring to light what engagement in race critical research is really about. The reflections on the original texts shift the debate from resourceful intellectual engagement to the complexities and inconclusiveness of critical research in the area of race, ethnicities, and racisms.

Authors offer revealing background information one sometimes reads in a preface, or, only in autobiographical materials. They explain the sociopolitical context of their writing, which political events or the kinds of political environments motivated them to write that particular kind of work or to engage in race critical research in general. Students are encouraged to see that scholarship can be a useful tool against dominance. Martin Barker's answer to the infamous speech of then UK cabinet minister Enoch Powell, predicting that immigrants would cause "rivers of blood," was *The New Racism*, a book that had significant impact on the debate on immigration and racism. Ruth Wodak, in Vienna, embarked on a series of research projects depicting racist discourse among political elites – out of deep rejection of the increasing support among the Austrians for neo-Nazi political parties. Less extreme, but no less harmful, conservatism in the US has sought in the 1980s and 1990s to dismantle affirmative action. In many respects, affirmative action represents little more than face value. Nevertheless, as Johanna Fernandez observes, Manning Marable's public intervention in defense of affirmative action has been critical.

The reflections also deal with the conceptual and theoretical problems to which authors were responding in the text. Michael Omi and Howard Winant were critical of the absence of "race" in theories of the state and the tendency in the broader literature on class relations to explain racism as a form of "false consciousness" among the white working class. Speaking to whiteness, David Roediger would argue half a decade later, is and has been central to the making of white working-class identity. His work is anchored in analyses of racism in the tradition of critical black perspectives on white domination in the United States. As we have argued, the making of critical research is an interactive process, where national, ethnic, regional, cultural, and disciplinary boundaries are acknowledged, challenged, redefined, or transcended. Drawing from insights developed in the United States as well as in Europe, Philomena Essed's work on everyday racism conceptualizes a bridge between grand system theories of race-ethnic relations and the mundane, often subtle ways in which dominance is expressed from day to day. David Theo Goldberg challenges the heart of philosophy and the history of knowledge in exposing racist undercurrents in the rise of modernity.

For authors themselves, it is sometimes difficult to qualify the impact of their work on others. Those who have been influenced by the texts have been more extended in their reflections on the theoretical and political impact of the text included. Saree Makdisi explains in a rich essay how dramatically Edward Said's text on Orientalism has shaped our insight on the extent to which scholars and writers are complicit in the production of specific versions of world history. We recommend Said's autobiography, *Out of Place*, from which one can read how his youth prepared Said to be perfectly positioned later to write a seminal text on Orientalism. Sue Kim observes about Chandra Mohanty's "Cartographies of Struggle: Third World Women and the Politics of Feminism" that this article has been very influential. What was unique at the time of its appearance was the global scope in critiquing Eurocentrism in western feminism. Mohanty shows among other things how a number of interlinking ordering principles – race, class, gender, and sexuality – have been articulated and manipulated by colonial and (gendered) forms of liberalism and multinational capitalism. Women of color have been at the forefront of developing, applying, and refining theories of intersectionality, while acknowledging, constraining, and empowering dimensions of different identities. Suzette Spencer offers a good example of how she has been able to use in her own research on maroon societies the probing analysis Toni Morrison employs to demonstrate currents of multiple identities.

We not only looked for original notes that have been widely embraced within race critical circles, but also for authors who had the foresight and honesty to be critical of certain directions in race critical theory. A case in point is Paul Gilroy, who criticized lingering essentialisms in antiracism. Vikki Bell explains in a concise and clear way how Gilroy eventually deepened the debate with his trenchant criticism of the reification within multiculturalism of culture as static traditions.

We asked authors whether they think relevant colleagues really understood their critical intervention. Maria Root, in putting squarely on the table the rights of people to acknowledge identification with more than one group of people only, has spoken to the hearts of many racially mixed people. Transcending racial ideological claims of categorizing and belonging, her work on the fluidity of identities speaks in particular to young and future generations for whom racial or ethnic identities are differently relevant than those who grew up at the center of what Du Bois has called the century of the color line. Maria Markus, in the same vein and drawing from her own experience of migration, encourages us not only to shift but to lift boundaries of taken-for-granted identifications. We believe that the twenty-first century will very much be about negotiating between different and overlapping interests and affiliations, about creating space for individuality in the fashioning of inter- and transcultural identifications.

In speaking to the issue of societal reaction to race critical work, the other side of the coin – the risks and dangers of doing critical research – become sharply pronounced. Teun A. van Dijk's account is unsettling, as it shows how colleagues and the media retaliated against his many critical analyses of racism in media discourse and among elites in general. After a witch-hunt for many years, he has distanced himself from the Netherlands. The political nature of the story is evident in the fact that outside of his native country he enjoys worldwide recognition for his work on racism.

A question only a few authors addressed is whether, in retrospect, they would be inclined to revise or modify their theoretical (political) contribution. Patricia Hill Collins testifies to the deepening of her understanding of empowerment – the aim to empower black women strongly motivated her in working on *Black Feminist Thought*. She has come to reject binary thinking, including those traces in her own work, while acknowledging more fluidity and overlap between black feminist thought and other bodies of knowledge.

Breaking with fixed positions, with mono-reductionisms, with local determinism, is exactly the way forward we have in mind in aspiring, in this volume, to reveal complex influences that run in all directions geographically and conceptually. Various authors in both parts of the book point to the need for a broader frame, to consider local national expressions of race and racism in terms also of the social control of migration flows, of concerns over global power as a result of the agglomeration of technologies and finance, and of the positioning of old and new centers of capital in the world system. This in turn raises questions about the tensions in conceiving race in relation to global and local conditions, about the intersection of dominant contemporary interests with older colonial orders, with new elites, and to account for the implications for rethinking race.

We conclude with a point of hope: It is ironic to note that modernity in establishing race as a concept of divide and in creating segregated disciplines has provided the very conditions to turn the waves. Race critical theory contains the very tools to show that disciplinary approaches are outdated, and by extension, that mono-disciplines are not part of a future of multi-identifications either. We believe that race critical theory will continue to break, both conceptually and methodologically, through barriers between disciplines and geographical locations, between genders and diverse populations.

Part I

*Conceptual Mapping,
in Chronological Order
(ca. 1980–2000)*

1

Imaginative Geography and Its Representations: Orientalizing the Oriental

Edward Said

Strictly speaking, Orientalism is a field of learned study. In the Christian West, Orientalism is considered to have commenced its formal existence with the decision of the Church Council of Vienne in 1312 to establish a series of chairs in "Arabic, Greek, Hebrew, and Syriac at Paris, Oxford, Bologna, Avignon, and Salamanca."[1] Yet any account of Orientalism would have to consider not only the professional Orientalist and his work but also the very notion of a field of study based on a geographical, cultural, linguistic, and ethnic unit called the Orient. Fields, of course, are made. They acquire coherence and integrity in time because scholars devote themselves in different ways to what seems to be a commonly agreed-upon subject matter. Yet it goes without saying that a field of study is rarely as simply defined as even its most committed partisans – usually scholars, professors, experts, and the like – claim it is. Besides, a field can change so entirely, in even the most traditional disciplines like philology, history, or theology, as to make an all-purpose definition of subject matter almost impossible. This is certainly true of Orientalism, for some interesting reasons.

To speak of scholarly specialization as a geographical "field" is, in the case of Orientalism, fairly revealing since no one is likely to imagine a field symmetrical to it called Occidentalism. Already the special, perhaps even eccentric attitude of Orientalism becomes apparent. For although many learned disciplines imply a position taken towards, say, *human* material (a historian deals with the human past from a special vantage point in the present), there is no real analogy for taking a fixed, more or less total geographical position towards a wide variety of social, linguistic, political, and historical realities. A classicist, a Romance specialist, even an Americanist focuses on a relatively modest portion of the world, not on a full half of it. But Orientalism is a field with considerable geographical ambition. And since Orientalists have traditionally occupied themselves with things Oriental (a specialist in Islamic law, no less than an expert in Chinese dialects or in Indian religions, is considered an Orientalist by people who call themselves Orientalists), we must learn to accept enormous, indiscriminate size plus an almost infinite capacity for subdivision as one of the chief characteristics of Orientalism – one that is evidenced in its confusing amalgam of imperial vagueness and precise detail.

All of this describes Orientalism as an academic discipline. The "ism" in Orientalism serves to insist on the distinction of this discipline from every other kind. The rule in its historical development as an academic discipline has been its increasing scope, not its greater selectiveness. Renaissance Orientalists like Erpenius and Guillaume Postel were primarily specialists in the languages of the Biblical provinces, although Postel boasted that he could get across Asia as far as China without needing an interpreter. By and large, until the mid-eighteenth century Orientalists were Biblical scholars, students of the Semitic languages, Islamic specialists, or, because the Jesuits had opened up the new study of China, Sinologists. The whole middle expanse of Asia was not academically conquered for Orientalism until, during the later eighteenth century, Anquetil-Duperron and Sir William Jones were able intelligibly to reveal the extraordinary riches of Avestan and Sanskrit. By the middle of the nineteenth century Orientalism was as vast a treasure-house of learning as one could imagine. There are two excellent indices of this new, triumphant eclecticism. One is the encyclopedic description of Orientalism roughly from 1765 to 1850 given by Raymond Schwab in his *La Renaissance orientale*.[2] Quite aside from the scientific discoveries of things Oriental made by learned professionals during this period in Europe, there was the virtual epidemic of Orientalia affecting every major poet, essayist, and philosopher of the period. Schwab's notion is that "Oriental" identifies an amateur or professional enthusiasm for everything Asiatic, which was wonderfully synonymous with the exotic, the mysterious, the profound, the seminal; this is a later transposition eastwards of a similar enthusiasm in Europe for Greek and Latin antiquity during the High Renaissance. In 1829 Victor Hugo put this change in directions as follows: "Au siècle de Louis XIV on était helléniste, maintenant on est orientaliste."[3] A nineteenth-century Orientalist was therefore either a scholar (a Sinologist, an Islamicist, an Indo-Europeanist) or a gifted enthusiast (Hugo in *Les Orientales*, Goethe in the *Westöstlicher Diwan*), or both (Richard Burton, Edward Lane, Friedrich Schlegel).

The second index of how inclusive Orientalism had become since the Council of Vienne is to be found in nineteenth-century chronicles of the field itself. The most thorough of its kind is Jules Mohl's *Vingt-sept Ans d'histoire des études orientales*, a two-volume logbook of everything of note that took place in Orientalism between 1840 and 1867.[4] Mohl was the secretary of the Société asiatique in Paris, and for something more than the first half of the nineteenth century Paris was the capital of the Orientalist world (and, according to Walter Benjamin, of the nineteenth century). Mohl's position in the Société could not have been more central to the field of Orientalism. There is scarcely anything done by a European scholar touching Asia during those twenty-seven years that Mohl does not enter under "études orientales." His entries of course concern publications, but the range of published material of interest to Orientalist scholars is awesome. Arabic, innumerable Indian dialects, Hebrew, Pehlevi, Assyrian, Babylonian, Mongolian, Chinese, Burmese, Mesopotamian, Javanese: the list of philological works considered Orientalist is almost uncountable. Moreover, Orientalist studies apparently cover everything from the editing and translation of texts to numismatic, anthropological, archaeological, sociological, economic, historical, literary, and cultural studies in every known Asiatic and North African civilization, ancient and modern. Gustave Dugat's *Histoire des orientalistes de l'Europe du XIIᵉ au XIXᵉ siècle* (1868–70)[5] is a selective history of major figures, but the range represented is no less immense than Mohl's.

Such eclecticism as this had its blind spots, nevertheless. Academic Orientalists for the most part were interested in the classical period of whatever language or society it was that they studied. Not until quite late in the century, with the single major exception of Napoleon's Institut d'Égypte, was much attention given to the academic study of the modern, or actual, Orient. Moreover, the Orient studied was a textual universe by and large; the impact of the Orient was made through books and manuscripts, not, as in the impress of Greece on the Renaissance, through mimetic artifacts like sculpture and pottery. Even the rapport between an Orientalist and the Orient was textual, so much so that it is reported of some of the early-nineteenth-century German Orientalists that their first view of an eight-armed Indian statue cured them completely of their Orientalist taste.[6] When a learned Orientalist traveled in the country of his specialization, it was always with unshakable abstract maxims about the "civilization" he had studied; rarely were Orientalists interested in anything except proving the validity of these musty "truths" by applying them, without great success, to uncomprehending, hence degenerate, natives. Finally, the very power and scope of Orientalism produced not only a fair amount of exact positive knowledge about the Orient but also a kind of second-order knowledge – lurking in such places as the "Oriental" tale, the mythology of the mysterious East, notions of Asian inscrutability – with a life of its own, what V. G. Kiernan has aptly called "Europe's collective day-dream of the Orient."[7] One happy result of this is that an estimable number of important writers during the nineteenth century were Oriental enthusiasts: It is perfectly correct, I think, to speak of a genre of Orientalist writing as exemplified in the works of Hugo, Goethe, Nerval, Flaubert, Fitzgerald, and the like. What inevitably goes with such work, however, is a kind of free-floating mythology of the Orient, an Orient that derives not only from contemporary attitudes and popular prejudices but also from what Vico called the conceit of nations and of scholars. I have already alluded to the political uses of such material as it has turned up in the twentieth century.

Today an Orientalist is less likely to call himself an Orientalist than he was almost any time up to World War II. Yet the designation is still useful, as when universities maintain programs or departments in Oriental languages or Oriental civilizations. There is an Oriental "faculty" at Oxford, and a department of Oriental studies at Princeton. As recently as 1959, the British government empowered a commission "to review developments in the Universities in the fields of Oriental, Slavonic, East European and African studies . . . and to consider, and advise on, proposals for future development."[8] The Hayter Report, as it was called when it appeared in 1961, seemed untroubled by the broad designation of the word *Oriental*, which it found serviceably employed in American universities as well. For even the greatest name in modern Anglo-American Islamic studies, H. A. R. Gibb, preferred to call himself an

Orientalist rather than an Arabist. Gibb himself, classicist that he was, could use the ugly neologism "area study" for Orientalism as a way of showing that area studies and Orientalism after all were interchangeable geographical titles.[9] But this, I think, ingenuously belies a much more interesting relationship between knowledge and geography. I should like to consider that relationship briefly.

Despite the distraction of a great many vague desires, impulses, and images, the mind seems persistently to formulate what Claude Lévi-Strauss has called a science of the concrete.[10] A primitive tribe, for example, assigns a definite place, function, and significance to every leafy species in its immediate environment. Many of these grasses and flowers have no practical use; but the point Lévi-Strauss makes is that mind requires order, and order is achieved by discriminating and taking note of everything, placing everything of which the mind is aware in a secure, refindable place, therefore giving things some role to play in the economy of objects and identities that make up an environment. This kind of rudimentary classification has a logic to it, but the rules of the logic by which a green fern in one society is a symbol of grace and in another is considered maleficent are neither predictably rational nor universal. There is always a measure of the purely arbitrary in the way the distinctions between things are seen. And with these distinctions go values whose history, if one could unearth it completely, would probably show the same measure of arbitrariness. This is evident enough in the case of fashion. Why do wigs, lace collars, and high buckled shoes appear, then disappear, over a period of decades? Some of the answer has to do with utility and some with the inherent beauty of the fashion. But if we agree that all things in history, like history itself, are made by men, then we will appreciate how possible it is for many objects or places or times to be assigned roles and given meanings that acquire objective validity only *after* the assignments are made. This is especially true of relatively uncommon things, like foreigners, mutants, or "abnormal" behavior.

It is perfectly possible to argue that some distinctive objects are made by the mind, and that these objects, while appearing to exist objectively, have only a fictional reality. A group of people living on a few acres of land will set up boundaries between their land and its immediate surroundings and the territory beyond, which they call "the land of the barbarians." In other words, this universal practice of designating in one's mind a familiar space which is "ours" and an unfamiliar space beyond "ours" which is "theirs" is a way of making geographical distinctions that *can be* entirely arbitrary. I use the word "arbitrary" here because imaginative geography of the "our land–barbarian land" variety does not require that the barbarians acknowledge the distinction. It is enough for "us" to set up these boundaries in our own minds; "they" become "they" accordingly, and both their territory and their mentality are designated as different from "ours." To a certain extent modern and primitive societies seem thus to derive a sense of their identities negatively. A fifth-century Athenian was very likely to feel himself to be nonbarbarian as much as he positively felt himself to be Athenian. The geographic boundaries accompany the social, ethnic, and cultural ones in expected ways. Yet often the sense in which someone feels himself to be not-foreign is based on a very unrigorous idea of what is "out there," beyond one's own territory. All kinds of suppositions, associations, and fictions appear to crowd the unfamiliar space outside one's own.

Almost from earliest times in Europe the Orient was something more than what was empirically known about it. At least until the early eighteenth century, as R. W. Southern has so elegantly shown, European understanding of one kind of Oriental culture, the Islamic, was ignorant but complex.[11] For certain associations with the East – not quite ignorant, not quite informed – always seem to have gathered around the notion of an Orient. Consider first the demarcation between Orient and West. It already seems bold by the time of the *Iliad*. Two of the most profoundly influential qualities associated with the East appear in Aeschylus's *The Persians*, the earliest Athenian play extant, and in *The Bacchae* of Euripides, the very last one extant. Aeschylus portrays the sense of disaster overcoming the Persians when they learn that their armies, led by King Xerxes, have been destroyed by the Greeks. The chorus sings the following ode:

> Now all Asia's land
> Moans in emptiness.
> Xerxes led forth, oh oh!
> Xerxes destroyed, woe woe!
> Xerxes' plans have all miscarried
> In ships of the sea.
> Why did Darius then

Bring no harm to his men
When he led them into battle,
That beloved leader of men from Susa?[12]

What matters here is that Asia speaks through and by virtue of the European imagination, which is depicted as victorious over Asia, that hostile "other" world beyond the seas. To Asia are given the feelings of emptiness, loss, and disaster that seem thereafter to reward Oriental challenges to the West; and also, the lament that in some glorious past Asia fared better, was itself victorious over Europe.

In *The Bacchae*, perhaps the most Asiatic of all the Attic dramas, Dionysus is explicitly connected with his Asian origins and with the strangely threatening excesses of Oriental mysteries. Pentheus, king of Thebes, is destroyed by his mother, Agave, and her fellow bacchantes. Having defied Dionysus by not recognizing either his power or his divinity, Pentheus is thus horribly punished, and the play ends with a general recognition of the eccentric god's terrible power. Modern commentators on *The Bacchae* have not failed to note the play's extraordinary range of intellectual and aesthetic effects; but there has been no escaping the additional historical detail that Euripides "was surely affected by the new aspect that the Dionysiac cults must have assumed in the light of the foreign ecstatic religions of Bendis, Cybele, Sabazius, Adonis, and Isis, which were introduced from Asia Minor and the Levant and swept through Piraeus and Athens during the frustrating and increasingly irrational years of the Peloponnesian War."[13]

The two aspects of the Orient that set it off from the West in this pair of plays will remain essential motifs of European imaginative geography. A line is drawn between two continents. Europe is powerful and articulate; Asia is defeated and distant. Aeschylus *represents* Asia, makes her speak in the person of the aged Persian queen, Xerxes' mother. It is Europe that articulates the Orient; this articulation is the prerogative, not of a puppet master, but of a genuine creator, whose life-giving power represents, animates, constitutes the otherwise silent and dangerous space beyond familiar boundaries. There is an analogy between Aeschylus's orchestra, which contains the Asiatic world as the playwright conceives it, and the learned envelope of Orientalist scholarship, which also will hold in the vast, amorphous Asiatic sprawl for sometimes sympathetic but always dominating scrutiny. Secondly, there is the motif of the Orient as insinuating danger. Rationality is undermined by Eastern excesses, those mysteriously attractive opposites to what seem to be normal values. The difference separating East from West is symbolized by the sternness with which, at first, Pentheus rejects the hysterical bacchantes. When later he himself becomes a bacchant, he is destroyed not so much for having given in to Dionysus as for having incorrectly assessed Dionysus's menace in the first place. The lesson that Euripides intends is dramatized by the presence in the play of Cadmus and Tiresias, knowledgeable older men who realize that "sovereignty" alone does not rule men;[14] there is such a thing as judgment, they say, which means sizing up correctly the force of alien powers and expertly coming to terms with them. Hereafter Oriental mysteries will be taken seriously, not least because they challenge the rational Western mind to new exercises of its enduring ambition and power.

But one big division, as between West and Orient, leads to other smaller ones, especially as the normal enterprises of civilization provoke such outgoing activities as travel, conquest, new experiences. In classical Greece and Rome geographers, historians, public figures like Caesar, orators, and poets added to the fund of taxonomic lore separating races, regions, nations, and minds from each other; much of that was self-serving, and existed to prove that Romans and Greeks were superior to other kinds of people. But concern with the Orient had its own tradition of classification and hierarchy. From at least the second century BC on, it was lost on no traveler or eastward-looking and ambitious Western potentate that Herodotus – historian, traveler, inexhaustibly curious chronicler – and Alexander – king warrior, scientific conqueror – had been in the Orient before. The Orient was therefore subdivided into realms previously known, visited, conquered, by Herodotus and Alexander as well as their epigones, and those realms not previously known, visited, conquered. Christianity completed the setting up of main intra-Oriental spheres: there was a Near Orient and a Far Orient, a familiar Orient, which René Grousset calls "l'empire du Devant,"[5] and a novel Orient. The Orient therefore alternated in the mind's geography between being an Old World to which one returned, as to Eden or Paradise, there to set up a new version of the old, and being a wholly new place to which one came as Columbus came to America, in order to set up a New World (although, ironically, Columbus himself thought that he discovered a new part of the Old World). Certainly neither of these Orients was purely one thing or the other: it is their vacillations, their tempting suggestiveness, their capacity for entertaining and confusing the mind, that are interesting.

Consider how the Orient, and in particular the Near Orient, became known in the West as its great complementary opposite since antiquity. There were the Bible and the rise of Christianity; there were travelers like Marco Polo who charted the trade routes and patterned a regulated system of commercial exchange, and after him Lodovico di Varthema and Pietro della Valle; there were fabulists like Mandeville; there were the redoubtable conquering Eastern movements, principally Islam, of course; there were the militant pilgrims, chiefly the Crusaders. Altogether an internally structured archive is built up from the literature that belongs to these experiences. Out of this comes a restricted number of typical encapsulations: the journey, the history, the fable, the stereotype, the polemical confrontation. These are the lenses through which the Orient is experienced, and they shape the language, perception, and form of the encounter between East and West. What gives the immense number of encounters some unity, however, is the vacillation I was speaking about earlier. Something patently foreign and distant acquires, for one reason or another, a status more rather than less familiar. One tends to stop judging things either as completely novel or as completely well known; a new median category emerges, a category that allows one to see new things, things seen for the first time, as versions of a previously known thing. In essence such a category is not so much a way of receiving new information as it is a method of controlling what seems to be a threat to some established view of things. If the mind must suddenly deal with what it takes to be a radically new form of life – as Islam appeared to Europe in the early Middle Ages – the response on the whole is conservative and defensive. Islam is judged to be a fraudulent new version of some previous experience, in this case Christianity. The threat is muted, familiar values impose themselves, and in the end the mind reduces the pressure upon it by accommodating things to itself as either "original" or "repetitious." Islam thereafter is "handled": its novelty and its suggestiveness are brought under control so that relatively nuanced discriminations are now made that would have been impossible had the raw novelty of Islam been left unattended. The Orient at large, therefore, vacillates between the West's contempt for what is familiar and its shivers of delight in – or fear of – novelty.

Yet where Islam was concerned, European fear, if not always respect, was in order. After Mohammed's death in 632, the military and later the cultural and religious hegemony of Islam grew enormously. First Persia, Syria, and Egypt, then Turkey, then North Africa fell to the Muslim armies; in the eighth and ninth centuries Spain, Sicily, and parts of France were conquered. By the thirteenth and fourteenth centuries Islam ruled as far east as India, Indonesia, and China. And to this extraordinary assault Europe could respond with very little except fear and a kind of awe. Christian authors witnessing the Islamic conquests had scant interest in the learning, high culture, and frequent magnificence of the Muslims, who were, as Gibbon said, "coeval with the darkest and most slothful period of European annals." (But with some satisfaction he added, "since the sum of science has risen in the west, it should seem that the Oriental studies have languished and declined."[16]) What Christians typically felt about the Eastern armies was that they had "all the appearance of a swarm of bees, but with a heavy hand . . . they devastated everything": so wrote Erchembert, a cleric in Monte Cassino in the eleventh century.[17]

Not for nothing did Islam come to symbolize terror, devastation, the demonic, hordes of hated barbarians. For Europe, Islam was a lasting trauma. Until the end of the seventeenth century the "Ottoman peril" lurked alongside Europe to represent for the whole of Christian civilization a constant danger, and in time European civilization incorporated that peril and its lore, its great events, figures, virtues, and vices, as something woven into the fabric of life. In Renaissance England alone, as Samuel Chew recounts in his classic study *The Crescent and the Rose*, "a man of average education and intelligence" had at his fingertips, and could watch on the London stage, a relatively large number of detailed events in the history of Ottoman Islam and its encroachments upon Christian Europe.[18] The point is that what remained current about Islam was some necessarily diminished version of those great dangerous forces that it symbolized for Europe. Like Walter Scott's Saracens, the European representation of the Muslim, Ottoman, or Arab was always a way of controlling the redoubtable Orient, and to a certain extent the same is true of the methods of contemporary learned Orientalists, whose subject is not so much the East itself as the East made known, and therefore less fearsome, to the Western reading public.

There is nothing especially controversial or reprehensible about such domestications of the exotic; they take place between all cultures, certainly, and between all men. My point, however, is to emphasize the truth that the Orientalist, as much as anyone in the European West who thought about or experienced the Orient, performed this kind of mental operation. But what is more important still is the limited vocabulary and imagery that impose themselves as a consequence. The reception of Islam in the West is a perfect case in point, and has been admirably studied by Norman Daniel. One constraint acting upon Christian thinkers who tried to understand Islam was an analogical one; since Christ is the basis of Christian faith, it was assumed – quite incorrectly – that Mohammed was to Islam as Christ was to Christianity. Hence the polemic name "Mohammedanism" given to Islam, and the automatic epithet "imposter" applied to Mohammed.[19] Out of such and many other misconceptions "there formed a circle which was never broken by imaginative exteriorisation. . . . The Christian concept of Islam was integral and self-sufficient."[20] Islam became an image – the word is Daniel's but it seems to me to have remarkable implications for Orientalism in general – whose function was not so much to represent Islam in itself as to represent it for the medieval Christian.

> The invariable tendency to neglect what the Qur'an meant, or what Muslims thought it meant, or what Muslims thought or did in any given circumstances, necessarily implies that Qur'anic and other Islamic doctrine was presented in a form that would convince Christians; and more and more extravagant forms would stand a chance of acceptance as the distance of the writers and public from the Islamic border increased. It was with very great reluctance that what Muslims said Muslims believed was accepted as what they did believe. There was a Christian picture in which the details (even under the pressure of facts) were abandoned as little as possible, and in which the general outline was never abandoned. There were shades of difference, but only with a common framework. All the corrections that were made in the interests of an increasing accuracy were only a defence of what had newly been realised to be vulnerable, a shoring up of a weakened structure. Christian opinion was an erection which could not be demolished, even to be rebuilt.[21]

This rigorous Christian picture of Islam was intensified in innumerable ways, including – during the Middle Ages and early Renaissance – a large variety of poetry, learned controversy, and popular superstition.[22] By this time the Near Orient had been all but incorporated in the common world-picture of Latin Christianity – as in the *Chanson de Roland* the worship of Saracens is portrayed as embracing Mahomet *and* Apollo. By the middle of the fifteenth century, as R. W. Southern has brilliantly shown, it became apparent to serious European thinkers "that something would have to be done about Islam," which had turned the situation around somewhat by itself arriving militarily in Eastern Europe. Southern recounts a dramatic episode between 1450 and 1460 when four learned men, John of Segovia, Nicholas of Cusa, Jean Germain, and Aeneas Silvius (Pius II), attempted to deal with Islam through *contraferentia*, or "conference." The idea was John of Segovia's: it was to have been a staged conference with Islam in which Christians attempted the wholesale conversion of Muslims. "He saw the conference as an instrument with a political as well as a strictly religious function, and in words which will strike a chord in modern breasts he exclaimed that even if it were to last ten years it would be less expensive and less damaging than war." There was no agreement between the four men, but the episode is crucial for having been a fairly sophisticated attempt – part of a general European attempt from Bede to Luther – to put a representative Orient in front of Europe, to *stage* the Orient and Europe together in some coherent way, the idea being for Christians to make it clear to Muslims that Islam was just a misguided version of Christianity. Southern's conclusion follows:

> Most conspicuous to us is the inability of any of these systems of thought [European Christian] to provide a fully satisfying explanation of the phenomenon they had set out to explain [Islam] – still less to influence the course of practical events in a decisive way. At a practical level, events never turned out either so well or so ill as the most intelligent observers predicted; and it is perhaps worth noticing that they never turned out better than when the best judges confidently expected a happy ending. Was there any progress [in Christian knowledge of Islam]? I must express my conviction that there was. Even if the solution of the problem remained obstinately hidden from sight, the statement of the problem became more complex, more rational, and more related to experience. . . . The scholars who labored at the problem of Islam in the Middle Ages failed to find the solution they sought and desired; but they developed habits of mind and powers of comprehension which, in other men and in other fields, may yet deserve success.[23]

The best part of Southern's analysis, here and elsewhere in his brief history of Western views of Islam, is his demonstration that it is finally Western ignorance which becomes more refined and complex, not some body of positive Western knowledge which increases in size and accuracy. For fictions have their own logic and their own dialectic of growth or decline. Onto the character of Mohammed in the Middle Ages was heaped a bundle of attributes that corresponded to the "character of the [twelfth-century] prophets of the 'Free Spirit' who did actually arise in Europe, and claim credence and collect followers." Similarly, since Mohammed was viewed as the disseminator of a false Revelation, he became as well the epitome of lechery, debauchery, sodomy, and a whole battery of assorted treacheries, all of which derived "logically" from his doctrinal impostures.[24] Thus the Orient acquired representatives, so to speak, and representations, each one more concrete, more internally congruent with some Western exigency, than the ones that preceded it. It is as if, having once settled on the Orient as a locale suitable for incarnating the infinite in a finite shape, Europe could not stop the practice; the Orient and the Oriental, Arab, Islamic, Indian, Chinese, or whatever, become repetitious pseudo-incarnations of some great original (Christ, Europe, the West) they were supposed to have been imitating. Only the source of these rather narcissistic Western ideas about the Orient changed in time, not their character. Thus we will find it commonly believed in the twelfth and thirteenth centuries that Arabia was "on the fringe of the Christian world, a natural asylum for heretical outlaws,"[25] and that Mohammed was a cunning apostate, whereas in the twentieth century an Orientalist scholar, an erudite specialist, will be the one to point out how Islam is really no more than second-order Arian heresy.[26]

Our initial description of Orientalism as a learned field now acquires a new concreteness. A field is often an enclosed space. The idea of representation is a theatrical one: the Orient is the stage on which the whole East is confined. On this stage will appear figures whose role it is to represent the larger whole from which they emanate. The Orient then seems to be, not an unlimited extension beyond the familiar European world, but rather a closed field, a theatrical stage affixed to Europe. An Orientalist is but the particular specialist in knowledge for which Europe at large is responsible, in the way that an audience is historically and culturally responsible for (and responsive to) dramas technically put together by the dramatist. In the depths of this Oriental stage stands a prodigious cultural repertoire whose individual items evoke a fabulously rich world: the Sphinx, Cleopatra, Eden, Troy, Sodom and Gomorrah, Astarte, Isis and Osiris, Sheba, Babylon, the Genii, the Magi, Nineveh, Prester John, Mahomet, and dozens more; settings, in some cases names only, half-imagined, half-known: monsters, devils, heroes; terrors, pleasures, desires. The European imagination was nourished extensively from this repertoire: between the Middle Ages and the eighteenth century such major authors as Ariosto, Milton, Marlowe, Tasso, Shakespeare, Cervantes, and the authors of the *Chanson de Roland* and the *Poema del Cid* drew on the Orient's riches for their productions, in ways that sharpened the outlines of imagery, ideas, and figures populating it. In addition, a great deal of what was considered learned Orientalist scholarship in Europe pressed ideological myths into service, even as knowledge seemed genuinely to be advancing.

A celebrated instance of how dramatic form and learned imagery come together in the Orientalist theater is Barthélemy d'Herbelot's *Bibliothèque orientale*, published posthumously in 1697, with a preface by Antoine Galland. [. . .] In such efforts as d'Herbelot's, Europe discovered its capacities for encompassing and Orientalizing the Orient. A certain sense of superiority appears here and there in what Galland had to say about his and d'Herbelot's *materia orientalia*; as in the work of seventeenth-century geographers like Raphael du Mans, Europeans could perceive that the Orient was being outstripped and outdated by Western science.[27] But what becomes evident is not only the advantage of a Western perspective: there is also the triumphant technique for taking the immense fecundity of the Orient and making it systematically, even alphabetically, knowable by Western laymen. When Galland said of d'Herbelot that he satisfied one's expectations he meant, I think, that the *Bibliothèque* did not attempt to revise commonly received ideas about the Orient. For what the Orientalist does is to *confirm* the Orient in his readers' eyes; he neither tries nor wants to unsettle already firm convictions. All the *Bibliothèque orientale* did was represent the Orient more fully and more clearly; what may have been a loose collection of randomly acquired facts concerning vaguely Levantine history, Biblical imagery, Islamic culture, place names, and so on were transformed into a rational Oriental panorama, from A to Z. Under the entry for Mohammed, d'Herbelot first supplied all of the Prophet's given names, then proceeded to confirm Mohammed's ideological and doctrinal value as follows:

This is the famous imposter Mahomet, Author and Founder of a heresy, which has taken on the name of religion, which we call Mohammedan. See entry under *Islam*.

The interpreters of the Alcoran and other Doctors of Muslim or Mohammedan Law have applied to this false prophet all the praises which the Arians. Paulicians or Paulianists, and other Heretics have attributed to Jesus Christ, while stripping him of his Divinity.[28]

"Mohammedan" is the relevant (and insulting) European designation; "Islam," which happens to be the correct Muslim name, is relegated to another entry. The "heresy . . . which we call Mohammedan" is "caught" as the imitation of a Christian imitation of true religion. Then, in the long historical account of Mohammed's life, d'Herbelot can turn to more or less straight narrative. But it is the *placing* of Mohammed that counts in the *Bibliothèque*. The dangers of free-wheeling heresy are removed when it is transformed into ideologically explicit matter for an alphabetical item. Mohammed no longer roams the Eastern world as a threatening, immoral debauchee; he sits quietly on his (admittedly prominent) portion of the Orientalist stage.[29] He is given a genealogy, an explanation, even a development, all of which are subsumed under the simple statements that prevent him from straying elsewhere.

Such "images" of the Orient as this are images in that they represent or stand for a very large entity, otherwise impossibly diffuse, which they enable one to grasp or see. They are also *characters*, related to such types as the braggarts, misers, or gluttons produced by Theophrastus, La Bruyère, or Selden. Perhaps it is not exactly correct to say that one *sees* such characters as the *miles gloriosus* or Mahomet the imposter, since the discursive confinement of a character is supposed at best to let one apprehend a generic type without difficulty or ambiguity. D'Herbelot's character of Mahomet is an *image*, however, because the false prophet is part of a general theatrical representation called *orientale* whose totality is contained in the *Bibliothèque*.

The didactic quality of the Orientalist representation cannot be detached from the rest of the performance. In a learned work like the *Bibliothèque orientale*. Which was the result of systematic study and research, the author imposes a disciplinary order upon the material he has worked on; in addition, he wants it made clear to the reader that what the printed page delivers is an ordered, disciplined judgment of the material. What is thus conveyed by the *Bibliothèque* is an idea of Orientalism's power and effectiveness, which everywhere remind the reader that henceforth in order to get at the Orient he must pass through the learned grids and codes provided by the Orientalist. Not only is the

Orient accommodated to the moral exigencies of Western Christianity; it is also circumscribed by a series of attitudes and judgments that send the Western mind, not first to Oriental sources for correction and verification, but rather to other Orientalist works. The Orientalist stage, as I have been calling it, becomes a system of moral and epistemological rigor. As a discipline representing institutionalized Western knowledge of the Orient, Orientalism thus comes to exert a three-way force, on the Orient, on the Orientalist, and on the Western "consumer" of Orientalism. It would be wrong, I think, to underestimate the strength of the three-way relationship thus established. For the Orient ("out there" towards the East) is corrected, even penalized, for lying outside the boundaries of European society, "our" world; the Orient is thus *Orientalized*, a process that not only marks the Orient as the province of the Orientalist but also forces the uninitiated Western reader to accept Orientalist codifications (like d'Herbelot's alphabetized *Bibliothèque*) as the *true* Orient. Truth, is short, becomes a function of learned judgment, not of the material itself, which in time seems to owe even its existence to the Orientalist.

This whole didactic process is neither difficult to understand nor difficult to explain. One ought again to remember that all cultures impose corrections upon raw reality, changing it from free-floating objects into units of knowledge. The problem is not that conversion takes place. It is perfectly natural for the human mind to resist the assault on it of untreated strangeness; therefore cultures have always been inclined to impose complete transformations on other cultures, receiving these other cultures not as they are but as, for the benefit of the receiver, they ought to be. To the Westerner, however, the Oriental was always *like* some aspect of the West; to some of the German Romantics, for example, Indian religion was essentially an Oriental version of Germano-Christian pantheism. Yet the Orientalist makes it his work to be always converting the Orient from something into something else: he does this for himself, for the sake of his culture, in some cases for what he believes is the sake of the Oriental. This process of conversion is a disciplined one: it is taught, it has its own societies, periodicals, traditions, vocabulary, rhetoric, all in basic ways connected to and supplied by the prevailing cultural and political norms of the West. And, as I shall demonstrate, it tends to become more rather than less total in what it tries to do, so much so that as one surveys Orientalism in the nineteenth and twentieth centuries the overriding impression is of Orientalism's insensitive schematization of the entire Orient.

How early this schematization began is clear from the examples I have given of Western representations of the Orient in classical Greece. How strongly articulated were later representations building on the earlier ones, how inordinately careful their schematization, how dramatically effective their placing in Western imaginative geography, can be illustrated if we turn now to Dante's *Inferno*. Dante's achievement in *The Divine Comedy* was to have seamlessly combined the realistic portrayal of mundane reality with a universal and eternal system of Christian values. What Dante the pilgrim sees as he walks through the Inferno, Purgatorio, and Paradiso is a unique vision of judgment. Paolo and Francesca, for instance, are seen as eternally confined to hell for their sins, yet they are seen as enacting, indeed living, the very characters and actions that put them where they will be for eternity. Thus each of the figures in Dante's vision not only represents himself but is also a typical representation of his character and the fate meted out to him.

"Maometto" – Mohammed – turns up in canto 28 of the *Inferno*. He is located in the eighth of the nine circles of Hell, in the ninth of the ten Bolgias of Malebolge, a circle of gloomy ditches surrounding Satan's stronghold in Hell. Thus before Dante reaches Mohammed, he passes through circles containing people whose sins are of a lesser order: the lustful, the avaricious, the gluttonous, the heretics, the wrathful, the suicidal, the blasphemous. After Mohammed there are only the falsifiers and the treacherous (who include Judas, Brutus, and Cassius) before one arrives at the very bottom of Hell, which is where Satan himself is to be found. Mohammed thus belongs to a rigid hierarchy of evils, in the category of what Dante calls *seminator di scandalo e di scisma*. Mohammed's punishment, which is also his eternal fate, is a peculiarly disgusting one: he is endlessly being cleft in two from his chin to his anus like, Dante says, a cask whose staves are ripped apart. Dante's verse at this point spares the reader none of the eschatological detail that so vivid a punishment entails: Mohammed's entrails and his excrement are described with unflinching accuracy. Mohammed explains his punishment to Dante, pointing as well to Ali, who precedes him in the line of sinners whom the attendant devil is splitting in two; he also asks Dante to warn one Fra Dolcino, a renegade priest whose sect advocated community of women and goods and who was accused of having a mistress, of what will be in store for him. It will not have been lost on the reader that Dante saw a parallel between Dolcino's and Mohammed's revolting sensuality, and also between their pretensions to theological eminence.

But this is not all that Dante has to say about Islam. Earlier in the *Inferno*, a small group of Muslims turns up. Avicenna, Averroës, and Saladin are among those virtuous heathens who, along with Hector, Aeneas, Abraham, Socrates, Plato, and Aristotle, are confined to the first circle of the Inferno, there to suffer a minimal (and even honorable) punishment for not having had the benefit of Christian revelation. Dante, of course, admires their great virtues and accomplishments, but because they were not Christians he must condemn them, however lightly, to Hell. Eternity is a great leveler of distinctions, it is true, but the special anachronisms and anomalies of putting pre-Christian luminaries in the same category of "heathen" damnation with post-Christian Muslims does not trouble Dante. Even though the Koran specifies Jesus as a prophet, Dante chooses to consider the great Muslim philosophers and king as having been fundamentally ignorant of Christianity. That they can also inhabit the same distinguished level as the heroes and sages of classical antiquity is an ahistorical vision similar to Raphael's in his fresco *The School of Athens*, in which Averroës rubs elbows on the academy floor with Socrates and Plato (similar to Fénelon's *Dialogues des morts* [1700–18], where a discussion takes place between Socrates and Confucius).

The discriminations and refinements of Dante's poetic grasp of Islam are an instance of the schematic, almost cosmological inevitability with which Islam and its designated representatives are creatures of Western geographical, historical, and above all, moral apprehension. Empirical data about the Orient or about any of its parts count for very little; what matters and is decisive is what I have been calling the Orientalist vision, a vision by no means confined to the professional scholar, but rather the common possession of all who have thought about the Orient in the West. Dante's powers as a poet intensify, make more rather than less representative, these perspectives on the Orient. Mohammed, Saladin, Averroës, and Avicenna are fixed in a visionary cosmology – fixed, laid out, boxed in, imprisoned, without much regard for anything except their "function" and the patterns they realize on the stage on which they appear.

[T]he Orientalist attitude [. . .] shares with magic and with mythology the self-containing, self-reinforcing character of a closed system, in which objects are what they are *because* they are what they are, for once, for all time, for ontological reasons that no empirical material can either dislodge or alter. The European encounter with the Orient, and specifically with Islam, strengthened this system of representing the Orient and, as has been suggested by Henri Pirenne, turned Islam into the very epitome of an outsider against which the whole of European civilization from the Middle Ages on was founded. The decline of the Roman Empire as a result of the barbarian invasions had the paradoxical effect of incorporating barbarian ways into Roman and Mediterranean culture, Romania; whereas, Pirenne argues, the consequence of the Islamic invasions beginning in the seventh century was to move the center of European culture away from the Mediterranean, which was then an Arab province, and towards the North. "Germanism began to play its part in history. Hitherto the Roman tradition had been uninterrupted. Now an original Romano-Germanic civilization was about to develop." Europe was shut in on itself: the Orient, when it was not merely a place in which one traded, was culturally, intellectually, spiritually *outside* Europe and European civilization, which, in Pirenne's words, became "one great Christian community, coterminous with the *ecclesia*. . . . The Occident was now living its own life."[30] In Dante's poem, in the work of Peter the Venerable and other Cluniac Orientalists, in the writings of the Christian polemicists against Islam from Guibert of Nogent and Bede to Roger Bacon, William of Tripoli, Burchard of Mount Syon, and Luther, in the *Poema del Cid*, in the *Chanson de Roland*, and in Shakespeare's *Othello* (that "abuser of the world"), the Orient and Islam are always represented as outsiders having a special role to play *inside* Europe.

Imaginative geography, from the vivid portraits to be found in the *Inferno* to the prosaic niches of d'Herbelot's *Bibliothèque orientale*, legitimates a vocabulary, a universe of representative discourse peculiar to the discussion and understanding of Islam and of the Orient. What this discourse considers to be a fact – that Mohammed is an imposter, for example – is a component of the discourse, a statement the discourse compels one to make whenever the name Mohammed occurs. Underlying all the different units of Orientalist discourse – by which I mean simply the vocabulary employed whenever the Orient is spoken or written about – is a set of representative figures, or tropes. These figures are to the actual Orient – or Islam, which is my main concern here – as stylized costumes are to characters in a play; they are like, for example, the cross that Everyman will carry, or the particolored costume worn by Harlequin in a *commedia dell'arte* play. In other words, we need not look for correspondence between the language used to depict the Orient and the Orient itself, not so much because the language is inaccurate but because it is not even trying to be accurate. What it is trying to do, as Dante tried to do in the *Inferno*, is at one and the same time to characterize the Orient as alien and to incorporate it schematically on a theatrical stage whose audience, manager, and actors are *for* Europe, and only for Europe. Hence the vacillation between the familiar and the alien; Mohammed is always the imposter (familiar, because he pretends to be like the Jesus we know) and always the Oriental (alien, because although he is in some ways "like" Jesus, he is after all not like him).

Rather than listing all the figures of speech associated with the Orient – its strangeness, its difference, its exotic sensuousness, and so forth – we can geheralize about them as they were handed down through the Renaissance. They are all declarative and self-evident; the tense they employ is the timeless eternal; they convey an impression of repetition and strength; they are always symmetrical to, and yet diametrically inferior to, a European equivalent, which is sometimes specified, sometimes not. For all these functions it is frequently enough to use the simple copula *is*. Thus, Mohammed *is* an imposter, the very phrase canonized in d'Herbelot's *Bibliothèque* and dramatized in a sense by Dante. No background need be given; the evidence necessary to convict Mohammed is contained in the "is." One does not qualify the phrase, neither does it seem necessary to say that Mohammed *was* an imposter, nor need one consider for a moment that it may not be necessary to repeat the statement. It *is* repeated, he *is* an imposter, and each time one says it, he becomes more of an imposter and the author of the statement gains a little more authority in having declared it. Thus Humphrey Prideaux's famous seventeenth-century biography of Mohammed is subtitled *The True Nature of Imposture*. Finally, of course, such categories as imposter (or Oriental, for that matter) imply, indeed require, an opposite that is neither fraudulently something else nor endlessly in need of explicit identification. And that opposite is "Occidental," or in Mohammed's case, Jesus.

Philosophically, then, the kind of language, thought, and vision that I have been calling Orientalism very generally is a form of radical realism; anyone employing Orientalism, which is the habit for dealing with questions, objects, qualities, and regions deemed Oriental, will designate, name, point to, fix what he is talking or thinking about with a word or phrase, which then is considered either to have acquired, or more simply to be, reality. Rhetorically speaking, Orientalism is absolutely anatomical and enumerative: to use its vocabulary is to engage in the particularizing and dividing of things Oriental into manageable parts. Psychologically, Orientalism is a form of paranoia, knowledge of another kind, say, from ordinary historical knowledge. These are a few of the results, I think, of imaginative geography and of the dramatic boundaries it draws. [. . .]

Notes

1   R. W. Southern, *Western Views of Islam in the Middle Ages* (Cambridge, Mass.: Harvard University Press, 1962), p. 72. See also Francis Dvornik, *The Ecumenical Councils* (New York: Hawthorn Books, 1961), pp. 65–6: "Of special interest is the eleventh canon directing that chairs for teaching Hebrew, Greek, Arabic and Chaldean should be created at the main universities. The suggestion was Raymond Lull's, who advocated learning Arabic as the best means for the conversion of the Arabs. Although the canon remained almost without effect as there were few teachers of Oriental languages, its acceptance indicates the growth of the missionary idea in the West. Gregory X had already hoped for the conversion of the Mongols, and Franciscan friars had penetrated into the depths of Asia in their missionary zeal. Although these hopes were not fulfilled, the missionary spirit continued to develop." See also Johann W. Fück, *Die Arabischen Studien in Europa bis in den Anfang des 20. Jahrhunderts* (Leipzig: Otto Harrassowitz, 1955).

2   Raymond Schwab, *La Renaissance orientale* (Paris: Payot, 1950). See also V.-V. Barthold, *La Découverte de l'Asie: Histoire de l'orientalisme en Europe et en Russie*, trans. B. Nikitine (Paris: Payot, 1947), and the relevant pages in Theodor Benfey, *Geschichte der Sprachwissenschaft und Orientalischen Philologie in Deutschland* (Munich: Gottafschen, 1869). For an instructive contrast see James T. Monroe, *Islam and the Arabs in Spanish Scholarship* (Leiden: E. J. Brill, 1970).

3   Victor Hugo, *Oeuvres poétiques*, ed. Pierre Albouy (Paris: Gallimard, 1964), 1: 580.

4   Jules Mohl, *Vingt-sept Ans d'histoire des études orientales: Rapports faits à la Société asiatique de Paris de 1840 à 1867*, 2 vols. (Paris: Reinwald, 1879–80).

5   Gustave Dugat, *Histoire des orientalistes de l'Europe du XIIe au XIXe siècle*, 2 vols. (Paris: Adrien Maisonneuve, 1868–70).

6   See René Gérard, *L'Orient et la pensée romantique allemande* (Paris: Didier, 1963), p. 112.

7   V. G. Kiernan, *The Lords of Human Kind: Black Man, Yellow Man and White Man in an Age of Empire* (Boston: Little, Brown & Co., 1969), p. 131.

8   University Grants Committee, *Report of the Sub-Committee on Oriental, Slavonic, East European and African Studies* (London: Her Majesty's Stationery Office, 1961).

9   H. A. R. Gibb, *Area Studies Reconsidered* (London: School of Oriental and African Studies, 1964).

10   See Claude Lévi-Strauss, *The Savage Mind* (Chicago: University of Chicago Press, 1967), chs. 1–7.

11   Southern, *Western Views of Islam*, p. 14.

12   Aeschylus, *The Persians*, trans. Anthony J. Podleck (Englewood Cliffs, NJ: Prentice-Hall, 1970), pp. 73–4.

13   Euripides, *The Bacchae*, trans. Geoffrey S. Kirk (Englewood Cliffs, NJ: Prentice-Hall, 1970), p. 3. For further discussion of the Europe-Orient distinction see Santo Mazzarino, *Fra oriente e occidente: Ricerche di storia greca arcaica* (Florence: La Nuova Italia, 1947), and Denys Hay, *Europe: The Emergence of an Idea* (Edinburgh: Edinburgh University Press, 1968).

14   Euripides, *Bacchae*, p. 52.

15   René Grousset, *L'Empire du Levant: Histoire de la question d'Orient* (Paris: Payot, 1946).

16   Edward Gibbon, *The History of the Decline and Fall of the Roman Empire* (Boston: Little, Brown & Co., 1855), 6: 399.

17   Norman Daniel, *The Arabs and Medieval Europe* (London: Longmans, Green & Co., 1975), p. 56.

18   Samuel C. Chew, *The Crescent and the Rose: Islam and England During the Renaissance* (New York: Oxford University Press, 1937), p. 103.

19   Norman Daniel, *Islam and the West: The Making of an Image* (Edinburgh: Edinburgh University Press, 1960), p. 33. See also James Kritzeck, *Peter the Venerable and Islam* (Princeton, NJ: Princeton University Press, 1964).

20   Daniel, *Islam and the West*, p. 252.

21   Ibid., pp. 259–60.

22   See for example William Wistar Comfort, "The Literary Rôle of the Saracens in the French Epic," *PMLA*, 55 (1940): 628–59.

23   Southern, *Western Views of Islam*, pp. 91–2, 108–9.

24   Daniel, *Islam and the West*, pp. 246, 96, and *passim*.

25   Ibid., p. 84.

26   Duncan Black Macdonald, "Whither Islam?" *Muslim World*, 23 (January 1933): 2.

27   Barthold, *La Découverte de l'Asie*, pp. 137–8.

28   Barthélemy d'Herbelot, *Bibliothèque orientale, ou Dictionnaire universel con-tenant tout ce qui fait connaître les peuples de l'Orient* (The Hague: Neaulme & van Daalen, 1777), 2: 648.

29   See also Montgomery Watt, "Muhammad in the Eyes of the West," *Boston University Journal*, 22, 3 (Fall 1974): 61–9.

30   Henri Pirenne, *Mohammed and Charlemagne*, trans. Bernard Miall (New York: W. W. Norton & Co., 1939), pp. 234, 283.

2

Race, Articulation, and Societies Structured in Dominance

Stuart Hall

The aim of this paper is to mark out a set of emergent questions and problems in the study of racially structured social formations, and to indicate where some new and important initiatives are developing. In order to do this, it is necessary to situate the breaks which these studies represent from the established field of study; this, in turn, requires a crude characterization of the field. I begin with such a crude sketch, at a very general level of abstraction – offering only passing apologies for the necessary simplification involved. The attempts to deal with the question of "race" directly or to analyze those social formations where race is a salient feature constitute, by now, a formidable, immense, and varied literature, which is impossible to summarize at all adequately. No justice can be done to this complexity and achievement here.

Something important about this field of inquiry can nevertheless be grasped by dividing many of the varied tendencies represented within it into two broad dominant tendencies. Each has generated a great variety of different studies and approaches. But the selection of these two tendencies is not wholly arbitrary. In many ways, they have come to be understood as opposed to one another. As is often the case with such theoretical oppositions, they can also be understood, in many respects, as inverted mirror images of one another. Each tries to supplement the weakness of the opposing paradigm by stressing the so-called "neglected element." In doing so, each points to real weaknesses of conceptualization and indicates, symptomatically, important points of departure for more adequate theorizations. Each, however, I suggest, is inadequate within the operative terms of its present theorization. The break thus constitutes a theoretical rupture, in part or in whole, with each of these dominant tendencies, and a possible restructuring of the theoretical field such as might enable important work of a new kind to begin.

For simplification's sake, the two tendencies may be called the "economic" and the "sociological." Let us begin with the first – the economic. A great range and variety of studies must, for convenience, be bundled together under this crude heading. These include both differences of emphasis and differences of conceptualization. Thus, some studies within this tendency concentrate on internal economic structures, within specific social formations (analyses of the economic and racial structures of South Africa would be a good example). Others are more concerned with relations between internal and external economic features, however these are characterized (developed/underdeveloped; imperialist/colonized; metropolitan/satellite, etc.). Or very different ways of conceptualizing the "economic" are involved, based on radically different economic premises or frameworks. For the purposes of this paper, I shall group together within this tendency – the pertinent differences will be dealt with later – those which are framed by neoclassical "development" economics (e.g., a dual sector analysis – capitalist and subsistence sectors); those which adopt a modernization or industrialization model (e.g., based on something like Rostow's theory of "stages of growth"); those, like the "dependency" theorists of the ECLA school, utilizing a radical theory of the economics of world underdevelopment; or those like Baran or Gunder Frank, who have employed a Marxist orientation (how classical it remains, as shall be seen, is a matter of continuing controversy). What allows of a characterization of these very different approaches as belonging to a single tendency is simply this: they take economic relations and structures to have an overwhelmingly determining effect on the social structures of such formations. Specifically, those social divisions which assume a distinctively racial or ethnic character can be attributed or explained principally with reference to economic structures and processes.

The second approach I have called sociological. Here again – rather tendentiously – a great variety of approaches are placed under a single rubric. Some concentrate on social relations between different racial or ethnic strata. Some deal more exclusively with cultural differences (ethnicity), of which race is only one, extreme case. Some pursue a more rigorously plural theory, derived from Furnivall and M. G. Smith and others of that school. Some are exclusively concerned with forms of political domination or disadvantage, based on the exploitation of racial distinctions. In the vast majority of these studies, race is treated as a social category. Biological conceptions of race have greatly receded in importance, though they have by no means wholly disappeared (for example: the revival of bio-sociology, and the reintroduction of biologically based theories, through the genetic principle, in the recent work of Jensen and Eysenck). The principal stress in this second tendency is on race or ethnicity as specifically social or cultural features of the social formations under discussion.

Again, what distinguishes the contributors to this school as belonging – for the purposes here alone – to a single tendency, is this: however they differ internally, the contributors to the sociological tendency agree on the autonomy, the nonreductiveness, of race and ethnicity as social features. These exhibit, they argue, their own forms of structuration, have their own specific effects, which cannot be explained away as mere surface forms of appearance of economic relations, nor adequately theorized by reducing them to the economic level of determination.

Here it can be seen how the two paradigms have been counterposed to one another, each correcting the weakness of its opposite. The first tendency, whether Marxist or not, gives an overall determinacy to the economic level. This, it is said, imparts a hard center – a materialist basis – to the otherwise soft-centeredness or culturalism of ethnic studies. The stress on the sociological aspects, in the second tendency, is then a sort of direct reply to this first emphasis. It aims to introduce a necessary complexity into the simplifying schemas of an economic explanation, and to correct against the tendency of the first towards economic reductionism. Social formations, the second tendency argues, are complex ensembles, composed of several different structures, none of which is reducible to the other. Thus, whereas the former tends to be monocausal in form, the latter tends to be pluralist in emphasis, even if it is not explicitly plural in the theoretical sense.

It will be seen that this debate reproduces, in micro, the larger, strategic debates which have marked out the field of social science in general in recent years. Consequently, developments in the latter, larger, field – whether they take racially structured social formations as their specific objects of inquiry or not – are bound to have theoretical effects for that region of study. Hence, the consequences of such breaks in the paradigms for the "sociological theories of race." The debate is not, however, exclusively a theoretical one. Differences of theoretical analysis and approach have real effects for the strategies of political transformation in such societies. If the first tendency is broadly correct, then what is often experienced and analyzed as ethnic or racial conflicts are really manifestations of deeper, economic contradictions. It is, therefore, to the latter that the politics of transformations must essentially be addressed. The second tendency draws attention to the actual forms and dynamic of political conflict and social tension in such societies – which frequently assume a racial or ethnic character. It points to the empirical difficulty of subsuming these directly into more classical economic conflicts. But if ethnic relations are not reducible to economic relations, then the former will not necessarily change if and when the latter do. Hence, in a political struggle, the former must be given their due specificity and weight as autonomous factors. Theory here, as always, has direct or indirect practical consequences.

Political circumstances – while not sufficient to account for the scientific value of these theories – also provide one of the conditions of existence for theory, and have effects for its implementation and appropriation. This has clearly been the case, even if restricted (as is done for a good section of this paper) primarily to Latin America and the Caribbean. The dual sector model – based on an export-led, import-substitution, foreign investment supported type of economic development – sponsored a long and disastrous period of national economic development, which further undermined the economic position of one country after another in the region. The theory of modernization was for long the economic cutting-edge of alliance-for-progress strategies in the continent. Versions of the "dependency" school have been harnessed, under different conditions, to the promotion of anti-imperialist, national-capitalist development of a radical type. The metropolitan/satellite theories of Gunder Frank and others were specifically developed in the context of the Cuban revolution and the strategies of Latin-American revolution elaborated in OLAS – represented, for example, in the resolutions to the 1962 Second Declaration of Havana. The whole field, indeed, provides an excellent case study of the necessary interconnexions between theory, politics, and ideology in social science.

Each tendency exhibits something of its own rational core. Thus, it may not be possible to explain away race by reference to the economic relations exclusively. But the first tendency is surely correct when it insists that racial structures cannot be understood adequately outside the framework of quite specific sets of economic relations. Unless one attributes to race a single, unitary, transhistorical character – such that wherever and whenever it appears it always assumes the same autonomous features, which can be theoretically explained, perhaps, by some general theory of prejudice in human nature (an essentialist argument of a classic type) – then one must deal with the historical specificity of race in the modern world. Here one is then obliged to agree that race relations are directly linked with economic processes: historically, with the epochs of conquest, colonization, and mercantilist domination, and currently, with the "unequal exchanges" which characterize the economic relations between developed metropolitical and "underdeveloped" satellite economic regions of the world economy. The problem here is not whether economic structures are relevant to racial divisions but how the two are theoretically connected. Can the economic level provide an adequate and sufficient level of explanation of the racial features of these social formations? Here, the second tendency enters its caveat. Similarly, the second tendency is surely correct to draw attention to the specificity of those social formations which exhibit distinctive racial or ethnic charactistics. The critique of economic reductionism is also, certainly, to the point. The problem here is to account for the appearance of this "something else" – these extra-economic factors and their place in the dynamic reproduction of such social formations. But these "real problems" also help us to identify what weaknesses are obscured by the inversions which each paradigm practices on the other. If the dominant tendency of the first paradigm is to attempt to command all differences and specificities within the framework of a simplifying economic logic, then that of the second is to stop short with a set of plural explanations which lack an adequate theorization, and which in the end are descriptive rather than analytic. This, of course, is to state the differences in their sharpest, and most oversimplified form. [. . .]

[By contrast,] the emergent theory of the "articulation of different modes of production" begins to deliver certain pertinent theoretical effects for an analysis of racism at the social, political, and ideological levels. It begins to deliver such effects – and this is the crucial point – not by deserting the level of analysis of economic relations (i.e., mode of production) but by posing it in its correct, necessarily complex, form. Of course, this may be a necessary, but not a sufficient starting point. [. . .]

The level of economic analysis, so redefined, may not supply sufficient conditions in itself for an explanation of the emergence and operation of racism. But, at least, it provides a better, sounder point of departure than those approaches which are obliged to desert the economic level, in order to produce "additional factors" which explain the origin and appearance of racial structuring at other levels of the social formation. In this respect, at least, the theoretical advances briefly outlined here have the merit of respecting what we would call two cardinal premises of Marx's "method." The materialist premise – that the analysis of political and ideological structures must be grounded in their material conditions of existence; and the historical premise – that the specific forms of these relations cannot be deduced, *a priori*, from this level but must be made historically specific "by supplying those further delineations which explain their *differentiae sp.*" Both premises are well expressed in one of the most justly famous passages from *Capital*: "The specific economic form, in which unpaid labour-surplus is pumped out of direct producers, determines the relationship of rulers and ruled, as it grows directly out of production itself and, in turn, reacts upon it as a determining element. Upon this, however, is founded the entire formation of the economic community which grows up out of the production relations themselves, thereby simultaneously its specific political form . . ." (the materialist premise). But "This does not prevent the same economic basis – the same from the standpoint of its main conditions – due to innumerable different empirical circumstances, natural environments, racial relations, external historical influences, etc., from showing infinite variations and gradations in appearance, which can be ascertained only by analysis of the empirically given circumstances" (the historical premise), (Marx, 1974, pp. 791–2). Both premises are indeed required, if the conditions of theoretical adequacy are to be met: each, on its own, is not sufficient. The first, without the second, may lead us straight back into the *impasse* of economic reductionism; the second, without the first, snares us in the toils of historical relativism. Marx's method, properly understood and applied, provides us with the conditions – though not, of course, the guarantee – of a theoretical adequacy which avoids both. [. . .]

The term articulation is a complex one, variously employed and defined in the literature here referred to. No clear consensus of conceptual definition can be said to have emerged so far. Yet it remains the site of a significant theoretical rupture (*coupure*) and intervention. This is the intervention principally associated with the work of Althusser and the "school" of structuralist Marxism. The term is widely employed, in a range of contexts, especially in the *For Marx* essays, and the succeeding volume, with Balibar, in *Reading Capital* (1965; 1970). At least two different applications are particularly relevant to our concerns here (though, interestingly, the term is not defined in the "Glossary," prepared by Ben Brewster and sanctioned by Althusser himself, which appeared in the English editions of both books). Aside from these particular usages, the term has a wider reference of both a theoretical and a methodological nature.

Foster-Carter correctly suggests that it is a metaphor used "to indicate relations of linkage and effectivity between different levels of all sorts of things" – though he might have added that these things require to be linked because, though connected, they are not the same. The unity which they form is thus not that of an identity, where one structure perfectly recapitulates or reproduces or even "expresses" another; or where each is reducible to the other; or where each is defined by the same determinations or have exactly the same conditions of existence; or even where each develops according to the effectivity of the same conditions of existence; or even where each develops according to the effectivity of the same contradiction (e.g., the "principal contradiction" so beloved, as the warrant and guarantee of all arguments, by so-called "orthodox" Marxists). The unity formed by this combination or articulation is always, necessarily, a "complex structure": a structure in which things are related, as much through their differences as through their similarities. This requires that the mechanisms which connect dissimilar features must be shown – since no "necessary correspondence" or expressive homology can be assumed as given. It also means – since the combination is a structure (an articulated combination) and not a random association – that there will be structured relations between its parts, i.e., relations of dominance and subordination. Hence, in Althusser's cryptic phrase, a "complex unity, structured in dominance."

Many of the classic themes of the Althusserian intervention are resumed in and through his various uses of this term: for example, his argument that Marx's "unity" is not the essentialist "expressive unity" to be found in Hegel, and that, therefore, Marx's dialectic is not merely an inversion, but a theoretical advance over Hegel. This is the critique against conceiving Marx's "totality" as an "expressive totality," which grounds Althusser's early critique of the attempts to rescue Marx's work from "vulgar materialism" by way of a detour through Hegelianism (see Althusser's *For Marx*, especially the chapter "On the Marxian dialectic"). It also founds Althusser's critique of the attempt to read Marx as if he meant that all the structures of a social formation could be reduced to an "expression" of the economic base; or as if all the instances of any historical conjuncture moved in a relation of direct correspondence with the terms of the "principal contradiction" (that of the "base," between forces and relations of production) – this is Althusser's critique (the opposite of that against Hegelian idealism) against "economic reductionism." Marx's "complex unity," Althusser argues, is neither that in which everything perfectly expresses or corresponds to everything else; nor that in which everything is reducible to an expression of "the Economic." It operates, instead, on the terrain of articulation. What we find, in any particular historical conjuncture (his example, in "Contradiction and overdetermination" in *For Marx*, is Russia, 1917) is not the unrolling of the "principal contradiction," evenly, throughout all the other levels of the social formation, but, in Lenin's terms, the "merger," "rupture," condensation of contradictions, each with its own specificity and periodization – "absolutely dissimilar currents, absolutely heterogeneous class interests, absolutely contrary political and social strivings" – which have "merged . . . in a strikingly 'harmonious' manner" (Lenin, *Letters from Afar*, No. 1). Such conjunctures are not so much "determined" as overdetermined, i.e., they are the product of an articulation of contradictions, not directly reduced to one another.

Althusser and Balibar, then, employ this general theoretical concept in a variety of different contexts. They conceive of a social formation as composed of a number of instances – each with a degree of "relative autonomy" from one another – articulated into a (contradictory) unity. The economic instance or level, itself, is the result of such a "combination": the articulation between forces and relations of production. In particular social formations, especially in periods of "transition," social formations themselves may be an "articulated combination" of different modes with specified, shifting terms of hierarchical ordering between them. The term also figures in the Althusserian epistemology, which insists that knowledge and the production of knowledge are not directly produced, as an empiricist reflection of the real "in thought" but have a specificity and autonomy of their own – thought, "established on and articulated to the real world of a given historical society" (Althusser and Balibar, 1970, p. 42). The scientific analysis of any specific social formation depends on the correct grasping of its principle of articulation: the "fits" between different instances, different periods and epochs, indeed different periodicities, e.g., times, histories. The same principle is applied, not only synchronically, between instances and periodizations within any "moment" of a structure, but also, diachronically, between different "moments." This connects with Althusser's objections to the notion of a given and necessary sequence of stages, with a necessary progression built into them. He insists on the nonteleological reading of Marx, on the notion of "a discontinuous succession of modes of production" (Althusser and Balibar, 1970, p. 204), whose combined succession – i.e., articulation through time – requires to be demonstrated. Indeed, "scientificity" itself is associated with "the problem of the forms of variation of the articulation" of the instances in every social structure (Althusser and Balibar, 1970, p. 207). The same is said of the relations between the economic and the political and ideological forms of their appearance. This, too, is thought on the analogy of an articulation between structures which do not directly express or mirror each other. Hence, the classical problem for Marxism – the problem of determinancy of the structure, the "determination in the last instance by the economic" (which distinguishes Marxism from other types of social scientific explanation) – is itself redefined as a problem of "articulation." What is "determined" is not the inner form and appearance of each level, but the mode of combination and the placing of each instance in an articulated relation to the other elements. It is this "articulation of the structure" as the global effect of the structure itself – or what has been called, by Balibar, the "matrix role of the mode of production" – which defines the Althusserian concept of determination: as a structural causality (Althusser and Balibar, 1970, p. 220). It is this conception, on the other hand, which has provided the basis for the critique by Hindess and Hirst (1975) of Althusser's "determinacy of articulation by the structure" as, itself, an "expressive totality" – a Spinozian eternity. Dealing with the example of the relation between feudal ground rent and the feudal relation of lordship and servitude, Balibar treats it as a reduced instance of the articulation of *two* different instances, an "economic" instance and a "political" instance. Likewise, Balibar defines the concept of mode of production as, itself, the result of a variant combination of elements (object of labor, means of labor, labor-power). What changes, in each epoch, is not the elements, which are invariant (in the definitional sense), but the way they are combined: their articulation. While it is not possible to "tell" the whole of the Althusserian intervention through the terms of a single concept, like articulation, it must be by now apparent that the concept has a wide and extensive reference in the works of the structuralist Marxists.

Though we cannot go into the theoretical and methodological background to the emergence of the concept, we can at least note, in passing, two pertinent provenances. The first is that of structuralist linguistics, which provided the master-model of a substantial part of the whole "structuralist" venture. Saussure, the "founder" of this school, who argued that language is not a reflection of the world but produces meaning through the articulation of linguistic systems upon real relations, insists that meaning is no mere "correlation between signifier and signified, but perhaps more essentially àn act of simultaneously cutting out two amorphous masses, two 'floating kingdoms' . . . language is the domain of *articulations*" (Barthes, 1967). More pertinent, perhaps, is the warrant which Althusser and others have found, in Marx's most extensive "methodological" text – the 1857 *Introduction to the Grundrisse* – for a theory of the social formation as what Marx himself calls an "articulated hierarchy" (*Gliederung*) – or, as Althusser translates him, "an organic hierarchized whole." "In all forms of society," Marx wrote, "it is a determinate production and its relations which assign every other production and its relations their rank and influence" (Marx, 1973). If this represents a slender warrant for the construction of the whole structuralist edifice, it is certainly clear that, in the text, Marx was decisively opposing himself to any notion of a simple identity between the different relations of capital (production, circulation, exchange, consumption). He spoke, at length, of the complexity of determinations between these relations, the sum of whose articulations, nevertheless, provided him (in this text) with the object of his inquiry (adequately constructed in a theoretical sense); and, in *Capital*, with the key to the unraveling of the necessarily complex nature of the relations between the different circuits operating within the capitalist mode (cf. Hall, 1973). This is the real burden of Marx's extensive criticisms in the 1857 *Introduction* against treating the different relations which compose the capitalist mode as a "regular syllogism" – an "immediate identity." "To regard society as one single subject is . . . to look at it wrongly; speculatively." "The conclusion we reach is not that production, distribution, exchange and consumption are identical, but that they all form the members of a totality of distinctions within a unity" (Marx, 1973). In the same way, there seems to be a clear warning issued against any simple notion of an evolutionary sequence or succession of stages in that development: "Their sequence is determined, rather, by their relation to one another in modern bourgeois society, which is precisely the opposite of that which seems to be their natural order or which corresponds to historical development. The point is not the historic position of the economic relations in the succession of different forms of society." This last point indicates what we would want to call (in addition to those already signaled) the third premise of Marx's method: the structural premise. It is, above all, the employment of the structural premise in the later, mature work of Marx, and the manner in which this has been appropriated and developed by Althusser and the structuralists, which produces, as one of its theoretical results, the extensive-intensive concept of articulation.

The term itself is by no means unproblematic, indicating here a certain approach, rather than providing in itself a theoretical resolution to the problems it indexes. It has been subjected to a searching critique. In itself, the term has an ambiguous meaning, for, in English, it can mean both "joining up" (as in the limbs of the body, or an anatomical structure) and "giving expression to" (cf. Foster-Carter, 1978). In Althusserian usage, it is primarily the first sense which is intended. There are, in any case, theoretical objections to the notion that one structure "gives expression to" another: since this would be tantamount to seeing the second structure as an epiphenomenon of the first (i.e., a reductionist conception), and would involve treating a social formation as an "expressive totality" – precisely the object of Althusser's initial critique of Hegelianism. Some notion of an "expressive" line – say, between the economic and political structures of a society – remains, even in Althusserian usage, but this is elaborated by other terms which break up or break into any residual sense of a perfect and necessary "correspondence." Thus, in addition to insisting on the specificity, the nonreductiveness, the "relative autonomy," of each level of the society, Althusser always uses such terms as "displacement," "dislocation," "condensation," in order to demonstrate that the "unity" which these different relations form is not univocal, but misleads through "overdetermination." Another criticism, then, is that the concept of "articulation" may simply leave two dissimilar things yoked together by a mere external or arbitrary connexion: what Marx once called "independent, autonomous neighbours . . . not grasped in their unity" (Marx, 1973, p. 90). Althusser attempts to overcome this "mere juxtaposition" by using the concept of "overdetermination," and by always speaking of "articulation" as involving hierarchical as well as lateral relations, i.e., relations of dominance and subordination (cf. Marx's discussion of money in different historical epochs, which does not "wade its way through all economic relations" but is defined by where it plays a "dominant" or a "subordinate" role). This, however, leads on to other criticisms. The schema, constructed around articulation, has, often with justice, been described as too "formalist." Thus, in the full-blown "structural causality" of Althusser and Balibar's *Reading Capital*, the "economic" determines "in the last instance" not substantively but principally by "giving the index of effectivity" in the structure to one or another level: i.e., in a *formal* way. (But Althusser retreats from some of these more formalist excesses (Althusser, 1976).) While the whole attempt to develop such an analysis is predicated on the need for an approach which is not reductive, it has been criticized as giving rise to a conception of "structure" which – since it contains within itself all the conditions of its own functioning – is itself that "expressive totality" which Althusser seeks to avoid (cf. Hindess and Hirst, 1975; Hirst, 1977). The framework is also open to the criticism that it leaves the internal elements of any "structural combination" unchanged, with change or transition being limited to the variations (different articulations) through which the "invariant elements" are combined. This weakens the historicity of the approach – contravening what we have called the historical premise of Marx's work (but again see Althusser, 1976). This notion of the variation between invariant elements has resulted in a very formalist way of defining a "mode of production" (following, especially, Balibar): so that some of the real advances made in attempting to ground analysis in a more developed and sophisticated understanding of modes of production and their combination can easily be vitiated by a sort of formalist hunt for one, separate, "mode of production" after another. Nevertheless, we would continue to insist on the potentially generative value of the term and its cognate concepts, which give us a start in thinking the complex unity and *differentiae specificae* of social formations, without falling back on a naive or "vulgar materialist" reductionism, on the one hand, or a form of sociological pluralism on the other.

So far, I have been speaking, exclusively, of the application of the term "articulation" to the economic structure of complex social formations. But I have also said that the social formation itself can be analyzed as an "articulated hierarchy." At the economic level, this may involve the articulation of a social formation around more than one mode of production. Some of the political and ideological features of such societies can then be explained with reference to this particular combination. But it is also possible to conceptualize the different levels of a social formation as an articulated hierarchy. Since we must assume no "necessary correspondence" – no perfect replication, homology of structures, expressive connexion – between these different levels, but are nevertheless required to "think" the relations between them as an "ensemble of relations" (marked by what Marx in his 1857 *Introduction*, when dealing with these issues, defined as the "law of uneven development") – then it is, once more, to the nature of the articulations between them to which we must turn. The attention – of a more detailed and analytic kind – to the nature of modes of production helps to ground these other aspects of the social formation more adequately at the level of the economic structures (the materialist premise). However, we cannot thereby deduce *a priori* the relations and mechanisms of the political and ideological structures (where such features as racism make a decisive reappearance) exclusively from the level of the economic. The economic level is the necessary but not sufficient condition for explaining the operations at other levels of the society (the premise of nonreductionism). We cannot assume an express relation of "necessary correspondence" between them (the premise of historical specificity). These are, as Marx put it, "a product of historical relations and possess their full validity only for and within these relations." This is an important, indeed a critical, qualification. It requires us to demonstrate – rather than to assume, *a priori* – what the nature and degree of "correspondence" is, in any specific historical case. Thus, through this opening, some of the criticisms which, as was noted earlier, are made from the perspective of "sociological" explanations – for example the requirement to be historically specific – begin to be met, within the framework of this seminal revision.

Here, however, different positions within the general problematic of "articulation" can be identified. Some theorists argue that all we can do is to deal with each level, in terms of its own specificity, and the "conditions of existence" which must be fulfilled for it to function (e.g., the economic relations of the capitalist mode require, as a condition of exis-tence, some extra-economic, juridical framework, which secures the "contract" between buyer and seller of labor power). But, it is argued, the internal forms and specificities of the extra-economic levels can neither be prescribed nor identified from the economic level which "requires it," as a formal necessity of its functioning. This is tantamount to a theory of the "autonomy" (not "relative autonomy") of the differ-ent levels (Hirst, 1977; Cutler, et al., 1977). This, however, fails to deal with social formations as a "complex unity" (Marx's "unity of many determinations"). [. . .]

Where, then, the relations between the different levels of a social for-mation are concerned, one needs additional concepts, i.e., to supply further determinations, to those which have been mobilized for the a-nalysis of the economic "mode of production" levels. And one needs to acknowledge that the economic level, alone, cannot prescribe what those levels will be like and how they will operate – even if their mech-anisms are not fully specifiable without attending to the level of the eco-nomic. Here, the work of Althusser and of the "Althusserians" – for example, Poulantzas's work on "the State" – requires to be supple-mented by the work of another Marxist theorist whose elaboration, at this level, constitutes a contribution to the development of a rigorously nonreductionist Marxism of the very first importance. This is the work of Gramsci. Gramsci's work is more fragmentary (much of it written in prison, under the eyes of the censor, in one of Mussolini's jails), far less "theorized" than that of Althusser. Gramsci has been formative for the development of Althusser's problematic: though, since in certain respects Gramsci remained a "historicist," the relationship between Althusser and Gramsci is a complex one. In a recent review of this rela-tionship, we have expressed it in terms of Gramsci providing the "limit case" of historicity for Marxist structuralism (Hall et al., 1977).

We cannot elaborate in any depth, here, on Gramsci's concepts (for a review, see: Hall et al., 1977; Anderson, 1977; Mouffe, 1978). The central concept in his work is that of hegemony. Hegemony is that state of "total social authority" which, at certain specific conjunctures, a specific class alliance wins, by a combination of "coercion" and "consent," over the whole social formation, and its dominated classes: not only at the economic level, but also at the level of political and ide-ological leadership, in civil, intellectual, and moral life as well as at the material level: and over the terrain of civil society as well as in and through the condensed relations of the State. This "authority and leadership" is, for Gramsci, not a given *a priori* but a specific historical "moment" – one of unusual social authority. It represents the product of a certain mastery of the class struggle, certainly, but it is still subject to the class struggle and the "relations of social forces" in society, of which its "unstable equilibrium" is only one, provisional, outcome or result. Hegemony is a state of play in the class struggle which has, therefore, to be continually worked on and reconstructed in order to be maintained, and which remains a contradictory conjuncture. The important point, for Gramsci, is that, under hegemonic conditions, the organization of consent (by the dominated classes to the "leadership" of the dominant class alliance) takes precedence (though it does not obliterate) the exercise of domination through coercion. In such conditions, the class struggle tends to assume the form, not of a "frontal assault" on the bastions of the State ("war of maneuver") but of a more protracted, strategic, and tactical struggle, exploiting and working on a number of different contradictions (Gramsci's "war of position"). A state of hegemony enables the ruling class alliance to undertake the enormous task of modifying, harnessing, securing, and elaborating the "superstructure" of society in line with the long-term requirements of the development of the mode of production – e.g., capital accumulation on an expanded scale. It enables such a class alliance to undertake the educative and formative tasks of raising the whole social formation to what he calls a "new level of civilization," favoring the expanded regime of capital. This is no immediate and direct imposition of the narrow, short-term, "corporate" class interests of a single class on society. It forges that unity between economic, political, and ideological objectives such that it can place "all the questions around which the struggle rages on a 'universal' not a corporative level, thereby creating a hegemony of a fundamental social group over a series of subordinate groups." This is what Gramsci calls the "educative and formative role of the State. . . . Its aim is always that of creating new and higher types of civilization; of adapting the 'civilization' and the morality of the broadest popular masses to the necessities of the continuous development of the economic apparatus of production" – the formation of a "national-popular will," based on a particular relationship between the dominant and dominated classes. This, then, depends, not on a presumed, necessary, or *a priori* correspondence between (economic) structure and (political and ideological) superstructures but precisely on those historically specific mechanisms – and the concrete analysis of those historical "moments" – through which such a formative relationship *between* structure and superstructures comes to be forged. For Gramsci, the object of analysis is always the specificity of this "structure–superstructure" complex – though as a historically concrete articulation. "It is the problem of the relations between structure and superstructure which must be accurately posed and resolved if the forces which are active in history . . . are to be correctly analysed." This is a rigorously nonreductionist conception: "How then could the whole system of superstructures be understood as distinctions within politics, and the introduction of the concept of distinction into a philosophy of praxis hence be justified? But can one really speak of a dialectic of distincts, and how is the concept of a circle joining the levels of the superstructure to be understood? Concept of 'historical bloc', i.e., . . . unity of opposites and distincts. Can one introduce the criterion of distinction into the structure too?" Gramsci, clearly, answers these questions in the affirmative. He is especially sharp against any form of vulgar economism: "It is therefore necessary to combat economism not only in the theory of historiography, but also and especially in the theory and practice of politics. In this field, the struggle can and must be carried on by developing the concept of hegemony." (All the quotes are from two essays in Gramsci, 1971.)

Gramsci's theoretical contribution has only begun, recently, to be recognized – though his role as an outstanding militant in Italian politics in the 1920s and 1930s has long been acknowledged. His analysis bears, in a specially rich and productive way, on the analysis of the great bourgeois social formations of a developed capitalist type in Europe – Western Europe, where a reductionist economistic analysis, clearly, will not suffice to account for the depth of the transformations involved. Perhaps for this very reason, he has been thought of as, *par excellence*, the Marxist theorist of "Western capitalism." His work has, therefore, hardly been applied or employed in the analysis of non-European formations. There are, however, very strong grounds for thinking that it may have particular relevance for non-European social formations – for three, separate reasons. First, Gramsci may help to counteract the overwhelming weight of economism (Marxist and non-Marxist) which has characterized the analysis of post-Conquest and "colonial" societies. Perhaps because the weight of imperialist economic relations has been so powerfully visible, these formations have virtually been held to be explainable by an application of "imperialism" as essentially a purely "economic" process. Second, these societies present problems as to the relation in the "structure–superstructure complex" equal in complexity to those about which Gramsci wrote. Naturally, no simple transfer of concepts would be advisable here: Gramsci would be the first to insist on historical specificity, on difference. Third, Gramsci viewed the problem of "hegemony" from within the specific history of the Italian social formation. This gave him a particular, and highly relevant, perspective on the problem. For long periods Italy was marked precisely by the absence of "hegemony": by an alliance of ruling classes governing through domination rather than through hegemonic class leadership (direction). So his work is equally relevant for societies in which, according to the rhythm and punctuation of the class struggle, there have been significant movements into and out of a phase of "hegemonic direction." Moreover, Italy was/is a society brutally marked by the law of uneven development: with massive industrial capitalist development to the North, massive underdevelopment to the South. This raises the question of how the contradictions of the Italian social formation are articulated through different modes of production (capitalist and feudal), and through class alliances which combine elements from different social orders. The problem of the State, and the question of strategic alliances between the industrial proletariat and the peasantry, the "play" of traditional and advanced ideologies, and the difficulties these provide in the formation of a "national-popular will" all make his analysis of Italy specially relevant to colonial societies.

Gramsci's work has recently been taken up and developed in a structuralist manner – especially in Althusser's essay on "Ideological State Apparatuses" (Althusser, 1971). This seminal essay differs from Gramsci's work, specifically, in posing the problem in terms of "reproduction." But the concerns which underlie this approach are not all that distant from those of Gramsci. The economic relations of production must themselves be "reproduced." This reproduction is not simply economic, but social, technical, and, above all, ideological. This is another way of putting Gramsci's observation that, to achieve its full development, capitalist social relations require to be coupled with an elaborate development and elaboration at the "noneconomic" levels of politics, civil society, and culture, through moral, intellectual, and ideological leadership. Althusser then shares with Gramsci a classical concern for the manner in which the "hegemony" of a ruling class alliance is secured, at these other levels, through a formative and educative class leadership or authority over the social formation as a whole. Both of them argue that this enlarged or expanded hegemony is specific to the institutions, apparatuses, and relations of the so-called "superstructures" of the State and civil society. Both Althusser and Gramsci, then, insist that ideology, while itself a contradictory site and stake in the class struggle, has a specific function in securing the conditions for the expanded reproduction of capital. It is, therefore, a pertinent, and distinctive level of struggle, where leadership is secured and contested: with mechanisms and sites of struggle "relatively autonomous." Both also maintain that "ideology" is not a simple form of false consciousness, to be explained as a set of myths or simple false constructions in the head. All societies require specific ideologies, which provide those systems of meaning, concepts, categories, and representations which make sense of the world, and through which men come to "live" (albeit unconsciously, and through a series of "misrecognitions"), in an imaginary way, their relation to the real, material conditions of their existence (which are only representable to them, as modes of consciousness, in and through ideology). Althusser sometimes tends to represent ideology as rather too functionally secured to the rule of the dominant classes: as if all ideology is, by definition, operative within the horizon of the "dominance ideas" of the ruling class. For Gramsci, ideologies are thought of in a more contradictory way – really, as sites and stakes in the class struggle. What interests Gramsci is how the existing ideologies – the "common sense" of the fundamental classes – which are themselves the complex result of previous moments and resolutions in the ideological class struggle, can be so actively *worked upon* so as to transform them into the basis of a more conscious struggle, and form of intervention in the historical process. Both insist, however, that ideologies are not simply "in the head," but are material relations – what Lenin called "ideological social relations" – which shape social actions, function through concrete institutions and apparatuses, and are materialized through practices. Gramsci insists on the process which transforms these great "practical ideologies" of fundamental social classes. Althusser, for his part, adds that ideologies operate by constituting concrete individuals as the "social subjects" of ideological discourses – the process of what, following Laclau, he calls "interpellating subjects." [See Althusser, 1971.] [. . .]

These theorists begin to give us the tentative elements by means of which we can attempt to construct a non-reductionist theory of the superstructural or extra-economic aspects of social formations – once again, powered through the use of the concept of articulation.

What I have tried to do in this paper is to document the emergence of a new theoretical paradigm, which takes its fundamental orientation from the problematic of Marx's, but which seeks, by various theoretical means, to overcome certain of the limitations – economism, reductionism, "a priorism," a lack of historical specificity – which have beset certain traditional appropriations of Marxism, which still disfigure the contributions to this field by otherwise distinguished writers, and which have left Marxism vulnerable and exposed to effective criticism by many different variants of economistic monism and sociological pluralism. This is a survey of an emergent field, not a comprehensive critical account. It must in no sense be assumed that the solutions attempted have been fully demonstrated, or that they are as yet adequately developed or without serious weaknesses and lacunae. With respect to those racially structured social formations, which form the principal objects of inquiry in this collection, the problematic has hardly begun to be applied. Thus all that I have been able to do is to indicate certain strategic points of departure in such a potential field of application, certain protocols of theoretical procedure. Specifically, there is as yet no adequate theory of racism which is capable of dealing with both the economic and the superstructural features of such societies, while at the same time giving a historically concrete and sociologically specific account of distinctive racial aspects. Such an account, sufficient to substitute those inadequate versions which continue to dominate the field, remains to be provided. Nevertheless, in the hope of sponsoring and promoting such a development, it might be useful to conclude with a brief outline of some of the theoretical protocols which – in my view, of necessity – must govern any such proposed investigation.

This would have to begin from a rigorous application of what I have called the premise of historical specificity. Racism is not dealt with a s a general feature of human societies, but with historically specific racisms. Beginning with an assumption of difference, of specificity rather than of a unitary, transhistorical or universal "structure." This is not to deny that there might well be discovered to be certain common features to all those social systems to which one would wish to attribute the designation, "racially structured." But – as Marx remarked about the "chaotic" nature of all abstractions which proceed at the level of the "in-general" exclusively – such a general theory of racism is not the most favorable source for theoretical development and investigation: "even though the most developed languages have laws and characteristics in common with the least developed, nevertheless, just those things which determine their development, i.e., the elements which are *not* general and common, must be separated out . . . so that in their unity . . . their essential difference is not forgotten" (Marx, 1973). Racism in general is a "rational abstraction" in so far as "it really brings out and fixes the common element and saves us repetition." Thus it may help to distinguish those social features which fix the different positions of social groups and classes on the basis of racial ascription (biologically or socially defined) from other systems which have a similar social function. However, "some determinations belong to all epochs, others only to a few. Some will be shared by the most modern epoch and the most ancient." This is a warning against extrapolating a common and universal structure to racism, which remains essentially the same, outside of its specific historical location. It is only as the different racisms are historically specified – in their difference – that they can be properly understood as "a product of historical relations and possess . . . full validity only for and within those relations." It follows that there might be more to be learned from distinguishing what, in common sense, appear to be variants of the same thing: for example, the racism of the slave South from the racism of the insertion of blacks into the "free forms" of industrial-capitalist development in the post-bellum North; or the racism of Caribbean slave societies from that of the metropolitan societies like Britain, which have had to absorb black workers into industrial production in the twentieth century.

In part, this must be because one cannot explain racism in abstraction from other social relations – even if, alternatively, one cannot explain it by reducing it to those relations. It has been said that there are flourishing racisms in precapitalist social formations. This only means that, when dealing with more recent social formations, one is required to show how thoroughly racism is reorganized and rearticulated with the relations of new modes of production. Racism within plantation slave societies in the mercantilist phase of world capitalist development has a place and function, means and mechanisms of its specific effectivity, which are only superficially explained by translating it out from these specific historical contexts into totally different ones. Finley (1969), Davis (1969, 1970), and others have argued that, though slavery in the Ancient World was articulated through derogatory classifications which distinguished between the enslaved and enslaving peoples, it did not necessarily entail the use of specifically racial categories, whilst plantation slavery almost everywhere did. Thus, there can be no assumed, necessary coincidence between racism and slavery as such. Precisely the differences in the roles which slavery played in these very different epochs and social formations may point us to the necessary ground for specifying what this specific coincidence between slavery and racism might secure. Where this coincidence does in fact appear, the mechanisms and effectivity of its functioning – including its articulation with other relations – need to be demonstrated, not assumed.

Again, the common assumption that it was attitudes of racial superiority which precipitated the introduction of plantation slavery needs to be challenged. It might be better to start from the opposite end – by seeing how slavery (the product of specific problems of labor shortage and the organization of plantation agriculture – supplied, in the first instance, by nonblack, indigenous labor, and then by white indentured labor) produced those forms of juridical racism which distinguish the epoch of plantation slavery. The elaboration of the juridical and property forms of slavery, as a set of enclaves within societies predicated on other legal and property forms, required specific and elaborate ideological work – as the history of slavery, and of its abolition, eloquently testifies. The same point may be made, *in extenso*, for all those explanations which ascribe racism-in-general to some universal functioning of individual psychology – the "racial itch," the "race instinct" – or explain its appearance in terms of a general psychology of prejudice. The question is not whether men-in-general make perceptual distinctions between groups with different racial or ethnic characteristics, but rather, what are the specific conditions which make this form of distinction socially pertinent, historically active? What gives this abstract human potentiality its effectivity, as a concrete material force? It could be said, for example, that Britain's long imperial hegemony, and the intimacy of the relationship between capitalist development at home and colonial conquest overseas, laid the trace of an active racism in British popular consciousness. Nevertheless, this alone cannot explain either the form and function which racism assumed, in the period of "popular imperialism" at the height of the imperialist rivalry towards the end of the nineteenth century, or the very different forms of indigenous racism, penetrating deep into the working class itself, which has been an emergent feature of the contact between black and white workers in the conditions of post-war migration. The histories of these different racisms cannot be written as a "general history" (Hall, 1978; Hall et al., 1978). Appeals to "human nature" are not explanations, they are an alibi.

One must start, then, from the concrete historical "work" which racism accomplishes under specific historical conditions – as a set of economic, political, and ideological practices, of a distinctive kind, concretely articulated with other practices in a social formation. These practices ascribe the positioning of different social groups in relation to one another with respect to the elementary structures of society; they fix and ascribe those positionings in ongoing social practices; they legitimate the positions so ascribed. In short, they are practices which secure the hegemony of a dominant group over a series of subordinate ones, in such a way as to dominate the whole social formation in a form favorable to the long-term development of the economic productive base. Though the economic aspects are critical, as a way of beginning, this form of hegemony cannot be understood as operating purely through economic coercion. Racism, so active at the level – "the economic nucleus" – where Gramsci insists hegemony must first be secured, will have or contract elaborate relations at other instances – in the political, cultural, and ideological levels. Yet, put in this (obviously correct) way, the assertion is still too *a priori*. How specifically do these mechanisms operate? What further determinations need to be supplied? Racism is not present, in the same form or degree, in all capitalist formations: it is not necessary to the concrete functioning of all capitalisms. It needs to be shown how and why racism has been specifically overdetermined by and articulated with certain capitalisms at different stages of their development. Nor can it be assumed that this must take one, single form or follow one necessary path or logic, through a series of necessary stages.

This requires us, in turn, to show its articulation with the different structures of the social formation. For example, the position of the slave in pre-emancipation plantation society was not secured exclusively through race. It was predominantly secured by the quite specific and distinctive productive relations of slave-based agriculture, and through the distinctive property status of the slave (as a commodity) and of slave labor-power (as united with its exerciser, who was not however its "owner"), coupled with legal, political, and ideological systems which anchored this relation by racial ascription. This coupling may have provided the ready-made rationale and framework for those structures of "informal racism" which became operative when "freed" black labor migrated northwards in the United States or into the "free village" system in the post-emancipation Caribbean. Yet the "coupling" operated in new ways, and required their own ideological work – as in the "Jim Crow" legislation of the 1880s and 1890s (Van Woodward, 1957). The reproduction of the low and ascribed status of black labor, as a specific fraction of the "free laboring" classes of industrial capitalism, was secured – with the assistance of a transformed racism, to be sure: but also through other mechanisms, which accomplished their structured positioning with respect to new forms of capital in new ways. In the latter case, pertinent struggles have developed which exploited the gaps, or worked directly on the contradictions between racial ascription and the official ideologies of "equal opportunity" which were simply not available to black slaves under a plantation system (Myrdal, 1962). We treat these differences as "essentially the same" at our peril. On the other hand, it does not follow that, because developed capitalism here functions predominantly on the basis of "free labor," the racial aspects of social relations can be assimilated, for all practical purposes, to its typical class relations (as does Cox (1970), despite his many pertinent observations). Race continues to differentiate between the different fractions of the working classes with respect to capital, creating specific forms of fracturing and fractioning which are as important for the ways in which they intersect class relations (and divide the class struggle, internally) as they are mere "expressions" of some general form of the class struggle. Politically and culturally, these combined and uneven relations between class and race are historically more pertinent than their simple correspondence.

At the economic level, it is clear that race must be given its distinctive and "relatively autonomous" effectivity, as a distinctive feature. This does not mean that the economic is sufficient to found an explanation of how these relations concretely function. One needs to know how different racial and ethnic groups were inserted historically, and the relations which have tended to erode and transform, or to preserve these distinctions through time – not simply as residues and traces of previous modes, but as active structuring principles of the present organization of society. Racial categories alone will not provide or explain these. What are the different forms and relations in which these racial fractions were combined under capital? Do they stand in significantly different relations to capital? Do they stand within an articulation of dif-

ferent modes of production? What are the relations of dissolution/con-
servation between them? How has race functioned to preserve and
develop these articulations? What are the functions which the dominated modes of production perform in the reproduction of the dominant
mode? Are these linked to it through the domestic reproduction of labor
power "below its value," the supply of cheap labor, the regulation of the
"reserve army of labor," the supply of raw materials, of subsistence agriculture, the hidden costs of social reproduction? The indigenous
"natural economies" of Latin America and the forms of semi-domestic
production characteristic of the Caribbean societies differ significantly,
among and between them, in this respect. The same is true even where
different ethnic fractions stand in the same sets of relations to capital.
For example, the position of black labor in the industrial North of the
United States and of black migration to post-war Britain show highly
distinctive patternings along racial lines: yet these situations are not
explicable without the concept of the "reserve army of labor." Yet it is
clear that blacks are not the only division within the "reserve army":
hence race is not the only mechanism through which its size and composition is regulated. In the United States, both white immigrants (e.g.,
European and Mexican) and women, and in Britain, both women and
the Irish have provided a significant alternative element (see Braverman,
1975; Castle and Kosack, 1973).

The either/or alternatives, surveyed in the opening parts of this
paper, are therefore seriously disabling, at a theoretical level, whether it
is "metropolitan" or "satellite" formations which are under discussion;
and whether it is historical or contemporary forms which are under
scrutiny. As I have recently argued (Hall et al., 1978), the structures
through which black labor is reproduced – structures which may be
general to capital at a certain stage of development, whatever the racial
composition of labor – are not simply "colored" by race: they work
through race. The relations of capitalism can be thought of as articulating classes in distinct ways at each of the levels or instances of the
social formation – economic, political, ideological. These levels are the
"effects" of the structures of modern capitalist production, with the necessary displacement of relative autonomy operating between them.
Each level of the social formation requires its own independent "means
of representation" – the means by which the class-structured mode of
production appears, and acquires effectivity at the level of the economic,
the political, the ideological class struggle. Race is intrinsic to the
manner in which the black laboring classes are complexly constituted

Black labor
race →
gender →
class →

at each of these levels. It enters into the way black labor, male and female, is distributed as economic agents at the level of economic practices, and the class struggles which result from it; and into the way the fractions of the black laboring classes are reconstituted, through the means of political representation (parties, organizations, community action centers, publications, and campaigns) as political forces in the "theater of politics" – and the political struggles which result; and the manner in which the class is articulated as the collective and individual "subjects" of emergent ideologies – and the struggles over ideology, culture and consciousness which result. This gives the matter or dimension of race, and racism, a practical as well as theoretical centrality to all the relations which affect black labor. The constitution of this fraction as a class, and the class relations which ascribe it, function as race relations. Race is thus, also, the modality in which class is "lived," the medium through which class relations are experienced, the form in which it is appropriated and "fought through." This has consequences for the whole class, not specifically for its "racially defined" segment. It has consequences in terms of the internal fractioning and division within the working class which, among other ways, are articulated in part through race. This is no mere racist conspiracy from above. For racism is also one of the dominant means of ideological representation through which the white fractions of the class come to "live" their relations to other fractions, and through them to capital itself. Those who seek, with effect, to disarticulate some of the existing syntaxes of class struggle (albeit of a corporatist or social-reformist kind) and to rearticulate class experience through the condensed interpellations of a racist ideological syntax are, of course, key agents in this work of ideological transformation – this is the ideological class struggle, pursued, precisely, through harnessing the dominated classes to capital by means of the articulation of the internal contradictions of class experience with racism. In Britain, this process has recently attained a rare and general pitch. But they succeed to the measure that they do because they are practicing on real contradictions within and inside the class, working on real effects of the structure (however these may be "misrecognized" through racism) – not because they are clever at conjuring demons, or because they brandish swastikas and read *Mein Kampf*.

Racism is, thus, not only a problem for blacks who are obliged to suffer it. Nor is it a problem only for those sections of the white working

class and those organizations infected by its stain. Nor can it be overcome, as a general virus in the social body, by a heavy dose of liberal
innoculation. Capital reproduces the class, including its internal contradictions, as a whole – structured by race. It dominates the divided
class, in part, through those internal divisions which have racism as one
of its effects. It contains and disables representative class institutions by
neutralizing them – confining them to strategies and struggles which
are race-specific, which do not surmount its limits, its barrier. Through
racism, it is able to defeat the attempts to construct alternative means
of representation which could more adequately represent the class as a
whole, or which are capable of effecting the unity of the class as a result:
that is, those alternatives which would adequately represent the class as
a whole – against capitalism, against racism. The sectional struggles,
articulated through race, instead, continue to appear as the necessary
defensive strategies of a class divided against itself, face-to-face with
capital. They are, therefore, also the site of capital's continuing hegemony over it. This is certainly not to treat racism as, in any simple sense,
the product of an ideological trick.

Nevertheless, such an analysis would need to be complemented by an
analysis of the specific forms which racism assumes in its ideological
functioning. Here, we would have to begin by investigating the different
ways in which racist ideologies have been constructed and made operative under different historical conditions: the racisms of mercantilist
theory and of chattel slavery; of conquest and colonialism; of trade
and "high imperialism"; of "popular imperialism" and of so-called
"post-imperialism." In each case, in specific social formations, racism as
an ideological configuration has been reconstituted by the dominant
class relations, and thoroughly reworked. If it has performed the function of that cementing ideology which secures a whole social formation
under a dominant class, its pertinent differences from other such hegemonic ideologies require to be registered in detail. Here, racism is particularly powerful and its imprint on popular consciousness especially
deep, because in such racial characteristics as color, ethnic origin,
geographical position, etc., racism discovers what other ideologies have
to construct: an apparently "natural" and universal basis in nature
itself. Yet, despite this apparent grounding in biological givens, outside
history racism, when it appears, has an effect on other ideological formations within the same society, and its development promotes a transformation of the whole ideological field in which it becomes operative.

It can, in this way, harness other ideological discourses to itself – for example, it articulates securely with the us/them structure of corporate class consciousness – through the mechanism previously discussed of connotative condensation. Its effects are similar to other ideologies from which, on other grounds, it must be distinguished: racisms also dehistoricize – translating historically specific structures into the timeless language of nature; decomposing classes into individuals and recomposing those disaggregated individuals into the reconstructed unities, the great coherences, of new ideological "subjects": it translates "classes" into "blacks" and "whites," economic groups into "peoples," solid forces into "races." This is the process of constituting new "historical subjects" for ideological discourses – the mechanism we encountered earlier, of forming new interpellative structures. It produces, as the natural and given "authors" of a spontaneous form of racial perception, the naturalized "racist subject." This is not an external function, operative only against those whom it disposes or disarticulates (renders silent). It is also pertinent for the dominated subjects – those subordinated ethnic groups or "races" which live their relation to their real conditions of existence, and to the domination of the dominant classes, in and through the imaginary representations of a racist interpellation, and who come to experience themselves as "the inferiors," *les autres*. And yet these processes are themselves never exempted from the ideological class struggle. The racist interpellations can become themselves the sites and stake in the ideological struggle, occupied and redefined to become the elementary forms of an oppositional formation – as where "white racism" is vigorously contested through the symbolic inversions of "black power." The ideologies of racism remain contradictory structures, which can function both as the vehicles for the imposition of dominant ideologies, and as the elementary forms for the cultures of resistance. Any attempt to delineate the politics and ideologies of racism which omit these continuing features of struggle and contradiction win an apparent adequacy of explanation only by operating a disabling reductionism.

In this field of inquiry, "sociological theory" has still to find its way, by a difficult effort of theoretical clarification, through the Scylla of a reductionism which must deny almost everything in order to explain something, and the Charybdis of a pluralism which is so mesmerized by "everything" that it cannot explain anything. To those willing to labor on, the vocation remains an open one.

Bibliography

Alavi, H. (1975). India and the Colonial Mode of Production. *Socialist Register*. Atlantic Highlands: Humanities.

Althusser, L. (1965). *For Marx*. London: Allan Lane.

——(1971). *Lenin and Philosophy and Other Essays*. London: New Left Books.

——(1976). *Essays in Self-criticism*. London: New Left Books.

——and Balibar, E. (1970). *Reading Capital*. London: New Left Books.

Anderson, P. (1977). The Antinomies of Antonio Gramsci. *New Left Review* (London), No. 100.

Banaji, J. (1977). Modes of Production in a Matrialist Conception of History. *Capital and Class*, No. 3.

Barthes, R. (1967). *Elements of Semiology*. London: Cape.

Beechey, V. (1978). The Ideology of Racism. Ph.D. Thesis, Oxford. Unpublished.

Bettelheim, C. (1972). Theoretical Comments. In A. Emmanuel, *Unequal Exchange*. London: New Left Books.

Bradby, B. (1975). Capitalist/Precapitalist Articulation. *Economy and Society* (London), Vol. 4, No. 2.

Braverman, H. (1975). *Labour and Monopoly Capital*. New York: Monthly Review Press.

Carchedi, G. (1977). *On the Economic Identification of Social Classes*. London: Routledge & Kegan Paul.

Castle, C. and Kosak, G. (1973). *Immigrant Workers and Class Structure in Western Europe*. London: Oxford University Press.

Clammer, J. (1975). Economic Anthropology and the Sociology of Development. In I. Oxall, T. Barnett, and D. Booth (eds.), *Beyond the Sociology of Development*. London: Routledge & Kegan Paul.

Cox, O. (1970). *Caste, Class and Race*. New York: Monthly Press Review.

Cutler, A. et al. (1977). *Marx's Capital and Capitalism Today*. London: Routledge & Kegan Paul.

Davis, D. B. (1969). Comparative Approach to American History: Slavery. In E. Genovese and L. Foner (eds.), *Slavery in the New World*. Englewood Cliffs: Prentice-Hall.

——(1970). *The Problem of Slavery in Western Culture*. Ithaca, NY: Cornell University Press.

Finley, M. (1969). The Idea of Slavery. In R. Genovese and L. Foner (eds.), *Slavery in the New World*. Englewood Cliffs: Prentice-Hall.

Fogel, R. and Engerman, S. (1974). *Time on the Cross*. Boston: Little, Brown & Co.

Foster-Carter, A. (1978). The Modes of Production Debate. *New Left Review* (London), No. 107.

Frank, G. (1969). *Capitalism and Underdevelopment in Latin America*. New York: Monthly Review Press.

Furtado, C. (1971). Dependencia externa y teoria economica. *El Trimestre Economico* (Mexico), April–June. (Translated by P. O'Brien. In I. Oxall, T. Barnett, and D. Booth (eds.), *Beyond the Sociology of Development*. London: Routledge & Kegan Paul.)

Genovese, E. (1965). *The Political Economy of Slavery*. New York: Vintage.

——(1970). *The World the Slaveholders Made*. New York: Vintage.

——(1971). *In Red and Black*. New York: Vintage.

——(1977). Reply to Criticism. *Medical History Review* (New York), Winter.

Gramsci, A. (1971). *Selections from the Prison Notebooks*. London: Lawrence & Wishart.

Hall, S. (1973). Marx's Notes on Methods: A Reading of "The 1857 Introduction." *Working Papers in Cultural Studies 6*. Birmingham.

——(1977). Continuing the Discussion. In UNESCO, *Race and Class in Post-colonial Society*. Paris.

——(1978). Pluralism, Race and Class in Caribbean Society. In UNESCO, *Race and Class in Post-colonial Society*. Paris.

——, Lumley, B., and McLennan, G. (1977). Politics and Ideology in A. Gramsci. *Working Papers in Cultural Studies 10*. Birmingham.

——et al. (1978). *Policing the Crisis*. London: Macmillan.

Hilton, R. (ed.) (1976). *The Transition from Feudalism to Capitalism*. London: New Left Books.

Hindess, B. and Hirst, P. (1975). *Pre-capitalist Modes of Production*. London: Routledge & Kegan Paul.

——and —— (1977). *Modes of Production and Social Formation*. Routledge & Kegan Paul.

Hirst, P. (1976). Althusser's Theory of Ideology. *Economy and Society* (London), Vol. 5, No. 4.

Johnson, R. et al. (1978). (a) The Problem of "a-priorism." (b) "The Histories" in Marx. Center for Cultural Studies. Birmingham. (Mimeographed papers.)

Kuper, L. (1974). *Race, Class and Power*. London: Duckworth.

Laclau, E. (1977). *Politics and Ideology in Marxist Theory*. London: New Left Books.

McLennan, G. (1976). Some Problems in British Marxist Historiography. Center for Cultural Studies, Birmingham. (Mimeographed.)

Marx, K. (1956). *Capital*. Vol. 2. London: Lawrence & Wishart.

——(1961). *Capital*. Vol. 1. Moscow: Foreign Languages Publishing House.

——(1964). *Precapitalist Economic Formations*, ed. E. Hobsbawm. London: Lawrence & Wishart.

——(1973). *Introduction to "The Grundisse."* London: Penguin.

——(1974). *Capital*. Vol. 3. London: Lawrence & Wishart.

Meillassoux, C. (1960). Essai d'interprétation du phénomène économique dans les sociétés traditionelles d'auto-subsistence. *Cahiers d'Études Africaines* (The Hague), Vol. 4.

——(1972). From Production to Reproduction. *Economy and Society* (London), VOl. 1, No. 1.

——(1974). Imperialism as a Mode of Reproduction of Labour Power. (Mimeographed.)

Mouffe, C. (1978). Introduction to a Selection of Essays on Gramsci. In preparation.

O'Brien, P. (1975). A Critique of Latin-American Dependency Theories. In I. Oxall, T. Barnett, and D. Booth (eds.), *Beyond the Sociology of Development*. London: Routledge & Kegan Paul.

O'Shea, A. (1978). A Critique of Laclau's Theory of Interpellation. Center for Cultural Studies, Birmingham. (Mimeographed.)

Oxall, I., Barnett, T., and Booth, D. (eds.) (1975). *Beyond the Sociology of Development*. London: Routledge & Kegan Paul.

Post, K. (1978). *Arise, Ye Starvelings*. In preparation.

Poulantzas, N. (1973). *Political Power and Social Classes*. London: New Left Books.

Rex, J. (1970). *Race Relations in Sociological Theory*. London: Weidenfeld & Nicolson.

——(1973). *Race, Colonialism and the City*. London: Routledge & Kegan Paul.

——(1978). New Nations and Ethnic Minorities. In UNESCO, *Race and Class in Post-colonial Societies*. Paris.

Rey, P.-P. (1971). *Colonialisme, néo-colonialisme, et transition au capitalisme*. Paris: Maspéro.

——(1973). *Les Alliances de Classes*. Paris: Maspéro.

——(1975). Reflections on the Lineage Mode of Production. *Critique of Anthropology*, No. 3.

——and Dupré, G. (1973). Reflections on the Pertinence of a Theory of Exchange. *Economy and Society* (London), Vol. 2, No. 2.

Rose, S., Hambley, J., and Haywood, J. (1973). Science, Racism and Ideology. *Socialist Register – 1973*. Atlantic Highlands: Humanities.

Schwarz, B. (1978). On Maurice Dobb. In R. Johnson, G. McLennan, and B. Schwarz, *Economy, history, concept*. Center for Cultural Studies, Birmingham.

Seddon, D. (1978). Introduction. *Relations of Production*. London: Cass.

Smith, M. G. (1965). *The Plural Society in the British West Indies*. Berkeley: University of California Press.

Terray, E. (1972). *Marxism and "Primitive Societies."* New York: Monthly Review Press.

Van den Berghe, P. (1965). *South Africa: A Study in Conflict*. Middletown, CT: Wesleyan University Press.

Van Woodward, C. (1957). *The Strange Career of Jim Crow*. London and New York: Oxford University Press.

Williams, E. (1966). *Capitalism and Slavery*. Chapel Hill: Russell.

Wolpe, H. (1972). Capitalism and Cheap Labour in South Africa. *Economy and Society* (London), Vol. 1, No. 4.

——(1975). The Theory of Internal Colonialism. In I. Oxall, T. Barnett, and D. Booth (eds.), *Beyond the Sociology of Development*. London: Routledge & Kegan Paul.

——(1976). The White Working Class in South Africa. *Economy and Society* (London), Vol. 5, No. 2.

——(1978). The Articulation of Modes of Production. Introduction to a Selection of Essays. In preparation.

3

Education and Liberation: Black Women's Perspective

Angela Y. Davis

Millions of Black people – and especially the women – were convinced that emancipation was "the coming of the Lord."[1]

> This was the fulfillment of prophecy and legend. It was the Golden Dawn, after chains of a thousand years. It was everything miraculous and perfect and promising.[2]

> There was joy in the South. It rose like perfume – like a prayer. Men stood quivering. Slim, dark girls, wild and beautiful with wrinkled hair, wept silently; young women, black, tawny, white and golden, lifted shivering hands, and old and broken mothers, black and gray, raised great voices and shouted to God across the fields and up to the rocks and the mountains.[3]

> A great song arose, the loveliest thing born this side of the seas. It was a new song . . . and its deep and plaintive beauty, its great cadences and wild appeal wailed, throbbed and thundered on the world's ears with a message seldom voiced by man. It swelled and blossomed like incense, improvised and born anew out of an age long past and weaving into its texture the old and new melodies in word and in thought.[4]

Black people were hardly celebrating the abstract principles of freedom when they hailed the advent of emancipation. As that "great human sob shrieked in the wind and tossed its tears upon the sea – free, free, free,"[5] Black people were not giving vent to religious frenzy. They knew exactly what they wanted: the women and the men alike wanted land, they wanted the ballot and "they were consumed with desire for schools."[6]

Like the young slave child Frederick Douglass, many of the four million people who celebrated emancipation had long since realized that "knowledge unfits a child to be a slave."[7] And like Douglass' master, the former slaveholders realized that "if you give a nigger an inch, he will take an ell. Learning will spoil the best nigger in the world."[8] Master Hugh's proscription notwithstanding, Frederick Douglass secretly continued his pursuit of knowledge. Soon he could write all the words from *Webster's Spelling-Book*, further perfecting his skill by examining the family Bible and other books in the clandestinity of the night. Of course, Frederick Douglass was an exceptional human being who became a brilliant thinker, writer, and orator. But his desire for knowledge was by no means exceptional among Black people, who had always manifested a deep-seated urge to acquire knowledge. Great numbers of slaves also wanted to be "unfit" for the harrowing existence they led. A former slave interviewed during the 1930s, Jenny Proctor recalled the *Webster's Spelling-Book* which she and her friends had surreptitiously studied.

> None of us was 'lowed to see a book or try to learn. They say we git smarter than they was if we learn anything, but we slips around and gits hold of that Webster's old blue-back speller and we hides it till 'way in the night and then we lights a little pine torch, and studies that spelling book. We learn it too. I can read some now and write a little too.[9]

Black people learned that emancipation's "forty acres and a mule" was a malicious rumor. They would have to fight for land; they would have to fight for political power. And after centuries of educational deprivation, they would zealously assert their right to satisfy their profound craving for learning. Thus, like their sisters and brothers all over the South, the newly liberated Black people of Memphis assembled and resolved that education was their first priority. On the first anniversary of the Emancipation Proclamation, they urged the Northern teachers to make haste and

> to bring their tents with them, ready for erection in he field, by the roadside, or in the fort, and not to wait for magnificent houses to be erected in time of war . . .[10]

The mystifying powers of racism often emanate from its irrational, topsy-turvy logic. According to the prevailing ideology, Black people were allegedly incapable of intellectual advancement. After all, they had been chattel, naturally inferior as compared to the white epitomes of humankind. But if they really were biologically inferior, they would have manifested neither the desire nor the capability to acquire knowledge. Ergo, no prohibition of learning would have been necessary. In reality, of course, Black people had always exhibited a furious impatience as regards the acquisition of education.

The yearning for knowledge had always been there. As early as 1787, Black people petitioned the state of Massachusetts for the right to attend Boston's free schools.[11] After the petition was rejected, Prince Hall, who was the leader of this initiative, established a school in his own home.[12] Perhaps the most stunning illustration of this early demand for education was the work of an African-born woman who was a former slave. In 1793 Lucy Terry Prince boldly demanded an audience before the trustees of the newly established Williams College for Men, who had refused to admit her son into the school. Unfortunately, the racist prejudices were so strong that Lucy Prince's logic and eloquence could not sway the trustees of this Vermont institution. Yet she aggressively defended her people's desire for – and right to – education. Two years later Lucy Terry Prince successfully defended a land claim before the highest court of the land, and according to surviving records, she remains the first woman to have addressed the Supreme Court of the United States.[13]

Seventeen ninety-three was also the year an ex-slave woman, who had purchased her freedom, established a school in the city of New York which was known as Katy Ferguson's School for the Poor. Her pupils, whom she recruited from the poorhouse, were both Black and white (twenty-eight and twenty, respectively)[14] and were quite possibly both boys and girls. Forty years later the young white teacher Prudence Crandall steadfastly defended Black girls' right to attend her Canterbury, Connecticut, school. Crandall persistently taught her Black pupils until she was dragged off to jail for refusing to shut down her school.[15] Margaret Douglass was another white woman who was imprisoned in Norfolk, Virginia, for operating a school for Black children.[16]

The most outstanding examples of white women's sisterly solidarity with Black women are associated with Black people's historical struggle for education. Like Prudence Crandall and Margaret Douglass, Myrtilla Miner literally risked her life as she sought to impart knowledge to young Black women.[17] In 1851, when she initiated her project to establish a Black teachers' college in Washington, DC, she had already instructed Black children in Mississippi, a state where education for Blacks was a criminal offense. After Myrtilla Miner's death, Frederick Douglass described his own incredulousness when she first announced her plans to him. During their first meeting he wondered about her seriousness in the beginning, but then he realized that

> the fire of enthusiasm lighted in her eye and that the true martyr spirit flamed in her soul. My feelings were those of mingled joy and sadness. Here I thought is another enterprise – wild, dangerous, desperate and impracticable, and destined only to bring failure and suffering. Yet I was deeply moved with admiration by the heroic purpose of the delicate and fragile person who stood or rather moved to and fro before me.[18]

It was not long before Douglass recognized that none of the warnings he issued to her – and not even the stories of the attacks on Prudence Crandall and Margaret Douglass – could shake her determination to found a college for Black women teachers.

> To me the proposition was reckless almost to the point of madness. In my fancy I saw this fragile little woman harassed by the law, insulted in the street, a victim of slaveholding malice and possibly beaten down by the mob.[19]

In Frederick Douglass' opinion, relatively few white people outside the anti-slavery activists would sympathize with Myrtilla Miner's cause and support her against the mob. This was a period, he argued, of diminishing solidarity with Black people. Moreover,

> the District of Columbia (was) the very citadel of slavery, the place most watched and guarded by the slave power and where humane tendencies were more speedily detected and sternly opposed.[20]

In retrospect, however, Douglass confessed that he did not really understand the depth of this white woman's individual courage. Despite the grave risks, Myrtilla Miner opened her school in the fall of 1851, and within a few months her initial six students had grown to forty. She taught her Black students passionately over the next eight years, simultaneously raising money and urging congressmen to support her efforts. She even acted as a mother to the orphan girls whom she brought into her home so that they might attend the school.[21]

As Myrtilla Miner struggled to teach and as her pupils struggled to learn, they all fought evictions, arson attempts, and the other misdeeds of racist stone-throwing mobs. They were supported by the young women's families and abolitionists such as Harriet Beecher Stowe, who donated a portion of the royalties she received from the sale of *Uncle Tom's Cabin*.[22] Myrtilla Miner may have been "frail," as Frederick Douglass observed, but she was definitely formidable, and was always able, at lesson time, to discover the eye of that racist storm. Early one morning, however, she was abruptly awakened by the odor of smoke and raging flames, which soon consumed her schoolhouse. Although her school was destroyed, the inspiration she provided lived on, and eventually Miner's Teachers College became a part of the District of Columbia public educational system.[23] "I never pass the Miner Normal School for colored girls," so Frederick Douglass confessed in 1883,

> without a feeling of self reproach that I could have said ought to quench the zeal, shake the faith, and quail the courage of the Noble woman by whom it was founded and whose name it bears.[24]

Sisterhood between Black and white women was indeed possible, and as long as it stood on a firm foundation – as with this remarkable woman and her friends and students – it could give birth to earthshaking accomplishments. Myrtilla Miner kept the candle burning that others before her, like the Grimke sisters and Prudence Crandall, had left as a powerful legacy. It could not have been a mere historical coincidence that so many of the white women who defended their Black sisters in the most dangerous of situations were involved in the struggle for education. They must have understood how urgently Black women needed to acquire knowledge – a lamp unto their people's feet and a light unto the path toward freedom.

Black people who did receive academic instruction inevitably associated their knowledge with their people's collective battle for freedom. As the first year of Black schooling in Cincinnati drew to a close, pupils who were asked "What do you think *most* about?" furnished these answers:

> 1st. We are going . . . to be good boys and when we get a man to get the poor slaves from bondage. And I am sorrow to hear that the boat of Tiskilwa went down with two hundred poor slaves . . . it grieves my heart so that I could faint in one minute. (seven-year-old)

> 2nd. . . . What we are studying for is to try to get the yoke of slavery broke and the chains parted asunder and slave holding cease for ever. . . . (twelve-year-old)

> 3rd. . . . Bless the cause of abolition. . . . My mother and step-father, my sister and myself were all born in slavery. The Lord did let the oppressed go free. Roll on the happy period that all nations shall know the Lord. We thank him for his many blessings. (eleven-year-old)

> 4th. . . . This is to inform you that I have two cousins in slavery who are entitled to their freedom. They have done everything that the will requires and now they won't let them go. They talk of selling them down the river. If this was your case what would you do? . . . (ten-year-old)[25]

The last surviving answer came from a sixteen-year-old attending this new Cincinnati school. It is an extremely fascinating example of the way the students gleaned a contemporary meaning from world history that was as close to home as the desire to be free.

> 5th. Let us look back and see the state in which the Britons and Saxons and Germans lived. They had no learning and had not a knowledge of letters. But now look, some of them are our first men. Look at King Alfred and see what a great man he was. He at one time did not know his a,b,c, but before his death he commanded armies and nations. He was never discouraged but always looked forward and studied the harder. I think if the colored people study like King Alfred they will soon do away the evil of slavery. I can't see how the Americans can call this a land of freedom where so much slavery is.[26]

As far as Black people's faith in knowledge was concerned, this sixteen-year-old child said it all.

This unquenchable thirst for knowledge was as powerful among the slaves in the South as among their "free" sisters and brothers in the North. Needless to say, the anti-literacy restrictions of the slave states were far more rigid than in the North. After the Nat Turner Revolt in 1831, legislation prohibiting the education of slaves was strengthened throughout the South. In the words of one slave code, "teaching slaves to read and write tends to dissatisfaction in their minds, and to produce insurrection and rebellion."[27] With the exception of Maryland and Kentucky, every Southern state absolutely prohibited the education of slaves.[28] Throughout the South, slaveholders resorted to the lash and the whipping post in order to counter their slaves' irrepressible will to learn. Black people wanted to be educated.

> The poignancy of the slaves' struggle for learning appeared everywhere. Frederika Bremer found a young woman desperately trying to read the Bible. "Oh, this book," she cried out to Miss Bremer. "I turn and turn over its leaves and I wish I understood what is on them. I try and try; I should be so happy if I could read, but I can not.[29]

Susie King Taylor was a nurse and teacher in the first Black regiment of the Civil War. In her autobiography she described her persistent efforts to educate herself during slavery. White children, sympathetic adults, as well as her grandmother, assisted her to acquire the skills of reading and writing.[30] Like Susie King's grandmother, numerous slave women ran great risks as they imparted to their sisters and brothers the academic skills they had secretly procured. Even when they were compelled to convene their schools during the late hours of the night, women who had managed to acquire some knowledge attempted to share it with their people.[31]

These were some of the early signs – in the North and South alike – of that post-emancipation phenomenon which DuBois called "a frenzy for schools."[32] Another historian described the ex-slaves' thirst for learning in these words:

> With a yearning born of centuries of denial, ex-slaves worshipped the sight and sound of the printed word. Old men and women on the edge of the grave could be seen in the dark of the night, poring over the Scripture by the light of a pine knot, painfully spelling out the sacred words.[33]

According to yet another historian,

> (M)any educators reported that they found a keener desire to learn among the Negro children of the Reconstruction South than among white children in the North.[34]

About half of the volunteer teachers who joined the massive educational campaign organized by the Freedman's Bureau were women. Northern white women went South during Reconstruction to assist their Black sisters who were absolutely determined to wipe out illiteracy among the millions of former slaves. The dimensions of this task were herculean: according to DuBois, the prevailing illiteracy rate was 95 percent.[35] In the histories chronicling the Reconstruction Era and in the historical accounts of the Women's Rights Movement, the experiences of Black and white women working together in the struggle for education have received sparse attention. Judging, however, from the articles in the *Freedman's Record*, these teachers undoubtedly inspired each other and were themselves inspired by their students. Almost universally mentioned in the white teachers' observations was the former slaves' unyielding commitment to knowledge. In the words of a teacher working in Raleigh, North Carolina, "[i]t is surprising to me to see the amount of suffering which many of the people endure for the sake of sending their children to school."[36] Material comfort was unhesitatingly sacrificed for the furtherance of educational progress:

> A pile of books is seen in almost every cabin, though there be no furniture except a poor bed, a table and two or three broken chairs.[37]

As teachers, the Black and white women seem to have developed a profound and intense mutual appreciation. A white woman working in Virginia, for example, was immensely impressed by the work of a Black woman teacher who had just emerged from slavery. It "seems almost a miracle," this white woman exclaimed, that " a colored woman, who had been a slave up to the time of the Surrender, would succeed in a vocation to her so novel."[38] In the reports she authored, the Black woman in question expressed sincere – though by no means servile – gratitude for the work of her "friends from the North."[39]

By the time of the Hayes Betrayal and the overthrow of Radical Reconstruction, the accomplishments in education had become one of the most powerful proofs of progress during that potentially revolutionary era. Fisk University, Hampton Institute, and several other Black colleges and universities had been established in the post-Civil War South.[40] Some 247,333 pupils were attending 4,329 schools – and these were the building blocks for the South's first public school system, which would benefit Black and white children alike. Although the post-Reconstruction period and the attendant rise of Jim Crow education drastically diminished Black people's educational opportunities, the impact of the Reconstruction experience could not be entirely obliterated. The dream of land was shattered for the time being and the hope for political equality waned. But the beacon of knowledge was not easily extinguished – and this was the guarantee that the fight for land and for political power would unrelentingly go on.

> Had it not been for the Negro school and college, the Negro would, to all intents and purposes, have been driven back to slavery. . . . His reconstruction leadership had come from Negroes educated in the North, and white politicians, capitalists and philanthropic teachers. The counter-revolution of 1876 drove most of these, save the teachers, away. But already, through establishing public schools and private colleges, and by organizing the Negro church, the Negro had acquired enough leadership and knowledge to thwart the worst designs of the new slave drivers.[41]

Aided by their white sister allies, Black women played an indispensable role in creating this new fortress. The history of women's struggle for education in the United States reached a true peak when Black and white women together led the post-Civil War battle against illiteracy in the South. Their unity and solidarity preserved and confirmed one of our history's most fruitful promises.

Notes

1   W. E. B. Du Bois, *Black Reconstruction in America* (Cleveland and New York: Meridian Books, 1964), ch. V.
2   Ibid., p. 122.
3   Ibid., p. 124.
4   Ibid.
5   Ibid.
6   Ibid., p. 123.

7   Frederick Douglass, *The Life and Times of Frederick Douglass* (New York: Collier; London: Collier-Macmillan, 1962), p. 79. Reprinted from the revised edition of 1892.

8   Ibid.

9   Mel Watkins and Jay David (eds.), *To Be a Black Woman: Portraits in Fact and Fiction* (New York: William Morrow and Co., 1970), p. 18.

10 Herbert Aptheker (ed.), *A Documentary History of the Negro People in the United States*, Vol. 1 (Secaucus. NJ: The Citadel Press, 1973), p. 493.

11 Ibid., p. 19.

12 Ibid.

13 Barbara Wertheimer, *We Were There: The Story of Working Women in America* (New York: Pantheon Books, 1977), pp. 35–6.

14 Gerda Lerner (ed.), *Black Women in White America: A Documentary History* (New York: Pantheon Books, 1972), p. 76.

15 See chapter 2.

16 Philip Foner (ed.), *The Life and Writings of Frederick Douglass*, Vol. 4 (New York: International Publishers, 1950), p. 553 (note 16).

17 Ibid., pp. 371ff.

18 Ibid., p. 372.

19 Ibid.

20 Ibid., p. 371.

21 Ibid.

22 Eleanor Flexner, *Century of Struggle: The Women's Rights Movement in the U.S.* (New York: Atheneum, 1973), p. 99.

23 Ibid., pp. 99–101.

24 Foner, *The Life and Writings of Frederick Douglass*, Vol. 4, p. 373.

25 Aptheker, *A Documentary History*, Vol. 1, pp. 157–8.

26 Ibid.

27 William Goodell, *The American Slave Code* (New York: American and Foreign Anti-Slavery Society, 1853), p. 321. Quoted in Stanley Elkins, *Slavery: A Problem in American Institutional and Intellectual Life*, 3rd edn, revised (Chicago and London: University of Chicago Press, 1976), p. 60.

28 Ibid.

29 Eugene D. Genovese, *Roll, Jordan, Roll: The World the Slaves Made* (New York: Pantheon Books, 1974), p. 565.

30 Lerner, *Black Women in White America*, pp. 27ff. and pp. 99ff.

31 Ibid., pp. 32ff.

32 Du Bois, *Black Reconstruction in America*, p. 123.

33 Lerone Bennett, *Before the Mayflower* (Baltimore: Penguin Books, 1969), p. 181.

34 William Z. Foster, *The Negro People in American History* (New York: International Publishers, 1970), p. 321.

35   Du Bois, *Black Reconstruction in America*, p. 638.
36   Lerner, *Black Women in White America*, p. 102.
37   Ibid., p. 103.
38   Ibid.
39   Ibid., pp. 104–5.
40   John Hope Franklin, *From Slavery to Freedom* (New York: Vintage Books, 1969), p. 308.
41   Du Bois, *Black Reconstruction in America*, p. 667.

4

The Problems with Racism

Martin Barker

Five days before the 1979 general election in Britain, the leader of the Conservatives, Margaret Thatcher, took part in a phone-in discussion on BBC Radio 4. In the course of the programme, she was challenged by a black listener to withdraw a statement she had made some months earlier. In a major speech she had said that Britain was being "swamped" by immigrants with alien cultures. Mrs Thatcher refused to withdraw, indeed reasserted the claim that "Some people do feel swamped if streets they have lived in for the whole of their lives are really now quite, quite different." The *Sun* newspaper, among others, reported this exchange the next day on its front page. On page two, the *Sun* took time to give its view, in preparation for the election, of the extreme right-wing National Front. They were described as "twisted little men," with views similar to Hitler's, with a mixture of "crackpot economics, jingoism and odious racialism." "Fortunately," said the editorial, "it no longer matters what these revolting people say." At last one of the major political parties had "grasped the immigration nettle"; and the paper went on to discuss the radio programme. "No reasonable person – black or white – could quarrel" with Tory plans for tightening the rules governing immigration. The proposals were fair, responsible, and humane. They were quite unlike the National Front's despicable attitudes. Indeed they were the best, perhaps the only, insurance against their foul propaganda.

Thus, the *Sun*. It was giving voice to a view that is perhaps the dominant one on this question: the National Front, Britain's most organized ultra-right-wing party, is overtly racist; it promotes hatred of black people; it plays on irrational fears, encourages prejudices. Racism is thus seen as a package of irrational beliefs: a prejudice. It is not a rational response in any sense of the word to problems that may be engendered by immigration, for example. From this same viewpoint a tough stand on immigration is a quite different matter: it is realistic and rational, based on facts and arguments; it has nothing to do with prejudice. In addition, a tough policy will allay the very emotions that the racists play on. Stop immigration and you stop the National Front. To say that people feel swamped by immigrants is just plain fact. And because the main political parties start out from facts of this sort they cannot be called racist. They do not encourage hatred, prejudice. The Conservatives may take a tough line on questions of immigration, but their policies – whether right or wrong – are part of a legitimate area of debate. Of course, there are differences between the main parties, but they are differences about policies, not over the fundamental issues. All have to begin from the facts of Britain's economic and political situation and from the reactions of ordinary people. They don't exploit emotions.

This is surely the most commonly presented view of the relation between the question of immigration in Britain and the question of racism. On such a view, perhaps the most important implication is a radical break between the racism of a body such as the National Front and the rest of the political spectrum. But the main ground of political debate, Conservative, Liberal, and Labour, is different from and separate from the racists. In particular, there is no case to be made that the main political parties have been responsible for the regrowth of racism, either as latent attitudes or as organized fascism. Or, perhaps in one way, they might be responsible: but by a sin of omission rather than of commission. If only, so the dominant view goes, the main political parties had been more definite and determined, less hesitant and more strict on immigration, there would not have been the chance for all those irrational hatreds and prejudices to take root. But this omission cannot be seen as a positive act giving comfort to racism. And now, as the *Sun* put it, it is being put right.

This book takes a different position. I will argue that just as dangerous as prejudices about other people, if not more so, are theories which result in justifications for keeping ourselves separate. Suppose a theory about human nature puts emphasis on how natural it is to feel hostility towards, or even just essentially different to, members of other populations. To my mind that is racist. Referring barriers between peoples to human nature is racist because of the way it suggests that national separatism is natural and inevitable. Such theories are all too common. The particular illustration of the lurking presence of such a theory that this book has picked out is from British Conservatism. But I am certain that it is not a phenomenon limited to Britain.

The purpose of using a detailed case-study of this nature is not just to criticize a particular political position. It is also to show how a theory about race can be concealed inside apparently innocent language. Its concealment enables it to provide form and structure to people's experiences and reactions, without displaying itself as a whole theory with big and dangerous implications. Only under certain conditions does it display itself as a fully theorized view of human nature. It is only by careful investigation, therefore, using many quotations, that the theory in the language can be exposed. Individual statements may otherwise only appear metaphorical. What should we make, for example, of an individual word such as "alien"? [T]his word regularly occurs as part of a web of concepts that make its use far more than merely colorful. It is not exaggeration, it is a theorization – but of what?

Coupled with the belief that racism is a matter of prejudice is another idea that this book seeks to criticize. It is common to define racism as asserting the superiority of one's own "race" over others. Strangely, this is a definition often proposed by both left and right. One committed anti-racist has typically argued:

> By "racism" is meant any claim of the natural superiority of one identifiable human population, group or race over another. By "scientific racism" is meant the attempt to use the language and some of the techniques of science in support of theories or contentions that particular human groups or populations are innately inferior to others in terms of intelligence, "civilisation" or other socially-defined attitudes. (Rose, 1976, p. 113)

This is not much different from a definition of racism offered from quite another point of the political compass:

> Racialism is the belief that intellectual, cultural and moral qualities are genetically transmitted among the main racial groupings of mankind, that racial groups can be graded according to these qualities as inferior, with the racialists' own group at the apex. (Sherman, 1978)

The author of this second definition is a regular columnist for the *Daily Telegraph* who frequently contributes on questions of immigration and race relations. In the terms that this book will seek to clarify, Sherman has undoubtedly given voice to racist opinions. In addition to examples used in chapter 2, it is worth quoting an article published in November 1979, on the "fiancés" question:

> Minor problems can encapsulate major principles. The Asian fiancés issue is the visible tip of a submerged but inescapable problem: the conflict between the instincts of the people and the intellectual fashions of the Establishment where British nationhood is concerned . . . The relationship between indigenous Britons and this country is inherently different from that of Asians and most other immigrant stock. Hence there are unassailable moral no less than political grounds for embodying these differences in law and practice wherever necessary . . . The law's job is to fit the facts. This obliges it to discriminate between marriages made in heaven and those arranged in Islamabad. (Sherman, 1979)

I have quoted this at length because, whilst making assertions that to me are evidently racist, Sherman has himself offered a definition of racism according to which he would not be a racist. It is a contention of this book that the prevalence of a definition of racism in terms of superiority/inferiority has helped conceal how common is a form of racism that does not need to make such assertions – indeed, can make a positive virtue out of not making them. It is indeed a myth about the past that racism has generally been of the superiority/inferiority kind.

The form of theory into which such words as "alien" have been placed, giving them wider and more explicit meaning, is a theory of xenophobia. The wish to exclude foreigners has been built up into a theory capable of operating at different levels. At one level, I have already suggested, the theory inhabits the language of political arguments. In those arguments ideas about the naturalness of xenophobia allow politicians to move between (selected) evidence, and policy-conclusions. The implicit concept acts as a "bridge," allowing individual experiences, particular bits of information and evidence, to be theorized, given status and significance. Emotional responses now seem justified by their very "naturalness."

This is a form of racism. It is racism because it sees as biological, or pseudo-biological, groupings that are the result of social and historical processes. It is, however, a much more subtle form of racism than that which we stereotypically recognize as such. It can refuse insults: it need never talk of "niggers," "wogs," or "coons." It does not need to see Jews as morally degenerate, or blacks as "jungle bunnies." None the less in subtle but effective ways it authorizes the very emotions of hostility that then get expressed in these terms. As one writer puts it, we may all share a common human nature, but part of that very shared nature is the natural tendency to form bounded social units and to differentiate ourselves from outsiders (see Desmond Morris 1971, p. 128).

The Problem of Ideology

This reference to Morris is intended to introduce a second, more explicit level at which this theory of xenophobia is to be found. There are traditions of ideas centered within biology that have come to just such conclusions. It is nothing new to realize that science can be used for dubious political ends. Social Darwinism has rightly been seen over many years as pseudo-knowledge, with political conclusions supportive of reactionary positions either implicit or explicit. I hope we will not soon forget the role of race-biology in Nazi Germany. But it is not satisfactory to stop simply at recognition of this fact. It is not even enough to show, as I shall, that Social Darwinism is now regrowing in new forms. For as Steven Rose has rightly said: "To understand the significance of the current revival of biological determinism, it is necessary to examine both its social and political history and the truth content of its present claims" (Rose 1979, p. 423). The difficulty is to know what is to be the relation between these two examinations.

Take a representative problem. A large part of this book is concerned with the nature of reductionist biology, that is, with biological accounts of species that interpret their behavior as functions of genetic or biochemical activity. In recent years, an important dispute has developed between those writers called the ethologists and a new group of opponents called sociobiologists. One spokesman for the latter has insisted that the dispute arose entirely within evolutionary biology as an academic discipline. And yet it can be argued that, despite the truth of this, ethology and sociobiology are equally but differently ideological. And the differences in their ideologies are in part a function of their different conceptions of evolutionary mechanisms – the very point over which their disputes have been hottest. Any attempt to explain the political or general ideological significance of their theories must, therefore, take centrally into account the specific nature of these theories.

Unfortunately, accounts of the ideological significance of such scientific theories have very often done exactly the opposite. Interpreters are apt to see the truth or falsity of a theory as distinct from its political content. Representative of such an approach is Erich Fromm's gloss on Konrad Lorenz, an ethologist, an associate of Desmond Morris and a man who [. . .] has both a dubious past and a controversial present:

> Perhaps Lorenz's neo-instinctivism was so successful not because his arguments are strong, but because people are so susceptible to them. What could be more welcome to people who are frightened and feel impotent to change the course leading to destruction, than a theory that assures us that violence stems from our animal nature, from an ungovernable drive for aggression, and that the best we can do, as Lorenz asserts, is to understand the law of evolution that accounts for the power of this drive? (Fromm, 1977, p. 22)

Note the way that Fromm separates the truth or falsity of Lorenz's theory, from its effect. The political significance lies in the latter. There are many difficulties with this view. It seems to see Lorenz and his co-thinkers inviting passivity, where I find much evidence that their ideas are the basis of a right-wing activism. It sees the ideological significance residing in ethology's general deterministic form. But then how are we to differentiate ethology from its rival, sociobiology? In general form, they correspond closely. But their view of the place of aggression is markedly different and has been the subject of a strong controversy. Should we write that off as an unimportant faction-fight between them? I think not.

The general trouble with analyses such as Fromm's is that they tempt us not to look closely enough at the structure of the ideas presented and the exact form of their claims, when assessing them for ideology. This book will start by taking the claims of such scientists seriously. In this way, I hope to avoid Fromm's trap and much of the debate that has gone on among the Left about the status of science. This debate has often revolved around the question of whether science can be seen as an independent set of social practices, seeking truth, capable of being objective and capable of being neutral in the knowledges they produce. One whole school has wanted to treat "science as social relations," claiming that all knowledge produced by scientists is necessarily marked in its form and content by the social relations within which it is produced. This has led to serious questioning of how much we can have use for concepts of truth in our understanding of science and its "discoveries."

I want to bypass this debate by taking my theorists at their own words. I am not offering a general theory of ideology, nor of science. If one is possible at all, we are not yet in a position to formulate it. Far too much discussion of ideology has been cavalier in its attitude to evidence and inspection of cases in detail. But my more limited approach does not involve accepting scientists' conclusions about their own work. It means only being prepared to accept that they are trying to do what they say they are trying to do. Take each one's project seriously and let us see where it leads. What are, for example, the implications of their various disagreements over evolutionary mechanisms and over the nature of aggression? By "living within" the structure of their ideas, we will be able to see the points at which they depart from their own procedures; and that, as we shall see, allows us to strengthen the case that their theories are not simply scientific, but simultaneously political. Approaching the problem of ideology in this circumscribed, uncommitted way will enable us to answer, or begin to answer, what to me is an interesting and important question: Why is it that racists, in search of justificatory arguments, have so often turned to biology? What is it in the nature of certain forms of biological argument that makes them so available to racist (and other reactionary) positions?

Racism and Philosophy

I want to test simultaneously the truth content of certain scientific claims and their ideological content. Such an approach will enable me to answer the question: In what senses may scientific ideas of this sort be called ideological? This is what can be contributed to an understanding and critique of racism from my competence as a philosopher. It is a project that may seem distant from many of the traditional concerns of philosophers. For a good many years, philosophers by and large saw themselves as not able to comment on practical issues. Philosophy answered metaquestions; it dealt with the clarification of concepts which would only secondarily have application to the problems of living. A widespread belief, for example, in a universal distinction between facts and values meant that moral and political decisions were not subject to much philosophical scrutiny. And sciences were primary, where philosophy was secondary, "ground-clearing."

There were always heretics who did not accept such a picture, even when it was at its height. But recent years have seen a progressive weakening of this (analytic) tradition, both in Britain and elsewhere. Some established philosophers have been prepared to reopen substantive enquiry in philosophy. A new generation of younger philosophers, many of them bitten deep with the experiences of the 1960s, have been prepared to go further. I hope this book is a contribution to the latters' attempts.

Among other things, I have had to conclude that the analytic tradition has distorted philosophy's own history. [. . .] I offer an account of the philosophy of David Hume. Hume was a racist, both in his personal attitudes and also in the content of his philosophy. His politics were high Tory, and, most important, the general political direction of his thought has been better grasped by some modern Conservative politicians than it has by the majority of philosophical commentators. Where philosophers have abstracted out his concerns with the nature of knowledge, or his discussions of ethics, a number of politicians have sensed how useful to them is the whole structure of his thought. The result of philosophers reading Hume abstractly has been particularly to miss the significance of his continual references to man's "original nature" as precursors of later biologistic views of a fixed human nature.

Obviously, however, the core of this study is directed at contemporary thought and problems. It constitutes an invitation to philosophers to use their skills in conceptual analysis to look much more closely at implicit theories, at the structures of argument used in "commonsense." There is so much serious work to be done, for instance, in considering the ways ideas of "need" are used in political and social welfare discussions. To do this would not be to abandon philosophy, but to extend it. For in truth, very little has been done by way of philosophical analysis of concepts such as "need."

In this study, the primary philosophical issue is evolution. It is a tragedy that, here again, so much philosophical enquiry is vitiated by never seeming to notice that a man called Charles Darwin once wrote an important book called *On the Origin of Species*. Much philosophizing on the nature of mind, self, purpose, and so on desperately needs a confrontation with the demands set up by evolutionary theory. This is not to say that evolutionary theory is a fixed science that dictates philosophical conclusions. But it is a set of parameters without which a lot of argument is worse than useless. We need an interplay between certain crucial Darwinian claims and philosophical analysis. For the theory of evolution contains concepts whose clarification must have very significant implications for our understanding of human beings. In this book I will only be opening up some lines that have appeared to me to be important: for example, a potential distinction within evolutionary biology between adaptiveness and adaptability. I have also queried the concept of genetic determination, showing how under definite circumstances it is self-defeating – thus making space for versions of the very concepts of mind, purpose, and intention into which philosophers have wanted to enquire. But evolutionary theory thus understood still conditions the forms that these are capable of taking.

Many other overtly philosophical issues have to arise in the course of this study of racism. Not least is the fact-value distinction. I have not dealt with this in the standard way. It is not obviously the most helpful way, to ask whether values are *ever* deducible from facts. That is probably an unanswerable question, since it assumes that in the examples we use we have found typical and generalizable conditions. If from these initial conditions we cannot derive value-conclusions, the assumption runs, we never can. I have, in this book, confronted one form of fact-value distinction which, because of the structure of concepts in which it occurs, cannot be maintained.

There is surely a lesson in this. Philosophy as a mode of enquiry could be greatly benefited if its practitioners relied more heavily on real, living examples. It was Gellner, I think, who wrote of the silly examples that philosophers use. It is not as if the world in which we live is short of real claims, arguments, and uses of ideas that are badly in need of evaluation.

Of course there are costs in committing oneself to the sort of philosophy that I have tried. The most important is that philosophy becomes political in many senses. It has to take a stand. This book is committed because of its philosophical stance to anti-racism, and many other specific political conclusions. I have long found worrying a tendency for philosophical formulations to appear neutral when they can afford comfort to definite political positions with which their authors undoubtedly would not sympathize. An example relevant to this book would be Wittgenstein's concept of a "form of life." This is his idea of a set of linguistic and other practices which, being like games, do not have any external criteria by which they may be judged. They contain their own criteria of validity; they are self-validating. This fits in remarkably closely with the idea within the new racism of a "way of life." But I know of no evidence that Wittgenstein, or Winch who elaborates a more or less Wittgensteinian position in the social field, is a racist. It is a matter of ideas which have a potential life beyond an author's expectations. But the life of the ideas is inherent in their nature, not an external accident.

Accepting that philosophy can be political must involve greater thought and care about the direction our analyses take. That is a part of breaking out of the hermetic world in which philosophers have thought they could live. [. . .]

References

Fromm, Erich (1977). *The Anatomy of Human Destructiveness*. Penguin.
Morris, Desmond (1971). *The Human Zoo*. Corgi.
Rose, Steven (1976). "Scientific Racism and IQ." In H. Rose and S. Rose (eds.), *The Political Economy of Science*. Macmillan.
——(1979). "Review of Allan Chase: The Legacy of Malthus." *Race and Class*, XX (4).
Sherman, Alfred (1978). "Why Britain Can't Be Wished Away." *Daily Telegraph*, September 8.
——(1979). "Britain is not Asia's Fiancé." *Daily Telegraph*, November 9.

5

A Genealogy of Modern Racism

Cornel West

The notion that black people are human beings is a relatively new discovery in the modern West. The idea of black equality in beauty, culture, and intellectual capacity remains problematic and controversial within prestigious halls of learning and sophisticated intellectual circles. The Afro-American encounter with the modern world has been shaped first and foremost by the doctrine of white supremacy, which is embodied in institutional practices and enacted in everyday folkways under varying circumstances and evolving conditions.[1]

My aim in this chapter is to give a brief account of the way in which the idea of white supremacy was constituted as an object of modern discourse in the West, without simply appealing to the objective demands of the prevailing mode of production, the political interests of the slave-holding class, or the psychological needs of the dominant white racial group. Despite the indispensable role these factors would play in a full-blown explanatory model to account for the emergence and sustenance of modern racism in the West, I try to hold these factors constant and focus solely on a neglected variable in past explanatory models – namely, the way in which the very structure of modern discourse *at its inception* produced forms of rationality, scientificity, and objectivity as well as aesthetic and cultural ideals which require the constitution of the idea of white supremacy.

This requirement follows from a logic endemic to the very structure of modern discourse. This logic is manifest in the way in which the controlling metaphors, notions, and categories of modern discourse produce and prohibit, develop and delimit, specific conceptions of truth and knowledge, beauty and character, so that certain ideas are rendered incomprehensible and unintelligible. I suggest that one such idea that cannot be brought within the epistemological field of the initial modern discourse is that of black equality in beauty, culture, and intellectual capacity. This act of discursive exclusion, of relegating this idea to silence, does not simply correspond to (or is not only reflective of) the relative powerlessness of black people at the time. It also reveals the evolving internal dynamics of the structure of modern discourse in the late seventeenth and eighteenth centuries in western Europe – or during the Enlightenment. The concrete effects of this exclusion and the intellectual traces of this silence continue to haunt the modern West: on the nondiscursive level, in ghetto streets, and on the discursive level, in methodological assumptions in the disciplines of the humanities.

I shall argue that the initial structure of modern discourse in the West "secretes" the idea of white supremacy. I call this "secretion" – the underside of modern discourse – a particular logical consequence of the quest for truth and knowledge in the modern West. To put it crudely, my argument is that the authority of science, undergirded by a modern philosophical discourse guided by Greek ocular metaphors and Cartesian notions, promotes and encourages the activities of observing, comparing, measuring, and ordering the physical characteristics of human bodies. Given the renewed appreciation and appropriation of classical antiquity, these activities are regulated by classical aesthetic and cultural norms. The creative fusion of scientific investigation, Cartesian epistemology, and classical ideals produced forms of rationality, scientificity, and objectivity which, though efficacious in the quest for truth and knowledge, prohibited the intelligibility and legitimacy of the idea of black equality in beauty, culture, and intellectual capacity. In fact, to "think" such an idea was to be deemed irrational, barbaric, or mad.

Theoretical Considerations: The Genealogical Approach

I call this inquiry a "genealogy" because, following the works of Friedrich Nietzsche and Michel Foucault, I am interested in the emergence (*Entstebung*) or the "moment of arising" of the idea of white supremacy within the modern discourse in the West.[2] This genealogy tries to address the following questions: What are the discursive conditions for the possibility of the intelligibility and legitimacy of the idea of white supremacy in modern discourse? How is this idea constituted within the epistemological field of modern discourse? What is the complex configuration of metaphors, notions, categories, and norms which produces and promotes such an object of modern discourse?

My genealogical approach subscribes to a conception of power that is neither simply based on individual subjects – e.g., heroes or great personages as in traditional historiography – nor on collective subjects – e.g., groups, elites, or classes as in revisionist and vulgar Marxist historiography. Therefore I do not believe that the emergence of the idea of white supremacy in the modern West can be fully accounted for in terms of the psychological needs of white individuals and groups or the political and economic interests of a ruling class. I will try to show that the idea of white supremacy emerges partly because of the powers within the structure of modern discourse – powers to produce and prohibit, develop and delimit, forms of rationality, scientificity, and objectivity which set perimeters and draw boundaries for the intelligibility, availability, and legitimacy of certain ideas.

These powers are subjectless – that is, they are the indirect products of the praxis of human subjects. They have a life and logic of their own, not in a transhistorical realm but within history alongside yet not reducible to demands of an economic system, interests of a class, or needs of a group. What I am suggesting is not a history without a subject propagated by the structuralist Marxist Louis Althusser, but rather a history made by the praxis of human subjects which often results in complex structures of discourses which have relative autonomy from (or is not fully accountable in terms of) the intentions, aims, needs, interests, and objectives of human subjects.[3]

I am further suggesting that there is no direct correspondence between nondiscursive structures, such as a system of production (or, in Marxist terms, an economic base), and discursive structures, such as theoretical formations (or, in Marxist terms, an ideological superstructure). Rather, there are powers immanent in nondiscursive structures and discursive structures.[4] Traditional, revisionist, and vulgar Marxist types of historiography focus primarily on powers within nondiscursive structures – e.g., powers of kings, presidents, elites, or classes – and reduce the powers within discursive structures to mere means for achieving the intentions, aims, needs, interests, and objectives of subjects in nondiscursive structures. This reductionism is not wrong; it is simply inadequate. It rightly acknowledges noteworthy concrete effects generated by the relationship between powers in discursive structures and those in nondiscursive structures, but it wrongly denies the relative autonomy of the powers in discursive structures and hence reduces the complexity of cultural phenomena.

The primary motivation behind such reductionism (such as personalistic analyses of race prejudice or orthodox Marxist accounts of racism) is to ensure an easy resolution of a highly complex problem, without calling into question certain fundamental assumptions that inform such resolutions. These fundamental assumptions, such as the subject-based conception of power, and easy resolutions, such as the elimination of race prejudice by knowledge or the abolition of racism under socialism, preclude theoretical alternatives and strategic options. In this way, these fundamental assumptions and hypothetical resolutions illustrate the effects of the powers immanent in certain liberal and Marxist discourses.

The Structure of Modern Discourse

I understand "the structure of modern discourse" to be the controlling metaphors, notions, categories, and norms that shape the predominant conceptions of truth and knowledge in the modern West. These metaphors, notions, categories, and norms are circumscribed and determined by three major historical processes: the scientific revolution, the Cartesian transformation of philosophy, and the classical revival.[5]

The scientific revolution is usually associated with the pioneering breakthroughs of Copernicus and Kepler in astronomy, Galileo and Newton in physics, and Descartes and Leibnitz in mathematics. These breakthroughs were pre-Enlightenment, most of them occurring during the seventeenth century, the so-called Age of Genius. The scientific revolution is noteworthy (to say the least) primarily because it signified the authority of science. This authority justified new modes of knowledge and new conceptions of truth and reality; it arose at the end of the era of pagan Christianity and set the framework for the advent of modernity.

The originary figures of the scientific revolution went beyond the Renaissance problematic – of finding a compromise formula which reconciled Christian and classical modes of thinking and living – yet stopped short of drawing thoroughly secular conclusions from their breakthroughs, that is, of waging intellectual war on natural religion and dogmatic theology. Galileo's Platonism and Newton's Socinianism illustrate this peculiar protomodern world view of making peace between science and religion.[6]

For our purposes, the scientific revolution is significant because it highlights two fundamental ideas: *observation* and *evidence*. These two ideas have played, in an isolated manner, a role in previous paradigms of knowledge in the West (since the times of Aristotle and Aristarchus). But the scientific revolution brought these ideas together in such a way that they have become the two foci around which much of modern discourse evolves. The modern concepts of hypothesis, fact, inference, validation, confirmation, and verification cluster around the ideas of observation and evidence.

The major proponents of the scientific revolution, or, more specifically, of the authority of science, were two philosophers, Francis Bacon and René Descartes. Bacon is noteworthy primarily because of his metaphilosophical honesty. For him, the aim of philosophy was to give humankind mastery over nature by means of scientific discoveries and inventions. He then promoted the philosophical importance of the inductive method as a means of arriving at general laws to facilitate this human mastery. Despite Bacon's acceptance of orthodox religion, his rejection of Copernican theory, and his lack of acquaintance with some of the major scientific discoveries of his time – e.g., the work of Andreas Vesalius on modern anatomy, William Gilbert on magnetism, or William Harvey (Bacon's own medical attendant) on the circulation of blood – Bacon's writings, especially *The Advancement of Learning*, did much to promote the authority of science.[7]

Descartes is highly significant because his thought provided the controlling notions of modern discourse: *the primacy of the subject and the preeminence of representation*. Descartes is widely regarded as the founder of modern philosophy not simply because his philosophical outlook was profoundly affected by the scientific revolution but, more important, because he associated the scientific aim of predicting and explaining the world with the philosophical aim of picturing and representing the world. In this view, the fruits of scientific research do not merely provide more useful ways for human beings to *cope* with reality; such research also yields a true *copy* of reality. Descartes's conception of philosophy as a tortuous move from the subject to objects, from the veil of ideas to the external world, from immediate awareness to extended substances, from self-consciousness to things in space, and ultimately from doubt to certainty was motivated primarily by an attempt to provide a theoretical basis for the legitimacy of modern science. Martin Heidegger made this crucial connection between Cartesian philosophy and modern science in his famous essay, "The Age of the World View":

> We are reflecting on the nature of modern science in order to find its metaphysical basis. What conception of the existent and what concept of truth cause science to become research?
>
> Understanding as research holds the existent to account on the question of how and how far it can be put at the disposal of available "representation." Research has the existent at its disposal if it can either calculate it in advance, in its future course, or calculate it afterwards as past. Nature and history become the object of expository representation. . . .
>
> This objectification of the existent takes place in re-presentation which aims at presenting whatever exists to itself in such a way that the calculating person can be secure, that is, certain of the existent. Science as research is produced when and only when truth has been transformed into such certainty of representation. In the metaphysics of Descartes the existent was defined for the first time as objectivity of representation, and truth as certainty of representation.[8]

Bacon and Descartes had basic differences: Bacon inductive orientation and Descartes the deductive viewpoint; Bacon the empiricist outlook and Descartes the rationalist (mathematical) perspective. Despite these differences, both of these propagandists of modern science agreed that scientific method provides a new paradigm of knowledge and that observation and evidence are at the center of scientific method. In *The New Organon*, Bacon likened his ideal natural philosopher to the bee, which collects "its material from the flowers of the garden and of the field" and digests it "by a power of its own." In his *Discourse on*

Method, Descartes set forth as a rule that "observations" become "the more necessary the further we advance in knowledge." And, as D'Alembert acknowledged in *The Encyclopedia*, both Bacon and Descartes "introduced the spirit of experimental science."[9]

The last major historical process that circumscribed and determined the metaphors, notions, categories, and norms of modern discourse was the classical revival. This classical revival – in response to medieval mediocrity and religious dogmatism – was initiated in the Early Renaissance (1300–1500), principally with humanist studies in Roman art and Latin literature, such as Giotto in painting, Petrarch in letters, and Dufay in music. This revival intensified during the High Renaissance (1500–1530), which Da Vinci, Raphael, Bramante, and the early Michelangelo in the arts; Ariosto, Rabelais, and Erasmus in literature; and Josquin and Lassus in music. The revival mellowed in the Mannerist era (1530–1600), as illustrated by El Greco, Tintoretto, and the later Michelangelo in the arts; Montaigne, Cervantes, and Shakespeare in literature; and Marenzio, Gabrieli, and Frescobaldi in music. The revival was strengthened in the Baroque period (1600–1750), as seen in the works of Velasquez and Rembrandt in the arts; Racine, Milton, and Vondel in literature; and Bach and Handel in music. The classical revival culminated in the neoclassical movement in the middle of the eighteenth century, with the paintings of David and Ingres, the lyrics of Hölderlin, the tragedies of Alfieri, the verse and prose of Landor, and the music of Haydn and Mozart. The Enlightenment revolt against the authority of the church and the search for models of unrestrained criticism led to a highly charged recovery of classical antiquity, and especially to a new appreciation and appropriation of the artistic and cultural heritage of ancient Greece.

For our purposes, the classical revival is important because it infuses Greek ocular metaphors and classical ideals of beauty, proportion, and moderation into the beginnings of modern discourse. Greek ocular metaphors – Eye of the Mind, Mind as Mirror of Nature, Mind as Inner Arena with its Inner Observer – dominate modern discourse in the West.[10] Coupled with the Cartesian notion of knowledge as inner representation, modern philosophical inquiry is saddled with the epistemological model of intellect (formerly Plato's and Aristotle's Nous, now Descartes's Inner Eye) inspecting entities modeled on retinal images, with the Eye of the Mind viewing representations in order to find some characteristic that would testify to their fidelity.

The creative fusion of scientific investigation, Cartesian philosophy, Greek ocular metaphors, and classical aesthetic and cultural ideals constitutes the essential elements of modern discourse in the West. In short, modern discourse rests upon a conception of truth and knowledge governed by an ideal value-free subject engaged in observing, comparing, ordering, and measuring in order to arrive at evidence sufficient to make valid inferences, confirm speculative hypotheses, deduce error-proof conclusions, and verify true representations of reality.

The Emergence of Modern Racism: The First Stage

The recovery of classical antiquity in the modern West produced what I shall call a "normative gaze," namely, an ideal from which to order and compare observations. This ideal was drawn primarily from classical aesthetic values of beauty, proportion, and human form and classical cultural standards of moderation, self-control, and harmony.[11] The role of classical aesthetic and cultural norms in the emergence of the idea of white supremacy as an object of modern discourse cannot be underestimated.

These norms were consciously projected and promoted by many influential Enlightenment writers, artists, and scholars, of whom the most famous was J. J. Winckelmann. In his widely read book, *History of Ancient Art*, Winckelmann portrayed ancient Greece as a world of beautiful bodies. He laid down rules – in art and aesthetics – that should govern the size of eyes and eyebrows, of collarbones, hands, feet, and especially noses. He defined beauty as noble simplicity and quiet grandeur. In a celebrated passage he wrote:

> As the depth of the ocean always remains calm however much the surface may be agitated, so does the expression in the figures of the Greeks reveal a great and composed soul in the midst of passions.[12]

Although Winckelmann was murdered in middle life, never set foot in Greece, and saw almost no original Greek art (only one exhibition of Greek art in Munich), he viewed Greek beauty and culture as the ideal or standard against which to measure other peoples and cultures.

Winthrop Jordan and Thomas Gossett have shown that there are noteworthy premodern racist viewpoints aimed directly and indirectly at nonwhite, especially black, people.[13] For example, in 1520 Paracelsus held that black and primitive peoples had a separate origin from Europeans. In 1591, Giordano Bruno made a similar claim, but had in mind principally Jews and Ethiopians. And Lucilio Vanini posited that Ethiopians had apes for ancestors and had once walked on all fours. Since theories of the separate origin of races were in disagreement with the Roman Catholic Church, Bruno and Vanini underwent similar punishment: both were burned at the stake. Of course, biblically based accounts of racial inferiority flourished, but the authority of the church prohibited the proliferation of nonreligious, that is, protomodern, accounts of racial inferiority.

What is distinctive about the role of classical aesthetic and cultural norms at the advent of modernity is that they provided an acceptable authority for the idea of white supremacy, an acceptable authority that was closely linked with the major authority on truth and knowledge in the modern world, namely, the institution of science. In order to see how this linkage took place, let us examine the categories and aims of the major discipline that promoted this authority, that is, those of natural history.

The principal aim of natural history is to observe, compare, measure, and order animals and human bodies (or classes of animals and human bodies) *based on visible, especially physical, characteristics.* These characteristics permit one to discern identity and difference, equality and inequality, beauty and ugliness among animals and human bodies.

The governing categories of natural history are preeminently *classificatory* categories – that is, they consist of various taxonomies in the form of tables, catalogs, indexes, and inventories which impose some degree of order or representational schema on a broad field of visible characteristics. *Observation* and *differentness* are the essential guiding notions in natural history. Foucault wrote:

> Natural history has as a condition of its possibility the common affinity of things and language with representation; but it exists as a task only in so far as things and language happen to be separate. It must therefore reduce this distance between them so as to bring language as close as possible to the observing gaze, and the things observed as close as possible

to words. Natural history is nothing more than the nomination of the
visible. . . .

Natural history . . . covers a series of complex operations that introduce the possibility of a constant order into a totality of representations.
It constitutes a whole domain of empiricity as at the same time describ-
able and orderable.[14]

The initial basis for the idea of white supremacy is to be found in the
classificatory categories and the descriptive, representational, order-
imposing aims of natural history. The captivity of natural history
to what I have called the "normative gaze" signifies the first stage
of the emergence of the idea of white supremacy as an object of
modern discourse. More specifically (and as Ashley Montagu has tire-
lessly argued), the genealogy of racism in the modern West is inseparable from the appearance of the classificatory category of race in
natural history.

The category of race – denoting primarily skin color – was first
employed as a means of classifying human bodies by François
Bernier, a French physician, in 1684. He divided humankind into
basically four races: Europeans, Africans, Orientals, and Lapps.[15] The
first authoritative racial division of humankind is found in the influential *Natural System* (1735) of the most preeminent naturalist of the
eighteenth century, Carolus Linnaeus. For Linnaeus, species were fixed
in number and kind; they were immutable prototypes. Varieties,
however, were members of a species that might change in appearance.
The members of a species produced fertile offspring; interfertility was
the test for the division of species. There were variations of kind within
a species; the races were a prime example. For Linnaeus, there were
four races: Homo Europaeus, Homo Asiaticus, Homo Afer, and Homo
Americanus.

Winthrop Jordan has argued that Linnaeus did not subscribe to a
hierarchical ranking of races but rather to "one chain of universal
being." Jordan states:

It was one thing to classify all living creation and altogether another to
arrange it in a single great hierarchy; and when Linnaeus undertook
the first of these tasks he was not thereby forced to attempt the latter. In
the many editions of the *Systema Naturae* he duly catalogued the various
kinds of men, yet never in a hierarchic manner.[16]

Yet it is quite apparent that Linnaeus implicitly evaluated the observable characteristics of the racial classes of people, especially those pertaining to character and disposition. For example, compare Linnaeus' description of the European with the African:

> European.   White, Sanguine, Brawny. Hair abundantly flowing. Eyes blue. Gentle, acute, inventive. Covered with close vestments. Governed by customs.
> African.   Black, Phlegmatic, Relaxed. Hair black, frizzled. Skin silky. Nose flat. Lips tumid, Women's bosom a matter of modesty. Breasts give milk abundantly. Crafty, indolent. Negligent. Anoints himself with grease. Governed by caprice.[17]

Linnaeus' use of evaluative terms revealed, at the least, an implicit hierarchy by means of personal preference. It also is important to note that he included some remarks about the African woman, but that he said nothing about the European woman (nor the American and Asiatic woman). It also is significant that in the 1750s when he first acknowledged that hybridization of species occurs, he chose black people and apes as the probable candidates, while restricting such unions to black women and male apes.

Georges Louis Leclerc de Buffon accepted hybridization without question in his famous *Natural History of Man* (1778). Although Buffon, like Linnaeus, viewed races as mere chance variations, he held that white was "the real and natural color of man." Black people and other races were variations of this natural color, yet somehow not members of a different species. He remained uncertain about the objective reality of species. Buffon believed that black skin was caused by hot climate and would change if the climate became colder. Although he was a fervent antislavery advocate, he claimed that black people had "little genius" and then added, "The unfortunate negroes are endowed with excellent hearts, and possess the seeds of every human virtue."[18]

The Emergence of Modern Racism: The Second Stage

In the works of Johann Friedrich Blumenbach, one of the founders of modern anthropology, the aesthetic criteria and cultural ideals of Greece began to come to the forefront. Like Linnaeus and Buffon,

Blumenbach held that all human beings belonged to the same species and that races were merely varieties. Yet contrary to the claims by Winthrop Jordan, Ashley Montagu, and Thomas Gossett concerning Blumenbach's opposition to hierarchic racial ranking or irritation at those who use aesthetic standards for such ranking, Blumenbach praised the symmetrical face as the most beautiful of human faces precisely because it approximated the "divine" works of Greek art, and specifically the proper anatomical proportions found in Greek sculpture.[19] Applying the classical ideal of moderation, he claimed that the more moderate the climate, the more beautiful the face. The net result was that since black people were farthest from the Greek ideal and located in extremely hot climates, they were, by implication, inferior in beauty to Europeans.

The second stage of the emergence of the idea of white supremacy as an object of modern discourse primarily occurred in the rise of phrenology (the reading of skulls) and physiognomy (the reading of faces). These new disciplines – closely connected with anthropology – served as an open platform for the propagation of the idea of white supremacy not principally because they were pseudo-sciences, but, more important, because these disciplines acknowledged the European value-laden character of their observations. This European value-laden character was based on classical aesthetic and cultural ideals.

Pieter Camper, the Dutch anatomist, made aesthetic criteria the pillar of his chief discovery: the famous "facial angle." Camper claimed that the "facial angle" – a measure of prognathism – permitted a comparison of heads of human bodies by way of cranial and facial measurements. For Camper, the ideal "facial angle" was a 100-degree angle which was achieved only by the ancient Greeks. He openly admitted that this ideal conformed to Winckelmann's classical ideal of beauty. Following Winckelmann, Camper held that Greek proportions and stature exemplified beauty and embodied perfection. Camper further held that a beautiful face, beautiful body, beautiful nature, beautiful character, and beautiful soul were inseparable. He tried to show that the "facial angle" of Europeans measured about 97 degrees and those of black people between 60 and 70 degrees, closer to the measurements of apes and dogs than to human beings.

Although many anthropologists readily accepted the "facial angle" as a scientific notion,[20] Camper made it clear that his aim was not simply to contribute to the new discipline of anthropology but also to promote the love of classical antiquity to young artists and sculptors. As George Mosse has noted, historians of race theories often overlook the fact that Camper and many subsequent theoreticians of race and racism were trained as artists and writers. Camper was a painter by training and, in fact, won the gold medal of the Amsterdam School of Art two years before he published his work on the "facial angle."[21]

Johann Kaspar Lavater, the father of physiognomy, explicitly acknowledged that the art of painting was the mother of his new discipline. Moreau, an early editor of Lavater's work, clearly noted that the true language of physiognomy was painting, because it spoke through images, equally to the eye and to the spirit.[22] This new discipline linked particular visible characteristics of human bodies, especially those of the face, to the character and capacities of human beings. This discipline openly articulated what many of the early naturalists and anthropologists tacitly assumed: *the classical ideals of beauty, proportion, and moderation regulated the classifying and ranking of groups of human bodies*. In short, physiognomy brought the "normative gaze" into daylight.

Lavater believed that the Greek statues were the models of beauty. His description of the desirable specimen – blue eyes, horizontal forehead, bent back, round chin, and short brown hair – resembled the beautiful person preferred by Camper. The common Greek ideals of beauty, though slightly distorted (to say the least), were the principal source of this "normative gaze." Lavater's new discipline was highly influential among scientists – for example, Jean Baptiste Porta, Christian Meiners – and artists. His close friend, the famous Goethe, aided him in editing and publishing his physiognomic formulations and findings and Sir Walter Scott, among others, popularized them in his novels.

Lavater's promotion of what I call the "normative gaze" consisted no longer of detailed measurements, as was the case with the naturalists, but rather of the visual glance. He wrote: "Trust your first quick impression, for it is worth more than what is usually called observation."[23] Therefore it is not surprising that Lavater put forth an elaborate theory of noses, the most striking member of the face. Neither is it surprising that subsequent classifications of noses, based on Lavater's formulations, associate Roman and Greek noses with conquerors and persons of refinement and taste.

The next and last step we shall consider in this genealogy of racism in late-seventeenth- and eighteenth-century Europe is the advent of phrenology, the new discipline which held that human character could be read through the shape of the human head. Franz Joseph Gall, a highly regarded German physician, argued in 1796 that the inner workings of the brain could be determined by the shape of the skull. For example, he associated an arched forehead with a penchant for metaphysical speculation; a skull arched at the rear with love of fame; and a skull large at the base with a criminal disposition. In the nineteenth century, when racist ideology was systematized, this new discipline took on a life of its own with Johann Kaspar Spurzheim, Anders Retzius, Carl Gustav Carus, and others; it also aided in allying modern racism with nationalism and repressed sexuality in bourgeois morality.

Theoretical Consequences: Restrictive Powers in Modern Discourse

A major example of the way in which the restrictive powers of modern discourse delimit theoretical alternatives and strategic options in regard to the idea of white supremacy is seen in writings of radical environmentalists of the period – those one would expect to be open to the idea of black equality in beauty, culture, and intellectual capacity. Yet even these progressive antislavery advocates remain captive to the "normative gaze."

The major opponent of predominant forms of a hierarchic ranking of races and the outspoken proponent of intermarriage in the United States during this era, Samuel Stanhope Smith, illustrates this captivity. In his day Smith stood at the pinnacle of American academia. He was president of Princeton University and an honorary member of the American Philosophical Society. He was awarded honorary degrees from Harvard and Yale. In his well-known *Essays* of 1787 (and revised in 1810) Smith argued that humankind constituted one species and that human variations could be accounted for in reference to three natural causes: "climate," "state of society," and "habits of living." He believed "that colour may be justly considered as an universal freckle."[24]

The "normative gaze" operative in Smith's viewpoint is located, as in Buffon, in the assumption that physical, especially racial, variations are always degenerate ones from an ideal state. For Smith, this ideal state consisted of highly civilized white people. As Winthrop Jordan notes, "Smith treated the complexion and physiognomy of the white man not merely as indication of superiority but as the hallmark of civilization."[25] Smith justified this ideal standard and legitimized his "normative gaze" by appealing to the classical ideals of beauty. In a patriotic footnote he wrote:

> It may perhaps gratify my countrymen to reflect that the United States occupy those latitudes that have ever been most favourable to the beauty of the human form. When time shall have accommodated the constitution of its new state, and cultivation shall have meliorated the climate, the beauties of Greece and Circasia may be renewed in America; as there are not a few already who rival those of any quarter of the globe.[26]

Smith's radical environmentalism (along with his adherence to Greek aesthetic ideals) led him to adopt the most progressive and sympathetic alternative which promotes the welfare of black people permissible within the structure of modern discourse: integration which *uplifts* black people, assimilation which *civilizes* black people, intermarriage which *ensures less Negroid features* in the next generation. For example, Smith wrote:

> The great difference between the domestic and field slaves gives reason to believe that, if they were perfectly free, enjoyed property, and were admitted to a liberal participation of the society rank and privileges of their masters, they would change their African peculiarities much faster.[27]

This theoretical alternative was taken to its logical consequence by the distinguished American antislavery advocate, publicizer of talented black writers, and eminent physician, Benjamin Rush. This logical consequence was the elimination of the skin color of black people. In a paper entitled "Observations Intended to Favour a Supposition that the Black Color (As it is called) of the Negroes is Derived From the Leprosy," Rush denounced the idea of white supremacy, then stated: "Is the color of Negroes a disease? Then let science and humanity combine their efforts and endeavor to discover a remedy for it."[28] In one bold stroke, Rush provided grounds for promoting abolitionism, opposing intermarriage (who wants to marry diseased persons!), and supporting the Christian unity of humankind. In his opinion, his viewpoint also maximized the happiness of black and white people:

> To encourage attempts to cure this disease of the skin in Negroes, let us recollect that by succeeding in them, we shall produce a large portion of happiness in the world. . . .
>   Secondly, we shall add greatly to their happiness, for however well they appear to be satisfied with their color, there are many proofs of their preferring that of the white people.[29]

Racism in the Enlightenment

The intellectual legitimacy of the idea of white supremacy, though grounded in what we now consider marginal disciplines (especially in its second stage), was pervasive. This legitimacy can be illustrated by the extent to which racism permeated the writings of the major figures of the Enlightenment. It is important to note that the idea of white supremacy not only was accepted by these figures, but, more important, it was accepted by them *without their having to put forward their own arguments to justify it*. Montesquieu and Voltaire of the French Enlightenment, Hume and Jefferson of the Scotch and the American Enlightenment, and Kant of the German Enlightenment not merely held racist views; they also uncritically – during this age of criticism – believed that the *authority* for these views rested in the domain of naturalists, anthropologists, physiognomists, and phrenologists.

Montesquieu's satirical remarks in *Spirit of the Laws* about black people (and his many revisions of these remarks) may seem to suggest an equivocal disposition toward the idea of white supremacy. Yet his conclusion leaned toward support of the idea:

> It is impossible for us to suppose that these beings should be men; because if we supposed them to be men, one would begin to believe we ourselves were not Christians.[30]

Voltaire's endorsement of the idea of white supremacy was unequivocal. In his essay "The People of America," he claimed that black people (and Indians) were distinct species from Europeans:

The Negro race is a species of men as different from ours as the breed of spaniels is from that of greyhounds. The mucous membrane, or network, which nature has spread between the muscles and the skin, is white in us and black or copper-colored in them. . . .

If their understanding is not of a different nature from ours, it is at least greatly inferior. They are not capable of any great application or association of ideas, and seemed formed neither for the advantages nor the abuses of philosophy.[31]

Hume's racism was notorious; it served as a major source of pro-slavery arguments and antiblack education propaganda. In his famous footnote to his essay "Of National Characteristics," he stated:

I am apt to suspect the negroes, and in general all the other species of men (for there are four or five different kinds) to be naturally inferior to the whites. There never was a civilized nation of any other complexion than white, nor even any individual eminent either in action or speculation. No ingenious manufactures amongst them, no arts, no sciences. . . .

In Jamaica indeed they talk of one negroe as a man of parts and learning; but 'tis likely he is admired for very slender accomplishments, like a parrot, who speaks a few words plainly.[32]

Jefferson arrived at mildly similar conclusions in his *Notes on Virginia*. Regarding the intellectual capacities of black people, he wrote:

Comparing them by their faculties of memory, reason, and imagination, it appears to me, that in memory they are equal to the whites; in reason much inferior . . . and that in imagination they are dull, tasteless and anomalous. . . . Never yet could I find that a black had uttered a thought above the level of plain narration; never see even an elementary trait of painting or sculpture.[33]

Finally, Kant, whose views were based heavily on Hume's claims, held that "the negroes of Africa have by nature no feeling that rises above the trifling." In his *Observations on the Feeling of the Beautiful and Sublime*, Kant noted:

Mr. Hume challenges anyone to cite a simple example in which a negro has shown talents, and asserts that among the hundreds of thousands of blacks who are transported elsewhere from their countries, although many of them have even been set free, still not a single one was ever found who presented anything great in art or science or any other praiseworthy quality, even though among the whites some continually rise aloft from the lowest rabble, and through superior gifts earn respect in the world. So fundamental is the difference between the two races of man, and it appears to be as great in regard to mental capacities as in color.[34]

Kant further revealed his racist views when, in reply to advice that a black person gave to Father Labat, he wrote,

And it might be that there was something in this which perhaps deserved to be considered; but in short, this fellow was quite black from head to foot, a clear proof that what he said was stupid.[35]

The Emergence of Modern Racism: Inevitable or Contingent?

The emergence of the idea of white supremacy as an object of modern discourse seems inevitable in that, besides the practical need to justify nonwhite domination (especially in the early nineteenth century), the only available theoretical alternative for the unhampered search for truth and knowledge in the modern West consisted of detailed observation, measurement, comparison, and ordering of the natural and human kingdom by autonomous subjects in the light of the aesthetic and cultural ideals of classical antiquity. Given the Enlightenment obsession with criticism, especially criticism of the church and religion, the past was divided into four major epochs:

the great river civilizations of the Near East; Ancient Greece and Rome; the Christian millennium; and modern times, beginning with the "revival of letters." These four epochs were rhythmically related to each other: the first and third were paired off as ages of myth, belief and superstition, while the second and fourth were ages of rationality, science and Enlightenment.[36]

The implications of Frank Snowden's thesis in his book *Blacks in Antiquity: Ethiopians in the Greco-Roman Experience* call into question the notion that the Enlightenment recovery of classical antiquity – its aesthetic and cultural ideals – inevitably required, on the discursive level, the emergence of the idea of white supremacy as an object of modern discourse. Snowden's thesis is that racial prejudice did not exist in classical antiquity. He claims that in the first major encounter in European records of black people in a predominantly white society the idea of black equality in beauty, culture, and intellectual capacity was seriously entertained. In regard to ideals of beauty, he notes that Herodotus called Ethiopians the most handsome people on earth; Philostratus spoke of charming Ethiopians with their strange color; Pseudo-Callisthenes held the black Queen of Meroë (visited by Alexander the Great) to be of wondrous beauty; and the poet Martial, though pursued by a woman whiter than snow, sought a "super-black" woman.[37] Snowden goes as far as to state: "On the whole . . . the number of expressed preferences for blackness and whiteness in classical literature is approximately equal."[38]

If Snowden's viewpoint is correct, two noteworthy issues arise. First, it permits us to accent the crucial role that the advent of modern science played in *highlighting the physical appearances of people in relation to what it is to be human, beautiful, cultured, and intelligent.* In this regard, the primacy of observation – the "gaze" character of scientific knowledge – may be as important as the classical ideals which are latent in such observations at the inception of modern discourse. Second, Snowden's claims require that I provide an account of why the Enlightenment revival of classical antiquity ignored or excluded black statues and the proportions and measurements of black figures as part of classical aesthetic ideals.

Snowden's thesis is highly plausible and extremely provocative, but I find it neither persuasive nor convincing. His claims are too exorbitant, but they do contain kernels of truth. Race indeed mattered much less in classical antiquity than it does in modern times. But race did matter in classical antiquity, as can be seen from the evidence meticulously gathered by Snowden, Sikes, Westermann, and others.[39] The crucial difference seems to be that racial differences were justified on cultural grounds in classical antiquity, whereas at the inception of modern discourse, racial differences are often grounded in nature, that is, ontology and later biology.

And even if race prejudice did not exist in classical antiquity, the minority status of black people in Greece and Rome still rendered black statues, proportions, and measurements marginal to cultural life. Hence, the black presence, though tolerated and at times venerated, was never an integral part of the classical ideals of beauty.

The emergence of the idea of white supremacy as an object of modern discourse seems contingent, in that there was no iron necessity at work in the complex configuration of metaphors, notions, categories, and norms that produce and promote this idea. There is an accidental character to the discursive emergence of modern racism, a kind of free play of discursive powers which produce and prohibit, develop and delimit the legitimacy and intelligibility of certain ideas within a discursive space circumscribed by the attractiveness of classical antiquity.

Yet even such claims about the contingency of the emergence of the idea of white supremacy in the modern West warrant suspicion. This is so because, as we noted earlier, this genealogical approach *does not purport to be an explanation of the rise of modern racism, but rather a theoretical inquiry into a particular neglected variable, i.e., the discursive factor, within a larger explanatory model.* This variable is significant because it not only precludes reductionist treatments of modern racism; it also highlights the cultural and aesthetic impact of the idea of white supremacy on black people. This inquiry accents the fact that the everyday life of black people is shaped not simply by the exploitative (oligopolistic) capitalist system of production but also by cultural attitudes and sensibilities, including alienating ideals of beauty.

The idea of white supremacy is a major bowel unleashed by the structure of modern discourse, a significant secretion generated from the creative fusion of scientific investigation, Cartesian philosophy, and classical aesthetic and cultural norms. Needless to say, the odor of this bowel and the fumes of this secretion continue to pollute the air of our postmodern times.

Notes

1   This second theoretical moment of Afro-American philosophy constitutes its Foucaultian elements: the exploration of the complex relationship between knowledge and power, discourse and politics. For a similar yet more ambitious project, see Edward Said, *Orientalism* (Pantheon Books,

1978). Note that my aim is not to endorse the discursive idealism of Michel Foucault, but rather to incorporate some of his powerful insights into a more sophisticated Marxist analysis of the emergence of modern racism. I have just embarked on a huge project that deepens my concern in this chapter into a full-fledged volume.

2   Friedrich Nietzsche, *On the Genealogy of Morals*, trans. Walter Kaufmann and R. J. Hollingdale (Vintage Books, 1967); Michel Foucault, "Nietzsche, Genealogy, History," in *Language, Counter-Memory, Practice: Selected Essays and Interviews*, trans. Donald F. Bouchard and Sherry Simon (Cornell University Press, 1977), pp. 139–64.

3   Cf. Louis Althusser, "Marx's Relation to Hegel," in his *Politics and History* (Schocken Books, 1972), pp. 181–3. For trenchant criticisms of Althusser, see Stanley Aronowitz, *The Crisis in Historical Materialism: Class, Politics, and Culture in Marxist Theory* (Praeger Publications, 1981), pp. 68–9, 120–1, 325–7.

4   This insight bears the stamp of Foucault's long-drawn-out quarrel with vulgar Marxism. See Michel Foucault, *The History of Sexuality*, Vol. 1, trans. Robert Hurley (Random House, 1980), pp. 92–8; *Power/Knowledge: Selected Interviews and Other Writings, 1972–1977*, ed. Colin Gordon (Pantheon Books, 1980), pp. 109–45.

5   For the "classicism plus science" view of the Enlightenment, see Peter Gay, *The Enlightenment: An Interpretation*, Vol. 1 (New York: Alfred Knopf, 1969), pp. 3–27, 313–21. For the importance of the Cartesian transformation of philosophy, see Richard Rorty's insightful metaphilosophical claims in *Philosophy and the Mirror of Nature* (Princeton: Princeton University Press, 1979), esp. pp. 8–12, 45–51, 54–69, 136–40.

6   This understanding of the Renaissance derives from Aby Warburg's notion of *Ausgleichsformel* (compromise formula); and for Galileo's and Newton's protomodern world views, see Gay, *The Enlightenment*, pp. 269–77.

7   Benjamin Farrington, *Francis Bacon: Philosopher of Industrial Science* (Collier Books, 1961), pp. 78–106; Bertrand Russell, *A History of Western Philosophy* (Simon & Schuster, 1945), p. 544.

8   Martin Heidegger, "The Age of the World View," trans. Marjorie Grene, *Boundary 2*, Vol. 4, No. 2 (Winter 1976), pp. 348–9.

9   Gay, *The Enlightenment*, pp. 310–11.

10 Rorty, *Philosophy and the Mirror of Nature*; M. H. Abrams, *The Mirror and the Lamp: Romantic Theory and the Critical Tradition* (Oxford: Oxford University Press, 1953).

11 This claim, as well as my general argument, derives in part from the seminal study by George L. Mosse, *Toward the Final Solution: A History of*

European Racism (Howard Fertig, 1978). This neglected work deserves much more attention than it has heretofore received.

12   Ibid., p. 10.

13   Winthrop Jordan, *White Over Black: American Attitudes Toward the Negro, 1550–1812* (New York: W. W. Norton, 1968), pp. 3–98; Thomas Gossett, *Race: The History of an Idea in America* (Dallas: Southern Methodist University Press, 1965), pp. 3–31.

14   Michel Foucault, *The Order of Things: An Archaeology of the Human Sciences* (Pantheon Books, 1970), pp. 132, 158.

15   Jordan, *White Over Black*, pp. 217–18; Gossett, *Race: The History of an Idea in America*, pp. 32–4; Ashley Montagu, "The Origin of the Concept of 'Race,'" in his *Man's Most Dangerous Myth: The Fallacy of Race*, 5th ed. (Oxford University Press, 1974), pp. 46ff.

16   Jordan, *White Over Black*, p. 220.

17   Ibid., pp. 220–1.

18   Gossett, *Race*, p. 36.

19   For their defenses of Blumenbach, see Jordan, *White Over Black*, pp. 223, 507; Gossett, *Race*, p. 39; Montagu, *Man's Most Dangerous Myth*, pp. 41–5. Support for my viewpoint is found in Mosse, *Toward the Final Solution*, pp. 11, 21.

20   Most notably in the United States, Dr John Augustine Smith, president of the College of William and Mary, and the famous naturalist Dr Samuel George Morton of Philadelphia – both fervent proponents of black inferiority. Jordan, *White Over Black*, pp. 505–6; Gossett, *Race*, pp. 58–9.

21   Mosse, *Toward the Final Solution*, p. 22.

22   Ibid., p. 25.

23   Ibid.

24   Jordan, *White Over Black*, pp. 486ff., 514.

25   Ibid., p. 515.

26   Ibid.

27   Ibid., pp. 515–16.

28   Ibid., p. 520.

29   Ibid.

30   David Brion Davis, *The Problem of Slavery in Western Culture* (Cornell University Press, 1966), p. 403.

31   Gossett, *Race*, p. 45.

32   Richard H. Popkin, "Hume's Racism," *The Philosophical Forum*, Vol. 9, Nos. 2–3, p. 213.

33   Jordan, *White Over Black*, pp. 436–7.

34   Popkin, "Hume's Racism," p. 218.

35   Ibid.

36   Gay, *The Enlightenment*, p. 34.

37   Frank M. Snowden, Jr, *Blacks in Antiquity: Ethiopians in the Greco-Roman Experience* (Belknap Press, 1970), pp. 178–9.
38   Ibid., p. 179.
39   E. E. Sikes, *The Anthropology of the Greeks* (London, 1914); W. L. Westermann, *The Slave Systems of Greek and Roman Antiquity, Memoirs of the American Philosophical Society*, Vol. 50 (1955), pp. xi–180; Moses Hadas, *Hellenistic Culture: Fusion and Diffusion* (Columbia University Press, 1959); Adrian N. Sherwin-White, *Racial Prejudice in Imperial Rome* (Cambridge University Press, 1967).

6

Of Mimicry and Man: The Ambivalence of Colonial Discourse

Homi Bhabha

Mimicry reveals something in so far as it is distinct from what might be called an itself that is behind. The effect of mimicry is camouflage. . . . It is not a question of harmonizing with the background, but against a mottled background, of becoming mottled – exactly like the technique of camouflage practised in human warfare.

> Jacques Lacan, "The Line and the Light," *Of the Gaze*[1]

It is out of season to question at this time of day, the original policy of a conferring on every colony of the British Empire a mimic representation of the British Constitution. But if the creature so endowed has sometimes forgotten its real significance and under the fancied importance of speakers and maces, and all the paraphernalia and ceremonies of the imperial legislature, has dared to defy the mother country, she has to thank herself for the folly of conferring such privileges on a condition of society that has no earthly claim to so exalted a position. A fundamental principle appears to have been forgotten or overlooked in our system of colonial policy – that of colonial dependence. To give to a colony the forms of independence is a mockery; she would not be a colony for a single hour if she could maintain an independent station.

> Sir Edward Cust, "Reflections on West African affairs . . . addressed to the Colonial Office," Hatchard, London 1839

The discourse of post-Enlightenment English colonialism often speaks in a tongue that is forked, not false. If colonialism takes power in the name of history, it repeatedly exercises its authority through the figures of farce. For the epic intention of the civilizing mission, "human and not wholly human" in the famous words of Lord Rosebery, "writ by the finger of the Divine"[2] often produces a text rich in the traditions of *trompe-l'œil*, irony, mimicry, and repetition. In this comic turn from the high ideals of the colonial imagination to its low mimetic literary effects mimicry emerges as one of the most elusive and effective strategies of colonial power and knowledge.

Within that conflictual economy of colonial discourse which Edward Said[3] describes as the tension between the synchronic panoptical vision of domination – the demand for identity, stasis – and the counter-pressure of the diachrony of history – change, difference – mimicry represents in *ironic* compromise. If I may adapt Samuel Weber's formulation of the marginalizing vision of castration,[4] then colonial mimicry is the desire for a reformed, recognizable Other, *as a subject of a difference that is almost the same, but not quite.* Which is to say, that the discourse of mimicry is constructed around an *ambivalence*; in order to be effective, mimicry must continually produce its slippage, its excess, its difference. The authority of that mode of colonial discourse that I have called mimicry is therefore stricken by an indeterminacy: mimicry emerges as the representation of a difference that is itself a process of disavowal. Mimicry is thus the sign of a double articulation; a complex strategy of reform, regulation, and discipline, which "appropriates" the Other as it visualizes power. Mimicry is also the sign of the inappropriate, however, a difference or recalcitrance which coheres the dominant strategic function of colonial power, intensifies surveillance, and poses an immanent threat to both "normalized" knowledges and disciplinary powers.

The effect of mimicry on the authority of colonial discourse is profound and disturbing. For in "normalizing" the colonial state or subject, the dream of post-Enlightenment civility alienates its own language of liberty and produces another knowledge of its norms. The ambivalence which thus informs this strategy is discernible, for example, in Locke's Second Treatise which *splits* to reveal the limitations of liberty in his double use of the word "slave": first simply, descriptively as the locus of a legitimate form of ownership, then as the trope for an intolerable, illegitimate exercise of power. What is articulated in that distance between the two uses is the absolute, imagined difference between the "Colonial" State of Carolina and the Original State of Nature.

It is from this area between mimicry and mockery, where the reforming, civilizing mission is threatened by the displacing gaze of its disciplinary double, that my instances of colonial imitation come. What they all share is a discursive process by which the excess or slippage produced by the *ambivalence* of mimicry (almost the same, *but not quite*) does not merely "rupture" the discourse, but becomes transformed into an uncertainty which fixes the colonial subject as a "partial" presence. By "partial" I mean both "incomplete" and "virtual." It is as if the very emergence of the "colonial" is dependent for its representation upon some strategic limitation or prohibition *within* the authoritative discourse itself. The success of colonial appropriation depends on a proliferation of inappropriate objects that ensure its strategic failure, so that mimicry is at once resemblance and menace.

A classic text of such partiality is Charles Grant's "Observations on the State of Society among the Asiatic Subjects of Great Britain" (1792),[5] which was only superseded by James Mills's *History of India* as the most influential early nineteenth-century account of Indian manners and morals. Grant's dream of an evangelical system of mission education conducted uncompromisingly in the English language was partly a belief in political reform along Christian lines and partly an awareness that the expansion of company rule in India required a system of subject formation – a reform of manners, as Grant put it – that would provide the colonial with "a sense of personal identity as we know it." Caught between the desire for religious reform and the fear that the Indians might become turbulent for liberty, Grant paradoxically implies that it is the "partial" diffusion of Christianity, and the "partial" influence of moral improvements which will construct a particularly appropriate form of colonial subjectivity. What is suggested is a process of reform through which Christian doctrines might collude with divisive caste practices to prevent dangerous political alliances. Inadvertently, Grant produces a knowledge of Christianity as a form of social control which conflicts with the enunciatory assumptions that authorize his discourse. In suggesting, finally, that "partial reform" will produce an empty form of "the *imitation* [my emphasis] of English manners which will induce them [the colonial subjects] to remain under our protection."[6] Grant mocks his moral project and violates the Evidence of Christianity – a central missionary tenet – which forbade any tolerance of heathen faiths.

The absurd extravagance of Macaulay's "Minute" (1835) – deeply influenced by Charles Grant's "Observations" – makes a mockery of Oriental learning until faced with the challenge of conceiving of a "reformed" colonial subject. Then, the great tradition of European humanism seems capable only of ironizing itself. At the intersection of European learning and colonial power, Macaulay can conceive of nothing other than "a class of interpreters between us and the millions whom we govern – a class of persons Indian in blood and colour, but English in tastes, in opinions, in morals and in intellect"[7] – in other words a mimic man raised "through our English School," as a missionary educationist wrote in 1819, "to form a corps of translators and be employed in different departments of Labour."[8] The line of descent of the mimic man can be traced through the works of Kipling, Foster, Orwell, Naipaul, and to his emergence, most recently, in Benedict Anderson's excellent work on nationalism, as the anomalous Bipin Chandra Pal.[9] He is the effect of a flawed colonial mimesis, in which to be Anglicized is *emphatically* not to be English.

The figure of mimicry is locatable within what Anderson describes as "the inner compatibility of empire and nation."[10] It problematizes the signs of racial and cultural priority, so that the "national" is no longer naturalizable. What emerges between mimesis and mimicry is a *writing*, a mode of representation, that marginalizes the monumentality of history, quite simply mocks its power to be a model, that power which supposedly makes it imitable. Mimicry *repeats* rather than *re-presents* and in that diminishing perspective emerges Decoud's displaced European vision of Sulaco in Conrad's *Nostromo* as:

> the endlessness of civil strife where folly seemed even harder to bear than its ignominy . . . the lawlessness of a populace of all colours and races, barbarism, irremediable tyranny. . . . America is ungovernable.[11]

Or Ralph Singh's apostasy in Naipaul's *The Mimic Men*:

> We pretended to be real, to be learning, to be preparing ourselves for life, we mimic men of the New World, one unknown corner of it, with all its reminders of the corruption that came so quickly to the new.[12]

Both Decoud and Singh, and in their different ways Grant and Macaulay, are the parodists of history. Despite their intentions and invocations they inscribe the colonial text erratically, eccentrically across a body politic that refuses to be representative, in a narrative that refuses to be representational. The desire to emerge as "authentic" through mimicry – through a process of writing and repetition – is the final irony of partial representation.

What I have called mimicry is not the familiar exercise of *dependent* colonial relations through narcissistic identification so that, as Fanon has observed,[13] the black man stops being an actional person for only the white man can represent his self-esteem. Mimicry conceals no presence or identity behind its mask: it is not what Césaire describes as "colonization-thingification"[14] behind which there stands the essence of the *présence Africaine*. The *menace* of mimicry is its *double* vision which in disclosing the ambivalence of colonial discourse also disrupts its authority. And it is a double vision that is a result of what I've described as the partial representation/recognition of the colonial object. Grant's colonial as partial imitator, Macaulay's translator, Naipaul's colonial politician as play-actor, Decoud as the scene setter of the *opéra bouffe* of the New World, these are the appropriate objects of a colonialist chain of command, authorized versions of otherness. But they are also, as I have shown, the figures of a doubling, the part-objects of a metonymy of colonial desire which alienates the modality and normality of those dominant discourses in which they emerge as "inappropriate" colonial subjects. A desire that, through the repetition of *partial presence*, which is the basis of mimicry, articulates those disturbances of cultural, racial, and historical difference that menace the narcissistic demand of colonial authority. It is a desire that reverses "in part" the colonial appropriation by now producing a partial vision of the colonizer's presence; a gaze of otherness, that shares the acuity of the genealogical gaze which, as Foucault describes it, liberates marginal elements and shatters the unity of man's being through which he extends his sovereignty.[15]

I want to turn to this process by which the look of surveillance returns as the displacing gaze of the disciplined, where the observer becomes the observed and "partial" representation rearticulates the whole notion of *identity* and alienates it from essence. But not before observing that even an exemplary history like Eric Stokes's *The English Utilitarians and India* acknowledges the anomalous gaze of otherness but finally disavows it in a contradictory utterance:

Certainly India played *no* central part in fashioning the distinctive qualities of English civilisation. In many ways it acted as a disturbing force, a
magnetic power placed at the periphery tending to distort the natural
development of Britain's character.[16] (My emphasis)

What is the nature of the hidden threat of the partial gaze? How does
mimicry emerge as the subject of the scopic drive and the object of colonial surveillance? How is desire disciplined, authority displaced?

If we turn to a Freudian figure to address these issues of colonial
textuality, that form of difference that is mimicry – *almost the same but
not quite* – will become clear. Writing of the partial nature of fantasy,
caught *inappropriately*, between the unconscious and the preconscious,
making problematic, like mimicry, the very notion of "origins," Freud
has this to say:

Their mixed and split origin is what decides their fate. We may compare
them with individuals of mixed race who taken all round resemble white
men but who betray their coloured descent by some striking feature or
other and on that account are excluded from society and enjoy none of
the privileges.[17]

Almost the same but not white: the visibility of mimicry is always produced at the site of interdiction. It is a form of colonial discourse that is
uttered *inter dicta*: a discourse at he crossroads of what is known and
permissible and that which though known must be kept concealed; a
discourse uttered between the lines and as such both against the rules
and within them. The question of the representation of difference is
therefore always also a problem of authority. The "desire" of mimicry,
which is Freud's "striking feature" that reveals so little but makes such
a big difference, is not merely that impossibility of the Other which
repeatedly resists signification. The desire of colonial mimicry – an interdictory desire – may not have an object, but it has strategic objectives
which I shall call the *metonymy of presence*.

Those inappropriate signifiers of colonial discourse – the difference
between being English and being Anglicized; the identity between
stereotypes which, through repetition, also become different; the discriminatory identities constructed across traditional cultural norms
and classifications, the Simian Black, the Lying Asiatic – all these are
metonymies of presence. They are strategies of desire in discourse that

make the anomalous representation of the colonized something other than a process of "the return of the repressed," what Fanon unsatisfactorily characterized as collective catharsis.[18] These instances of metonymy are the nonrepressive productions of contradictory and multiple belief. They cross the boundaries of the culture of enunciation through a strategic confusion of the metaphoric and metonymic axes of the cultural production of meaning.

In mimicry, the representation of identity and meaning is rearticulated along the axis of metonymy. As Lacan reminds us, mimicry is like camouflage, not a harmonization of repression of difference, but a form of resemblance, that differs from or defends presence by displaying it in part, metonymically. Its threat, I would add, comes from the prodigious and strategic production of conflictual, fantastic, discriminatory "identity effects" in the play of a power that is elusive because it hides no essence, no "itself." And that form of *resemblance* is the most terrifying thing to behold, as Edward Long testifies in his *History of Jamaica* (1774). At the end of a tortured, negrophobic passage, that shifts anxiously between piety, prevarication, and perversion, the text finally confronts its fear; nothing other than the repetition of its resemblance "in part': "[Negroes] are represented by all authors as the vilest of human kind, to which they have little more pretension of resemblance *than what arises from their exterior forms*" (my emphasis).[19]

From such a colonial encounter between the white presence and its black semblance, there emerges the question of the ambivalence of mimicry as a problematic of colonial subjection. For if Sade's scandalous theatricalization of language repeatedly reminds us that discourse can claim "no priority," then the work of Edward Said will not let us forget that the "ethnocentric and erratic will to power from which texts can spring"[20] is itself a theater of war. Mimicry, as the metonymy of presence, is, indeed, such an erratic, eccentric strategy of authority in colonial discourse. Mimicry does not merely destroy narcissistic authority through the repetitious slippage of difference and desire. It is the process of the *fixation* of the colonial as a form of cross-classificatory, discriminatory knowledge within an interdictory discourse, and therefore necessarily raises the question of the *authorization* of colonial representations; a question of authority that goes beyond the subject's lack of priority (castration) to a historical crisis in the conceptuality of colonial man as an *object* of regulatory power, as the subject of racial, cultural, national representation.

"This culture . . . fixed in its colonial status," Fanon suggests, "[is] both present and mummified, it testified against its members. It defines them in fact without appeal."[21] The ambivalence of mimicry – almost but not quite – suggests that the fetishized colonial culture is potentially and strategically an insurgent counter-appeal. What I have called its "identity-effects" are always crucially *split*. Under cover of camouflage, mimicry, like the fetish, is a part-object that radically revalues the normative knowledges of the priority of race, writing, history. For the fetish mimes the forms of authority at the point at which it deauthorizes them. Similarly, mimicry rearticulates presence in terms of its "otherness," that which it disavows. There is a crucial difference between this *colonial* articulation of man and his doubles and that which Foucault describes as "thinking the unthought"[22] which, for nineteenth-century Europe, is the ending of man's alienation by reconciling him with his essence. The colonial discourse that articulates an *interdictory* otherness is precisely the "other scene" of this nineteenth-century European desire for an authentic historical consciousness.

The "unthought" across which colonial man is articulated is that process of classificatory confusion that I have described as the metonymy of the substitutive chain of ethical and cultural discourse. This results in the *splitting* of colonial discourse so that two attitudes towards external reality persist; one takes reality into consideration while the other disavows it and replaces it by a product of desire that repeats, rearticulates "reality" as mimicry.

So Edward Long can say with authority, quoting variously Hume, Eastwick, and Bishop Warburton in his support, that: "Ludicrous as the opinion may seem I do not think that an orangutang husband would be any dishonour to a Hottentot female."[23]

Such contradictory articulations of reality and desire – seen in racist stereotypes, statements, jokes, myths – are not caught in the doubtful circle of the return of the repressed. They are the effect of a disavowal that denies the differences of the other but produces in its stead forms of authority and multiple belief that alienate the assumptions of "civil" discourse. If, for a while, the ruse of desire is calculable for the uses of discipline soon the repetition of guilt, justification, pseudo-scientific theories, superstition, spurious authorities, and classifications can be seen as the desperate effort to "normalize" *formally* the disturbance of a discourse of splitting that violates the rational, enlightened claims of its enunciatory modality. The ambivalence of colonial authority repeatedly turns from *mimicry* – a difference that is almost nothing but not quite – to *menace* – a difference that is almost total but not quite. And in that other scene of colonial power where history turns to farce and presence to "a part" can be seen the twin figures of narcissism and paranoia that repeat furiously, uncontrollably.

In the ambivalent world of the "not quite/not white," on the margins of metropolitan desire, the *founding objects* of the Western world become the erratic, eccentric, accidental *objets trouvés* of the colonial discourse – the part-objects of presence. It is then that the body and the book lose their part-objects of presence. It is then that the body and the book lose their representational authority. Black skin splits under the racist gaze, displaced into signs of bestiality, genitalia, grotesquerie, which reveal the phobic myth of the undifferentiated whole white body. And the holiest of books – the Bible – bearing both the standard of the cross and the standard of empire finds itself strangely dismembered. In May 1817 a missionary wrote from Bengal:

> Still everyone would gladly receive a Bible. And why? – that he may lay it up as a curiosity for a few pice; or use it for waste paper. Such it is well known has been the common fate of these copies of the bible. . . . Some have been bartered in the markets, others have been thrown in snuff shops and used as wrapping paper.[24]

Notes

1 J. Lacan, "The Line and the Light," in his *The Four Fundamental Concepts of Psychoanalysis*, trans. Alan Sheridan (London: The Hogarth Press and the Institute of Psycho-Analysis, 1977), p. 99.

2 Cited in E. Stokes, *The Political Ideas of English Imperialism* (Oxford: Oxford University Press, 1960), pp. 17–18.

3 E. Said, *Orientalism* (New York: Pantheon Books, 1978), p. 240.

4 S. Weber, "The Sideshow, or: Remarks on a Canny Moment," *Modern Language Notes*, Vol. 88, No. 6 (1973), p. 112.

5 C. Grant, "Observations on the State of Society among the Asiatic Subjects of Great Britain," *Sessional Papers of the East India Company*, Vol. X, No. 282 (1812–13).

6 Ibid., ch. 4, p. 104.

7 T. B. Macaulay, "Minute on Education," in W. Theodore de Bary (ed.), *Sources of Indian Tradition*, Vol. II (New York: Columbia University Press, 1958), p. 49.

8   Mr Thomason's communication to the Church Missionary Society, September 5, 1819, in *The Missionary Register*, 1821, pp. 54–5.

9   B. Anderson, *Imagined Communities* (London: Verso, 1983), p. 88.

10   Ibid., pp. 88–9.

11   J. Conrad, *Nostromo* (London: Penguin, 1979), p. 161.

12   V. S. Naipaul, *The Mimic Men* (London: Penguin, 1967), p. 146.

13   F. Fanon, *Black Skin, White Masks* (London: Paladin, 1970), p. 109.

14   A. Césaire, *Discourse on Colonialism* (New York: Monthly Review Press, 1972), p. 21.

15   M. Foucault, "Nietzsche, Genealogy, History," in his *Language, Counter-Memory, Practice*, trans. D. F. Bouchard and S. Simon (Ithaca: Cornell University Press, 1977), p. 153.

16   E. Stokes, *The English Utilitarians and India* (Oxford: Oxford University Press, 1959), p. xi.

17   S. Freud, "The Unconscious" (1915), *SE*, XIV, pp. 190–1.

18   Fanon, *Black Skin, White Masks*, p. 103.

19   E. Long, *A History of Jamaica*, 1774, Vol. II, p. 353.

20   E. Said, "The Text, the World, the Critic," in J. V. Harari (ed.), *Textual Strategies* (Ithaca: Cornell University Press, 1979), p. 184.

21   F. Fanon, "Racism and Culture," in his *Toward the African Revolution*, trans. H. Chevalier (London: Pelican, 1967), p. 44.

22   M. Foucault, *The Order of Things* (New York: Pantheon Books, 1971), part II, ch. 9.

23   Long, *History of Jamaica*, p. 364.

24   *The Missionary Register*, May 1817, p. 186.

7

Racial Formation

Michael Omi and Howard Winant

What is Race?

There is a continuous temptation to think of race as an *essence*, as
something fixed, concrete, and objective. And there is also an opposite
temptation: to imagine race as a mere *illusion*, a purely ideological
construct which some ideal nonracist social order would eliminate.
It is necessary to challenge both these positions, to disrupt and reframe
the rigid and bipolar manner in which they are posed and debated,
and to transcend the presumably irreconcilable relationship between
them.

The effort must be made to understand race as an unstable and
"decentered" complex of social meanings constantly being transformed
by political struggle. With this in mind, let us propose a definition: *race
is a concept which signifies and symbolizes social conflicts and interests by
referring to different types of human bodies.* Although the concept of race
invokes biologically based human characteristics (so-called "pheno-
types"), selection of these particular human features for purposes of
racial signification is always and necessarily a social and historical
process. In contrast to the other major distinction of this type, that of
gender, there is no biological basis for distinguishing among human
groups along the lines of race.[1] Indeed, the categories employed to differentiate among human groups along racial lines reveal themselves,

upon serious examination, to be at best imprecise, and at worst completely arbitrary.

If the concept of race is so nebulous, can we not dispense with it? Can we not "do without" race, at least in the "enlightened" present? This question has been posed often, and with greater frequency in recent years.[2] An affirmative answer would of course present obvious practical difficulties: it is rather difficult to jettison widely held beliefs, beliefs which moreover are central to everyone's identity and understanding of the social world. So the attempt to banish the concept as an archaism is at best counterintuitive. But a deeper difficulty, we believe, is inherent in the very formulation of this schema, in its way of posing race as a *problem*, a misconception left over from the past, and suitable now only for the dustbin of history.

A more effective starting point is the recognition that despite its uncertainties and contradictions, the concept of race continues to play a fundamental role in structuring and representing the social world. The task for theory is to explain this situation. It is to avoid both the utopian framework which sees race as an illusion we can somehow "get beyond," and also the essentialist formulation which sees race as something objective and fixed, a biological datum.[3] Thus we should think of race as an element of social structure rather than as an irregularity within it; we should see race as a dimension of human representation rather than an illusion. These perspectives inform the theoretical approach we call racial formation.

Racial Formation

We define *racial formation* as the sociohistorical process by which racial categories are created, inhabited, transformed, and destroyed. Our attempt to elaborate a theory of racial formation will proceed in two steps. First, we argue that racial formation is a process of historically situated *projects* in which human bodies and social structures are represented and organized. Next we link racial formation to the evolution of hegemony, the way in which society is organized and ruled. Such an approach, we believe, can facilitate understanding of a whole range of contemporary controversies and dilemmas involving race, including the nature of racism, the relationship of race to other forms of differences, inequalities, and oppression such as sexism and nationalism, and the dilemmas of racial identity today.

From a racial formation perspective, race is a matter of both social structure and cultural representation. Too often, the attempt is made to understand race simply or primarily in terms of only one of these two analytical dimensions.[4] For example, efforts to explain racial inequality as a purely social structural phenomenon are unable to account for the origins, patterning, and transformation of racial difference.

Conversely, many examinations of racial difference – understood as a matter of cultural attributes à la ethnicity theory, or as a society-wide signification system, à la some poststructuralist accounts – cannot comprehend such structural phenomena as racial stratification in the labor market or patterns of residential segregation.

An alternative approach is to think of racial formation processes as occurring through a linkage between structure and representation. Racial *projects* do the ideological "work" of making these links. *A racial project is simultaneously an interpretation, representation, or explanation of racial dynamics, and an effort to reorganize and redistribute resources along particular racial lines.* Racial projects connect what race *means* in a particular discursive practice and the ways in which both social structures and everyday experiences are racially *organized*, based upon that meaning. Let us consider this proposition, first in terms of large-scale or macro-level social processes, and then in terms of other dimensions of the racial formation process.

Racial formation as a macro-level social process

To *interpret the meaning of race is to frame it social structurally.* Consider, for example, this statement by Charles Murray on welfare reform:

> My proposal for dealing with the racial issue in social welfare is to repeal every bit of legislation and reverse every court decision that in any way requires, recommends, or awards differential treatment according to race, and thereby put us back onto the track that we left in 1965. We may argue about the appropriate limits of government intervention in trying to enforce the ideal, but at least it should be possible to identify the ideal: Race is not a morally admissible reason for treating one person differently from another. Period.[5]

Here there is a partial but significant analysis of the meaning of race: it is not a morally valid basis upon which to treat people "differently from one another." We may notice someone's race, but we cannot act upon that awareness. We must act in a "color-blind" fashion. This analysis of the meaning of race is immediately linked to a specific conception of the role of race in the social structure: it can play no part in government action, save in "the enforcement of the ideal." No state policy can legitimately require, recommend, or award different status according to race. This example can be classified as a particular type of racial project in the present-day US – a "neoconservative" one.

Conversely, *to recognize the racial dimension in social structure is to interpret the meaning of race*. Consider the following statement by the late Supreme Court Justice Thurgood Marshall on minority "set-aside" programs:

> A profound difference separates governmental actions that themselves are racist, and governmental actions that seek to remedy the effects of prior racism or to prevent neutral government activity from perpetuating the effects of such racism.[6]

Here the focus is on the racial dimensions of *social structure* – in this case of state activity and policy. The argument is that state actions in the past and present have treated people in very different ways according to their race, and thus the government cannot retreat from its policy responsibilities in this area. It cannot suddenly declare itself "color-blind" without in fact perpetuating the same type of differential, racist treatment.[7] Thus, race continues to signify difference and structure inequality. Here, racialized social structure is immediately linked to an interpretation of the meaning of race. This example too can be classified as a particular type of racial project in the present-day US – a "liberal" one.

To be sure, such political labels as "neoconservative" or "liberal" cannot fully capture the complexity of racial projects, for these are always multiply determined, politically contested, and deeply shaped by their historical context. Thus, encapsulated within the neoconservative example cited here are certain egalitarian commitments which derive from a previous historical context in which they played a very different role, and which are rearticulated in neoconservative racial discourse precisely to oppose a more open-ended, more capacious conception of the meaning of equality. Similarly, in the liberal example,

Justice Marshall recognizes that the contemporary state, which was formerly the architect of segregation and the chief enforcer of racial difference, has a tendency to reproduce those patterns of inequality in a new guise. Thus he admonishes it (in dissent, significantly) to fulfill its responsibilities to uphold a robust conception of equality. These particular instances, then, demonstrate how racial projects are always concretely framed, and thus are always contested and unstable. The social structures they uphold or attack, and the re-presentations of race they articulate, are never invented out of the air, but exist in a definite historical context, having descended from previous conflicts. This contestation appears to be permanent in respect to race.

These two examples of contemporary racial projects are drawn from mainstream political debate; they may be characterized as center-right and center-left expressions of contemporary racial politics.[8] We can, however, expand the discussion of racial formation processes far beyond these familiar examples. In fact, we can identify racial projects in at least three other analytical dimensions: first, the political spectrum can be broadened to include radical projects, on both the left and right, as well as along other political axes. Second, analysis of racial projects can take place not only at the macro-level of racial policy-making, state activity, and collective action, but also at the micro-level of everyday experience. Third, the concept of racial projects can be applied across historical time, to identify racial formation dynamics in the past. [. . .]

To summarize the argument so far: the theory of racial formation suggests that society is suffused with racial projects, large and small, to which all are subjected. This racial "subjection" is quintessentially ideological. Everybody learns some combination, some version, of the rules of racial classification, and of her own racial identity, often without obvious teaching or conscious inculcation. Thus are we inserted in a comprehensively racialized social structure. Race becomes "common sense" – a way of comprehending, explaining, and acting in the world. A vast web of racial projects mediates between the discursive or representational means in which race is identified and signified on the one hand, and the institutional and organizational forms in which it is routinized and standardized on the other. These projects are the heart of the racial formation process.

Under such circumstances, it is not possible to represent race discursively without simultaneously locating it, explicitly or implicitly, in a social structural (and historical) context. Nor is it possible to organize, maintain, or transform social structures without simultaneously engaging, once more either explicitly or implicitly, in racial signification. Racial formation, therefore, is a kind of synthesis, an outcome, of the interaction of racial projects on a society-wide level. These projects are, of course, vastly different in scope and effect. They include large-scale public action, state activities, and interpretations of racial conditions in artistic, journalistic, or academic fora,[9] as well as the seemingly infinite number of racial judgments and practices we carry out at the level of individual experience.

Since racial formation is always historically situated, our understanding of the significance of race, and of the way race structures society, has changed enormously over time. The processes of racial formation we encounter today, the racial projects large and small which structure US society in so many ways, are merely the present-day outcomes of a complex historical evolution. [. . .]

From Science to Politics

As a result of prior efforts and struggles, we have now reached the point of fairly general agreement that race is not a biologically given but rather a socially constructed way of differentiating human beings. While a tremendous achievement, the transcendence of biologistic conceptions of race does not provide any reprieve from the dilemmas of racial injustice and conflict, nor from controversies over the significance of race in the present. Views of race as socially constructed simply recognize the fact that these conflicts and controversies are now more properly framed on the terrain of politics. By privileging politics in the analysis which follows we do not mean to suggest that race has been displaced as a concern of scientific inquiry, or that struggles over cultural representation are no longer important. We do argue, however, that race is now a preeminently political phenomenon. Such an assertion invites examination of the evolving role of racial politics in the US. This is the subject to which we now turn.

Dictatorship, Democracy, Hegemony

For most of its existence both as European colony and as an independent nation, the US was a *racial dictatorship*. From 1607 to 1865 – 258 years – most nonwhites were firmly eliminated from the sphere of politics.[10] After the Civil War there was the brief egalitarian experiment of Reconstruction which terminated ignominiously in 1877. In its wake followed almost a century of legally sanctioned segregation and denial of the vote, nearly absolute in the South and much of the Southwest, less effective in the North and far West, but formidable in any case.[11] These barriers fell only in the mid-1960s, a mere quarter-century ago. Nor did the successes of the black movement and its allies mean that all obstacles to their political participation had now been abolished. Patterns of racial inequality have proven, unfortunately, to be quite stubborn and persistent.

It is important, therefore, to recognize that in many respects, racial dictatorship is the norm against which all US politics must be measured. The centuries of racial dictatorship have had three very large consequences: first, they defined "American" identity as white, as the negation of racialized "otherness" – at first largely African and indigenous, later Latin American and Asian as well.[12] This negation took shape in both law and custom, in public institutions and in forms of cultural representation. It became the archetype of hegemonic rule in the US. It was the successor to the conquest as the "master" racial project.

Second, racial dictatorship organized (albeit sometimes in an incoherent and contradictory fashion) the "color line" rendering it the fundamental division in US society. The dictatorship elaborated, articulated, and drove racial divisions not only through institutions, but also through psyches, extending up to our own time the racial obsessions of the conquest and slavery periods.

Third, racial dictatorship consolidated the oppositional racial consciousness and organization originally framed by maroonage[13] and slave revolts, by indigenous resistance, and by nationalisms of various sorts. Just as the conquest created the "native" where once there had been Pequot, Iroquois, or Tutelo, so too it created the "black" where once there had been Asante or Ovimbundu, Yoruba or Bakongo.

The transition from a racial dictatorship to a racial democracy has been a slow, painful, and contentious one; it remains far from complete. A recognition of the abiding presence of racial dictatorship, we contend, is crucial for the development of a theory of racial formation in the US. It is also crucial to the task of relating racial formation to the broader context of political practice, organization, and change.

In this context, a key question arises: in what way is racial formation related to politics as a whole? How, for example, does race articulate with other axes of oppression and difference – most importantly class and gender – along which politics is organized today?

The answer, we believe, lies in the concept of *hegemony*. Antonio Gramsci – the Italian communist who placed this concept at the center of his life's work – understood it as the conditions necessary, in a given society, for the achievement and consolidation of rule. He argued that hegemony was always constituted by a combination of coercion and consent. Although rule can be obtained by force, it cannot be secured and maintained, especially in modern society, without the element of consent. Gramsci conceived of consent as far more than merely the legitimation of authority. In his view, consent extended to the incorporation by the ruling group of many of the key interests of subordinated groups, often to the explicit disadvantage of the rulers themselves.[14] Gramsci's treatment of hegemony went even farther: he argued that in order to consolidate their hegemony, ruling groups must elaborate and maintain a popular system of ideas and practices – through education, the media, religion, folk wisdom, etc. – which he called "common sense." It is through its production and its adherence to this "common sense," this ideology (in the broadest sense of the term), that a society gives its consent to the way in which it is ruled.[15]

These provocative concepts can be extended and applied to an understanding of racial rule. In the Americas, the conquest represented the violent introduction of a new form of rule whose relationship with those it subjugated was almost entirely coercive. In the US, the origins of racial division, and of racial signification and identity formation, lie in a system of rule which was extremely dictatorial. The mass murders and expulsions of indigenous people, and the enslavement of Africans, surely evoked and inspired little consent in their founding moments.

Over time, however, the balance of coercion and consent began to change. It is possible to locate the origins of hegemony right within the heart of racial dictatorship, for the effort to possess the oppressor's tools – religion and philosophy in this case – was crucial to emancipation (the effort to possess oneself). As Ralph Ellison reminds us, "The slaves often took the essence of the aristocratic ideal (as they took Christianity) with far more seriousness than their masters."[16] In their language, in their religion with its focus on the Exodus theme and on Jesus's tribulations, in their music with its figuring of suffering, resistance, perseverance, and transcendence, in their interrogation of a political philosophy which sought perpetually to rationalize their bondage in a supposedly "free" society, the slaves incorporated elements of racial rule into their thought and practice, turning them against their original bearers.

Racial rule can be understood as a slow and uneven historical process which has moved from dictatorship to democracy, from domination to hegemony. In this transition, hegemonic forms of racial rule – those based on consent – eventually came to supplant those based on coercion. Of course, before this assertion can be accepted, it must be qualified in important ways. By no means has the US established racial democracy at the end of the century, and by no means is coercion a thing of the past. But the sheer complexity of the racial questions US society confronts today, the welter of competing racial projects and contradictory racial experiences which Americans undergo, suggests that hegemony is a useful and appropriate term with which to characterize contemporary racial rule.

Our key theoretical notion of racial projects helps to extend and broaden the question of rule. Projects are the building blocks not just of racial formation, but of hegemony in general. Hegemony operates by simultaneously structuring and signifying. As in the case of racial opposition, gender- or class-based conflict today links structural inequity and injustice on the one hand, and identifies and represents its subjects on the other. The success of modern-day feminism, for example, has depended on its ability to reinterpret gender as a matter of both injustice and identity/difference.

Today, political opposition necessarily takes shape on the terrain of hegemony. For from ruling principally through exclusion and coercion (though again, these are hardly absent), hegemony operates by including its subjects, incorporating its opposition. *Pace* both Marxists and liberals, there is no longer any universal or privileged region of political action or discourse.[17] Race, class, and gender all represent potential antagonisms whose significance is no longer given, if it ever was.

Thus race, class, and gender (as well as sexual orientation) constitute "regions" of hegemony, areas in which certain political projects can take shape. They share certain obvious attributes in that they are all "socially constructed," and they all consist of a field of projects whose common feature is their linkage of social structure and signification.

Going beyond this, it is crucial to emphasize that race, class, and gender are not fixed and discrete categories, and that such "regions" are by no means autonomous. They overlap, intersect, and fuse with each other in countless ways. Such mutual determinations have been illustrated by Patricia Hill Collins's survey and theoretical synthesis of the themes and issues of black feminist thought.[18] They are also evident in Evelyn Nakano Glenn's work on the historical and contemporary racialization of domestic and service work.[19] In many respects, race is gendered and gender is racialized. In institutional and everyday life, any clear demarcation of specific forms of oppression and difference is constantly being disrupted.

There are no clear boundaries between these "regions" of hegemony, so political conflicts will often invoke some or all these themes simultaneously. Hegemony is tentative, incomplete, and "messy." For example, the 1991 Hill-Thomas hearings, with their intertwined themes of race and gender inequality, and their frequent genuflections before the altar of hard work and upward mobility, managed to synthesize various race, gender, and class projects in a particularly explosive combination.[20]

What distinguishes political opposition today – racial or otherwise – is its insistence on identifying itself and speaking for itself, its determined demand for the transformation of the social structure, its refusal of the "common sense" understandings which the hegemonic order imposes. Nowhere is this refusal of "common sense" more needed, or more imperilled, than in our understanding of racism.

What is Racism?

Since the ambiguous triumph of the civil rights movement in the mid-1960s, clarity about what racism means has been eroding. The concept entered the lexicon of "common sense" only in the 1960s. Before that, although the term had surfaced occasionally,[21] the problem of racial injustice and inequality was generally understood in a more limited fashion, as a matter of prejudiced attitudes or bigotry on the one hand,[22] and discriminatory practices on the other.[23] Solutions, it was believed, would therefore involve the overcoming of such attitudes, the achievement of tolerance, the acceptance of "brotherhood," etc., and the passage of laws which prohibited discrimination with respect to access to public accommodations, jobs, education, etc. The early civil rights movement explicitly reflected such views. In its espousal of integration and its quest for a "beloved community" it sought to overcome racial prejudice. In its litigation activities and agitation for civil rights legislation it sought to challenge discriminatory practices.

The later 1960s, however, signaled a sharp break with this vision. The emergence of the slogan "black power" (and soon after, of "brown power," "red power," and "yellow power"), the wave of riots that swept the urban ghettos from 1964 to 1968, and the founding of radical movement organizations of nationalist and Marxist orientation, coincided with the recognition that racial inequality and injustice had much deeper roots. They were not simply the product of prejudice, nor was discrimination only a matter of intentionally informed action. Rather, prejudice was an almost unavoidable outcome of patterns of socialization which were "bred in the bone," affecting not only whites but even minorities themselves.[24] Discrimination, far from manifesting itself only (or even principally) through individual actions or conscious policies, was a structural feature of US society, the product of centuries of systematic exclusion, exploitation, and disregard of racially defined minorities.[25] It was this combination of relationships – prejudice, discrimination, and institutional inequality – which defined the concept of racism at the end of the 1960s.

Such a synthesis was better able to confront the political realities of the period. Its emphasis on the structural dimensions of racism allowed it to address the intransigence which racial injustice and inequality continued to exhibit, even after discrimination had supposedly been outlawed[26] and bigoted expression stigmatized. But such an approach also had clear limitations. As Robert Miles has argued, it tended to "inflate" the concept of racism to a point at which it lost precision.[27] If the "institutional" component of racism were so pervasive and deeply rooted, it became difficult to see how the democratization of US society could be achieved, and difficult to explain what progress had been made. The result was a leveling critique which denied any distinction between the Jim Crow era (or even the whole *longue durée* of racial dictatorship since the conquest) and the present. Similarly, if the prejudice component of racism were so deeply inbred, it became difficult to account for the evident hybridity and interpenetration that characterizes civil society in the US, as evidenced by the shaping of popular culture, language, and style, for example. The result of the "inflation" of the concept of racism was thus a deep pessimism about any efforts to overcome racial barriers, in the workplace, the community, or any other sphere of lived experience. An overly comprehensive view of racism, then, potentially served as a self-fulfilling prophecy.

Yet the alternative view – which surfaced with a vengeance in the 1970s – urging a return to the conception of racism held before the movement's "radical turn," was equally inadequate. This was the neo-conservative perspective, which deliberately restricted its attention to injury done to the individual as opposed to the group, and to advocacy of a color-blind racial policy.[28] Such an approach reduced race to ethnicity,[29] and almost entirely neglected the continuing organization of social inequality and oppression along racial lines. Worse yet, it tended to rationalize racial injustice as a supposedly natural outcome of group attributes in competition.[30]

The distinct, and contested, meanings of racism which have been advanced over the past three decades have contributed to an overall crisis of meaning for the concept today. Today, the absence of a clear "common sense" understanding of what racism means has become a significant obstacle to efforts aimed at challenging it. Bob Blauner has noted that in classroom discussions of racism, white and nonwhite students tend to talk past one another. Whites tend to locate racism in color consciousness and find its absence color-blindness. In so doing, they see the affirmation of difference and racial identity among racially defined minority students as racist. Nonwhite students, by contrast, see racism as a system of power, and correspondingly argue that blacks, for example, cannot be racist because they lack power. Blauner concludes that there are two "languages" of race, one in which members of racial minorities, especially blacks, see the centrality of race in history and everyday experience, and another in which whites see race as "a peripheral, nonessential reality."[31]

Given this crisis of meaning, and in the absence of any "common sense" understanding, does the concept of racism retain any validity? If so, what view of racism should we adopt? Is a more coherent theoretical approach possible? We believe it is.

We employ racial formation theory to reformulate the concept of racism. Our approach recognizes that racism, like race, has changed over time. It is obvious that the attitudes, practices, and institutions of the epochs of slavery, say, or of Jim Crow, no longer exist today. Employing a similar logic, it is reasonable to question whether concepts of racism which developed in the early days of the post-civil rights era, when the limitations of both moderate reform and militant racial radicalism of various types had not yet been encountered, remain adequate to explain circumstances and conflicts a quarter-century later.

Racial formation theory allows us to differentiate between race and racism. The two concepts should not be used interchangeably. We have argued that race has no fixed meaning, but is constructed and transformed sociohistorically through competing political projects, through the necessary and ineluctable link between the structural and cultural dimensions of race in the US. This emphasis on projects allows us to refocus our understanding of racism as well, for racism can now be seen as characterizing some, but not all, racial projects.

A racial project can be defined as *racist* if and only if it *creates or reproduces structures of domination based on essentialist*[32] *categories of race.* Such a definition recognizes the importance of locating racism within a fluid and contested history of racially based social structures and discourses. Thus there can be no timeless and absolute standard for what constitutes racism, for social structures change and discourses are subject to rearticulation. Our definition therefore focuses instead on the "work" essentialism does for domination, and the "need" domination displays to essentialize the subordinated.

Further, it is important to distinguish racial awareness from racial essentialism. To attribute merits, allocate values or resources to, and/or represent individuals or groups on the basis of racial identity should not be considered racist in and of itself. Such projects may in fact be quite benign.

Consider the following examples: first, the statement, "Many Asian Americans are highly entrepreneurial"; second, the organization of an association of, say, black accountants.

The first racial project, in our view, signifies or represents a racial category ("Asian Americans") and locates that representation within the social structure of the contemporary US (in regard to business, class issues, socialization, etc.). The second racial project is organizational or social structural, and therefore must engage in racial signification. Black accountants, the organizers might maintain, have certain common experiences, can offer each other certain support, etc. Neither of these racial projects is essentialist, and neither can fairly be labeled racist. Of course, racial representations may be biased or misinterpret their subjects, just as racially based organizational efforts may be unfair or unjustifiably exclusive. If such were the case, if for instance in our first example the statement in question were "Asian Americans are naturally entrepreneurial," this would by our criterion be racist. Similarly, if the effort to organize black accountants had as its rationale the raiding of clients from white accountants, it would by our criterion be racist as well.

Similarly, to allocate values or resources – let us say, academic scholarships – on the basis of racial categories is not racist. Scholarships are awarded on a preferential basis to Rotarians, children of insurance company employees, and residents of the Pittsburgh metropolitan area. Why then should they not also be offered, in particular cases, to Chicanos or Native Americans?

In order to identify a social project as racist, one must in our view demonstrate a link between essentialist representations of race and social structures of domination. Such a link might be revealed in efforts to protect dominant interests, framed in racial terms, from democratizing racial initiatives.[33] But it might also consist of efforts simply to reverse the roles of racially dominant and racially subordinate.[34] There is nothing inherently white about racism.[35]

Obviously a key problem with essentialism is its denial, or flattening, of differences within a particular racially defined group. Members of subordinate racial groups, when faced with racist practices such as exclusion or discrimination, are frequently forced to band together in order to defend their interests (if not, in some instances, their very lives). Such "strategic essentialism" should not, however, be simply equated with the essentialism practiced by dominant groups, nor should it prevent the interrogation of internal group differences.[36]

Without question, any abstract concept of racism is severely put to the test by the untidy world of reality. To illustrate our discussion, we analyze the following examples, chosen from current racial issues because of their complexity and the rancorous debates they have engendered:

- Is the allocation of employment opportunities through programs restricted to racially defined minorities, so-called "preferential treatment" or affirmative action policies, racist? Do such policies practice "racism in reverse"? We think not, with certain qualifications. Although such programs necessarily employ racial criteria in assessing eligibility, they do not generally essentialize race, because they seek to overcome specific socially and historically constructed inequalities.[37] Criteria of effectiveness and feasibility, therefore, must be considered in evaluating such programs. They must balance egalitarian and context-specific objectives, such as academic potential or job-related qualifications. It should be acknowledged that such programs often do have deleterious consequences for whites who are not personally the source of the discriminatory practices the programs seek to overcome. In this case, compensatory measures should be enacted to vitiate the charge of "reverse discrimination."[38]
- Is all racism the same, or is there a distinction between white and nonwhite versions of racism? We have little patience with the argument that racism is solely a white problem, or even a "white disease."[39] The idea that nonwhites cannot act in a racist manner, since they do not possess "power," is another variant of this formulation.[40]

  For many years now, racism has operated in a more complex fashion than this, sometimes taking such forms as self-hatred or self-aggrandizement at the expense of more vulnerable members of racially subordinate groups.[41] Whites can at times be the victims of racism – by other whites or nonwhites – as is the case with anti-Jewish and anti-Arab prejudice. Furthermore, unless one is prepared to argue that there has been no transformation of the US racial order over the years, and that racism consequently has remained unchanged – an essentialist position *par excellence* – it is difficult to contend that racially defined minorities have attained no power or influence, especially in recent years.

Having said this, we still do not consider that all racism is the same. This is because of the crucial importance we place in situating various "racisms" within the dominant hegemonic discourse about race. We have little doubt that the rantings of a Louis Farrakhan or Leonard Jeffries – to pick two currently demonized black ideologues – meet the criteria we have set out for judging a discourse to be racist. But if we compare Jeffries, for example, with a white racist such as Tom Metzger of the White Aryan Resistance, we find the latter's racial project to be far more menacing than the former's. Metzger's views are far more easily associated with an essentializing (and once very powerful) legacy: that of white supremacy and racial dictatorship in the US, and fascism in the world at large. Jeffries's project has far fewer examples with which to associate: no more than some ancient African empires and the (usually far less bigoted) radical phase of the black power movement.[42] Thus black supremacy may be an instance of racism, just as its advocacy may be offensive, but it can hardly constitute the threat that white supremacy has represented in the US, nor can it be so easily absorbed and rearticulated in the dominant hegemonic discourse on race as white supremacy can. All racisms, all racist political projects, are not the same. [. . .]

Parallel to the debates on the concept of race, recent academic and political controversies about the nature of racism have centered on whether it is primarily an ideological or structural phenomenon. Proponents of the former position argue that racism is first and foremost a matter of beliefs and attitudes, doctrines and discourse, which only then give rise to unequal and unjust practices and structures. Advocates of the latter view see racism as primarily a matter of economic stratification, residential segregation, and other institutionalized forms of inequality which then give rise to ideologies of privilege.

[. . .] We believe it is crucial to disrupt the fixity of these positions by simultaneously arguing that ideological beliefs have structural consequences, and that social structures give rise to beliefs. Racial ideology and social structure, therefore, mutually shape the nature of racism in a complex, dialectical, and overdetermined manner.

Even those racist projects which at first glance appear chiefly ideological turn out upon closer examination to have significant institutional and social structural dimensions. For example, what we have called "far right" projects appear at first glance to be centrally ideological. They are rooted in biologistic doctrine, after all. The same seems to hold for certain conservative black nationalist projects which have deep commitments to biologism.[43] But the unending stream of racist assaults initiated by the far right, the apparently increasing presence of skinheads in high schools, the proliferation of neo-Nazi computer bulletin boards, and the appearance of racist talk shows on cable access channels, all suggest that the organizational manifestations of the far right racial projects exist and will endure.[44] [. . .]

By contrast, even those racisms which at first glance appear to be chiefly structural upon closer examination reveal a deeply ideological component. For example, since the racial right abandoned its explicit advocacy of segregation, it has not seemed to uphold – in the main – an ideologically racist project, but more primarily a structurally racist one. Yet this very transformation required tremendous efforts of ideological production. It demanded the rearticulation of civil rights doctrines of equality in suitably conservative form, and indeed the defense of continuing large-scale racial inequality as an outcome preferable to (what its advocates have seen as) the threat to democracy that affirmative action, busing, and large-scale "race-specific" social spending would entail.[45] [. . .]

In summary, the racism of today is no longer a virtual monolith, as was the racism of yore. Today, racial hegemony is "messy." The complexity of the present situation is the product of a vast historical legacy of structural inequality and invidious racial representation, which has been confronted during the post-World War II period with an opposition more serious and effective than any it had faced before. [. . .]

Notes

1   This is not to suggest that gender is a biological category while race is not. Gender, like race, is a social construct. However, the biological division of humans into sexes – two at least, and possibly intermediate ones as well – is not in dispute. This provides a basis for argument over gender divisions – how "natural," etc. – which does not exist with regard to race. To ground an argument for the "natural" existence of race, one must resort to philosophical anthropology.

2   "The truth is that there are no races, there is nothing in the world that can do all we ask race to do for us. . . . The evil that is done is done by the concept, and by easy – yet impossible – assumptions as to its application." (Kwame Anthony Appiah, *In My Father's House: Africa in the Philosophy of Culture* (New York: Oxford University Press, 1992).) Appiah's eloquent and learned book fails, in our view, to dispense with the race concept, despite its anguished attempt to do so; this indeed is the source of its author's anguish. We agree with him as to the nonobjective character of race, but fail to see how this recognition justifies its abandonment. This argument is developed below.

3   We understand essentialism as *belief in real, true human, essences, existing outside or impervious to social and historical context.* We draw this definition, with some small modifications, from Diana Fuss, *Essentially Speaking: Feminism, Nature, & Difference* (New York: Routledge, 1989), p. xi.

4   Michael Omi and Howard Winant, "On the Theoretical Status of the Concept of Race," in Warren Crichlow and Cameron McCarthy (eds.), *Race, Identity, and Representation in Education* (New York: Routledge, 1993).

5   Charles Murray, *Losing Ground: American Social Policy, 1950–1980* (New York: Basic Books, 1984), p. 223.

6   Justice Thurgood Marshall, dissenting in *City of Richmond v. J. A. Croson Co.*, 488 US 469 (1989).

7   See, for example, Derrick Bell, "Remembrances of Racism Past: Getting Past the Civil Rights Decline," in Herbert Hill and James E. Jones, Jr (eds.), *Race in America: The Struggle for Equality* (Madison: The University of Wisconsin Press, 1993), pp. 75–6; Gertrude Ezorsky, *Racism and Justice: The Case for Affirmative Action* (Ithaca: Cornell University Press, 1991), pp. 109–11; David Kairys, *With Liberty and Justice for Some: A Critique of the Conservative Supreme Court* (New York: The New Press, 1993), pp. 138–41.

8   Howard Winant has developed a tentative "map" of the system of racial hegemony in the US circa 1990, which focuses on the spectrum of racial projects running from the political right to the political left. See Winant, "Where Culture Meets Structure: Race in the 1990s," in idem, *Racial Conditions: Politics, Theory, Comparisons* (Minneapolis: University of Minnesota Press, 1994).

9   We are not unaware, for example, that publishing this work is in itself a racial project.

10 Japanese, for example, could not become naturalized citizens until passage of the 1952 McCarran-Walter Act. It took over 160 years, since the passage of the Law of 1790, to allow all "races" to be eligible for naturalization.

11   Especially when we recall that until around 1960, the majority of blacks, the largest racially defined minority group, lived in the South.

12   Toni Morrison, *Playing in the Dark: Whiteness and the Literary Imagination* (Cambridge, MA: Harvard University Press, 1992); Richard Drinnon, *Facing West: The Metaphysics of Indian-Hating and Empire-Building* (Minneapolis: University of Minnesota Press, 1980); Michael Paul Rogin, *Fathers and Children: Andrew Jackson and the Subjugation of the American Indian* (New York: Knopf, 1975).

13   This term refers to the practice, widespread throughout the Americas, whereby runaway slaves formed communities in remote areas, such as swamps, mountains, or forests, often in alliance with dispossessed indigenous peoples.

14   Antonio Gramsci, *Selections from the Prison Notebooks*, edited and translated by Quintin Hoare and Geoffrey Nowell Smith (New York: International Publishers, 1971), p. 182.

15   Anne Showstack Sassoon, *Gramsci's Politics*, 2nd ed. (London: Hutchinson, 1987); Sue Golding, *Gramsci's Democratic Theory: Contributions to Post-Liberal Democracy* (Toronto: University of Toronto Press, 1992).

16   Ralph Ellison, *Shadow and Act* (New York: New American Library, 1966), p. xiv.

17   Chantal Mouffe makes a related argument in "Radical Democracy: Modern or Postmodern?" in Andrew Ross (ed.), *Universal Abandon: The Politics of Postmodernism* (Minneapolis: University of Minnesota Press, 1988).

18   Patricia Hill Collins, *Black Feminist Thought: Knowledge, Consciousness, and the Politics of Empowerment* (New York and London: Routledge, 1991).

19   Evelyn Nakano Glenn, "From Servitude to Service Work: Historical Continuities in the Racial Division of Paid Reproductive Labor," *Signs: Journal of Women in Culture & Society*, Vol. 18, No. 1 (Autumn 1992).

20   Toni Morrison (ed.), *Race-ing Justice, En-gendering Power: Essays on Anita Hill, Clarence Thomas, and the Construction of Social Reality* (New York: Pantheon, 1992).

21   For example, in Magnus Hirschfeld's prescient book, *Racism* (London: Victor Gollancz, 1938).

22   This was the framework employed in the crucial study of Myrdal and his associates; see Gunnar Myrdal, *An American Dilemma: The Negro Problem and Modern Democracy*, 20th Anniversary Edition (New York: Harper and Row, 1962 [1944]). See also the articles by Thomas F. Pettigrew and George Frederickson in Pettigrew et al., *Prejudice: Selections from The Harvard Encyclopedia of American Ethnic Groups* (Cambridge, MA: The Belknap Press of Harvard University, 1982).

23   On discrimination, see Frederickson in ibid. In an early essay which explicitly sought to modify the framework of the Myrdal study, Robert K. Merton
recognized that prejudice and discrimination need not coincide, and
indeed could combine in a variety of ways. See Merton, "Discrimination
and the American Creed," in R. M. McIver (ed.), *Discrimination and National
Welfare* (New York: Harper and Row, 1949).

24   Gordon W. Allport, *The Nature of Prejudice* (Cambridge, MA: Addison-
Wesley, 1954) remains a classic work in the field; see also Philomena
Essed, *Understanding Everyday Racism: An Interdisciplinary Theory*
(Newbury Park, CA: Sage, 1991). A good overview of black attitudes
toward black identities is provided in William E. Cross, Jr, *Shades of Black:
Diversity in African-American Identity* (Philadelphia: Temple University
Press, 1991).

25   Stokely Carmichael and Charles V. Hamilton first popularized the notion
of "institutional" forms of discrimination in *Black Power: The Politics of Liberation in America* (New York: Vintage, 1967), although the basic concept
certainly predated that work. Indeed, President Lyndon Johnson made a
similar argument in his 1965 speech at Howard University:

> But freedom is not enough. You do not wipe away the scars of cen-
> turies by saying: Now you are free to go where you want, do as you
> desire, and choose the leaders you please.
>
> You do not take a person who, for years, has been hobbled by
> chains and liberate him (*sic*), bring him up to the starting line of a
> race and then say, "You are free to compete with all the others," and
> still justly believe that you have been completely fair.
>
> Thus it is not enough just to open the gates of opportunity. All
> our citizens must have the opportunity to walk through those gates.
>
> This is the next and more profound stage of the battle for civil
> rights. We seek not just freedom but opportunity – not just legal
> equity but human ability – not just equality as a right but equality
> as a fact and as a result. (Lyndon B. Johnson, "To Fulfill These
> Rights," reprinted in Lee Rainwater and William L. Yancey, *The
> Moynihan Report and the Politics of Controversy* (Cambridge, MA: MIT
> Press, 1967, p. 125).)

This speech, delivered at Howard University on June 4, 1965, was written
in part by Daniel Patrick Moynihan. A more systematic treatment of the
institutional racism approach is David T. Wellman, *Portraits of White
Racism* (New York: Cambridge University Press, 1977).

26   From the vantage point of the 1990s, it is possible to question whether discrimination was ever effectively outlawed. The federal retreat from the

agenda of integration began almost immediately after the passage of civil rights legislation, and has culminated today in a series of Supreme Court decisions making violation of these laws almost impossible to prove. See Ezorsky, *Racism and Justice*; Kairys, *With Liberty and Justice for Some*. As we write, the Supreme Court has further restricted antidiscrimination laws in the case of *St. Mary's Honor Center v. Hicks*. See Linda Greenhouse, "Justices Increase Workers' Burden in Job-Bias Cases," *The New York Times*, June 26, 1993, p. 1.

27   Robert Miles, *Racism* (New York and London: Routledge, 1989), esp. ch. 2.

28   The *locus classicus* of this position is Nathan Glazer, *Affirmative Discrimination: Ethnic Inequality and Public Policy*, 2nd ed. (New York: Basic Books, 1978); for more recent formulations, see Murray, *Losing Ground*; Arthur M. Schlesinger, *The Disuniting of America: Reflections on a Multicultural Society* (New York: W. W. Norton, 1992).

29   See chapter 1.

30   Thomas Sowell, for example, has argued that one's "human capital" is to a large extent culturally determined. Therefore the state cannot create a false equality which runs counter to the magnitude and persistence of cultural differences. Such attempts at social engineering are likely to produce negative and unintended results: "If social processes are transmitting real differences – in productivity, reliability, cleanliness, sobriety, peacefulness [!] – then attempts to impose politically a very different set of beliefs will necessarily backfire" (Thomas Sowell, *The Economics and Politics of Race: An International Perspective* (New York: Quill, 1983), p. 252).

31   Bob Blauner "Racism, Race, and Ethnicity: Some Reflections on the Language of Race" (unpublished manuscript, 1991).

32   Essentialism, it will be recalled, is understood as belief in real, true human essences, existing outside or impervious to social and historical context.

33   An example would be the "singling out" of members of racially defined minority groups for harsh treatment by authorities, as when police harass and beat randomly chosen ghetto youth, a practice they do not pursue with white suburban youth.

34   For example, the biologistic theories found in Michael Anderson Bradley, *The Iceman Inheritance: Prehistoric Sources of Western Man's Racism, Sexism, and Aggression* (Toronto: Dorset, 1978), and in Frances Cress Welsing, *The Isis (Yssis) Papers* (Chicago: Third World Press, 1991).

35   "These remarks should not be interpreted as simply an effort to move the gaze of African-American studies to a different site. I do not want to alter one hierarchy in order to institute another. It is true that I do not want to encourage those totalizing approaches to African-American scholarship

which have no drive other than the exchange of dominations – dominant Eurocentric scholarship replaced by dominant Afrocentric scholarship. More interesting is what makes intellectual domination possible; how knowledge is transformed from invasion and conquest to revelation and choice; what ignites and informs the literary imagination, and what forces help establish the parameters of criticism." (Toni Morrison, *Playing in the Dark*, p. 8; emphasis original.)

36   Lisa Lowe states: "The concept of 'strategic essentialism' suggests that it is possible to utilize specific signifiers of ethnic identity, such as Asian American, for the purpose of contesting and disrupting the discourses that exclude Asian Americans, while simultaneously revealing the internal contradictions and slippages of Asian Americans so as to insure that such essentialisms will not be reproduced and proliferated by the very appara- tuses we seek to disempower." Lisa Lowe, "Heterogeneity, Hybridity, Multiplicity: Marking Asian American Differences," *Diaspora*, Vol. 1, No. 1 (Spring 1991), p. 39.

37   This view supports Supreme Court decisions taken in the late 1960s and early 1970s, for example in *Griggs v. Duke Power*, 401 US 424 (1971). We agree with Kairys that only "[F]or that brief period in our history, it could accurately be said that governmental discrimination was prohibited by law" (Kairys, *With Liberty and Justice For Some*, p. 144).

38   This analysis draws on Ezorsky, *Racism and Justice*.

39   See, for example, Judy H. Katz, *White Awareness: Handbook for anti-Racism Training* (Norman: University of Oklahoma Press, 1978).

40   The formula "racism equals prejudice plus power" is frequently invoked by our students to argue that only whites can be racist. We have been able to uncover little written analysis to support this view (apart from Katz, ibid., p. 10), but consider that it is itself an example of the essentializing approach we have identified as central to racism. In the modern world, "power" cannot be reified as a thing which some possess and others don't, but instead constitutes a relational field. The minority student who boldly asserts in class that minorities cannot be racist is surely not entirely pow- erless. In all but the most absolutist of regimes, resistance to rule itself implies power.

41   To pick but one example among many: writing before the successes of the civil rights movement, E. Franklin Frazier bitterly castigated the collabo- ration of black elites with white supremacy. See Frazier, *Black Bourgeoisie: The Rise of a New Middle Class in the United States* (New York: The Free Press, 1957).

42   Interestingly, what they share most centrally seems to be their anti- semitism.

43   Racial teachings of the Nation of Islam, for example, maintain that whites are the product of a failed experiment by a mad scientist.

44   Elinor Langer, "The American Neo-Nazi Movement Today," *The Nation*, July 16/23, 1990.

45   Such arguments can be found in Nathan Glazer, *Affirmative Discrimination*, Charles Murray, *Losing Ground*, and Arthur M. Schlesinger, Jr., *The Disuniting of America*, among others.

8

Preface to Dominance Without Hegemony: History and Power in Colonial India

Ranajit Guha

This book is made up of modified versions of three essays written in 1986–7 and published between 1988 and 1992. All three connect with our project, *Subaltern Studies*, and refer back to and develop certain positions I have taken up there. That project made its debut by announcing its revisionist aims for studies on colonial India. However, in doing so, it did not claim any novelty. Ours was not the first or only intervention to express discontent about the state of South Asian historiography and social sciences and provoke debates about it. Debates of this kind had already started in the nineteenth century, when Indian intellectuals put on record their first public, though cautious and loyalist, criticism of the colonial administration and have continued ever since as one variety or another of a whole range of liberal-imperialist and liberal-nationalist tendencies. In spite of their differences in other respects, these tendencies have been unanimous in the assumption that the power relations of colonial rule were contained in an integrated and unified field with all the ideologies and political practices of the period articulated within a single domain.

Subaltern Studies made its debut by questioning that assumption and arguing that there was no such unified and singular domain of politics and the latter was, to the contrary, structurally split between an elite and a subaltern part, each of which was autonomous in its own way. Much of what we have to say has indeed been concerned with documenting the existence of these two distinct but interacting parts as well as with arguing why such a structural split between them was historically necessary.

However, by questioning that monistic conception we immediately and inevitably raised a question about the nature of the colonial state itself. For all those tendencies I have mentioned had proceeded from a thoroughly unexamined belief that the so-called unitary character of politics was nothing other than the effect of the homogenizing function of colonialism.

This notion of colonialism as a homogenizing force is fundamental to both of the dominant historiographies – neocolonialist and nationalist. The former characterizes it in positive terms as either a cultural or an institutional force. According to one of its versions, the colonial regime politicized India by the introduction of liberal education, and the ideas and activities of a Western-educated elite in the course of its collaboration with the raj were all that was there to Indian politics. According to another version, which superseded the first, it was not so much the metropolitan liberal culture as the colonial administration itself which created a political arena for the natives by involving them in a scramble for rewards in the form of privileges and power in governmental institutions developed by the raj.

Whichever version one takes, it is the civilizing or institutionalizing function of the regime that figures as the generative impulse of Indian politics and its unifying force in this neocolonialist view. The nationalist standpoint shares the same assumption, but turns it to its own advantage by defining the content and character of politics simply in terms of the indigenous elite's response to colonial rule and the sum of all the ideas and activities by which it dealt with the government of the day.

Between these two interpretations the question of power was reduced to an elite contest with no room left in it for the South Asian people except as an inert mass deployed by the dominant elements to serve their own ends according to strategies of their own invention. We took notice of this omission in an inaugural statement in *Subaltern Studies I* (Delhi: Oxford University Press, 1982) thus:

What is clearly left out of this un-historical historiography is the *politics of the people*. For parallel to the domain of elite politics there existed throughout the colonial period another domain of Indian politics in

which the principal actors were not the dominant groups of the indigenous society or the colonial authorities but the subaltern classes and
groups constituting the mass of the labouring population and the intermediate strata in town and country – that is, the people. This was an
autonomous domain, for it neither originated in elite politics nor did its
existence depend on the latter.

Underlying the exclusive and elitist approach is an idea which has
prevailed in historiography since the rise of the Italian city-states and
has continued through the Enlightenment until the emergence of the
modern nation-states nearer our time. This is the idea that with the
ascendancy of the bourgeoisie in Western Europe all of the power relations of civil society have everywhere been so fully assimilated to those
of the state that the two may be said to have coincided in an undifferentiated and integrated space where alone such relations have situated
and articulated themselves ever since. It has been possible therefore for
historical scholarship that has fed on this theorem for centuries and
made it into the stuff of academic common sense to represent power in
its most generalized form as Civil Society = Nation = State.

To say and demonstrate, as we have done, that the domain of
politics is not unitary but structurally split is of course to spoil the ele-
gance of this equation at once. However, by doing so, we take it upon
ourselves to redefine how these three terms relate to each other in such
a domain. Our attempt to face up to that task leads directly, as indicated
above, to the question: "What is colonialism and what is a colonial
state?"

Questions like these have of course been asked before. An answer to
one or another of them is indeed presupposed in all that has ever been
written about British rule in South Asia. This has been so since the
first histories of the subcontinent were published by the East India
Company's servants as early as the 1770s and has continued to be the
case until today with the imperial theme established firmly as an object
of academic research and teaching. Yet the progress of scholarship
during the last two hundred years has done little to challenge or even
seriously interrogate such presuppositions. In fact, they have hardly
moved from where Bolts and Verelst had left them standing as a set of
necessary, if invisible, prejudices which the passage of time has allowed
to merge unobtrusively in the background of historical discourse.
Thanks to an amazing oversight characteristic of academic work of all

kinds irrespective of their points of view, the notion of a unitary political domain has survived until now even the mutually opposed readings of the Indian past from imperialist and nationalist points of view.

We take the enigma of that oversight common to both of those rival ideologies as our point of departure and go on to suggest that the colonial state in South Asia was very unlike and indeed fundamentally different from the metropolitan bourgeois state which had sired it. The difference consisted in the fact that the metropolitan state was hegemonic in character with its claim to dominance based on a power relation in which the moment of persuasion outweighed that of coercion, whereas the colonial state was nonhegemonic with persuasion outweighed by coercion in its structure of dominance. Indeed, we have argued that the originality of the South Asian colonial state lay precisely in this difference: a historical paradox, it was an autocracy set up and sustained in the East by the foremost democracy of the Western world. And since it was nonhegemonic, it was not possible for that state to assimilate the civil society of the colonized to itself. We have defined the character of the colonial state therefore as a *dominance without hegemony*.

The consequence of this paradox for the political culture of colonial India was to generate an original alloy from the fusion and overdetermination of two distinct paradigms – an originality which has been witness to the historic failure of capital to realize its universalizing tendency under colonial conditions, and the corresponding failure of the metropolitan bourgeois culture to dissolve or assimilate fully the indigenous culture of South Asia in the power relations of the colonial period. We have followed up these considerations by reflecting on the character of colonialist historiography and shown how it has sought to endow colonialism with a spurious hegemony denied it by history.

Dominance without hegemony has a nationalist aspect as well. This follows from the structural split in politics and the coexistence of its two domains. As it has been put in the statement cited above, "The coexistence of these two domains or streams, which can be sensed by intuition and proved by demonstration as well, was the index of an important historical truth, that is, the *failure of the Indian bourgeoisie to speak for the nation*. There were vast areas in the life and consciousness of the people which were never integrated into their hegemony."

That failure is self-evident from the difficulty which has frustrated the bourgeoisie in its effort so far at winning a hegemonic role for itself even after half a century since the birth of a sovereign Indian nation-state. The predicament continues to grow worse, and by current showing should keep students of contemporary South Asia busy for years to come. For our part we have concentrated, in what follows, on two important moments of its career under the raj which anticipated its accession to power by mobilization and by historiography. What was at issue in both respects was its desire for recognition in its claim to speak for the people constituted as a nation and to challenge thereby any pretensions the alien rulers had to represent the colonized. A rivalry between an aspirant to power and its incumbent, this was in essence a contest for hegemony.

Our approach to these problems picks its way through historiography, as the readers will notice no doubt from the signs displayed all over the text and the arguments these refer to. We have taken this particular course not out of any conviction that this is the only possible way of asking questions about colonialism and the colonial state. One could have formulated the same or very similar questions deductively following the classical models of political philosophy (whose influence, especially that of Hobbes, Machiavelli, and Montesquieu, on the development of our own argument should be obvious to all) or any of their latter-day adaptations in academic work on the modern state-systems. But we have decided on the historiographical approach primarily because it helps us to combine the advantages of the classical theories with a consideration of history as writing.

The importance of the latter for our problematic is hard to exaggerate. For at a certain level the question of power in colonial South Asia or anywhere else in a land under foreign occupation can be phrased succinctly as "Who writes the history of the subjugated people?" In the Indian instance that question resonates with one that agitated the very first architects of the empire as they asked, "Who is the king of Bengal?" As Warren Hastings and Philip Francis were both thoughtful enough to declare in response, the East India Company's claim to such "kingship" derived entirely from the right of conquest. For all that was involved in such a claim, ranging from the assumption of statutory authority to act as *Diwan* to grabbing the produce of the land and converting it by the most predatory means into mercantile wealth, rested simply and exclusively on the power of the sword.

What we have tried to point out here is how that sword conferred a "right" on the pen as well. It was conquest which empowered the conquerors to impose on the colonized a past written from the colonizer's point of view and uphold that writing as foundational to the law of the land. Our attempt to inform this study of colonialism by the pathos of a purloined past is therefore not so much a matter of professional convenience as a strategy to situate the writing of a conquered people's history by conquerors at the very heart of the question of one nation's oppression by another.

To think the colonial condition of rulership and historiography together in this manner is of course to think of the second term too as a force. To do so would not be to raise the power of the pen to that of the gun by *utprekṣā* – the figure of Sanskrit poetics which allows a thing to be elevated fancifully, if absurdly on occasions, to the likeness of something superior to it. Rather, it would be to put on record the effect of an *atideśa* – a metonymic extension by which statist concerns forced their way into historical interpretation, allowing a colonial dominance to overflow and appropriate a writing culture of the colonized.

But such extension did not come about as a simple laterality. The force of that writing culture was destined to acquire a vertical thrust as well. For it enlisted the colonized too as interpreters of their own past and created the conditions for an Indian historiography of India. However, as discussed in these pages, such an agenda for the reclamation of an appropriated past could in no way be adequate to its concept without wrenching itself away from its liberal-imperialist armature, without in fact arming itself with a genuinely anti-imperialist critique for which it did not, alas, have either the strength or the motivation yet. It was precisely such debility that frustrated whatever was there as a desire for power underlying the first historical discourses informed by an Indian point of view. In so far as any nationalist claim to speak for a people's past was hegemonic by implication, it would be sometime yet for that claim to be fully upheld by historiography. [. . .]

9

Defining Black Feminist Thought

Patricia Hill Collins

Widely used yet rarely defined, Black feminist thought encompasses diverse and contradictory meanings. Two interrelated tensions highlight issues in defining Black feminist thought. The first concerns the thorny question of who can be a Black feminist. One current response, explicit in Patricia Bell Scott's (1982b) "Selected Bibliography on Black Feminism," classifies all African-American women, regardless of the content of our ideas, as Black feminists. From this perspective, living as Black women provides experiences to stimulate a Black feminist consciousness. Yet indiscriminately labeling all Black women in this way simultaneously conflates the terms *woman* and *feminist* and identifies being of African descent – a questionable biological category – as being the sole determinant of a Black feminist consciousness. As Cheryl Clarke points out, "I criticized Scott. Some of the women she cited as 'black feminists' were clearly not feminist at the time they wrote their books and still are not to this day" (1983, p. 94).

The term *Black feminist* has also been used to apply to selected African-Americans – primarily women – who possess some version of a feminist consciousness. Beverly Guy-Sheftall (1986) contends that both men and women can be "Black feminists" and names Frederick Douglass and William E. B. Du Bois as prominent examples of Black male feminists. Guy-Sheftall also identifies some distinguishing features of Black feminist ideas: namely, that Black women's experiences with both racial and gender oppression that result in needs and problems distinct from white women and Black men, and that Black women must struggle for equality both as women and as African-Americans. Guy-Sheftall's definition is helpful in that its use of ideological criteria fosters a definition of Black feminist thought that encompasses both experiences and ideas. In other words, she suggests that experiences gained from living as African-American women stimulate a Black feminist sensibility. But her definition is simultaneously troublesome because it makes the biological category of Blackness the prerequisite for possessing such thought. Furthermore, it does not explain why these particular ideological criteria and not others are the distinguishing ones.

The term Black feminist has also been used to describe selected African-American women who possess some version of a feminist consciousness (Beale, 1970; hooks, 1981; Barbara Smith, 1983; White, 1984). This usage of the term yields the most restrictive notion of who can be a Black feminist. The ground-breaking Combahee River Collective (1982) document, "A Black Feminist Statement," implicitly relies on this definition. The Collective claims that "as Black women we find any type of biological determinism a particularly dangerous and reactionary basis upon which to build a politic" (p. 17). But in spite of this statement, by implying that only African-American women can be Black feminists, they require a biological prerequisite for race and gender consciousness. The Collective also offers its own ideological criteria for identifying Black feminist ideas. In contrast to Beverly Guy-Sheftall, the Collective places a stronger emphasis on capitalism as a source of Black women's oppression and on political activism as a distinguishing feature of Black feminism.

Biologically deterministic criteria for the term *black* and the accompanying assumption that being of African descent somehow produces a certain consciousness or perspective are inherent in these definitions. By presenting race as being fixed and immutable – something rooted in nature – these approaches mask the historical construction of racial categories, the shifting meaning of race, and the crucial role of politics and ideology in shaping conceptions of race (Gould, 1981; Omi and Winant, 1986). In contrast, much greater variation is afforded the term feminist. Feminists are seen as ranging from biologically determined – as is the case in radical feminist thought, which argues that only women can be feminists – to notions of feminists as individuals who have undergone some type of political transformation theoretically achievable by anyone.

Though the term Black feminist could also be used to describe any individual who embraces Black feminist ideas, the separation of biology from ideology required for this usage is rarely seen in the works of Black women intellectuals. Sometimes the contradictions among these competing definitions can be so great that Black women writers use all simultaneously. Consider the following passage from Deborah McDowell's essay "New Directions for Black Feminist Criticism":

> I use the term here simply to refer to Black female critics who analyze the works of Black female writers from a feminist political perspective. But the term can also apply to any criticism written by a Black woman regardless of her subject or perspective – a book written by a male from a feminist or political perspective, a book written by a Black woman or about Black women authors in general, or any writings by women. (1985, p. 191)

While McDowell implies that elite white men could be "black feminists," she is clearly unwilling to state so categorically. From McDowell's perspective, whites and Black men who embrace a specific political perspective, and Black women regardless of political perspective, could all potentially be deemed Black feminist critics.

The ambiguity surrounding current perspectives on who can be a Black feminist is directly tied to a second definitional tension in Black feminist though: the question of what constitutes Black feminism. The range of assumptions concerning the relationship between ideas and their advocates as illustrated in the works of Patricia Bell Scott, Beverly Guy-Sheftall, the Combahee River Collective, and Deborah McDowell leads to problems in defining Black feminist theory itself. Once a person is labeled a "Black feminist," then ideas forwarded by that individual often become defined as Black feminist thought. This practice accounts for neither changes in the thinking of an individual nor differences among Black feminist theorists.

A definition of Black feminist thought is needed that avoids the materialist position that being Black and/or female generates certain experiences that automatically determine variants of a Black and/or feminist consciousness. Claims that Black feminist thought is the exclusive province of African-American women, regardless of the experiences and worldview of such women, typify this position. But a definition of Black feminist thought must also avoid the idealist position that ideas can be evaluated in isolation from the groups that create them. Definitions claiming that anyone can produce and develop Black feminist thought risk obscuring the special angle of vision that Black women bring to the knowledge production process.

The Dimensions of a Black Women's Standpoint

Developing adequate definitions of Black feminist thought involves facing this complex nexus of relationships among biological classification, the social construction of race and gender as categories of analysis, the material conditions accompanying these changing social constructions, and Black women's consciousness about these themes. One way of addressing the definitional tensions in Black feminist thought is to specify the relationship between a Black women's standpoint – those experiences and ideas shared by African-American women that provide a unique angle of vision on self, community, and society – and theories that interpret these experiences.[1] I suggest that Black feminist thought consists of specialized knowledge created by African-American women which clarifies a standpoint of and for Black women. In other words, Black feminist thought encompasses theoretical interpretations of Black women's reality by those who live it.

This definition does not mean that all African-American women generate such thought or that other groups do not play a critical role in its production. Before exploring the contours and implications of this working definition, understanding five key dimensions of a Black women's standpoint is essential.

The core themes of a Black women's standpoint

All African-American women share the common experience of being Black women in a society that denigrates women of African descent. This commonality of experience suggests that certain characteristic themes will be prominent in a Black women's standpoint. For example, one core theme is a legacy of struggle. Katie Cannon observes, "throughout the history of the United States, the interrelationship of white supremacy and male superiority has characterized the Black woman's reality as a situation of struggle – a struggle to survive it two contradictory worlds simultaneously, one white, privileged, and oppressive, the other black, exploited, and oppressed" (1985, p. 30). Black women's vulnerability to assaults in the workplace, on the street, and at home has stimulated Black women's independence and self-reliance.

In spite of differences created by historical era, age, social class, sexual orientation, or ethnicity, the legacy of struggle against racism and sexism is a common thread binding African-American women. Anna Julia Cooper, a nineteenth-century Black woman intellectual, describes Black women's vulnerability to sexual violence:

> I would beg . . . to add my plea for the *Colored Girls* of the South: – that large, bright, promising fatally beautiful class . . . so full of promise and possibilities, yet so sure of destruction; often without a father to whom they dare apply the loving term, often without a stronger brother to espouse their cause and defend their honor with his life's blood; in the midst of pitfalls and snares, waylaid by the lower classes of white men, with no shelter, no protection. (Cooper, 1892, p. 240)

Yet during this period Black women struggled and built a powerful club movement and numerous community organizations (Giddings, 1984, 1988; Gilkes, 1985).

Age offers little protection from this legacy of struggle. Far too many young Black girls inhabit hazardous and hostile environments. In 1975 I received an essay entitled "My World" from Sandra, a sixth-grade student who was a resident of one of the most dangerous public housing projects in Boston. Sandra wrote, "My world is full of people getting rape. People shooting on another. Kids and grownups fighting over girls-friends. And people without jobs who can't afford to get a education so they can get a job . . . winos on the streets raping and killing little girls." Her words poignantly express a growing Black feminist sensibility that she may be victimized by racism and poverty. They also reveal her awareness that she is vulnerable to rape as a gender-specific form of sexual violence. In spite of her feelings about her community, Sandra not only walked the streets daily but managed safely to deliver three younger siblings to school. In doing so she participated in a Black women's legacy of struggle.

This legacy of struggle constitutes one of several core themes of a Black women's standpoint. Efforts to reclaim the Black feminist intellectual tradition are revealing Black women's longstanding attention to a series of core themes first recorded by Maria W. Stewart (Richardson, 1987). Stewart's treatment of the interlocking nature of race, gender, and class oppression, her call for replacing denigrated images of Black womanhood with self-defined images, her belief in Black women's activism as mothers, teachers, and Black community leaders, and her sensitivity to sexual politics are all core themes advanced by a variety of Black feminist intellectuals.

Variation of responses to core themes

The existence of core themes does not mean that African-American women respond to these themes in the same way. Diversity among Black women produces different concrete experiences that in turn shape various reactions to the core themes. For example, when faced with stereotypical, controlling images of Black women, some women – such as Sojourner Truth – demand, "ain't I a woman?" By deconstructing the conceptual apparatus of the dominant group, they invoke a Black women's legacy of struggle. In contrast, other women internalize the controlling images and come to believe that they are the stereotypes (Brown-Collins and Sussewell, 1986).

A variety of factors explain the diversity of responses. For example, although all African-American women encounter racism, social class differences among African-American women influence how racism is experienced. A young manager who graduated with honors from the University of Maryland describes the specific form racism can take for middle-class Blacks. Before flying to Cleveland to explain a marketing plan for her company, her manager made her go over it three or four times in front of him so that she would not forget *her* marketing plan. Then he explained how to check luggage at an airport and how to reclaim it. "I just sat at lunch listening to this man talking to me like I was a monkey who could remember but couldn't think," the Black female manager recalled. When she had had enough, she responded, "I asked him if he wanted to tie my money up in a handkerchief and put a note on me saying that I was an employee of this company. In case

I got lost I would be picked up by Traveler's Aid, and Traveler's Aid would send me back" (Davis and Watson, 1985, p. 86). Most middle-class Black women do not encounter such blatant incidents, but many working-class Blacks do. For both groups the racist belief that African-Americans are less intelligent than whites remains strong.

Sexual orientation provides another key factor. Black lesbians have identified homophobia in general and the issues they face living as Black lesbians in homophobic communities as being a major influence on their angle of vision of everyday events (Shockley, 1974; Lorde, 1982, 1984; Clarke et al., 1983; Barbara Smith, 1983). Beverly Smith describes how being a lesbian affected her perceptions of the wedding of one of her closest friends: "God, I wish I had one friend here. Someone who knew me and would understand how I feel. I am masquerading as a nice, straight, middle-class Black 'girl'" (1983, p. 172). While the majority of those attending the wedding saw only a festive event, Beverly Smith felt that her friend was being sent into a form of bondage.

Other factors such as ethnicity, region of the country, urbanization, and age combine to produce a web of experiences shaping diversity among African-American women. As a result, it is more accurate to discuss a Black *women's* standpoint than a Black *woman's* standpoint.

The interdependence of experience and consciousness

Black women's work and family experiences and grounding in traditional African-American culture suggest that African-American women as a group experience a world different from that of those who are not Black and female. Moreover, these concrete experiences can stimulate a distinctive Black feminist consciousness concerning that material reality.[2] Being Black and female may expose African-American women to certain common experiences, which in turn may predispose us to a distinctive group consciousness, but it in no way guarantees that such a consciousness will develop among all women or that it will be articulated as such by the group.

Many African-American women have grasped this connection between what one does and how one thinks. Hannah Nelson, an elderly Black domestic worker, discusses how work shapes the perspectives of

African-American and white women: "Since I have to work, I don't really have to worry about most of the things that most of the white women I have worked for are worrying about. And if these women did their own work, they would think just like I do – about this, anyway" (Gwaltney, 1980, p. 4). Ruth Shays, a Black inner-city resident, points out how variations in men's and women's experiences lead to differences in perspective. "The mind of the man and the mind of the woman is the same" she notes, "but this business of living makes women use their minds in ways that men don' even have to think about" (Gwaltney, 1980, p. 33).

This connection between experience and consciousness that shapes the everyday lives of all African-American women pervades the works of Black women activists and scholars. In her autobiography, Ida B. Wells describes how the lynching of her friends had such an impact on her worldview that she subsequently devoted much of her life to the antilynching cause (Duster 1970). Sociologist Joyce Ladner's (1972) *Tomorrow's Tomorrow*, a groundbreaking study of Black female adolescence, emerged from her discomfort with the disparity between the teachings of mainstream scholarship and her experiences as a young Black woman in the South. Similarly, the transformed consciousness experienced by Janie, the light-skinned heroine of Zora Neale Hurston's (1937) classic *Their Eyes Were Watching God*, from obedient granddaughter and wife to a self-defined African-American woman, can be directly traced to her experiences with each of her three husbands. In one scene Janie's second husband, angry because she served him a dinner of scorched rice, underdone fish, and soggy bread, hits her. That incident stimulates Jenie to stand "where he left her for unmeasured time" and think. Her thinking leads to the recognition that "her image of Jody tumbled down and shattered . . . she had an inside and an outside now and suddenly she knew how not to mix them" (p. 63).

Consciousness and the struggle for a self-defined standpoint

African-American women as a group may have experiences that provide us with a unique angle of vision. But expressing a collective, self-defined Black feminist consciousness is problematic precisely because dominant groups have a vested interest in suppressing such thought.[3] As Hannah Nelson notes, "I have grown to womanhood in a world where the saner

you are, the madder you are made to appear" (Gwaltney, 1980, p. 7).
Ms Nelson realizes that those who control the schools, media, and other
cultural institutions of society prevail in establishing their viewpoint as
superior to others.

An oppressed group's experiences may put its members in a position
to see things differently, but their lack of control over the ideological
apparatuses of society makes expressing a self-defined standpoint more
difficult. Elderly domestic worker Rosa Wakefield assesses how the standpoints of the powerful and those who serve them diverge:

> If you eats these dinners and don't cook 'em, if you wears these clothes
> and don't buy or iron them, then you might start thinking that the good
> fairy or some spirit did all that. . . . Black folks don't have no time to be
> thinking like that. . . . But when you don't have anything else to do, you
> can think like that. It's bad for your mind, though. (Gwaltney, 1980,
> p. 88)

Ms Wakefield has a self-defined perspective growing from her experiences that enables her to reject the standpoint of more powerful groups.
And yet ideas like hers are typically suppressed by dominant groups.
Groups unequal in power are correspondingly unequal in their ability
to make their standpoint known to themselves and others.

Individual African-American women have long displayed varying
types of consciousness regarding our shared angle of vision. By aggre-
gating and articulating these individual expressions of consciousness,
a collective, focused group consciousness becomes possible. Black
women's ability to forge these individual, unarticulated, yet potentially
powerful expressions of everyday consciousness into an articulated, self-
defined, collective standpoint is key to Black women's survival. As Audre
Lorde points out, "it is axiomatic that if we do not define ourselves for
ourselves, we will be defined by others – for their use and to our detriment" (1984, p. 45).

One fundamental feature of this struggle for a self-defined standpoint
involves tapping sources of everyday, unarticulated consciousness that
have traditionally been denigrated in white, male-controlled institutions. For Black women, the struggle involves embracing a consciousness that is simultaneously Afrocentric and feminist. What does this
mean?

Research in African-American Studies suggests that an Afrocentric worldview exists which is distinct from and in many ways opposed to a Eurocentric worldview (Okanlawon, 1972; Asante, 1987; Myers, 1988). Standard scholarly social constructions of blackness and race define these concepts as being either reflections of quantifiable, biological differences among humans or residual categories that emerged in response to institutionalized racism (Lyman, 1972; Bash, 1979; Gould, 1981; Omi and Winant, 1986). In contrast, even though it often relies on biological notions of the "race," Afrocentric scholarship suggests that "blackness" and Afrocentricity reflect longstanding belief systems among African peoples (Diop, 1974; Richards, 1980; Asante, 1987). While Black people were forced to adapt these Afrocentric belief systems in the face of different institutional arrangements of white domination, the continuation of an Afrocentric worldview has been fundamental to African-Americans' resistance to racial oppression (Smitherman, 1977; Webber, 1978; Sobel, 1979; Thompson, 1983). In other words, being Black encompasses *both* experiencing white domination *and* individual and group valuation of an independent, longstanding Afrocentric consciousness.

African-American women draw on this Afrocentric worldview to cope with racial oppression. But far too often Black women's Afrocentric consciousness remains unarticulated and not fully developed into a self-defined standpoint. In societies that denigrate African ideas and peoples, the process of valuing an Afrocentric worldview is the result of self-conscious struggle.

Similar concerns can be raised about the issue of what constitutes feminist ideas (Eisenstein, 1983; Jaggar, 1983). Being a biological female does not mean that one's ideas are automatically feminist. Self-conscious struggle is needed in order to reject patriarchal perceptions of women and to value women's ideas and actions. The fact that more women than men identify themselves as feminists reflects women's greater experience with the negative consequences of gender oppression. Becoming a feminist is routinely described by women (and men) as a process of transformation, of struggling to develop new interpretations of familiar realities.

The struggles of women from different racial/ethnic groups and those of women and men within African-American communities to articulate self-defined standpoint represent similar yet distinct processes. While race and gender are both socially constructed categories, constructions of gender rest on clearer biological criteria than do constructions of race. Classifying African-Americans into specious racial categories is considerably more difficult than noting the clear biological differences distinguishing females from males (Patterson, 1982). But though united by biological sex, women do not form the same type of group as do African-Americans, Jews, native Americans, Vietnamese, or other groups with distinct histories, geographic origins, cultures, and social institutions. The absence of an identifiable tradition uniting women does not mean that women are characterized more by differences than by similarities. Women do share common experiences, but the experiences are not generally the same type as those affecting racial and ethnic groups (King, 1988). Thus while expressions of race and gender are both socially constructed, they are not constructed in the same way. The struggle for an Afrocentric feminist consciousness requires embracing both an Afrocentric worldview and a feminist sensibility and using both to forge a self-defined standpoint.[4] [. . .]

Who Can Be a Black Feminist? The Centrality of Black Women Intellectuals to the Production of Black Feminist Thought

I aim to develop a definition of Black feminist thought that relies exclusively neither on a materialist analysis – one whereby all African-American women by virtue of biology become automatically registered as "authentic Black feminists" – nor on an idealist analysis whereby the background, worldview, and interests of the thinker are deemed irrelevant in assessing his or her ideas. Resolving the tension between these two extremes involves reassessing the centrality Black women intellectuals assume in producing Black feminist thought. It also requires examining the importance of coalitions with Black men, white women, people of color, and other groups with distinctive standpoints. Such coalitions are essential in order to foster other groups' contributions as critics, teachers, advocates, and disseminators of a self-defined Afrocentric feminist standpoint.

Black women's concrete experiences as members of specific race, class, and gender groups as well as our concrete historical situations necessarily play significant roles in our perspectives on the world. No standpoint is neutral because no individual or group exists unembedded in the world. Knowledge is gained not by solitary individuals but by Black women as socially constituted members of a group (Narayan, 1989). These factors all frame the definitional tensions in Black feminist thought.

Black women intellectuals are central to Black feminist thought for several reasons. First, our experiences as African-American women provide us with a unique standpoint on Black womanhood unavailable to other groups. It is more likely for Black women as members of an oppressed group to have critical insights into the condition of our own oppression than it is for those who live outside those structures. One of the characters in Frances Ellen Watkins Harper's 1892 novel, *Iola Leroy*, expresses this belief in the special vision of those who have experienced oppression:

> Miss Leroy, out of the race must come its own thinkers and writers. Authors belonging to the white race have written good books, for which I am deeply grateful, but it seems to be almost impossible for a white man to put himself completely in our place. No man can feel the iron which enters another man's soul. (Carby, 1987, p. 62).

Only African-American women occupy this center and can "feel the iron" that enters Black women's souls, because we are the only group that has experienced race, gender, and class oppression as Black women experience them. The importance of Black women's leadership in producing Black feminist thought does not mean that others cannot participate. It does mean that the primary responsibility for defining one's own reality lies with the people who live that reality, who actually have those experiences.

Second, Black women intellectuals provide unique leadership for Black women's empowerment and resistance. In discussing Black women's involvement in the feminist movement, Sheila Radford-Hill points out the connections among self-definition, empowerment, and taking actions in one's own behalf:

> Black women now realize that part of the problem within the movement was our insistence that white women do for/with us what we must do for/with ourselves: namely, frame our own social action around our own agenda for change. . . . Critical to this discussion is the right to organize

on one's own behalf. . . . Criticism by black feminists must reaffirm this
principle. (1986, p. 162)

Black feminist thought cannot challenge race, gender, and class oppression without empowering African-American women. "Oppressed people
resist by identifying themselves as subjects, by defining their reality,
shaping their new identity, naming their history, telling their story,"
notes bell hooks (1989, p. 43). Because self-definition is key to individual and group empowerment, using an epistemology that cedes the
power of self-definition to other groups, no matter how well-meaning,
in essence perpetuates Black women's subordination. As Black feminist
sociologist Deborah K. King succinctly states, "Black feminism asserts
self-determination as essential" (1988, p. 72).

Stressing the importance of Black women's centrality to Black feminist thought does not mean that all African-American women exert this
leadership. While being an African-American woman generally provides the experiential base for an Afrocentric feminist consciousness,
these same conditions suppress its articulation. It is not acquired as a
finished product but must continually develop in relation to changing
conditions.

Bonnie Johnson emphasizes the importance of self-definition. In her
critique of Patricia Bell Scott's bibliography on Black feminism, she challenges both Scott's categorization of all works by Black women as being
Black feminist and Scott's identification of a wide range of African-
American women as Black feminists: "Whether I think they're feminists
is irrelevant. *They* would not call themselves feminist" (Clarke et al.,
1983, p. 94). As Patrice L. Dickerson contends, "a person comes into
being and knows herself by her achievements, and through her efforts
to become and know herself, she achieves" (personal correspondence,
1988). Here is the heart of the matter. An Afrocentric feminist consciousness constantly emerges and is part of a self-conscious struggle to
merge thought and action.

Third, Black women intellectuals are central in the production
of Black feminist thought because we alone can create the group
autonomy that must precede effective coalitions with other groups.
This autonomy is quite distinct from separatist positions whereby Black
women withdraw from other groups and engage in exclusionary politics. In her introduction to *Home Girls, A Black Feminist Anthology*,
Barbara Smith describes this difference: "Autonomy and separatism are

fundamentally different. Whereas autonomy comes from a position of strength, separatism comes from a position of fear. When we're truly autonomous we can deal with other kinds of people, a multiplicity of issues, and with difference, because we have formed a solid base of strength" (1983, p. xl). Black women intellectuals who articulate an autonomous, self-defined standpoint are in a position to examine the usefulness of coalitions with other groups, both scholarly and activist, in order to develop new models for social change. However, autonomy to develop a self-defined, independent analysis does not mean that Black feminist thought has relevance only for African-American women or that we must confine ourselves to analyzing our own experiences. As Sonia Sanchez points out, "I've always known that if you write from a black experience, you're writing from a universal experience as well . . . I know you don't have to whitewash yourself to be universal" (in Tate, 1983, p. 142).

While Black feminist thought may originate with Black feminist intellectuals, it cannot flourish isolated from the experiences and ideas of other groups. The dilemma is that Black women intellectuals must place our own experiences and consciousness at the center of any serious efforts to develop Black feminist thought yet not have that thought become separatist and exclusionary. bell hooks offers a solution to this problem by suggesting that we shift from statements such as "I am a feminist" to those such as "I advocate feminism." Such an approach could "serve as a way women who are concerned about feminism as well as other political movements could express their support while avoiding linguistic structures that give primacy to one particular group" (1984, p. 30).

By advocating, refining, and disseminating Black feminist thought, other groups – such as Black men, white women, white men, and other people of color – further its development. Black women can produce an attenuated version of Black feminist thought separated from other groups. Other groups cannot produce Black feminist thought without African-American women. Such groups can, however, develop self-defined knowledge reflecting their own standpoints. But the full actualization of Black feminist thought requires a collaborative enterprise with Black women at the center of a community based on coalitions among autonomous groups.

Coalitions such as these require dialogues among Black women intellectuals and within the larger African-American women's community.

Exploring the common themes of a Black women's standpoint is an important first step. Moreover, finding ways of handling internal dissent is especially important for the Black women's intellectual community. Evelynn Hammond describes how maintaining a united front for whites stifles her thinking: "What I need to do is challenge my thinking, to grow. On white publications sometimes I feel like I'm holding up the banner of black womanhood. And that doesn't allow me to be as critical as I would like to be" (in Clarke et al., 1983, p. 104). Cheryl Clarke observes that she has two dialogues: one with the public and the private ones in which she feels free to criticize the work of other Black women. Clarke states that the private dialogues are the ones that "have changed my life, have shaped the way I feel . . . have mattered to me" (p. 103).

Coalitions also require dialogues with other groups. Rather than rejecting our marginality, Black women intellectuals can use our outsider-within stance as a position of strength in building effective coalitions and stimulating dialogue. Barbara Smith suggests that Black women develop dialogues based on a "commitment to principled coalitions, based not upon expediency, but upon our actual need for each other" (1983, p. xxxiii). Dialogues among and coalitions with a range of groups, each with its own distinctive set of experiences and specialized thought embedded in those experiences, form the larger, more general terrain of intellectual and political discourse necessary for furthering Black feminism. Through dialogues exploring how relations of domination and subordination are maintained and changed, parallels between Black women's experiences and those of other groups become the focus of investigation.

Dialogue and principled coalition create possibilities for new versions of truth. Alice Walker's answer to the question of what she felt were the major differences between the literature of African-Americans and whites offers a provocative glimpse of the types of truths that might emerge through an epistemology based on dialogue and coalition. Walker did not spend much time considering this question, since it was not the difference between them that interested her, but, rather, the way Black writers and white writers seemed to be writing one immense story, with different parts of the story coming from a multitude of different perspectives. In a conversation with her mother, Walker refines this epistemological vision: "I believe that the truth about any subject only comes when all sides of the story are put together, and all their different meanings make one new one. Each writer writes the missing parts to the other writer's story. And the whole story is what I'm after" (1983, p. 49). Her mother's response to Walker's vision of the possibilities of dialogues and coalitions hints at the difficulty of sustaining such dialogues under oppressive conditions: " 'Well, I doubt if you can ever get the *true* missing parts of anything away from the white folks,' my mother says softly, so as not to offend the waitress who is mopping up a nearby table; 'they've sat on the truth so long by now they've mashed the life out of it' " (1983, p. 49).

What Constitutes Black Feminism?
The Recurring Humanist Vision

A wide range of African-American women intellectuals have advanced the view that Black women's struggles are part of a wider struggle for human dignity and empowerment. In an 1893 speech to women, Anna Julia Cooper cogently expressed this alternative worldview:

> We take our stand on the solidarity of humanity, the oneness of life, and the unnaturalness and injustice of all special favoritisms, whether of sex, race, country, or condition. . . . The colored woman feels that woman's cause is one and universal; and that . . . not till race, color, sex, and condition are seen as accidents, and not the substance of life; not till the universal title of humanity to life, liberty, and the pursuit of happiness is conceded to be inalienable to all; not till then is woman's lesson taught and woman's cause won – not the white woman's nor the black woman's, not the red woman's but the cause of every man and of every woman who has writhed silently under a mighty wrong. (Loewenberg and Bogin, 1976, pp. 330–1)

Like Cooper, many African-American women intellectuals embrace this perspective regardless of particular political solutions we propose, our fields of study, or our historical periods. Whether we advocate working through separate Black women's organizations, becoming part of women's organizations, working within existing political structures, or supporting Black community institutions, African-American women intellectuals repeatedly identify political actions such as these as a *means* for human empowerment rather than ends in and of themselves. Thus

the primary guiding principle of Black feminism is a recurring humanist vision (Steady, 1981, 1987).[5]

Alice Walker's preference for the term womanist, a term she describes
as "womanist is to feminist as purple is to lavender," addresses this
notion of the solidarity of humanity. To Walker, one is "womanist" when
one is "committed to the survival and wholeness of entire people,
male and female." A womanist is "not a separatist, except periodically
for health" and is "traditionally universalist, as is 'Mama, why are we
brown, pink, and yellow, and our cousins are white, beige, and black?'
Ans.: 'Well, you know the colored race is just like a flower garden, with
every color flower represented'" (1983, p. xi). By redefining all people
as "people of color," Walker universalizes what are typically seen as individual struggles while simultaneously allowing space for autonomous
movements of self-determination.

In assessing the sexism of the Black nationalist movement of the
1960s, Black feminist lawyer Pauli Murray identifies the dangers inherent in separatism as opposed to autonomy, and also echoes Cooper's
concern with the solidarity of humanity:

> The lesson of history that all human rights are indivisible and that the
> failure to adhere to this principle jeopardizes the rights of all is particu-
> larly applicable here. A built-in hazard of an aggressive ethnocentric
> movement which disregards the interests of other disadvantaged groups
> is that it will become parochial and ultimately self-defeating in the face of
> hostile reactions, dwindling allies, and mounting frustrations. . . . Only
> a broad movement for human rights can prevent the Black Revolution
> from becoming isolated and can insure ultimate success. (Murray, 1970,
> p. 102)

Without a commitment to human solidarity, suggests Murray, any
political movement – whether nationalist, feminist, or anti-elitist – may
be doomed to ultimate failure.

bell hooks's analysis of feminism adds another critical dimension
that must be considered: namely, the necessity of self-conscious struggle against a more generalized ideology of domination:

> To me feminism is not simply a struggle to end male chauvinism or a
> movement to ensure that women will have equal rights with men; it is a
> commitment to eradicating the ideology of domination that permeates

Western culture on various levels – sex, race, and class, to name a few – and a commitment to reorganizing U.S. society so that the self-development of people can take precedence over imperialism, economic expansion, and material desires. (hooks, 1981, p. 194)

Former assemblywoman Shirley Chisholm also points to the need for self-conscious struggle against the stereotypes buttressing ideologies of domination. In "working toward our own freedom, we can help others work free from the traps of their stereotypes," she notes. "In the end, antiblack, antifemale, and all forms of discrimination are equivalent to the same thing – antihumanism. . . . We must reject not only the stereotypes that others have of us but also those we have of ourselves and others" (1970. p. 181).

This humanist vision is also reflected in the growing prominence of international issues and global concerns in the works of contemporary African-American women intellectuals (Lindsay, 1980; Steady, 1981, 1987). Economists Margaret Simms and Julianne Malveaux's 1986 edited volume, *Slipping through the Cracks: The Status of Black Women*, contains articles on Black women in Tanzania, Jamaica, and South Africa. Angela Davis devotes an entire section of her 1989 book, *Women, Culture, and Politics*, to international affairs and includes essays on Winnie Mandela and on women in Egypt. June Jordan's 1985 volume, *On Call*, includes essays on South Africa, Nicaragua, and the Bahamas. Alice Walker writes compellingly of the types of links these and other Black women intellectuals see between African-American women's issues and those of other groups: "To me, Central America is one large plantation; and I see the pepole's struggle to be free as a slave revolt" (1988, p. 177).

The words and actions of Black women intellectuals from different historical times and addressing markedly different audiences resonate with a strikingly similar theme of the oneness of all human life. Perhaps the most succinct version of the humanist vision in Black feminist thought is offered by Fannie Lou Hamer, the daughter of sharecroppers, and a Mississippi civil rights activist. while sitting on her porch, Ms Hamer observed, "Ain' no such thing as I can hate anybody and hope to see God's face" (Jordan, 1981, p. xi).

Taken together, the ideas of Anna Julia Cooper, Pauli Murray, bell hooks, Alice Walker, Fannie Lou Hamer, and other Black women intellectuals too numerous to mention suggest a powerful answer to the question "What is Black feminism?" Inherent in their words and deeds is a definition of Black feminism as a process of self-conscious struggle that empowers women and men to actualize a humanist vision of community.

Notes

1   For discussions of the concept of standpoint, see Hartsock (1983a, 1983b), Jaggar (1983), and Smith (1987). Even though I use standpoint epistemologies as an organizing concept in this volume, they remain controversial. For a helpful critique of standpoint epistemologies, see Harding (1986). Haraway's (1988) reformulation of standpoint epistemologies approximates my use here.

2   Scott (1985) defines consciousness as the symbols, norms, and ideological forms people create to give meaning to their acts. For de Lauretis (1986), consciousness is a process, a "particular configuration of subjectivity . . . produced at the intersection of meaning with experience. . . . Consciousness is grounded in personal history, and self and identity are understood within particular cultural contexts. Consciousness . . . is never fixed, never attained once and for all, because discursive boundaries change with historical conditions" (p. 8).

3   The presence of a Black women's culture of resistance (Terborg-Penn, 1986; Dodson and Gilkes, 1987) that is both Afrocentric and feminist challenges two prevailing interpretations of the consciousness of oppressed groups. One approach claims that subordinate groups identify with the powerful and have no valid independent interpretation of their own oppression. The second assumes the oppressed are less human than their rulers, and are therefore less capable of interpreting their own experiences (Rollins, 1985; Scott, 1985). Both approaches see any independent consciousness expressed by oppressed groups as being either not of their own making or inferior to that of the dominant group. More important, both explanations suggest that the alleged lack of political activism on the part of oppressed groups stems from their flawed consciousness of their own subordination.

4   Even though I will continue to use the term *Afrocentric feminist thought* interchangeably with the phrase *Black feminist thought*, I think they are conceptually distinct.

5   My use of the term *humanist* grows from an Afrocentric historical context distinct from that criticized by Western feminists. I use the term to tap an Afrocentric humanism as cited by West (1977–8), Asante (1987), and

Turner (1984) and as part of the Black theological tradition (Mitchell and Lewter, 1986; Cannon, 1988). See Harris (1981) for a discussion of the humanist tradition in the works of three Black women writers. See Richards (1990) for a discussion of African-American spirituality, a key dimension of Afrocentric humanism. Novelist Margaret Walker offers one of the clearest discussions of Black humanism. Walker claims: "I think it is more important now to emphasize humanism in a technological age than ever before, because it is only in terms of humanism that society can redeem itself. I believe that mankind is only one race – the human race. There are many strands in the family of man – many races. The world has yet to learn to appreciate the deep reservoirs of humanism in all races, and particularly in the Black race" (Rowell, 1975, p. 12).

References

Asante, Molefi Kete (1987). *The Afrocentric Idea*. Philadelphia: Temple University Press.

Bash, Harry H. (1979). *Sociology, Race and Ethnicity*. New York: Gordon and Breach.

Beale, Frances (1970). "Double Jeopardy: To Be Black and Female." In Toni Cade (Bambara) (ed.), *The Black Woman: An Anthology*. New York: Signet, pp. 90–100.

Brown-Collins, Alice and Sussewell, Deborah Ridley (1986). "The Afro-American Women's Emerging Selves." *Journal of Black Psychology*, 13 (1), pp. 1–11.

Cannon, Katie G. (1985). "The Emergence of a Black Feminist Consciousness." In Letty M. Russell (ed.), *Feminist Interpretations of the Bible*. Philadelphia: Westminster Press, pp. 30–40.

——(1988). *Black Womanist Ethics*. Atlanta: Scholars Press.

Carby, Hazel (1987). *Reconstructing Womanhood: The Emergence of the Afro-American Woman Novelist*. New York: Oxford University Press.

Chisholm, Shirley (1970). *Unbought and Unbossed*. New York: Avon.

Clarke, Cheryl (1983). "The Failure to Transform: Homophobia in the Black Community." In Barbara Smith (ed.), *Home Girls: A Black Feminist Anthology*. New York: Kitchen Table Press, pp. 197–208.

——, Gomez, Jewell L., Hammonds, Evelyn, Johnson, Bonnie, and Powell, Linda (1983). "Conversations and Questions: Black Women on Black Women Writers." *Conditions: Nine*, 3 (3), pp. 88–137.

The Combahee River Collective (1982). "A Black Feminist Statement." In Gloria T. Hull, Patricia Bell Scott, and Barbara Smith (eds.), *But some of Us Are Brave*. Old Westbury, NY: Feminist Press, pp. 13–22.

Cooper, Anna Julia (1892). *A Voice from the South; By a Black Woman of the South*. Xenia, OH: Aldine Printing House.

Davis, George, and Watson, Glegg (1985). *Black Life in Corporate America*. New York: Anchor.

de Lauretis, Teresa (1986). "Feminist Studies/Critical Studies: Issues, Terms, and Contexts." In Teresa de Lauretis (ed.), *Feminist Studies/Critical Studies*. Bloomington: Indiana University Press, pp. 1–19.

Diop, Cheikh (1974). *The African Origin of Civilization: Myth or Reality*. New York: L. Hill.

Dodson, Jualyne E. and Gilkes, Cheryl Townsend (1987). "Something Within: Social Change and Collective Endurance in the Sacred World of Black Christian Women." In Rosemary Reuther and R. Keller (eds.), *Women and Religion in America, Volume 3: 1900–1968*. New York: Harper and Row, pp. 80–130.

Duster, Alfreda M. (ed.) (1970). *Crusade for Justice: The Autobiography of Ida B. Wells*. Chicago: University of Chicago Press.

Eistenstein, Hester (1983). *Contemporary Feminist Thought*. Boston: G. K. Hall.

Giddings, Paula (1984). *When and Where I Enter . . . The Impact of Black Women on Race and Sex in America*. New York: William Morrow.

——(1988). *In Search of Sisterhood: Delta Sigma Theta and the Challenge of the Black Sorority Movement*. New York: William Morrow.

Gilkes, Cheryl Townsend (1985). " 'Together and in Harness': Women's Traditions in the Sanctified Church." *Signs*, 10 (4), pp. 678–99.

Gould, Stephen Jay (1981). *The Mismeasure of Man*. New York: W. W. Norton.

Guy-Sheftall, Beverly (1986). "Remembering Sojourner Truth: On Black Feminism." *Catalyst* (Fall), pp. 54–7.

Gwaltney, John Langston (1980). *Drylongso, A Self-portrait of Black America*. New York: Vintage.

Haraway, Donna (1988). "Situated Knowledges: The Science Question in Feminism and the Privilege of Partial Perspective." *Feminist Studies*, 14 (3), pp. 575–99.

Harding, Sandra (1986). *The Science Question in Feminism*. Ithaca, NY: Cornell University Press.

Harris, Trudier (1981). "Three Black Women Writers and Humanism: A Folk Perspective." In R. Baxter Miller (ed.), *Black American Literature and Humanism*. Lexington: University of Kentucky Press, pp. 50–74.

Hartsock, Nancy M. (1983a). "The Feminist Standpoint: Developing the Ground for a Specifically Feminist Historical Materialism." In Sandra Harding and Merrill B. Hintikka (eds.), *Discovering Reality*. Boston: D. Reidel, pp. 283–310.

——(1983b). *Money, Sex and Power*. Boston: Northeastern University Press.

hooks, bell (1981). *Ain't I a Woman: Black Women and Feminism*. Boston: South End Press.

—— (1984). *From Margin to Center*. Boston: South End Press.

—— (1989). *Talking Back: Thinking Feminist, Thinking Black*. Boston: South End Press.

Hurston, Zora Neale [1937] (1969). *Their Eyes Were Watching God*. Greenwich, CT: Fawcett.

Jaggar, Alison M. (1983). *Feminist Politics and Human Nature*. Totawa, NJ: Rowman and Allanheld.

Jordan, June (1981). *Civil Wars*. Boston: Beacon.

King, Deborah K. (1988). "Multiple Jeopardy, Multiple Consciousness: The Context of a Black Feminist Ideology." *Signs*, 14 (1), pp. 42–72.

Ladner, Joyce (1972). *Tomorrow's Tomorrow*. Garden City, NY: Doubleday.

Lindsay, Beverly (ed.) (1980). *Comparative Perspectives of Third World Women: The Impact of Race, Sex, and Class*. New York: Praeger.

Loewenberg, Bert J. and Bogin, Ruth (eds.) (1976). *Black Women in Nineteenth-century American Life*. University Park: Pennsylvania State University Press.

Lorde, Audre (1982). *Zami, A New Spelling of My Name*. Trumansberg, NY: The Crossing Press.

—— (1984). *Sister Outsider*. Trumansberg, NY: The Crossing Press.

Lyman, Stanford M. (1972). *The Black American in Sociological Thought: A Failure of Perspective*. New York: Capricorn.

McDowell, Deborah E. (1985). "New Directions for Black Feminist Criticism." In Elaine Showalter (ed.), *The New Feminist Criticism*. New York: Pantheon, pp. 186–99.

Mitchell, Henry H. and Lewter, Nicholas Cooper (1986). *Soul Theology: The Heart of American Black Culture*. San Francisco: Harper and Row.

Murray, Pauli (1970). "The Liberation of Black Women." In Mary Lou Thompson (ed.), *Voices of the New Feminism*. Boston: Beacon, pp. 87–102.

Myers, Linda James (1988). *Understanding an Afrocentric World View: Introduction to an Optimal Psychology*. Dubuque, IA: Kendall/Hunt.

Narayan, Uma (1989). "The Project of Feminist Epistemology: Perspectives from a Nonwestern Feminist." In Alison M. Jaggar and Susan R. Bordo (eds.), *Gender/Body/Knowledge: Feminist Reconstructions of Being and Knowing*. New Brunswick, NJ: Rutgers University Press, pp. 256–69.

Okanlawon, Alexander (1972). "Africanism – A Synthesis of the African World-view." *Black World*, 21 (9), pp. 40–4, 92–7.

Omi, Michael and Winant, Howard (1986). *Racial Formation in the United States: From the 1960s to the 1980s*. New York: Routledge and Kegan Paul.

Patterson, Orlando (1982). *Slavery and Social Death*. Cambridge, MA: Harvard University Press.

Radford-Hill, Sheila (1986). "Considering Feminism as a Model for Social Change." In Teresa de Lauretis (ed.), *Feminist Studies/Critical Studies*. Bloomington: Indiana University Press, pp. 157–72.

Richards, Dona (1980). "European Mythology: The Ideology of 'Progress.'" In Molefi Kete Asante and Abdulai Sa. Vandi (eds.), *Contemporary Black Thought*. Beverly Hills, CA: Sage, pp. 59–79.

—— (1990). "The Implications of African-American Spirituality." In Molefi Kete Asante and Kariamu Welsh Asante (eds.), *African Culture: The Rhythms of Unity*. Trenton, NJ: Africa World Press, pp. 207–31.

Richardson, Marilyn (ed.) (1987). *Maria W. Stewart, America's First Black Woman Political Writer*. Bloomington: Indiana University Press.

Rollins, Judith (1985). *Between Women, Domestics and Their Employers*. Philadelphia: Temple University Press.

Rowell, Charles H. (1975). "An Interview with Margaret Walker." *Black World*, 25 (2), pp. 4–17.

Scott, James C. (1985). *Weapons of the Weak: Everyday Forms of Peasant Resistance*. New Haven, CT: Yale University Press.

Scott, Patricia Bell (1982b). "Selected Bibliography on Black Feminism." In Gloria T. Hull, Patricia Bell Scott, and Barbara Smith (eds.), *But Some of Us Are Brave*. Old Westbury, NY: Feminist Press, pp. 23–36.

Shockley, Ann Allen (1974). *Loving Her*. Tallahassee, FL: Naiad Press.

Smith, Barbara (1983). "Introduction." In Barbara Smith (ed.), *Home Girls: A Black Feminist Anthology*. New York: Kitchen Table Press, pp. xix–lvi.

Smith, Beverly (1983). "The Wedding." In Barbara Smith (ed.), *Home Girls: A Black Feminist Anthology*. New York: Kitchen Table Press, pp. 171–6.

Smith, Dorothy (1987). *The Everyday World as Problematic*. Boston: Northeastern University Press.

Smitherman, Geneva (1977). *Talkin and Testifyin: The Language of Black America*. Boston: Houghton Mifflin.

Sobel, Mechal (1979). *Trabelin' On: The Slave Journey to an Afro-Baptist Faith*. Princeton: Princeton University Press.

Steady, Filomina Chioma (1981). "The Black Woman Cross-culturally: An Overview." In Filomina Chioma Steady (ed.), *The Black Woman Cross-culturally*. Cambridge, MA: Schenkman, pp. 7–42.

—— (1987). "African Feminism: A Worldwide Perspective." In Rosalyn Terborg-Penn, Sharon Harley, and Andrea Benton Rushing (eds.), *Women in Africa and the African Diaspora*. Washington, DC: Howard University Press, pp. 3–24.

Tate, Claudia (ed.) (1983). *Black Women Writers at Work*. New York: Continuum Publishing.

Terborg-Penn, Rosalyn (1986). "Black Women in Resistance: A Cross-cultural Perspective." In Gary Y. Okhiro (ed.), *In Resistance: Studies in African, Caribbean and Afro-American History*. Amherst: University of Massachusetts Press, pp. 188–209.

Thompson, Robert Farris (1983). *Flash of the Spirit: African and Afro-American Art and Philosophy*. New York: Vintage.

Turner, James E. (1984). "Foreword: Africana Studies and Epistemology: A Discourse in the Sociology of Knowledge." In James E. Turner (ed.), *The Next Decade: Theoretical and Research Issues in African Studies*. Ithaca, NY: Cornell University Africana Studies and Research Center, pp. v–xxv.

Walker, Alice (1983). *In Search of Our Mothers' Gardens*. New York: Harcourt Brace Jovanovich.

——(1988). *Living by the Word*. New York: Harcourt Brace Jovanovich.

Webber, Thomas L. (1978). *Deep Like the Rivers*. New York: W. W. Norton.

West, Cornel (1977–8). "Philosophy of the Afro-American Experience." *Philosophical Forum*, 9 (2–3), pp. 117–48.

White, E. Frances (1984). "Listening to the Voices of Black Feminism." *Radical America*, 18 (2–3), pp. 7–25.

10

Everyday Racism: A New Approach to the Study of Racism

Philomena Essed

Confronted with a problem as complex as racism, we cannot afford to let ourselves be constrained by the boundaries of specific disciplines. This makes the study of racism more complicated but also more challenging. [. . .]

Many studies have identified the mechanisms of racism at a societal level, but few have revealed its pervasive impact on the daily experiences of Blacks. The impetus for this study emerged from the need to make visible the lived experience of racism and, more specifically, to analyze Black perceptions about racism in everyday life. This approach presupposes that Black people's knowledge about racism is socially relevant. Du Bois (1969) was among the first to point out that, over the generations, Blacks in the United States developed a "double consciousness." This idea is premised on the view that Blacks are familiar with dominant group interpretations of reality and, therefore, have knowledge of racist ideas and interpretations of reality. With their sense of history, through communication about racism within the Black community, and by testing their own experiences in daily life, Black people can develop profound and often sophisticated knowledge about the reproduction of racism. These qualities make Black definitions of racism interesting as an object for academic inquiry.

This study has also been prompted by the slow progress of the social sciences in the development of interdisciplinary studies of racism. By and large traditional boundaries between different disciplines were reproduced in studies of racism. Thus there is little connection between social psychological and sociological approaches, between theories of the cognitive and structural components of racism. Within sociology controversies between "macro" and "micro" paradigms have frustrated theories that integrate structural and interactional dimensions of racism.

Racism is defined as inherent in culture and social order. It is argued in this study that racism is more than structure and ideology. As a process it is routinely created and reinforced through everyday practices. With this view in mind I earlier introduced the concept of "everyday racism" (Essed, 1984), which connects structural forces of racism with routine situations in everyday life. It links ideological dimensions of racism with daily attitudes and interprets the reproduction of racism in terms of the experience of it in everyday life. Through a detailed theoretical analysis, this study articulates new sets of meanings in the concept of everyday racism.

Everyday Racism, Experiences, and Accounts

Before we proceed to a more explicit analysis of everyday racism, it is useful to begin with a more informal characterization of this notion. The "everyday" has been addressed as a problematic, in particular in philosophy, phenomenology, ethnomethodology, and also recently in social psychology. The notion of "everyday" is often used to refer to a familiar world, a world of practical interest, a world of practices we are socialized with in order to manage in the system. In our everyday lives sociological distinctions between "institutional" and "interactional," between ideology and discourse, and between "private" and "public" spheres of life merge and form a complex of social relations and situations.

Everyday racism is racism, but not all racism is everyday racism. The concept of everyday racism counters the view, prevalent in particular in the Netherlands, that racism is an individual problem, a question of "to be or not to be a racist." The crucial criterion distinguishing racism from everyday racism is that the latter involves only systematic, recurrent, familiar practices. The fact that it concerns repetitive practices indicates that everyday racism consists of practices that can be generalized.

Because everyday racism is infused into familiar practices, it involves socialized attitudes and behavior. Finally, its systematic nature indicates that everyday racism includes cumulative instantiation. These arguments make clear that the notion of everyday racism is defined in terms of practices prevalent in a given system. Note that practices are not just "acts" but also include complex relations of acts and (attributed) attitudes.

Experience is a central concept in this study. Experiences are a suitable source of information for the study of everyday racism because they include personal experiences as well as vicarious experiences of racism. In addition the notion of experience includes general knowledge of racism, which is an important source of information to qualify whether specific events can be generalized. These experiences of racism are made available for academic inquiry through accounts – that is, verbal reconstructions of experiences. I argue in this study that reconstructions of experiences in such accounts provide the best basis for the analysis of the simultaneous impact of racism in different sites and in different social relations. Accounts of racism locate the narrators as well as their experiences in the social context of their everyday lives, give specificity and detail to events, and invite the narrator to carefully qualify subtle experiences of racism. [. . .]

Conceptualizing Racism as a Process

The fallacies of "institutional" and "individual" racism

My approach to racism draws on structural theories of racism. I have, however, tried to overcome some of the shortcomings of earlier studies. One major problem was the distinction between institutional and individual racism. It places the individual outside the institutional, thereby severing rules, regulations, and procedures from the people who make and enact them, as if it concerned qualitatively different racism rather than different positions and relations through which racism operates.

The notion of "institutional racism" is a central concept in many structural approaches. Whereas Carmichael and Hamilton (1967), Knowles and Prewitt (1969), and others rightly went beyond Myrdal's definition of racism as a moral dilemma (Myrdal, 1944/1972), and beyond the Kerner Report's list of conditions of Black riots (Kerner Commission, 1968/1988), the distinction between so-called individual racism and institutional racism is not unproblematic. The notion of the "institutional" is notoriously difficult in sociology because it has been given various meanings. Some researchers use the terms *institution* and *institutional* to identify structuring relations of the ruling apparatus organized around different functions. This definition of *institutional* has been used in various European studies to narrow the problem of racism down to "institutional discrimination." Usually these approaches have a pragmatic orientation that underrates the power of ideology in the structuring of racism in society (e.g., Daniel, 1968/1971; Smith, 1977).

The term *individual racism* is a contradiction in itself because racism is by definition the expression or activation of group power. Some authors tried to find alternative solutions to set apart "institutional racism" against "other racism." Brandt (1986, p. 101) distinguishes between interactional racism and institutional racism, but he does not make clear why this is an improvement over the usual distinction between "individual" and "institutional" racism. However, he introduces another interesting concept, namely, "systemic racism." The systemic realization of institutional racism he refers to in terms of "day-to-day interactions" within institutions (Brandt, 1986, p. 102). In an excellent article Rowe (1977, p. 1) speaks in this context of "microinequities," which she defines as "destructive, but practicably-speaking non-actionable, aspects of the environment." Systemic racism "marks the meeting point between structural and interactional forms of racism and exists within the specificity of the 'ethos' or sociocultural environment of the organization" (p. 102). Brandt (1986, p. 102) contends that the systemic is also structural. However, he does not further work out his idea of systemic racism, which, therefore, remains rather vague. He also insists on defining systemic racism in terms of "institutional racism." Compared with many other studies, this notion probably comes closest to the meaning of everyday racism, which is the interweaving of racism in the fabric of the social system. Still the notion of everyday racism transcends the traditional distinctions between institutional and individual racism.

Everyday racism has two obvious constituent elements. One part pertains to the notion of racism and the other to the notion of "everyday." To understand experiences of everyday racism, the following concepts must be implemented: (a) the notion of racism, (b) the notion of every-day, (c) the notion of everyday racism, (d) the idea of experience, and (e) the notion of accounts of racism. The notions of racism, everyday, and everyday racism are discussed first. [. . .]

Racism: A Working Definition

My critique of structural studies of racism has already suggested that a working definition of racism must acknowledge the macro (structural-cultural) properties of racism as well as the micro inequities perpetuat-ing the system. It must take into account the constraining impact of entrenched ideas and practices on human agency, but it must also acknowledge that the system is continually construed in everyday life and that, under certain conditions, individuals resist pressures to conform to the needs of the system. Traditional sociological approaches have defined macro structures as more or less independent of the prac-tices in daily life. Moreover macrosociologists usually consider institu-tions and structures as somehow above the mundane level of practice and experience. My intention to go beyond macro social facts in address-ing practice and the social reality of racism has been inspired, initially, by phenomenology, symbolic interactionism, ethnomethodology, and cognitive sociology. These interpretative and micro orientations empha-size from various points of view the active nature of human conduct and try to understand its meaning, reasons, and experience (Berger and Luckmann, 1966; Blumer, 1969; Brittan, 1973; Cicourel, 1973; Douglas, 1970/1974; Garfinkel, 1967; Goffman, 1959, 1961, 1967, 1969, 1974; Helle and Eisenstadt, 1985; Leiter, 1980; Luckmann, 1978; Mehan and Wood, 1975; Rogers, 1983; Schutz, 1970). More sig-nificant to my approach have become, however, recent developments in social theory that try to overcome the rigorous distinction between micro and macro approaches (Alexander et al., 1987; Collins, 1981a, 1983; Fielding, 1988; Giddens, 1984; Knorr-Cetina and Cicourel, 1981). This is not, of course, to imply any necessary agreement among these authors. A problem with most of the work mentioned is, however, that it is useful in theorization but lacks adequate implementation, espe-cially when applied to the area of racism.

Despite these limitations two major attempts to integrate macro and micro dimensions of the system are particularly important for my purposes. The aggregation hypothesis advanced by Collins (1981b) contends that macrosociological reality is composed of aggregates of micro situations. The representation hypothesis (Cicourel, 1981), which comes close to the aggregation hypothesis, argues that macro social facts, or structures, are produced in interactions. These theoretical frameworks emphasize the role of routine and repetitive practices in the making of social structures. However, I depart to a certain degree from these approaches by giving greater weight to the mutual interdependence of macro and micro dimensions of racism. From a macro point of view, racism is a system of structural inequalities and a historical process, both created and re-created through routine practices. *System* means reproduced social relations between individuals and groups organized as regular social practices (Giddens, 1981). From a micro point of view, specific practices, whether their consequences are intentional or unintentional, can be evaluated in terms of racism only when they are consistent with (our knowledge of) existing macro structures of racial inequality in the system. In other words, structures of racism do not exist external to agents – they are made by agents – but specific practices are by definition racist only when they activate existing structural racial inequality in the system.

Racism as power

Racism then is defined in terms of cognitions, actions, and procedures that contribute to the development and perpetuation of a system in which Whites dominate Blacks. Note that racial domination, as I pointed out earlier, interacts with dynamic forces of gender and class domination. [. . .]

Domination constitutes a special case of power. To conceptualize how racism, as a complex system of power, shapes the ways in which social relations and practices are actually experienced by Blacks, I draw on major insights of some people who have worked on the notion of power. However, I do not necessarily adopt the whole conceptual framework of these works. The concept of power I use is based on two different meanings derived from Arendt (1970) and Lukes (1974). The combination of their perceptions of power is useful to integrate macro and micro dimensions of racism. Arendt (1970) argues that power is never the property of an individual. It belongs to a group as long as the group stays together. Therefore, power pertains to the human ability not only to act but to act in concert. This view of power is relevant to the study of racism for the following reasons: It enables us to conceptualize relations between White and Black individuals in terms of power relations, for they are representatives of groups with relatively more and relatively less power. This implies that the consciously or unconsciously felt security of belonging to the group in power, plus the expectation that other group members will give (passive) consent, empowers individual members of the dominant group in their acts or beliefs against the dominated group.

The extent to which the expectation of group consensus is a relevant source of empowerment is understood better when we take the following concrete example. The current norm that racism is "wrong" has a certain disempowering impact on individual members of the dominant group. Today the almost universal rejection of racism is often experienced by Whites as a restriction. They feel that they can no longer express what they feel about Blacks because others will accuse them of racism. This is experienced as an unfair situation. [. . .] As Solomos (1989, p. 137) puts it, "Today, the most strident voices in the mass media and in academic discourse are raised not against racism but against . . . antiracism." The experiences of Blacks testify to the implied indifference among Whites to racism.

Group power exists as long as the group stays together against the "others." This introduces the second characteristic of power as a quality of the group. Arendt's view of power provides a basis for understanding the crucial role of racist ideologies, not only as rationalization of existing inequalities but also as determinants of future uniformity of action. This means that ideology is the binding element between practices involving different actors and situations. To keep the group intact it is necessary to cultivate ideologies supporting the idea of innate group differences based on "race" or ethnicity. Group power can only empower individuals when they have a sense of group membership. Therefore, it is necessary to keep alive a permanent sense of "us" (dominant group) as opposed to "them" (dominated groups). This point is elaborated at length in Memmi (1983) and Barker (1981). Here Lukes would speak of exercising influence to achieve and to maintain consensus (Lukes, 1974, p. 3). When dominant group members implicitly or explicitly rely on group consensus in support of anti-Black actions, they make use of an important power resource.

It is difficult to define where the determinism of group power ends and the exercise of power by individuals begins. From a macro point of view racism only exists as a specific variant of group power. From a micro point of view racism as group power only exists because it was created and is maintained through individuals. Because racism is a form of power, it must be assumed that it involves conflict of interests between two parties. At this point Lukes's notion of power is important (Lukes, 1974).

Lukes's notion of power is particularly useful in understanding situations where conflict between groups is not openly acknowledged as such. He sees as the central quality of power the attempt to successfully secure people's compliance by overcoming or averting their opposition. Exercising power over other people affects them, through action or inaction, in a manner contrary to their interests, whether or not those who exercise power are aware of the success or consequences of their practices and whether or not the other party is aware of the power being exercised over him or her. [. . .] Dominant group members often control without there being any overt, actual disagreement. [. . .]

The domination of Blacks may be described as "systemic domination" (Fay, 1987, p. 123), which means that it is through the pattern of organization of the system as a whole that dominance is reproduced. Thus Whites can dominate Blacks without the former necessarily being aware of the ways in which the system is so structured that it is their interests rather than those of Blacks that are met. Lukes relates the exercise of power to responsibility when (a) such an exercise involves the assumption that the exerciser(s) could have acted differently (b) where, if unaware of the consequences of their action or inaction, they could have found out about them (Lukes, 1974, pp. 55–6). This point, the attribution of responsibility not only for action but also for inaction, is very important in the analysis of contemporary racism. A main problem today is inaction among the dominant group (detachment from racial issues and from Blacks) and, more specifically, passive tolerance of racism.

Although a working definition of racism must include the structuring role of ideology in coordinating uniformity of action, individual or group differences may also be important. It may be assumed that individuals are involved differently in the (re)production of everyday racism through their gender- and class-determined functions and positions in society. These differences are largely determined by the location of power in structural relations and in specific situations. The degree of power is determined by, among other things, the number of people affected by its exercise (Goldman, 1972, pp. 191–2). The racist practices of those who have power of position (authority) and power of property, as compared with those who do not have such power, are similar in nature but different in impact. Conversely research suggests that alternative arrangements, or antiracist strategies, are more successful when sanctioned by relevant authorities in the situation (Jones, 1988, p. 127). This does not mean that people with power that "rightfully belongs to the incumbent of any social role or organizational office possessing authority" (Lenski, 1966, p. 250) practice racism independently of those who do not have such power. Racism practiced by authorities is substantially supported by the fact that other members of the dominant racial group are more likely to tolerate than to challenge negative beliefs and practices against dominated groups. Alternatively authorities who choose to take responsibility for racism can use the power of their position to influence the views of others and to resist protest from subordinates in the implementation of alternative arrangements. Furthermore others can choose to challenge authorities who use power of position to practice racism. Hence a working definition of racism must be able to account for the dynamics of tolerance of racism and challenge to racism. In view of these arguments it can be concluded that, the more access to power in the system, the more consequences racist practices of agents have. The more access agents have to knowledge about the nature of domination, the more responsible they are for the outcome of their practices.

Apart from factors structuring the impact of racism and the question of responsibility, it is also necessary to make a clear distinction between the structural beneficiaries of racism and the actual agents of racism in everyday situations. That is, the dominant group structurally benefits from racism. This holds true for all its members, whether or not they willingly accept this. Of course there may be different interests at stake along class and gender lines. Nevertheless it must not be assumed that all Whites are agents of racism and all Blacks only the victims. Such a rigid definition of the problem ignores the psychology of being oppressed (Fanon, 1967; Meulenbelt, 1985) as well as the role of Blacks who work for what Mullard (1986b) calls the institution of ethnic exchange and those who may be involved in the formulation and enactment of racist policies. Conversely it is also relevant to take into account the many dominant group members who incidentally or frequently oppose racism, whether in small or in significant ways (Mullard, 1984; Terry, 1975). Dominant group members who take a clear stand against racism, or who otherwise identify with the Black cause, may under certain circumstances become substitute targets of racism. This problem obviously deserves more attention, but that is beyond the purpose of this study.

Given these arguments, and keeping in mind that "race" is an ideological construction with structural expressions (racialized or "ethnicized" structures of power), racism must be understood as ideology, structure, and process in which inequalities inherent in the wider social structure are related, in a deterministic way, to biological and cultural factors attributed to those who are seen as a different "race" or "ethnic" group. "Race" is called an *ideological construction*, and not just a social construction, because the idea of "race" has never existed outside of a framework of group interest. As a nineteenth-century pseudoscientific theory, as well as in contemporary "popular" thinking, the notion of "race" is inherently part of a "model" of asymmetrically organized "races" in which Whites rank higher than "non-Whites." Furthermore racism is a *structure* because racial and ethnic dominance exists in and is reproduced by the system through the formulation and application of rules, laws, and regulations and through access to and the allocation of resources. Finally racism is a *process* because structures and ideologies do not exist outside the everyday practices through which they are created and confirmed. These practices both adapt to and themselves contribute to changing social, economic, and political conditions in society. [. . .]

The Notion of Everyday Racism

Theories about the meaning of "the everyday" have been developed in the fields of philosophy, phenomenology, social psychology, symbolic interactionism, and ethnomethodology, where it has often been referred to intuitively as a "known in common world" (Zimmerman and Pollner, 1970, p. 85), a "familiar world, a world taken for granted" (Luckmann, 1970/1978, p. 275). The tendency to use metaphors and other associations instead of more precise descriptions or definitions when talking about the everyday is amazing considering, for instance, that everyday explanations have been quite a popular topic of recent publications in the area of social cognition theory (e.g., Antaki, 1981, 1988a; Semin and Gergen, 1990). In the social psychology of everyday explanations, the idea of "everyday" is often associated with vague notions such as the "ordinary" (Antaki, 1988b, p. 1) or "common sense" (Furnham, 1990). Others write about everyday cognitions without giving any further explanation or just broadly characterize the concept as the opposite of the "scientific" (Carugati, 1990; Groeben, 1990; Semin, 1990) or as the opposite of the philosophical world, in which philosophy belongs to the "highest spheres of culture," and everyday life stands for the "most trivial and commonplace sphere" (Lefebvre, 1971, p. 116). Intuitive associations like these represent specific characteristics of "the everyday," but they cannot be used as a basis for a theory of everyday racism.

I do not intend to conceptualize the notion of "the everyday" in terms of a philosophy of everyday life (Heller, 1984) – a study in itself – but in terms of the categories and social relations operative in everyday life (Smith, 1987) and in terms of the characteristics of everyday life (Heller, 1984). Such a qualification of the everyday is sufficient for the purposes of this study, namely, to distinguish between "everyday racism" and "experiences of everyday racism." With these arguments in mind the following tentative proposals for the analysis of "everyday life" are relevant in understanding racism as a process operative in everyday life.

Meaning and characteristics of everyday life

Everyday life always takes place in and relates to the immediate environment of a person. It is a world in which we are located physically and socially. The content and structure of everyday life are not necessarily the same for all individuals in society. It can also be different in different periods of a person's life. Obviously everyday life for a university professor who is also the mother of three children has similarities, but also differences, when compared with the life of a university professor without children or that of a mother who has a job as a bank teller. Everyday life is the direct reproduction of the person embedded in social relations. This assumption is included in Heller's (1984, p. 3) definition of "everyday life" as "the aggregate of those individual reproduction factors which . . . make social reproduction possible." Everyday life is not only reproductive of persons but also of the positions of persons in social relations and of social relations themselves.

The everyday world is a world in which one must learn to maneuver and a world that one must learn to handle. Without a minimum knowledge of how to cope in everyday life, one cannot handle living in society. This at least includes knowledge of language, norms, customs and rules, and knowledge to use the means and resources that make living possible (or successful) in a given environment, determined by factors of class, gender, profession, and so on (Heller, 1984). This knowledge includes expectations and "scripts" (Schank and Abelson, 1977) of everyday situations.

The fundamental stock of knowledge needed to cope in everyday life is transmitted by each generation to its successors. Knowledge used in everyday life is not restricted to knowledge that can be derived directly from the everyday environment. Knowledge used in everyday life can also include scientific knowledge communicated by the mass media or through education. In other words, the system is internalized in everyday life through socialization processes. The everyday is based on expectations and conditions that are taken for granted. Without these expectations the everyday cannot be managed. Garfinkel's experiments showed that the undermining, by others, of taken-for-granted conditions in everyday life is upsetting and unbearable for individuals subjected to these experiments (Garfinkel, 1967). Conversely individuals who are seen as unable to cope with "the everyday" are stigmatized as "mentally ill." These arguments do not mean to suggest that the everyday is static. It remains possible for individuals to transcend the limits of the everyday. People who reject what is seen as "normal' often become agents of change. Given these considerations the notion of "the everyday" can be tentatively defined as *socialized meanings making practices immediately definable and uncontested so that, in principle, these practices can be managed according to (sub)cultural norms and expectations.* These practices and meanings belong to our familiar world and usually involve routine or repetitive practices. Therefore, they can be expected and generalized for specific relations and situations. This addition is important in distinguishing the everyday from the noneveryday – that is, the incidental, unfamiliar, that is neither generalizable nor taken for granted. [. . .]

Characteristics and structure of everyday racism

The structure of everyday racism must be seen as a complex of practices made operative in race and ethnic relations. Race relations in this sense are a process present in and activated at the everyday level as well as prestructured in a way that transcends the control of individual subjects. Everyday racism is the integration of racism into everyday situations through practices (cognitive and behavioral, see below) that activate underlying power relations. This process must be seen as a continuum through which the integration of racism into everyday practices becomes part of the expected, of the unquestionable, and of what is seen as normal by the dominant group. When racist notions and actions infiltrate everyday life and become part of the reproduction of the system, the system reproduces everyday racism. [. . .]

Analogous to everyday life, everyday racism is heterogeneous in its manifestations but at the same time structured by forces toward uniformity. Everyday racism is a complex of practices operative through heterogeneous (class and gender) relations, present in and producing race and ethnic relations. Such relations are activated and reproduced as practices. Everyday racism is locked into the underlying dynamics of relations and forces of racial and ethnic domination and governed by the powers to which they give rise. For the purpose of this study, racial and ethnic domination can be implemented as interlocking forces of oppression and repression coordinated and unified by ideological constructions. These interlocking forces represent at the same time micro and macro dimensions of racism. From a micro point of view oppression can be implemented as creating structures of racial and ethnic inequality through situated practices (oppression). Racial inequality can only be maintained when other forces operate to secure compliance and to prevent, manage, or break opposition (repression). Seen from this point of view the macro structures of domination are already contextualized in racial ideologies implicitly or explicitly familiar to the subjects who reinforce racial inequality through repression. Uniformity of oppressive and repressive practices is coordinated ideologically through socialization and the constant actualization, through the media and other channels of communication, of images, opinions, and versions of reality legitimizing the status quo.

The firm interlocking of forces of domination operates in a way that makes it hard to escape its impact on everyday life. Although individual men or women may work out strategies to break away from particular oppressive relations or situations, and frequently oppose racism, as members of an oppressed group, they remain locked into the forces of the system, unless enough counterpressure develops to unlock these forces and to transform the machinery of the system that produces racial and ethnic inequality. This explains, as will be shown later in more detail, why everyday racism cannot be reduced to incidents or to specific events. Everyday racism is the process of the system working through multiple relations and situations. Once we understand that in a racist society, race and ethnicity can operate through any social relation, when we recognize the racial or ethnic dimensions in particular relationships, it becomes possible to speak of everyday racism as the situational activation of racial or ethnic dimensions in particular relations in a way that reinforces racial or ethnic inequality and contributes to new forms of racial and ethnic inequality. This view is parallel to Omi and Winant's (1986, pp. 61–2) theory of racial formation – the process

> by which social, economic, and political forces determine the content and importance of racial categories, and by which they are in turn shaped by racial meanings. Crucial to this formulation is the treatment of race as a central axis of social relations which cannot be subsumed or reduced to some broader category of conception.

They argue, however, that racial dimensions of a particular relationship or social practice are never given automatically, whereas in my view this dimension is always present when racial meaning can be given to previously nonracial relationships. Of course the particular content of systems of racial meanings can change historically, but the presence of a system of racial meanings is a permanent feature of European culture that has been consistently activated throughout the United States in the past few centuries and in the Netherlands in more recent times. Social relations are racialized (or ethnicized) when they represent racially or ethnically identified differences in position and power. Because "race" is an organizing principle of many social relations, the fundamental social relations of society are racialized relations. However, it is only when these racial or ethnic dimensions of social relations are called upon or activated through practice that racial and ethnic relations are created, reinforced, or reproduced. In other words, even when specific relations are racialized and when these relations underlie and structure social situations, racism does not necessarily have to occur in a specific time or place.

Everyday racism does not exist in the singular but only as a complex – as interrelated instantiations of racism. Each instantiation of everyday racism has meaning only in relation to the whole complex of relations and practices. Thus expressions of racism in one particular social relation are related to all other racist practices and can be reduced to the fundamental structuring forces of everyday racism: oppression, repression, and legitimation.

Given these arguments, everyday racism can be defined as *a process in which (a) socialized racist notions are integrated into meanings that make practices immediately definable and manageable, (b) practices with racist implications become in themselves familiar and repetitive, and (c) underlying racial and ethnic relations are actualized and reinforced through these routine or familiar practices in everyday situations.*

This discussion implies that people are involved differently in the process of everyday racism according to gender, class, status, and other factors determining the content and structure of their everyday lives. It also must be emphasized that the process of everyday racism operates not only through direct interaction with Blacks but also through indirect contact. This becomes clear when we consider the role of, for instance, policymakers or journalists in the process of everyday racism. In the immediate practice of their everyday lives, policymakers formulate and enact rules and conditions that reinforce existing racial injustice, even when they do not directly interact with Blacks in making these policies. Similarly racist newspaper articles are part of the process of everyday racism, whether or not based on direct interaction with Blacks. Finally it should be stressed that not all racism is everyday racism. The concept of everyday racism distinguishes the reproduction of racism through routine and familiar practices from incidental and uncommon expressions of racism. Of course the content of everyday racism is not static. It changes with the changing relations and practices through which the system is reproduced as a racist system. This will be illustrated later in the discussion of differences in the experience of everyday racism in the United States and in the Netherlands.

Specific agents can be involved in different ways, through different situations, in the reproduction of racism in everyday life. Given the ubiquity of sites and relations through which racism operates, it would hardly be possible to monitor the process of racism in a systematic way with traditional methods involving surveys or observation. In the experiences of Black communities, everyday racism does not exist in the singular but only in the plural form. It is a coherent complex of oppression continuously present and systematically activated personally through encounters, vicariously through the experiences of other Blacks, through the media, and through the daily awareness of racial injustice in society. An experiential point of view, therefore, enables us to examine the simultaneous manifestations of racism reproduced in multiple situations. [. . .]

References

Alexander, J., Giesen, B., Münch, R., and Smelser, N. (eds.) (1987). *The Micro–Macro Link*. Berkeley: University of California Press.

Antaki, C. (ed.) (1981). *The Psychology of Ordinary Explanations of Social Behaviour*. London: Academic Press.

——(ed.) (1988a). *Analysing Everyday Explanation*. London: Sage.

——(1988b). "Explanations, Communication and Social Cognition." In C. Antaki (ed.), *Analysing Everyday Explanation*. London: Sage, pp. 1–14.

Arendt, H. (1970). "Communicative Power." In S Lukes (ed.), *Power*. Oxford: Blackwell, pp. 59–74.

Barker, M. (1981). *The New Racism*. London: Junction.

Berger, P. L. and Luckmann, T. (1966). *The Social Construction of Reality*. Harmondsworth: Penguin.

Blumer, H. (1969). *Symbolic Interaction*. Englewood Cliffs, NJ: Prentice-Hall.

Brandt, G. L. (1986). *The Realization of Anti-racist Teaching*. London: Falmer.

Brittan, A. (1973). *Meanings and Situations*. London: Routledge and Kegan Paul.

Carmichael, S. and Hamilton, C. (1967). *Black Power*. New York: Vintage.

Carugati, F. F. (1990). "Everyday Ideas, Theoretical Models and Social Representations: The Case of Intelligence and its Development." In G. R. Semin and K. J. Gergen (eds.), *Everyday Understanding*. London: Sage, pp. 130–50.

Cicourel, A. V. (1973). *Cognitive Sociology: Language and Meaning in Social Interaction*. New York: Free Press.

——(1981). "Notes on the Integration of Micro- and Macro-levels of analysis." In K. Knorr-Cetina and A. V. Cicourel (eds.), *Advances in Social Theory and Methodology*. Boston: Routledge and Kegan Paul, pp. 51–80.

Collins, R. (1981a). "On the Micro-foundations of Macro-sociology." *American Journal of Sociology*, 86, pp. 984–1014.

——(1981b). "Micro-translation as a Theory-building Strategy." In K. Knorr-Cetina and A. V. Cicourel (eds.), *Advances in Social Theory and Methodology*. Boston: Routledge and Kegan Paul, pp. 81–108.

——(1983). "Micro-methods as a Basis for Macro-sociology." *Urban Life*, 12, pp. 184–202.

Daniel, W. W. (1971). *Racial Discrimination in England*. Harmondsworth: Penguin. (Original work published 1968.)

Douglas, J. D. (ed.) (1974). *Understanding Everyday Life*. London: Routledge and Kegan Paul. (Original work published 1970.)

Du Bois, W. E. B. (1969). *The Souls of Black Folk*. New York: New American Library.

Essed, P. (1984). *Alledaags Racisme*. Amsterdam: Sara. [*Everyday Racism*: Claremont, CA: Hunter House, 1990.]

Fanon, F. (1967). *Black Skins, White Masks*. New York: Grove.

Fay, B. (1987). *Critical Social Science*. Cambridge: Polity.

Fielding, N. G. (ed.) (1988). *Actions and Structure*. London: Sage.

Furnham, A. (1990). "Commonsense Theories of Personality." In G. R. Semin and K. J. Gergen (eds.), *Everyday Understanding*. London: Sage, pp. 176–203.

Garfinkel, H. (1967). *Studies in Ethnomethodology*. Englewood Cliffs, NJ: Prentice-Hall.

Giddens, A. (1981). "Agency, Institution, and Time–Space Analysis." In K. Knorr-Cetina and A. V. Cicourel (eds.), *Advances in Social Theory and Methodology*. Boston: Routledge and Kegan Paul.

——(1984). *The Constitution of Society*. Cambridge: Polity (in association with Blackwell, Oxford).

Goffman, E. (1959). *The Presentation of Self in Everyday Life*. New York: Doubleday.

——(1961). *Encounters*. Indianapolis: Bobbs-Merrill.

——(1967). *Interaction Ritual*. Garden City, NY: Doubleday.

——(1969). *Stategical Interaction*. Philadelphia: University of Pennsylvania Press.

——(1974). *Frame Analysis*. New York: Harper and Row.

Goldman, A. (1972). "Toward a Theory of Social Power." In S. Lukes (ed.), *Power*. Oxford: Blackwell, pp. 156–202.

Groeben, N. (1990). "Subjective Theories and the Explanation of Human Action." In G. R. Semin and K. J. Gergen (eds.), *Everyday Understanding*. London: Sage, pp. 19–44.

Helle, H. J. and Eisenstadt, S. N. (eds.) (1985). *Micro Sociology*. London: Sage.

Heller, A. (1984). *Everyday Life*. London: Routledge and Kegan Paul.

Jones, J. M. (1988). "Racism in Black and White: A Bicultural Model of Reaction and Evolution." In P. Katz and D. Taylor (eds.), *Eliminating Racism*. New York: Plenum.

Kerner Commission (1988). *Report of the National Advisory Commission on Civil Disorders*. New York: Pantheon. (Original work published 1968.)

Knorr-Cetina, K. and Cicourel, A. V. (eds.) (1981). *Advances in Social Theory and Methodology*. Boston: Routledge and Kegan Paul.

Knowles, L. and Prewitt, K. (1969). *Institutional Racism in America*. Englewood Cliffs, NJ: Prentice-Hall.

Lefebvre, H. (1971). *Everyday Life in the Modern World*. New York: Harper.

Leiter, K. (1980). *A Primer on Ethnomethodology*. New York: Oxford University Press.

Lenski, G. (1966). "Power and Privilege." In S. Lukes (ed.), *Power*. Oxford: Blackwell, pp. 241–52.

Luckmann, B. (1978). "The Small Life-worlds of Modern Man." In T. Luckmann (ed.), *Phenomenology and Sociology*. Harmondsworth: Penguin, pp. 275–90. (Original work published 1970.)

Luckmann, T. (ed.) (1978). *Phenomenology and Sociology*. Harmondsworth: Penguin.

Lukes, S. (1974). *Power: A Radical View*. London: Macmillan.

Mehan, H. and Wood, H. (1975). *The Reality of Ethnomethodology*. New York: John Wiley.

Memmi, A. (1983). *Racisme hoezo?* [Racism, What Do You Mean?]. Nijmegen: Masusa.

Meulenbelt, A. (1985). *De ziekte bestrijden, niet de patient* [To Combat the Disease, Rather than the Patient]. Amsterdam: van Gennep.

Mullard, C. (1984). *Anti-racist Education: The Three O's*. London: National Association for Multi-racial Education.

——(1986b). "An Etharchy in the Making." Paper presented to the International Sociological Association, New Delhi, August 19.

Myrdal, G. (1972). *An American Dilemma*. New York: Random House. (Original work published by Pantheon, 1944.)

Omi, M. and Winant, H. (1986). *Racial Formation in the United States*. New York: Routledge and Kegan Paul.

Rogers, M. F. (1983). *Sociology, Ethnomethodology, and Experience: A Phenomenological Critique*. Cambridge: Cambridge University Press.

Rowe, M. P. (1977). "The Saturn's Rings Phenomenon: Micro-inequities and Unequal Opportunity in the American Economy" (preprint). In P. Bourne and V. Parness (eds.), *Proceedings*. Santa Cruz: University of California.

Schank, R. C. and Abelson, R. (1977). *Scripts, Plans, Goals and Understanding*. Hillsdale, NJ: Lawrence Erlbaum.

Schutz, A. (1970). *On Phenomenology and Social Relations*. Chicago: University of Chicago Press.

Semin, G. R. (1990). "Everyday Assumptions, Language and Personality." In G. R. Semin and K. J. Gergen (eds.), *Everyday Understanding*. London: Sage, pp. 151–75.

Semin, G. R. and Gergen, K. J. (eds.) (1990). *Everyday Understanding*. London: Sage.

Smith, B. (1977). *Toward a Black Feminist Criticism*. New York: Out and Out Books.

Smith, D. E. (1987). *The Everyday World as Problematic*. Toronto: Toronto University Press.

Solomos, J. (1989). *Race and Racism in Contemporary Britain*. London: Macmillan.

Terry, R. W. (1975). *For Whites Only*, revised edition. Grand Rapids, MI: Eerdmans.

Zimmerman, D. H. and Pollner, M. (1970). "The Everyday World as a Phenomenon." In J. D. Douglas (ed.), *Understanding Everyday Life*. London: Routledge and Kegan Paul, pp. 80–103.

11

Cartographies of Struggle: Third World Women and the Politics of Feminism

Chandra T. Mohanty

[. . .]

Definitions: Third World Women and Feminism

Unlike the history of Western (white, middle-class) feminisms, which has been explored in great detail over the last few decades, histories of third world women's engagement with feminism are in short supply. There is a large body of work on "women in developing countries," but this does not necessarily engage feminist questions. There is now a substantial amount of scholarship on women in liberation movements, or on the role and status of women in individual cultures. However, this scholarship also does not necessarily engage questions of feminist historiography. Constructing such histories often requires reading against the grain of a number of intersecting progressive discourses (e.g., white feminist, third world nationalist, and socialist), as well as the politically regressive racist, imperialist, sexist discourses of slavery, colonialism, and contemporary capitalism. The very notion of addressing what are often internally conflictual histories of third world women's feminisms under a single rubric, in one (admittedly introductory) essay, may seem ludicrous – especially since the very meaning of the term *feminism* is continually contested. For, it can be argued, there are no simple ways of representing these diverse struggles and histories. Just as it is difficult to speak of a singular entity called "Western feminism," it is difficult to generalize about "third world feminisms." But just as we have chosen to foreground "third world women" as an analytical and political category in the title of this collection, I want to recognize and analytically explore the links among the histories and struggles of third world women against racism, sexism, colonialism, imperialism, and monopoly capital. I am suggesting, then, an "imagined community" of third world oppositional struggles. "Imagined" not because it is not "real" but because it suggests potential alliances and collaborations across divisive boundaries, and "community" because in spite of internal hierarchies within third world contexts, it nevertheless suggests a significant, deep commitment to what Benedict Anderson, in referring to the idea of the nation, calls "horizontal comradeship."[1] [. . .]

The idea of imagined community is useful because it leads us away from essentialist notions of third world feminist struggles, suggesting political rather than biological or cultural bases for alliance. Thus, it is not color or sex which constructs the ground for these struggles. Rather, it is the *way* we think about race, class, and gender – the political links we choose to make among and between struggles. Thus, potentially, women of all colors (including white women) can align themselves with and participate in these imagined communities. However, clearly our relation to and centrality in particular struggles depend on our different, often conflictual, locations and histories.

Third world women as social category

As I argue in my essay ("Under Western Eyes") [. . .], scholars often locate "third world women" in terms of the underdevelopment, oppressive traditions, high illiteracy, rural and urban poverty, religious fanaticism, and "overpopulation" of particular Asian, African, Middle Eastern, and Latin American countries. Corresponding analyses of "matriarchal" black women on welfare, "illiterate" Chicana farmworkers, and "docile" Asian domestic workers also abound in the context of the US. Besides being normed on a white, Western (read progressive/modern)/non-Western (read backward/traditional) hierarchy, these analyses freeze third world women in time, space, and history. For example, in analyzing indicators of third world women's status and roles, Momsen and Townsend (1987) designate the following categories of analysis: life expectancy, sex ratio, nutrition, fertility, income-generating activities, education, and the new international division of labor. Of these, fertility issues and third world women's incorporation into multinational factory employment are identified as two of the most significant aspects of "women's worlds" in third world countries.

While such descriptive information is useful and necessary, these presumably "objective" indicators by no means exhaust the meaning of women's day-to-day lives. The everyday, fluid, fundamentally historical and dynamic nature of the lives of third world women is here collapsed into a few frozen "indicators" of their well-being. Momsen and Townsend (1987) state that in fact fertility is the most studied aspect of women's lives in the third world. This particular fact speaks volumes about the predominant representations of third world women in social-scientific knowledge production. And our representations of third world women circumscribe our understanding and analysis of feminism as well as of the daily struggles women engage in in these circumstances.

For instance, compare the analysis of "fertility" offered by Momsen and Townsend (as a "social indicator" of women's status) with the analysis of population policy and discussions on sexuality among poor Brazilian women offered by Barroso and Bruschini in this volume. By analyzing the politics of family planning in the context of the Brazilian women's movement, and examining the way poor women build collective knowledge about sex education and sexuality, Barroso and Bruschini link state policy and social movements with the politics of everyday life, thus presenting us with a dynamic, historically specific view of the struggles of Brazilian women in the barrios. I address some of these methodological questions in more detail later on. For the present, however, suffice it to say that our definitions, descriptions, and interpretations of third world women's engagement with feminism must necessarily be simultaneously historically specific and dynamic, not frozen in time in the form of a spectacle.

Thus, if the above "social indicators" are inadequate descriptions/ interpretations of women's lives, on what basis do third world women form any constituency? First, just as "Western women" or "white women" cannot be defined as coherent interest groups, "third world women" also do not constitute any automatic unitary group. Alliances and divisions of class, religion, sexuality, and history, for instance, are necessarily internal to each of the above "groups." Second, ideological differences in understandings of the social mediate any assumption of a "natural" bond between women. After all, there is no logical and necessary connection between being "female" and becoming "feminist."[2] Finally, defining third world women in terms of their "problems" or their "achievements" in relation to an imagined free white liberal democracy effectively removes them (and the "liberal democracy") from history, freezing them in time and space.

A number of scholars in the US have written about the inherently *political* definition of the term *women of color* (a term often used interchangeably with *third world women*, as I am doing here).[3] This is a term which designates a political constituency, not a biological or even sociological one. It is a sociopolitical designation for people of African, Caribbean, Asian, and Latin American descent, and native peoples of the US. It also refers to "new immigrants" to the US in the last decade – Arab, Korean, Thai, Laotian, etc. What seems to constitute "women of color" or "third world women" as a viable oppositional alliance is a *common context of struggle* rather than color or racial identifications. Similarly, it is third world women's oppositional *political* relation to sexist, racist, and imperialist structures that constitutes our potential commonality. Thus, it is the common context of struggles against specific exploitative structures and systems that determines our potential political alliances. [. . .]

Why feminism?

[. . .] Before proceeding to suggest the structural, historical parameters which lead to third world women's particular politics, it is important to understand how women in different sociocultural and historical locations formulate their relation to feminism. The term *feminism* is itself questioned by many third world women. Feminist movements have been challenged on the grounds of cultural imperialism, and of shortsightedness in defining the meaning of gender in terms of middle-class, white experiences, and in terms of internal racism, classism, and homophobia. All of these factors, as well as the falsely homogeneous representation of the movement by the media, have led to a very real suspicion of "feminism" as a productive ground for struggle. Nevertheless third world women have always engaged with feminism, even if the label has been rejected in a number of instances. [. . .]

Third world women's writings on feminism have consistently focused on (1) the idea of the simultaneity of oppressions as fundamental to the experience of social and political marginality and the grounding of feminist politics in the histories of racism and imperialism; (2) the crucial role of a hegemonic state in circumscribing their/our daily lives and survival struggles; (3) the significance of memory and writing in the creation of oppositional agency; and (4) the differences, conflicts, and contradictions internal to third world women's organizations and communities. In addition, they have insisted on the complex inter-relationships between feminist, antiracist, and nationalist struggles. In fact, the challenge of third world feminisms to white, Western feminisms has been precisely this inescapable link between feminist and political liberation movements. In fact, black, white, and other third world women have very different histories with respect to the particular inheritance of post-fifteenth-century Euro-American hegemony: the inheritance of slavery, enforced migration, plantation and indentured labor, colonialism, imperial conquest, and genocide. Thus, third world feminists have argued for the rewriting of history based on the *specific* locations and histories of struggle of people of color and postcolonial peoples, and on the day-to-day strategies of survival utilized by such peoples. [. . .]

Contexts: History, the State, and Relations of Rule

Do third world feminisms share *a* history? Surely the rise of the post-1947 women's movement in India is historically different from the emergence of black feminist politics in the UK or the US? The major *analytic* difference in the writings on the emergence of white, Western, middle-class liberal feminism and the feminist politics of women of color in the US is the contrast between a singular focus on gender as a basis for equal rights, and a focus on gender in relation to race and/or class as part of a broader liberation struggle. Often the singular focus of the former takes the form of definitions of femininity and sexuality in relation to men (specifically white privileged men).

Hurtado's (1989) analysis of the effects of the different relationships of white middle- and upper-class women and working-class women and women of color to privileged white men is relevant here in understanding the conditions of possibility of this singular focus on gender. Hurtado argues that it is the (familial) closeness of white (heterosexual) women to white men, and the corresponding social distance

of women of color from white men, that leads to the particular historical focus of white women's feminist movements. Since the relationships
of women of color to white men are usually mediated by state institutions, they can never define feminist politics without accounting for this
mediation. For example, in the arena of reproductive rights, because of
the race- and class-based history of population control and sterilization
abuse, women of color have a clearly ambivalent relation to the "abortion rights" platform. For poor women of color, the notion of a
"woman's right to choose" to bear children has always been mediated
by a coercive, racist state. Thus, abortion rights defined as a *woman's*
right vs. men's familial control can never be the only basis of feminist
coalitions across race and class lines. For many women of color, reproductive rights conceived in its broadest form, in terms of familial
male/female relationships, but also, more significantly, in terms of institutional relationships and state policies, must be the basis for such coalitions. Thus, in this instance, gender defined as male/female domestic
relations cannot be a singular focus for feminists of color. However,
while Hurtado's suggestion may explain partially the exclusive focus on
gender relationships in (heterosexual) white women's movements,
this still does not mean that this unitary conceptualization of gender is
an adequate ground for struggle for white middle- and upper-class
feminists.

In fact, in terms of *context*, the history of white feminism is not very
different from the history of the feminisms of third world women: all of
these varied histories emerge *in relation to* other struggles. Rich, layered
histories of the second wave of white feminism in the US incorporate its
origins in the civil rights and new left movements. However, often in discussion such origins, feminist historians focus on "gender" as the sole
basis of struggle (the feminist part) and omit any discussion of the racial
consolidation of the struggle (the white part). The best histories and
analyses of the second waves of US white feminism address the construction of whiteness in relation to the construction of a politicized
gender consciousness.[4] Thus, it is not just third world women who are
or should be concerned about race, just as feminism is not just the
purview of women (but of women *and* men). Ann Russo argues just this
point in her essay in this collection. Drawing on her own feminist trajectory as a white woman, she situates the urgency for white women to
react to racism with *outrage* rather than the usual guilt or defensiveness.
In other words, Russo suggests that racism is as much an issue for white

people as for people of color, and in specifying outrage as the crucial response, she suggests how white people are implicated in racial formations, without losing sight of the hierarchies of power based on color and race.

Above all, gender and race are *relational* terms: they foreground a relationship (and often a hierarchy) between races and genders. To define feminism purely in gendered terms assumes that our consciousness of being "women" has nothing to do with race, class, nation, or sexuality, just with gender. But no one "becomes a woman" (in Simone de Beauvoir's sense) purely because she is female. Ideologies of womanhood have as much to do with class and race as they have to do with sex. Thus, during the period of American slavery, constructions of white womanhood as chaste, domesticated, and morally pure had everything to do with corresponding constructions of black slave women as promiscuous, available plantation workers. It is the intersections of the various systemic networks of class, race, (hetero)sexuality, and nation, then, that position us as "women." Herein lies a fundamental challenge for feminist analysis once it takes seriously the location and struggles of third world women, and this challenge has implications for the rewriting of all hegemonic history, not just the history of people of color. [. . .]

The state, citizenship, and racial formation

Unlike the colonial state, the gender and racial regimes of contemporary liberal capitalist states operate through the ostensibly "unmarked" discourses of citizenship and individual rights. In contrast to the visible racialized masculinity of nineteenth- and early twentieth-century territorialist imperialism, white capitalist patriarchies institute relations of rule based on a liberal citizenship model with its own forms of knowledge and impersonal bureaucracies. According to R. W. Connell, the contemporary Euro-American state operates through the setting up of a "gender regime": a regime whereby the state is the primary organizer of the power relations of gender.[5] In other words, the state delimits the boundaries of personal/domestic violence, protects property, criminalizes "deviant" and "stigmatized" sexuality, embodies masculinized hierarchies (e.g., the gendered bureaucracy of state personnel), structures collective violence in the police force, prisons, and wars, and sometimes allows or even invites the countermobilization of power.

While imperial rule was constructed on the basis of a sharp sexual division of labor whereby (white) masculinity was inseparable from social authority and masculine adventure was followed by masculinized rule, the notion of citizenship created by bourgeois liberal capitalism is predicated on an impersonal bureaucracy and a hegemonic masculinity organized around the themes of rationality, calculation, and orderliness. Thus, Connell argues, contemporary liberal notions of citizenship are constitutively dependent on and supported by the idea of the patriarchal household, and formulated around the notion of a "rationalized" hegemonic masculinity (in contrast to the violent masculinity of colonial rule or of the military). This rationalized masculinity is evident in the bureaucratic sexual division of labor of people employed by the state: 80 to 90 percent of the political elite, civil-service bureaucracy (railways, maritime services, power, and construction), judiciary, and military are male, while women are overwhelmingly employed in the human services (education, nursing, social work, etc.) and secretarial arms of the state. [. . .]

Historically, (white) feminist movements in the West have rarely engaged questions of immigration and nationality (one exception is Britain, which has a long history of black feminist organizing around such issues). In any event, I would like to suggest that analytically these issues are the contemporary metropolitan counterpart of women's struggles against colonial occupation in the geographical third world. In effect, the construction of immigration and nationality laws, and thus of appropriate racialized, gendered citizenship, illustrates the continuity between relationships of colonization and white, masculinist, capitalist state rule.

In an important study of US racial trajectories, Michael Omi and Howard Winant[6] introduce the idea of "racial formation," which "refer[s] to the process by which social, economic and political forces determine the content and importance of racial categories, and by which they are in turn shaped by racial meanings" (Omi and Winant, 1986, p. 61). Omi and Winant maintain that in the contemporary United States, race is one of the central axes of understanding the world. Particular racial myths and stereotypes change, but the underlying presence of a racial meaning system seems to be an anchoring point of American culture. While racial formation is a matter of the dynamic between individual identities and collective social structures, the racial parameters of the US state include citizenship and naturalization laws, and social and welfare policies and practices which often arise as a response to oppositional movements. Historically, citizenship and immigration laws and social policies have always been connected to economic agendas, and to the search for cheap labor. These state practices are anchored in the institutions of slavery, capitalist neocolonialism, and, more recently, monopoly, multinational capitalism. Thus, racism is often the product of a colonial situation, although it is not limited to it. Blacks and Latinos in the US, Asians and West Indians in Britain, and North Africans in France, all share similarly oppressive conditions and the status of second-class citizens.

A comparison of the history of the immigration of white people and of the corresponding history of slavery and indentured labor of people of color in the US indicates a clear pattern of racialization tied to the ideological and economic exigencies of the state. White men were considered "free labor" and could take a variety of jobs. At the same time, black men and women were used as slave labor to develop the agriculture of the South, and Mexican-Americans were paid much lower wages than whites for their work in the mines, railroads, lumber camps, oil extraction, and agriculture in the Southwest. These relations of inequality are the context for the entry of US women of color into the labor force – usually in domestic or laundry work, or slave labor in the fields. In part it is this history of low-wage, exploitative occupations which have been the purview of US third world women which contributes to the racist definitions they must endure vis-à-vis a dominant white, middle-class, professional culture.

In effect, then, citizenship and immigration laws are fundamentally about defining insiders and outsiders. The US Naturalization Law of 1790, the state's original attempt to define citizenship, maintained that only free, "white" immigrants could qualify. It took the Walter-McCarran Act of 1952 to grant Japanese-Americans US citizenship. Racial categorization has remained very fluid throughout the nineteenth and twentieth centuries, dependent on labor needs. For instance, in the nineteenth century there were three racial categories: white, Negro, and Indian. Mexicans were legally accorded the status of "free white persons" after the 1848 treaty of Guadalupe Hidalgo, while a California Supreme Court ruled in 1854 that the Chinese, who were a major source of cheap labor on the West Coast, were to be considered "Indian" (Omi and Winant, 1986, p. 75). [. . .]

The first law explicitly based on nationality was the 1882 Chinese Exclusion Act. The 1907 Gentlemen's Agreement curtailed Japanese and Korean immigration, the 1917 Act restricted Asian Indian immigration, the 1924 Oriental Exclusion Act terminated all labor immigration from mainland Asia, while the 1934 Tydings-McDuffie Act restricted Filipino immigration to the US. Citizenship through naturalization was denied to all Asians from 1924 to 1943. Beginning in 1943, and until the mid-1960s, when immigration laws were liberalized, the state instituted a quota system for Asian immigrants. Quotas were available only for professionals with postsecondary education, technical training, and specialized experience. Thus, the replacement of the "yellow peril" stereotype by a "model minority" stereotype is linked to a particular history of immigration laws which are anchored in the economic exigencies of the state and systemic inequalities.

In the contemporary American context, the black/white line is rigidly enforced. This is evident even in the recent legal cases on affirmative action, where the very basis for affirmative action as a form of collective retribution is being challenged on grounds of "reverse discrimination," an argument based on individual rather than collective demands. These arguments are made and upheld in spite of the ostensibly liberal, pluralist claims of the American state.[7] On the other hand, racial categorization in Brazil varies along a black/white color continuum which signifies status and privilege differences. Similarly, in South Africa, Chinese people have the same status as Asians (or "coloreds"), while Japanese are referred to as "honorary whites." Omi and Winant's notion of racial formation allows us to account for the historical determinants of these ideological definitions of race.

The most developed discussion of the state's regulation of third world peoples through immigration and naturalization laws can be found in the UK. Third world feminists in Britain position the racist state as a primary focus of struggle. British nationality and immigration laws define and construct "legitimate" citizenship – an idea which is constitutively racialized and gender-based. Beginning in the 1950s, British immigration laws were written to prevent black people (commonwealth citizens from Africa, Asia, the Far East, Cyprus, and the Caribbean) from entering Britain, thus making the idea of citizenship meaningless. These laws are entirely constructed around a racist, classist ideology of a patriarchal nuclear family, where women are never accorded subject status but are always assumed to be legal appendages of men.[8] For instance, the 1968 Commonwealth Immigrants Act, in which ancestry was decisive, permitted only black men with work permits to enter Britain and assumed that men who were the "heads of families" could send for their "wives," but not vice versa. The focus on familial configurations also indicates the implicit heterosexual assumptions written into these laws. Women can be defined only (a) in relation to men, and (b) through the heterosexual nuclear family model. Similar, the 1981 British Nationality Act translated immigration legislation into nationality law whereby three new kinds of race- and gender-specific citizenships were created: British citizenship, dependent territories citizenship, and British overseas citizenship.

The effects of this act on women's citizenship were substantial: it took away the automatic right of women married to British men to register as citizens; it disenfranchised all children born in Britain who were originally entitled to automatic citizenship (children were entitled to citizenship only if one of their parents was born or settled in Britain); and it allowed British (white) women to pass on citizenship to children born abroad for the first time in history. Thus, as the Women, Immigration and Nationality Group (WING) argues, immigration and nationality laws in Britain are a feminist issue, as they explicitly reflect the ideology of (white) women as the reproducers of the nation. [. . .]

Finally, racial formation takes its most visibly violent and repressive form in Apartheid South Africa. Here, the very language of apartheid (and of course the denial of "citizenship" to black people) – "separate but equal development," "White areas vs. Bantustans (less than 13 percent of the land)," black women workers as "superfluous appendages" – encapsulates the material force of ideological definitions of race. Working-class solidarity across racial lines is impossible because of racialization:

> the racist ideology of South Africa is an explicit, systematic, holistic ideology of racial superiority – so explicit that it makes clear that the White working class can only maintain its standard of living on the basis of a Black underclass, so systematic as to guarantee that the White working class will continue to remain a race for itself, so holistic as to ensure that the color line is the power line is the poverty line. (Sivanandan, 1981, p. 300)

This equation of the color line with the power line with the poverty line[9] encapsulates the contours of racial formation under apartheid, and it is this context that determines the particular emergence of the struggles of South African women: struggles around racial, political, and economic liberation, work, domestic life, housing, food, and land rights. Racist ideology has the hegemonic capacity to define the terms whereby people understand themselves and their world. The project of decolonization thus involves the specification of race in political, economic, and ideological terms, for the meanings of race are necessarily shaped as much in collective and personal practice (identity politics) as by the state (colonial or contemporary capitalist). [. . .]

By analyzing the discourse and concept of citizenship as constructed through immigration and nationality laws, I have attempted a specification of the gender and racial regime of the contemporary Euro-American liberal democratic state and its relations of rule. The fact that notions of sexuality (morality of women), gender (familial configurations), and race ("Oriental") are implicitly written into these laws (a) indicates the reason why this particular aspect of the contemporary state is a crucial context for third world women's feminist struggles, and (b) provides a method of feminist analysis which is located at the intersections of systemic gender, race, class, and sexual paradigms as they are regulated by the liberal state. This discussion suggests the relationships between the economic exigencies of the state (the original reason for migration/immigration) and its gender and racial regimes.

Multinational production and social agency

Questions of gender and race take on a new significance in the late twentieth century, when, as a consequence of the massive incorporation of third world women into a multinational labor force and into domestic service, feminist theorists are having to rethink such fundamental concepts as the public/private distinction in explanations of women's oppression. Indeed, questions pertaining to the situation of "third world" women (both domestic and international), who are often the most exploited populations, are some of the most urgent *theoretical* challenges facing the social and political analysis of gender and race in postindustrial contexts. Of course, no discussion of the contemporary contexts of third world women's engagement with feminism could omit a sketch of the massive incorporation and proletarianization of these women in multinational factories. While this location is not just a "social indicator" of third world women's economic and social status (Momsen and Townsend, 1987), it is a significant determinant of the micropolitics of daily life and self-constructions of massive numbers of third world women employed in these factories. In fact, the 1960s expansion of multinational export-processing labor-intensive industries to the third world and the US/Mexican border is the newest pernicious form of economic and ideological domination.

World market factories relocate in search of cheap labor, and find a home in countries with unstable (or dependent) political regimes, low levels of unionization, and high unemployment. What is significant about this particular situation is that it is young third world women who overwhelmingly constitute the labor force. And it is these women who embody and personify the intersection of sexual, class, and racial ideologies. Faye Harrison's essay in this volume clarifies some of these intersections of multinational capital, work, and third world women's location by analyzing women in the urban informal economy in Jamaica. Placing Jamaica within the paradigm of "development studies," Harrison suggests a model for understanding the sex- and class-based contradictions in the lives of poor working women in Kingston slums.

Numerous feminist scholars have written about the exploitation of third world women in multinationals.[10] While there are a number of studies which provide information on the mobilization of racist and (hetero)sexist stereotypes in recruiting third world women into this labor force, relatively few studies address questions of the social agency of women who are subjected to a number of levels of capitalist discipline. In other words, few studies have focused on women workers as *subjects* – as agents who make choices, have a critical perspective on their own situations, and think and organize collectively against their oppressors. Most studies of third world women in multinationals locate them as victims of multinational capital as well as of their own "traditional' sexist cultures. [. . .]

An analysis of the employment of third world women workers by multinational capital in terms of ideological constructions of race, gender, and sexuality in the very definition of "women's work" has significant repercussions for feminist cross-cultural analysis. In fact, questions pertaining to the social agency of third world women workers may

well be some of the most challenging questions facing feminist organizing today. By analyzing the sexualization and racialization of women's
work in multinational factories, and relating this to women's own ideas
of their work and daily life, we can attempt a definition of self and collective agency which takes apart the idea of "women's work" as a
naturalized category. Just as notions of "motherhood" and "domestic-
ity" are historical and ideological rather than "natural" constructs, in
this particular context, ideas of "third world women's work" have their
basis in social hierarchies stratified by sex/gender, race, and class.
Understanding these constructions in relation to the state and the
international economy is crucial because of the overwhelming employment of third world women in world market factories, sweatshops, and
home work. Thus, this forms another important context for understanding the systemic exploitation of poor third world women, and provides a potential space for cross-national feminist solidarity and
organizing. [. . .]

Consciousness, identity, writing

[. . .] This section foregrounds the interconnections of consciousness,
identity, and writing and suggests that questions of subjectivity are
always multiply mediated through the axes of race, class/caste, sexuality, and gender. I do not provide a critique of identity politics here, but I
do challenge the notion "I am, therefore I resist!" That is, I challenge the
idea that simply being a woman, or being poor or black or Latino, is sufficient ground to assume a politicized oppositional identity. In other
words, while questions of identity are crucially important, they can
never be reduced to automatic self-referential, individualist ideas of the
political (or feminist) subject. Three of the essays in this volume, Barbara
Smith's essay on black lesbians in contemporary fiction, Lourdes
Torres's essay on US Latina autobiographies, and Nellie Wong's largely
autobiographical essay on "coming to consciousness" in a classist,
heterosexist, racist culture, address these questions at differing levels.
Issues of self and consciousness are central to each of the three essays,
and each writer subtly emphasizes the importance of *writing* in the production of self- and collective consciousness.

This section focuses on life story-oriented written narratives, but this
is clearly only one, albeit important, context in which to examine the
development of political consciousness. Writing is itself an activity

which is marked by class and ethnic position. However, testimonials, life stories, and oral histories are a significant mode of remembering and recording experience and struggles. Written texts are not produced in a vacuum. In fact, texts which document third world women's life histories owe their existence as much to the exigencies of the political and commercial marketplace as to the knowledge, skills, motivation, and location of individual writers.

For example, critics have pointed to the recent proliferation of experientially oriented texts by third world women as evidence of "diversity" in US feminist circles. Such texts now accompany "novels" by black and third world women in Women's Studies curricula. However, in spite of the fact that the growing demand among publishers for culturally diverse life (hi)stories indicates a recognition of plural realities and experiences as well as a diversification of inherited Eurocentric canons, often this demand takes the form of the search for more "exotic" and "different" stories in which individual women write as truth-tellers, and authenticate "their own oppression," in the tradition of Euro-American women's autobiography. In other words, the mere proliferation of third world women's texts, in the West at least, owes as much to the relations of the marketplace as to the conviction to 'testify" or "bear witness." Thus, the existence of third world women's narratives in itself is not evidence of decentering hegemonic histories and subjectivities. It is the way in which they are read, understood, and located institutionally which is of paramount importance. After all, the point is not just "to record" one's history of struggle, or consciousness, but how they are recorded; the way we read, receive, and disseminate such imaginative records is immensely significant. It is this very question of reading, theorizing, and locating these writings that I touch on in the examples below.

The consolidation and legitimation of testimonials as a form of Latin American oral history (history from below) owes as much to the political imperatives of the Cuban revolution as to the motivations and desires of the intellectuals and revolutionaries who were/are the agents of these testimonials. The significance of representing "the people" as subjects of struggle is thus encapsulated in the genre of testimonials, a genre which, unlike traditional autobiography, is constitutively public, and collective (for and of the people).[11]

Similarly, in the last two decades, numerous publishing houses in different countries have published autobiographical, or life story-oriented, texts by third world feminists. This is a testament to the role of publishing houses and university and trade presses in the production, reception, and dissemination of feminist work, as well as to the creation of a discursive space where (self-)knowledge is produced by and for third world women. Feminist analysis has always recognized the centrality of rewriting and remembering history. This is a process which is significant not merely as a corrective to the gaps, erasures, and misunderstandings of hegemonic masculinist history, but because the very practice of remembering and rewriting leads to the formation of politicized consciousness and self-identity. Writing often becomes the context through which new political identities are forged. It becomes a space for struggle and contestation about reality itself. If the everyday world is not transparent and its relations of rule, its organizations and institutional frameworks, work to obscure and make invisible inherent hierarchies of power (Smith, 1987), it becomes imperative that we rethink, remember, and utilize our lived relations as a basis of knowledge. Writing (discursive production) is one site for the production of this knowledge and this consciousness.

Written texts are also the basis of the exercise of power and domination. This is clear in Barbara Harlow's (1989) delineation of the importance of literary production (narratives of resistance) during the Palestinian Intifada. Harlow argues that the Israeli state has confiscated both the land and the *childhood* of Palestinians, since the word *child* has not been used for twenty years in the official discourse of the Israeli state. This language of the state disallows the notion of Palestinian "childhood," thus exercising immense military and legal power over Palestinian children. In this context, Palestinian narratives of childhood can be seen as narratives of resistance, which write childhood, and thus selfhood, consciousness, and identity, back into daily life. Harlow's analysis also indicates the significance of written or recorded history as the basis of the constitution of memory. In the case of Palestinians, the destruction of all archival history, the confiscation of land, and the rewriting of historical memory by the Israeli state mean that not only must narratives of resistance undo hegemonic recorded history, but they must also *invent* new forms of encoding resistance, of remembering.

Honor Ford-Smith,[12] in her introduction to a book on "life stories of Jamaican women,' encapsulates the significance of this writing:

The tale-telling tradition contains what is most poetically true about our struggles. The tales are one of the places where the most subversive elements of our history can be safely lodged, for over the years the tale tellers convert fact into images which are funny, vulgar, amazing or magically real. These tales encode what is overtly threatening to the powerful into covert images of resistance so that they can live on in times when overt struggles are impossible or build courage in moments when it is. To create such tales is a collective process accomplished within a community bound by a particular historical purpose. . . . They suggest an altering or redefining of the parameters of political process and action. They bring to the surface factors which would otherwise disappear or at least go very far underground. (Sistren with Ford-Smith, 1987, pp. 3–4)

I have quoted this passage at length because it suggests a number of crucial elements of the relation of writing, memory, consciousness, and political resistance: (a) the codification of covert images of resistance during nonrevolutionary times; (b) the creation of a communal (feminist) political consciousness through the practice of storytelling; and (c) the redefinition of the very possibilities of political consciousness and action through the act of writing. One of the most significant aspects of writing against the grain in both the Palestinian and the Jamaican contexts is thus the invention of spaces, texts, and images for encoding the history of resistance. Therefore, one of the most significant challenges here is the question of decoding these subversive narratives. Thus, history and memory are woven through numerous genres: fictional texts, oral history, poetry, as well as testimonial narratives – not just what counts as scholarly or academic ("real?") historiography. [. . .]

Ford-Smith's discussion also suggests an implicit challenge to the feminist individualist subject of much of liberal feminist theory, what Norma Alarcon, in a different context, calls "the most popular subject of Anglo-American feminism . . . an autonomous, self-making, self-determining subject who first proceeds according to the *logic of identification* with regard to the subject of consciousness, a notion usually viewed as the purview of man, but now claimed for women" (Alarcon, 1989, p. 3). Alarcon goes on to define what she calls the "plurality of self" of women of color as subject in the text *This Bridge Called My Back* (1981) in relation to the feminist subject of Anglo-American feminism. Both Ford-Smith and Alarcon suggest the possibility, indeed the *necessity*, of conceptualizing notions of collective selves and consciousness as the political practice of historical memory and writing by women of color and third world women. This writing/speaking of a multiple consciousness, one located at the juncture of contests over the meanings of racism, colonialism, sexualities, and class, is thus a crucial context for delineating third world women's engagement with feminisms. This is precisely what Gloria Anzaldúa refers to as a "mestiza consciousness" (Anzaldúa, 1987).[13]

A mestiza consciousness is a consciousness of the borderlands, a consciousness born of the historical collusion of Anglo and Mexican cultures and frames of reference. It is a plural consciousness in that it requires understanding multiple, often opposing ideas and knowledges, and negotiating these knowledges, not just taking a simple counterstance. [. . .]

This notion of the uprooting of dualistic thinking suggests a conceptualization of consciousness, power, and authority which is fundamentally based on knowledges which are often contradictory. For Anzaldúa, a consciousness of the borderlands comes from a recentering of these knowledges – from the ability to see ambiguities and contradictions clearly, and to act collectively, with moral conviction. Consciousness is thus simultaneously singular and plural, located in a theorization of being "on the border." Not any border – but a historically specific one: the US/Mexican border. Thus, unlike a Western, postmodernist notion of agency and consciousness which often announces the splintering of the subject, and privileges multiplicity in the abstract, this is a notion of agency born of history and geography. It is a theorization of the materiality and politics of the everyday struggles of Chicanas. [. . .]

To summarize, this essay on "third world women and the politics of feminism" is divided into two parts: questions of definition, and questions of context. The first part delineates the urgency and necessity to rethink feminist praxis and theory within a cross-cultural, international framework, and discusses (a) the assumption of third world women as a social category in feminist work, and (b) definitions and contests over feminism among third world women. The second part suggests five provisional contexts for understanding third world women's engagement with feminism. The first tree chart political and historical junctures: decolonization and national liberation movements in the third world, the consolidation of white, liberal capitalist patriarchies in Euro-America, and the operation of multinational capital within a global economy.

The last section focuses on discursive contexts: [. . .] on storytelling or autobiography (the practice of writing) as a discourse of oppositional consciousness and agency. Again, these are necessarily partial contexts meant to be suggestive rather than comprehensive – this is, after all, one possible cartography of contemporary struggles. And it is admittedly a cartography which begs numerous questions and suggests its own gaps and fissures. However, I write it in an attempt to "pivot' the center of feminist analyses, to suggest new beginnings and middles, and to argue for more finely honed historical and context-specific feminist methods. I also write it out of the conviction that we must be able and willing to theorize and engage the feminist politics of third world women, for these are the very understandings we need to respond seriously to the challenges of race an our postcolonical condition. [. . .]

Notes

I thank Satya Mohanty and Jacqui Alexander for their thoughtful and incisive comments on this essay. I remain indebted to my students at Oberlin College, whose enthusiastic engagement with the politics of feminism continually challenges me to clarify and refine my own thinking about the issues in this introduction. Teaching about these issues has made it possible to write about them.

1   Benedict Anderson, *Imagined Communities: Reflections on the Origin and Spread of Nationalism* (New York: Verso Books, 1983), esp. pp. 11–16. [. . .]

2   I argue this point in detail in an earlier essay on the politics of experience entitled "Feminist Encounters: Locating the Politics of Experience,' *Copyright*, 1 (Fall 1987), pp. 30–44.

3   See, for instance, Chela Sandoval's work on the construction of the category "Women of Color" in the US, and her theorization of oppositional consciousness in "Women Respond to Racism: A Report on the National Women's Studies Association Conference, Storrs, Connecticut," Occasional Paper Series, Oakland: Center for Third World Organizing, 1983; and her "Towards a Theory of Oppositional Consciousness: U.S. Third World Feminism and the U.S. Women's Movement," unpublished manuscript, 1988. Norma Alarcon offers an important conceptualization of third world women as subjects in her essay "The Theoretical Subject(s) of *This Bridge Called My Back* and Anglo-American Feminism," in Gloria Anzaldúa (ed.), *Making Face, Making Soul/Haciendo caras: Creative and Critical Perspectives by Women of Color* (San Francisco: Aunt Lute Books, 1990). See also essays in Moraga and Anzaldúa (1983), Trinh

T. Minh-Ha (1989), hooks (1984), and Anzaldúa (1987) for similar conceptualizations.

4   A number of white feminists have provided valuable analyses of the construction of "whiteness" in relation to questions of gender, class, and sexuality within feminist scholarship. See especially Biddy Martin's work on lesbian autobiography (1988); Elizabeth Spelman's book *Inessential Woman: Problems of Exclusion in Feminist Theory* (Boston: Beacon, 1989); Katie King's "Producing Sex, Theory and Culture: Gay/Strait ReMappings in Contemporary Feminism," in M. Hirsch and E. Fox Keller (eds.), *Conflicts in Feminism* (forthcoming); and Ruth Frankenberg's dissertation on the social construction of whiteness.

5   R. W. Connell, *Gender and Power* (Stanford: Stanford University Press, 1987), esp. pp. 125–32; and R. W. Connell, "The State in Sexual Politics: Theory and Appraisal," unpublished manuscript, 1989. For a radical feminist analysis of the state, see Catherine MacKinnon, *Towards a Feminist Theory of the State* (Cambridge MA: Harvard University Press, 1989); see also Sylvia Walby, *Patriarchy at Work* (Cambridge: Polity Press, 1986); C. Burton, *Subordination* (Sydney: Allen and Unwin, 1985); K. E. Ferguson, *The Feminist Case against Bureaucracy* (Philadelphia: Temple University Press, 1984); Sue Ellen M. Charlton et al., *Women, the State, and Development* (Albany: SUNY Press, 1989); F. Anthias and N. Yuval-Davis, *Women and the State* (London: Macmillan, 1990).

6   M. Omi and H. Winant, *Racial Formation in the United States: From the 1960s to the 1980s* (New York and London: Routledge and Kegan Paul, 1986). See also Howard Winant's recent essay "Postmodern Racial Politics: Difference and Inequality," in *Socialist Review*, 90, no. 1 (1990), pp. 121–47. For similar discussion of racial formation in the British context, see Paul Gilroy, *There Ain't No Black in the Union Jack* (Cambridge: Polity Press, 1987).

7   See Z. Eisenstein, *The Female Body and the Law* (Berkeley: University of California Press, 1988), esp. ch. 4 for a discussion of the pluralist nature of the US state.

8   Women, Immigration and Nationality Group, *Worlds Apart: Women under Immigration and Nationality Law* (London and Sydney: Pluto Press, 1985).

9   A. Sivanandan, "Race, Class and Caste in South Africa: An Open Letter to No Sizwe," *Race and Class*, 22, no. 3 (1981), pp. 293–301; see also his recent essay "All That Melts into Air Is Solid: The Hokum of the New Times," *Race and Class*, 31, no. 3 (1990), pp. 1–30.

10 See especially essays in J. Nash and M. P. Fernandez-Kelly (eds.), *Women, Men and the International Division of Labor* (Albany: State University of New York Press, 1983); see also M. Patricia Fernandez-Kelly, *For We Are Sold, I*

and My People: Women and Industry in Mexico's Frontier (Albany: State University of New York Press, 1983); E. Leacock and H. Safa (eds.), *Women's Work: Development and the Division of Labor by Gender* (South Hadley, MA: Bergin and Garvey, 1986); Saskia Sassen, *The Mobility of Labor and Capital* (New York: Cambridge University Press, 1988); and L. Beneria and C. Stimpson (eds.), *Women, Households and the Economy* (New Brunswick: Rutgers University Press, 1987).

11   Doris Sommer makes this point in her excellent essay "Not Just a Personal Story: Women's *Testimonios* and the Plural Self,' in Bella Brodzki and Celeste Schenck (eds.), *Life/Lines: Theorizing Women's Autobiography* (Ithaca: Cornell University Press, 1988), pp. 107–30. My discussion of testimonies draws on Sommer's analysis.

12   Sistren with Honor Ford-Smith, *Lionhart Gal: Life Stories of Jamaican Women* (Toronto: Sister Vision Press, 1987). Another text which raises similar questions of identity, consciousness, and history is *I, Rigoberta Menchu, an Indian Woman in Guatemala* (London: Verso Books, 1984).

13   For texts which document the trajectory of third world women's consciousness and politics, see also the recent publications of the following feminist publishers: Firebrand Press, Crossing Press, Spinsters/Aunt Lute, Zed Press, South End Press, Women's Press, and Sheba Feminist Publishers.

References

Alarcon, Norma (1989). "The Theoretical Subject(s) of *This Bridge Called My Back* and Anglo-American Feminism." In H. Calderon and J. D. Saldivar (eds.), *Chicana Criticism in a Social Context*. Durham: Duke University Press.

Anderson, Benedict (1983). *Imagined Communities: Reflections on the Origin and Spread of Nationalism*. New York: Verso Books.

Anthias, F. and Yuval Davis, N. (1990). *Women and the State*. London: Macmillan.

Anzaldúa, Gloria (1987). *Borderlands/La Frontera*. San Francisco: Spinsters/Aunt Lute.

——(ed.) (1990). *Making Face, Making Soul/Haciendo caras: Creative and Critical Perspectives by Women of Color*. San Francisco: Aunt Lute Books.

Asian Women United of California (eds.) (1989). *Making Waves: An Anthology of Writings by and about Asian American Women*. Boston: Beacon Press.

Beneria, L. and Stimpson, C. (eds.) (1987). *Women, Households and the Economy*. New Brunswick: Rutgers University Press.

Bhabha, J. et al. (1985). *Worlds Apart: Women under Immigration and Nationality Law*. London: Pluto Press.

Blassingame, John (1979). *The Slave Community: Plantation Life in the Antebellum South*. New York: Oxford University Press.

Bryan, B. et al. (1985). *The Heart of the Race*. London: Virago.

Burton, C. (1985). *Subordination*. Sydney: Allen and Unwin.

Callaway, Helen (1987). *Gender, Culture, and Empire: European Women in Colonial Nigeria*. Urbana: University of Illinois Press.

Charlton, Sue Ellen M., Everett, J., and Staudt Kathleen (eds.) (1989). *Women, the State, and Development*. Albany: SUNY Press.

Chowdhry, Prem (1989). "Customs in a Peasant Economy: Women in Colonial Haryana." In KumKum Sangari and Sudesh Vaid (eds.), *Recasting Women: Essays in Colonial History*. New Delhi: Kali Press, pp. 302–36.

Clifford, J. and Marcus, G. (eds.) (1986). *Writing Culture: The Poetics and Politics of Ethnography*. Berkeley: University of California Press.

Connell, R. W. (1987). *Gender and Power*. Stanford: Stanford University Press.

Davis, Miranda (1981). *Third World/Second Sex, Vol. 1*. London: Zed Press.

——(1987). *Third World/Second Sex, Vol. 2*. London: Zed Press.

Eisenstein, Zillah (1988). *The Female Body and the Law*. Berkeley: University of California Press.

Etienne, Mona and Leacock, Eleanor (eds.) (1980). *Women and Colonization*. New York: Praeger.

Ferguson, K. E. (1984). *The Feminist Case against Bureaucracy*. Philadelphia: Temple University Press.

Fernandez-Kelly, M. P. (1983). *For We Are Sold, I and My People: Women and Industry in Mexico's Frontier*. Albany: SUNY Press.

Fox-Genovese, Elizabeth (1988). *Within the Plantation Household: Black and White Women of the Old South*. Chapel Hill: University of North Carolina Press.

Genovese, Eugene (1979). *From Rebellion to Revolution: Afro-American Slave Revolts in the Making of the Modern World*. Boston: Beacon Press.

Giddings, Paula (1984). *When and Where I Enter: The Impact of Black Women on Race and Sex in America*. New York: William Morrow.

Gilroy, Paul (1987). *There Ain't No Black in the Union Jack*. Cambridge: Polity Press.

Grewal, S. et al. (1988). *Charting the Journey: Writings by Black and Third World Women*. London: Sheba Feminist Publishers.

Harlow, B. (1989). "Narrative in Prison: Stories from the Palestinian Intifada." *Modern Fiction Studies*, 35, no. 1, pp. 29–46.

Higginbotham, Elizabeth (1983). "Laid Bare by the System: Work and Survival for Black and Hispanic Women." In A. Swerdlow and H. Lessinger (eds.), *Class, Race and Sex: The Dynamics of Control*. Boston: G. K. Hall, pp. 200–215.

hooks, bell (1984). *Feminist Theory: From Margin to Center*. Boston: South End Press.

——(1988). *Talking Back: Thinking Feminist, Thinking Black*. Boston: South End Press.

Hurtado, Aida (1989). "Relating to Privilege: Seduction and Rejection in the Subordination or White Women and Women of Color." *Signs*, 14, no. 4, pp. 833–55. *I, Rigoberta Menchu, an Indian Woman in Guatemala* (1984). London: Verso Books.

Jayawardena, Kumari (1986). *Feminism and Nationalism in the Third World*. London: Zed Press.

Jones, Jacqueline (1985). *Labor of Love, Labor of Sorrow: Black Women, Work, and the Family from Slavery to the Present*. New York: Random House.

King, Katie (1990). "Producing Sex, Theory and Culture: Gay/Straight ReMappings in Contemporary Feminism." In M. Hirsch and E. Fox-Keller (eds.), *Conflicts in Feminism*. New York: Methuen (forthcoming).

Kishwar, M. and Vanita, R. (eds.) (1984). *In Search of Answers: Indian Women's Voices from Manushi*. London: Zed Press.

Latin American and Caribbean Women's Collective (1977). *Slaves of Slaves*. London: Zed Press.

Leacock, E. and Safa, H. (eds.) (1986). *Women's Work: Development and the Division of Labor by Gender*. South Hadley, MA: Bergin and Garvey.

Liddle, J. and Joshi, R. (1986). *Daughters of Independence: Gender, Caste and Class in India*. London: Zed Press.

Lorde, Audre (1984). *Sister Outside*. Freedom, CA: Crossing Press.

MacKinnon, Catherine (1989). *Towards a Feminist Theory of the State*. Cambridge: Harvard University Press.

Marcus, G. and Fischer, M. (1986). *Anthropology as Cultural Critique*. Chicago: University of Chicago Press.

Martin, Biddy (1988). "Lesbian Identity and Autobiographical Difference(s)." In B. Brodzki and C. Schenck (eds.), *Life/Lines: Theorizing Women's Autobiography*. Ithaca: Cornell University Press, pp. 77–106.

Mascia-Lees, F. E. et al. (1989). "The Postmodernist Turn in Anthropology: Cautions from a Feminist Perspective." *Signs*, 15, no. 1, pp. 7–33.

Mohanty, Chandra Talpade (1987). "Feminist Encounters: Locating the Politics of Experience." *Copyright*, 1, pp. 30–44.

——and Mohanty, Satya P. (1990). "Contradictions of Colonialism." *The Women's Review of Books*, 7, no. 6, pp. 19–21.

Mohanty, Satya P. (1989). "Kipling's Children and the Color Line." *Race and Class* 31, no. 1, pp. 21–40.

——(1991). *Literary Theory and the Claims of History*. Oxford: Basil Blackwell.

Momsen, J. H. and Townsend, J. (1987). *Geography of Gender in the Third World*. New York: SUNY Press.

Moore, H. (1988). *Feminism and Anthropology*. Oxford: Basil Blackwell.

Moraga, C. and Anzaldúa, G. (eds.) (1983). *This Bridge Called My Back: Writings by Radical Women of Color*. New York: Kitchen Table: Women of Color Press.

Nash, J. and Fernandez-Kelly, M. P. (eds.) (1983). *Women, Men and the International Division of Labor*. Albany: SUNY Press.

O'Hanlon, R. (1988). "Recovering the Subject: Subaltern Studies and Histories of Resistance in Colonial South Asia." *Modern Asian Studies*, 22, no. 1, pp. 189–224.

Okohiro, G. Y. (ed.) (1986). *In Resistance: Studies in African, Caribbean and Afro-American History*. Amherst: University of Massachusetts Press.

Omi, M. and Winant, H. (1986). *Racial Formation in the United States, from the 1960s to the 1980s*. New York: Routledge and Kegan Paul.

Ong, Aihwa (1987). *Spirits of Resistance and Capitalist Discipline: Factory Women in Malaysia*. Albany: SUNY Press.

Popkin, Richard (1974). "The Philosophical Bases of Modern Racism." *Journal of Operational Psychiatry*, 5, no. 2.

Reiter, Rayna (ed.) (1975). *Toward an Anthropology of Women*. New York: Monthly Review Press.

Rollins, Judith (1987). *Between Women: Domestics and Their Employers*. New Brunswick: Rutgers University Press.

Sandoval, Chela (1983). "Women Respond to Racism: A Report on the National Women's Studies Association Conference, Storrs, Connecticut." Occasional Paper Series, Oakland, Center for Third World Organizing.

Sangari, KumKum and Vaid, Sudesh (eds.) (1989). *Recasting Women: Essays in Collonial History*. New Delhi: Kali Press.

Scott, Joan W. (1986). "Gender: A Useful Category of Historical Analysis." *American Historical Review*, 91, no. 5, pp. 1053–75.

Sistren with Ford-Smith, Honor (1987). *Lionhart Gal: Life Stories of Jamaican Women*. Toronto: Sister Vision Press.

Sivanandan, A. (1981). "Race, Class and Caste in South Africa: An Open Letter to No Sizwe." *Race and Class*, 22, no. 3, pp. 293–301.

——(1990). "All That Melts into Air Is Solid: The Hokum of the New Times." *Race and Class*, 31, no. 3, pp. 1–30.

Smith, Dorothy (1987). *The Everyday World as Problematic: A Feminist Sociology*. Boston: Northeastern University Press.

Sommer, Doris (1988). "Not Just a Personal Story: Women's *Testimonios* and the Plural Self." In B. Brodzki and C. Schenck (eds.), *Life/Lines: Theorizing Women's Autobiography*. Ithaca: Cornell University Press, pp. 107–30.

Spelman, Elizabeth (1989). *Inessential Woman: Problems of Exclusion in Feminist Theory*. Boston: Beacon Press.

Spillers, Hortense (1987). "Mama's Baby, Papa's Maybe: An American Grammar Book." *Diacritics*, Summer 1987.

Spivak, G. C. (1987). *In Other Worlds: Essays in Cultural Politics*. New York: Methuen.

Stree Shakti Sangathana (1990). *We Were Making History: Women and the Telengana Uprising*. London: Zed Press.

Trinh T. Minh-ha (1989). *Women, Native Other*. Bloomington: Indiana University Press.

Walby, Sylvia (1985). *Patriarchy at Work*. Cambridge: Polity Press.

Winant, Howard (1990). "Postmodern Racial Politics: Difference and Inequality." *Socialist Review* 90, no. 1, pp. 121–47.

12

The Nation Form: History and Ideology

Etienne Balibar

> ... a "past" that has never been present, and which never will be.
>
> Jacques Derrida, *Margins of Philosophy*

[...]

Producing the People

A social formation only reproduces itself as a nation to the extent that, through a network of apparatuses and daily practices, the individual is instituted as *homo nationalis* from cradle to grave, at the same time as he or she is instituted as *homo œconomicus, politicus, religiosus* ... That is why the question of the nation form, if it is henceforth an open one, is, at bottom, the question of knowing under what historical conditions it is possible to institute such a thing: by virtue of what internal and external relations of force and also by virtue of what symbolic forms invested in elementary material practices? Asking this question is another way of asking oneself to what transition in civilization the nationalization of societies corresponds, and what are the figures of individuality between which nationality moves.

The crucial point is this: What makes the nation a "community"? Or rather, in what way is the form of community instituted by the nation distinguished specifically from other historical communities?

Let us dispense right away with the antitheses traditionally attached to that notion, the first of which is the antithesis between the "real" and the "imaginary" community. *Every social community reproduced by the functioning of institutions is imaginary*, that is to say, it is based on the projection of individual existence into the weft of a collective narrative, on the recognition of a common name and on traditions lived as the trace of an immemorial past (even when they have been fabricated and inculcated in the recent past). But this comes down to accepting that, under certain conditions, *only* imaginary communities are real.

In the case of national formations, the imaginary which inscribes itself in the real in this way is that of the "people." It is that of a community which recognizes itself in advance in the institution of the state, which recognizes that state as "its own" in opposition to other states and, in particular, inscribes its political struggles within the horizon of that state – by, for example, formulating its aspirations for reform and social revolution as projects for the transformation of "its national state." Without this, there can be neither "monopoly of organized violence" (Max Weber), nor "national-popular will" (Gramsci). But such a people does not exist naturally, and even when it is tendentially constituted, it does not exist for all time. No modern nation possesses a given "ethnic" basis, even when it arises out of a national independence struggle. And, moreover, no modern nation, however "egalitarian" it may be, corresponds to the extinction of class conflicts. The fundamental problem is therefore to produce the people. More exactly, it is to make the people produce itself continually as national community. Or again, it is to produce the effect of unity by virtue of which the people will appear, in everyone's eyes, "as a people," that is, as the basis and origin of political power.

Rousseau was the first to have explicitly conceived the question in these terms, "What makes a people a people?" Deep down, this question is no different from the one which arose a moment ago: How are individuals nationalized or, in other words, socialized in the dominant form of national belonging? Which enables us to put aside from the outset another artificial dilemma: it is not a question of setting a collective identity against individual identities. *All identity is individual*, but there is no individual identity that is not historical or, in other words, constructed within a field of social values, norms of behavior, and collective symbols. Individuals never identify with one another (non even in the "fusional" practices of mass movements or the "intimacy" of affective relations), nor, however, do they ever acquire an isolated identity, which is an intrinsically contradictory notion. The real question is how the dominant reference points of individual identity change over time and with the changing institutional environment.

To the question of the historical production of the people (or of national individuality) we cannot merely be content to rely with a description of conquests, population movements, and administrative practices of "territorialization." The individuals destined to perceive themselves as the members of a single nation are either gathered together externally from diverse geographical origins, as in the nations formed by immigration (France, the USA) or else are brought mutually to recognize one another within a historical frontier which contained them all. The people is constituted out of various populations subject to a common law. In every case, however, a model of their unity must "anticipate" that constitution: the process of unification (the effectiveness of which can be measured, for example, in collective mobilization in wartime, that is, in the capacity to confront death collectively) presupposes the constitution of a specific ideological form. It must at one and the same time be a mass phenomenon and a phenomenon of individuation, must effect an "interpellation of individuals as subjects" (Althusser) which is much more potent than the mere inculcation of political values or rather one that integrates this inculcation into a more elementary process (which we may term "primary") of fixation of the affects of love and hate and representation of the "self." That ideological form must become an *a priori* condition of communication between individuals (the "citizens") and between social groups – not by suppressing all differences, but by relativizing them and subordinating them to itself in such a way that it is the symbolic difference between "ourselves" and "foreigners" which wins out and which is lived as irreducible. In other words, to use the terminology proposed by Fichte in his *Reden an die deutsche Nation* of 1808, the "external frontiers" of the state have to become "internal frontiers" or – which amounts to the same thing – external frontiers have to be imagined constantly as a projection and protection of an internal collective personality, which each of us carries within ourselves and enables us to inhabit the space of the state as a place where we have always been – and always will be – "at home."

What might that ideological form be? Depending on the particular circumstances, it will be called patriotism or nationalism, the events which promote its formation or which reveal its potency will be recorded and its origin will be traced back to political methods – the combination of "force" and "education" (as Machiavelli and Gramsci put it) – which enable the state to some extent to fabricate public consciousness. But this fabrication is merely an external aspect. To grasp the deepest reasons for its effectiveness, attention will turn then, as the attention of political philosophy and sociology has turned for three centuries, towards the analogy of *religion*, making nationalism and patriotism out to be a religion – if not indeed *the* religion – of modern times.

Inevitably, there is some truth in this – and not only because religions, formally, in so far as they start out from "souls" and individual identities, institute forms of community and prescribe a social "morality"; but also because theological discourse has provided models for the idealization of the nation and the sacralization of the state, which make it possible for a bond of sacrifice to be created between individuals, and for the stamp of "truth" and "law" to be conferred upon the rules of the legal system.[1] Every national community must have been represented at some point or another as a "chosen people." Nevertheless, the political philosophies of the Classical Age had already recognized the inadequacy of this analogy, which is equally clearly demonstrated by the failure of the attempts to constitute "civil religions," by the fact that the "state religion" ultimately only constituted a transitory form of national ideology (even when this transition lasted for a long time and produced important effects by superimposing religious on national struggles) and by the interminable conflict between theological universality and the universality of nationalism.

In reality, the opposite argument is correct. Incontestably, national ideology involves ideal signifiers (first and foremost the very *name* of the nation or "fatherland") on to which may be transferred the sense of the sacred and the affects of love, respect, sacrifice, and fear which have cemented religious communities; but that transfer only takes place because *another type* of community is involved here. The analogy is itself based on a deeper difference. If it were not, it would be impossible to understand why national identity, more or less completely integrating the forms of religious identity, ends up tending to replace it, and forcing it itself to become "nationalized."

Fictive Ethnicity and Ideal Nation

I apply the term "fictive ethnicity" to the community instituted by the nation-state. This is an intentionally complex expression in which the term fiction, in keeping with my remarks above, should not be taken in the sense of a pure and simply illusion without historical effects, but must, on the contrary, be understood by analogy with the *persona ficta* of the juridical tradition in the sense of an institutional effect, a "fabrication." No nation possesses an ethnic base naturally, but as social formations are nationalized, the populations included within them, divided up among them or dominated by them are ethnicized – that is, represented in the past or in the future *as if* they formed a natural community, possessing of itself an identity of origins, culture, and interests which transcends individuals and social conditions.[2]

Fictive ethnicity is not purely and simply identical with the *ideal nation* which is the object of patriotism, but it is indispensable to it, for, without it, the nation would appear precisely only as an idea or an arbitrary abstraction; patriotism's appeal would be addressed to no one. It is fictive ethnicity which makes it possible for the expression of a preexisting unity to be seen in the state, and continually to measure the state against its "historic mission" in the service of the nation and, as a consequence, to idealize politics. By constituting the people as a fictively ethnic unity against the background of a universalistic representation which attributes to each individual one – and only one – ethnic identity and which thus divides up the whole of humanity between different ethnic groups corresponding potentially to so many nations, national ideology does much more than justify the strategies employed by the state to control populations. It inscribes their demands in advance in a sense of belonging in the double sense of the term – both what it is that makes one belong to oneself and also what makes one belong to other fellow human beings. Which means that one can be interpellated, as an individual, *in the name of* the collectivity whose name one bears. The naturalization of belonging and the sublimation of the ideal nation are two aspects of the same process.

How can ethnicity be produced? And how can it be produced in such a way that it does not appear as fiction, but as the most natural of origins? History shows us that there are two great competing routes to this: language and race. Most often the two operate together, for only their complementarity makes it possible for the "people" to be represented as an absolutely autonomous unit. Both express the idea that the national character (which might also be called its soul or its spirit) is immanent in the people. But both offer a means of transcending actual individuals and political relations. They constitute two ways of rooting historical populations in a fact of "nature" (the diversity of languages and the diversity of races appearing predestined), but also two ways of giving a meaning to their continued existence, of transcending its contingency. By force of circumstance, however, at times one or the other is dominant, for they are not based on the development of the same institutions and do not appeal to the same symbols or the same idealizations of the national identity. The fact of these different articulations of, on the one hand, a predominantly linguistic ethnicity and, on the other, an ethnicity that is predominantly racial has obvious political consequences. For this reason, and for the sake of clarity of analysis, we must begin by examining the two separately.

The language community seems the more abstract notion, but in reality it is the more concrete since it connects individuals up with an origin which may at any moment be actualized and which has as its content the *common act* of their own exchanges, of their discursive communication, using the instruments of spoken language and the whole, constantly self-renewing mass of written and recorded texts. This is not to say that that community is an immediate one, without internal limits, any more than communication is in reality "transparent" between all individuals. But these limits are always relative: even if it were the case that individuals whose social conditions were very distant from one another were never in direct communication, they would be bound together by an uninterrupted chain of intermediate discourses. They are not isolated – either *de jure* or *de facto*.

We should, however, certainly not allow ourselves to believe that this situation is as old as the worth itself, It is, on the contrary, remarkably recent. The old empires and the *Ancien Régime* societies were still based on the juxtaposition of linguistically separate populations, on the superimposition of mutually incompatible "languages" for the dominant and the dominated and for the sacred and profane spheres. Between these there had to be a whole system of translations.[3] In modern national formations, the translators are writers, journalists, and politicians, social actors who speak the language of the "people" in a way that seems all the more natural for the very degree of distinction they thereby bring to it. The translation process has become primarily one of internal translation between different "levels of language." Social differences are expressed and relativized as different ways of speaking the national language, which supposes a common code and even a common norm.[4] This latter is, as we know, inculcated by universal schooling, whose primary function it is to perform precisely this task.

That is why there is a close historical correlation between the national formation and the development of school as "popular" institutions, not limited to specialized training or to elite culture, but serving to underpin the whole process of the socialization of individuals. That the school should also be the site of the inculcation of a nationalist ideology – and sometimes also the place where it is contested – is a secondary phenomenon, and is, strictly speaking, a less indispensable aspect. Let us simply say that schooling is the principal institution which produces ethnicity as linguistic community. It is not, however, the only one: the state, economic exchange, and family life are also schools in a sense, organs of the ideal nation recognizable by a common language which belongs to them "as their own." For what is decisive here is not only that the national language should be recognized as the official language, but, much more fundamentally, that it should be able to appear as the very element of the life of a people, the *reality* which each person may appropriate in his or her own way, without thereby destroying its identity. There is no contradiction between the instituting of *one* national language and the daily discrepancy between – and clash of – "class languages" which precisely are not different languages. In fact, the two things are complementary. All linguistic practices feed into a single "love of the language" which is addressed not to the textbook norm nor to particular usage, but to the "mother tongue" – that is, to the ideal of a common origin projected back beyond learning processes and specialist forms of usage and which, by that very fact, becomes the metaphor for the love fellow nationals feel for one another.[5]

One might then ask oneself, quite apart from the precise historical questions which the history of national languages poses – from the difficulties of their unification or imposition, and from their elaboration into an idiom that is both "popular" and "cultivated" (a process which we know to be far from complete today in all nation-states, in spite of the labors of their intellectuals with the aid of various international bodies) – *why the language community is not sufficient* to produce ethnicity.

Perhaps this has to do with the paradoxical properties which, by virtue of its very structure, the linguistic signifier confers on individual identity. In a sense, it is always in the element of language that individuals are interpellated as subjects, for every interpellation is of the order of discourse. Every "personality" is constructed with words, in which law, genealogy, history, political choices, professional qualifications, and psychology are set forth. But the linguistic construction of identity is by definition *open*. No individual "chooses" his or her mother tongue or can "change" it at will. Nevertheless, it is always possible to appropriate several languages and to turn oneself into a different kind of bearer of discourse and of the transformations of language. The linguistic community induces a terribly constraining ethnic memory (Roland Barthes once went so far as to call it "fascist"), but it is one which none the less possesses a strange plasticity: it immediately naturalizes new acquisitions. It does so *too quickly* in a sense. It is a collective memory which perpetuates itself at the cost of an individual forgetting of "origins." The "second generation" immigrant – a notion which in this context acquires a structural significance – inhabits the national language (and through it the nation itself) in a manner as spontaneous, as "hereditary" and as imperious, so far as affectivity and the imaginary are concerned, as the son of one of those native heaths which we think of as so very French (and most of which not so long ago did not even have the national language as their daily parlance). One's "mother" tongue is not necessarily the language of one's "real" mother. The language community is a community *in the present*, which produces the feeling that it has always existed, but which lays down no destiny for the successive generations. Ideally, it "assimilates" anyone, but holds no one. Finally, it affects all individuals in their innermost being (in the way in which they constitute themselves as subjects), but its historical particularity is bound only to interchangeable institutions. When circumstances permit, it may serve different nations (as English, Spanish, and even French do) or survive the "physical" disappearance of the people who used it (like "ancient" Greek and Latin or "literary" Arabic). For it to be tied down to the frontiers of a particular people, it therefore needs an extra degree [*un supplément*] of particularity, or a principle of closure, of exclusion.

This principle is that of being part of a common race. But here we must be very careful not to give rise to misunderstandings. All kinds of somatic or psychological features, both visible and invisible, may lend themselves to creating the fiction of a racial identity and therefore to representing natural and hereditary differences between social groups either within the same nation or outside its frontiers. I have discussed elsewhere, as have others before me, the development of the marks of race and the relation they bear to different historical figures of social conflict. What we are solely concerned with here is the symbolic kernel which makes it possible to equate race and ethnicity ideally, and to represent unity of race to oneself as the origin or cause of the historical unity of a people. Now, unlike what applied in the case of the linguistic community, it cannot be a question here of a practice which is really common to *all* the individuals who form a political unit. We are not dealing with anything equivalent to communication. What we are speaking of is therefore a second-degree fiction. This fiction, however, also derives its effectiveness from everyday practices, relations which immediately structure the "life" of individuals. And, most importantly, whereas the language community can only create equality between individuals by simultaneously "naturalizing" the social inequality of linguistic practices, the race community dissolves social inequalities in an even more ambivalent "similarity"; it ethnicizes the social difference which is an expression of irreconcilable antagonisms by lending it the form of a division between the "genuinely" and the "falsely" national.

I think we may cast some light on this paradox in the following way. The symbolic kernel of the idea of race (and of its demographic and cultural equivalents) is the schema of genealogy, that is, quite simply the idea that the filiation of individuals transmits from generation to generation a substance both biological and spiritual and thereby inscribes them in a temporal community known as "kinship." That is way, *as soon as* national ideology enunciates the proposition that the individuals belonging to the same people are interrelated (or, in the prescriptive mode, that they should constitute a circle of extended kinship), we are in the presence of this second mode of ethnicization.

The objection will not doubt be raised here that such a representation characterizes societies and communities which have nothing national about them. But, it is precisely on this point that the particular innovation hinges by which the nation form is articulated to the modern idea of race. This idea is correlative with the tendency for "private" genealogies, as (still) codified by traditional systems of preferential marriage and lineage, to disappear. The idea of a racial community makes its appearance when the frontiers of kinship dissolve at the level of the clan, the neighborhood community, and, theoretically at least, the social class, to be imaginarily transferred to the threshold of nationality: that is to say, when nothing prevents marriage with any of one's "fellow citizens" whatever, and when, on the contrary, such a marriage seems the only one that is "normal" or "natural." The racial community has a tendency to represent itself as one big family or as the common envelope of family relations (the community of "French," "American," or "Algerian" families).[6] From that point onward, each individual has his/her family, whatever his/her social condition, but the family – like property – becomes a contingent relation between individuals. [. . .]

These historical differences in no sense impose any necessary outcome – they are rather the stuff of political struggles – but they deeply modify the conditions in which problems of assimilation, equality of rights, citizenship, nationalism, and internationalism are posed. One might seriously wonder whether in regard to the production of fictive ethnicity, the "building of Europe" – to the extent that it will seek to transfer to the "Community" level functions and symbols of the nation-state – will orientate itself *predominantly* towards the institution of a "European co-lingualism" (and if so, adopting which language) or *predominantly* in the direction of the idealization of "European demographic identity" conceived mainly in opposition to the "southern populations" (Turks, Arabs, Blacks).[7] Every "people," which is the product of a national process of ethnicization, is forced today to find its own means of going beyond exclusivism or identitarian ideology in the world of transnational communications and global relations of force. Or rather: every individual is compelled to find in the transformation of the imaginary of "his" or "her" people the means to leave it, in order to communicate with the individuals of other peoples with which he or she shares the same interests and, to some extent, the same future.

Notes

1   On all these points, the work of Kantorowicz is clearly of crucial significance: see *Mourir pour la patrie et autres textes* (Paris: PUF, 1985).

2   I say "included within them," but I should also add "or excluded by them," since the ethnicization of the "others" occurs simultaneously with that of the "nationals": there are no longer any historical differences other than ethnic ones (thus the Jews also have to be a "people"). On the ethnicization of colonized populations, see J.-L. Amselle and E. M'Bokolo, *Au cœur de l'ethnie: ethnies, tribalisme et Etat en Afrique* (Paris: La Découverte, 1985).

3   Ernest Gellner, *Nations and Nationalism* (Oxford: Blackwell, 1983) and Benedict Anderson, *Imagined Communities* (London: Verso, 1983), whose

analyses are as opposed as materialism" and "idealism," both rightly stress this point.

4 See Renée Balibar, *L'Institution du français. Essai sur le colingualisme des Carolingiens à la République* (Paris: PUF, 1985).

5 Jean-Claude Milner offers some very stimulating suggestions on this point, though more in *Les Noms indistincts* (Paris: Seuil, 1983), pp. 43 *et seq.* than in *L'Amour de la langue* (Paris: Seuil, 1978). On the "class struggle"/"language struggle" alternative in the USSR at the point when the policy of "socialism in one country" became dominant, see F. Gadet, J.-M. Gaymann, Y. Mignot, and E. Roudinesco, *Les Maîtres de la langue* (Paris: Maspero, 1979).

6 Let us add that we have here a sure *criterion* for the commutation between racism and nationalism: every discourse on the fatherland or nation which associates these notions with the "defense of the family" – not to speak of the birth rate – is already ensconced in the universe of racism.

7 Right at the heart of this alternative lies the following truly crucial question: will the administrative and educational institutions of the future "United Europe" accept Arabic, Turkish, or even certain Asian or African languages on an equal footing with French, German, and Portuguese, or will those languages be regarded as "foreign"?

13

Turning the Tables: Antisemitic Discourse in Post-war Austria

Ruth Wodak

It would be absurd to deny that many Austrians responded to some extent to the Nazis' racial propaganda; however, when they saw how anti-semitism was actually put into practice, they were cured. One could safely say that sympathy for the persecuted Jews eradicated antisemitism in Austria. I do not believe that this issue will ever again assume even the slightest importance.

Leopold Figl, the first elected Federal Chancellor of the
Austrian Second Republic[1]

[The international press] is dominated by the World Jewish Congress. This is well known.

Kurt Waldheim[2]

If it had been meant seriously, the Austrian Chancellor's optimism after 1945 was unfounded. In fact, Figl must have known better, since he had been present at meetings of the Council of Ministers immediately after 1945, where antisemitic sentiments were expressed by some other members of the government in conjunction with the debate about reparations payments to Austrian Jews who had survived the Shoa (see Knight, 1988). Figl's disingenuous remark can thus be regarded as but a further element designed to buttress Austria's positive image in the world.

Almost forty years later, public discourse about Jews in Austria in the course of the "Waldheim affair" recalled earlier times and gave rise to a great deal of concern in the Jewish community organization (*Gemeinde*).[3] The immediate occasion for this was the criticism which Jewish organizations, among others, directed against Kurt Waldheim, then campaigning for the Austrian presidency, and his hitherto hidden past. The Waldheim affair has exposed the tenuousness of official Austria's post-war *Lebenslüge* about the widespread complicity of Austrians in the Nazi abomination, and the attendant denials of the existence of antisemitic prejudice in the post-war period this entailed (see Gruber and de Cillia, 1989; Wodak 1989a, 1990a, b, c; Wodak and de Cillia, 1988).

On the one hand, after 1945 the open expression of anti-Jewish hostility is subject to a public political taboo. Instead, one enumerates the Jewish friends one has or praises those Jews who contributed so much to Austrian culture (the standard "philo-Semitic" discourse; cf. Stern, 1989). On the other hand, one expresses despair at not being allowed to criticize individual Jews. These predominantly foreign Jews are described as "dishonorable" or worse, and they stand as representatives for Jews as a whole.

Within the limited scope of this paper, it is impossible to consider all aspects of the question of who speaks or writes in an antisemitic way for or to whom in what form and to what effect.[4] I therefore begin with a brief sketch of the historical-sociological context of post-war antisemitism in Austria and indicate the register (both in terms of form and content) of antisemitic prejudice currently possible in contemporary Austria.

A New Antisemitism in Austria?

The Austrian sociologist Bernd Marin (Bunzl and Marin, 1983) has characterized antisemitism in Austria after 1945 as an "antisemitism without Jews," since Jews constitute only 0.1 percent of the Austrian population (in Vienna, 0.5 percent). Moreover, antisemitism is stronger in those areas where Jews no longer live and where previously practically no Jews had lived, and among people who neither have had nor have any personal contact with Jews. In addition, according to Marin, it is an "antisemitism without antisemites," since prejudice against Jews has been publicly forbidden and tabooed. Nevertheless, there is still "antisemitism in politics."

Whatever general validity Marin's thesis had prior to 1986, the results of our study suggest that Marin's findings are applicable to the period since then only with significant modifications.

The taboo against open expressions of explicitly antisemitic beliefs, for example, which Marin posited in an abstract form, has remained, but the means of circumventing it linguistically have extended its boundaries in such a way that the taboo itself appears to have lost some of its significance. Anti-Jewish prejudices which had remained hidden began to surface and were increasingly found in public settings. Quantitative sociological studies (Bunzl and Marin, 1983; Weiss, 1987; Kienzl and Gehmacher, 1987)[5] have continually confirmed that a relatively high percentage of the Austrian population is open to antisemitic resentment.

The persistence of antisemitic attitudes is then ascribed to a small group of right-wing radicals. The number of such (radical) antisemites can thus be carefully delimited, and their numbers be shown to be falling. "Antisemitism" is also frequently identified with a purely racial variety of anti-Jewish prejudice, which is equated with Nazism or with the Nazi extermination of the Jews, effectively excluding or minimizing other antisemitic traditions in Austria, such as the Christian or the Christian social traditions.

If one looks at the history of the political parties in the Austrian First Republic, for example, it is clear that the line dividing the different currents of antisemitism was indistinct. There has remained a reservoir of antisemitic prejudice from which, appropriately packaged, one could (and can) draw as occasion required. Since 1945, moreover, new motives for antisemitism have arisen. What the German Jewish author Henrik Broder said about the Germans is certainly applicable to the Austrians as well: they will never forgive the Jews for Auschwitz. The collapse of the Third Reich forced many, in Austria as in Germany, to confront the extent of the Nazi crimes. Doubts, guilt feelings, the need to justify or rationalize one's behavior encouraged the development of strategies for "dealing with the past": playing down the events themselves, denying all knowledge of them, transforming the victims into the causes of present woes (by not letting bygones be bygones, i.e., by simply continuing to exist). Moreover, since the Moscow Declaration[6] offered Allied support to Austria's claim to have been (collectively) the first "victim" of Hitlerite aggression, such reversals could draw upon an especially potent legitimation.

This putative victim status made it also possible to deny any responsibility which went beyond individual crimes; the new search for identity could produce a stronger feeling of nationalism, which in turn reinforced a specific definition of insiders and outsiders, of "us" and "them."

Since 1945, there have been intermittent scandals involving antisemitic prejudice. In 1967, for example, the openly antisemitic outpourings of Thaddeus Borodajkiewicz, economics professor in Vienna, led to protests by both his opponents and supporters. At one of these, one of Borodajkiewicz's opponents was killed by the economic professor's neo-Nazi supporters. This was the occasion for a bipartisan demonstration against political violence, but no corresponding campaign against his views. Borodajkiewicz himself was forced into early retirement (see Welzig, 1985). In the 1970 national assembly electoral campaign, posters of the candidate of the Austrian's People's Party for chancellor, Josef Klaus, emphasized that he, unlike his opponent Bruno Kreisky, whose Jewish origins were only too well known, was "a genuine Austrian" (see Wodak and de Cillia, 1988). Simon Wiesenthal's publication in 1975 of material about the leader of the Freedom Party,[7] Friedrich Peter, ostensibly linking him to massacres carried out by the SS-unit to which he had belonged, was the occasion for a spate of public invective against Wiesenthal led by Bruno Kreisky. Kreisky insinuated, for example, that Wiesenthal had been a Gestapo informer. Another Kreisky comment, in an interview with a foreign journalist, "if the Jews are a people, they are a lousy [mies] people," moreover, could in this context only serve to provide Jewish "cover" for hostilities against Wiesenthal by those less schooled in the dialectical complexities of Kreisky's views.[8] Against the wave of antisemitic hostilities unleashed by the events of 1986, however, those prior scandals appear as minor affairs indeed.

Antisemitism in post-war Austria must therefore be viewed chiefly in relation to the various ways employed in dealing with alleged or real guilt, with alleged or actual accusations about the Nazi past. Both the large, traditional reservoir of antisemitic prejudice as well as a general, traditional discourse of collective experiences and attitudes provide discursive remedies, while several new topoi have been added. The forms of expression are very different, manifest or latent, explicit or very indirect. But each and every one appears to be a discourse of justification (or varieties of justification and defense).

Antisemitic Stereotypes (Prejudice Content)

Of the many clichés and contents of prejudice that are associated with Jews, we will only list the four that occurred most frequently in 1986. We cannot deal in detail with the historical underpinnings of these prejudices, but refer readers to the literature as a source for the unusual features and uniqueness of the "antisemitic syndrome" (see, inter alia, Adorno, 1973; Allport, 1987; Heinsohn, 1988; Poliakov, 1987; Pulzer, 1966; Wodak, 1990).

1   *Christian antisemitism.* According to this prejudice, Jews are regarded as the murderers of Christ, as traitors. Christian antisemitism was found especially in the mass media in 1986 (in the press and also in the semipublic sphere). These prejudices have the longest and most consistent history in Austria, being deeply embedded in the collective experience and in the "collective subconscious" (Erdheim, 1984).

2   *The "dishonest" or "dishonorable" Jew, the "tricky Jew".* This prejudice has its origins in Judas' betrayal of Christ. On the other hand, this view is also based on economic stereotypes: in the Middle Ages Jews were responsible for lending money at interest (they were excluded from most other occupations). This cliché was used repeatedly with reference to the World Jewish Congress (WJC) in the course of the Waldheim debate in 1986.

3   *The Jewish conspiracy.* The Jews in the world dominate or control the international press, the banks, political power and capital, and they are planning the world conspiracy, e.g., the "campaign" against Waldheim or against Austria (see Mitten, 1991; Wodak, 1990a).[9]

4   *Jews are privileged.* This new prejudice relates directly to the Holocaust. The Jews who "emigrated" and thereby were able to avoid a far worse fate have no reason to complain. Emigration is not especially terrible, and Jews who were not in concentration camps have no grounds to be angry in any case.

The "Fear of Revenge"

The collapse of the Third Reich in 1945 gave rise to several additional reasons for fearing the wrath of the "vengeful Jew." One was the fear of the discovery of war crimes and the persecution and conviction of war criminals. Another was the fear that the stolen ("aryanized") property could be demanded back. Finally, there was fear that the exiles would merely wish to return to their homeland. Not only would they possibly want their property back or take legal action against their former persecutors, but they might become dominant and again "over-judaize" certain professions.

Feelings of guilt can be easily transformed into aggression towards those whose mere presence is an implicit "attack." One reacts defensively or by turning the tables on the victims themselves.

Attack is the Best Defense: The Discourse of Justification

There are various possible ways of dealing with or reacting to such an attack, be it real or imagined. We have distinguished macro-strategies, i.e., basic (conscious or unconscious, planned or spontaneous, or irrational) alternatives in social behavior from the micro-strategies dependent on them (linguistic realizations).[10]

One reaction to perceived criticism is actually to deal openly with it, to show regret or remorse, to reappraise one's actions and accept blame in certain cases or qualify one's responsibility in others. This, however, rarely occurs, for such arguments usually take place in situations that are rife with conflict and pent-up emotions. And it is in these that the strategies we discovered become the means for transporting prejudice. One can attempt to impede the discussion, for example, or to ignore the situation (i.e., "let sleeping dogs lie").

If this strategy does not work, the controversial event can be trivialized. In this way the persons involved, i.e., the perpetrators of these acts, are rendered harmless (i.e., there were not many, one does not know them, etc.), or a euphemism is employed to describe the acts themselves, for example in the use of "emigration" to describe "expulsion." Such a trivialization can manifest itself in different ways, either by rationalization (i.e., there are really objective reasons for antisemitism); by accusing someone else (i.e., someone else is guilty, too); by shifting the blame (i.e., it was someone else's fault), by personalizing it (i.e., only one individual is to blame); or by depersonalizing it altogether (i.e., somebody was to blame), or by making fun of the accusations (i.e., the attackers exaggerate and dramatize them in an unacceptable way). Guilt as such is not, in principle, denied, but rather rendered meaningless.

Apart from merely shifting responsibility for events on to named or unnamed persons, the disavowal of personal knowledge or involvement can also involve a mechanism of victim–victimizer reversal, or the designation of a scapegoat in the case of group conflict (the enemy from the outside). In an argument among individuals, the blame can by mutual agreement be placed on someone who is not present. The defamation and debasement of the opponent belongs to this group of micro-strategies, since this makes blaming the victim, i.e., the victim –victimizer reversal, especially easy. In this case, possible feelings of guilt are transformed into aggression and into a counterattack. This mechanism explains, for example, how the "Kreisky–Peter–Wiesenthal affair" eventually became merely the "Wiesenthal affair" (see Wodak et al., 1990).

Yet another alternative is to deny the guilt in principle. Accusations and attacks are distorted or invented and ascribed to opponents who had not made them, at least not in the form alleged. A systematic distortion of the facts takes place. One is thus justified in protecting oneself or planning counterattacks against such "infamous" attacks. In this way a second reality is constructed, a portrayal of an enemy against which every measure of defense is permissible.

Anti-Jewish (Antisemitic) Language Use: The Pervasiveness of Antisemitic Prejudice in Public Life in Austria

The degree of threat and hostility towards Jews expressed in language can vary greatly: different forms and different degrees of directness and boldness can be differentiated according to context and speaker. In analyzing the material, four hierarchical levels of anti-semitic statements were identified which correspond to the different individual strategies of justification. A connection can be seen between the content of prejudice, political context, setting, speaker, and form of expression.

Level 1. Trivialization and relativization of antisemitism and the uniqueness of the Holocaust (putting the blame on someone else, generalizing). This occurred in totally formal and official contexts such as news broadcasts and informational programmes on Austrian radio and television. The issues of a world conspiracy and Christian issues dominate on this level.

Level 2. Statements with the content: "antisemitism is the Jews' own fault" (victim–victimizer reversal). Such remarks are packaged differently (as direct accusations, as threats, or as insinuations) and occur in many contexts, especially in semipublic ones (i.e., broadcast interviews or in TV discussions) and finally also in the memorial vigil (anonymous discussions on the street, in the center of town, June 1987, due to a memorial vigil dedicated to the victims of World War II) (see Wodak, 1990a, b). Greed, dishonesty, and vindictiveness constitute the contents of additional prejudice.

Level 3. All traditional antisemitic prejudices appear: (a) implicit (stories, allusions); or (b) explicit (generalizations). This requires either less formal contexts or especially protected (well-known) figures. This level corresponds to the third macro-strategy of justification discourse, the systematic distortion and the creation of a stereotyped image of one's opponent (*Feindbild*).

Level 4. Direct and open abuse of Jews. Such labels appeared – if at all – only in anonymous settings, in the memorial vigil, for example, or in complaint calls to the Austrian television network. Outside of such settings the perceived public sanctions against such statements would restrict their occurrence almost completely.

A qualitative text analysis, however, cannot restrict itself to the linguistic level alone. The way in which the types of content are presented and the patterns of argumentation which always appear are of equal significance. They contribute to the organization of the whole text and influence the use of certain linguistic devices. All macro-strategies fit into the patterns of justification identified above, from denial to reversal and counterattack. Before we look at an example from a formal situation, we would like to present several typical forms of antisemitic language behavior from varying contexts, all of them from the Waldheim electoral campaign of 1986 (de Cillia et al., 1987; Mitten et al., 1989).

Predication and assertion

Predication and assertion ascribe certain characteristics to people and groups of people. They are an important linguistic device for constructing a dichotomous world, which in turn functions to make judgments concerning "insiders" and "outsiders" or "them" and "us." Predications can also assume the character of abuse, according to the context and explicitness of the four hierarchical levels. "That whippersnapper, General Secretary Singer . . . the private club with that bombastic name, World Jewish Congress . . . the wheeling and dealing of the first president of the club, N. Goldmann, with the Arabs, the arch-enemy of the Jewish state" (*Neue Kronen Zeitung (NKZ)*, April 2, 1986).

An excerpt quoted from a press conference of the Jewish *Gemeinde* in Vienna on June 18, 1986 is given below. It represents a collage of statements by spokespersons of the Austrian People's Party and serves as an example for the device of predication and the content of dishonesty:[11]

> Untrustworthy and dishonorable methods. Dishonorable members of the World Jewish Congress. Untrustworthy – dishonorable and full of hate. Lies – deception and breaking promises – having no culture and simplistic and unfounded hate. The crying of the puppets of the World Jewish Congress motivated by hate and the need for admiration. Assassins. Mafia of slanderers. The epitome of baseness. Bribed witnesses. Methods of the mafia. Astoundingly stupid. Dirty self-aggrandizement campaigns. The habitual slanderer Singer.

Allusions

Allusions can be manifested in very different ways, for example by means of citations, formal text construction, word choice, vagueness. All forms of allusion, however, share the characteristic that the connection between two contents is established implicitly rather than explicitly, and assumes previous knowledge on the part of the audience. Consequently, the responsibility for the interpretation is shifted onto the readers, who are believed to know the background of the insinuation (for example, "dishonorable lot" [*ehrlose Gesellen*]).

In a letter which Karl Hödl, then vice-mayor of Linz, wrote on May 12, 1987 to Edgar Bronfman, the president of the World Jewish Congress, we find Christian antisemitism transmitted in the form of allusions. The writer of the letter makes a comparison between Bronfman as a Jew and Hödl as an "Austrian, Christian, and trained jurist," who must "defend himself" against "infamous attacks" – thus as a representative for Waldheim and all Austrians. The letter also contains an analogy between Waldheim's persecution by the World Jewish Congress (WJC) and the Jews' handing over of Jesus to the Romans. Finally, Hödl contrasts the revengeful Judaism of the Old Testament to a (forgiving) Christianity: "An eye for an eye, a tooth for a tooth is not our European attitude. The basic Talmudic tendency to preach in the whole world is left up to them and theirs." Similar analogies between the murder of Christ and the critique of Waldheim were found in a series of newspaper commentaries from 1986 and 1987 (e.g., Wodak et al., 1990; Wodak, 1990c).

Quotations (discourse representation)

Quotations are an ever-recurring part of antisemitic language use. It is precisely this form of argumentation that has the appearance of being especially objective and rational. Quotations often enable a speaker or author to transport antisemitic prejudice without having to take responsibility for the statement. This is especially true of quotations by generally recognized authorities and, in the special case of antisemitic argumentation, of quotations by Jews, which are intended to reinforce the argument ("alibi Jews" such as Kreisky, Wiesenthal, etc.). In addition to deflecting authorial responsibility, quotations can be employed to cloak extreme antisemitism, while the quotations themselves can serve as allusions in the sense noted above. Decisive in this case is the specific way in which the statements of a third person are reported.

The term "discourse representation" has been suggested for this basic aspect of media coverage (Hak, 1987). Not only the text that was actually expressed in the course of the coverage, but also the situation in the text at hand was almost always reported as well. Newspapers and the Austrian radio broadcasting company (ORF) made the most frequent use of this technique (cf. the example below), and the cases varied according to content and explicitness, and corresponded to the hierarchical levels 1–3.[12]

Case Studies

Scenes from a noonday news programme – a case study

The WJC held a press conference in New York on March 25, 1986. To a certain extent this constituted a turning-point in the Waldheim affair, especially because the entire country of Austria felt as if it had been attacked. Almost the entire programme (always a full hour from 12–1 o'clock every day except Sunday) was devoted to important aspects of the "campaign" or to an alleged "interference" in Austria's internal affairs and to commentaries on these subjects. In the evening news programme, a telephone interview with Waldheim was broadcast. A wide variety of views were obtained from important representatives of the political scene in Austria (Wodak, 1989b, c). The representatives of the WJC were the only ones who were not interviewed. A summary of press reports was read, as was a commentary on a "discussion about anti-semitism," a formulation which is itself a euphemism.[13]

The situation on March 25, 1986 – what really happened?

On March 22, 1986, the WJC published the CROWCASS listing (Central Registry of War Criminals and Security Suspects) which showed that after 1945 Waldheim had been sought by the US Army for alleged war crimes. This list also recorded (as it turned out mistakenly) that Waldheim had served in the counterintelligence section (Abwehr) or Army Group E, which the press release of the WJC duly noted. At its press conference in New York three days later, March 25, historian Robert Herzstein produced documents which showed that Waldheim had served in the military intelligence section (Ic) rather than the counter-intelligence section (Abwehr).[14]

At this latter press conference, neither Herzstein nor the WJC referred to Waldheim as "an officer in the Abwehr," as the evidence Herzstein presented showed the CROWCASS listing to have been mistaken.

The reporting in the Austrian media on March 25 amalgamated these two press conferences (as well as an interview with WJC leaders which had been published on March 24). The general tone was defensive, as though all Austrians had been implicated by the link between

Waldheim and the Abwehr. This is the element that was focused on and distorted; the WJC, as well as Herzstein, wee portrayed as having referred to Waldheim as an officer in the Abwehr (see also Mitten, 1991).

It thus became possible to defend oneself against an untrue accusation, and this in turn justified in advance any and all counterattacks. At the same time, the "accusations" and substantiated facts which the WJC or Herzstein actually raised were swept under the rug. With few exceptions, the Austrian media became passive supporters of the "campaign with 'the campaign,'" i.e., the Waldheim propaganda line, merely by their (at least) sloppy handling of statements and documents. [. . .]

The press conference of the WJC took place as scheduled that afternoon (CET). At this conference no mention was made of Waldheim in connection with the Abwehr. On the evening news programme *Abendjournal* Waldheim was interviewed via telephone about the allegations the WJC had ostensibly made about him:

> *Interviewer*:   You've heard the report from our New York correspondent about the press conference the World Jewish Congress gave today. Uh we can uh summarize uh these accusations approximately like this: it can be proven that you were a Nazi; you lied for forty years; you knew about and personally took part in partisan activities – all are accusations that are diametrically opposed to the positions you have previously held.
>
> *Waldheim*:   Yes, I categorically deny these accusations. Uh, the former Chancellor Kreisky has also already explained that these accusations by the uh World Jewish Congress have to do with, and I quote, with "monstrous baseness" [*ungeheure Niedertracht*].

Following this exchange, Waldheim offered a lengthy justification based on the themes of "doing one's duty" and having served in the Wehrmacht, "just like hundreds of thousands of other Austrians." Kreisky thus serves as Waldheim's "alibi" Jew, and by quoting Kreisky, Waldheim can shift the responsibility for the defamation away from himself. Waldheim's own "carelessness" about his past is pursued by neither Waldheim nor any of the other politicians who were quoted. The description of Waldheim as an officer in the Abwehr (contained in the CROWCASS listing, and reported – once – by the WJC), is central to his justification. He can legitimately dismiss this one accusation; all others are thereby similarly dismissed or simply ignored. Towards the end of the interview Waldheim is asked:

> Dr Waldheim, would it be correct to summarize your statements in the fol-
> lowing way: there is nothing correct, nothing true in what the World
> Jewish Congress publicized in New York today?'
> *Waldheim*:   I wouldn't say that. Well, the fact, that I was seen uh there and
> was present there, is true. . . .

After this vague and euphemistic explanation, Waldheim again very
strongly denies accusations, especially those that were never made.

> One last question, Dr Waldheim: You continue to maintain that you
> knew nothing about the deportation of Jews, specifically about those from
> Thessaloniki?
> *Waldheim*:   I continue to maintain this. There is no reason to change my
> statement.

The interviewer does not address the principal questions raised by the
WJC, but is railroaded into discussing details considered (by Waldheim)
to be relevant. In this way, Waldheim's justification is the absolute and
uncontested conclusion for the official ORF news on this day.

Conclusions

All the politicians interviewed in these two radio news programmes
employed similar strategies: trivializations, denial, and finally cutting
off the discussion when the discussion dealt with Austria's Nazi past;
distortion, defamation, and preemptive defense against charges still
unknown when the discussion dealt with the WJC. The introductory
passages and interviewers' questions reinforced this discourse. The
order of speakers interviewed in the programme, i.e., Hacker's incon-
spicuous position between Kreisky and Graff, made the opposing arguments relatively ineffective. The diversion and avoidance strategies were
successful: the discussion no longer had to do with Waldheim's past, but
rather with Waldheim as Austria. It was not about post-war Austria and
antisemitism, but about the WJC, their accusations which, in addition,
had been systematically distorted.

The scapegoat strategy, "Iudeus ex machina" (see Wodak, 1989a)
and the construction of this *Feindbild* can be clearly seen *in actu* in
this news broadcast. The premiss is we-discourse, which all the politicians without exception used. One defends oneself against foreign countries and their interference in Austria's internal affairs. In this way the

criticism of Waldheim's dealings with his past was transformed into a plot against Austria contrived by vengeful Jews seeking admiration. When such a reality is constructed by influential politicians in a public forum such as a news broadcast, it is not surprising that antisemitism is expressed much more explicitly in other contexts (such as the memorial vigil).

Did 1986 change anything? Has the antisemitic language use become more obvious? Antisemitic prejudices are ubiquitous in Austria. Since 1986, however, some taboos have fallen away in certain public realms, especially in the media. Although the more subtle expressions of prejudice are usual in such formal contexts, certain persons are entitled to employ cruder or more blatant forms in such contexts as well, conjuring up images of an enemy by reverting at the same time to a mystified past and to Austria's sham existence. The connection between justification and counterattack, between guilt and the construction of a *Feindbild*, is ineluctable.

Notes

I would like to thank Michael Agar, Gerhard Botz, Teun van Dijk, and Richard Mitten for their very useful comments and criticism on earlier drafts of this article, as well as Ardith Meier and Richard Mitten for their help in translating and editing this paper. The details of the whole study are published in Wodak et al. (1990).

1   Interview with the *Shanghai Echo*, quoted in *Der Neue Weg*, no 10, the beginning of June 1947, p. 11.
2   "Comment expliquez-vous que la presse internationale ait été aussi largement critique envers vous? (Il s'emporte.) Mais parce qu'elle est dominée par le Congrès juif mondial, c'est bien connu!" Interview with Claire Trean, *Le Monde*, May 3, 1986.
3   In Austria, religions have institutions recognized in law which record the number of members. The "Israelitische Kultusgemeinde" is the official representative of Austrian Jews. There is no Anglo-American equivalent, and the term "Jewish Community" is conventionally not restricted to those who officially declare themselves Jews on religious grounds. For this paper, when this particular Jewish institution in Austria is meant, the German *Gemeinde* is employed.
4   Two case studies which were part of the project "Sprache und Vorurteil" (Language and Prejudice) were able to shed some light on the Waldheim affair and on an earlier dispute between Simon Wiesenthal, then Austrian

Chancellor Bruno Kreisky, and the then head of the Austrian Freedom Party (FPÖ) Friedrich Peter. Both affairs were examined qualitatively in public and semiformal settings. The whole register of the forms and contents of antisemitic prejudice could be identified in both. This register appears continuous: an appropriate prejudice is sought and found according to situation. The project report (Wodak et al., 1990; Projecktteam "Sprache und Vorurteil," 1989) includes all the data as well as the theoretical and methodological approaches employed in the study.

5 Questionnaires and standardized interviews, and telephone surveys even more so, have serious limitations in prejudice research, since especially in the area of taboos it is almost impossible to obtain opinions and attitudes; therefore, the studies differ from each other. Hilde Weiss' questionnaire appears to be sophisticated and she reaches several important conclusions. Other opinion surveys already fail in their formulation of the questions (cf. in detail regarding this, Projektteam "Sprache und Vorurteil," 1989).

6 The Moscow Declaration, issued by the foreign ministers of the US, Great Britain, and the Soviet Union in October 1943, included the statement that Austria "was the first victim of Hitler's typical policy of aggression."

7 Between 1945 to 1949, former members of what were termed "more incriminated" Nazi organizations were disenfranchised as part of the de-Nazification policy. In the 1949 elections, the Union of Independents, which reorganized the (German) "nationally inclined," captured 20 seats. The Freedom Party [*Freiheitliche Partei Österreichs*] was formed in 1954 out of the Union of Independents. Friedrich Peter was chairman of the FPÖ in 1975. For background on this "affair" see van Amerongen (1977); Wodak et al. (1990).

8 Kreisky's own conception of nationhood derives from the Austrian Socialist theorist Otto Bauer. Bauer's criterion for a nation was that it be a "community of fate" (*Schicksalsgemeinschaft*). Neither Bauer, who died in 1938, nor Kreisky would concede that the Jews are a nation. This in itself is a legitimate position to defend, and Kreisky's pejorative and contemptuous aside probably referred to the difficulty of the Jews conforming to his (unspecified) criteria of nationhood. This, however, in no way mitigates the charge of irresponsibility, and, in the context, would easily be seen as pandering to the anti-Wiesenthal hostilities of the FPÖ voters.

9 One example from our data illustrates this point. The then leader of the People's Party, Alois Mock, said the following in an interview on *Zeit im Bild*, a TV-news broadcast on June 5, 1986: "That guy Singer travels around the world and, aided by the pressure of the international media, suddenly demands that one look at documents from the archives that have been available for forty years. Many say okay, we can take a look at

them. We are not going to risk the pressure and the argument with the men who were even able to place the large international media at their disposal in an unprecedented manhunt [*Menschenhatz*]" (*Zeit im Bild*, June 5, 1986).

10   For the entire range of these, of which only a few representative samples can be offered here, see Projektteam (1989). Regarding the concept of "strategy," see ibid., ch. 7.2 (cf. also Lutz and Wodak, 1987).

11   The entire interview illustrates numerous strategies of justification (see Wodak et al., 1990).

12   For other examples of such linguistic realizations, especially from the semi-public and anonymous spheres, see Projektteam (1989). We have limited ourselves here to those patterns which are actually found in the example passage. The hierarchy of explicitness mentioned above contains the full range of possible antisemitic forms of expression.

13   The complete context, analysis, and text can be found in Wodak et al. (1990). Here, the most important politicians are presented as well as the supplementary comments made by the moderator. The Austrian radio station is a state monopoly (ORF). This example shows better than most others how reality is distorted and how the *Feindbild Jud* was constructed.

14   For the purpose of this article it is sufficient to note his service. The Abwehr section of Army Group E could have brought Waldheim *ceteris paribus* closer to activities judged criminal by the Military Tribunal at Nuremberg than would have his duties in the military intelligence. For details on this point, see Kurz et al. (1988).

References

Adorno, T. W. (1973). *Studien zum autoritären Charakter*. Frankfurt/Main: Suhrkamp.

Allport, G. W. (1987). *The Nature of Prejudice*. Reading, MA: Addison-Wesley.

Botz, G. (1987). "Stufen der Ausgliederung der Juden aus der Gesellschaft. Die österreichischen Juden vom 'Anschluß' zum 'Holocaust.'" *Zeitgeschichte*, 9/10 (June/July), pp. 359–78.

Bunzl, J. and Marin, B. (1983). *Antisemitismus in Österreich*. Innsbruck: Inn-Verlag.

De Cillia, R., Mitten, R., and Wodak, R. (1987). "Von der Kunst, antisemitisch zu sein," in Exhibition catalogue *Heilige Gemeinde Wien. Die Sammlung Max Berger im historischen Museum der Stadt Wien*, pp. 94–107. Vienna: Historisches Museum.

Erdheim, M. (1984). *Die gesellschaftliche Produktion des Unbewußten*. Frankfurt/Main: Suhrkamp.

Gruber, H. and de Cillia, R. (1989). "Menschenfresser aller Länder vereinigt euch! Antisemitische Stereotype in den österreichischen Medien seit 1986." *Journal für Sozialforschung* 29 (2), pp. 215–43.

Hak, T. (1987). "Discourse Representation in Media Discourse." Manuscript. Amsterdam.

Heinsohn, G. (1988). *Was ist Antisemitismus? Der Ursprung von Monotheismus und Judehaß – Warum Antizionismus?* Frankfurt/Main: Scarabäus bei Eichborn.

Kienzl, H. and Gehmacher, E. (eds.) (1987). "Antisemitismus in Österreich. Eine Studie der österreichischen demoskopischen Institute." Vienna: Nationalbank.

Knight, R. (ed.) (1988). *"Ich bin dafür, die Sache in die Länge zu ziehen." Die Wortprotokolle der österreichischen Bundesregierung von 1945 bis 1952 über die Entschädigung der Juden.* Frankfurt/Main: Athenäum.

Kurz, H., Collins, J., Vanwelkenhuysen, J., Fleming, G., Fleischer, H., Wallach, J., and Messerschmidt, M. (1988). *Der Bericht der internationalen Historikerkommission* February 8, 1988, supplement to *Profil*, February 15, 1988.

Lutz, B. and Wodak, R. (1987). *Information für Informierte. Linguistische Studien zu Verständlichkeit und Verstehen von Hörfunknachrichten.* Vienna: Akademie der Wissenschaften.

Mitten, R. (1991). *The Politics of Antisemitic Prejudice. The Waldheim Phenomenon in Austria.* Boulder, CO: West View Press (in press).

Mitten, R., Wodak, R., and de Cillia, R. (1989). "Sprechen Sie antisemitisch." *Sprachreport*, 2, pp. 3–11.

Poliakov, L. (1987). *Geschichte des Antisemitismus. Emanzipation und Rassenwahn.* Worms: Jüdischer Verlag Athenäum.

Projektteam "Sprache und Vorurteil" (1989). " 'Wir sind alle unschuldige Täter.' Studien zum antisemitischen Diskurs im Nachkriegsösterreich," 2 vols., final report. Vienna: Institut für Sprachwissenschaft.

Pulzer, P. G. (1966). *Die Entstehung des politischen Antisemitismus in Deutschland und Österreich 1867–1914.* Stuttgart: Gütersloh.

Stern, F. (1989). "The Whitewashing of the Yellow Badge: Antisemitism and Philosemitism in West Germany." Dissertation, Tel Aviv.

van Amerongen, M. (1977). *Kreisky und seine unbewältigte Vergangenheit.* Graz: Styria.

Weiss, H. (1987). *Antisemitische Vorurteile in Österreich.* Vienna: Braumüller.

Welzig, E. (1985). *Die 68er. Karrieren einer rebellischen Generation.* Vienna, Cologre, and Graz: Böhlau.

Wodak, R. (1989a). "Iudeus ex Machina." *Grazer Linguistische Studien,* 32, pp. 153–80.

Wodak, R. (1989b). "1968 – The Power of Political Jargon: A Club-2 Discussion," in R. Wodak (ed.), *Language, Power and Ideology*. Amsterdam: Benjamins, pp. 137–65.

Wodak, R. (ed.) (1989c). *Language, Power and Ideology*. Amsterdam: Benjamins.

Wodak, R. (1990a). "Some of My Best Friends are Jewish." *Patterns of Prejudice* (in press).

Wodak, R. (1990b). "Alles schonmal da gewesen? Gespräche bei der Mahnwache," in A. Holl (ed.), *Aus Menschen werden Monster* (in press).

Wodak, R. (1990c). "Opfer der Opfer? Der 'alltägliche Antisemitismus' in Österreich – erste qualitative soziolinguistische Überlegungen," in W. Bergmann and R. Erb (eds.), *Antisemitismus in der politischen Kultur nach 1945*. Opladen: Westdeutscher Verlag, pp. 292–319.

Wodak, R. and de Cillia, R. (1988). *Sprache und Antisemitismus*, vol. 3: Ausstellungskatalog. Vienna: Mitteilungen des Instituts für Wissenschaft und Kunst.

Wodak, R., Nowak, P., Pelikan, J., Gruber, H., de Cillia, R., and Mitten, R. (1990). "Wir sind alle unschuldige Täter!" *Diskurshistorische Studien zum Nachkriegsantisemitismus*. Frankfurt/Main: Suhrkamp.

14

The End of Antiracism

Paul Gilroy

The task of developing a radical critique of the moralistic excesses practiced in the name of "antiracism" is an urgent task today. The absurdities of antiracist orthodoxy have become a target of critique by the right (Honeyford, 1988; Lewis, 1988), and have formed a backdrop to the bitter debates that have surrounded the publication of *The Satanic Verses*. The dictatorial character of antiracism, particularly in local government, has itself become an important theme within the discourse of popular racism.

These assaults on the fundamental objective of antiracism and the attendant practice of multiculturalism in education, social work, and other municipal services have passed largely unanswered and vocal political support for antiracism has been hard to find. This is partly because the cadre of antiracism professionals which was created during the boom years of radicalism on the rates has lost its collective tongue: its political confidence has been drained away. There has been little support from independent black defense organizations and authentic community groups whose actions go far beyond the narrow categories in which antiracism can operate. Meanwhile, many of the ideological gains of Thatcherite conservatism have dovetailed neatly with the shibboleths of black nationalism – self-reliance and economic betterment through thrift, hard work, and individual disciplines. The impact of this resolutely conservative and often authoritarian political ideology can be felt right across the field of social and economic policy where an ideal-ized and homogenized vision of "The Black Community" is the object of a discourse that urges it to take care of its own problems and assume the major burden of managing its own public affairs. That is not a wholly negative development, but in the new atmosphere it creates antiracist initiatives can only appear to be a patronizing and unaccept-able form of special pleading. Apart from these important changes, spe-cialized antiracist work within the local state has been increasingly identified as an embarrassment by the Labour Party for whom political commitments to antiracism and multiculturalism are apparently a vote loser.

These developments have created political inertia in what was once an antiracist *movement*. The political forces which once made that move-ment move are now enveloped in a catastrophe that has two distinct dimensions. Firstly, there is a crisis of organizational forms. In the absence of mass mobilization around antiracist aims, it has been impos-sible to construct structures that could span the gulf between the elements of the movement which are outside the local state and the residues which are dedicated to remaining within it. This problem is also conveyed in the considerable rift that has opened up between those sec-tions which are ideologically committed to the Labour Party and those which are indifferent if not actively opposed to it. Secondly, and more importantly for what follows, there is a crisis of the political language, images, and cultural symbols which this movement needs in order to develop its self-consciousness and its political programme. This problem with the language of antiracism is acutely expressed by the lack of clarity that surrounds the term "antiracism" itself. It includes the diffi-culties involved in producing a coherent definition of racism (cf. Miles, 1989) as well as the tension that appears from the need to link an account of the racialization of social and political structures and dis-courses with an understanding of individual action and institutional behavior.

For all its antipathy to the new racism of the New Right, the com-monsense ideology of antiracism has also drifted towards a belief in the absolute nature of ethnic categories and a strong sense of the in-surmountable cultural and experiential divisions which, it is argued, are a feature of racial difference. I have argued elsewhere that these ideological failures have been compounded firstly by a reductive conception of culture and secondly by a culturalist conception of race and ethnic identity (Gilroy, 1987). This has led to a position where politically opposed groups are united by their view of race exclusively in terms of culture and identity rather than politics and history. Culture and identity are part of the story of racial sensibility but they do not exhaust that story. At a theoretical level "race" needs to be viewed much more contingently, as a precarious discursive construction. To note this does not, of course, imply that it is any less real or effective politically.

It is possible, then, that the idea of antiracism has been so discredited that it is no longer useful. It is certain that we have to devise ways to move beyond antiracism as it is presently constituted. I must emphasize that I am thinking not of antiracism as a political objective, or a goal which emerges alongside other issues from the daily struggles of black people, from the practice of community organizations and voluntary groups, even from the war of position which must be waged inside the institutions of the state. I am not talking about the ongoing struggle towards black liberation, for there is much more to the emancipation of blacks than opposition to racism. I am thinking instead of antiracism as a much more limited project defined simply, even simplistically, by the desire to do away with racism.

The antiracism I am criticizing trivializes the struggle against racism and isolates it from other political antagonisms – from the contradiction between capital and labor, from the battle between men and women. It suggests that racism can be eliminated on its own because it is readily extricable from everything else. Yet in Britain, "race" cannot be understood if it is falsely divorced from other political processes or grasped if it is reduced to the effect of these other relations. Antiracism in this sense is a phenomenon which grew out of the political openings created by the 1981 riots. In the years since then, antiracists have become a discrete and self-contained political formation. Their activism is now able to sustain itself independently of the lives, dreams, and aspirations of the majority of blacks from whose experience they derive their authority to speak.

To criticize antiracism necessitates understanding racism and being able to locate the politics of "race" from which it springs. Analyzing what racism does in our society means, first of all, claiming "race" and racism back from the margins of British politics. Racism is not epiphenomenal. Yet just as racism itself views black settlers as an external, alien visitation, antiracism can itself appear to be tangential to the main business of the political system as a whole.

The apparent marginality of race politics is often an effect of a fundamental tension inherent in antiracist organizing. A tension exists between those strands in antiracism which are primarily antifascist and those which work with a more extensive and complex sense of what racism is in contemporary Britain. This simplistic antifascist emphasis attempts to mobilize the memory of earlier encounters with the fascism of Hitler and Mussolini. The racists are a problem because they are descended from the brown- and black-shirted enemies of earlier days. To oppose them is a patriotic act; their own use of national flags and symbols is nothing more than a sham masking their terroristic inclinations.

The price of overidentifying the struggle against racism with the activities of these extremist groups and grouplets is that however much of a problem they may be in a particular area (and I am not denying the need to combat their organizing) they are exceptional. They exist on the fringes of political culture and for the foreseeable future are destined to have only tenuous and intermittent relationships with respectability. They are a threat but not the only threat. There is more to contemporary racism than the violence they perpetrate. We shall see in a moment that there are problems with the nationalism which goes hand in hand with this outlook.

A more productive starting point is provided by focusing on racism in the mainstream and seeing "race" and racism not as fringe questions but as a volatile presence at the very center of British politics, actively shaping and determining the history not simply of blacks, but of this country as a whole at a crucial stage in its development.

The importance of racism in contemporary politics betrays something about the nature of the painful transition this country, and the overdeveloped world as a whole, is undergoing. The almost mystical power of race and nation on the political stage conveys something about the changing nature of class relations, the growth of state authoritarianism, the eclipse of industrial production, the need to maintain popular support for militarism and exterminism and the end of the nation-state as a political form.

The highly charged politics of national identity that have been occasioned by these developments have been transposed into a higher, shriller key by current concern over the appeal of a wide pan-European disposition tailored to the new range of possibilities that flow from tighter political and economic integration of the European Economic Community. This potentially post-national European consciousness has racial referents of its own. It is however felt by elements of both left and right to pose a threat to the sovereignty and cultural integrity of the United Kingdom. Whether it is possible to generate a political discourse capable of articulating the distinctive needs and historical experiences of black Europeans remains to be seen. Though the rich legacy of an extensive black presence on this continent suggests that it may be possible for many commentators, the terms "black" and "European" remain categories which mutually exclude each other.

Racism and the Ideology of Antiracism

The first question I want to ask of contemporary antiracism is whether it does not collude in accepting that the problems of "race" and racism are somehow peripheral to the substance of political life. My view, which locates racism in the core of politics, contrasts sharply with what can be called the coat-of-paint theory of racism (Gilroy, 1987). This is not, in fact, a single theory but an approach which sees racism on the outside of social and political life – sometimes the unwanted blemish is the neo-fascists, sometimes it is immigration laws, other times it is the absence of equal opportunities – yet racism is always located on the surface of other things. It is an unfortunate excrescence on a democratic policy which is essentially sound and it follows from this that, with the right ideological tools and political elbow grease, racism can be dealt with once and for all, leaving the basic structures and relations of British economy and society essentially unchanged.

Though not always stated openly, the different permutations of this view underpin much of contemporary antiracism. I think there are particular problems posed by the fact that this type of theory is intrinsic to equal opportunities initiatives. The coat-of-paint approach is doubly mistaken because it suggests that fundamental issues of social justice, democracy, and political and economic power are not raised by the struggle against racial subordination.

Seeing racism as determining rather than determinate, at the center rather than in the margins, also means accepting that Britain's crisis is centrally and emphatically concerned with notions of race and national identity. It has been held together, punctuated and periodized by racial politics – immigration, the myriad problems of the riotous "inner city" and by the loony left. These terms are carefully coded and they are significant because they enable people to speak about race without mentioning the word. The frequent absence of any overt reference to "race" or hierarchy is an important characteristic of the new types of racism with which we have to deal. This kind of coded language has created further strategic problems for antiracism. It is easy to call Mr Honeyford, the Bradford headteacher, a racist and to organize against him on that basis but less easy to show precisely how and why this is the case.

We must be prepared to focus unsentimentally on antiracism's inability to respond to other distinctive aspects of these new forms of racism. Apart from the way that racial meanings are inferred rather than stated openly, these new forms are distinguished by the extent to which they identify race with the terms "culture" and "identity," terms which have their own resonance in antiracist orthodoxy. The new racism has a third important feature which enables it to slip through the rationalist approach of those who, with the best will in the world, reduce the problem of racism to the sum of power and prejudice. This is the closeness it suggests between the idea of race and the ideas of nation, nationality, and national belonging.

We increasingly face a racism which avoids being recognized as such because it is able to link "race" with nationhood, patriotism, and nationalism, a racism which has taken a necessary distance from crude ideas of biological inferiority and superiority and now seeks to present an imaginary definition of the nation as a unified *cultural* community. It constructs and defends an image of national culture – homogeneous in its whiteness yet precarious and perpetually vulnerable to attack from enemies within and without. The analogy of war and invasion is increasingly used to make sense of events.

This is racism that answers the social and political turbulence of crisis and crisis management by the recovery of national greatness *in the imagination*. Its dreamlike construction of our sceptered isle as an ethnically purified one provides a special comfort against the ravages of decline. It has been a key component in the ideological and political processes which have put the "Great" back in Britain. The symbolic restoration of greatness has been achieved in part through the actual expulsion of blacks and the fragmentation of their households, which is never far from page three in the tabloids.

The shock of decline has induced Britons to ask themselves a question first posed by Enoch Powell: What kind of people are we? The emphasis on culture and the attendant imagery of the nation composed of symmetrical family units contributes to a metaphysics of Britishness which has acquired racial referents. I can illustrate this by referring to a poem which was part of a racist leaflet circulated in Haringey during the 1987 election. It was illustrated by a picture of Bernie Grant, the black Labour candidate, with the hairy body of a gorilla. It read:

> Swing along with Bernie, it's the very natural thing
> He's been doing it for centuries and now he thinks he's king
> He's got a little empire and he doesn't give a jot
> But then the British are a bloody tolerant lot
> They'll let him swing and holler hetero-homo-gay
> And then just up and shoot him in the good old British way.

These lines signify a powerful appropriation of the rights and liberties of the freeborn Briton so beloved of the new left. The rhyme's historical references demonstrate how completely blackness and Britishness have been made into mutually exclusive categories, incompatible identities. The problems which Bernie represents are most clearly visible against the patterned backdrop of the Union Jack. The picture of him as a gorilla was necessary on the leaflet because the words make no overt mention of his race. The crime which justifies lynching him is a form of treason, not racial inferiority.

This culturalist variety of racism and the cultural theory of "race" difference linked to it hold that the family supplies the units, the building blocks from which the national community is constructed. This puts black women directly in the firing line: firstly, because they are seen as playing a key role in reproducing the alien culture, and, secondly, because their fertility is identified as excessive and therefore threatening.

It has become commonplace to observe that the precious yet precarious Churchillian, stiff-upper-lip culture which only materializes in the midst of national adversity – underneath the arches, down in the air-raid shelters where Britannia enjoyed her finest hours – is something from which blacks are excluded. The means of their exclusion is identified in the colorful deviancy which is produced by their pathological family forms. Pathology and deviancy are the qualities which define distinct and insubordinate black cultures. This applies in different yet parallel ways to both Afro-Caribbean and Asian populations, whose criminality violates the law – the supreme achievement of British civilization.

Deviancy, so the argument runs, has its roots in generational conflict which appears along cultural lines. The antisocial activities of the "Holy Smokes" in west London's Asian gangland are, in a sense, parallel to the barbarous misdemeanors of the Afro-Caribbean Yardies on London's proliferating frontlines. The "racial" criminal subcultures of each group are seen to wantonly violate the laws and customs which express the civilization of the national community and in so doing provide powerful symbols which express black difference as a whole. To be a street criminal is therefore to fulfill cultural destiny.

For a long while, the crime question provided the principal means to underscore the *cultural* concerns of this new nationalist racism. Its dominance helped us to understand where the new racism began in Powell's bloody nightmare of the aged white woman pursued through the streets by black children. However, crime has been displaced recently at the center of race politics by another issue which points equally effectively to the incompatibility of different cultures supposedly sealed off from one another forever along ethnic lines. This too used images of the black child to make its point – the cultural sins of the fathers will be visited on their children. Where once it was the main streets of the decaying inner city which hosted the most fearsome encounter between Britons and their most improbable and intimidating other – black youth – now it is the classrooms and staffrooms of the inner-city school which frame the same conflict and provide the most potent terms with which to make sense of racial difference.

The publication of *Antiracism: An Assault on Education and Value*, the book of essays edited by Frank Palmer (1987), confirmed the fact that the school has become the principal element in the ideology with which the new right have sought to attack antiracism. While it is important not to be mesmerized by the gains and strengths of the new right – as many radicals are – it is essential to understand *why* their burgeoning anti-antiracism has focused upon education. From their perspective, schools are repositories of the authentic national culture which they transmit between generations. They mediate the relation of the national community to its youthful subjects – future citizens.

Decaying school buildings provide a ready image for the nation in microcosm. The hard-fought changes which antiracists and multiculturalists have wrought on the curriculum mirror the bastardization of genuine British culture. Antiracism initiatives that literally denigrate educational standards are identified as an assault on the traditional virtues of British education. This cultural conflict is a means through which power is transposed and whites become a voiceless ethnic minority oppressed by totalitarian local authority antiracism. The racists are redefined as the black racists and Mr Honeyford, dogged defender of freedom, is invited to Number 10 Downing Street for consultation. In the *Independent* of July 23, 1987 Baroness Cox argues that black parents are motivated to demand their own separate schools not by dissatisfaction or frustration with the way that racism is institutionalized in state education, but because they want "a good old-fashioned British education" for their children.

I think we have to recognize that the effect of these images and the conflicts from which they spring in Brent or Bradford has been to call into question any antiracist or multicultural project in education and indeed the idea of antiracism in general. The new racism's stress on cultural difference and its absolutist conception of ethnicity have other significant effects. It is now not only a feature of the relationship between blacks and whites. It enters directly into the political relations between the different groups which, in negotiating with each other, promise to construct a unified black community from their diversity.

The potentially unifying effects of their different but complementary experiences of racism are dismissed, while the inclusive and openly politicized definitions of "race" which were a notable feature of the late 1970s have been fragmented into their ethnic components, first into Afro-Caribbean and Asian and then into Pakistani, Bangladeshi, Bajan, Jamaican, and Guyanese in a spiral. This boiling down of groups into their respective ethnic essences is clearly congruent with the nationalist concerns of the right, but it is also sanctioned by the antiracist orthodoxy of the left and by many voices from within the black communities themselves which have needed no prompting to develop their own fascination with ethnic differences and thus reduce political definitions of "race" to a narcissistic celebration of culture and identity.

I have argued that antiracism has been unable to deal with the new forms in which racism has developed. In particular, it has been incapable of showing how British cultural nationalism becomes a language of race. The power of this patriotic political language is there for all to behold. It puts the vital populist force into those processes for which "Thatcherism" serves as a reasonable shorthand term. However, it does not appear to be the exclusive property of the right. Its magical populist appeal will tempt political pragmatists of all hues. I am afraid there are segments of the left who are especially envious of its capacity to animate the groups which were once regarded as their traditional supporters. Unfortunately, Labour's blustering "patriotism of freedom and fairness," like its recent attempts to "take crime seriously," is no less saturated with racial connotations than the Conservative versions of these arguments. This is not to say that the right and left are necessarily the same, but rather that they converge at key points and share an understanding of what is involved in the politics of "race."

The Bernie poem seamlessly knitted together images invoking empire, sovereignty, and sexuality, with a concluding exhortation to violence. There is nothing about this combination of themes which marks it out as the exclusive preserve of the right. It is another example of how the racism which ties national culture to ethnic essences, which sees custom, law, and constitution, schools and courts of justice beset by corrosive alien forces, has moved beyond the grasp of the old left/right distinction.

This populist character of the new racism works across class lines as well as within them. It can link together disparate and formally opposed groups, leading them to discover the morbid pleasures of seeing themselves as "one nation." It transmits the idea of the British people as the *white people*. While Labour seeks to simply snatch the language of one nation from the Tories, the danger here can only grow and it is compounded because it is by no means clear how far a reconstituted and emphatically "un-loony" socialism may go in negotiating its own language of toughness on immigration and nationality, even perhaps on humane socialist repatriation. [. . .]

Racial Justice and Civil Society

I think it is important to concede that what we can loosely call the anti-antiracist position associated with sections of the new right and with populist politics has fed on crucial ambiguities in antiracist and multi-cultural initiatives.

The definition of racism as the sum of prejudice and power can be used to illustrate these problems. Power is a relation between social groups, not a possession to be worn like a garment or flaunted like an antiracist badge. Prejudice suggests conscious action if not actual choice. Is this an appropriate formula? The most elementary lessons involved in studying ideas and consciousness seem to have been forgotten. Racism, like capitalism as a whole, rests on the mystification of social relations – the necessary illusions that secure the order of public authority.

There are other aspects of what has become a multiculturalist or antiracist orthodoxy which can be shown to replicate in many ways the *volkish* new right sense of the relationship between race, nation, and culture – kin blood and ethnic identity. I have already mentioned how the left and right distinction has begun to evaporate as formally opposed groups have come to share a sense of what race is. These problems are even more severe when elements of the black community have themselves endorsed this understanding. Here I am thinking of the definition of race exclusively in terms of culture and identity which ties certain strands in antiracism to the position of some of the new right ideologues.

By emphasizing this convergence I am not saying that culture and identity are unimportant, but challenging the routine reduction of race to them alone which obscures the inherently political character of the term. The way in which culture is itself understood provides the key to grasping the extraordinary convergence between left and right, antiracist and avowedly racist over precisely what race and racism add up to.

At the end of the day, an absolute commitment to cultural insiderism is as bad as an absolute commitment to biological insiderism. I think we need to be theoretically and politically clear that no single culture is hermetically sealed off from others. There can be no neat and tidy pluralistic separation of racial groups in this country. It is time to dispute with those positions which, when taken to their conclusions, say "there is no possibility of shared history and no human empathy." We must beware of the use of ethnicity to wrap a spurious cloak of legitimacy around the speaker who invokes it. Culture, even the culture which defines the groups we know as races, is never fixed, finished, or final. It is fluid, it is actively and continually made and remade. In our multicultural schools the sound of the steel pan may evoke Caribbean ethnicity, tradition, and authenticity, yet they originate in the oil drums of the Standard Oil Company rather than the mysterious knowledge of ancient African griots.

These theoretical problems are most visible and at their most intractable in the area of fostering and adoption policy. Here, the inflated rhetoric and culturalist orthodoxies of antiracism have borne some peculiar fruit. The critique of the pathological views of black family life that were so prevalent in Social Services during the late 1970s and early 1980s has led directly to an extraordinary idealization of black family forms. Antiracist orthodoxy now sees them as the only effective repositories of authentic black culture and as a guaranteed means to transmit all the essential skills that black children will need if they are to "survive" in a racist society without psychological damage. "Same-race" adoption and fostering for "minority ethnics" is presented as an unchallenged and seemingly unchallengeable benefit for all concerned. It is hotly defended with the same fervor that denounces white demands for "same-race" schooling as a repellent manifestation of racism. What is most alarming about this is not its inappropriate survivalist tone, the crudity with which racial identity is conceived, nor even the sad inability to see beyond the conservation of racial identities to possibility of their transcendence. It is the extraordinary manner in which the pathological imagery has simply been inverted so that it forms the basis of a pastoral view which asserts the strength and durability of black family life and, in present circumstances, retreats from confronting the difficult issues which result in black children arriving in care in the first place. The contents of the racist pathology and the material circumstances to which it can be made to correspond are thus left untouched. The tentacles of racism are everywhere, except in the safe haven which a nurturing black family provides for delicate, fledgling racial identities.

The Forces of Antiracism

I want to turn now to the forces which have grouped around the antiracist project and to the question of class. There is a problem here in that much of the certainty and confidence with which the term has been used have collapsed along with the secure lifetime employment which characterized industrial capitalism. Today, for example, I think it means next to nothing to simply state that blacks are working class when we are likely to be unemployed and may not recognize our experience and history in those areas of political life where an appeal to class is most prominent. Class politics do not, in any case, enjoy a monopoly of political radicalism. Obviously people still belong to classes, but belief in the decisive universal agency of the dwindling proletariat is something which must be dismissed as an idealist fantasy. Class is an indispensable instrument in analyzing capitalism, but it contains no ready-made plan for its overcoming. We must learn to live without a theological faith in the working class as either a revolutionary or an antiracist agent.

There is a major issue here, but I want to note it and move on to consider a different aspect of how race and class intersect. A more significant task for class analysis is comprehending the emergence of a proto-middle-class grouping narrowly constituted around the toeholds which some blacks have been able to acquire in the professions, mostly those related directly to the welfare state itself – social work, teaching, and now antiracist bureaucracies. A Marxist writer would probably identify this group as the first stirrings of a black petite bourgeoisie. I do not think this grouping or grouplet is yet a class either in itself or for itself and it may never become one. For one thing it is too small; for another it is too directly dependent on the state institutions which pay its wages. But it is with this group that antiracism can be most readily identified and we need to examine it on its own terms and in its relationship to other more easily identifiable class groupings. It is obviously in an uncomfortably contradictory position – squeezed between the expectations of the bureaucracies on which it relies and its political affiliation to the struggles of the mass of blacks which it is called upon to mediate, translate, and sometimes police. It is caught between the demands of bureaucratic professionalism and the emotive pull of ethnic identification.

This not-yet-class plays a key role in organizing the political forces of antiracism centered on local authorities. It involves three opposed tendencies which have evolved an uneasy symbiosis. They are not wholly discrete. The campaign for autonomous Black Sections in the Labour Party, for example, involves elements of each of them. First, there is the equal opportunities strand, which has its roots in the social democratic "race" interventions of the 1960s. It has also borrowed heavily from the experience of Afro-America's shift into electoral politics – the black mayors' movement and so on. This tendency is proud and secure in its bureaucratic status and it identifies equality (antiracism) with efficiency and good management practice. Policy questions dominate political ones and antiracism emerges from the production of general blueprints which can be universally applied. Of course, equal opportunities afford an important interface between struggles around race and gender and they can be a locus of possible alliances. However, in the context of local authorities these initiatives can also host a competition between different political forces over which of them is going to take immediate priority. We should therefore be wary of collapsing antiracism let alone black emancipation into equal opportunities.

The second tendency is what used to be called Black nationalism but is now fragmented into multiple varieties, each with its own claim to ethnic particularity. It is now emphatically culturalist rather than political, each ethnic or national group arguing for cultural relativism in the strongest form. Very often, these mutually unintelligible and exclusive ethnic cultures just happen to be the same as the groups which common sense tells us are "races." Perversely and ironically, this tendency has happily coexisted with old-style Labourism for which ethnic absolutism and cultural relativism have provided on obvious means to rationalize and balance its funding practices.

The third tendency is the most complex. It unendingly reiterates the idea that class is race, race is class and is both black and white. Its spokespeople have sought refuge from interethnic conflict in some of the more anachronistic formulae of socialist class politics. For them class is the thing which will unify the diverse and end the polyphonic ethnobabble in the new municipal Tower of Babel. Class remains synonymous with organized labor, regardless of the fact that in the context of local authorities organized labor is not always very radical. This tendency overlooks the role which the bureaucratic hierarchy plays in coercing the actually existing working class into antirace line. So far its class-based line has been almost exclusively animated by a critique of race awareness training – a practical strategy which has been thrown up in the grating between the first two tendencies. This is an important issue, but it is nonetheless the most gestural and superficial aspect of deeper problems, namely culturalism and ethnic absolutism. This tendency has mistaken the particular for the general – racism awareness training is a symptom, not a cause in its own right.

Apart from their conceit, these diverse yet interdependent groupings share a statist conception of antiracism. In making the local state the main vehicle for advancing antiracist politics they have actively confused and confounded the black community's capacity for autonomous self-organization. Here, we must make an assessment of the politics of funding community organizations and the dependency which that creates.

There is every likelihood that the versions of antiracism I have criticized will wither away as the local state structures on which they have relied are destroyed by the conflict with central government. But antiracist activities encapsulate one final problem which may outlive them. This is the disastrous way in which they have trivialized the rich complexity of black life by reducing it to nothing more than a response to racism. More than any other issue this operation reveals the extent of the antiracists' conceptual trading with the racists and the results of embracing their culturalist assumptions. Seeing in black life nothing more than an answer to racism means moving on to the ideological circuit which makes us visible in two complementary roles – the problem and the victim.

Antiracism seems very comfortable with this idea of blacks as victims. I remember one simplistic piece of Greater London Council propaganda which said "We are all either the victims or the perpetrators of racism." Why should this be so? Suffering confers no virtue on the victim; yesterday's victims are tomorrow's executioners. I propose that we reject the central image of ourselves as victims and install instead an alternative conception which sees us as an active force working in many different ways for our freedom from racial subordination. The plural is important here for there can be no single or homogeneous strategy against racism because racism itself is never homogeneous. It varies, it changes, and it is *always* uneven. The recent history of our struggles has shown how people can shrink the world to the size of their communities and act politically on that basis, expressing their dissent in the symbolism of disorderly protest while demanding control over their immediate conditions. However you feel about the useless violence of these eruptions, it was the riotous protests of 1981 which created the space in which political antiracism became on option.

We must accept that for the years immediately ahead these struggles will be essentially defensive and probably unable to make the transition to more stable, totalizing forms of politics. But the challenge we face is the task of linking these immediate local concerns together across the international division of labor, transcending national boundaries, turning our back on the state, and using all the means at our disposal to build a radical, democratic movement of civil society. This kind of activity could be called the micro-politics of race, though in practice, as where we align ourselves with the struggles of our brothers and sisters in South Africa, it is more likely to prove the micro-politics of race's overcoming.

References

Gilroy, P. (1987). *There Ain't No Black in the Union Jack*. London: Hutchinson.
Honeyford, R. (1988). *Integration or Disintegration*. London: Claridge Press.
Lewis, R. (1988). *Anti-Racism: A Mania Exposed*. London: Quartet.
Miles, R. (1989). *Racism*. London: Routledge & Kegan Paul.
Palmer, F. (1987). *Antiracism: An Assault on Education and Value*. London: Sherwood Press.

15

Black Matters

Toni Morrison

These chapters put forth an argument for extending the study of American literature into what I hope will be a wider landscape. I want to draw a map, so to speak, of a critical geography and use that map to open as much space for discovery, intellectual adventure, and close exploration as did the original charting of the New World – without the mandate for conquest. I intend to outline an attractive, fruitful, and provocative critical project, unencumbered by dreams of subversion or rallying gestures at fortress walls.

I would like it to be clear at the outset that I do not bring to these matters solely or even principally the tools of a literary critic. As a reader (before becoming a writer) I read as I had been taught to do. But books revealed themselves rather differently to me as a writer. In that capacity I have to place enormous trust in my ability to imagine others and my willingness to project consciously into the danger zones such others may represent for me. I am drawn to the ways all writers do this: the way Homer renders a heart-eating cyclops so that our hearts are wrenched with pity; the way Dostoevsky compels intimacy with Svidrigailov and Prince Myshkin. I am in awe of the authority of Faulkner's Benjy, James's Maisie, Flaubert's Emma, Melville's Pip, Mary Shelley's Frankenstein – each of us can extend the list.

I am interested in what prompts and makes possible this process of entering what one is estranged from – and in what disables the foray, for purposes of fiction, into corners of the consciousness held off and away from the reach of the writer's imagination. My work requires me to think about how free I can be as an African-American women writer in my genderized, sexualized, wholly racialized world. To think about (and wrestle with) the full implications of my situation leads me to consider what happens when other writers work in a highly and historically racialized society. For them, as for me, imagining is not merely looking or looking at; nor is it taking oneself intact into the other. It is, for the purposes of the work, *becoming*.

My project rises from delight, not disappointment. It rises from what I know about the ways writers transform aspects of their social grounding into aspects of language, and the ways they tell other stories, fight secret wars, limn out all sorts of debates blanketed in their text. And rises from my certainty that writers always know, at some level, that they do this.

For some time now I have been thinking about the validity or vulnerability of a certain set of assumptions conventionally accepted among literary historians and critics and circulated as "knowledge." This knowledge holds that traditional, canonical American literature is free of, uninformed, and unshaped by the four-hundred-year-old presence of, first, Africans and then African-Americans in the United States. It assumes that this presence – which shaped the body politic, the Constitution, and the entire history of the culture – has had no significant place or consequence in the origin and development of that culture's literature. Moreover, such knowledge assumes that the characteristics of our national literature emanate from a particular "Americanness" that is separate from and unaccountable to this presence. There seems to be a more or less tacit agreement among literary scholars that, because American literature has been clearly the preserve of white male views, genius, and power, those views, genius, and power are without relationship to and removed from the overwhelming presence of black people in the United States. This agreement is made about a population that preceded every American writer of renown and was, I have come to believe, one of the most furtively radical impinging forces on the country's literature. The contemplation of this black presence is central to any understanding of our national literature and should not be permitted to hover at the margins of the literary imagination.

These speculations have led me to wonder whether the major and championed characteristics of our national literature – individualism, masculinity, social engagement versus historical isolation; acute and ambiguous moral problematics; the thematics of innocence coupled with an obsession with figurations of death and hell – are not in fact responses to a dark, abiding, signing Africanist presence. It has occurred to me that the very manner by which American literature distinguishes itself as a coherent entity exists because of this unsettled and unsettling population. Just as the formation of the nation necessitated coded language and purposeful restriction to deal with the racial disingenuousness and moral frailty at its heart, so too did the literature, whose founding characteristics extend into the twentieth century, reproduce the necessity for codes and restriction. Through significant and underscored omissions, startling contradictions, heavily nuanced conflicts, through the way writers peopled their work with the signs and bodies of this presence – one can see that a real or fabricated Africanist presence was crucial to their sense of Americanness. And it shows.

My curiosity about the origins and literary uses of this carefully observed, and carefully invented, Africanist presence has become an informal study of what I call American Africanism. It is an investigation into the ways in which a nonwhite, Africanlike (or Africanist) presence or persona was constructed in the United States, and the imaginative uses this fabricated presence served. I am using the term "Africanism" not to suggest the larger body of knowledge on Africa that the philosopher Valentine Mudimbe means by the term "Africanism," nor to suggest the varieties and complexities of African people and their descendants who have inhabited this country. Rather I use it as a term for the denotative and connotative blackness that African peoples have come to signify, as well as the entire range of views, assumptions, readings, and misreadings that accompany Eurocentric learning about these people. As a trope, little restraint has been attached to its uses. As a disabling virus within literary discourse, Africanism has become, in the Eurocentric tradition that American education favors, both a way of talking about and a way of policing matters of class, sexual license, and repression, formations and exercises of power, and meditations on ethics and accountability. Through the simple expedient of demonizing and reifying the range of color on a palette, American Africanism makes it possible to say and not say, to inscribe and erase, to escape and engage, to act out and act on, to historicize and render timeless. It provides a way of contemplating chaos and civilization, desire and fear, and a mechanism for testing the problems and blessings of freedom.

The United States, of course, is not unique in the construction of Africanism. South America, England, France, Germany, Spain – the cultures of all these countries have participated in and contributed to some aspect of an "invented Africa." None has been able to persuade itself for long that criteria and knowledge could emerge outside the categories of domination. Among Europeans and the Europeanized, this shared process of exclusion – of assigning designation and value – has led to the popular and academic notion that racism is a "natural," if irritating, phenomenon. The literature of almost all these countries, however, is now subject to sustained critiques of its racialized discourse. The United States is a curious exception, even though it stands out as being the oldest democracy in which a black population accompanied (if one can use that word) and in many cases preceded the white settlers. Here in that nexus, with its particular formulations, and in the absence of real knowledge or open-minded inquiry about Africans and African-Americans, under the pressures of ideological and imperialistic rationales for subjugation, an American brand of Africanism emerged: strongly urged, thoroughly serviceable, companionably ego-reinforcing, and pervasive. For excellent reasons of state – because European sources of cultural hegemony were dispersed but not yet valorized in the new country – the process of organizing American coherence through a distancing Africanism became the operative mode of a new cultural hegemony.

These remarks should not be interpreted as simply an effort to move the gaze of African-American studies to a different site. I do not want to alter one hierarchy in order to institute another. It is true that I do not want to encourage those totalizing approaches to African-American scholarship which have no drive other than the exchange of dominations – dominant Eurocentric scholarship *replaced* by dominant Afrocentric scholarship. More interesting is what makes intellectual domination possible; how knowledge is transformed from invasion and conquest to revelation and choice; what ignites and informs the literary imagination, and what forces help establish the parameters of criticism.

Above all I am interested in how agendas in criticism have disguised themselves and, in so doing, impoverished the literature it studies. Criticism as a form of knowledge is capable of robbing literature not only of its own implicit and explicit ideology but of its ideas as well; it can dismiss the difficult, arduous work writers do to make an art that becomes and remains part of and significant within a human landscape. It is important to see how inextricable Africanism is or ought to be from the deliberations of literary criticism and the wanton, elaborate strategies undertaken to erase its presence from view.

What Africanism became for, and how it functioned in, the literary imagination is of paramount interest because it may be possible to discover, through a close look at literary "blackness," the nature – even the cause – of literary "whiteness." What is it *for?* What parts do the invention and development of whiteness play in the construction of what is loosely described as "American"? If such an inquiry ever comes to maturity, it may provide access to a deeper reading of American literature – a reading not completely available now, not least, I suspect, because of the studied indifference of most literary criticism to these matters.

One likely reason for the paucity of critical material on this large and compelling subject is that, in matters of race, silence and evasion have historically ruled literary discourse. Evasion has fostered another, substitute language in which the issues are encoded, foreclosing open debate. The situation is aggravated by the tremor that breaks into discourse on race. It is further complicated by the fact that the habit of ignoring race is understood to be a graceful, even generous, liberal gesture. To notice is to recognize an already discredited difference. To enforce its invisibility through silence is to allow the black body a shadowless participation in the dominant cultural body. According to this logic, every well-bred instinct argues *against noticing* and forecloses adult discourse. It is just this concept of literary and scholarly moeurs (which functions smoothly in literary criticism, but neither makes nor receives credible claims in other disciplines) that has terminated the shelf life of some once extremely well-regarded American authors and blocked access to remarkable insights in their works.

These moeurs are delicate things, however, which must be given some thought before they are abandoned. Not observing such niceties can lead to startling displays of scholarly lapses in objectivity. In 1936 an American scholar investigating the use of Negro so-called dialect in the works of Edgar Allan Poe (a short article clearly proud of its racial equanimity) opens this way: "Despite the fact that he grew up largely in the south and spent some of his most fruitful years in Richmond and Baltimore, Poe has little to say about the darky."[1]

Although I know this sentence represents the polite parlance of the day, that "darky" was understood to be a term more acceptable than "nigger," the grimace I made upon reading it was followed by an alarmed distrust of the scholar's abilities. If it seems unfair to reach back to the 1930s for samples of the kind of lapse that can occur when certain manners of polite repression are waived, let me assure you equally egregious representations of the phenomenon are still common.

Another reason for this quite ornamental vacuum in literary discourse on the presence and influence of Africanist peoples in American criticism is the pattern of thinking about racialism in terms of its consequences on the victim – of always defining it assymetrically from the perspective of its impact on the object of racist policy and attitudes. A good deal of time and intelligence has been invested in the exposure of racism and the horrific results on its objects. There are constant, if erratic, liberalizing efforts to legislate these matters. There are also powerful and persuasive attempts to analyze the origin and fabrication of racism itself, contesting the assumption that it is an inevitable, permanent, and eternal part of all social landscapes. I do not wish to disparage these inquiries. It is precisely because of them that any progress at all has been accomplished in matters of racial discourse. But that well-established study should be joined with another, equally important one: the impact of racism on those who perpetuate it. It seems both poignant and striking how avoided and unanalyzed is the effect of racist inflection on the subject. What I propose here is to examine the impact of notions of racial hierarchy, racial exclusion, and racial vulnerability and availability on nonblacks who held, resisted, explored, or altered those notions. The scholarship that looks into the mind, imagination, and behavior of slaves is valuable. But equally valuable is a serious intellectual effort to see what racial ideology does to the mind, imagination, and behavior of masters.

Historians have approached these areas, as have social scientists, anthropologists, psychiatrists, and some students of comparative literature. Literary scholars have begun to pose these questions of various national literatures. Urgently needed is the same kind of attention paid to the literature of the western country that has one of the most resilient Africanist populations in the world – a population that has always had a curiously intimate and unhingingly separate existence within the dominant one. When matters of race are located and called attention to in American literature, critical response has tended to be on the order of a humanistic nostrum – or a dismissal mandated by the label "political." Excising the political from the life of the mind is a sacrifice that has proven costly. I think of this erasure as a kind of trembling hypochondria always curing itself with unnecessary surgery. A criticism that needs to insist that literature is not only "universal" but also "race-free" risks lobotomizing that literature, and diminishes both the art and the artist.

I am vulnerable to the inference here that my inquiry has vested interests; that because I am an African-American and a writer I stand to benefit in ways not limited to intellectual fulfillment from this line of questioning. I will have to risk the accusation because the point is too important: for both black and white American writers, in a wholly racialized society, there is no escape from racially inflected language, and the work writers do to unhobble the imagination from the demands of that language is complicated, interesting, and definitive.

Like thousands of avid but nonacademic readers, some powerful literary critics in the United States have never read, and are proud to say so, *any* African-American text. It seems to have done them no harm, presented them with no discernible limitations in the scope of their work or influence. I suspect, with much evidence to support the suspicion, that they will continue to flourish without any knowledge whatsoever of African-American literature. What is fascinating, however, is to observe how their lavish exploration of literature manages *not* to see meaning in the thunderous, theatrical presence of black surrogacy – an informing, stabilizing, and disturbing element – in the literature they do study. It is interesting, not surprising, that the arbiters of critical power in American literature seem to take pleasure in, indeed relish, their ignorance of African-American texts. What is surprising is that their refusal to read black texts – a refusal that makes no disturbance in their intellectual life – repeats itself when they reread the traditional, established works of literature worthy of their attention.

It is possible, for example, to read Henry James scholarship exhaustively and never arrive at a nodding mention, much less a satisfactory treatment, of the black woman who lubricates the turn of the plot and becomes the agency of moral choice and meaning in *What Maisie Knew*. Never are we invited to a reading of "The Beast in the Jungle" in which that figuration is followed to what seems to me its logical conclusion. It is hard to think of any aspect of Gertrude Stein's *Three Lives* that has not been covered, except the exploratory and explanatory uses to which she puts the black woman who holds center stage in that work. The urgency and anxiety in Willa Cather's rendering of black characters are liable to be missed entirely; no mention is made of the problem that race causes in the technique and the credibility of her last novel, *Sapphira and the Slave Girl*. These critics see no excitement or meaning in the tropes of darkness, sexuality, and desire in Ernest Hemingway or in his cast of black men. They see no connection between God's grace and Africanist "othering" in Flannery O'Connor. With few exceptions, Faulkner criticism collapses the major themes of that writer into discursive "mythologies" and treats the later works – whose focus is race and class – as minor, superficial, marked by decline.

An instructive parallel to this willed scholarly indifference is the centuries-long, hysterical blindness to feminist discourse and the way in which women and women's issues were read (or unread). Blatant sexist readings are on the decline, and where they still exist they have little effect because of the successful appropriation by women of their own discourse.

National literatures, like writers, get along the best way they can, and with what they can. Yet they do seem to end up describing and inscribing what is really on the national mind. For the most part, the literature of the United States has taken as its concern the architecture of a *new white man*. If I am disenchanted by the indifference of literary criticism toward examining the range of that concern, I do have a lasting resort: the writers themselves.

Writers are among the most sensitive, the most intellectually anarchic, most representative, most probing of artists. The ability of writers to imagine what is not the self, to familiarize the strange and mystify the familiar, is the test of their power. The languages they use and the social and historical context in which these languages signify are indirect and direct revelations of that power and its limitations. So it is to them, the creators of American literature, that I look for clarification about the invention and effect of Africanism in the United States.

My early assumptions as a reader were that black people signified little or nothing in the imagination of white American writers. Other than as the objects of an occasional bout of jungle fever, other than to provide local color or to lend some touch of verisimilitude or to supply a needed moral gesture, humor, or bit of pathos, blacks made no appearance at all. This was a reflection, I thought, of the marginal impact that blacks had on the lives of the characters in the work as well as the creative imagination of the author. To imagine or write otherwise, to situate black people throughout the pages and scenes of a book like some government quota, would be ludicrous and dishonest.

But then I stopped reading as a reader and began to read as a writer. Living in a racially articulated and predicated world, I could not be alone in reacting to this aspect of the American cultural and historical condition. I began to see how the literature I revered, the literature I loathed, behaved in its encounter with racial ideology. American literature could not help being shaped by that encounter. Yes, I wanted to identify those moments when American literature was complicit in the fabrication of racism, but equally important, I wanted to see when literature exploded and undermined it. Still, those were minor concerns. Much more important was to contemplate how Africanist personae, narrative, and idiom moved and enriched the text in self-conscious ways, to consider what the engagement meant for the work of the writer's imagination.

How does literary utterance arrange itself when it tries to imagine an Africanist other? What are the signs, the codes, the literary strategies designed to accommodate this encounter? What does the inclusion of Africans or African-Americans do to and for the work? As a reader my assumption had always been that nothing "happens": Africans and their descendants were not, in any sense that matters, *there*; and when they were there, they were decorative – displays of the agile writer's technical expertise. I assumed that since the author was not black, the appearance of Africanist characters or narrative or idiom in a work could never be *about* anything other than the "normal," unracialized, illusory white world that provided the fictional backdrop. Certainly no American text of the sort I am discussing was ever written *for* black people – no more than *Uncle Tom's Cabin* was written for Uncle Tom to read or be persuaded by. As a writer reading, I came to realize the obvious: the subject of the dream is the dreamer. The fabrication of an Africanist persona is reflexive; an extraordinary meditation on the self; a powerful exploration of the fears and desires that reside in the writerly conscious. It is an astonishing revelation of longing, of terror, of perplexity, of shame, of magnanimity. It requires hard work *not* to see this.

It is as if I had been looking at a fishbowl – the glide and flick of the golden scales, the green tip, the bolt of white careening back from the gills; the castles at the bottom, surrounded by pebbles and tiny, intricate fronds of green; the barely disturbed water, the flecks of waste and food, the tranquil bubbles traveling to the surface – and suddenly I saw the bowl, the structure that transparently (and invisibly) permits the ordered life it contains to exist in the larger world. In other words, I began to rely on my knowledge of how books get written, how language arrives; my sense of how and why writers abandon or take on certain aspects of their project. I began to rely on my understanding of what the linguistic struggle requires of writers and what they make of the surprise that is the inevitable concomitant of the act of creation. What became transparent were the self-evident ways that Americans choose to talk about themselves through and within a sometimes allegorical, sometimes metaphorical, but always choked representation of an Africanist presence.

I have made much here of a kind of willful critical blindness – a blindness that, if it had not existed, could have made these insights part of our routine literary heritage. Habit, manners, and political agenda have contributed to this refusal of critical insight. A case in point is Willa Cather's *Sapphira and the Slave Girl*, a text that has been virtually jettisoned from the body of American literature by critical consensus.

References to this novel in much Cather scholarship are apologetic, dismissive, even cutting in their brief documentation of its flaws – of which there are a sufficient number. What remains less acknowledged is the source of its flaws and the conceptual problems that the book both poses and represents. Simply to assert the failure of Cather's gifts, the exhaustion of her perception, the narrowing of her canvas, evades the obligation to look carefully at what might have caused the book to fail – if "failure" is an intelligent term to apply to any fiction. (It is as if the realms of fiction and reality were divided by a line that, when maintained, offers the possibility of winning but, when crossed, signals the inevitability of losing.)

I suspect that the "problem" of *Sapphira and the Slave Girl* is not that it has a weaker vision or is the work of a weaker mind. The problem is trying to come to terms critically and artistically with the novel's concerns: the power and license of a white slave mistress over her female slaves. How can that *content* be subsumed by some other meaning? How can the story of a white mistress be severed from a consideration of race and the violence entailed in the story's premise?

If *Sapphira and the Slave Girl* neither pleases nor engages us, it may be enlightening to discover why. It is as if this last book – this troublesome, quietly dismissed novel, very important to Cather – is not only about a fugitive but is itself a fugitive from its author's literary estate. It is also a book that describes and inscribes its narrative's own fugitive flight from itself.

Our first hint of this flight appears in the title, *Sapphira and the Slave Girl*. The girl referred to is named Nancy. To have called the book "Sapphira and Nancy" would have lured Cather into dangerous deep water. Such a title would have clarified and drawn attention immediately to what the novel obscures even as it makes a valiant effort at honest engagement: the sycophancy of white identity. The story, briefly, is this.

Sapphira Colbert, an invalid confined to her chair and dependent on slaves for the most intimate services, has persuaded herself that her husband is having or aching to have a liaison with Nancy, the pubescent daughter of her most devoted female slave. It is clear from the beginning that Mistress Colbert is in error: Nancy is pure to the point of vapidity; Master Colbert is a man of modest habits, ambition, and imagination.

Sapphira's suspicions, fed by her feverish imagination and by her leisure to have them, grow and luxuriate unbearably. She forms a plan. She will invite a malleable lecherous nephew, Martin, to visit and let his nature run its course: Nancy will be seduced. The purpose of arranging the rape of her young servant is to reclaim, for purposes not made clear, the full attentions of her husband.

Interference with these plans comes from Sapphira's daughter, Rachel, estranged from her mother primarily for her abolitionist views but also, we are led to believe, because Sapphira does not tolerate opposition. It is Rachel who manages to effect Nancy's escape to the north and freedom, with the timid help of her father, Mr Colbert. A reconciliation of all of the white characters takes place when the daughter loses one of her children to diphtheria and is blessed with the recuperation of the other. The reconciliation of the two key black characters is rendered in a postscript in which many years later Nancy returns to see her aged mother and recount her post-flight adult narrative to the author, a child witnessing the return and the happiness that is the novel's denouement. The novel was published in 1940, but has the shape and feel of a tale written or experienced much earlier.

This précis in no way does justice to the novel's complexities and its problems of execution. Both arise, I believe, not because Cather was failing in narrative power, but because of her struggle to address an almost completely buried subject: the interdependent working of power, race, and sexuality in a white woman's battle for coherence.

In some ways this novel is a classic fugitive slave narrative: a thrilling escape to freedom. But we learn almost nothing of the trials of the fugitive's journey because the emphasis is on Nancy's fugitive state within the household *before her escape*. And the real fugitive, the text asserts, is the slave mistress. Furthermore, the plot escapes the author's control and, as its own fugitive status becomes clear, is destined to point to the hopelessness of excising racial considerations from formulations of white identity.

Escape is the central focus of Nancy's existence on the Colbert farm. From the moment of her first appearance, she is forced to hide her emotions, her thoughts, and eventually her body from pursuers. Unable to please Sapphira, plagued by the jealousy of the darker-skinned slaves, she is also barred from help, instruction, or consolation from her own mother, Till. That condition could only prevail in a slave society where the mistress can count on (and an author can believe the reader does not object to) the complicity of a mother in the seduction and rape of her own daughter. Because Till's loyalty to and responsibility for her mistress is so primary, it never occurs and need not occur to Sapphira that Till might be hurt or alarmed by the violence planned for her only child. That assumption is based on another – that slave women are not mothers; they are "natally dead," with no obligations to their offspring or their own parents.

This breach startles the contemporary reader and renders Till an unbelievable and unsympathetic character. It is a problem that Cather herself seems hard put to address. She both acknowledges and banishes this wholly unanalyzed mother–daughter relationship by inserting a furtive exchange between Till and Rachel in chapter 10:

> Till asked in a low, cautious murmur: "You ain't heard nothin', Miss Rachel?"
>
> "Not yet. When I do hear, I'll let you know. I saw her into good hands, Till. I don't doubt she's in Canada by this time, amongst English people."
>
> "Thank you, mam, Miss Rachel. I can't say no more. I don't want them niggers to see me cryin'. If she's up there with the English folks, she'll have some chance."[2]

The passage seems to come out of nowhere because there has been nothing in a hundred or so pages to prepare us for such maternal concern. "You ain't heard nothin'?" Till asks of Rachel. Just that – those four words – meaning: Is Nancy all right? Did she arrive safely? Is she alive? Is anybody after her? All of these questions lie in the one she does manage to ask.

Surrounding this dialogue is the silence of four hundred years. It leaps out of the novel's void and out of the void of historical discourse on slave parent–child relationships and pain. The contemporary reader is relieved when Till finally finds the language and occasion to make this inquiry about the fate of her daughter. But nothing more is made of it. And the reader is asked to believe that the silence surrounding the inquiry as well as its delay are due to Till's greater concern about her status among dark-skinned "field" niggers. Clearly Cather was driven to create the exchange not to rehabilitate Till in our readerly eyes but because at some point the silence became an unbearable violence, even in a work full of violence and evasion. Consider the pressures exerted by the subject: the need to portray the faithful slave; the compelling attraction of exploring the possibilities of one woman's absolute power over the body of another woman; confrontation with an uncontested assumption of the sexual availability of black females; the need to make credible the bottomless devotion of the person on whom Sapphira is totally dependent. It is after all *hers*, this slave woman's body, in a way that her own invalid flesh is not. These fictional demands stretch to breaking all narrative coherence. It is no wonder that Nancy cannot think up her own escape and must be urged into taking the risk.

Nancy has to hide her interior life from hostile fellow slaves *and* her own mother. The absence of camaraderie between Nancy and the other slave women turns on the device of color fetish – the skin-color privilege that Nancy enjoys because she is lighter than the others and therefore enviable. The absence of mother love, always a troubling concern of Cather's, is connected to the assumption of a slave's natal isolation. These are bizarre and disturbing deformations of reality that normally lie mute in novels containing Africanist characters, but Cather does not repress them altogether. The character she creates is at once a fugitive within the household and a sign of the sterility of the fiction-making imagination when there is no available language to clarify or even name the source of unbelievability.

Interestingly, the other major cause of Nancy's constant state of flight is wholly credible: that she should be unarmed in the face of the nephew's sexual assault and that she alone is responsible for extracting herself from the crisis. We do not question her vulnerability. What becomes titillating in this wicked pursuit of innocence – what makes it something other than an American variant of *Clarissa* – is the racial component. The nephew is not even required to court or flatter Nancy. After an unsuccessful reach for her from the branches of a cherry tree, he can, and plans to, simply arrive wherever she is sleeping. And since Sapphira has ordered her to sleep in the hall on a pallet, Nancy is forced to sneak away in the dark to quarters where she may be, but is not certain to be, safe. Other than Rachel, the proabolitionist, Nancy has access to no one to whom she can complain, explain, object, or from whom she can seek protection. We must accept her total lack of initiative, for there are no exits. She has no recourse – except in miserable looks that arouse Rachel's curiosity.

Nor is there any law, if the nephew succeeds in the rape, to entertain her complaint. If she becomes pregnant as a result of the violence, the issue is a boon to the economy of the estate, not an injury to it. There is no father or, in this case, "stepfather" to voice a protest on Nancy's behalf, since honor was the first thing stripped from the man. He is a "capon," we are told, given to Till so that she will have no more children and can give her full attention and energy to Mistress Sapphira.

Rendered voiceless, a cipher, a perfect victim, Nancy runs the risk of losing the reader's interest. In a curious way, Sapphira's plotting, like Cather's plot, is without reference to the characters and exists solely for the ego-gratification of the slave mistress. This becomes obvious when we consider what would have been the consequences of a successful rape. Given the novel's own terms, there can be no grounds for Sapphira's thinking that Nancy can be "ruined" in the conventional sense. There is no question of marriage to Martin, to Colbert, to anybody. Then, too, why would such an assault move her slave girl outside her husband's interest? The probability is that it would secure it. If Mr Colbert is tempted by Nancy the chaste, is there anything in slavocracy to make him disdain Nancy the unchaste?

Such a breakdown in the logic and machinery of plot construction implies the powerful impact race has on narrative – and on narrative strategy. Nancy is not only the victim of Sapphira's evil, whimsical scheming. She becomes the unconsulted, appropriated ground of Cather's inquiry into what is of paramount importance to the author: the reckless, unabated power of a white woman gathering identity unto herself from the wholly available and serviceable lives of Africanist others. This seems to me to provide the coordinates of an immensely important moral debate.

This novel is not a story of a mean, vindictive mistress; it is the story of a desperate one. If concerns a troubled, disappointed woman confined to the prison of her defeated flesh, whose social pedestal rests on the sturdy spine of racial degradation; whose privileged gender

has nothing that elevates it except color, and whose moral posture collapses without a whimper before the greater necessity of self-esteem,
even though the source of that esteem is a delusion. For Sapphira too is
a fugitive in this novel, committed to escape: from the possibility of
developing her own adult personality and her own sensibilities; from
her femaleness; from motherhood; from the community of women; from
her body.

She escapes the necessity of inhabiting her own body by dwelling on
the young, healthy, and sexually appetizing Nancy. She has transferred
its care into the hands of others. In this way she escapes her illness,
decay, confinement, anonymity, and physical powerlessness. In other
words, she has the leisure and the instruments to construct a self; but
the self she constructs must be – is conceivable only as – white. The surrogate black bodies become her hands and feet, her fantasies of sexual
ravish and intimacy with her husband, and, not inconsiderably, her sole
source of love.

If the Africanist characters and their condition are removed
from the text of Sapphira and the Slave Girl we will not have a
Miss Havisham immured or in flames. We have nothing: no
process of deranged self-construction that can take for granted
acquiescence in so awful an enterprise; no drama of limitless
power. Sapphira can hide far more successfully than Nancy. She
can, and does, remain outside the normal requirements of adult
womanhood because of the infantilized Africanist population at her
disposal.

The final fugitive in Cather's novel is the novel itself. The plot's own
plotting to free the endangered slave girl (of no apparent interest, as we
have seen, to the girl's mother or her slave associates) is designed for
quite other purposes. It functions as a means for the author to meditate
on the moral equivalence of free white women and enslaved black
women. The fact that these equations are designed as mother–daughter
pairings and relationships leads to the inescapable conclusion that
Cather was dreaming and redreaming her problematic relationship with
her own mother.

The imaginative strategy is a difficult one at best, an impossible one
in the event – so impossible that Cather permits the novel to escape from
the pages of fiction into nonfiction. For narrative credibility she substi-
tutes her own determination to force the equation. It is an equation that
must take place outside the narrative.

Sapphira and the Slave Girl turns at the end into a kind of memoir, the author's recollection of herself as a child witnessing the return, the reconciliation, and an imposed "all rightness" in untenable, outrageous circumstances. The silenced, acquiescent Africanist characters in the narrative are not less muzzled in the epilogue. The reunion – the drama of it, like its narrative function – is no more the slave characters' than their slave lives have been. The reunion is literally stage-managed for the author, now become a child. Till agrees to wait until little Willa is at the doorway before she permits herself the first sight she has had of her daughter in twenty-five years.

Only with Africanist characters is such a project thinkable: delayed gratification for the pleasure of a (white) child. When the embrace is over, Willa the white child accompanies the black mother and daughter into their narrative, listening to the dialogue but intervening in it at every turn. The shape and detail and substance of their lives are hers, not theirs. Just as Sapphira has employed these surrogate, serviceable black bodies for her own purposes of power without risk, so the author employs them in behalf of her own desire for a *safe* participation in loss, in love, in chaos, in justice.

But things go awry. As often happens, characters make claims, impose demands of imaginative accountability over and above the author's will to contain them. Just as Rachel's intervention foils Sapphira's plot, so Cather's urgent need to know and understand this Africanist mother and daughter requires her to give them center stage. The child Cather listens to Till's stories, and the slave, silenced in the narrative, has the final words of the epilogue.

Yet even, or especially, here where the novel ends Cather feels obliged to gesture compassionately toward slavery. Through Till's agency the elevating benevolence of the institution is invoked. Serviceable to the last, this Africanist presence is permitted speech only to reinforce the slaveholders' ideology, in spite of the fact that it subverts the entire premise of the novel. Till's voluntary genuflection is as ecstatic as it is suspicious.

In returning to her childhood, at the end of her writing career, Cather returns to a very personal, indeed private experience. In her last novel she works out and toward the meaning of female betrayal as it faces the void of racism. She may not have arrived safely, like Nancy, but to her credit she did undertake the dangerous journey.

Notes

1   Killis Campbell, "Poe's Treatment of the Negro and of the Negro Dialect," *Studies in English*, 16 (1936), p. 106.
2   Willa Cather, *Sapphira and the Slave Girl* (New York: Alfred A. Knopf, 1940), p. 249.

16

Modernity, Race, and Morality

David Theo Goldberg

[. . .] Moral discourse has both reflected and refined social relations, centrally defining changed images of social subjectivity across time and place. Indeed, the differences between these images are suggested by the syntax of their basic terms: We are virtuous; we sin; we have obligations; we bring about or effect utility; we are the bearers of rights. I have indicated initial ways in which historically dominant pictures of moral nature have been key in forming both social self-conception and the figure of the Other: what each agent at some conjuncture could be, expect, and achieve. And the forms of exclusion each enables are perfectly general. In so far as they exclude at all, they may do so in terms of varying forms of related group membership: class, ethnicity, gender, national or religious affiliation. The form I am centrally interested in here is racial. My concern is to see how, in fact, racial exclusions have been effected, what their relations are to these other forms of exclusion, how they have been legitimated and may disturbingly be justified in terms of the historically prevailing conception of moral subjectivity.

Race, Morality, and Subjectivity

[. . .] Race *is* a morally irrelevant category in the Greek social formation, but on empirical grounds not normative ones. There are no exactly *racial* exclusions in the classical Greek social formation, for there is no racial conception of the social subject. While things were more complex at a later time, I want to suggest that this is also the case for the medieval experience. The word "race" is sometimes used in translation of classical and medieval texts, but the term translated is almost invariably "species," and what is intended conceptually is not *race* but *peoples* or *man* generically.[1] I do not mean to deny that discriminatory exclusions were both common and commonly rationalized in various ways in Greek and medieval society, only that these exclusions and their various rationalizations did not assume racialized form. The concept of *race* enters European social consciousness more or less explicitly in the fifteenth century. Indeed, the first recorded reference to the sense of Europe as a collective "we" is in papal letters of the mid-fifteenth century, the first recorded usage of "race" shortly after that. It is only from this point on that social differentiation begins increasingly to take on a specifically racial sense. Not only did the Greeks have no concept for racial identification, strictly speaking they had no conception of race. There is considerable evidence of ethnocentric and xenophobic discrimination in Greek texts, of claims to *cultural* superiority, yet little evidence that these claimed inequalities were generally considered to be biologically determined.[2] In the absence of both the term and the conception, the social sense of self and other can hardly be said to be racially conceived nor the social formation to be one properly considered racist. [. . .]

In medieval thought, by contrast, individuals and groups were conceived as the subjects of theological categories, and discriminatory characterization and exclusion came to serve a different order. There appear in medieval literature and art representations of a range of strange, exotic beings, often falling between the human and the animal. These representations in part refer to and are influenced by mythological figures in early Western literature and art. Nevertheless, they were also tenuously imagined and invented on the preconceived basis of observing those dramatically different both among themselves (for example, deformed births) and elsewhere. In the first century AD, Pliny the Elder (who is thought to have died of asphyxiation in the volcanic destruction of Pompeii) constructed a catalog of these human and quasi-human figures that remained influential throughout the medieval period.[3] The more extreme mythological and fabulous figures listed by Pliny include the Amyctyrae or "unsociable" who have lips protruding so far as to serve as sun umbrellas; Amazons, or women who cut off their right breasts so as to shoot arrows more accurately; the Blemmyae, or men in the deserts of Libya whose heads are literally on their chests; giants; Hippopodes or "horse-footed" men; horned men, and so on. Pliny also listed those peoples whose identities were established on geographical or physical or cultural grounds. They included Albanians, Ethiopians, and pygmies but also speechless, gesturing men, many types of hairy men and women, troglodytes or cave dwellers, ichthiophagi or fish-eaters, "wife-givers," and so on. Clearly, peoples were often constructed on the basis of some combination of these various categories.[4]

In general, the exotic peoples of the Middle Ages were referred to as *monstra* (monstrous). As the duality in Pliny's catalog suggests, the category of *monstrum* was subject to two interpretations: on one hand, the prophetic but awful births of defective individuals, and on the other, strange and usually mythological people. Defective births were deemed an ominous sign of the destruction of celestial and earthly order. Observers were thus overcome by awe, repulsion, and fear of the implied threat to spiritual life and the political state. This concern translated into vigorous debates about the proper treatment of strangers, both in religious terms (could they be baptized and so saved as rational creatures having a soul) and in political terms (how were they to be treated juridically). Some insisted that human form is the mark of rationality and by extension of civil liberty, of the capacity to follow the law. Pygmies, for example, were deemed to represent a stage in the development of man, a step below humanity in the great chain of being, higher than apes but lacking true reason. True reason was thought to consist in the Aristotelian ability to formulate syllogisms and derive conclusions from universals. Pygmies were considered capable only of speaking instinctively, from the perception of particulars and not from universals. They thus lacked the discipline of rationally controlling instinct and imagination. [. . .]

This defining of humanity in relation to rationality clearly prefaces modernity's emphasis on rational capacity as a crucial differentia of racial groups. The concern in medieval thought with rationally defined categories of inclusion and exclusion seems to mirror later racial categorizations. However, while the medieval experience furnished models that modern racism would assume and transform according to its own lights, we need to proceed with care in labeling this medieval *racism*. As we have seen, there was no explicit category of race or of racial differentiation – no thinking, that is, of the subject in explicitly racial terms. More fundamentally, the place such exclusions occupy in medieval thought is very different than the space of racial thought in modernity. Late medieval experience was marked by increasing contact with peoples geographically, culturally, and, seemingly, physically different from people of familiar form. Over time, then, the Plinian categories grew increasingly empty. The folk monster of the earlier period was replaced by a new category, the *Savage Man*. This figure was usually pictured as naked, very hairy though without facial or feet fur, apelike but not an ape, carrying a large club or tree trunk (a version, perhaps, of what later would become modernity's cartoon characterization of the caveman dragging off "his" woman by her hair).[5]

The generic image of the savage represented violence, sexual license, a lack of civility and civilization, an absence of morality or any sense of it. Thus, with the psychological interiorizing of the moral space in late medieval thinking, the savage man came to represent the wild man within – sin or lack of reason, the absence of discipline, culture, civilization, in a word, morality – that confronts each human being. The Other that requires repression, denial, and disciplinary constraint was taken first and foremost to be the irrational other in us, and only by extension did it come to refer to those not ruled over (or lacking the capacity to be so ruled) by the voice of Reason, the purveyor of the Natural Law. It follows that the primary forms of discrimination were against non-Christians, or infidels: Those subjects who were seen to fail in constraining themselves appropriately would either have discipline imposed upon them or be excluded from God's city. [. . .] In short, medieval exclusion and discrimination were religious at root, not racial.

If premodernity lacked any conceiving of the differences between human beings as racial differences, modernity comes increasingly to be defined by and through race. The shift from medieval premodernity to modernity is in part the shift from a religiously defined to a racially defined discourse of human identity and personhood. Medieval discourse had no catalog of racial groupings, no identification of individuals or groups (or animals for that matter) in terms of racial membership; by the mid-nineteenth century, on the other hand, Disraeli could declare without fanfare in *Tancred* that "all is race". In three and a half centuries the world had of course become dramatically different, and a central strand of that difference was the growing impression of race upon human self-identity and upon identification, human and animal.

The influential classical ethnographers Pliny and Strabo had both thought the equatorial regions unfit for human habitation. This view crumbled in the late fifteenth century, first as West Africa was explored, conquered, and its peoples enslaved by the Spanish and Portuguese, and then as the New World was created, subjugated, and plundered. The sixteenth century thus marks the divide in the rise of race consciousness. Not only does the concept of race become explicitly and consciously applied but also one begins to see racial characterization emerging in art as much as in politico-philosophical and economic debates. [. . .]

By the seventeenth century, whatever tensions might have existed between the racial and the religious as modes of identity and identification had largely been resolved in favor of the former. Imperatives of European empire and expansion entailed territorial penetration, population regulation, and labor exploitation. The institution of racialized slave labor in spite of, indeed, in the name of Las Casas's Christian humanism seemed necessary for exploiting the natural resources offered by the new territories. Nevertheless, it is important to notice that slavery turned also and fundamentally on the conception of indigenous peoples as a natural resource, as part of the spoils acquired in the victorious but "just wars" of colonial expansion. Witness Velasquez's haunting painting, *The Servant* (1618–22), and the gigantic black marble statues of four Moor slaves, a monument to the Doge Giovanni Pesaro, that stand guard over the side door of the Church of Santa Maria dei Frati in Venice. So though it is in part true that "[r]acial terms mirror the political process by which populations of whole continents were turned into providers of coerced surplus labor,"[6] any reductive account of racial categorization and subjugation should be rejected. For while slavery may be explained largely (though not nearly exhaustively) in economic terms, one must insist in asking why it was at this time that racial difference came to define fitness for enslavement and why some kinds of racial difference rather than others. After all, strictly economic determinations should be indiscriminate in exploiting anyone capable of work. Racial definition and discourse, I am suggesting, have from their outset followed an independent set of logics, related to and intersecting with economic, political, legal, and cultural considerations, to be sure, but with assumptions, concerns, projects, and goals that can properly be identified as their own. Emergence of racial difference on its own terms as a significant feature of social definition could then be invoked as the rationalized grounds for enslavement. The peculiarities of this claimed difference – their brutishness and barbarism – delivered those so racialized up to enslavement.

Consider here John Locke's philosophical reflections on race, slavery, property, the just war, and their influence on the emerging Enlightenment. The opening sentence of Locke's justly famous *First Treatise on Government* (published in 1689 but probably written in the early years of that decade) unmistakably rejects slavery or property in other persons as a justifiable state of civil society, rejects it interestingly as un-English and ungentlemanly. Human beings are free, and equally so, in virtue of equal endowment in and command by rationality. Many commentators have pointed out that Locke seems to contradict this repudiation of slavery in the name of liberty, equality, and rationality both in his comments on slavery in the *Second Treatise* and in his practice as a colonial administrator. In the *Second Treatise*, Locke specifies the conditions under which he considers slavery justifiable, namely, for persons otherwise facing death, as in a just war when the captor may choose to delay the death of the captured by enslaving them. As secretary to the Carolina Proprietors (South Carolina), Locke played a key role in drafting both that colony's Fundamental Constitution of 1669 and the Instructions to Governor Nicholson of Virginia. The former considered citizens to "have absolute power over [their] negro slaves," and the latter considered the enslavement of negroes justifiable because prisoners of a just war who had "forfeited [their] own Life . . . by some Act that deserves Death." Locke considered the slave expeditions of the Royal Africa Company to be just wars in which the "negroes" captured had forfeited their claim to life.[7]

Locke committed no inconsistency here. Moreover, his view on this point actually reflected widely held European presuppositions about the nature of racial others, and by extension about human subjectivity. First, it is a basic implication of Locke's account that anyone behaving irrationally is to that degree a brute and should be treated as an animal or machine. Hence, rationality is a mark of human subjectivity and so a condition of the necessity to be extended full moral treatment.[8] Rational capacity, in other words, sets the limit upon the natural equality of all those beings ordinarily taken to be human. [. . .]

Locke is representative of the late seventeenth century, and not just of English empiricists at the time. [. . .] Locke's influence upon the Enlightenment is pervasive, not just on empiricists like Hume. Emphasis upon the autonomy and equality of rational subjects is a constitutive feature of eighteenth-century thought, though qualified by the sorts of racial limits on its extension that we have identified as a condition of Locke's conception. This is not to endorse the error that empiricism is solely responsible for Enlightenment racial exclusion. The contemporaneous innatism of Leibniz's rationalism, for example, is clearly reflected in his remark that "the greater and better part of humanity gives testimony to these instincts [of conscience] . . . one would have to be as brutish as the American savages to approve their customs which are more cruel than those of wild animals."[9] This should give pause to anyone accepting Bracken and Chomsky's claim that rationalism offers "a modest conceptual barrier to racism." Empiricism encouraged the tabulation of perceivable differences between peoples and from this it deduced their natural differences. Rationalism proposed initial innate distinctions (especially mental ones) to explain the perceived behavioral disparities. This contrast between Lockean empiricism and Leibnizean rationalism on the nature of racialized subjectivity and the implications for the domain of the moral stand as prototype of the contrast between two great philosophical representatives of the Enlightenment, Hume and Kant, half a century later.

Subjugation perhaps properly defines the order of the Enlightenment: subjugation of nature by human intellect, colonial control through physical and cultural domination, and economic superiority through mastery of the laws of the market. The confidence with which the culture of the West approached the world to appropriate it is reflected in the constructs of science, industry, and empire that principally represent the wealth of the period. This "recovery of nerve," as Gay aptly calls it, was partly a product of the disintegration of customary social hierarchies and their replacement by egalitarian sentiment, as much as it was accompanied by them. This recovered confidence was both expressed in and a consequence of the epistemological drive to name the emergent set of conditions, to analyze, to catalog, and to map them.[10] The scientific catalog of racial otherness, the variety of racial alien, was a principal product of this period.

The emergence of independent scientific domains of anthropology and biology in the Enlightenment defined a classificatory order of racial groupings – subspecies of *Homo sapiens* – along correlated physical and cultural matrices. Enlightenment thinkers were concerned to map the physical and cultural transformations from prehistorical savagery in the state of nature to their present state of civilization of which they took themselves to be the highest representatives. Assuming common origin, biology set out in part to delineate the natural causes of human difference in terms primarily of climatic variation. Anthropology was initially concerned to catalog the otherness of cultural practices. However, as it became increasingly identified as "the science of peoples without history," anthropology turned primarily to establishing the physical grounds of racial difference.

Thus, general categories like "exotic," "oriental," and "East" emerged, but also more specific ones like "Negro," "Indian," and "Jew" (as racial and not merely religious other), and modes of being like "negritude," along with epistemological subdisciplines like "sinology." Where the exotic of the medieval order had been placed in times past or future, the exotic of the Enlightenment occupied another geography, namely, the East or South, places indicative of times gone. Indeed, these spatial distinctions defined differences within the order of the exotic. Those of the East were acknowledged to have civilization, language, and culture. But, generically, the East was a place of violence and lascivious sensuality, the rape of which was thus invited literally as much as it was metaphorically. Africa to the south, by contrast, was the Old World of prehistory: Supposedly lacking language and culture, the Negro was increasingly taken to occupy a rung apart on the ladder of being, a rung that as the eighteenth century progressed was thought to predate humankind. In cataloging the variety of racial aliens, however, Enlightenment science simultaneously extended racial self-definition to the West: Western Europeans were similarly classified on the hierarchical scale moving upward from dark-skinned and passionate Southern Europeans to fair-skinned and rational Northerners. The catalog of national characters emerged in lock step with the classification of races. Racial and national identities, it could be said, are identities of anonymity, identities of distance and alienation, at once prelude to and expression of the drive to marginalize and exclude, to dominate, and to exploit.

Now the Enlightenment consolidation of racialized discourse in terms of the scientific and philosophical was also effected on the basis of the eighteenth-century resurrection of classical values of beauty[11] and their similitude with the criteria of value in the classical economic tradition. Equilibrium and utility functioned in classical economic theory in ways analogous to proportion, symmetry, and refinement for classical aesthetics. Both sets of criteria determined an order of balance and harmony established on the basis of the geometric model. Beauty, for classical aesthetics, was a property possession of which determined subjects' ontological value, just as possession of economic goods for classical economics created utility. Possession of property was a sign of wealth, a measure of what the agent was capable of appropriating in the face of competition.[12] To lack the "natural" qualities of classical beauty was to be poor; and as with *laissez faire* economic theory, this was considered the subject's own responsibility. By the late eighteenth century, beauty was established in terms of racial properties: fair skin, straight hair, orgnathous jaw, skull shape and size, well-composed bodily proportions, and so on. To fail to possess these traits was considered a fault of inheritance, much as heirs were identified to maintain wealth within the confines of the family bloodline. So, following Locke's lead, as economic poverty (lack of property ownership or the means of production) inevitably led subjects to work for pittances in factories and mines, "racial poverty" was taken to justify property in persons.

Thus, natural qualities of beauty and perfection were supposed to be established on *a priori* grounds of racial membership. Aesthetic value solidified into natural law, which in the eighteenth century was considered as compelling as the laws of nature, economics, and morality precisely because they were all deemed to derive from the same rational basis. It is for this reason that many natural historians, biologists, and anthropologists at the time classified humankind not simply on grounds of physical criteria like size and shape, climate, or environment but according to the aesthetic values of beauty or deformity.[13] These aesthetic values of bodily beauty were established as the mode of determining the individual's place in the racial, and therefore social, hierarchy; and perceived intellectual ability or its lack were considered to reveal inherent racial differences in mental capacity. Blacks were quite frequently represented in eighteenth-century European portrait painting and, as with Joseph Wright's *Two Girls and a Negro Servant* (ca. 1769–70), most often in subservient and demeaning fashion. Paintings like John Wootton's *The Racehorse Lamprey* or Bartholomew Dandridge's *Young Girl with Dog and Negro Boy* represent childish and so mentally immature black slaves in positions explicitly or implicitly analogous to the master's or mistress's horse or dog. The racialized relations of social power are reflected in and reproduced by the aesthetics of popular portraiture at the time.[14]

Those critics committed to the moral irrelevance of race tend to assume that racists inevitably combine these two strains, aesthetic values and natural qualities, into a spurious causal principle. If racists are inherently committed to such spurious causal presuppositions, sophisticated Enlightenment philosophers must have claimed that racial membership defines both one's degree of beauty and one's intellectual capacity. It would follow that where an observer knows either one's intellectual or aesthetic standing, the other may be deduced. Nevertheless, this fails to recognize that more careful racial theorists have sometimes expressed other forms of racial thinking.

David Hume, for example, had begun to think of mind and nature as merely *correlated* in various ways. Hume distinguished between the moral and physical determinants of national character. The latter are those physical elements like climate and air that eighteenth-century monogenists so readily supposed to be the sole determinants of perceived human difference. By moral causes, Hume meant social considerations like custom, government, economic conditions, and foreign relations that influence the mind and manners of a people. Hume insisted that national characters are a function almost completely of moral causes. Thus, Jews in general were "fraudulent" (Hume was careful enough to emphasize that what we now call stereotypes admit to exceptions); Arabs "uncouth and disagreeable"; modern Greeks "deceitful, stupid, and cowardly" in contrast with both the "ingenuity, industry, and activity" of their ancestors and the "integrity, gravity, and bravery" of their Turkish neighbors. Superior to all others were the English, in large part because they benefited from their governmental mixture of monarchy, aristocracy, and bourgeois democracy. In general, Hume agreed with the earlier judgments of Bacon and Berkeley that inhabitants of the far north and of the tropics were inferior to inhabitants of more temperate regions (mainly Central Europe) owing in large part, however, not to physical causes but to matters of habit like industry and sexual moderation.

While *national* differences for Hume were social, *racial* differences were inherent. All "*species* of men" other than whites (and especially the "Negro") were "*naturally* inferior to the whites." Hume's justification of this footnoted claim was empirical: Only whites had produced anything notable and ingenious in the arts or sciences, and even the most lowly of white peoples (ancient Germans, present Tartars) he thought had something to commend them. "Negroes," even those living in Europe, had no accomplishments they could cite. Like Locke, the only probable explanation of this "fact" Hume could find was an original natural difference between "the breeds." Thus, Hume concluded, "In Jamaica they talk of one negroe as a man of parts and learning; but tis likely he is admired for very slender accomplishments, like a parrot, who speaks few words plainly."[15] Inherent nature admits of no exceptions.

Like Hume, Kant proceeded from a catalog of national characters to a characterization of racial difference.[16] Where Hume had identified the English as superior among all national characters, Kant predictably elevated Germans above all others, finding in them a synthesis of the English intuition for the sublime and the French feeling for the beautiful; Germans were thus thought to avoid the excesses of either extreme. Of the peoples of the Orient (what Kant elsewhere calls the Mongolian race[17]), the Arabs were deemed most noble ("hospitable, generous, and truthful" but troubled by an "inflamed imagination" that tends to distort), followed by the Persians (good poets, courteous, with fine taste), and the Japanese (resolute but stubborn). Indians and Chinese, by contrast, were dominated in their taste by the grotesque and monstrous, with the former committed to the "despotic excess" of *sati*.

Nevertheless, compared to Negroes, Oriental races fared relatively well in Kant's scheme.[18] Kant's remarks about "Negroes" and their position in relation to his moral theory need to be read against the general discourse of racialized subjects that defined the Enlightenment. "Savages" are wanting in "moral understanding," and Negroes" in Kant's view are the most lacking of all "savages." (American Indians – "honorable, truthful, and honest" – were considered the least lacking of "savages."[19] As a moral rationalist Kant turned Hume's empiricist endorsement of racial subordination into an *a priori* principle:

So fundamental is the difference between [the Negro and White] races of man, and it appears to be as great in regard to mental capacities as in

color. . . . The blacks are vain in the Negro way, and so talkative that they
must be driven apart from each other by thrashings.[20]

Hume's correlation of race and nature was reworked by Kant back into
a strictly causal relation. This enabled him to conclude logically that
"the fellow was quite black from head to foot, *a clear proof* that what he
said was stupid."[21] Kant could therefore consider himself to have derived
a "Negro's stupidity" from the fact of his blackness.

This outcome of Kant's reckoning is perhaps less surprising if
we recall that he had set out assuming the acceptability of "commonsense morality" in the Judeo-Christian tradition, and as we have seen
racial differentiation and subordination were basic to it at the time.
So in establishing the justificatory conditions for commonsense moral
value, Kant would also be justifying racially defined discrimination.
One way for Enlightenment philosophers committed to moral notions
of equality and autonomy to avoid inconsistency on the question of
racialized subordination was to deny the rational capacity of blacks,
to deny the very condition of their humanity. This implication is borne
out even if we interpret in generous ways the Enlightenment commitment to universalistic moral principles. It is true that vigorous
movements emerged at the time opposing race-based slavery, movements that justified their opposition precisely in the name of universalist
Enlightenment ideals.[22] We should recognize, though, that this resistance, valuable as it may have been at the time, presupposed and
reproduced recognition of racial difference. And the standard by which
any measure of equality was set remained uniform and unchanged:
It was, namely, European and Western. Local values became fixed as
universal; in issuing moral commands autonomous agents may impose
upon others their own principles and impose them in the name of
universality and objectivity. Cloaking themselves in the name of the
natural, the certain, and the timeless, racial discrimination and exclusion imprinted themselves as naturally given and so as inoffensive and
tolerable.

If there is any content to the charge of cultural chauvinism, it
does not lie simply in the refusal to recognize the values of other (in
this case non-European and non-Western) cultures; it lies also in the
refusal to acknowledge influences of other cultures on one's own while
insisting on one's own as representing the standards of civilization

and moral progress. This became the nineteenth-century modernist legacy of the Enlightenment project, and it was in the name of the principle of utility emerging from the Enlightenment that this was carried forward.

The principle of utility, that morality is a matter of producing "the greatest happiness of the greatest number," furnishes no principled restriction of racially discriminatory, exclusionary, or violent acts, policies, or institutions. In weighing up utility, the theory insists on treating each social subject affected equally and impartially, and it therefore rejects paternalistic expressions. Subjects are considered the best judges of their own happiness, of the goals they set themselves, and of what they take their happiness to consist in. Utilitarianism, for example, does not exclude anyone as a proper object of obligatory aid: On the face of it, strangers and aliens have as much claim to aid as those at hand.

There are severe limits to utilitarian benevolence and self-determination. First, we mostly find ourselves better able to aid those we know, whose needs we are more readily able to identify, empathize with, and satisfy. So utilitarian considerations are strongly likely to have us aid those in close proximity to us, spatially and culturally. But there are more straightforwardly racial delimitations on the principle's applicability. [. . .] [So,] Bentham and his followers admitted racial difference as having at least secondary influence on utility. "Race" or "lineage" was treated in Humean fashion not as climatically determined but as "operating chiefly through the medium of moral, religious, sympathetic and antipathetic biases."[23] This interpretation exercised great influence on British colonial bureaucracy, indeed, through the direct hand of James and John Stuart Mill.

It has often been pointed out that were the calculus of pleasure and pain to establish it, slavery and severe racist treatment of a minority by a majority would be obliged by utilitarian consideration. The acceptability of slavery and racism turn for utilitarianism on the number of beneficiaries and the extent of their benefits from such practices and institutions. [. . .]

The same paternalistic logic was used by both James and John Stuart Mill and their administrative followers to justify colonial rule, namely, the general civilizing and utilitarian benefits of capitalist development for the sake of the colonized so as to broaden the scope of the latter's liberty. James Mill entered service with the East Indies Company first as Assistant Examiner (from 1819) and eleven years later as Examiner in the chief executive office. As such, he effectively became the most powerful Indian administrator of his day. In these capacities he was able to institute the principles of administration for India that he had insisted on in his celebrated *History of British India*. Here, Mill attacked the "hideous state" of "Hindu and Muslim civilization" that prevailed in India. Like the Chinese, Indians were found to be "tainted with the vices of insincerity, dissembling, treacherous . . . disposed to excessive exaggeration . . . cowardly and unfeeling . . . in the highest degree conceited . . . and full of affected contempt for others. Both are, in the physical sense, disgustingly unclean in their persons and houses." Indians and Chinese, in short, were found completely lacking in morality. This state of affairs Mill ascribed to underlying political causes, namely, the shortcomings of "oriental despotism." Incapable of representative democracy, Mill recommended that the Indian government should thus submit to the benevolent direction of the British Parliament.[24]

John Stuart Mill followed his father into colonial service in 1823, conducting the correspondence with India in the Department of Native States, one of the Company's important divisions. He later succeeded the older Mill as Examiner, remaining with the Company until its abolition shortly after the Indian Rebellion of 1857–8. Echoing his father, John Stuart insisted that India required direction by colonial government – recall that he deemed the principles of *On Liberty* applicable only where civilized conditions ensured the settling of disputes by rational discussion. Like his appeal to those who have experienced both sorts of pleasure in proving the qualitative superiority of the "higher" kind over the "lower," the younger Mill's distinction between civilized and uncivilized peoples implicitly invoked the standard of the white European. Unlike his father, Mill acknowledged – in principle, if not in fact – that India should exercise self-government once it had assumed civilized forms of social life, and he saw nothing in the nature of its people to prevent it from developing in this direction.[25]

Both James and John Stuart Mill thus viewed natives as children or childlike, to be directed in their development by rational, mature administrators concerned with maximizing the well-being of all. Natives ought not to be brutalized, to be sure, nor enslaved but directed – administratively, legislatively, pedagogically, and socially. Paternalistic colonial administration was required in their view until the governed sufficiently mature and throw off the shackles of their feudal condition and thinking and are then to assume the civilized model of reasoned self-government. It was therefore in the name of the natives' own happiness, their future good defined in utilitarian terms, that they should have been willing to accept this state of affairs. This conclusion is established, in Taylor's fitting phrase, by utilitarianism's "homogeneous universe of rational calculation."[26] Though each sentient subject is in principle equal, "civilized" subjects furnish the criterion of calculation and hence control the outcome. Application of the utilitarian method facilitates the drive for power and control, the subjugative drive of/over physical and human nature that is central to the modernist legacy of the Enlightenment.

For utilitarians, accordingly, nothing in principle save a subject's good intention stands in the way of racially discriminatory or exclusionary undertakings. And though intentions are on John Stuart Mill's own admission relevant to judgments of character, they are irrelevant to establishing the rightness or wrongness of any act. Indeed, even judgments of intention and character are a matter of racial definition in a social milieu in which the bishop of Kentucky could unself-consciously declare that "instinct and reason, history and philosophy, science and revolution alike cry out against the degradation of the race by the commingling of the tribe which is the highest [whites] with that which is the lowest [blacks] in the scale of development" (1883).[27] Not only does the principle of utility offer no effective delimitation of discriminatory exclusion; we have seen how such exclusion was mandated by its staunchest proponents in the name of the principle itself. Utilitarianism rationalized nineteenth-century racial rule in two related senses, then: It laid claim to a justification of racialized colonialism, and it systematized its institution.

Where utility fails the application of "rights" has been thought to succeed. Articulation of the concept in various important ways can be traced back to the seventeenth century, and the contemporary emphasis upon legal and moral rights needs to be understood in light of this tradition. The American and French revolutions, torch-bearers of the Enlightenment, both licensed influential doctrines of rights.[28] Nevertheless, the great popular authority the concept of *rights* has come to exercise in defining the space of social subjectivity and especially the effectivity it has enjoyed in combatting racial discourse both followed World War II. The (self-)conception of the social subject predominantly as the bearer of rights – that is, in the name of those rights vested in and borne by the subject – has only come to prevail in the latter half of the twentieth century. It is pertinent, then, that the contemporaneous critical attack on racial discourse and definition has been authorized in terms of rights: witness, most notably, the United Nations Declaration on Human Rights, the Civil Rights movement in the United States, and the various United Nations statements on race.

In recent history, insistence on rights has served as a rallying point for the oppressed and given pause to oppressors. By contrast, oppression has been carried out not in virtue of a commitment to rights but under the banner of their denial. This suggests the semantic relation between "rights" and "justice" that is attributable to their common derivation from the Latin *jus*: A right is what is (considered) at least in the context just. Even where justice and so rights are naturalized, as in the history of their initial co(e)mergence ("natural rights," the "rights of man," "human rights"), there were considered to be limitations on their referential range, a range which by extension was also naturalized. Slaves, as we have seen, fell outside this scope, and the criteria of enslavability and rights-applicability were racialized.

So rights are in their very formulation relative to their *social* recognition and institution. In this sense, they are never absolute or universal: Rights exist and empower, if at all and even where they claim universality, only on the basis of some socially constructed and civil system already established by a specific process of politics and law.[29] It follows that even where a discourse of rights purports to include and embrace, in its application and range of reference it is open to circumscription and constriction. The reformulation of moral space in the twentieth century in terms of radically atomized and isolated individuals vested with rights on the basis only of their contractual relations has made conflicts of rights and dispute resolution central to moral and legal (self-)conception. In this culture of bureaucratic individualism, utility defines the bureaucratic rationality, and rights service the social invention of the autonomous moral individual.[30] Racialized and national identifications have served as modernist compensations for the merely "agglomerative" and instrumental social identities that this radically individualist and atomistic order entails.[31] Rights-assertion, accordingly, has come to refract these social identities, "delimiting certain others as 'extrinsic' to rights entitlement." The objects of the contractual arrangement, those excluded from this contract or from contracting as such, have no rights.[32]

Subjects assume value, then, only in so far as they are bearers of rights; and they are properly vested with rights only in so far as they are imbued with value. The rights others as a matter of course enjoy are yet denied people of color because black, brown, red, and yellow subjectivities continue to be disvalued; and the devaluation of these subjectivities delimits at least the applicability of rights or restricts their scope of application that people of color might otherwise properly claim. "Where one's experience is rooted not just in a 'sense' of illegitimacy but in *being* illegitimate,"[33] in literally being outside the law, the rights to which one might appeal are erased. The space in which a subject might construct rights and their conceivable range of possibility are severely circumscribed.

Part of the difficulty with rights-application is the conflict it not only implicitly presupposes but also that it serves in part to generate. This conflict may assume either conceptual or substantive form. Conceptually, by a right one subject may intend a liberty, another a claim, or entitlement, or power. Substantively, one person's liberty may conflict with another's, or one's liberty or claim with another's entitlement or power, and so on. Where these conflicts are racialized, whatever gains and losses or inclusions and exclusions there are will be exacerbated, magnified, emphasized, and accentuated. [. . .]

Long and bitter struggles have undermined both the nonracial and the racialized conditions for the justification of property rights in human beings. Nevertheless, there continue to be conflicts between subjects' interpretations and assertion of rights, conflicts deepened in assuming racialized form. The US Civil Rights Act of 1964 promoted preferential treatment programs for those suffering racial discrimination. The claim to be treated preferentially, subject to qualifying conditions, and the entitlement to be admitted to colleges or hired preferentially generated the counterclaim a decade later of reverse discrimination suffered as a result by whites. Preferential treatment programs, it was charged, violate the right of all to equal opportunity: entitlement right of one subject conflicting with entitlement or claim right of another, each in the context assuming racial definition.

Similarly, the right of all to protected speech may be taken to entail the right (liberty) of racist expression, at least in the nonpublic domain, but not the (claim or entitlement) right or empowerment to be shielded from such expression. This turns on the standard but questionable interpretation of racist expression as merely offensive, never harmful.

For reasons of this sort MacIntyre condemns rights, like utility, as a moral fiction. Moral fictions purport to furnish us with an objective and impersonal criterion of morality but in practice do not.[34] The primary concepts in terms of which social subjectivity has been set in our moral tradition are fictive in this way. That they are open to abusive interpretation and application is a function of their inherently social character. [. . .]

The centrality of moral notions to social and self-conception enables and constrains actions of certain kinds. It also makes possible those basic categories of distinction between self and other that promote and sustain thinking in the terms of exclusionary discrimination. In this sense, *formal* moral notions of any kind are perniciously fictive in respect to racial and racializing discourse (whatever their redeeming value in authorizing or constraining some kinds of expression and disciplining subjects). This fictive character has to do with the nature of the moral concepts themselves, and with their role in fixing social subjectivity. They serve to naturalize the concept of race, to render it basic to modernity's (and so far, at least in transformed form, to postmodernity's) common sense.

As Hobbes noted, a moral order permits those expressions it does not explicitly prohibit. In the case of discriminatory exclusions it can be concluded more strongly that what the moral order fails explicitly to exclude it implicitly authorizes. The moral formalism of modernity establishes itself as the practical application of rationality, as "the rational language and the language of rationality"[35] in its practical application. Modernist moralism is concerned principally with a complete, rationally derived system of self-justifying moral reasons logically constructed from a single basic principle. But in ignoring the social fabric and concrete identities in virtue of which moral judgment and reason are individually effective, in terms of which the very content of the moral categories acquires its sense and force, moral modernity fails to recognize the series of exclusions upon which the state of modernity is constituted.[36] So though the formal principles of moral modernity condemn and discourage some racist expressions, they fail, and fail necessarily, to condemn and discourage such expressions exhaustively. Indeed, where they fail in this way, they extend discriminatory racialized expression either indirectly and inadvertently by seeming to condone and approve what they do not explicitly disapprove, or directly by enabling racialized expression and effectively authorizing discriminatory racial exclusions on the basis of the principle of moral reason itself.

This colonizing of the moral reason of modernity by racialized categories has been effected for the most part by constituting racial others outside the scope of morality. This has been done not by denying the social and so moral relevance of racial identity but by taking race as a central expression of the language of "thick description." This is the culturally developed and articulated language of everyday and intellectual life in terms of which morality is lived out, the thick description in terms of which the moral notions apply or fail to apply, and in terms of which discriminations are made and acquire legitimacy.[37]

I have stressed that the primary principles of our moral tradition – virtue, sin, autonomy and equality, utility, and rights – are delimited in various ways by the concept of *race*. It should be clear that one could make out the same argument for moral method, that is, whether the moral principles are produced out of and so justified by appeal to social contract, or pure reason in its practical application, or to the appeal to consequences, or to the standards of a community tradition. In each case, race is conceptually able to insinuate itself into the terms of the moral analysis, thereby delimiting by definition the scope of the moral. Thus, the racializing paradox of liberal modernity is firmly established: Liberalism's commitment to principles of universality is practically sustained only by the reinvented and rationalized exclusions of racial particularity. [. . .]

Notes

1   See, for example, the translation of Aristotle's *Politics*, line 1252a27 in Aristotle (1946); Marco Polo's *Travels* (written in Latin in the early fourteenth century) speaks in the English translation (1958, p. 258) of "a race of men"; and Sir John Mandeville's *Travels* (written in Latin around 1346) refers in the English translation (1983, p. 137) to both "races" and

"peoples." Despite the title of his book, Sherwin-White (1970) more or less admits that the prevailing form of discrimination by Romans against those who were not amounts not to "racial prejudice" but to ethnocentrism. J. B. Friedman's characterization in the title of his book (1981) of the medieval *monstra* as races has been widely influential. Thus, Mason (1990) refers indiscriminately in terms of race to characterizations of monstrous beings as early as those of Hellenistic Greeks and as late as those in the eighteenth century of "Europeans" and "non-Europeans" (particularly American Indians) alike. Indeed, there is a sense in which the term "race" carries Mason's undertaking to establish an overarching structural identity for all such characterizations, to establish synchronic rules of ethnocentric reference. In each of these cases, the conception of race emerging with modernity is inappropriately being read back by contemporary scholars via translation and imposed interpretation into premodern texts.

2   Cf. Hall (1989), p. ix.

3   J. B. Friedman calls the figures so cataloged "Plinian *races*" but this again imposes "race" retrospectively upon a form of thinking for which the concept was not yet available. Cf. J. B. Friedman (1981), esp. ch. 1. Friedman's account has been influential not only in its phenomenology of medieval monstrous representations but in the unquestioned contemporary acceptance that the figures so characterized were at the time *racially* conceived. See, for example, Mason (1990), pp. 18, 32.

4   J. B. Friedman (1981), pp. 9–15.

5   For accounts of the genealogy of the Wild Man, see Mason (1990), pp. 45ff.; Taussig (1987); and Dudley and Novak (1972).

6   Wolf (1981), pp. 380–1.

7   Locke (1960), I, #1, II, #22–4. See also the editor's footnote to II, #24, Gay (1969), II, pp. 409–10, and Higginbotham (1978), pp. 163–4. The percentage of people of African descent in the population of the Carolinas was greater than in any other of the North American colonies at the time.

8   Locke (1960), I, #58, II, #172. Locke's indictment of slavery in the *First Treatise* covers only natural slavery. Underlying his justification of enslavement as a result of war lies Locke's labor theory of value, a forerunner of both Adam Smith's and Marx's, which distinguishes between those who improve what they mix their labor with, who are thereby rational, and those ("savages" in the "state of nature") who simply collect, who thereby merely survive. Cf. Hulme and Jordanova (1990), pp. 29–30.

9   Leibniz (1981), I, ii, #17; see also I, i, #76, 84.

10   Cf. Gay (1969), p. 8; G. S. Rousseau and Porter (1989), pp. 1–2.

11   Cf. Mosse (1979), pp. 10–11, 21–2; West (1982), pp. 53–4, 58–9.

12   Locke (1960), *Second Treatise*, #25–51.

13 Mosse and others have documented in detail this aesthetic tendency by Enlightenment theorists of race such as Buffon, Camper, and Lavater and the influence upon their work by art historian J. J. Winckelmann. Cf. Mosse (1979), pp. 1–29; West (1982), pp. 53–9; Gossett (1965), pp. 32–9; Jordan (1968), pp. 3–95.

14 For a fuller analysis of this tendency, see Debydeen (1985), pp. 17–40, and esp. pp. 32–3.

15 Hume (1964), pp. 244–58.

16 See section IV, "Of National Characteristics" of Kant (1960), pp. 97–116.

17 Kant (1950), p. 18.

18 In 1794 William Robertson listed Indians with most Europeans as "commercial peoples." See Marshal (1989), pp. 54–5.

19 J.-J. Rousseau's view, by contrast, is notable for the absence of a catalog of national characters and pernicious characterization of racial others. Indeed, Rousseau's "noble savage" and "primitive man" are positively portrayed as having desirable, uncorrupted characteristics. But these concepts are exemplified for Rousseau by American and African indigenes, and they form part of the Enlightenment discourse of exoticism. The pre-civilized and primitive lack reason and autonomy, and so they cannot be party to the general will and civil society.

20 Kant (1960), p. 111.

21 Ibid., p. 113. My emphasis. Some may object that this is an early, pre-Critical and so immature work, and that this sort of reasoning does not appear in the Critical and especially moral writings with which it is inconsistent. It need only be pointed out in response that similar sentiments are expressed by Kant in his essay on race in 1775 and repeated again in his philosophical anthropology of 1791. The latter are hardly products of an immature mind.

22 See, for example, Higginbotham (1978), pp. 377ff.; Gates (1990), pp. 320–3; Dabydeen (1985), pp. 46–7.

23 Bentham (1907), pp. 310–11, n. 1; and pp. 62–3.

24 J. Mill (1820), vol. 2, pp. 135, 166–7; cf. Stokes (1959), pp. 48, 53–4.

25 Stokes (1959), pp. 48, 298–9.

26 Taylor (1989), p. 83.

27 Quoted in Stember (1976), p. 38.

28 The degree to which racial others were perceived inhuman rendered them outside the scope both of the Bill of Rights (the first ten Amendments to the US Constitution ratified by the end of 1791) and the Declaration of the Rights of Man in France (1789). The US Constitution made the principle of exclusion explicit: A slave was declared to be but three-fifths a person. While some constitutional commentators are quick to point out that this clause was explicitly (and so only) for the sake of taxation and represen-

tation, this reading rubs up against the opening constitutional claim that declares all human beings to be born equal. Reading the three-fifths clause as presupposing a principle of dehumanization renders it consistent with claims of inherent human equality.

29   Mackie (1977), p. 174; cf. MacIntyre (1981), p. 65.
30   MacIntyre (1981), p. 68.
31   Cf. Taylor (1989), p. 413.
32   P. J. Williams (1987), p. 424.
33   Ibid., p. 417.
34   MacIntyre (1981), p. 68.
35   Grillo (1989), p. 6.
36   Taylor (1989), pp. 76–7; B. Williams (1985), pp. 116–17; Foucault (1988), pp. 146, 150–1.
37   Geertz (1973).

References

Aristotle (1946). *The Basic Works of Aristotle*, ed. R. McKeon. New York: Random House.

Bentham, Jeremy [1823] (1907). *An Introduction to the Principles of Morals and Legislation*. Oxford: Clarendon Press.

Dabydeen, David (1985). *Hogarth's Blacks: Images of Blacks in Eighteenth Century English Art*. Denmark: Dangaroo Press.

Dudley, Edward and Novak, Maximilian E. (eds.) (1972). *The Wild Man Within: An Image from the Renaissance to Romanticism*. Pittsburgh: University of Pittsburgh Press.

Foucault, Michel (1988). "The Political Technologies of Individuals." In L. H. Martin, H. Gluckman, and P. Hutton (eds.), *Technologies of the Self*. Minneapolis: University of Minnesota Press.

Friedman, John B. (1981). *The Monstrous Races in Medieval Art and Thought*. Cambridge, MA: Harvard University Press.

Gates, Henry Louis Jr. (1990). "Critical Remarks." In David Theo Goldberg (ed.), *Anatomy of Racism*. Minneapolis: University of Minnesota Press.

Gay, Peter (1969). *The Enlightenment: An Interpretation*, 2 vols. New York: Alfred Knopf.

Geertz, Clifford (1973). *The Interpretation of Culture*. New York: Basic Books.

Gossett, Thomas (1965). *Race: The History of an Idea in America*. Dallas: Southern Methodist University Press.

Grillo, R. D. (1989). *Dominant Languages: Language and Hierarchy in Britain and France*. Cambridge: Cambridge University Press.

Hall, Edith (1989). *Inventing the Barbarian*. Oxford: Clarendon Press.

Higginbotham, A. Leon (1978). *In the Matter of Color, Race and the American Legal Process: The Colonial Period.* Oxford: Oxford University Press.

Hulme, Peter and Jordanova, Ludmilla (1990). *The Enlightenment and its Shadows.* London: Routledge.

Hume, David [1748] (1964). "Of National Characters." In *The Philosophical Works*, ed. T. H. Green and T. H. Grose III. Aalen: Scientia Verlag.

Jordan, Winthrop (1968). *White Over Black: American Attitudes Towards the Negro, 1550–1812.* New York: W. W. Norton.

Kant, Immanuel [1775] (1950). "On the Different Races of Man." In Earl W. Count (ed.), *This is Race.* New York: Henry Schuman.

——[1763] (1960). *Observations on the Feeling of the Beautiful and the Sublime*, trans. J. T. Goldthwait. Berkeley: University f California Press.

Leibniz, Gottfried (1981). *New Essays on Human Understanding*, trans. P. Remnant and J. Bennett. Cambridge: Cambridge University Press.

Locke, John [1689] (1960). *Two Treatises of Government*, ed. Peter Laslett. New York: Mentor Books.

MacIntyre, Alasdair (1981). *Whose Justice? Which Rationality?* South Bend: University of Notre Dame Press.

Mackie, John (1977). *Ethics: Inventing Right and Wrong.* Harmondsworth: Penguin.

Mandeville, John (1983). *The Travels of Sir John Mandeville*, trans. C. W. R. D. Mosley. Harmondsworth: Penguin.

Marshal, P. J. (1989). "Taming the Exotic: The British in India in the Seventeenth and Eighteenth Centuries." In G. S. Rousseau and Roy Porter (eds.), *Exoticism in the Enlightenment*, Manchester: Manchester University Press.

Mason, Peter (1990). *Deconstructing America: Representations of the Other.* London: Routledge.

Mill, James (1820). *History of British India*, 2nd edn. London.

Mosse, George (1979). *Toward the Final Solution.* New York: Howard Fertig.

Polo, Marco (1958). *The Travels*, trans. R. Latham. Harmondsworth: Penguin.

Rousseau, G. S. and Porter, Roy (eds.) (1989). *Exoticism in the Enlightenment.* Manchester: Manchester University Press.

Sherwin-White, A. N. (1970). *Racial Prejudice in Imperial Rome.* Cambridge: Cambridge University Press.

Stember, Charles Herbert (1976). *Sexual Racism.* New York: Harper Colophon.

Stokes, Eric (1959). *The English Utilitarians and India.* Oxford: Clarendon Press.

Taussig, Michael (1987). *Shamanism, Colonialism and the Wild Man.* Chicago: Chicago University Press.

Taylor, Charles (1989). *Sources of the Self.* Cambridge, MA: Harvard University Press.

West, Cornel (1982). *Prophesy Deliverance! An Afro-American Revolutionary Christianity.* Philadelphia: Westminster Press.

Williams, Bernard (1985). *Ethics and the Limits of Philosophy*. Cambridge, MA: Harvard University Press.

Williams, Patricia J. (1987). "Alchemical Notes: Reconstructed Ideals from Deconstructed Rights." *Harvard Civil Rights–Civil Liberties Review*, 22, 2 (Spring), pp. 401–34.

Wolf, Eric (1981). *Europe and the People Without History*. Berkeley: University of California Press.

17

Denying Racism: Elite Discourse and Racism

Teun A. van Dijk

Introduction

Within a larger research framework that studies the ways white people speak and write about minorities, this chapter examines one major strategy in such discourse, viz., the denial of racism. The prototype of such denials is the well-known disclaimer: "I have nothing against blacks, but . . ."

Discourse plays a prominent role in the reproduction of racism. It expresses, persuasively conveys, and legitimates ethnic or racial stereotypes and prejudices among white group members, and may thus form or confirm the social cognitions of other whites. This is particularly true for various forms of elite discourse, since the elites control or have preferential access to the major means of public communication, e.g., through political, media, educational, scholarly, or corporate discourse. Without alternative sources of information or opinion formation, the white public at large may have few resources for resistance against such prevailing messages that preformulate the ethnic consensus. Our (informal) discourse analytical approach is embedded

Parts of this paper were presented at conferences in Amsterdam, Coventry, and Duisburg in 1991. A longer version of this chapter, "Discourse and the Denial of Racism," was published in *Discourse and Society*, 3 (1992), pp. 87–118.

within this complex sociocognitive and sociopolitical framework, which will not be spelled out here (for details, see van Dijk, 1984, 1987, 1991, 1993).

The Forms and Functions of Racism Denials

The many forms denials of racism may take are part of a well-known overall discourse and interaction strategy, viz., that of positive self-presentation or keeping face (Brown and Levinson, 1987; Goffman, 1967; Tedeschi, 1981). Given general social norms that prohibit explicit discrimination and outgroup derogation, white group members usually do not want to be seen as "racists." When they want to say something negative about minorities, they will tend to use denials, disclaimers, or other forms that are intended to avoid a negative impression with their listeners or their readers. That is denials have the function of blocking negative inferences of the recipients about the attitudes of the speaker or writer. Such denials may not only be personal, but especially in elite discourse, they may also pertain to "our" group in general: "We British (Dutch, French) are not racist . . ." That is in talk about minorities, white people often speak as dominant group members.

Denials come in many guises. In general, a denial presupposes a real or potential accusation, reproach, or suspicion of others about one's present or past actions or attitudes, and asserts that such attacks against one's moral integrity are not warranted. That is, denials may be a move in a strategy of *defense*, as well as part of the strategy of positive self-presentation. Thus speakers may not only deny the incriminated (verbal or other) act itself, but also its underlying intentions, purposes, or attitudes, or its noncontrolled consequences: "I did not do/say that," "I did not do/say that on purpose," "That is not what I meant," "You got me wrong," etc. Since lack of specific intentions may diminish responsibility, denials of intentions are a well-known move in defenses against accusations of legal or moral transgression, and typical in denials of discrimination. Thus journalists often deny prejudiced intentions of biased news reports about minorities, e.g., by claiming to have only written "the truth," or by denying responsibility for the effects of their coverage upon the attitudes of the audience.

Another way to avoid negative impressions is to play down, trivialize, or generally to mitigate the seriousness, extent, or consequences of one's negative actions, for instance by using euphemisms in the description of such actions. Indeed, they may deny that their acts or attitudes are negative in the first place. "Telling the truth" may thus be the typical euphemism of those accused of saying or writing derogatory things about minorities. Similarly, even the very term "racism" may thus be declared taboo, for instance in the Netherlands and Germany, where the term is seen to apply only to overt right-wing racism (or to racism abroad), and considered to be "exaggerated" or totally out of place for the more "moderate" or "modern" (Dovidio and Gaertner, 1986) forms of everyday racism, especially among the elites. Instead, if at all, the terms "discrimination," "resentment," or "xenophobia" are used to describe various manifestations of such everyday racism (for an analysis of such events of everyday racism, see Essed, 1991).

Instead of directly or indirectly denying accusations or suspicions of bias or racist attitudes, white people may of course also have recourse to *justifications*, more or less according to the following pattern of argumentation: "I did express a negative judgment, but it was justified in this case, and that does not mean I am a racist" (for various strategies of such justifications, see, e.g., Antaki, 1988; Scott and Lyman, 1968; Tedeschi and Reiss, 1981). Such justifications also play a prominent role in strategies of excuses (Cody and McLaughlin, 1988), for instance in political discourse about immigration: "That we restrict immigration is not because we are racist, but because we want (a) not to worsen the situation of the other immigrants, (b) avoid further unemployment, (c) avoid (white) popular resentment, etc." Justifications may also go one step further and blame the victim: "If they don't get a better education, and engage in crime (drugs), no wonder blacks don't get jobs or are being discriminated against" (Ryan, 1976).

Denials may also transfer the charge to others: "I have nothing against blacks, but my neighbors (customers, etc.) . . ." Ultimately, denials may also reverse the charges and accuse the accuser for having (intentionally) misunderstood the actor/speaker, for having accused the actor/speaker without grounds, or even for being intolerant: "Not WE, but THEY are the real racists." Such reversals are typical for right-wing attacks against antiracists (Murray, 1986; van Dijk, 1991).

Denials not only have discursive and interactional functions at the level of interpersonal communication. We have already stressed that they also have social implications: they are intended to "save face" for the whole ingroup. They express ingroup allegiances and white group solidarity, defend "us" against "them," that is, against minorities and (other) antiracists. They mark social boundaries and reaffirm social and ethnic identities, and self-attribute moral superiority to their own group.

At the same time, denials of racism have a *sociopolitical function*. Denials challenge the very legitimacy of antiracist analysis, and thus are part of the politics of ethnic management: as long as a problem is being denied in the first place, the critics are ridiculed, marginalized, or delegitimated: denials debilitate resistance. As long as racism is denied, there is no need for official measures against it, for stricter laws, regulations, or institutions to combat discrimination, or moral campaigns to change the biased attitudes of whites. By selectively attributing "racism" only to the extreme right, the mainstream parties and institutions at the same time define themselves as being "not racists." "After all [so the argument goes], discrimination is officially prohibited by law, and punished by the courts, so there is no problem, and there is nothing else we can do. We are a tolerant country. There may be incidental acts of discrimination, but that does not make our society or country 'racist.'"

It is this overall social and political myth in which denials function. They thus play a role in the manufacture of the ethnic consensus and, indirectly, contribute to the legitimation of white group dominance, that is to the reproduction of racism. Finally, denials of racism and affirmation of tolerance also have a cultural function when "our" or "western" norms and values are contrasted with those of other, "intolerant" cultures, such as Islam, with the obvious implication that "our" culture is superior (Said, 1981). Such implications, which were prominent during the Rushdie affair and the Gulf War, function within the broader culturalization of modern racism, and its transformation into ethnicism.

Analyzing Denials

Against this very succinctly sketched theoretical framework, let us now examine various forms of denial in different discourse genres. Although denials, such as the widespread disclaimer mentioned above, "I have nothing against . . . but . . . ," are also prevalent in everyday conversations about ethnic affairs (for details, see van Dijk, 1984, 1987), we shall focus only on elite discourse, viz., on the press and on parliamentary discourse. Note though that many dominant properties of such elite discourses also influence everyday talk and opinions about ethnic affairs: similar topics are being discussed (viz., problems, for us, of immigration, crime, deviance, cultural deviance, and ethnic relations), and even similar modes of argumentation, such as the denials that are part of the overall strategies of positive ingroup presentation. In the remainder of this chapter, we shall only focus on these denials (for other properties of elite discourse on ethnic affairs, see van Dijk, 1991, 1993).

The Press

Although discrimination is often covered in the press, though usually defined as incidental, racism is denied in many ways. First of all, racism is usually elsewhere: in the past (during slavery or segregation), abroad (apartheid in South Africa), politically at the far right (racist parties), and socially at the bottom (poor inner cities, skinheads). This is true for both the liberal and the conservative press. This means that it never applies to "us," that is, the moderate mainstream, let alone to the liberal left or to the elites. Those who accuse "us" of racism are therefore severely attacked in much of the conservative press or simply ignored or marginalized in the more liberal press, especially when the press itself is the target of critical analysis. Racism, thus, if discussed at all, is explained away by restricting its definition to old-style, aggressive, ideological racism based on notions of racial superiority. Everyday forms of cultural racism, or ethnicism, are at most characterized as intolerance or xenophobia, which may even be blamed on the victim.

Positive self-presentation

The semantic basis of denial is "truth" as the writer sees it. The denial of racism in the press, therefore, presupposes that the journalist or columnist believes that his or her own group or country is essentially "tolerant" towards minorities or immigrants. Positive self-presentation, thus, is an important move in journalistic discourse, and should be seen as the argumentative denial of the accusations of antiracists:

> (1) (Handsworth.) Contrary to much doctrine, and acknowledging a small malevolent fascist fringe, this is a remarkably tolerant society. But tolerance would be stretched were it to be seen that enforcement of law adopted the principle of reverse discrimination. (*Daily Telegraph*, Editorial, September 11, 1985)

This example not only asserts or presupposes white British "tolerance," but at the same time defines its boundaries. Tolerance might be interpreted as a position of weakness, and therefore it should not be "stretched" too far, lest "every terrorist," "criminal," or other immigrants, take advantage of it. Affirmative action or liberal immigration laws, thus, can only be seen as a form of reverse discrimination, and hence as a form of self-destruction of white Britain. Ironically, therefore, this example is self-defeating because of its internal contradictions: It is not tolerance *per se* that is aimed at, but rather the limitations preventing its "excesses."

Denial and counter-attack

Having constructed a positive self-image of white Britain, the conservative and tabloid press in particular engages in attacks against those who hold a different view, at the same time defending those who agree with its position, as was the case during the notorious Honeyford affair (Honeyford was headmaster of a Bradford school who was suspended, then reinstated, and finally let go with a golden handshake, after having written articles on multicultural education which most of the parents of his mostly Asian students found racist). The attacks on the antiracists often embody denials of racism:

> (2) (Reaction of "race lobby" against Honeyford.) Why is it that this lobby have chosen to persecute this man . . . It is not because he is a racist; it is precisely because he is not a racist, yet has dared to challenge the attitudes, behaviour and approach of the ethnic minority professionals. (*Daily Telegraph*, September 6, 1985)

(3) (Worker accused of racism.) The really alarming thing is that some of these pocket Hitlers of local government are moving into national politics. It's time we set about exposing their antics while we can. Forewarned is forearmed. (*Daily Mail*, Editorial, October 26, 1985)

These examples illustrate several strategic moves in the press campaign against antiracists. First, as we have seen above, denial is closely linked to the presupposition of "truth": Honeyford is presented as defending the "truth," viz., the failure and the anti-British nature of multiculturalism.

Secondly, consequent denials often lead to the strategic move of reversal: Not we are the racists, *they* are the "true racists." This reversal also implies, thirdly, a reversal of the charges: Honeyford, and those who sympathize with him, are the victims, not his Asian students and their parents. Consequently, the antiracists are the enemy: *they* are the ones who persecute innocent, ordinary British citizens, they are the ones who are intolerant. Therefore, victims who resist their attackers may be defined as folk heroes, who "dare" the "antiracist brigade." Ultimately, as in example (3), the charges may be fully reversed, viz., by identifying the symbolic enemy precisely with the categories of their own attacks: they are intolerant, they are totalitarian "pocket Hitlers."

Moral blackmail

One element that was very prominent in the Honeyford affair, as well as in similar cases, was the pretense of censorship: The antiracists not only ignore the "truth" about multicultural society, they also prevent others (us) from telling the truth. Repeatedly, thus, journalists and columnists argue that this "taboo" and this "censorship" must be broken in order to be able to tell the "truth," as was the case after the disturbances in Tottenham:

(4) (Tottenham.) The time has come to state the truth without cant and without hypocrisy . . . the strength to face the facts without being silenced by the fear of being called racist. (*Daily Mail*, October 9, 1985, column by Linda Lee-Potter)

Such examples also show that the authors feel morally blackmailed, while at the same time realizing that to "state the truth," meaning "to say negative things about minorities," may well be against the prevalent norms of tolerance and understanding. Clamoring for the "truth" thus expresses a dilemma, even if the dilemma is only apparent: the apparent dilemma is a rhetorical strategy to accuse the opponent of censorship or blackmail, not the result of moral soul-searching and a difficult decision. After all, the same newspapers extensively to write negative things about young blacks, and never hesitate to write what they see as the "truth." Nobody "silences" them, and the taboo is only imaginary. On the contrary, the right-wing press in Britain reaches many millions of readers.

Subtle denials

Denials are not always explicit. There are many ways to express doubt, distance, or nonacceptance of statements or accusations by others. When the official Commission for Racial Equality (CRE) in 1985 published a report on discrimination in the UK, outright denial of the facts would hardly be credible. Other discursive means, such as quotation marks, and the use of words like "claim" or "allege," presupposing doubt on the part of the writer, may be employed in accounting for the facts, as is the case in the following editorial of the *Daily Telegraph*:

> (5) In its report which follows a detailed review of the operation of the 1976 Race Relations Act, the Commission claims that ethnic minorities continue to suffer high levels of discrimination and disadvantage. (*Daily Telegraph*, August 1, 1985)

Such linguistic tricks do not go unnoticed, as we may see in the following reaction to this passage in a letter from Peter Newsam, then director of the CRE:

> (6) Of the Commission you say "it claims that ethnic minorities continue to suffer high levels of discrimination and disadvantage." This is like saying that someone "claims" that July was wet. It was. And it is also a fact supported by the weight of independent research evidence that discrimination on racial grounds, in employment, housing and services, remains at a disconcertingly high level. (*Daily Telegraph*, August 7, 1985)

Denials, thus, may be subtly conveyed by expressing doubt or distance. Therefore, the very notion of "racism" usually appears between quotation marks, especially also in the headlines. Such scare quotes are not merely a journalistic device for reporting opinions or controversial points of view. If that were the case, the opinions with which the newspaper happens to agree would also have to be put between quotation marks, which is not always the case. Rather, apart from signaling journalistic doubt and distance, the quotation marks also connote "unfounded accusation." The use of quotation marks around the notion of racism has become so much routine, that even in cases where the police or the courts themselves established that racism was involved in a particular case, the conservative press may maintain the quotation marks out of sheer habit.

Mitigation

Our conceptual analysis of denial has already shown that denial may also be implied by various forms of mitigation, such as toning down, using euphemisms or other circumlocutions that minimize the act itself or the responsibility of the accused. In the same editorial of the *Daily Telegraph* we quoted above, we find the following statement:

> (7) (CRE report.) No one would deny the fragile nature of race relations in Britain today or that there is misunderstanding and distrust between parts of the community. (*Daily Telegraph*, Editorial, August 1, 1985)

Thus instead of inequality or racism, race relations are assumed to be "fragile," whereas "misunderstanding and distrust" are also characteristic of these relations. Interestingly, this passage also explicitly denies the prevalence of denials, and therefore might be read, as such, as a concession: There are problems. However, the way this concession is rhetorically presented by way of various forms of mitigation, suggests, in the context of the rest of the same editorial, that the concession is apparent. Such apparent concessions are another major form of disclaimer in discourse about ethnic relations, as we also have them in statements like: "There are also intelligent blacks, but . . ." or "I know that minorities sometimes have problems, but . . ." Note also that in the example from the *Daily Telegraph* the mitigation not only appears in the use of euphemisms, but also in the *redistribution of responsibility*, and hence in the denial of blame. It is not we (whites) who are mainly responsible for the tensions between the communities, but everybody is, as is suggested by the use of the impersonal existential phrase: "*There is misunderstanding . . .*" Apparently, one effective move of denial is either to dispute the responsible agency, or to conceal the agency.

Parliamentary Discourse

In close symbiosis with the mass media, politics plays a prominent role in the definition of the ethnic situation. In western Europe, decision-making by the administration and the bureaucracy, and parliamentary debates in the 1980s and 1990s, increasingly deal with ethnic affairs, immigration, and refugees. Persistent social inequalities, unemployment, affirmative action, educational "disadvantage," popular resentment against immigration, and the arrival of "waves" of new refugees from the south, are among the major topics on the political agenda, which are "made public," and possibly emphasized, by the press, and thus by the population at large. Note that since parliamentary speeches are for the record, and usually written in advance, we should not normally expect, except by right-wing speakers, overt derogation of minority groups. However, since restrictions on immigration or refusals to legislate in favor of minorities need to be legitimated we may nevertheless expect negative other-presentation of immigrants, refugees, or minorities. These subtle forms of derogation, in turn, require the usual forms of positive self-presentation, and hence of denial. Let us give some examples from parliamentary debates in the UK, France, Germany, the Netherlands, and the USA (for detail, see van Dijk, 1993). We shall not identify the individual speakers: here we are only interested, more generally, in official forms of talk about ethnic minorities.

Nationalist self-glorification

Parliament is the prime forum for nationalistic rhetoric. This is particularly true when international norms and values, such as democracy, equal rights, and tolerance are involved. Accusations of racism in such a context may easily be heard as a moral indictment of the nation as a whole, and are therefore permitted, though resented, only in partisan debates, in which one party accuses the other of racism. After all, as we have seen, racism is always elsewhere, and always a property of the others.

> (8) I believe that we are a wonderfully fair country. We stick to the rules unlike some foreign Governments. (UK)

> (9) Our country has long been open to foreigners, a tradition of hospitality going back, beyond the revolution, to the *ancien régime*. (France)

> (10) I know no other country on this earth that gives more prominence to the rights of resident foreigners as does this bill in our country. (Germany)

> (11) There are so many great things about our country, all the freedoms that we have, speech, religion, the right to vote and choose our leaders and of course our greatness lies in our mobility, the ability to each and every one of us, regardless of the circumstances of our birth, to rise in American society, to pursue our individual dreams. (USA)

Although nationalist rhetoric may differ in different countries (it is usually more exuberant in France and in the USA, for instance), the basic strategy of positive self-presentation appears in all Houses: we are fair, respect human rights, have a long tradition of tolerance, etc. It is not uncommon to hear in each parliament that at least some representatives think of their own country as the most liberal, freedom-loving, democratic etc. in the world.

Fair, but . . .

Such self-glorification, especially when introducing a debate on minorities or immigration, has various functions in parliamentary discourse. For those groups or parties that oppose legislation in favor of minorities or immigrants, positive self-presentation often functions as a disclaimer, that is, as an introduction for a BUT, followed by arguments in favor of special restrictions, as is also the case in the following fragment from a radio interview with the Dutch Prime Minister, Ruud Lubbers:

(12) In practice, we should come to opportunities and possibilities for them, but in practice we should also come to a less soft approach. There should be a line like: we also hold them responsible [literally: "we address them"].

Elsewhere we find a nearly routine combination of fairness on the one hand, and firmness, realism, pragmatism etc. On the other hand:

(13) If we are to work seriously for harmony, non-discrimination, and equality of opportunity in our cities, that has to be accompanied by firm and fair immigration control. (UK)

(14) It belongs to this fair balance of interests that the further immigration of foreigners must be limited, because for each society there are limits to the ability and the readiness to integrate. (Germany)

(15) This substitute offers the House of Representatives an opportunity to enact a landmark civil rights bill that is both fair and pragmatic. (USA)

This remarkably similar rhetoric of fairness ("fair, but strict" etc.) in the different countries also seeks to combine two opposed ideological or political aims, viz., the humanitarian values of tolerance or hospitality on the one hand, and the commonsense values of "realism" on the other hand. In other words, the humanitarian aims are recognized, but at the same time they are rejected as being too idealistic, and therefore unpractical in the business of everyday political management and decision-making. The reference to fairness also serves as an element in a "balance," viz., in order to mitigate the negative implications of proposed legislation, such as limitations on further immigration in the European debates, and limitations on the 1990 Civil Rights Bill (eventually vetoed by President Bush) in the USA. Fairness in such rhetoric usually is supported by the claim that the (restrictive) measures are always "in their own best interests."

Denial of racism

In such a political context of public impression management, the denial of racism plays a prominent role. Whatever the political orientation or party involved, including the extremist right, all parliamentarians emphatically reject any accusation or suggestion of prejudice, discrimination, or racism. Indeed, the more racist the opinions professed, the more insistent are the denials of racism, as may be apparent in the following quote from a representative of the Front National in the French *Assemblée Nationale*:

> (16) We are neither racist nor xenophobic. Our aim is only that, quite naturally, there be a hierarchy, because we are dealing with France, and France is the country of the French.

Note that an implicit but ("only") follows the denial. The speaker (the leader of the Front National, Le Pen, himself) even claims that it is "natural" to have a hierarchy between the "own group," the French, and the immigrants. This assignment of a "natural" right to a superior position is at the heart of racist ideologies.

Besides the discursive and political strategy of populism, which is very prominent in such debates ("The people would resent it," "You should listen to what ordinary French, English . . . people say"), we also find the element of *euphemism*: we are not racist, only worried. Here is a more sophisticated example of such a strategy:

> (17) The French are not racist. But, facing this continuous increase of the foreign population in France, one has witnessed the development, in certain cities and neighbourhoods, of reactions that come close to xenophobia. In the eyes of the French unemployed man, for instance, the foreigner may easily become a rival, towards whom a sentiment of animosity may threaten to appear.

Following the usual "but," we do not find, as in other disclaimers, a negative statement about immigrants, but rather an explanation of the reaction of the "common man" (women are apparently not involved). Note that the way this explanation is formulated ("continuous increase," "rival") suggests understanding, if not an excuse, as in the usual accounts of racism in terms of economic competition. The denial of racism itself is rather complex, however. It is a denial that holds for the French in general. It is followed by a partial concession, duly limited by heavy mitigation and hedging ("coming close to xenophobia," "a sentiment of animosity may threaten to appear"), as well as limited in place ("in certain cities"). In other words, prejudice, discrimination, and racism are local incidents, and should also be seen as being provoked by continuous immigration, arguments we also found in the right-wing British press.

When restrictive measures are being debated, those who support them feel impelled to remind their audience, and the public at large, that such political decisions have nothing to do with prejudice or racism:

> (18) I hope that people outside, whether they are black or white and wherever they come from, will recognize that these are not major changes resulting from prejudice. (UK)

Such denials need argumentative support. Saying only that the measures are "fair" may be seen as too flimsy. Therefore they are often followed by the moves we have found earlier, such as concern for the inner cities. Note that such arguments also imply a move of transfer: we are not racist, but the poor people in the inner cities are, and we should avoid exacerbating the mood of resentment among the population at large. This argument is rather typical of what we have called "elite racism," which consistently denies racism among the own elite group, but recognizes that others, especially poor white people, may fail to be as tolerant.

Denial and reproach

In the analysis of the British press, we have found that denials of racism easily transform into attacks against antiracists. Such a strategy may also be found in parliamentary discourse. Thus, conservative representatives will not accept accusations or even implicit suggestions that their stricter immigration or ethnic minority policies are categorized as racist by other politicians. Since the official norm is "that we are all tolerant citizens," such allegations are declared unacceptable:

> (19) Addressing myself to the people of the left, I repeat again that we are
> . . . I have noted in your words, my God, terms such as racism and xenophobia, that those who do not support your proposals would be judged with the same terms. It should be understood once and for all: we are not racists because we combat your text. (France)

> (20) Well, now can we also agree this afternoon that you can have different philosophies about how to achieve through law civil rights

and equal opportunities for everybody without somehow being anti-civilrights or being a racist or something like that. (USA)

One interesting case may be found in a German debate on the new aliens bill. When one of the Green Party representatives qualifies the provisions of the bill as "racist," a term that is as unusual in official German discourse as it is in the Netherlands, other representatives are shocked:

> (21) A chill ran down my back when our colleague . . . said that this bill was a form of institutionalized racism. Whereas the older ones among us had to live twelve years under institutionalized racism, ladies and gentlemen, I beg you, and in particular our younger colleagues, to show respect for these terrible experiences, and not to introduce such concepts to our everyday political business.

In other words, evaluations in terms of racism are limited only to the Nazi past, and are banned from official political discourse. At most, the term *Ausländerfeindlichkeit* (literally: animosity against foreigners) may be used. "Racism" thus is by definition too strong, if only because the present situation cannot be compared to the monstrosities of the Nazis. A similar attitude exists in the Netherlands, where racism is also avoided as a term in public (political, media) discourse because it is understood only in terms of extremist, right-wing ideologies of racial superiority.

Reversal

Although moderate reproaches directed against antiracist delegates are not uncommon in parliament, reversal is rather exceptional. However, it is quite typical for right-wing party representatives, such as those of the Front National in France. Being routinely accused, also explicitly, of racism, they go beyond mere denial, and reverse the charges. For them, this means that the others, and especially the socialists, allegedly letting is so many immigrants and granting them equal rights, are guilty of what they call "anti-French racism":

> (22) There exists a form of racism, my dear colleagues [interruptions] that is passed over silently, but of which the manifestations nowadays

reach an insupportable level and a scope that should concern us: that is the anti-French racism.

Another way of reversing the charges is to accuse the antiracists of being themselves responsible for creating racism in the country, if only by not listening to the people and by letting in so many non-European immigrants:

(23) Well, France today, according to what those creatures of the whole world tell us who often have come to take refuge in our country . . . France is the least racist country that exists in the world. We can't tolerate to hear it said that France is a racist country . . . In this respect, this law proposal, because of the debate that takes place at this moment, secretes and fabricates racism!

These examples taken from several western parliaments show that although the debate may be couched in less extremist terms than in much of the right-wing or tabloid press, or in everyday conversations, rather similar strategies and moves are used to talk about ethnic affairs. Most characteristic of this kind of political discourse is not merely the nationalist self-praise, but also the strategic management of impression: whatever we decide, we are fair. Since, especially in Europe, ethnic minorities, let alone new immigrants and refugees, have virtually no political power, this "balancing act" of presenting policies as "firm but fair" is obviously addressed primarily to the dominant white public at large. When defined as humane without being too soft, thus, the government and its supporting parties may be acceptable as essentially reasonable: "We take energetic measures, but we are not racist."

In other words, besides managing impressions, such political discourse also manages its own legitimation by manufacturing consent on ethnic policies, and at the same time manages the politics of ethnic affairs, immigration, and international relations.

Conclusions

Racism, defined as a system of racial and ethnic inequality, can survive only when it is daily reproduced through multiple acts of exclusion, inferiorization, or marginalization. Such acts need to be sustained by an ideological system and by a set of attitudes that legitimate difference and dominance. Discourse is the principal means for the construction and reproduction of this sociocognitive framework. At the same time, there are norms and values of tolerance and democratic humanitarianism, which may be felt to be inconsistent with biased attitudes and negative text and talk about minorities. To manage such contradictions, white speakers engage in strategies of positive self-presentation in order to be able credibly to present the "others" in a negative light. Disclaimers, mitigations, euphemisms, transfers, and many other forms of racism denial are the routine moves in social face-keeping, so that ingroup members are able to come to terms with their own prejudices. At the same time, these denials of racism have important social and political functions, e.g., in the management of ethnic affairs and the delegitimation of resistance. We have seen that, especially in elite discourse, for instance in the media and in the legislature, the "official" versions of own-group tolerance, and the rejection of racism as an implied or explicit accusation, are crucial for the self-image of the elite as being tolerant, understanding leaders. However, we have also seen how these strategies of denial at the same time confirm their special role in the formulation and the reproduction of racism.

References

Antaki, C. (ed.) (1988). *Analysing Everyday Explanation: A Casebook of Methods.* London: Sage.

Brown, P. and Levinson, S. C. (1987). *Politeness: Some Universals in Language Use.* Cambridge: Cambridge University Press.

Cody, M. J. and McLaughlin, M. L. (1988). "Accounts on Trial: Oral Arguments in Traffic Court." In C. Antaki (ed.), *Analysing Everyday Explanation: A Casebook of Methods.* London: Sage.

Dovidio, J. F. and Gaertner, S. L. (eds.) (1986). *Prejudice, Discrimination and Racism.* New York: Academic Press.

Essed, P. (1991). *Understanding Everyday Racism.* Newbury Park, CA: Sage.

Goffman, E. (1967). *The Presentation of Self in Everyday Life.* Harmondsworth: Penguin.

Murray, N. (1986). " 'Anti-racists' and Other Demons: The Press and Ideology in Thatcher's Britain." *Race and Class,* 27 (3), pp. 1–20.

Ryan, W. (1976). *Blaming the Victim,* revised edition. New York: Vintage.

Said, E. (1981). *Covering Islam: How the Media and the Experts Determine How We See the Rest of the World.* New York: Pantheon.

Scott, M. B. and Lyman, S. M. (1968). "Accounts: Inquiries in the Social Construction of Reality." *American Sociological Review*, 33, pp. 46–62.

Tedeschi, J. T. (ed.) (1981). *Impression Management. Theory and Social Psychological Research.* New York: Academic Press.

——and Reiss, M. (1981). "Identities, the Phenomenal Self, and Laboratory Research." In J. T. Tedeschi (ed.), *Impression Management. Theory and Social Psychological Research.* New York: Academic Press.

van Dijk, T. A. (1984). *Prejudice in Discourse.* Amsterdam: Benjamins.

——(1987). *Communicating Racism.* Newbury Park, CA: Sage.

——(1991). *Racism and the Press.* London: Routledge.

——(1993). *Elite Discourse and Racism.* Newbury Park, CA: Sage.

18

Whiteness and Ethnicity in the History of "White Ethnics" in the United States

David Roediger

Barbara Fields has recently argued that the absence of the term *white people* in the United States Constitution "is not surprising [since] in a legal document . . . slang of that kind would be hopelessly imprecise." Nonetheless, the first Congress convened under that Constitution voted in 1790 to require that a person be "white" in order to become a naturalized citizen of the US. Predictably enough, the hopeless imprecision of the term left the courts with impossible problems of interpretation that stretched well into the twentieth century. As Robert T. Devlin, United States Attorney at San Francisco, understated it in 1907: "There is considerable uncertainty as to just what nationalities come within the term 'white person.'" The courts thus discovered in the early part of this century what historians have belatedly learned in its latter stages: that the social fiction of race defies rigorous definition. If science were to determine whiteness, problems proliferated because ethnological wisdom constantly changed. In particular, modern ethnology shunned the word *white* and used instead terms like *caucasian* and *Aryan*, which were not current when the legislation was passed in 1790. Moreover, science tended to classify Syrians and Asian Indians as caucasians, a view that clashed with the commonsense view of federal naturalization officials and of some judges bent on excluding them as nonwhites.

If the ground were shifted to culture and geography as determinants of who was white, the inconvenient fact was that these standards too had evolved messily over time. The Pennsylvania jurist Oliver B. Dickinson acutely noted, "Although the original 1790 statute probably was not intended to include the Latin races . . . later immigration expanded the term to cover Latin Europeans," and still later southeastern Europeans came to be included. Color differences were so varied within so-called "races" as to preclude the possibility that whiteness could have literally been measured by (absence of) pigmentation. The 1923 Supreme Court decision to deny naturalization to Bhagat Singh Thind marked the culmination of a process by which the legal system, in the words of Joan M. Jensen, "rejected science, history, legal precedent and logic to put the Constitution at the disposal of a legal fiction called 'the common man'" – an invented figure who knew that Asian Indians were not white. Between 1923 and 1927, sixty-five Asian Indians suffered denaturalization in the wake of the Thind decision. Lower courts had naturalized them as white immigrants, but under the test of "common understanding" they had become nonwhite.[1]

If the legal and social history of Jim Crow often turned on the question "Who was Black?" the legal and social history of immigration often turned on the question "Who was white?" And yet, amidst the large and sophisticated literature on ethnic consciousness and Americanization among immigrants, we know very little about how the Irish and Italians, for example, became white; about how the Chinese and Japanese became nonwhite; or about how groups like Asian Indians and Mexican Americans were at least partly identified as white before becoming nonwhite.[2]

The recent outpouring of historical writing on the social construction of whiteness as a racial category and as an identity opens the possibility of closing this gap in the historical literature and of undertaking a full reconsideration of the relationship between race and ethnicity in US history.[3] Until now, most objections to the conflation of the category of race with that of ethnicity have turned on the quite reasonable point that, historically, civilly, and structurally, racial minorities have not been treated in a relevantly similar way to those immigrants who came to be identified as "white ethnics." Richard Williams's elegant *Hierarchical Structures and Social Value* has recently pushed this argument to the fascinating conclusion that in the US ethnicity is made possible by race – that ethnicity is a social status assigned to those immigrants who, though slotted into low-wage jobs, were *not* reduced to the slavery or systematic civil discrimination that "racial" minorities suffered. But however compelling the case that racial oppression has not equalled ethnic oppression, another challenge deserves to be made to analyses that do not sharply differentiate between race and ethnicity as ideological categories. *Among whites*, racial identity (whiteness) and ethnic identity are distinct, and this article will argue, often counterposed, forms of consciousness.[4]

This latter distinction, and its importance, becomes clearer as we look at a recent passage from the distinguished legal historian William Forbath's *Law and the Shaping of the American Labor Movement*. Forbath aptly summarizes the position of the "new labor history" on why US labor is not so "exceptional" by world standards in its historical lack of class consciousness. He writes, "Ethnic division is the other principle factor in the traditional exceptionalism story. In any revised account, ethnic and racial cleavages will surely remain central. However, the new labor historians have discovered that ethnic identities and affiliations were not as corrosive of class-based identities and actions as we tend to assume."[5] The sliding here from an argument about ethnicity to one about race and ethnicity and back to one about ethnicity is significant. Surely, as the work of Wayne Broehl, Earl Lewis, Vicki Ruiz, Victor Greene, Robin D. G. Kelley, and others shows, specific white ethnic (that is, Polish American, Irish American, and so on), African American and Mexican American cultural forms and institutions often undergirded class mobilization in the US past.[6] But what happens when we remember that racial identity also means *whiteness*? The central point of much of the recent writing on the instances of attempts to organize specifically as white workers – in hate strikes and campaigns for Oriental exclusionism, for example – is how fully such mobilization played into the emergence of a narrow, brittle, and at best craft-conscious labor movement. Ethnicity is one thing in this case, and whiteness quite another.

"Racial identities are not only Black, Latino, Asian, Native American and so on," Coco Fusco has written, "they are also white. To ignore white ethnicity is to redouble its hegemony by naturalizing it." Fusco's comment is breathtakingly clear in its recognition of the need to explore the social construction of white identities, but her use of the term *white ethnicity* introduces interesting complications with regard to how white Americans have historically come to think of themselves as white. Fusco uses white ethnicity in the same sense as one might use *white racial identity*, illustrating a long tendency in US scholarship to conflate race and ethnicity. But *white ethnicity* has also meant, at least for the last forty years, the consciousness of a distinct identity among usually second- or third-generation immigrants who both see themselves and are seen as racially white and as belonging to definable ethnic groups. And the complications do not end there. As Barry Goldberg and Colin Greer have observed, this "white ethnicity," which gained force in major cities from the 1950s onwards in opposition to racial integration of neighborhoods, was not just a heading grouping together specific ethnic identities (Greek American, Polish American, Italian American, and so on) but a "pan-ethnic" ideology that "did not emphasize cultural distinction but the shared values of a white immigrant heritage." Thus it was possible to become more self-consciously "white ethnic," but less self-consciously Greek, Polish, or Italian at the same time.[7]

Though the phrase *white ethnic* trips off the tongue easily today, the relationship between whiteness and ethnicity is in no sense simple, not now and certainly not historically. This essay attempts to survey some of the historical complexities of the interplay of racial and ethnic consciousness among whites in the US. Its very preliminary nature qualifies it as less a survey of what we know about this understudied topic than as a survey of what we do not know. Although we badly need studies of how "nonwhite" ethnic groups became so defined – indeed, in effect became "races" – the focus here is on the process of "becoming white" with material on nonwhiteness largely included to illuminate that process.

The Not-Yet-White Ethnic

Alex Haley's epilogue to Malcolm X's *Autobiography* features a rivetting scene in which Malcolm admires European children newly arrived at a US airport and predicts that they are soon to use their first English word: *nigger*. The force of the passage lies in its dramatic rendering of the extent to which European immigrants became not just Americans but specifically *white* Americans and of the apparent ease with which they did so.[8] As important as the telescoped, long-range historical truth in the passage is, it also leads us to miss – as most historians have missed – the dramatic, tortuous subplots of immigration history via which, as James Baldwin has written, arriving Europeans "became white."[9]

The history of what John Bukowczyk has called the "not-yet-white ethnic" remains to be written. Its writing will sharply focus our attention on the fact that immigrants could be Irish, Italian, Hungarian, and Jewish, for example, without being white. Many groups now commonly termed part of the "white" or "white ethnic" population were in fact historically regarded as nonwhite, or of debatable racial heritage, by the host American citizenry. In the mid-nineteenth century, the racial status of Catholic Irish incomers became the object of fierce, extended debate. The "simian" and "savage" Irish only gradually fought, worked, and voted their ways into the white race in the US. Well into the twentieth century, Blacks were counted as "smoked Irishmen" in racist and anti-Irish US slang. Later, sometimes darker, migrants from Southern and Eastern Europe were similarly cast as nonwhite. The nativist folk wisdom that held that an Irishman was a Black, inside out, became transposed to the reckoning that the turning inside out of Jews produced "niggers." Factory managers spoke of employees distinctly as Jews and as "white men," though the "good Jew" was sometimes counted as white. Poorer Jews were slurred as Black with special frequency. Indeed a 1987 Supreme Court decision used the record of Jews having been seen as a distinct race in the nineteenth century as precedent to allow a Jewish group to sue under *racial* discrimination statutes. Stock anti-Black humor was pressed into service as anti-Semitic, anti-Czech, and, later, anti-Polish humor. Slavic "Hunkies" were nonwhite in steel towns. Among "white" miners defending their "American towns" in Arizona mining areas, not only the Chinese and Mexicans, but also Eastern and Southern Europeans, were termed nonwhite. As the leading scholar of nativism, John Higham, has observed, "In all sections [of the US] native-born and northern European laborers called themselves "white men" to distinguish themselves from the southern Europeans whom they worked beside."[10]

Of course none of this implies, as the modern white ethnics' historical memories and invented traditions often do, that the immigrant experience was parallel to that of African Americans, except for the more successful outcome, arising from determination and effort. Not-yet-white immigrants consistently had a more secure claim to citizenship, to civil rights and political power, and a greater opportunity to choose to pass as whites, especially in seeking jobs. The duration of "not-yet-whiteness," as measured against that of racial oppression in the US, was quite short. In Joe Eszterhaus's much-better-than-the-movie labor novel, *F.I.S.T.*, set in and after the 1930s, the Afro-Polish freight-handler Lincoln Dombrowsky is plagued by a boss who "kept after him, hitting his buzzer. Calling him 'polack' as if he were saying 'nigger.' "[11] Readers understand that the implied use of the latter term greatly added to the sting of the former. It is, as Lawrence Joseph's withering review of the recent collection *Devil's Night* by the Michigan-raised Israeli writer Ze'ev Chafets, maintains, "silly" for Chafets to portray himself as a "nonwhite" in writing about Detroit. Chafets's self-described "bad hair" and "swarthy skin" notwithstanding, Joseph argues, "In America, blacks cannot choose which racial side they're on; in America, Chafets can."[12] To write the history of the whitening of the not-yet-white ethnic thus requires close attention to change over time. In reconstructing that history we may, for example, not only develop an appreciation for why the pioneer labor researcher David Saposs consistently referred to anti-Slavic and anti-Southern European prejudice as "race prejudice" as late as the 1920s but also a sense of the problems raised by his and others doing so. Further complexity arises when we cease to regard racial and ethnic identities as categories into which individuals simply are "slotted," as Williams's *Hierarchical Structures* has it, and begin to see whiteness as in part a category into which people place themselves.[13] James Baldwin's point that Europeans arrived in the US and became white – "by deciding they were white" – powerfully directs our attention to the fact that white ethnics, while they lived under conditions not of their own choosing, by and large chose whiteness, and even struggled to be recognized as white.

We urgently need studies of how and why this choice was made by specific immigrant groups. It is not strictly true that, as Baldwin argues, "no one was white before he or she came to America." In a few cities providing significant numbers of migrants, such as London, there was a significant Black population and a developing sense of whiteness within the working class before immigration. White Cuban immigrants brought to the US a sense of the importance of race, though one not nearly as finely honed as that present in the US. We need also to know far more about folk beliefs regarding Blacks in areas like Ireland, Germany, and Slavic Europe. The extent to which, as Williams argues, English anti-Irish oppression was racism rather than ethnic prejudice – or to which anti-Sicilian oppression in Italy or anti-Gypsy and anti-Semitic oppression in Europe involved a kind of race-thinking – deserves consideration in accounting for the development of a sense of whiteness among immigrants to the US. Robbie McVeigh's astute comments on "anti-traveler" ideas as a source of racism in Ireland begin such studies penetratingly. Nonetheless, in its broad outline Baldwin's point is hardly assailable. Norwegians, for example, did not spend a great deal of time and energy in Norway thinking of themselves as white. As the great Irish nationalist and antiracist Daniel O'Connell thundered to Irish Americans who increasingly asserted their whiteness in the 1840s, "It was not in Ireland you learned this cruelty."[14]

But neither was whiteness *immediately* learned in the United States. At times a strong sense of ethnic identity could cut *against* the development of a white identity. Thus Poles in the Chicago stockyards community initially saw the post-World War I race riots there as an affair between the whites and the Blacks, with Poles separate and uninvolved. The huge numbers of "birds of passage" – migrants working for a time in the US and then returning home – were probably less than consumed by a desire to build a white American identity. That the native population questioned their whiteness may also have led immigrants to a sense of apartness from white America and occasionally to a willingness to sympathize and fraternize with African Americans. The best-studied example of the dynamics of such solidarity and mixing is that of the Italian (and especially Sicilian) immigrant population in the late nineteenth and early twentieth centuries, especially in Louisiana – a "not-yet-white" population both in the view of white Louisianans, and in its self-perception. Many Black Louisianans, according to Hodding Carter, Sr's *Southern Legacy*, "made unabashed distinctions between Dagoes and white folks and treated [Italians] with a friendly, first-name familiarity." White natives also made such distinctions, counting "black dagoes" as neither Black nor white. If Paola Giordano exaggerated in treating Italian Louisianans unequivocally as a group that "associated freely with the Blacks, going clearly against the accepted social order," he did so only slightly. The associations of Blacks and Italians took place at peddlers' carts, in the cane fields, in the timber camps, and in the halls and bars where jazz was made.[15] Italian–Black solidarity was also strikingly present, albeit alongside its opposite, in New York City and, from Buffalo to California, Italians suffered from racial typing and what Micaela di Leonardo calls "racist oppression."[16]

The Italian and Polish examples are far from isolated ones of mixing and solidarity. However vexed the record of relations between African Americans and Jews, the history record of solidarity with Black civil rights causes by radical and mainstream Jewish organizations and individuals is clear. The important Ukrainian American paper *Svoboda Cbob' OAA* included militant antilynching articles and even homages to John Brown. Roger Horowitz's work on interracial unionism in meatpacking identifies Croatian American workers in Kansas City as "among white packinghouse workers" the group most clearly committed to interracialism. He attributes this commitment to the Croats sharing oppression with Blacks as they worked "at the bottom end of the employment ladder [and] chafed under mistreatment by German foremen who called them 'Hunky' rather than their . . . name." Raymond Mohl's and Neil Betten's research on Gary, Indiana shows examples of positive Black–Greek associations. In Houston, such interracial contacts were not pronounced, as Greek Americans quickly learned Jim Crow. But the Greek community also long continued to differentiate itself from *i aspri* (that is, "the whites"), a term often used disparagingly. The Mississippi Chinese, whose racial status was the object of contention over decades but who arguably eventually became accepted as white, also frequently socially mixed with and married Blacks in the early years after migrating. Even some Irish were "not yet white" in their own eyes, and not just in the eyes of nativists, in the 1820s and 1830s and mixed considerably with free Blacks.

As the term *not-yet-white ethnic* implies, many of these patterns of association of immigrants and Blacks were ephemeral. Moreover, it was quite possible for immigrants and African Americans not to see their interactions in Black–white terms but nonetheless to regard each other with suspicion and even hatred, much as rival immigrant groups did at times. Still the patterns are important in that they signal that the "white ethnic" developed historically and that he or she was certainly not white because of his or her ethnicity. Indeed at times of great identification with homeland and ethnicity, immigrants' identification with whiteness was often minimal.

Americanization or Whitening?

Malcolm X therefore had a great deal of the story right when he argued that in the process of Americanizing European immigrants acquired a sense of whiteness and of white supremacy. As groups made the transition from Irish in America or Poles in America to Irish Americans or Polish Americans, they also became white Americans. In doing so they became white ethnics but also became less specifically ethnic, not only because they sought to assimilate into the broad category of American but also because they sought to be accepted as white rather than as Irish or Polish. In the Irish case this seeking of whiteness involved constructing a pan-white identity in which Irish Americans struggled to join even the *English* in the same racial category. In Ireland, it goes without saying, there was little talk of the common whiteness uniting Anglo-Saxon and Celtic peoples.

Nonetheless the precise relationships among Americanization, whiteness and loss of specific ethnicity are extremely complex. One complicating factor is that immigrants at times developed significant contacts with Black culture, and through those contacts maintained elements of their own ethnic cultures that resonated with Black culture, even as they embraced whiteness. The haunting example of the blacked-up Irish minstrel, singing songs of lost land and exile, is, as Leni Sloan has tellingly observed, an extreme case of the phenomenon. The essence of minstrelsy was the whiteness – not specific ethnicity – beneath the mask, but elements of Irish memory and culture were perversely maintained in blackface. Alexander Saxton's fine World War II labor novel *Bright Web in the Darkness* provides a more modest and modern example. Its hero, the young union militant Tom O'Regan, notices that his wife-to-be is standing with a Black student when he picks her up from a welding class. "So," O'Regan asks, "who's the smoked Irishman?" Sensing disapproval, he adds, "Oh, it's only a joke, Sally, don't act so huffy. After all, I'm an Irishman . . . like you're all the time telling me." Saxton here picks up on the combination of racism, defensiveness, and a certain desire to keep alive comparisons of Black and Irish that runs through Irish American retellings of "Paddy and the Slave" jokes.[17] Still more recently, as Donald Tricarico has shown, the most self-consciously "proud because we're Italian" segment of New York City youth culture has "generously appropriated" African American styles in forming a "guido" subculture. Deriding assimilationist "wannabes," Guidos, some-times called B-boys, have adopted the anti-Italian slur "Guinea" – a term perfectly illustrative of the "not-yet-white" period of Italian American history – as their preferred form of address. They have become able hiphop musicians. Nonetheless, Tricarico adds, Guidos on other levels "resist identification with Black youth" and "bite the hand that feeds them style."[18]

Moreover, partial identification with African American culture can-not simply be connected to a defense of specific ethnicity against the cultural homogeneity or the emptiness of white American culture. It may well be that, as the music historian Ronald Morris has argued, Sicil-ians playing jazz in New Orleans embraced Black music because "Sicil-ians were like black people in seeing music as a highly personalized affair . . . born of collective experience." But in the playing, Sicilians not only retained this sensibility but contributed to creating a new American art form, though far from a white American one. Louis Prima, the second-generation Italian American jazz great, may have rebelled out of some sense of ethnic pride when forced to learn to play the violin in the clas-sical tradition "as a means of cultural assimilation." But when he picked up the horn and discovered Louis Armstrong, he moved into a wide and great Black and American tradition in a career that took him to the most famous "white" clubs in New York City, to the Apollo in Harlem, the Howard in Washington, DC, and the palatial hotels of Las Vegas, but, out of principle, not to segregated Southern venues. The same might be said of Chicago's ethnic jazzmen, especially those in and around the Austin High Gang, who fled the homogenizing influences of suburban culture and assimilationism and preserved much of the best of immigrant resistance to routinization via an identification with African American culture, even as they helped innovate within an American music. The best modern example is undoubtedly Johnny Otis, the important bluesman and West Coast music promoter. Otis, born of Greek immigrant parents who ran small stores in Black neighbor-hoods, chose the vibrancy of African American life over what he saw as the relative stagnation of white American mass culture and then pio-neered in forms of rock and roll, which much changed US culture and the world's.

The examples of Prima and Otis suggest that it was at least possible to become an American, rather than to become a white American, and that through participation in an "incontestably mulatto" American culture a greater part of that which was vital in immigrant culture was capable of being preserved and developed than by assimilating to white Americanism. However, such glorious subplots in immigration history remain subplots. In particular, political mobilization around the claiming of white Americanism by immigrants was far more constant and powerful than the episodic claiming of a nonracial Americanism – as perhaps in the case of the early CIO or the Knights of Columbus's response to the resurgence of Anglo-Saxonism after World War I with the antiracist "Gifts of American peoples" initiatives. The very claiming of a place in the US legally involved, as the Asian Indian example shows, a claiming of whiteness.

But more than that, immigrants often were moved to struggle to equate whiteness with Americanism in order to turn arguments over immigration from the question of who was foreign to the question of who was white. Nativists frequently favorably compared the long-established Black population with the newcoming immigrant one as an argument to curtail the rights of the latter. Abolitionists made the same comparison to buttress the case for African American freedom. Blacks at times used their long-established tenure in America to argue that they should be protected against "invading" Italians or Chinese or at least placed on a par with the immigrants.

Immigrants could not win on the question of who was foreign. They lost as long as the issue was whether, as Jack London put it, "Japs" and "Dagoes" would usurp the jobs and privileges of "real Americans."[19] The new immigrant was often viewed by the host population as a threat to "our [American] jobs." But if the issue somehow became defending "white man's jobs" or a "white man's government," the not-yet-white ethnic could gain space by deflecting debate from nativity, a hopeless issue, to race, an ambiguous one. The first dramatic example of this phenomenon was the embrace of Democratic Party appeals to an "American race" of "white men" by the huge masses of Catholic Irish arriving in the antebellum US. If whiteness made for Americanity and if the Irish could qualify as white, nativist arguments suffered greatly. It was even possible for the Irish to campaign for an Irish monopoly of New York City longshore jobs under the cover of agitation for an "all-white waterfront."[20] After the Civil War, the newcoming Irish would help lead the movement to bar the relatively established Chinese from

California, with their agitation for a "white man's government" serving to make race, and not nativity, the center of the debate and to prove the Irish white. "What business has the likes of him over here?" a recent Irish settler in California asked regarding resident Chinese. The question made sense only if whiteness conferred a right to settle. Sixty years later, the despised newcoming internal migrants, the "Okies," would similarly seek to establish their claims as more fit to be Californian than long-established Californians by turning to questions of race. One new arrival from Oklahoma asked, "Just who built California?" before misanswering his own question: "Certainly not the Chinese, Japanese, Hindus, etc."[21]

"Shared" Oppression and the Claiming of Whiteness

The process by which "not yet" and "not quite" white ethnics, whose own status as white Americans was sharply questioned, came to stress that their whiteness made them Americans shows how fraught with problems are those interpretations that posit that "shared" oppression should have caused new immigrants to ally with African Americans. It was not just that the oppression of new working-class immigrants differed from that of African Americans but that even very similar experiences of oppression could cause new immigrants to grasp for the whiteness at the margins of their experiences rather than concentrating on the ways in which they shared much in daily life with African Americans. It seems to me worth investigating whether the immigrant groups with sufficient numbers of small businessmen to be identified as "trading minorities" – for example, Jews, New Orleans Italians, Syrians, the Mississippi Chinese, and Greeks – had greater opportunity to develop a positive sense of nonwhite identity, and even to cross over into African American culture, than did more overwhelmingly proletarian new immigrant groups. Certainly, as the tragedy of African American relations with Korean merchants today suggests, trading minorities with businesses in the Black community often have developed a sense of distance from, or hostility towards, the neighborhoods in which they trade, and vice versa. But it is also precisely those "trading minorities" that have produced some of the nation's best transgressors of the color line and race traitors, from Louis Prima to Johnny Otis. Of course, proximity to the Black community at his family's store mattered in the case of Otis, but more broadly the very distance between the ways trading minorities were stereotyped and the ways wageworking ethnic groups were stereotyped afforded a certain assurance that, however much they might be termed nonwhite, trading minorities were not in danger of being branded "niggers." As Carey McWilliams noted, the trading minority was usually seen as "not . . . lazy but . . . too industrious," as "not . . . incapable of learning but . . . too knowing."[22] If members of such minorities (like the broader middle class today) often developed superficial or even exploitative relations with African American culture, they also may have been able to borrow more confidently from Blacks without fearing that they would be cast as "white niggers" and their jobs as "nigger work" – an anxiety that the white working poor seldom escaped.[23]

Different dynamics characterized proletarian new immigrants' relations to African Americans, producing at once greater social proximity and a greater desire for distance. In his 1914 volume *The Old World and the New*, the nativist sociologist E. A. Ross approvingly quoted expert testimony from a physician who held that "the Slavs are immune to certain kinds of dirt. They can stand what would kill a white man." Slavs had excellent reasons to want out from under such a stereotype, which not only declared them nonwhite but gave free rein to employers hiring them as laborers (and to native-born skilled workers hiring them as helpers) to place them in the dirtiest and most unhealthy jobs. In such positions Slavic workers would be said to be "working like niggers" and would, like the most exploited Jews, Sicilians, or Louisiana creoles elsewhere, face further questioning of their whiteness based on the very fact of their hard and driven labor. Such sharing of oppression with Blacks doubtless made many Slavs question whether they wanted to be white Americans, but at the same time bitter knowledge of how Blacks fared made whiteness that much more attractive. In the case of working-class Italian Americans in and around Harlem, *proximity* of position, language, culture, and appearance made for an especially sharp need to establish that Puerto Rican migrants were of another race while cultural and color *differences* allowed for more tolerance toward Haitians, and even to the perception that Haitians were "not black."[24]

Thus the logic of class propelled Slavs and other not-yet-white ethnics at once in both of the directions of appreciating that which they had in common with African Americans *and* of denying the same. At times, it may simply have been that job competition made Slavs conscious of the potentialities of their possible whiteness. However, much more subtle processes could also be at play, as is illustrated by the rich testimony regarding both the possibility of rejecting whiteness and the attractions of claiming it from a Slovak woman from Bridgeport, Connecticut interviewed by the Federal Writers Project in the 1930s:

> I always tell my children not [to] play with the nigger-people's children, but they always play with them just the same. I tell them that the nigger children are dirty and that they will get sick if they play. I tell them they could find some other friends that are Slovaks just the same. This place now is all spoiled, and all the people live like pigs because the niggers they come and live here with the decent white people and they want to raise up their children with our children. If we had some place for the children to play I'm sure that the white children they would not play with the nigger children. . . . All people are alike – that's what God says – but just the same it's no good to make our children play with the nigger children because they are too dirty.

Ivan Greenberg, whose fine dissertation includes this important passage, observes that the very "'dirty' stereotype" long used to abuse immigrants was turned by Slovak and Italian Bridgeport residents against Blacks and criticism of white ethnics was thus deflected if not defused.[25]

It would of course be simplistic to suppose that whiteness and white supremacy were embraced and forwarded by not-yet-white ethnics simply as a public relations ploy to shore up their own group image. What gave force, poignancy, and pathos to the process of choosing whiteness was that it not only enabled the not-yet-white ethnics to live more easily with the white American population but to live more easily with themselves and with the vast changes industrial capitalist America required of them. I have argued this case in some detail with regard to Irish Americans in my book *Wages of Whiteness*, but other later-coming groups also came to grips with their own (forced) acceptance of time discipline, loss of contact with nature, and regimented work by projecting "primitive" values onto "carefree" African Americans. Thus a resident in the Italian-Slavic enclave studied by

Greenberg combined racism and envy in holding that Blacks had it easier than "white" workers:

> the nigger people can stay up to 3 o'clock in the morning playing and dancing and they don't have to worry about going to work. . . . We [white] poor people can't even have a good time one time a week. . . . The nigger people have a holiday every day in the week.

The tremendously conflicted emotional decision of white ethnics to abandon urban neighborhoods – and, as Robert Orsi observes, often to abandon parents and grandparents in the city – was similarly softened by the development of a historical memory emphasizing that "black crime" moved white ethnics to the suburbs by "driving them out" of the center city, though the timing of mass suburbanization hardly fits such a pattern.[26]

Other dimensions of the ways in which whiteness was constructed among immigrants remain so shrouded by mystery and inattention from historians as to be perfectly illustrative of the fact that at this stage we are much better placed to report on our ignorance rather than our knowledge of the history of white ethnic consciousness. In closing, it is worth evoking a particularly rich passage in William Attaway's great 1941 proletarian novel *Blood on the Forge*, which suggests not only how far we have to go in understanding that history but also how well worth the effort developing such an understanding can be. Attaway describes the reaction of Irish workers in a foundry after a Black worker, Big Mat, had knocked out a "hayseed" before he could hit an Irishman. Mat was "the hero of the morning" and drew praise for being both a model "colored worker" and for being more than Black. The boss melter, a "big Irishman" in charge of five furnaces, took the former line of praise: "Never had a colored helper work better on the hearth . . . do everythin' the melter tell him to do and take care of the work of a whole crew if he ain't held back." Other Irish workers on the gang conferred the title "Black Irish" on Mat. One "grinned" that "Lots of black fellas have Irish guts." Another added, "That black fella make a whole lot better Irisher than a hunky or a ginny. They been over here twenty years and still eatin' garlic like it's as good as stew meat and potatoes," before "glanc[ing] sharply around to see if any of the foreigners had heard him." But Big Mat did not celebrate his newfound acceptance. He made no answer when called Black Irish but instead "full of savage pressure," took refuge in the "pleasant thought" of animals "tearing at each other" and hurried away to the dogfights.[27] Some of this arresting scene is familiar: the social construction of race; the question of whether "foreigners" merit inclusion over African Americans; the combination of a commitment to specific (Irish) ethnicity and a lack of reference to whiteness; and the importance of timing, in that the Irish are by now natives, not newcomers.

But much is also unsettling. There is little grandeur in the breaking down of race lines here, in part because the break is a superficial and momentary one, based on Mat's temporary status as model "colored worker." Moreover, the very thing that makes Mat such a model to the more privileged Irish workers and bosses – a supposed loyal willingness to do anything for his superiors if not "held back" – is bound to define him as a "nigger" in the eyes of the "hunkies and ginnies" on the gang. In this scene at least, Attaway shows us a workplace that does not bridge distinctions between African Americans and white ethnics but tragically recasts such distinctions. What should perhaps be most unsettling to us as historians is how little prepared we are to judge how typical this scene was at the shopfloor level and how it was experienced by the "colored workers," the not-yet-white ethnics, and the white ethnics who built America. Until we follow the example of the recent and brilliant work on Italian Americans by Robert Orsi and develop a history of American immigration that "puts the issues and contests of racial identity and difference at its center," we are likely to remain puzzled.[28]

Notes

1   Barbara Fields, "Slavery, Race and Ideology in the United States of America," *New Left Review*, no. 181 (May–June 1990), p. 99; Joan M. Jensen, *Passage from India: Asian Indian Immigrants in North America* (New Haven, CT, 1988), pp. 246–69.

2   Sarah Deutsch, *No Separate Refuge: Culture, Class, and Gender on an Anglo-Hispanic Frontier in the American Southwest, 1880–1940* (New York, 1987).

3   On whiteness, see Vron Ware, *Beyond the Pale: White Women, Racism and History* (London, 1992); David R. Roediger, *The Wages of Whiteness: Race*

and the Making of the American Working Class (London, 1991); Alexander Saxton, *The Rise and Fall of the White Republic: Class Politics and Mass Culture in Nineteenth-Century America* (London, 1991). For prominent and otherwise useful studies continuing the conflation (and confusion) of race and ethnicity, see Werner Sollors, *Beyond Ethnicity: Consent and Descent in American Culture* (New York, 1986), and Orlando Patterson, *Ethnic Chauvinism: The Reactionary Impulse* (New York, 1977).

4   Richard Williams, *Hierarchical Structures and Social Value: The Creation of Black and Irish Identities in the United States* (New York, 1990), p. 2.

5   William Forbath, *Law and the Shaping of the American Labor Movement* (Cambridge, MA, 1991), p. 23.

6   Victor Greene, *The Slavic Community on Strike: Immigrant Labor in Pennsylvania Anthracite* (South Bend, IN, 1968); Earl Lewis, *In Their Own Interests: Race, Class and Power in Twentieth-Century Norfolk, Virginia* (Berkeley, CA, 1991); Robin D. G. Kelley, *Hammer and Hoe: Alabama Communists during the Great Depression* (Chapel Hill, NC, 1990); Wayne Broehl, Jr, *The Molly Maguires* (London, 1968); Vicki L. Ruiz, *Cannery Workers, Cannery Lives: Mexican Women, Unionization and the California Processing Industry, 1930–1950* (Albuquerque, NM, 1987).

7   Coco Fusco, as quoted in bell hooks, "Representing Whiteness: Seeing Wings of Desire," *Z*, 2 (March 1989), p. 39.

8   Malcolm X with Alex Haley, *The Autobiography of Malcolm X* (New York, 1984), p. 399.

9   James Baldwin, "On Being 'White' . . . And Other Lies," *Essence* (April, 1984), pp. 90, 92.

10 John Higham, *Strangers in the Land: Patterns of American Nativism, 1860–1925* (New York, 1963), p. 173.

11 Joe Eszterhaus, *F.I.S.T.* (New York, 1978), p. 88.

12 Lawrence Joseph, "Can't Forget the Motor City," *Nation*, December 17, 1990, pp. 775–6.

13 Certainly many African Americans have chosen and choose to be Black as well, but in doing so they identify at least as much with African American national culture as with racial ideology. One would be hard pressed to find such a specifically white American *culture*. Indeed, in its extreme forms identification with whiteness represents a cutting off of oneself from what Albert Murray calls America's "incontestably mulatto" culture. In its production of identity through negation ("We are not Black"), and in the record of behavior it has called forth, whiteness in the US is best regarded as an *absence* of culture. In this it fundamentally differs from African Americanity and from specific "white" ethnicities. See Murray, *The Omni Americans* (New York, 1983), and Baldwin, "On Being 'White.'"

14   Quoted in George Potter, *To the Garden Door: The Story of the Irish in Ireland and America* (Boston, 1960), p. 372.

15   Carter, *Southern Legacy* (Baton Rouge, LA, 1950), pp. 105–6; Paola Giordano, "Italian Immigration in the State of Louisiana," *Italian Americana* (Fall–Winter 1977), p. 172; George Cunningham, "The Italian: A Hindrance to White Solidarity in Louisiana 1890–1893," *Journal of Negro History*, 50 (January 1965), esp. pp. 24–6; Jean Scarpaci and Garry Boulard, "Blacks, Italians and the Making of New Orleans Jazz," *Journal of Ethnic Studies*, 16 (Spring 1988), pp. 53–66. Compare, however, Arnold Shankman, "This Menacing Influx: Afro Americans on Italian Immigration in the South, 1880–1915," *Mississippi Quarterly* (Winter 1977–8); Robert Orsi, "The Religious Boundaries of an Inbetween People: Street *Feste* and the Problem of the Dark-Skinned Other in Italian Harlem, 1920–1990," *American Quarterly*, 44 (September 1992), pp. 314–18 and 342 n. 3.

16   Virginia Yans-McLaughlin, *Family and Community: Italian Immigrants in Buffalo, 1880–1930* (Ithaca, NY, 1971), pp. 113–14; Micaela di Leonardo, *The Varieties of Ethnic Experience* (Ithaca, NY, 1984), p. 24 n. 16.

17   "Irish Mornings and African Days on the Old Minstrel Stage: An Interview with Leni Sloan," *Callahan's Irish Quarterly*, 2 (Spring 1982), pp. 49–53.

18   Donald Tricarico, "Guido: Fashioning an Italian-American Youth Style," *Journal of Ethnic Studies*, 19 (Spring 1991), esp. pp. 56–7. The portrayals of Italian Americans in Spike Lee's *Do the Right Thing* and *Jungle Fever* are fascinating in this regard. While in *Jungle Fever* love relationships between Italian Americans and African Americans are connected in part with desires on the part of members of the former group to escape confining aspects of Italian American culture, Lee also shows, with uncommon clarity and no romanticizing, the ways in which a sense of Italian Americanity depends, in inner New York City at least, on imitating African American culture and exploring ethnicity specifically in counterpoint to African Americanity.

19   London, as quoted in Alexander Saxton, *The Indispensable Enemy: Labor and the Anti-Chinese Movement in California* (Berkeley, CA, 1971), p. 211.

20   See Roediger, *Wages of Whiteness*, pp. 140–4.

21   James N. Gregory, *American Exodus: The Dust Bowl Migration and Okie Culture in California* (New York, 1989), pp. 164–9, with the quote from p. 165.

22   Carey McWilliams, *A Mask for Privilege: Anti-Semitism in America* (Westport, CT, 1979 [1948]), pp. 163–9, esp. p. 164.

23   On *nigger work* and *white niggers*, see Roediger, *Wages of Whiteness*, pp. 129–30, and pp. 68 and 145 respectively.

24   Quoted in Stanley Lieberson, *A Piece of the Pie: Black and White Immigrants since 1880* (Berkeley, CA, 1980), p. 25.

25   Ivan Greenberg, "Class Culture and Generational Change: Immigrant Families in Two Connecticut Industrial Cities during the 1930s," Ph.D. dissertation, City University of New York, 1990, pp. 76–7, includes the quote.

26   Ibid., p. 78 for the quote.

27   William Attaway, *Blood on the Forge* (New York, 1987 [1941]), pp. 122–3.

28   Orsi, "Inbetween People," p. 335.

19

Affirmative Action and the Politics of Race

Manning Marable

The triumph of "Newtonian Republicanism" is not a temporary aberration: it is the culmination of a thirty-year ideological and political war
against the logic of the reforms of the 1960s. Advocates of civil rights,
affirmative action, and other policies reflecting left-of-center political
values must recognize how and why the context for progressive reform
has fundamentally changed. And, instead of pleasant-sounding but
simplistic defenses of "affirmative action as it is," we need to do some
hard thinking about the reasons why several significant constituencies
which have greatly benefited from affirmative action have done relatively little to defend it. We need to recognize what the critical theoretical and strategic differences are which separate liberals and progressives
on how to achieve a nonracist society. And we urgently need to reframe
the context of the political debate, taking the initiative away from the
right.

The first difficulty in developing a more effective progressive model for
affirmative action goes back to the concept's complex definition, history,
and political evolution. "Affirmative action" *per se* was never a law, or
even a coherently developed set of governmental policies designed to
attack institutional racism and societal discrimination. It was instead
a series of presidential executive orders, civil-rights laws, and governmental programs regarding the awarding of federal contracts, fair
employment practices and licenses, with the goal of uprooting bigotry.

Historically, at its origins, it was designed to provide some degree of compensatory justice to the victims of slavery, Jim Crow segregation, and institutional racism. This was at the heart of the Civil Rights Act of 1866, which stated that "all persons within the jurisdiction of the United States shall have the same right in every State and Territory, to make and enforce contracts, to sue, be parties, give evidence, and to the full and equal benefit of all laws and proceedings for the security of persons and property as is enjoyed by white citizens."

During the Great Depression, the role of the federal government in protecting the equal rights of black Americans was expanded again through the direct militancy and agitation of black people. In 1941, socialist and trade-union leader A. Philip Randolph mobilized thousands of black workers to participate in the "Negro March on Washington Movement," calling upon the administration of Franklin D. Roosevelt to carry out a series of reforms favorable to civil rights. To halt this mobilization, Roosevelt agreed to sign Executive Order 8802, which outlawed segregationist hiring policies by defense-related industries that held federal contracts. This executive order not only greatly increased the number of African-Americans who were employed in wartime industries, but also expanded the political idea that government could not take a passive role in the dismantling of institutional racism.

This position was reaffirmed in 1953, by President Harry S. Truman's Committee on Government Contract Compliance, which urged the Bureau of Employment Security "to act positively and affirmatively to implement the policy of nondiscrimination in its functions of placement counseling, occupational analysis and industrial services, labor market information, and community participation in employment services." Thus, despite the fact that the actual phrase, "affirmative action," was not used by a chief executive until President John F. Kennedy's Executive Order 11246 in 1961, the fundamental idea of taking proactive steps to dismantle prejudice has been around for more than a century.

What complicates the current discussion of affirmative action is that historically liberals and progressives were at odds over the guiding social and cultural philosophy which should inform the implementation of policies on racial discrimination. Progressives like W. E. B. Du Bois were convinced that the way to achieve a nonracist society was through the development of strong black institutions, and the preservation of

African-American cultural identity. The strategy of Du Bois was reflected in his concept of "double consciousness," that black American identity was simultaneously African and American, and that dismantling racism should not require the aesthetic and cultural assimilation of blackness into white values and social norms. The alternative to the Du Boisian position was expressed by integrationist leaders and intellectuals like Walter White, Roy Wilkins, Bayard Rustin, and Kenneth Clark. They, too, fought to destroy Jim Crow. But their cultural philosophy for the Negro rested on "inclusion" rather than pluralism. They deeply believed that the long-term existence of separate all-black institutions was counterproductive to the goal of a "color-blind" society, in which racial categories would become socially insignificant or even irrelevant to the relations of power. Rustin, for instance, personally looked forward to the day when Harlem would cease to exist as a segregated, identifiably black neighborhood. Blacks should be assimilated or culturally incorporated into the mainstream.

My central criticism of the desegregationist strategy of the "inclusionists" (Rustin, White, Wilkins, et al.) is that they consistently confused "culture" with "race," underestimating the importance of fostering black cultural identity as an essential component of the critique of white supremacy. The existence of separate black institutions or a self-defined, all-black community was not necessarily an impediment to interracial cooperation and multicultural dialogue. Nevertheless, both desegregationist positions from the 1930s onward were expressed by the organizations and leadership of the civil-rights movement. These divisions were usually obscured by a common language of reform, and a common social vision which embraced color-blindness as an ultimate goal. For example, both positions are reflected in the main thrust of the language in the Civil Rights Act of 1964, which declared that workplace discrimination on the basis of "race, color, religion, sex or national origin" should be outlawed. However, the inclusionist orientation of Wilkins, Rustin and company is also apparent in the 1964 Act's assertion that it should not be interpreted as having to require any employers "to grant preferential treatment to any individual or to any group."

Five years later, after Richard Nixon's narrow victory for the presidency, it was the Republicans' turn to interpret and implement civil-rights policy. The strategy of Nixon had a profound impact upon the political culture of America, and continues to have direct consequences within the debates about affirmative action today. Through the counterintelligence program of the FBI, the Nixon administration vigorously suppressed the radical wing of the black movement. Second, it appealed to the racial anxieties and grievances of George Wallace voters, recruiting segregationists like Jesse Helms and Strom Thurmond into the ranks of the Republican Party. On affirmative action and issues of equal opportunity, however, Nixon's goal was to utilize a liberal reform for conservative objectives, the expansion of the African-American middle class, which might benefit the Republican Party. Under Nixon in 1969, the federal government authorized what became known as the "Philadelphia Plan." This program required federal contractors to set specific goals for minority hiring. As a result, the number of racial minorities in the construction industry increased from 1 to 12 percent. The Nixon administration supported provisions for minority set-asides to promote black and Hispanic entrepreneurship; it placed Federal Reserve funds in black-owned banks. Nixon himself publicly praised the concept of "Black Power," carefully interpreting it as "black capitalism."

It was under the moderate conservative aegis of the Nixon–Ford administrations of 1969–77 that the set of policies which we identify with "affirmative action" was implemented nationally in both the public and private sectors. Even after the 1978 Bakke decision, in which the Supreme Court overturned the admission policy of the University of California at Davis, which had set aside 16 out of 100 medical-school openings for racial minorities, the political impetus for racial reform was not destroyed. What did occur, even before the triumph of reaction under Reagan in the early 1980s, was that political conservatives deliberately usurped the "color-blind" discourse of many liberals from the desegregation movement. Conservatives retreated from the Nixonian strategy of utilizing affirmative-action tools to achieve conservative political goals, and began to appeal to the latent racist sentiments within the white population. They cultivated the racist mythology that affirmative action was nothing less than a rigid system of inflexible quotas which rewarded the incompetent and the unqualified (who happened to be nonwhite) at the expense of hard-working, tax-paying Americans (who happened to be white). White conservatives were able to define "merit" in a manner that would reinforce white male privilege, but in an inverted language which would make the real victims of discrimination appear to be the "racists." It was, in retrospect, a brilliant political maneuver. And the liberals were at a loss in fighting back effectively precisely because they lacked a consensus internally about the means and goals for achieving genuine equality. Traditional "liberals," like Morris Dees of the Southern Poverty Law Center, who favored an inclusionist "color-blind" ideology of reform, often ended up inside the camp of racial reactionaries, who cynically learned to manipulate the discourse of fairness.

The consequences of these shifts and realignments within American political culture by the 1990s on how to achieve greater fairness and equality for those who have experienced discrimination were profound. In general, most white Americans have made a clear break from the overtly racist Jim Crow segregationist policies of a generation ago. They want to be perceived as being "fair" toward racial minorities and women, and they acknowledge that policies like affirmative action are necessary to foster a more socially just society. According to the March 17–19, 1995 *USA Today*/CNN/Gallup poll, when asked, "Do you favor or oppose affirmative-action programs," 53 percent of whites polled expressed support, compared to only 36 percent who opposed. Not surprisingly, African-Americans expressed much stronger support: 72 percent for affirmative-action programs to only 21 percent against. Despite widespread rhetoric that the vast majority of white males have supposedly lost jobs and opportunities due to affirmative-action policies, the poll indicated that only 15 percent of all white males believe that "they've lost a job because of affirmative-action policies."

However, there is a severe erosion of white support for affirmative action when the focus is more narrowly on specific steps or remedies addressing discrimination. For example, the *USA Today*/CNN/Gallup poll indicates that only 30 percent of whites favor the establishment of gender and racial "quotas" in businesses, with 68 percent opposed. Conversely, two-thirds of all African-Americans expressed support for "quotas" in business employment, with only 30 percent opposed. When asked whether quotas should be created "that require schools to admit a certain number of minorities and women," 61 percent of whites were opposed, with 35 percent in favor. Nearly two-thirds of all whites would also reject policies which "require private businesses to set up specific goals and timetables for hiring women and minorities if there were not government programs that included hiring quotas." On the issue of implementing government-supported initiatives for social equality, most black and white Americans still live in two distinct racial universes.

It is not surprising that "angry white men" form the core of those who are against affirmative action. What is striking, however, is the general orientation of white American women on this issue. White women have been overwhelmingly the primary beneficiaries of affirmative action. Millions of white women have gained access to educational and employment opportunities through the implementation and enforcement of such policies. But most of them clearly do not share the political perspectives of African-Americans and Hispanics on this issue, nor do they perceive their own principal interests to be at risk if affirmative-action programs were to be abandoned by the federal government or outlawed in the courts. For example, in the same *USA Today*/CNN/Gallup poll, only 8 percent of all white women stated that their "colleagues at work or school privately questioned" their qualifications due to affirmative action, compared to 19 percent of black women and 28 percent of black men. Fewer than one in five white women polled defined workplace discrimination as a "major problem," compared to 41 percent of blacks and 38 percent of Latinos. Some 40 percent of the white women polled described job discrimination as "not being a problem" at all. These survey results may help to explain why middle-class-oriented liberal feminist leaders and constituencies have been relatively less vocal than African-Americans in the mobilization to defend affirmative action.

A quarter of a century of affirmative-action programs, goals, and timetables has clearly been effective in transforming the status of white women in the labor force. It is certainly true that white males still dominate the upper ranks of senior management: while constituting 47 percent of the nation's total workforce, white males constitute 95 percent of all senior managerial positions at the rank of vice-president or above. However, women of all races now constitute about 40 percent of the total workforce overall. As of the 1990 census, white women held nearly 40 percent of all middle-management positions. While their median incomes lag behind those of white males, over the past twenty years white women have gained far greater ground in terms of real earnings than black or Hispanic males in the labor force. In this context, civil-rights advocates and traditional defenders of affirmative action must ask themselves whether the majority of white American women actually perceive their material interests to be tied to the battles for income equity and affirmative action that most blacks and Latinos, women and men alike, continue to fight for.

We should also recognize that, although all people of color suffer in varying degrees from the stigmatization of racism and economic disadvantage within American society, they do not have the same material interests or identify themselves with the same politics as the vast majority of African-Americans. For example, according to the 1990 census, the mean on-the-job earnings for all American adults totaled $15,105. Blacks' mean on-the-job annual earnings came to $10,912; Native Americans', $11,949; Hispanics', $11,219. But it is crucial to disaggregate social categories like "Hispanics" and "Asian Americans" to gain a true picture of the real material and social experiences within significant populations of color.

About half of all Hispanics, according to the Bureau of the Census, term themselves "white," regardless of their actual physical appearance. Puerto Ricans in New York City have lower median incomes than African-Americans, while Argentines, a Hispanic group which claims benefits from affirmative-action programs, have mean on-the-job incomes of $15,956 per year. The Hmong, immigrants from Southeast Asia, have mean on-the-job incomes of $3,194; in striking contrast, the Japanese have annual incomes higher than those of whites. None of these statistics negates the reality of racial domination and discrimination in terms of social relations, access to employment opportunities, or job advancement. But they do tell us part of the reason why no broad coalition of people of color has coalesced behind the political demand for affirmative action; various groups interpret their interests narrowly in divergent ways, looking out primarily for themselves rather than addressing the structural inequalities within the social fabric of the society as a whole.

So where do progressives and liberals go from here, given that the right has seized the political initiative in dismantling affirmative action, minority economic set-asides, and the entire spectrum of civil-rights reforms? We must return to the theoretical perspectives of Du Bois, with some honest dialogue about why race relations have soured so profoundly in recent years. Affirmative action was largely responsible for a significant increase in the size of the black middle class; it opened many professional and managerial positions to blacks, Latinos, and women for the first time. But in many other respects, affirmative action can and should be criticized from the left, not because it was "too liberal" in its pursuit and implementation of measures to achieve equality, but because it was "too conservative. " It sought to increase representative numbers of minorities and women within the existing structure and arrangements of power, rather than challenging or redefining the institutions of authority and privilege. As implemented under a series of presidential administrations, liberal and conservative alike, affirmative action was always more concerned with advancing remedial remedies for unequal racial outcomes than with uprooting racism as a system of white power.

Rethinking progressive and liberal strategies on affirmative action would require sympathetic whites to acknowledge that much of the anti-affirmative-action rhetoric among Democrats is really a retreat from a meaningful engagement on issues of race, and that the vast majority of Americans who have benefited materially from affirmative action have not been black at all. A Du Boisian strategy on affirmative action would argue that, despite the death of legal segregation a generation ago, we have not yet reached the point where a color-blind society is possible, especially in terms of the actual organization and structure of white power and privilege. Institutional racism is real, and the central focus of affirmative action must deal with the continuing burden of racial inequality and discrimination in American life.

There are many ways to measure the powerful reality of contemporary racism. For example, a 1994 study of the Office of Personnel Management found that African-American federal employees are more than twice as likely to be dismissed as their white counterparts. Blacks are likely to be fired at much higher rates than whites in jobs where they constitute a significant share of the labor force: for example, black clerk typists are 4.7 times more likely to be dismissed than whites, and black custodians 4.1 times more likely to be fired. Discrimination is also rampant in capital markets. Banks continue policies of "red lining," denying loans in neighborhoods which are largely black and Hispanic. And even after years of affirmative-action programs, blacks and Latinos remain grossly underrepresented in a wide number of professions. For example, African-Americans and Hispanics represent 12.4 percent and 9.5 percent respectively of the US adult population. But of all American physicians, blacks account for barely 4.2 percent, and Latinos 5.2 percent. Among engineers, blacks represent 3.7 percent, Latinos 3.3 percent; among lawyers, blacks account for 3.3 percent, Latinos 3.1 percent; and for all university and college professors, blacks made up 5 percent, Latinos 2.9 percent. As Jesse Jackson observed in a speech before the National Press Club, while native-born white males constitute only one-third of the US population, they constitute 80 percent of all tenured professors, 92 percent of the Forbes 400 chief executive officers, and 97 percent of all school superintendents.

If affirmative action is to be criticized, it should be on the grounds that it has not gone far enough in transforming the actual power relations between black and white within US society. More evidence for this is addressed in a new book by sociologists Melvin Oliver and Thomas Shapiro, *Black Wealth/White Wealth*. They point out that "the typical black family has eleven cents of wealth for every dollar owned by the typical white family." Even middle-class African-Americans – people who often benefited from affirmative action – are significantly poorer than whites who earn identical incomes. If housing and vehicles owned are included in the definition of "net wealth," the median middle-class African-American family has only $8,300 in total assets, to $56,000 for the comparable white family. Why are blacks at all income levels much poorer than whites in terms of wealth? African-American families not only inherit much less wealth, they are affected daily by institutional inequality and discrimination. For years they were denied life-insurance policies by white firms. They are still denied home mortgages at twice the rate of similarly qualified white applicants. African-Americans are less likely to receive government-backed home loans.

Given the statistical profile of racial inequality, liberals must reject the economistic temptation to move away from "race-conscious remedies" to "race-neutral" reforms defined by income or class criteria. Affirmative action has always had a distinct and separate function from antipoverty programs. Income and social class inequality affect millions of whites, Asian Americans, Latinos, and blacks alike, and programs which expand employment, educational access, and social-service benefits based on narrowly defined economic criteria are absolutely essential. The impetus for racism is not narrowly "economic" in origin. Racial prejudice is still a destructive force in the lives of upper-middle-class, college-educated African-Americans, as well as poor blacks, and programs designed to address the discrimination they feel and experience collectively every day must be grounded in the context of race. However, affirmative action is legitimately related to class questions, but in a different way. A truly integrated workplace, where people of divergent racial backgrounds, languages, and cultural identities learn to interact and respect each other, is an essential precondition for building a broadly pluralistic movement for radical democracy. The expanded implementation of affirmative action, despite its liberal limitations, would assist in creating the social conditions essential for pluralistic coalitions for full employment and more progressive social policies.

What is required among progressives is not a reflective, uncritical defense of affirmative action, but a recognition of its contradictory evolution and conceptual limitations, as well as its benefits and strengths. We need a thoughtful and innovative approach in challenging discrimination which, like that of Du Bois, reaffirms the centrality of the struggle against racism within the development of affirmative-action measures. We must build upon the American majority's continued support for affirmative action, linking the general public's commitment to social fairness with creative measures that actually target the real patterns and processes of discrimination which millions of Latinos and blacks experience every day. And we must not be pressured by false debate to choose between race or class in the development and framing of public policies to address discrimination. A movement toward the long-term goal of a "color-blind" society, the deconstruction of racism, does not mean that we become "neutral" about the continuing significance of race in American life.

As the national debate concerning the possible elimination of affirmative action defines the 1996 presidential campaign, black and progressive Americans must reevaluate their strategies for reform. In recent years we have tended to rely on elections, the legislative process, and the courts to achieve racial equality. We should remember how the struggle to dismantle Jim Crow segregation was won. We engaged in economic boycotts, civil disobedience, teach-ins, freedom schools, "freedom rides," community-based coalitions, and united fronts. There is a direct relationship between our ability to mobilize people in communities to protest and the pressure we can exert on elected officials to protect and enforce civil rights. Voting is absolutely essential, but it isn't enough. We must channel the profound discontent, the alienation, and the anger which presently exist in the black community toward constructive, progressive forms of political intervention and resistance. As we fight for affirmative action, let us understand that we are fighting for a larger ideal: the ultimate elimination of race and gender inequality, the uprooting of prejudice and discrimination, and the realization of a truly democratic America.

20

A Bill of Rights for Racially Mixed People

Maria P. P. Root

Countless number of times I have fragmented and fractionalized myself in order to make the *other* more comfortable in deciphering my behavior, my words, my loyalties, my choice of friends, my appearance, my parents, and so on. And given my multiethnic history, it was hard to keep track of all the fractions, to make them add up to one whole. It took me over 30 years to realize that fragmenting myself seldom served a purpose other than to preserve the delusions this country has created around race.

Reciting the fractions to the *other* was the ultimate act of buying into the mechanics of racism in this country. Once I realized this, I could ask myself other questions. How exactly does a person be one fourth, one eighth, or one half something? To fragment myself and others, "she is one half Chinese and one half white," or "he is one quarter Native, one quarter African American, and one half Spanish" was to unquestioningly be deployed to operate the machinery that disenfranchised myself, my family, my friends, and others I was yet to meet.

This chapter is based upon a keynote address given by invitation of the University of California at Santa Barbara's student group, Variations, for the Second Annual California Statewide Multiracial Conference held at UC Santa Barbara, April 15, 1994. Carla Bradshaw's and Christine Hall's comments were helpful in the refinement of this manuscript.

At some deep psychological level, the mechanics of oppression derive from insecurities. When oppression is directed at whole groups of people, the mechanics are similar regardless of the type of oppression. First, a system of beliefs is constructed to preserve the self-interests of a group that has economic and judicial power. These beliefs are then spread by word of mouth. Second, data are collected, often by respected, intelligent people, to establish the beliefs as factual so that those in power may continue to think of themselves as moral and ethical. Together, the beliefs and data are used to rationalize superiority of one group over another. This rationalization justifies the fourth and last mechanism, social distance; social distance makes it easier to depersonalize and dehumanize the group that is viewed as inferior, so that there are few if any opportunities to observe oneself in the *other*. Together, social distance, rationalization, biased facts, and entrenched attitudes about race relegate multiracial individuals to object status, unconnected to humanity. Subsequently, otherwise sensitive, intelligent people and relieved of the moral obligation to resist or object to oppressive thought or action.

Most systematic oppression is based in paranoid delusions – a tightly gathered system of beliefs and rationalizations and biased data gathering that create a fractured and illusionary reality that allows one to stave off one's fears, even unconscious ones. Racism is the result of a delusion about the meaning of differences in the service of coping with disproportionate fears of inferiority to or harm by the *other*. Racism is simultaneously ambivalent, arbitrary, and rigid. Thus, a phenotypically European person with an African American parent is seen as black, whereas a person who looks phenotypically white with two parents of European ancestry can be judged as white. Millions of people have been unwittingly drafted into collaboration with an insidious destruction of human life and spirit. Deep in our psyches, racism feeds on crumbs of ignorance, insecurity, and fear.

Irrationality and economic incentive guide changes in the meaning of race (Omi and Winant, 1986; Takaki, 1993), rather than a moral incentive toward bettering the collective society. Therefore the boundaries and labels defining the disenfranchised by race shift over time, as demonstrated by the history of the US Census (Lee, 1993). The purpose of the classification system, which insists on clean lines between groups, always remains the same: to establish and maintain a social hierarchy in which the creators and enforcers of the system occupy a superior berth. Consequently, members of some group are always "deserving" of inferior status, until they are arbitrarily elevated to a higher status or a change in status provides economic advantage to those in power.

Although the mechanics of racism seem to start with those in power, the system is also maintained by the oppressed's internalization of the mechanics; for example, an insistence on singular ethnic or racial loyalties, colorism, and discrimination against multiracial people across all ethnic and racial groups in this country. Paradoxically, this internalization of the mechanics of oppression is a version of the hostage syndrome observed in prisoners of war. Prisoners take on characteristics of their captors and even defend their behaviors as their plight and ability to make sense out of an irrational reality are integrally linked with survival.

When race is constructed through the mechanics of racism, oppression chokes multiracial people from all sides (Root, 1990). This throttling and stifling takes many forms: forced to fit into just one category from school registration to US Census surveys; affiliations forced with oppressive questions (e.g., "Which one are you?"); forced to "act right," "think right," and "do right" in order to belong; and forced to prove ethnic legitimacy in order to have an identity in an ethnically diverse society.

Chao (in press) thinks of racism as the "original sin" in America. Ironically, the descendants of the Europeans who came to the United States spawned the delusion around race (Spickard, 1992), replete with one-drop rules of hypodescent, classification of a biracial child's race by mother's race to increase slave holdings and absolve white slavemasters of paternal responsibility, anti-Asian legislation, displacement of Native Americans, and so on. Unquestionably, race is invidiously intertwined with most major US institutions and social policies. For example, consider the power the US Bureau of the Census has in reconstructing race every ten years. It would also have considerable power to slowly deconstruct race.

Unfortunately, the oppressive squeeze created by the mechanics of racism has historically relegated multiracial people to deviant status or "mistakes," has minimized our contributions to society (despite the evidence), and/or has ignored our existence. Subsequently, the human rights of a growing segment of the US population are compromised by the imaginary borders between social races.

The Bill of Rights proposed in this chapter was developed in the historical context of three interacting factors and the social forces that enable them:

1   a critical number of multiracial people of an age and in positions to give voice to concerns and injustices;
2   a biracial baby boom; and
3   a continued social movement to dismantle racism.

The affirmation of rights below reflects *resistance, revolution,* and ultimately *change* for the system that has weakened the social, moral, and spiritual fiber of this country. This chapter offers a set of affirmations or "rights" as reminders to break the spell of the delusion that creates race to the detriment of us all. (See Bill of Rights, p. 7.)

Resistance

Resistance is a political act. It is also a nonviolent strategy for changing a status quo that perpetuates race wars and violates civil rights. To resist means that one does not accept the belief system, the data as they are presented, or the rationalizations used to perpetuate the status quo around race relations. In fact, the final test case that overturned all remaining state laws against interracial marriage in 1967 (*Loving v. Virginia*) came about because two individuals, Mildred Jetters and Perry Loving, resisted the laws prohibiting interracial marriage. Subsequently, the Supreme Court invoked an interpretation of the 14th Amendment to repeal these laws because they interfered with a basic civil liberty in this country, the pursuit of happiness.

Resistance also means refusing to fragment, marginalize, or disconnect ourselves from people and from ourselves. This is accomplished by refusal to uncritically apply to others the very concepts that have made

Bill of Rights for Racially Mixed People

I have the right
    not to justify my existence in this world
    not to keep the races separate within me
    not to be responsible for people's discomfort with my physical
        ambiguity
    not to justify my ethnic legitimacy

I have the right
    to identify myself differently than strangers expect me to identify
    to identify myself differently than how my parents identify me
    to identify myself differently than my brothers and my sisters
    to identify myself differently in different situations

I have the right
    to create a vocabulary to communicate about being multiracial
    to change my identity over my lifetime – and more than once
    to have loyalties and identify with more than one group of people
    to freely choose whom I befriend and love

some of us casualties of race wars. Four assertions listed following the Bill of Rights embody this resistance.

I have the right not to justify my existence in this world

Multiracial people blur the boundaries between races, the "us" and "them." They do not fit neatly into the observer's schema of reality. Questions such as "What are you?" "How did your parents meet?" and "Are your parents married?" indicate the stereotypes that make up the schema by which the *other* attempts to make meaning of the multiracial person's existence.

Many people still have a limited understanding of the racially mixed person's place in society. Images abound of slave masters raping black women, US military men carrying on sexually illicit relationships with Asian women during wars along the Pacific rim, and rebels and curiosity seekers having casual affairs.

The multiracial person's existence challenges the rigidity of racial lines that are a prerequisite for maintaining the delusion that race is a scientific fact. The multiracial person may learn to cope with these questions by asking questioners why they want to know or how this information will be useful, or by simply refusing to answer.

I have the right not to keep the races separate within me

The original racial system has been transformed and embedded into our country's political system by both the oppressors and the oppressed. A five-race framework adopted by the Federal Office of Management and Budget drives the categories of racial classification throughout the United States (Sanjek, 1994), leaving no room to acknowledge self-identified multiracial people.

Resistance means asking yourself the questions, Do I want to fit into a system that does not accommodate my reality? What would I be fitting into? What is the price? Will I have to be less than a whole person? Change often requires the presentation of extremely different realities and strategies (Freire, 1994) in order to break free from rigid realities. Multiracial people have a place and a purpose at this point in history to cross the borders built and maintained by delusion by creating emotional/psychic earthquakes in the social system. Declaring multiple racial affiliations and/or ethnic identities may have this effect on other people.

The biracial baby boom, the debate over racial classification for upcoming decennial census taking, and contemporary research on biracial children clarify the question: What about the children? This question is based on the belief that race dictates differences in human needs and problem solving, that racial differences are irreconcilable. To prove otherwise, the biracial or multiracial person challenges the delusional biases upon which racism is maintained.

I have the right not to be responsible for people's discomfort with my physical ambiguity

The physical ambiguity of many multiracial people, as well as mistaken identifications about their heritage, clearly challenges the notion of "pure race." The physical look of some racially mixed people is a catalyst for psychological change in how race is understood and employed. For example, many Eurasians are misidentified as Latino or Native Americans. Some words, such as *exotic*, referring to the physical appearance of multiracial people, may be used as tools to reduce discomfort. Unfortunately, such terms declare social distance between people in the guise of something special or positive being offered (Bradshaw, 1992; Root, 1994a).

Jean-Paul Sartre (trans. 1976) suggests that people define self in terms of the subjective experience of the *other*. In this case, multiracial people are the inkblot test for the *other's* prejudices and fears.

I have the right not to justify my ethnic legitimacy

Tests of ethnic legitimacy are always power struggles, demonstrating the internalization of oppressive mechanisms. They employ social distance through the use of rationalized interpretation of behavior understood within an oppressive system of beliefs. These tests serve purposes of increasing divisiveness around ethnicity and delusions around race. These tests usually require that multiracial people exaggerate caricatures of ethnic and racial stereotypes. Those who initiate such struggles usually win, because they create the rules – or change the rules to suit themselves. Anyone who unquestioningly accepts these tests, begging for acceptance, remains a prisoner of the system (Freire, 1970). Belonging remains fragile.

The existence of multiracial individuals requires that the common definition of ethnicity be revised. Specifically, race must not be synonymous with it. We must also challenge the notion that multiracial people will be the harbingers of doom to ethnic solidarity or ethnic continuity. Research shows that ethnicity to some extent is dynamic over time and that multiracial people are variable to the degree to which they are ethnically identified (Mass, 1992; Stephan, 1992).

Revolution

Everyone who enters into an interracial relationship or is born of racially different heritages is conscripted into a quiet revolution. People who voluntarily cross the border are often viewed in such strong terms as "race traitors," a sure sign that they have unwittingly created an emotional/psychic earthquake with emotional reverberations. They have refused to confirm the reality predicated on a belief in racial immutability and segregation at the most intimate level. Their resistance suggests that another reality exists. This suggests choice. Choice is frightening for some – often because it opens the door to the unknown in social relations and redefines self in relation to others.

The second set of four assertions further challenges the social construction of race in relationships. The individual has the right to resist this oppressive construction, as Paulo Freire (1970) observes:

> [The] marginal [person] has been expelled from and kept outside of the social system. . . . Therefore, the solution to their problem is not to become "beings inside of" but . . . [people] freeing themselves; for in reality, they are not marginal to the structure, but oppressed . . . [people] within it. (pp. 10–11)

I have the right to identify myself differently than strangers expect me to identify

Asserting this right meets with tremendous social resistance in the form of comments such as, "You can't be . . ." or "You don't look . . ." Such declarations of self-identity challenge the classification schema of the reactor. The declaration also exposes the rules that this person follows. More and more people took this tack in responding to the 1990 US Census question about race. Almost a quarter of a million people wrote in a multiracial identifier (Waters, 1994).

I have the right to identify myself differently than my parents identify me

Parents are not usually aware of the identity tasks their multiracial children face unless they, too, are multiracial. Parents often will racially identify a child in a way that they feel will make for the most welcome reception of their child socially – this means not challenging social convention but usually acquiescing to our country's rules around race, which enforce singular racial identities.

Sometimes race is avoided as a topic because parents do not know how to talk about it without pain. Sometimes they assume their ability to transcend racial barriers affords a certain protection for their off-spring. Parents can support the identity process by inviting conversations about race so that the illogical rules can be exposed and children can be explicitly taught how to take care of themselves as potential targets of racism (Greene, 1990; Miller and Miller, 1990). Parents' invitations for conversations in which they attempt to understand how and why their multiracial children identify themselves the way they do promote self-esteem and foster respect and psychological intimacy. These conversations in any household support revolutionary change.

I have the right to identify myself differently than my brothers and my sisters

Siblings can have different experiences and different goals and purposes that guide them and shape their experiences of themselves in the world. It is possible that gender influences how one comes to experience multiraciality, although this link is not yet clear.

I have the right to identify myself differently in different situations

Many biracial and multiracial people identify themselves differently in different situations, depending on what aspects of identity are salient. This "situational ethnicity" is often misinterpreted. In the novel, *The Crown of Columbus*, by Louise Erdrich and Michael Dorris (1991), one of the main characters, Vivian, a mixed-blood Native American woman, describes this process as watering whatever set of her ethnic roots needs it most. This changing of foreground and background does not usually represent confusion, but it may confuse someone who insists that race is an imperturbable fact and synonymous with ethnicity. The essence of who one is as a person remains the same. Changeability is a familiar process for most people, if they consider the roles by which they identify themselves in different situations: child, parent, lover, employee, student, friend, and so on.

Situational ethnicity is a natural strategy in response to the social demands of a situation for multiethnically and multiracially identified people. For example, participants in Stephan's (1992) research on people of Asian European heritage in Hawaii and people of Hispanic European mixed ethnic heritage in New Mexico usually gave more than one identity in replying to questions about how they experienced their own identity in five different contexts. Only 26 percent of people with mixed Japanese heritage, 11 percent of those with several different ethnic heritages in Hawaii, and 56 percent of people of mixed Hispanic heritage gave the same identification in each of the five s ituations posed. Funderburg's (1994) research on black and white biracial Americans reveals some similar process and exposes the formidable resistance and reluctance of outsiders to accept multiple ethnic identification.

Change

The third set of assertions frees us further from the constrictions of racialized existences created by delusional beliefs and rationalizations. It directs change to build upon previous and current willingness to resist social convention and its implicit rules around race. It removes one of the most insidious barriers to collective power, social distance, and attempts to replace it with connection.

Connection is never accomplished through fear. Fear drives racism and other injustices. Connection is gained through the possession of respect, esteem, and love for oneself and others. Connection acknowledges that our social fates are intertwined and our present and future are dependent on how we interact with one another now. It is predicated on an appreciation for differences that is destructive to "racist unity" (C. K. Bradshaw, personal communication, January 1995). Connection, wholeness, and a sense of belonging decrease the likelihood that one can commit atrocities against another human being.

I have the right to create a vocabulary to communicate about being multiracial

Society's vocabulary for race relations, the experience of being racialized, and the attempt to break free from concepts embedded in vocabulary requires some new terms. We must all take time and responsibility to reexamine vocabulary that has depicted racialized experience, the way Daniel (1992b) has done with his examination of the concept of "passing."

It is important to think about the meaning and origin of the terms that we use to refer to ourselves. New terms are necessarily being created by multiracial people as a step toward empowerment (Root, Introduction, this volume). Self-labeling is empowerment (Helms, 1990a). It is a proclamation of existence.

I have the right to change my identity over my lifetime –
and more than once

Identity is dynamic on the surface, whereas the core maintains some constancy. Identity is shaped by interpersonal, global, and spiritual experiences that are personally interpreted. This interpretation, however, is guided by cultural values. Thus it is possible to change one's identity over a lifetime as part of the process of clarifying or declaring who one is (Root, 1990). This is an extended conceptualization of situational ethnicity. The process of identity change may reflect a shift from a passive acceptance of the identity that society expects one to accept to a proactive exploration and declaration of who one believes oneself to be – and this may include identifying differently in different situations (Stephan, 1992). Ironically, these identities can even be the same, although the process is different (Root, 1990).

I have the right to have loyalties and identify with more than
one group of people

You have the right to loyalties and identification with more than one group of people. In fact, this fosters connections and bridges, broadening one's worldview, rather than perpetuating "us" versus "them" schisms and antagonisms. The allegiance to a greater number and variety of people increases the individual's sense of connection. The sense of connection makes it less likely that people will hurt one another by ignorance or malice. We are all empowered by connection. *The more connected we feel, the less threatening differences feel.*

I have the right to freely choose whom I befriend and love

Who the racially mixed person chooses to befriend, and particularly love, does not necessarily declare his or her racial identity or ethnic loyalty. The social folklore that racially mixed people tend to "outmarry" is a statement of the rules of the social order including hypodescent, singular allegiances, and us versus them mentality. One has the right to judge people as individuals, to know that skin color, hair texture, or eye, nose, and mouth shapes are not what measures endurance during times of hardship in love and friendship. Connection, respect, and willingness to understand, compromise, and negotiate make relationships work.

I hope this Bill of Rights exposes how insidiously entwined the mechanics of oppression are in our everyday lives – systematic beliefs, biased data or interpretation of data, rationalization, and ultimately social distance. Oppression always fragments people, as energy and attention are diverted from the experience of wholeness. A society that creates race as a difference to contend with places inordinate importance on this difference in the most negative of ways. It obscures important facts about the essence of an individual. Subsequently, instead of being seen as a *dependent* variable, the result of conditions, race is now often manipulated in the daily news, daily conversations about the motives of individuals, and in research as an *independent* variable.

If we resist this fragmentation, if we revolutionize the way we think about identity and the self in relationship to the *other*, we begin to free ourselves from an oppressive structure. When we refuse to fragment ourselves or others, then we become capable of embracing the humanity in ourselves and in others. We become less fearful, less judgmental, and less subject to defining ourselves by other's opinions of us. Then we can approach differences with respect and wonderment rather than with fear. It is respect that gives us the courage for resistance, revolution, and change in tackling racial boundaries for changing race relations.

References

Bradshaw, C. K. (1992). "Beauty and the Beast: On Racial Ambiguity." In M. P. P. Root (ed.), *Racially Mixed People in America*. Newbury Park, CA: Sage, pp. 77–90.

Chao, C. A. (in press). "A Bridge Over Troubled Waters: Being Eurasian in the U.S. of A." In J. Adleman and G. Enguidanos-Clark (eds.), *Racism in the Lives of Women: Testimony, Theory, and Guides to Antiracist Practice*. New York: Haworth.

Daniel, G. R. (1992b). "Passers and Pluralists: Subverting the Racial Divide." In M. P. P. Root (ed.), *Racially Mixed People in America*. Newbury Park, CA: Sage, pp. 91–107.

Freire, P. (1970). *Pedagogy of the Oppressed*. New York: Seabury.

——(1994). *Pedagogy of Hope*. New York: Continuum.

Funderburg, L. (1994). *Black, White, Other: Biracial Americans Talk About Race and Identity*. New York: William Morrow.

Greene, B. (1990). "What Has Gone Before: The Legacy of Racism and Sexism in the Lives of Black Mothers and Daughters." *Women and Therapy*, 9, pp. 207–30.

Helms, J. E. (1990a). *Black and White Racial Identity: Theory, Research and Practice*. New York: Greenwood.

Lee, S. (1993). "Racial Classifications in the U.S. Census: 1890–1990." *Ethnic and Racial Studies*, 16 (1), pp. 75–94.

Mass, A. (1992). "Interracial Japanese Americans: The Best of Both Worlds or the End of the Japanese American Community?" In M. P. P. Root (ed.), *Racially Mixed People in America*. Newbury Park, CA: Sage, pp. 265–79.

Miller, R. and Miller, B. (1990). "Mothering the Biracial Child: Bridging the Gaps Between African American and White Parenting Styles." *Women and Therapy*, 10 (1–2), pp. 169–79.

Omi, M. and Winant, H. (1986). *Racial Formation in the United States: From the 1960s to the 1980s*. New York: Routledge and Kegan Paul.

Root, M. P. P. (1990). "Resolving 'Other' Status: Identity Development of Biracial Individuals." In L. Brown and M. P. P. Root (eds.), *Complexity and Diversity in Feminist Theory and Therapy*. New York: Haworth, pp. 185–205.

——(1994a). "Mixed-race Women." In L. Comas-Díaz and B. Greene (eds.), *Women of Color: Integrating Ethnic and Gender Identities in Psychotherapy*. New York: Guilford, pp. 455–78.

Sanjek, R. (1994). "Intermarriage and the Future of Races in the United States." In S. Gregory and R. Sanjek (eds.), *Race*. New Brunswick, NJ: Rutgers University Press, pp. 103–30.

Sartre, J.-P. (1976). *Critique of Dialectical Reasoning: Theory of Practical Ensembles*, trans. A. Sheridan-Smith. London: New Left Books.

Spickard, P. R. (1992). "The Illogic of American Racial Categories." In M. P. P. Root (ed.), *Racially Mixed People in America*. Newbury Park, CA: Sage, pp. 12–23.

Stephan, C. W. (1992). "Mixed-heritage Individuals: Ethnic Identity and Trait

Characteristics." In M. P. P. Root (ed.), *Racially Mixed People in America*. Newbury Park, CA: Sage, pp. 50–63.

Takaki, R. (1993). *A Different Mirror: A History of Multicultural America*. Boston: Little, Brown.

Waters, M. C. (1994). "The Social Construction of Race and Ethnicity: Somes Examples from Demography." Paper presented at *American Diversity: A Demographic Challenge for the Twenty-first Century*, Center for Social and Demographic Analysis Conference, SUNY, Albany, April.

21

Racial Histories and Their Regimes of Truth

Ann Laura Stoler

[. . .]

Introduction

This paper is an effort to identify how contemporary scholars write about the history of racisms and the assumptions about racial thinking that they bring to those histories. I am interested in the analytic "grids of intelligibility" that underwrite their narratives, thus not with that object identified as "racism" (how it has manifested itself in different time and place), but rather with scholarly accounts of its emergence, its datings and its unique and recurrent attributes. Nor is this primarily an attempt to locate those more "truthful" stories about racism from those which are not (though I suppose I harbor some subliminal hope that this is what I can do), but rather to first step back and identify some features of racism's contemporary antiracist historiography.

I am interested in the "regimes of truth" that inform Euro-American accounts of racisms and the political investments that those of us who write those accounts have in them. By Foucault's definition these regimes are not "the ensemble of truths" but rather the "ensemble of rules according to which the true and the false are separated and specific effects of power [are] attached to the true" (Foucault, 1980, pp. 131–2). While still some way from identifying those "rules," the questions I pose push in that direction: What truth-claims inform our accounts, on what grounds do we take some accounts to be more credible and sensible than others, how do we imagine racisms to be secured, and what originary myths do we assign to them?

A hallmark feature of contemporary scholarship is a willingness – some might say an insistence – to acknowledge that there is no single object called racism, but a plurality of racisms which are not rehearsals of one another but distinct systems of practice and belief. Within this frame, historically different meanings are attached to the concept of "race" and the racisms they entail. Recognition of plurality in part stems from the attribution of racisms' conditions of origin to different events and different contexts. What is more surprising are the number of features these varied accounts hold in common and that, in view of their disparate foci, would seem unlikely to recur. So a basic question: Are these recurrences derived from the fact that these accounts share a common object, that is, racism, as we might expect, or rather from the common assumptions underlying the scholarship? Is there something to learn about the nature of racisms from discrepancies and commonalties in the stories we tell about them? Perhaps more troubling: Are these antiracist histories so much a part and product of racial discourse that they are, despite intention, subject to its regimes of truth? [. . .]

I start from a basic observation: that the profusion of historical research on the emergence of what Omi and Winant aptly refer to as "racial formations" has turned on specifying the changing political semantics of race and how the race concept has been mobilized differently in structuring specific racisms and their hierarchies of difference (Omi and Winant, 1986). Focused on the social construction of racial taxonomies and their naturalization, some have sought to identify the convergence of racisms with specific labor regimes: with slavery, with expanding capitalism, or with the bureaucratic normalizing technologies of modern states. Some have identified racism not as an aberrant feature of, and exception to, the establishment of liberalism and democratic rights but as a founding principle of them. Others have argued that 1800, not the 1600s, marks racism's emergence, identifying its critical articulation with nationalism and the ascendancy of bourgeois hegemony in its modern form (Mosse, 1985). My interest is less in the "accuracy" of these different datings than in their plurality and why such a range is possible.

I offer several arguments; one, that some of the patterned ways in which contemporary racism is understood are predicated on flattened, reductive histories of what racisms once looked like, so that, two, when scholars distinguish between racisms of past and present, they often imply that racisms once existed in more overt and pristine form. Third, I take this "flattening" not to be arbitrary, but contingent on a basic and historically problematic contrast between a biologized, physiological and somatic racism of the past held up as fundamentally distinct from a more nuanced culturally coded and complex racism of the present. Four, I hold that this contrast is central to how "the new racism" is marked as a more "insidious," "silently sophisticated," "subtle" and therefore "novel" phenomenon.[1] Finally, I suggest that this disposition towards the past rests on a scholarly quest for origins, for the "original" moment in which the dye of race was cast. That search in part shapes the particular forms that antiracist histories of racisms take: sometimes written as narratives of "original sin," sometimes as narratives that describe innocuous cultural representations of difference "before the (racial) fall." In both cases, histories of racism often appear as narratives of redemption. [. . .]

If racisms always entail an interpretation of the relationship between the seen and the unseen, construed historically in however many different ways, then we who write those histories must reckon with the two ways of knowing implied. In one, the "truth" of race is understood as grounded in somatically observable, *dependable* differences; in the other, the "truth" of racial membership is not visually secured at all. Surface perceptions are unreliable and membership is dependent on privileged knowledge of "hidden properties" of human kinds, of those secreted in their depths.

What follows from these epistemic standpoints are different stories: racism is either so pervasive because difference is so palpable and "obvious," or lethal because it is not. Antiracist histories may either expose the nineteenth-century fiction of somatic fixities or the fiction of nonvisual essentialist ones. In both cases the target is racism's reliance on the artifice of fixed and immutable racial types. Both accounts turn on "proving" the porousness of race as a concept, and/or the permeability of racial categories. Both accounts confront, and are designed to debunk, the false stability of racial taxonomies on the premise that such an analytic assault undermines one of racism's foundational fictions and serves as an effective antiracist strategy.

If the attack on immutability is one cornerstone of antiracist histories, what I would call an "ocular obsession" is another. In the latter, the power of racisms resides in a visual "common sense" about human kinds. It is the power of the gaze on which racial knowledge is thought to build and on which its resiliency is seen to rest. No one would deny that racisms call on the visual, but visual "common sense" is not an historical constant. It has played a minor part in some folk and scientific theories of race, a more prominent one in others. In whichever version, however, such theories rarely, if ever, have been about somatics alone. What is striking about the nineteenth-century imperial fields in which racial discourses were honed and thrived is in some ways counterintuitive to how we as scholars have construed the historical making of race and the part essentialism plays in it: racial memberships were based not only on a nonvisible set of criteria, but on the assessment of a *changing* set of features that made up a racial essence. Among these changing properties were cultural competencies, moral civilities and affective sensibilities that were poorly secured by chromatic indices, and not by color-based taxonomies or visual markers.

Rather than choose between these approaches, we might do better to explore the disparity between the "seen" and the "unseen," the interpretive space such a tension provides and what it enables. One line of my argument should become clear: that the ambiguity of those sets of relationships between the somatic and the inner self, the phenotype and the genotype, pigment shade and psychological sensibility are not slips in, or obstacles to, racial thinking but rather conditions for its proliferation and possibility.

Originary Myths and Common(Sense) Themes

Among the competing theories about when racisms emerge, and the commonalities that distinctively different and dissonant approaches to racism share, some are more obvious than others. I offer a number here not because they are comprehensive and definitively "right," but for more strategic reasons: (1) because these repetitions in explanation have been ignored; and (2) because their juxtaposition forces a troubling question: why does such *patterned* ambiguity pervade our historical narratives? Finally, I point to similarities in explanation to broach a more important observation: contrary renderings of racisms from varied time and place may not reveal the incompatibility of these accounts, but rather may reflect the "polyvalent mobility" of racial discourse and the tenacious significance of it.

Two striking features emerge in the historiography of racism by focusing on historians' narratives rather than on the history of the changing meanings of race: one is the wide range of different datings provided for racisms' moment of emergence, and the other is the sheer quantity of different explanations offered for them. Just to provide some sense of this range, I list below in no particular order, nor with careful attention to disciplinary context, some examples.

Harry Bracken has argued that seventeenth-century empiricism "and the rise of manipulative models of man" made it more possible to think about different species of humans and was "decisive" in racism's historical emergence (Bracken, 1973). Cornel West underscores that the "idea of white supremacy" emerged out of the powers of a modern discourse to "produce and prohibit, develop and delimit forms of rationality, scientificity, and objectivity . . . which draw boundaries for the intelligibility, availability and legitimacy of certain ideas" (West, 1982). Etienne Balibar has turned our attention to the fact that universalism and racism are more than "complementary" but rather "contraries affecting one another from the inside" (Balibar, 1994, p. 199).

Collette Guillaumin's account of racism's origins focuses on the rise of individuality and some bounded notion of the "ownership of the self" that "gave rise to the legal expression of racial membership" (Guillaumin, 1995). The decline of monarchy and destruction of the naturalized social hierarchies that absolutism endorsed prompted the forging of new naturalized collectivities and new disciplines that could account for them. These new disciplines could give credence to the belief that group membership was organic, based on distinct somatic and psychological traits that differently (but still naturally) "carved nature at its joints." In a similar vein, John Rex attributes racist beliefs to the decline of a legal system upholding inequalities and the sanctions to back it. He posits "that the doctrine of equality of economic opportunity [of economic liberalism] and that of racial superiority and inferiority are complements of one another" (Rex, 1980, p. 131).

George Mosse traces racism's "foundations" to "the Enlightenment" – as do many others – and to "the religious revival of the eighteenth century" (Mosse, 1978, p. 3). For Uday Mehta racism is an exclusionary principle theoretically inherent in, and crucial to, the development of a liberal politics (Mehta, 1990). By Zygmunt Bauman's account, extreme racism, modernity, bureaucratic culture, and the civilizing process are historically and organically bound (Bauman, 1989). David Goldberg too cites race as "one of the central conceptual inventions of modernity," embodying the "liberal paradox" that as "modernity commits itself to progressive idealized principles of liberty, equality and fraternity . . . there is a multiplication of racial identities and the sets of exclusions they prompt and rationalize, *enable*, and sustain" (Goldberg, 1993, p. 6; my emphasis). For Foucault, modern racism is a product of the normalizing rise of "biopower" and fundamental to the technology of *all* modern biopolitical states – be they capitalist, fascist or socialist ones.[2] This is obviously not an exhaustive list but the point I want to make should be clear. How can the emergence/articulation/development of empiricism, universalism, capitalism, modernity, liberalism, the Enlightenment, state structure, and slavery, all account for the rise of racism? [. . .]

Racial "theory" in these accounts is thought to reside with those who truck in high science and high politics, by and large confined to those who do "theory" with a capital "T." But there is little agreement about which forms of knowledge and political organization are critical in the making of racisms and which are not. For liberalism, universalism and cultural relativism – while frequently seen as the culprits – rarely occupy the same explanatory ground. Sometimes they are treated as bodies of belief whose own conception gives rise to racism, other times as conjectural moments that caused and consolidated racialized practices, and elsewhere as progressive political principles gone awry that may still, when righted, yield plausible strategies for racism's eradication.

What is at issue here? Either these scholars are not talking about the same phenomenon (the definitions of racism differ), or these are indeed complementary correlations, not causal connections. Or is it that the propensity to think in racial terms is a preserved possibility, activated, but not accounted for, by these historical sightings? (Hirschfeld, 1996). Or is it something inherent to racism as a discursive formation that facilitates how it welds itself to such varied projects? There are other narrative themes that might help frame the questions we should address.

Related to these disparate accounts above is another equally compelling feature in racism's historiography: namely, how frequently different datings – from the seventeenth to the twentieth centuries – are cited as the moment of its "true" emergence. Whether that date coincides with the advent of slavery, as Barbara Fields suggests, or with the decline of it, as Thomas Holt deftly argues, whether with the emergence of modernity and liberalism or with the making of modern nation-states, what stands out is that in such different periods racism is characterized as "new" by those analyzing it (Fields, 1982; Holt, 1992).

[. . .] But this "newness" of racism may be more than a case of scholarly misrecognition and mistaken identity. This appearance of newness may index something more, something crucial to the ease with which racial discourse harnesses itself to reformist projects.

This points to another problem. If racisms so often appear new, they also appear as frequently *renewed* for the same contexts, if not for the same authors. As often as scholars recount the uniqueness of racism's invention, they remind us that these racisms can only be called "new" because there are earlier ones from which they emerged and of which they are a part (Bjorgo and Witte, 1993). Thus even while the "newness" of racism is heralded, racisms are treated as systems of thinking and practice that build on primordial loyalties, that have deep and tenacious historical roots, that are vestiges of entrenched conflicts (as in Leon Poliakov's *Aryan Myth*), that tap atavistic psychological associations of color, contamination and pollution (as in Winthrop Jordan's repeatedly cited account in *White over Black*) that are readily available to service new social stratigraphies and classifications.

Rather than attempt to reconcile these contradictory claims, it may be more useful to take another tack: one which questions whether these competing claims are not evidence of a fundamental feature of the ways in which racial discourses work though sedimented and familiar cultural representations of difference as they simultaneously tap into and feed the emergence of new ones.[3] Thus the very "relevance" of racial distinctions, that which makes them speakable, common sense, comfortably incorporated and easily heard, may derive from the dense set of prior representations on which they build and in turn recast.[4] [. . .]

If racial discourses draw on the past as they harness themselves to new visions and projects, then at least one observation follows: by this reasoning, students of the history of racism should not expect consensus on whether they are witness to a legacy of the past or the emergence of a new phenomenon all together precisely because racial discourse operates in a mobile discursive field that at once contains and produces the two. As Foucault insisted in his 1976 Collège de France lectures on the subject, these are discourses of vacillations with dynamic motility. Racial discourses produce new truths and ruptures as they fold into and recuperate old ones.[5] [. . .]

For if Foucault is right that one of the defining features of racism is its "polyvalent mobility," that it may vacillate and be embraced by those opposed to and beleaguered by the state at one moment and become an intergral part of the technologies of state rule at another, then the fact that racial discourses contain and coexist with a range of political agendas is not a contradiction but a fundamental historical feature of their *nonlinear*, spiraling political genealogies.

[. . .] Foucault offers something more. He signals attention not only to the fact of their mobility, but to one compelling reason for it; namely, that racial discourses contain both "erudite" and "subjugated" knowledge, and thus genealogically build on the concerns of those privileged purveyors of truth, those with "erudite knowledge" as well as those whose knowledge has been disqualified or denied access to the realm of valorized knowledge.[6] Or as he puts it more succinctly: racial discourse has not, as often assumed, always positioned itself as a narrative/history of those allied with state power, but at different historical moments as a *contre-histoire* – a "counternarrative/history" of those contesting the state's legitimate claims to rule. Within his frame, historical accounts of racism matter very much for they are not outside racism's relations of power but fundamental to their making.[7] By Foucault's account, racial discourse operates at different levels in the micromanagement of individual bodies and the macromanagement of the body politic. But as a discursive formation, its tactical qualities are more quixotic still, for it moves as easily between different political projects as it seizes upon *different* elements of earlier discourses reworked for new political ends.[8]

These features of mobility are useful to keep in mind when we look to another exemplary paradox in the historiography of racism: namely, the "comfortable" fit students of racism repeatedly find between racism and conservative political agendas. There is no denying that connection; however, it is striking how much less we have attended to the ways in which racial discourses can and do harness themselves with frequent success to progressive ones.

Not all students of racisms' histories limit themselves to racisms' conserving and conservative impulses and strategies. Decades ago, Edmund Morgan argued that American republican notions of freedom were forged by asserting the distinctions of race. David Roediger more recently has argued convincingly that a discourse on "whiteness" not only enabled working-class formation in the nineteenth century, but that working-class "assertions of white freedom" and struggles against capitalist disciplinary strategies were made in the language of race (Roediger, 1991, p. 49).

Notwithstanding such exceptions, a common historiographic assumption is that racial discourse is a discourse of those with power (or those trying to maintain their hold) rather than a "dense transfer point of it"; more specifically, that the subjects of scholarly enquiry – racists – are ill-educated, close-minded conservatives, and/or ill-intentioned but well-heeled ones. As Pierre-Andre Taguieff argues, much of the antiracist discourse in France posits racism as a pathological response of those labeled "racist" (thereby simply inverting the racist claims that the designated Other is "pathologically" oversexed and psychologically lazy), deflecting attention from the "well-meaning" larger society in which racism is widespread, nurtured and maintained.[9] Racism is construed historically as a set of social practices embraced by reactionary members of a changing body politic. Even those who argue that liberalism gives rise to a racialized politics of exclusion often do so by arguing that racism is a *reactive* strategy, cemented by those upper or lower classes invested in guarding themselves against incursions on their extensive privilege (i.e., the rich), or limited power (i.e., "poor whites").

Paradoxically then, racism is treated as a set of power relations instigated by those who rule, but more fundamentally embraced in its more virulent forms by those who do not. Thus, there is another foundational fiction; racist excess, like sexual excess, is a result of the unbridled passions of ordinary folk, not those endowed with the civilities of well-educated white men.[10]

This view does more than shift effortlessly between the identification of individual and social pathologies. It prompts an analytic move that reappears in the historiography of racism of the seventeenth to the twentieth centuries. Namely, it associates racism's emergence with "disorder," whether it takes on social, moral, political or economic form. When strongly put, the causal arrow from "disorder" to racism is directly drawn. For example, Karen Newman attributes the racialized discourse in Shakespeare's *Othello* not only to the fear of "masterless men" (of persons out of place) but to fears of the Other crescendoing in a moment of "challenges to traditional notions of order and degree" (Newman, 1987, p. 47). Michael Banton draws on Winthrop Jordan to point to a seventeenth-century British society "in ferment," to the preponderance again of "masterless men" who provoked anxieties about the "apparent dissolution of social and moral controls" (Banton, 1977, p. 14; see also Jordan, 1968). Hannah Arendt saw racialized accounts of the social order emerging with an aristocracy whose privileges were fast being encroached upon by an increasingly mobile and wealthy bourgeoisie: In her account, it was not the fear of "masterless men" but fear of a masterful bourgeoisie usurping both positions of power and what defined morality (Arendt, 1948).[11] For the colonical context of the Dutch East Indies, I too have worked off the assumption that the intensification of racialized policies was a response to "crises of control," to the colonial state's fear that disorderly moral conduct was a form of political subversion (Stoler, 1991). Recent analyses of the "new racism" turn on similar arguments: namely, that racism is a response to the social and economic disorders, dislocations and anonymities produced by postmodern capitalism, and responsive to a disjuncture between expectations and an attenuation of entitlements (Goldberg, 1993, p. 70).

While all of these may accurately mark the particular moments that intensify racialized accounts, "disorder" in itself accounts for too little, and too much. More importantly, it is already a key term and justification for segregating and racialized policies and thus a tautology to suggest that it can account for that of which it is already a part. As Bauman argues, the image of the "conceptual Jew" in Nazi Germany as *visqueux* (slimy) represented not only boundary transgression but "chaos and devastation" (Bauman, 1989, pp. 39–40). The demand for "order" and the normalization and/or elimination and expulsion of those who threatened it – what Foucault has called a "defense of society against itself," and what Balibar calls a defense of a society's "interior frontiers" – is a leitmotif in the discourse of state racism, not an explanation of it.

On the Tactical Mobility of Racial Discourse

I frequently have used the term "discourse" here but should clarify that I do not intend it in the generic sense it is used in so much of what is labeled the "discursive turn" today. I want to stay closer to the analytic work I think Foucault did in defining what constitutes a "discursive formation." In fact, the pat gloss of "discourse" to designate a unified and coherent field of statements (as in the ubiquitous term "colonial discourse") ignores most of what Foucault had to say about discourse and is a pretty accurate description of what it is not. In *The Archaeology of Knowledge* he writes:

> [A discursive formation is marked by] the different possibilities that it opens of reanimating already existing themes, of arousing opposed strategies, of giving way to irreconcilable interests, of making it possible, with a particular set of concepts, to play different games. Rather than seeking the permanence of themes, images and opinions through time, rather than retracing the dialectic of their conflicts in order to individualize groups of statements, could one not rather mark out the dispersion of the points of choice, and define prior to any options, to any thematic preference, a field of strategic possibilities? (Foucault, 1972, pp. 36–7)

Could our current understanding of racism as a discursive formation be any further from this definition? Contemporary use fails to capture three crucial elements: (1) that it is mobile; (2) that it does *not* display constant or consistent political interests; and (3) that it lacks thematic unity. Viewed in this way, we should not expect the "racial discourse" of the Dutch in late nineteenth-century Java or among the LePenist constituency in turn of the twenty-first century France to reveal a common set of intentions, consequences, and/or themes. A discourse is racial not because it displays shared political interests but rather because it delineates a field and set of conditions in which it becomes impossible to talk about sexuality, class membership, morality, and childrearing without talking about race (Foucault, 1972, p. 144).

This notion of "polyvalent mobility" pushes us to another apparent contradiction in racial discourse that has gone unaddressed. While much of the historiography of racism has focused on how modern racisms build upon, recruit, and take hold of old loyalties and preexisting senses of commonality and difference in the service of new political projects, it pays less sustained attention to how racisms recuperate and invent past legacies that provide utopian visions of the future. At one level, this too is uncontroversial. Historians have discussed the social hygiene campaigns of the Nazi state and US sterilization laws at the high moment of eugenics as programs forged in the spirit and language of a new social order. My point, however, is that racial discourses, even in their more muted forms, are more broadly utopian and are not the futuristic fantasies of racist demagogues alone. Racism does not "dream of eternal contaminations . . . outside of history" as Ben Anderson once wrote, but rather promises to move society forward through a return to the past (Anderson, 1983). Pat Robertson's "new world order" is a diagnostic of today's troubles and a blueprint for the future (Robertson, 1991). LePen's National Front in France has not gained 30 percent of the votes in local elections only from skinheads and closet reactionaries. The current platform of the National Front is embraced precisely by those who see themselves as anti-elitist, antistate, populist, and conservatively progressive (Taguieff, 1990b). The Front's most recent and successful slogan "Neither Right, nor Left, but French" captures the sophisticated tactical mobility of its claims (Joffrin, 1995).

The nationalist and patriotic appropriations of racial discourse have been explored by students of racism for some time and I will not go into them here (see, e.g., Balibar, 1994; Eley and Suny, 1996). But one aspect of that relationship is relevant to note: much current analysis argues that racism today differs from earlier variants because it explicitly encourages those embracing its principles to see themselves not as racists, but as protectors of the national patrimony, as "true" and patriotic citizens of the United States, England, Germany, or France. Whether committed to individual rights, "the right to difference," or, as LePen urges, the "right to a national preference," accounts of contemporary racism note how easily a discourse of (individual) rights and rational behavior serves racial discourse, producing a political and psychological grid in which racial thinking, rationality and rights go hand in hand.[12] In the "illiberal" politics of D'Souza, who contends that racism is dead and the discourse about it should be as well, the taxi-driver who passes three men of color to pick up one who is white is doing nothing racist, but acting on the basis of reasoned, rational choice (D'Souza, 1995).

The observation that racists in the postmodern era are encouraged not to see themselves as such may capture something significant about how racial discourses operate today, but it again flattens history in the service of a spurious contrast; namely that earlier racisms did nothing of the sort, that those racisms were candidly embraced by their advocates. But this is a caricature of colonial racial sensibilities, not a description of them. Dutch colonials in Indonesia in the late nineteenth and early twentieth centuries were not alone in adamantly declaring that they did *not* subscribe to racism and emphatically did subscribe to the equality of human rights.

When we as scholars take such high profile racists as Gobineau, Madison Grant, and Vacher Lapouge as exemplars of racial reasoning, we miss the force field in which racial discourses have thrived. Focus on such extreme figures dissuades questioning the nuanced ways in which *homo europeaus* was discursively constructed, culturally maintained and secured as much in sexual and domestic arrangements within the family as in public discourse outside it.

The point is important because a central tenet in analyses of the "new racism" is that it occupies a different and more intimate location than earlier racisms, "above all, in family life" (Gilroy, 1987, p. 43). Paul Gilroy, for example, has argued that "families are therefore not only the nation in microcosm, its key components, but act as the means to turn social processes into natural, instinctive ones" (p. 43). But such assessments place subtle state interventions on the side of the postcolonial, and Manichean, blunt racisms on the other. When Gilroy states that "the new racism is primarily concerned with mechanisms of inclusion and exclusion," it should not be surprising that some students of colonial racisms are given pause (p. 45). Attention to the relationship between inclusions and exclusions are not new to contemporary racism but to the concerns and language of scholars studying them. Colonial racisms were explicitly preoccupied with the politics of exclusion, with the making of adults and children into racialized beings, with educating their racially cued comportements, moral sentiments and desires in ways that were invariably "about" bourgeois respectability, "civility," and culture and less explicitly "about" race.

What is more, this notion that being racist was once more acceptable than it is today feeds off a prevailing myth in stories of modern racism's origins; namely, that race was once a notion perceived as fixed and natural, in Winant's words, "as constant as a southern star." Thus even such an astute historian as Michael Adas contends that there was little racism in the field of colonial technology and science until the late nineteenth century on the grounds that the "notion [that] biological factors were responsible for Europe's achievement and global dominance was not [yet] widely argued" and that European colonials shared a belief in the "improvability" of Asian and African populations. Part of his "proof" is that "the connections between innate physical characteristics and moral or intellectual capabilities remained ill-defined even in the most systematic of the racist tracts" (Adas, 1989, p. 274). Such a reading of racism assumes a developmental model in which racism only emerges as dominant when the linkages between the physical and psychological are definitively specified, scientifically validated and easy, if not to prove, at least to grasp.[13]

Adas's account rests on a basic assumption of much antiracist discourse of the post-war period: namely, that if we can disprove the credibility of race as a scientific concept, we can dismantle the power of racism itself – that racisms rise and fall on the scientific credibility of the concept of race. Not only can racisms thrive without such certainty, racial discourses proliferate and produce new relations of power and knowledge in the contest over which of these linkages are "true" or "false." Thus, for example, the fact that phrenology – the theory that a person's character and intelligence could be deduced from the shape of the skull – was quickly discredited in the nineteenth century as an accurate measure of racial endowment did nothing to undermine the discussion of, and attention riveted on, the relationship between physical measurements and mental aptitude. On the contrary, phrenology provided a placeholder in which the search for a relationship between phenotype and genotype was not disqualified, but only its specific coordinates. What is important is that the search for a link could remain an active and reasonable quest in scientific and folk theories of race.

On Fixities and Fluidities in Racial Discourse

The premise underwriting Adas's historical account, that nineteenth-century racisms were first and foremost about biology, surfaces in analyses of racisms today: not that race was once ambiguous but that it was once a clear concept, and that past racisms were dependent on it. Contra that prevailing wisdom (of those such as Winant, by no means alone in making such a blanket claim), colonial concepts of "race" have had more the consistency and constancy of the Milky Way – perceptible boundaries from a distance but made up of a moving constellation of parts of changing intensity – and less the fixity of a southern star. This adherence to a notion of fixity rests on the assumption that fixity was rooted in a commonly shared biological model of race, that some notion of "immutability" was crucial to it, and that race was a concept unproblematically conceived as "natural." But as George Stocking once noted, Lamarckian notions that acquired traits could be inheritable, and that human variation was responsive to environmental conditions were as much a part of nineteenth-century racial thinking and practice as those focused more squarely on the immutability and permanence of traits (Stocking, 1968, pp. 234–69). [. . .]

I have made this argument elsewhere and only repeat it here to underscore that the porousness we assign to the contemporary concept of race may be a fluidity fundamental to the concept itself and not a hallmark of our postmodern moment. Histories of racisms that narrate a shift from the fixed and biological to the cultural and fluid impose a progression that poorly characterizes what racisms looked like in the nineteenth century and therefore have little to say about what distinguishes racisms today. Donald Kinder and Lynn Sanders's claim in their new book *Divided by Color* (1996), that there is a new form of racial prejudice in the United States less concerned with genes than with "moral character," is only accurate if we imagine that earlier racisms were built solely on genotypes and physiologies. Racist perceptions and policies founded on the notion that the racialized Other is somehow "behaving badly" or "undeserving" of poor relief, too indolent to work, indeed "spoiled" by the charity of state aid, have a very long political genealogy.

The complex legal machinations and political strategies by which racial membership has been redefined and realigned in any number of historical contexts – from the nineteenth-century Dutch East Indies and French Indochina to twentieth-century South Africa, Latin America, and the United States – should alert us to the fact that nineteenth-century racism was not built on the sure-footed classifications of science but on a potent set of cultural and affective criteria whose malleability was a key to the flexible scale along which economic privileges could be cordoned off and social entitlements reassigned. Racial taxonomies that included Japanese and Chinese as "European" at one colonial moment and not another, that placed children, regardless of color, who were acknowledged by their father in the category of European while excluding those fairskinned children who were not, suggests that race is a "moving" and resilient category in strategic, nonincidental ways.

This is not to suggest that notions of "fixity" do not underwrite racial logics. My point is that the current emphasis on the fluidity we now observe in the making of racial categories may not be the trenchant postcolonial critique we take it to be. It merely signals our somewhat belated recognition that the force of racial discourse is precisely in the double-vision it allows, in the fact that it combines notions of fixity and fluidity in ways that are basic to its dynamic.[14] That we who study the history of racism are so committed to documenting fluidity may have more to do with the sorts of political narratives of renouncement and thus of redemption we are intent to tell.[15] The "proof" that racial categories are fluid and not fixed confirms our political convictions that they can and should be undone. [. . .]

This does not undermine the notion that essentialist thinking and practices are operative. Rather it suggests that essentialisms are not secured by fixed traits but by substitutable and interchangeable sets of them. Basic to nineteenth-century European discourses on racial essence was an explicit debate about where that immutable essence was located, a disquiet about its vulnerability but rarely a belief in no essence at all. Essentialist thinking may rest not on a psychological commitment to permanence, but rather on the fact that those attributes that make it up have moving and fungible parts.

Racial Epistemologies

[. . .] I have argued here that we need to attend to a more complicated epistemic field. The force of racisms is not found in the alleged fixity of visual knowledge, nor on essentialism itself, but on the *malleability* of the criteria of psychological dispositions and moral sensibilities that the visual could neither definitively secure nor explain. In considering that a critical feature of racial discourse may be its "polyvalent mobility," I am not suggesting that racism is everywhere and nowhere, arbitrarily allied, infinitely adaptable or, in David Goldberg's words, an "empty vaccum." I am more interested in exploring the ways in which racisms take on the form of other things, wrap themselves around heated issues, descend upon political pulse points, appear as reasoned judgments, beyond sentiment, as they penetrate impassioned bodies.

In turning to inconsistencies and disparities in debates that ostensibly were not about race at all, we may better capture the specific ways in which that mobility was realized and the consequences of it. It is neither somatics nor essentialism that give racisms their force. It is rather the always ambiguous relationship between the two and the interpretive space that ambiguity affords that confers on racial discourse its dynamic motility. A notion of essence does not necessarily rest on immovable parts but on the strategic inclusion of different attributes, of a changing constellation of features and a changing weighing of them. Racial discourses do seem to have some patterned ways – some "southern stars" – by which they lodge themselves in different historical moments and define power relations between groups: our accounts of those histories do so as well. The question is whether those "stars" to which we ascribe certainty in accounting for racisms past and present, and those "stars" that provide for the continuing significance and salience of racisms, are yet shared.

One way to bring racisms' histories and our accounts of those histories into better line is to attend closer to the disparities in both our stories of origin and in the range of attributes by which we consider racisms should be defined. Instead of reconciling these discrepancies, I take them as telling signs. The tension between fluidity and fixity in racial discourse, between the seen and the unseen, between the appearance of racisms as always "new" and "renewed" at the same time, may signal something powerful about the force field in which such discourses thrive.

In that force field, the histories of racisms we write fold back into a field of radicalized practices that make up a broader set of racial genealogies. These racisms are transformed not only by the different moments in which they are instantiated – suggesting that racisms, like nationalisms, may have modular features. Our scholarly interpretations of those instantiations themselves become preserved possibilities providing these discourses of power with new inspirations and new locations that may nourish their expansive, polysemic and contingent qualities.

By calling into question how we write histories of racism and in suggesting that our accounts often read as narratives of redemption, I am not suggesting that we give up on the task of writing racisms' counter-histories, but rather that we attend more carefully to the politics that underwrite why we tell the historical stories we do and to the epistemic principles to which we subscribe. It is more histories of the present we need – not less – to appreciate what political invest-ments have made histories of racism in the post-civil rights 1970s look so different from (and sometimes similar to) histories of racism in the multicultural 1980s, and from histories of racism written under the specter of the New Right's sophisticated cultural politics that so fiercely denies that racism – and therefore any antiracist effort – matters today.

Notes

1   For the starkest examples of this position, that is, that contemporary racism is distinguished by its strong cultural coding, see Taguieff (1990a) and Gilroy (1987) who writes:

> It will be argued that [the new racism's] novelty lies in the capacity to link discourses of patriotism, nationalism, xenopho-bia, Englishness, Britishness, militarism and gender difference into a complex system which gives "race" its contemporary meaning. (p. 43)

2   On the relationship between state racism and biopower see Foucault's (1991) final 1976 Collège de France lecture and my discussion of it (Stoler, 1995, pp. 80–8).
3   On "dominant, residual and emergent" features of cultural systems see Williams (1977, pp. 121–7).
4   On theories of relevance see Sperber and Wilson (1986).
5   See my discussion of these lectures (Stoler, 1995, pp. 62–94). Only three of the 1976 Collège de France lectures have been published (the first two in English, the final one in French). While the first two have been available in English for sometime (see Foucault, 1980), they have never been treated in the context of the corpus of which they are a part, that is, as

the introductory lectures to the seminar Foucault devoted specifically to "the origins of modern racism."

6 Some students of racism's histories refer to racial discourse's "imperialistic" qualities in the sense that it may be taken up by, and take over the content of, other constructions of difference like that of caste in India where the contemporary debate on caste is so often framed in racial terms (see Dumont, 1963). Thus in noting racism's "tactical mobility" at issue is not only that it can harness to different projects within Europe, but as importantly, that it can be harnessed by other social movements to validate and substantiate the importance of their claims. On the hazards of so doing, see Anthony Appiah's (1992) discussion of the negritude movement in Africa that, he argues, not only "begins with the assumption of the racial solidarity of the Negro" but that "racism . . . could only be countered by accepting the categories of race" (p. 6).

7 For Foucault's discussion of racial discourse as a *contre-histoire*, see Stoler (1995, pp. 68–9, 73–80).

8 One could argue that all potent political symbols ("equality," "freedom," "individual rights," "social justice") are necessarily polyvalent, endowed with amorphous qualities that guarantee their resilience over space, context and time, properties ensuring that their potency will not be lost in local translation. One important difference between these very abstract concepts and that of race is the ways in which the latter descends into any particularity, not as a superimposition that can later be unpeeled, not as a general principle diluted in a specific context, but rather as a discourse that takes on the shape of other social distinctions with an almost miasmic quality.

9 As Taguieff writes:

> [antiracism works off the premise that] racism only exists among "racists," patently, labeled, declared or recognized as such in public space. Situated, localised, identified in the singular figure of the political "barbarian" of the late 20th century, racism thus can be combatted in the same way one fights against organized groups menacing the public order: i.e., through police repression and by judicial sanction. Prohibit and dissolve. (p. xi)

Racism as an attribute of individual and/or social pathology has a long genealogy. Most early psychological work on racism, certainly Adorno et al. (1982 [1950]), tried to mark it as the pathological outcome of a dysfunctional childhood.

10 In colonial documents and the analyses of colonial racism derived from them, poor, "decivilized'" whites are targeted as both the most ardent sup-

porters of racism and subversive of it. In addition, it is white women whose jealous passions and confinement in narrow-minded milieus bring racism to the colonies. For an analysis of the colonial debates and historical commentaries on this issue, see Stoler (1989, 1991). On the "unbridled passions" of subaltern European men, see Stoler (1995, pp. 179–80). Note that both colonial assessments and the historiography on the rise of racism converge on the similar point that "the problem" of intensified racism was related to the sexual appetites of subaltern European men. In a similar vein, Feagin and Vera (1995, p. 116) note that racial violence may be perpetrated by "less-educated whites," but the conditions for it are managed by the white middle class.

11   On others who make similar analyses, see Stoler (1995, pp. 77–8).

12   See, for example, Stanley Fish's (1995) Op-ed piece on racism and individual rights. Many defenders of affirmative action attempt to counter the current assault on it by pointing to the ways in which a discourse of individual rights is invoked to support a retreat from government support for affirmative action.

13   Adas's account is sensitive to the fact that "race" had a wide range of ambiguous meanings; nevertheless, a fixed notion of *racism*, not race, remains untouched by that observation.

14   My use of "double-vision" here is not to be confused with the sense in which DuBois used that term at the turn of the century.

15   On the politics of sentiment on which liberal empathy builds, see Ellison (1996).

References

Adas, M. (1989). *Machines as the Measure of Man: Science, Technology, and Ideologies of Western Dominance*. Ithaca, NY: Cornell University Press.

Adorno, T. W., Frenkel-Brunswik, E., Levinson, D., and Sanford, N. (1982) [1950]. *The Authoritarian Personality*. New York: W. W. Norton.

Anderson, B. (1983). *Imagined Communities*. London: Verso.

Appiah, A. (1992). *My Father's House: Africa in the Philosophy of Culture*. New York: Oxford University Press.

Arendt, H. (1948). *The Origins of Totalitarianism*. New York: Harcourt and Brace.

Balibar, E. (1994). "Racism as Universalism." In *Masses, Classes, Ideas*. New York: Routledge.

Banton, M. (1977). *The Idea of Race*. London: Tavistock.

Bauman, Z. (1989). *Modernity and the Holocaust*. Ithaca, NY: Cornell University Press.

Bjorgo, T. and Witte, R. (eds.) (1993). "Introduction." In *Racist Violence in Europe*. New York: St Martin's Press.

Bracken, H. M. (1973). "Essence, Accident and Race." *Hermathena*, 116 (Winter), pp. 81–96.

Curtin, P. (1964). *The Image of Africa: British Ideas and Action, 1780–1850*, Volume I. Madison: University of Wisconsin Press.

Di Leonardo, M. (1996). "Patterns of Culture Wars." *Nation*, April 8.

D'Souza, D. (1995). *The End of Racism*. New York: Free Press.

Dumont, L. (1963). *Homo Hierarchiehus*. Chicago: University of Chicago Press.

Eley, G. and Suny, R. (eds.) (1996). *Becoming National*. New York: Oxford University Press.

Ellison, E. (1996). "A Short History of Liberal Guilt." *Critical Inquiry*, 22 (Winter), pp. 344–71.

Ezekiel, R. (1995). *The Racist Mind*. New York: Viking.

Feagin, J. and Vera, H. (1995). *White Racism*. London: Routledge.

Fields, B. (1982). "Ideology and Race in American History." In J. M. Kousser and J. M. McPherson (eds.), *Region, Race, and Reconstruction*. New York, pp. 143–77.

Foucault, M. (1972). *The Archaeology of Knowledge*. New York: Pantheon.

——(1977). "Nietzsche, Geneology, History." In *Language, Counter-Memory*, ed. D. Bouchard. Ithaca, NY: Cornell University Press.

——(1980). "Truth and Power." In *Power/Knowledge: Selected Interviews and Other Writings, 1972–1977*, ed. C. Gordon. New York: Pantheon.

——(1991). "Faire vivre et laisser mourir: la naissance du racisme." *Les Temps Modernes* (February), pp. 37–61.

Gilroy, P. (1987). *"There Ain't no Black in the Union Jack": The Cultural Politics of Race and Nation*. Chicago: University of Chicago Press.

Goldberg, D. (1993). *Racist Culture: Philosophy and the Politics of Meaning*. Oxford: Blackwell.

Guillaumin, C. (1995). "The Idea of Race and Its Elevation to Autonomus, Scientific and Legal Status (1980)." In *Racism, Sexism, Power and Ideology*. London: Routledge.

Hirschfeld, L. (1996). *Race in the Making: Cognition, Culture and the Child's Construction of Human Kinds*. Cambridge, MA: MIT Press.

Holt, T. (1992). *The Problem of Freedom*. Baltimore, MD: Johns Hopkins University Press.

Joffrin, L. (1995). "Ce que les Lepenistes ont dans la tête." *Nouvel Observateur*, December 7–13, No. 1622.

Jordon, W. (1968). *White over Black*. Chapel Hill: University of North Carolina Press.

Kinder, D. and Sanders, L. (1996). *Divided by Color: Racial Politics and Democratic Ideals*. Chicago: University of Chicago Press.

Mehta, U. (1990). "The Liberal Politics of Exclusion." *Politics and Society*, 18 (4), pp. 427–545.

Morgan, E. (1975). *American Slavery, American Freedom*. New York: Norton.

Mosse, G. (1978). *Toward the Final Solution*. Madison: University of Wisconsin Press.

——(1985). *Nationalism and Sexuality*. Madison: University of Wisconsin Press.

Newman, K. (1987). "'And Wash the Ethiop White': Feminity and the Monstrous in *Othello*." In J. E. Howard and M. F. O'Connor (eds.), *Shakespeare Reproduced: The Text in the History and Ideology*. New York: Methuen.

Omi, M. and Winant, H. (1986). *Racial Formations in the United States: From the 1960s to the 1980s*. New York: Routledge.

Rabinow, P. (1986). "Representations are Social Facts: Modernity and Postmodernity in Anthropology." In J. Clifford and G. Marcus (eds.), *Writing Culture: The Poetics and Politics of Ethnography*. Berkeley: University of California Press, pp. 234–61.

Rex, J. (1980). "The Theory of Race Relations – A Weberian Approach." In *Sociological Theories: Race and Colonialism*. Paris: UNESCO.

Roediger, D. (1991). *Wages of Whiteness*. London: Verso.

Robertson, P. (1991). *The New World Order*. Dallas, TX: Word Publishing.

Sperber, D. and Wilson, D. (1986). *Relevance: Communication and Cognition*. Cambridge, MA: Harvard University Press.

Stoler, A. L. (1989). "Rethinking Colonial Categories." *Comparative Studies in Society and History*, 13 (1), pp. 134–61.

——(1991). "Carnal Knowledge and Imperial Power." In M. di Leonardo (ed.), *Gender at the Crossroads of Knowledge: Feminist Anthropology in a Postmodern Era*. Berkeley: University of California Press, pp. 51–101.

——(1995). *Race and the Education of Desire: Foucault's "History of Sexuality" and the Colonial Order of Things*. Durham, NC: Duke University Press.

——(1996). "A Sentimental Education: Native Servants and Cultivation of European Children in the Netherlands Indies." In L. Sears (ed.), *Fantasizing the Feminine in Indonesia*. Durham, NC: Duke University Press, pp. 71–91.

——(1992). "Sexual Affronts and Racial Frontiers: European Identities and the Cultural Politics of Exclusion in Colonial Southeast Asia." *Comparative Studies in Society and History*, 34 (3), pp. 514–51.

Stocking, G. (1986). *Race, Culture, and Evolution: Essays in the History of Anthropology*. Chicago: University of Chicago Press.

Taguieff, P.-A. (1990a). *La Force du prejugé*. Paris: La Découverte.

——(1990b). "The Doctrine of the National Front in France (1972–1989): A 'Revolutionary' Program? Ideological Aspects of a Nationalist-

Populist Mobilzation." *New Political Science*, 16–17 (Fall/Winter), pp. 29–70.

——(1994). *Les Fins de l'antiracisme*. Paris: Editions Michalon.

West, C. (1982). *Prophesy/Deliverance: An Afro-American Revolutionary Christianity*. Philadelphia, PA: Westminster Press.

Williams, R. (1977). *Marxism and Literature*. London: Oxford.

22

Cultural Pluralism and the Subversion of the "Taken-for-Granted" World

Maria R. Markus

Cultural pluralism is an indisputable fact for most countries today. How particular societies and their members deal with it, however, is a different question altogether and the answer to it cannot be reduced to any singular model. Differentiation occurs not only on the level of policies but, due to the different sources of such pluralism, it also produces different responses on the level of everyday life and practices of consociates within various societies.

While the pluralism in question may, of course, refer to differently generated cultures, I am limiting myself here to cultural differentiations rooted in national/ethnic or racial identifications only. There are at least two distinct facets of culture that are relevant here. On the one hand, there is a layer of culture which is rooted directly in the form of life into which one is born, that is, in everyday practices and relations within which initial personal identities are formed and links with others – the "community" between the participants – are established in an unreflective way. On the other hand, there is a more abstract level of culture which consists of intellectually and reflectively generated systems of beliefs, norms, and organized traditions ("moral maps"), providing evaluative standards for different modes of life or their components. In establishing such a map, the past is not only mobilized and interpreted but also reconstructed, or even invented. This work constructs a "collective memory" as a vital link between the given collective's past and future, thus uniting its whole as an "imagined community." While this certainly does not always lead to the constitution of a separate state, or to the constitution of a state at all, it may be instrumental in this process for which it provides both justification and secular legitimation and from which, in turn, it receives institutional support, facilitating the reproduction of the privileged forms of life.[1] Although there has rarely existed a nation-state composed of a single ethnic/national group,[2] various exclusionary mechanisms at work in the definition of citizenship rights and assimilationist policies often ensured the relatively homogeneous composition of nation-states. This, together with the liberal democratic principle of equality of all citizens and the subdivision of social life into public and private spheres (with the basic differences being relegated to the latter), have previously made it relatively easy to misrecognize this aspect of the nation-state and assume its basic neutrality in respect of ethnic, cultural, religious etc., differences of its citizens.

This is certainly no longer the case. Cultural identities encompassed within the borders of each state have become, as a rule, not only more pluralized and diversified but also more vocal and thus more visible.

The sources of this increased pluralization are many. They include, on the one hand, those cases when certain groups of population, although differing quite radically from the nation-forming majority in terms of concrete life practices (and often possessing separate languages or dialects), did not – at the time of the formation of the nation-state on their territory – thematize their own separate identities, that is, did not develop the second mentioned layer of culture. The factors contributing to the "self-awakening" of these groups of population are again numerous and cannot be reduced simply to a reaction against the exclusionary policies exercised by the dominant nation *vis-à-vis* these groups, although this has often been the case. Paradoxically, the results of assimilationist policies could equally contribute to such a process: they often lead to the emergence of a stratum of "indigenous intellectuals" as the most likely elaborators and propagators of the second mentioned type of culture and thus the heralds of the autonomous presence for the hitherto marginalized groups.[3]

A special case is constituted here by those indigenous groups whose territory has been colonized through mostly violent conquest often leading to decimation of the indigenous population, destruction of their native ways of life and cultures, and in each case to their marginalization. Furthermore, such a "self-awakening" is often either a product or a by-product of the processes of so-called globalization or internationalization. This may emerge as a conscious strategy at "reembedding" social institutions and relations which are increasingly separated from the local context of social interactions (Giddens, 1990), but may also be a more-or-less spontaneous response to these processes, or even – as some authors suggest (see e.g., Robertson, 1995) – constitute their organic part ("glocalization").

The other major source of such pluralization is, and always has been, the forced or voluntary migration which has recently become enormously intensified, due partly to the already mentioned processes of globalization but also, and no less importantly, to wars, famine, political oppression or emerging nationalisms.[4] In addition, it is not only people who migrate. Boundaries and frontiers of nations and "nation-states" are also occasionally redrawn, they also "migrate," locating different ethnic groups within new cultural and political contexts. There is a number of historical and recent examples of such processes, some implications of which are elaborated by Rainer Bauböck (Bauböck, in this volume).[5]

These two factors, increased migration and activation of indigenous groups, bring to light an unresolved tension or even conflict between the theoretical universality of democratic citizenship and the particularity of cultural identities.

The ethical/cultural neutrality of the state as a political community which is supposed to ensure the equality of all its citizens, together with the recognition and guarantee of their individual rights as private persons to pursue different goals, to choose different lifestyles, to belong to different religious denominations, voluntary organizations and so on, constitutes one of the basic principles of liberal democracy. It has, however, never been fully realized and its interpretations have also varied considerably through history. Moreover, it has become increasingly clear in the current debates (see e.g., Taylor, 1994; Kis, 1996), such a neutrality, at least in its radical form, cannot be effectively achieved and perhaps ought not to be striven for, not without further qualification.

Why isn't Neutrality Possible?[6]

In the most general terms, we can point firstly to the fact that the state, among other functions, has to fulfill the task of integration and coordination of society. This task requires a number of decisions in which the "ethnic origin" of the state and its grounding in a particular culture come to the fore, even if some concessions for minority groups are introduced. For example, decisions concerning the choice of "official language" (or even languages) of the particular country, which is necessary and which, as a rule, is quite logically defined as the language of the majority. Similarly, core decisions concerning school curricula, decisions about public holidays or recently challenged definitions of family. As the two last examples demonstrate, even such characteristics, constitutive of the very idea of a democratic state as its separation from religion, cannot be consistently realized. It is worth adding that the very division between the private and public and their concrete contents are not only culturally differentiated but are subject matters of an ongoing political contestation by different groups and movements.

Furthermore, another task of the democratic state: to ensure equality of all citizens as citizens, that is, to equalize their chances of active participation in citizenship, often demands some forms of affirmative action, or even special legislation, in respect of particular groups of citizens, that is, measures which go beyond or, in any case, differ from the general welfare policy of the state.[7]

So, while in a multicultural society the state cannot identify itself with any single ethnic group, but has to represent the political community as a whole, it also has to take into account the differences in actual conditions of equal citizenship between different groups and orient its policies towards their equalization.

All these considerations lead to the conclusion that the impartiality of the state and its desirability ought to be evaluated selectively, examining how far it contributes to the reduction of the privileged position of the majority where it is detrimental to the cultural heritage and cultural identities of other groups. For the political system ought to increase the opportunities of all citizens to participate equally in shaping the institutional/legal framework of political community as a whole without endangering individual freedom of choice.

What, However, Does This Mean Practically?

On the one hand, Stuart Hall is right to insist that the "rights of citizenship and the incommensurabilities of cultural difference both ought to be respected and that one cannot be made a condition of the other" (Hall, 1993, p. 360). On the other hand, however, the question arises whether in practice the exercise of citizenship can be radically divorced from the cultural "situatedness" (location) or identification of citizens.

It is generally recognized that the exercise of democratic citizenship requires a certain degree of social cohesiveness, a certain level of social integration or solidarity, which in the nation-state has been traditionally produced by the construction of "national culture." If such a cohesion is indeed necessary, the question is what can possibly substitute for this type of bond in a multicultural society, encompassing not only relatively closely related but often also quite incommensurable cultures?

Different models have emerged practically or have been formulated theoretically in response to this question (Schöpflin, 1995; Tamir, 1993; Kymlicka, 1995; Kis, 1996). Apart from straightforward assimilation, which is now to a large degree compromised and cannot be openly pursued as a requirement for citizenship in democratic societies, there are different models of integration, federation or consociationalism.

One of the more challenging current theoretical propositions in this respect is J. Habermas' notion of "constitutional patriotism" as a shared political culture of a society, separate (although not independent) from the plurality of "lifeworld cultures" present in any given society (Habermas, 1992a, 1992b, 1994). Habermas elaborates this conception with a critical reference to the variegated conceptions of communitarianism, above all in response to Charles Taylor's interpretation of liberalism. While accepting some points of Taylor's critique of the individualistic version of citizenship, he considers the communitarian model too restrictive from the point of view of the individual, as it directly links political culture with the substantive aspirations of particular communities and demands the individual's identification with these goals. This – he argues – could lead to the "normalizing" intervention of community, restricting the autonomy of individuals in choosing and leading their own lives.[8] In Taylor's understanding, the solidarity and cohesion of a political community is grounded in the concept of "common good," which in a multicultural society can emerge only out of the selective "fusion of horizons" of different cultures, or out of the equally selective[9] expansion of the horizon of the "host culture" (Taylor, 1994, p. 62). In contrast, Habermas defines the cohesion and integration of political community as grounded primarily in the democratic interpretation of the constitutional principles: as a cohesion which depends upon a common political culture and not upon an ethical-cultural form of life as a whole (Habermas, 1992b, p. 17). Such a common political culture of deliberative democracy is based, for Habermas, on a "formal universalism." This is understood as a normatively grounded procedure relating to the principles and mechanisms of democratic deliberation in which citizens as individuals embedded in various cultural forms of life and/or as members of groups representing these differentiated forms confront each other to negotiate issues of common interest. Acceptance of the framework of the political culture so understood is considered to be a normative requirement for all citizens and it is safeguarded by the legal structure of the country. Such a "political acculturation," however, does not involve, according to this conception, the necessity of giving up the person's particular cultural identification. "The same universalistic content must in each case be appropriated from out of one's own cultural form of life," says Habermas in his interview with J. M. Ferry (Habermas, 1992a, p. 241). Citizens are not abstract beings moving only in the political sphere. They are socialized and live within different cultural traditions and continuously redefine their identities through identification with various collectivities or communities and/or with different cultural traditions. Personal identities are thus deeply interwoven with collective identities of various sorts, including different ethnic groups, which themselves are also in a process of gradual transformation. The various cultural identifications of citizens constitute the net of "nodal points" against which the ethical-political discourses and, with that, an interpretation and reinterpretation of their self-understanding is negotiated and renegotiated. "If the population of citizens as a whole shifts, this horizon will change as well" (Habermas, 1994, p. 126).

This, of course, also means that on the one hand, political culture is not static, but continually evolving and that, on the other hand, it is not only dependent upon the constituency of the political community, but itself also contributes to the process of cultural identity formation. In this latter respect at least, despite their polemic, Habermas' proposal to some degree resembles Taylor's conception. More importantly, however, it also foregrounds the gravity of problems connected to the attempts to separate, analytically and – even more so – practically, the lifeworld-embedded plural cultures and the common political culture understood as a mutual respect for basic rights. Yet, this distinction, as noted earlier, is important and consequential. Namely, if the political order is indistinguishable from the particular, cultural preferences concerning the good life, then the nation's right to restrict the intake of migrants (not only numerically, but first of all culturally), or to demand their more-or-less full acculturation, in a defense of its own integrity, would be at least understandable, however problematic it otherwise might be. If, however, the integrity of the nation can be defined primarily in terms of a shared political culture, then all that could be required from the immigrants would be "the assimilation to the way in which the autonomy of the citizens is institutionalized in the recipient society and the way the 'public use of reason' is practiced here" (Habermas, 1994, p. 138).

While such an uncoupling of the two forms of culture does make the prospect of maintaining a certain minimum of social integration without culturally restrictive or assimilationist policies of immigration more promising, this division is beset by its own difficulties and provokes new challenges.

These challenges are connected above all with the already-mentioned interplay between the political culture and the pluralized cultural forms, of life, with the practical difficulty of separating the two. Participation in political culture requires certain resources which not all individuals and, for that matter, not all communities are in possession of. Furthermore, it also requires a degree of "fusion of horizons," which would enable the participants to enter common deliberations. How such a fusion can be achieved and what it may encompass are in a sense the central issues here. From this point of view two questions are particularly relevant: "who participates" (who is in a position to participate) and "what do those who participate bring into the common discourse." Both are closely related to the cultures within which the initial identities of citizens are formed and which provide them with a point of reference. Ethical-political decisions are an unavoidable part of common debates, and therefore present a two-sided challenge to participants.

On the one hand, it is a challenge to those who attempt to make their entry into the already-established political culture of the country and, on the other hand, to the majority culture's self-understanding, which is reflected in this culture. This challenge – as Habermas points out – "becomes all the greater, the more profound are the religious, racial, or ethnic differences or the historical-cultural disjunctions to be bridged" (Habermas, 1994, p. 118). The extension of the challenge involved here, however, is not limited to variations in cultural commensurability or incommensurability. Even more crucial from this point of view is the ability and willingness of the bearers of different cultural identities to maintain the intersubjective aspect of the process of identity formation, keeping it both internally reflexive and open to external questioning. According to Habermas, it requires from different groups and individuals a recognition that culture and identity are open, historical formations and that traditions, although partly given, are (and ought to be) selectively appropriated and interpreted, and perhaps even given up, if they contradict "one's own life-project." It is necessary that "one be able to relativize one's own way of life *vis-à-vis* other forms of life, that one be prepared to grant strangers and others the same rights as oneself and that one does not insist on universalizing one's own identity" (Habermas, 1992a, pp. 243, 240). This refers to majority culture as well as to endogenous minorities and migrant minorities in the diaspora. All three, although mostly for different reasons, are susceptible to essentialization of their own cultural identity and to closure which endangers the potential inclusiveness of political culture as one of the main integrative mechanisms in modern society. All three are prone, in one way or another, to conceptualize their identity as fixed and sharply delineated.

In the above-mentioned paper, Stuart Hall makes this point very emphatically: "Since cultural diversity" – writes Hall – "is, increasingly, the fate of the modern world, and ethnic absolutism a regressive feature of late-modernity, the greatest danger now arises from forms of national and cultural identity – new or old – which attempt to secure their identity by adopting closed versions of culture or community and by refusal to engage (. . .) with the difficult problems that arise from trying to live with difference" (Hall, 1993, p. 361).

While Hall refers here to such a tendency among the "dominant white cultures," the observation is valid for the broad spectrum of cultural differentiation, although – as I have already noted – the reasons for it are quite variegated. In the case of endogenous minorities, like the Aboriginal people in Australia (whose form of life has been destroyed at its very basis) the tendency to secure identity through closure is often associated with mobilization. Aboriginal communities attempt to reorganize without being absorbed by the social structures that tend to allocate them nothing but a marginalized position. Obviously, for all minorities the common and principal reason for such a stance is a self-defensive reaction against the insensitivity or, sometimes, arrogance of the majority culture and its hegemonic position in the societies in question.

But there is yet another aspect of the minority's experience which may produce such a closure. At the beginning of this paper, I distinguished two facets of culture which underlie the cultural identities of ethnic communities: the "pre-reflexive" (or nonreflexive) layer and the more-or-less systematized elaboration of the group's traditions, beliefs and norms. The first is grounded directly in everyday life practices, ways of doing things and arranging relationships, representing the "taken-for-granted" social reality with its ontological security and the handed-down recipes, which are shared in the community as "thinking-as-usual" patterns of life (Schütz, 1964). For most societies modernity has weakened this aspect of culture considerably by practically breaking up the slow flow of unnoticeable changes into more spectacular "turning points" and ruptures, but it has survived in more traditional societies, in rural areas, in sleepy "middletowns." The second layer, in so far as it is explicitly elaborated, is in no sense deduced from the first, but it must somehow refer to it and legitimize it as an ethically appropriate way of life. There must be some sort of congruency between the two.

What is happening with migration or, for that matter, with the colonization of indigenous cultures, is that this "pre-reflexive" layer is shattered and fragmented, losing its "taken-for-granted" character.

Migrants or indigenous people can, of course, try to sustain certain traditions, customs, forms of interpersonal intercourse, but these are no longer built into life conduct as a whole, which can be integrally connected to society at large. For this latter connection – as effectuated through work, through children's education, through dealings with market and bureaucracy, through "external" social relationships – demands, as a rule, other patterns of behavior. These are naturally the processes that set off the phenomena of so-called "hybridization" of cultures, to the more promising aspects of which I shall return in a moment.

But hybridization does not necessarily mean "blurring the boundaries." It could easily mean a further "closing off," in response to the new conditions which make the group particularly vulnerable. A type of closure may already occur at this level. Bhikhu Parekh aptly and beautifully describes such experience, which may result in cutting off the external world and creating an illusory, "suspended" existence within the simplified and thus fragmentarily "fundamentalized" code of rules. "There is a past, which is then ruptured and to which the present bears little relation. That leads to self-fragmentation, a painful state which one copes with by hoping that the present is only an aberration and that the future will either reconcile the past and present, or represent a happy return to the romanticized past (. . .) What you recreate in a new environment is never the same as what you left behind. What was a richly-nuanced body of beliefs and practices gets abbreviated into a set of abstract formulae, and a tradition degenerates into an ideology" (Bhabha and Parekh, 1989, p. 25). It is exactly such an "abbreviation" that often goes on in the second layer of culture, which strives to survive without being able to reconnect or to establish its congruency with the broader spectrum of everyday life practices.

Under such conditions, the ability and willingness of the group to engage in self-reflection and self-rejuvenation is easily abandoned to the mentality of the "besieged," when the group: "lacks the courage to critically reinterpret its fundamental principles, lest it opens the door to 'excessive' reinterpretation. It then turns its fundamentals into fundamentalism, it declares them inviolate and reduces them to a neat and easily-enforceable package of beliefs and rituals" (Bhabha and Parekh 1989, p. 25).

If any generalizations are here in place, it could be said that the less resourceful, the more besieged and the less confident in its future the group is, the more likely it is to mummify its past and to present it as the essence of its existence which cannot be questioned or altered.

Of course, such a "defensive" attitude is not the only strategy employed by cultural minorities, individuals or groups, attempting to find their place in society at large. Some groups actively attempt to appropriate the new reality, to engage in common discourses and to make their own mark. In other words, not just to expose themselves passively to the spontaneous ongoing process of hybridization, facilitated grossly by such common structures as market, bureaucracy and the other institutionalized forms of intercourse, but to participate consciously in this process, turning it into mutual "self-presentation," from which may result an expansion or even "fusion of the horizons" enabling rational democratic debate within the political sphere.

Many migrant communities gradually develop a mode of life equally distant from both assimilation and tradition. There are some almost anecdotal cases of such blends, like the new hybrid language spoken by a small community in Victoria, Australia, which is a mixture of Italian and English, that cannot be understood either by new Italian migrants or by native English speakers (Baggio, 1989). There is also a number of other, perhaps more meaningful examples, especially in the sphere of art: popular music, film and so on. In any case, a conscious search for a better alternative than either assimilation or closure is undoubtedly emerging in a number of forms within collective ways of life and is even more widespread on the individual level. For while migration – even where voluntary – always involves pain and loss, it is also considered by many to offer a chance of a new beginning, of a more autonomous construction of the self, rendering possible a choice among cultural patterns to be selectively incorporated into their development. Or as Breytenbach puts it, despite all the feelings of loss, uncertainty and alienation, "exile is a chance, a break, an escape, a challenge (. . .) To be in exile is to be free to imagine or to dream a past and the future of this past" (Breytenbach, 1991, pp. 71, 73). But he also acknowledges that it is a "difficult craft," hoping it is also a useful one (not just for oneself), because there is no more "homecoming." "The exile never returns" – he or she always remains a stranger. While there is an increasing number of strangers around us, and to be one has its own merits and functions, it is, at the same time, not an easy way to be. Bauman is right, noting: "it is not for everyone that the dismantling of constraints is experienced as liberation, for some it is experienced as loss: and what has been lost reveals itself, in retrospect, as identity" (Bauman, 1995, p. 149). Not everyone has the strength and the necessary resources to blend one's own identity anew.

It goes without saying that there are usually more options open to migrants than to marginalized indigenous populations in search for their place in society, mainly because in the migrants' case the voluntary aspect of their resettlement undoubtedly plays some role. In contrast, the lack of choice in the case of indigenous populations influences the shaping of relationships, for example, between the white population of Australia and the Australian Aboriginal people. The hurt is deep and the distrust widespread. Moreover, both played a mobilizing role in raising the self-consciousness and self-organization of Aboriginal people, and cultural closure has functioned here as one of the liberating instruments of these processes. The two histories of Australia were "written" in parallel, they did not even confront, but rather ignored each other. The programme of reconciliation is an attempt to confront the "other" history and to learn from it, but the learning is slow and new hurts are often created. Not guilt, but responsibility for the enduring consequences of the conquest have to be accepted by all nonindigenous citizens of the country today. This must not be dependent upon whether or not the Aboriginal tribes massacred each other before colonization, whether they were practicing infanticide or what their social malaises are today. But this also means that these topics ought not to be taboos either.

If it is true that the vitality of a culture depends upon its reflexivity, then this is perhaps Australia's chance on "both sides of the fence" and therefore a common one too. For, if up to this point I was speaking about the closures created by cultural minorities, this in no way means that it is only migrants or indigenous groups that create closures in cultural encounters. Majority cultures are no less prone to be exclusionary and no less unwilling to respond to the unsettling presence of the "stranger" with a critical examination of their own assumptions, beliefs and customs. In this case, it is not so much existential insecurity that prompts the closures, although this type of motive is often palpably present in racially motivated movements and ideologies which attempt to hide their sentiments behind "rationalized" arguments. But the presence of strangers is unsettling and "subversive" to these cultures above all because it often makes visible such composite elements that previously went unnoticed or unreflected upon. It is like a magnifying glass or a huge mirror in which suddenly the hidden wrinkles appear, making us aware that we are perhaps uglier (or at least look older) than we thought (or hoped). Linda Nicholson in her critical evaluation of Taylor's essay speaks about her understanding of the "recognition debate," according to which the "more challenging voices are not those saying 'recognize my worth' but rather those saying, 'let my presence make you aware of the limitations of what you have so far judged to be true and of worth'" (Nicholson, 1996, p. 10). Those are exactly the voices that majority cultures often attempt to silence through their own closures created through two basic mechanisms: inclusion as assimilation and exclusion as marginalization.

Hybridization does not necessarily result in increased homogenization or cultural uniformity. It does not create a uniform mixed culture which would then become the dominant or commonly accepted one. Rather it is about the further pluralization of critical perspectives and ways of life. Hybrids constitute a "species" in their own right. Speaking of "displaced peoples" and "dislocated cultures," Stuart Hall makes the point that, while "struggling in one sense at the margins of modernity, they are at the leading edge of what is destined to become the truly representative 'late-modern' experience. They are the product of the cultures of hybridity." He considers this notion essentially different from the "old internationalist grand narrative, from the superficiality of old style pluralism where no boundaries are crossed, and from the trendy nomadic voyaging of the postmodern or simplistic version of global homogenization – one damn thing after another or the difference that does not make the difference. These 'hybrids' retain strong links to and identification with the traditions and places of their 'origin' (. . .) They bear the traces of particular cultures, traditions, languages, systems of beliefs, texts and histories which have shaped them. But they are also obliged to come to terms with and to make something new of the cultures they inhabit, without simply assimilating to them. They are not and will never be unified culturally in the old sense, because they are inevitably the products of several interlocking histories and cultures, belonging at the same time to several 'homes' – and thus to no one particular home" (Hall, 1993, p. 362).

Jan Nedeveen Pieterse quotes Rowe and Schelling who, with respect to cultural forms, define hybridization as "the ways in which forms become separated from existing practices and recombine with new forms in new practices" (Pieterse, 1995, p. 48). Hybridization is thus not about the "blurring of the cultural boundaries," rather it is about the crossing of these boundaries in potentially endless combinations of the new and the old. Hybrids are crossing the boundaries between minority cultures as well as between the culture of majority and that of minorities. In this way, they "destabilize the established hierarchy of centre and margin, hegemony and minority" and perhaps, even more importantly, they contribute to the "deterritorialization" and "disessentialization" of the very concept of culture (ibid., pp. 56, 62, 63). This latter is a crucial point for understanding the process of hybridization as providing the most appropriate basis for a democratic polity, for which the ability "to relativize one's own lifeworld with regard to other lifeworlds" is a central one. In order to recapture this potential of the process of hybridization as the reinforcement of democratic political culture and to bring these two forms of social integration into accord, it is necessary to go beyond the spontaneity of the hybridization process and to transform it into a conscious self-reflective achievement, to move on from the hybridity of culture into a culture of hybridity. The most important result of such a transformation would be exactly such a disessentialization of the concept of identity in all its varieties, a recognition that identity is never accomplished, ready, or one-dimensional. Such a recognition would allow us to move beyond the spontaneous level of hybridization to a more reflexive one, based on autonomous choices rather than merely on the shelter of being defined by one's "myth of origin."

Needless to say that the issue of access to the requisite material and symbolic resources is a crucial one for this process. This includes, among others, an access to the public sphere or spaces in which this process can be played out both internally, within a particular group, and externally, between different groups. No group should feel vulnerable to the extent they can see no future other than that leading back to the past. The most important condition of doing away with a mentality of the "besieged" is to end the siege. This of course places a special responsibility on "majority cultures." Only this can bring us closer to establishing a common political culture of citizenship, which would be able to utilize the whole gamut of the cultural resources of its constitutive hybrids.

Notes

1   This is not to say that these two facets of culture exhaust the variety of meanings attached to this concept, some of which are radically divorced from, or even stand in opposition to, any ethnic/national reference.

2   According to Walker Connor (1994), a survey of the 132 entities considered to be states in 1971 demonstrated that only slightly over 9 percent of these can be justifiably described as nation-states; close to a further 19 percent, despite containing some important minority with about 90 percent of more or less homogeneous population, can approximate the nation-state concept. In the largest group of almost 30 percent, however, the "core nation" accounts for less than half of the population.

3   The case of the Kurds in Turkey demonstrates well the multiplicity of the possible motifs for separatist movements (see e.g., Kupchan, 1995).

4   The scope of this increase is well illustrated by Australia, where by now close to 40 percent of population consists of first- and second-generation migrants with 270 countries of origin. This is especially significant when we take into account that in the 1940s 90 percent of the Australian population was born in Australia and most migrants were from an English-speaking background. Australia, for a number of reasons, is obviously quite exceptional in this respect, but the phenomenon itself is widespread. Habermas, for example, mentions that 26 percent of Frankfurt's population today consists of "foreigners" (Habermas, 1994, p. 144).

5   The history of the industrial belt of Lorraine in France which changed its "nationality" and official language five times in a century is only one past example (Hobsbawm, 1996). The redistribution of the territories after the wars and after the dissolution of colonialism is another. But such phenomena are no less common today (see former Yugoslavia, former Soviet Union and so on).

6   Even in the little volume edited by Amy Gutmann (1994), there is a whole gamut of answers to this question, proposing different formulations or reformulations of this principle, see e.g., Taylor versus Walzer versus Habermas versus Appiah. Given the complexity of the issue, I can only present it here in a very simplified form.

7   In the Australian context, the recognition of Aboriginal people's native title, which is in a sense an attempt to "integrate indigenous societies into the legal and economic structure of the country", is not "adding" any preferential treatment for Aborigines but rather poses the issue of redressing their hitherto effected discrimination (see e.g., Patton, 1995).

8   K. A. Appiah, for example, in his contribution to the Taylor volume (Appiah, 1994), makes some strong observations concerning the oppressive charac-

ter of the ready-made scripts of behavior for member of different communities, who often identify themselves with several such communities, and with none in the totality of their identity.

9   Taylor makes it clear that we should not create for ourselves illusions about the universal applicability of liberalism. He emphasizes that "liberalism is not a possible meeting ground for all cultures, but is the political expression of one range of cultures, and quite incompatible with other ranges (. . .) It shouldn't claim complete cultural neutrality. Liberalism is also a fighting creed" (Taylor, 1994, p. 62).

References

Appiah, K. Anthony (1994). "Identity, Authenticity, Survival," in Ch. Taylor et al., *Multiculturalism: Examining the Politics of Recognition*. Princeton: Princeton University Press.

Baggio, R. A. (1989). *The Shoe in my Cheese. Immigrant Family Experience*. R. A. Baggio, Australia.

Bauman, Zygmunt (1995). "Searching for Centre that Holds," in M. Featherstone et al. (eds.), *Global Modernities*. London: Sage.

Bhabha, Homi and Parekh, Bhikhu (1989). "Identities on Parade. A Conversation," *Marxism Today*, June, pp. 23–9.

Breytenbach, Breyten (1991). "The Long March from Hearth to Heart," *Social Research*, 58 (1), pp. 69–83.

Connor, Walker (1994). "A Nation is a Nation, is a State, is an Ethnic Group, is a . . . ," in J. Hutchinson and A. D. Smith (eds.), *Nationalism, Oxford Reader*. Oxford: Oxford University Press.

Giddens, Anthony (1990). *The Consequences of Modernity*. Cambridge: Polity Press.

Gutmann, A. (ed.) (1994). *Multiculturalism: Examining the Politics of Recognition*. Princeton: Princeton University Press.

Habermas, Jürgen (1992a). *Autonomy and Solidarity*, ed. Peter Dews, revised edition. London: Verso.

——(1992b). "Citizenship and National Identity," *Praxis International*, 12 (1), pp. 1–19.

——(1994). "Struggles for Recognition in the Democratic Constitutional State," in Ch. Taylor et al., *Multiculturalism: Examining the Politics of Recognition*. Princeton: Princeton University Press.

Hall, Stuart (1993). "Culture, Community, Nation," *Cultural Studies*, 7 (3), pp. 349–63.

Hobsbawm, E. (1996). "Identity Politics and the Left," *New Left Review*, 217.

Jordens, Ann-Mari (1995). *Redefining Australians*. Sydney: Hale and Iremonger.

Kis, János (1996). "Beyond Nation State," *Social Research*, 63 (1), pp. 191–245.

Kupchan, Charles, A. (1995). "Introduction: Nationalism Resurgent," in Ch. A. Kupchan (ed.), *Nationalism and Nationalities in the New Europe*. Ithaca: Cornell University Press.

Kymlicka, Will (1995). *Multicultural Citizenship*. Oxford: Oxford University Press.

Nicholson, Linda (1996). "To Be or not to Be: Charles Taylor and the Politics of Recognition," *Constellations*, 3 (1), pp. 1–16.

Patton, Paul (1995). "Mabo and Australian Society," *The Australian Journal of Anthropology*, 6 (1–2), pp. 83–94.

Pieterse, Jan Nedeveen (1995). "Globalization as Hybridization," in M. Featherstone et al. (eds.), *Global Modernities*. London: Sage.

Robertson, Roland (1995). "Glocalization: Time–Space and Homogeneity–Heterogeneity," in M. Featherstone et al. (eds.), *Global Modernities*. London: Sage.

Schöpflin, George (1995). "Nationalism and Ethnicity in Europe, East and West," in Ch. A. Kupchan (ed.), *Nationalism and Nationalities in the New Europe*. Ithaca: Cornell University Press.

Schütz, A. (1964). *Collected Papers*, Volume 2, ed. M. Natanson. The Hague: Martinus Nijhoff.

Tamir, Y. (1993). *Liberal Nationalism*. Princeton: Princeton University Press.

Taylor, Charles (1994). "The Politics of Recognition," in A. Gutman (ed.), *Multiculturalism: Examining the Politics of Recognition*. Princeton: Princeton University Press.

Part II

Reflections, in Thematic Order (1999–2000)

Histories and Values

23

Reflections on "The Nation Form: History and Ideology" (E. Balibar)

Etienne Balibar

Generally speaking, I am not very fond of commenting on my own writings (although I understand that it could be useful for students to have this kind of information), but in this case there is an additional difficulty. The chapter David and Philomena have included here is not from a collection of my own essays, or, conversely, from an edited volume with multiple authors, but forms part of a book published jointly with Immanuel Wallerstein (first French edition 1988, English version 1991). We are both very attached to this collaboration, and I think that my contributions particularly, although written as autonomous pieces, are meaningful only in light of that background, intended as part of an intellectual and political dialogue.

I had met Wallerstein personally in 1981 in India. We discovered that although we did not have exactly the same training, neither did we belong to the same traditions in theoretical thought (apart from a broad reference to "Marxism," or rather, "critical Marxism," which we had in common, but which for neither of us was exclusive), we did share a number of mutual interests. When our paths crossed again in Paris in 1983, we asked each other: "What are your current interests?" I replied: "Racism and nationalism" – this was the period when the French National Front was increasing its influence considerably in French politics, acquiring something like a "mass base" – and Immanuel said: "Ethnicity." At this time it was becoming clearer – at least to those few who could look that far ahead – that, with the end of the Cold War in view, some of the "antisystemic" functions of the popular movements of exploited people would be taken over by "ethnic revival" and "national identity" movements, albeit with "ambivalent" results. This was also a time when the dubious results of "affirmative action" in the US were becoming more obvious, prompting conservatives, with increasing influence in some states, to call for its rejection.

As a result of these converging interests combining theory and politics, Immanuel and I established a joint seminar at the Maison des Sciences de l'Homme in Paris which lasted for three years (1985–7). At the end of this period we decided to publish a book together, to which we gave the form of a "fictive" dialogue because we wanted to mirror the real dialogue that had taken place in the sessions (and which has continued since then, although it has taken other forms). Consequently, Immanuel made a choice from among various essays of his, which he had been using as material for his oral contributions to the seminar, and I gave a written form to my own contributions and amended them. Then we tried to arrange all this material according to a meaningful plan, in which the "critical" confrontation between, for instance, the analysis of the "capitalist world-economy" with its political and ideological functions and the "structuralist" problematic of the ideological formations would bear some fruit and raise some issues.*

It is not our task to evaluate the reception of our ideas (which may be direct or indirect: a book is not a commodity). All I can say is that we were not dissatisfied that the book has found its original location in an environment where the questions of "race," "nation," and "social groups" (time and again referred to as "class structures" in Marxist or post-Marxist terms) have become very active. We certainly do not want to take sole credit for having anticipated the great importance the question of "national identity" has assumed today, for we were not the only ones to have done so. What rather shocks us is the extent of the intellectual effort that still needs to be made in order to take a grip on the history we are living and which we have the ambition of "creating."

---

* Etienne and Immanuel kindly allowed us to include and edit the remainder of this essay from the new Introduction to the second French edition (1997), as it touches reflectively upon political and conceptual concerns underlying their work. We are grateful to Nora Abusitta, who generously agreed, on very short notice, to translate the introduction from the French. [*Editors' note*]

In our second French edition (1997) we examine four methodological orientations that we have partially outlined elsewhere. We find no reason to renounce these orientations, regardless of the transformations and rectifications to which experience might lead us. Second, we have not tried to deny differences in cultures, histories, or affiliation by submerging them in a homogeneous globality. On the contrary, we have tried to understand their origin and study their political function, both ambivalent (in the uses to which they could be subject) and changing (as new tendencies and new power relations have emerged), prompting us to give more attention to the questions of migration and borders. Borders are multiplying and their defenses fortified, thus assuming a collective affect and losing their essential social function. These are, and probably will be, the challenges to a practical political democracy.

Third, conscious of the extent of the differences between the situations in the "North" and the "South" (and also of the fact that it is very difficult to attempt to trace a geographic border between these poles), we wanted to emphasize that the problems of identity or ethnicity are not the privilege of either side. Indeed, these contrasting situations belong to the same world. In addition, the North has no more entered a "post-national" era than the South is confined to a "pre-national" one. Together (and through each other) they are confronted by the incompleteness and the crisis in the "nation-form," and thus the crisis of the state that nurtured its construction. This diagnosis would have been reinforced had we closely examined the religious coloration of "ambiguous identities," an approach unfortunately absent from the essays that make up the book, *Race, Nation, Class*.

Finally, by going as far as confronting our own partly conflicting analysis we wanted to prove that we believe neither in purely "economic" explanations (which we undoubtedly abused in the past), nor in purely "ideological" explanations (which are now strengthened by the rise of individualism). Meanwhile, the miracle method does not lie in an eclectic juxtaposition of opposing points of view as in capital accumulation laws on a global scale, the hermeneutic of collective symbols or cultural national and religious expressions. Complete understanding will only be achieved through the study of the singularity of historical situations, starting from the specificity of their contradictions and the constraints imposed on them by the global structures to which they belong.

These hypothetical considerations would undoubtedly not stand on their own. However, books cannot be rewritten. They last for a certain time, long enough for other books and their authors to exhaust their suggestions and to take over. This is what we hope to achieve.

24

Reflections on "Racial Histories and Their Regimes of Truth" (A. Stoler)

Ann Laura Stoler

"Racial Histories and Their Regimes of Truth" was called "gutsy" by one of its readers but I see it rather as an uncomfortable and impatient response to the several fields in which I worked – and to my uneasy participation in them. At its writing in 1995, my research was focused in the Dutch colonial archives and on the construction of racial categories, my teaching on colonialism and the comparative history of racisms, my conceptual frame that of critical history, cultural theory, coupled with a long-standing commitment to questioning the politics of knowledge production then reinspired by Foucault.

At several registers, the essay represents a convergence and confrontation of these domains. Some of its questions were directly prompted by what I saw as a disturbing discrepancy between how race figured in the nineteenth-century colonial archives in which I worked and in postcolonial scholarship that I drew on, wrote, and my students read. Other questions about racial epistemologies emerged from seemingly disparate sites. On the one hand, from a decade of tracking the widening popular appeal of France's National Front, its racist platform and far-right politics; on the other, from an interest in racial regimes that drew me increasingly to read on the margins of cognition, the history of science and philosophy. I was convinced that hard questions about how we think we know what we know about race – what "grids of intelligibility" underwrite racist arguments, what regimes of truth underwrite racist claims – were too quickly set aside by historians and those drawing on their work. The essay was an attempt to understand this epistemological smugness about race – and why it was so.

Politically the mid-1990s was a confident moment for postcolonial studies. Its students were rethinking colonial representations of difference and gaining new insights about the contemporary cultural dynamics of race. For those working on racial formations in colonial contexts it was exhilarating as well. Our (social constructionist) research agendas felt subversive of racisms by their very nature. We set out to show that racial categories were invented not given, were protean and porous not fixed. Nothing about racism was written in biology or stone: if it was invented, it could be undone. There was political satisfaction in such accounts, redemption in the stories we told ourselves. Those working on postcolonial conditions seemed convinced that they knew about colonial "effects" – some seemed to think it was unnecessary to study the colonial at all. Ironically, postcolonial studies was often so sure of the colonial order of things that it seemed to be developing into a less, rather than more, historically grounded project.

This essay was my reaction to that trend, an effort to unsettle the neat historical narratives that portrayed the "new racisms" as rooted in culture as opposed to the "purer" and earlier racisms rooted in biology. In retrospect, I perhaps painted the canvas too broadly. But the notion that there was a flattening out of colonial histories is one to which I still firmly hold. At the very least, these observations added grist to my sense that we knew less than we thought about colonial and contemporary racisms, their discursive properties, their mobile forms and recursive genealogies.

The essay was, then, partly a response to a conceptual and pedagogic dilemma. I had been teaching on the histories of racisms for some time and each year as I honed a larger corpus of materials, I found it more difficult to teach. A graduate seminar that began as an exploration of racisms' varied properties turned into a different course, on both the development of racisms and on the nature of its historiography. The essay's argument that a search for racisms' origins both shapes and is shaped by how we think about race in the present and what we imagine is effective antiracist scholarship today grew out of that context. The essay, like the seminar, was an effort to make sense of, rather than dismiss, the profusion of conflicting claims about racism's origins and its sundry properties made by scholars whose work I respected and engaged.

I was not suggesting that good politics alone makes good history but rather that those of us engaged in writing racisms' histories need to think more about the stories we tell and why we want to tell them. Such a critique might be guided by what Foucault called "the art of reflective insolence," insolence toward our well-crafted narratives about racisms' "culprits," and insolence toward the ways of knowing race on which those accounts depend. Instead an "effective history" might attend to the "minute deviations" in what is agreed to be "true," to the "reversals" in the criteria of what counts as a truth about race and what does not.

Unlike much academic writing where feedback is postponed by long publication delays, responses to "Racial Histories" came quickly: from challenging interdisciplinary audiences but also from a seasoned and sharp set of readers who were asked to comment on the piece before it went to press. My comments here profit from their pointed and perceptive questions.

Some readers have charged that my focus on discourse detracts from a focus on racial domination. I would disagree. Taking discursive formations seriously is a way of broaching head on the fact that how we speak and what is unspeakable in written and oral form shape the categories of exclusion and inclusion in which racisms are built. Attention to discursive formations opens to an engagement with the cultural and political rationalities that make certain statements renderable as speech, with what discursive practices produce the conditions of possibility for why some statements are taken as adequate truth-claims and not others. Attention to the formation of discursive practices is just that, about practices that are culturally sedimented as enduring truths but that are cultural constructions of specific historical moments. Others have battled long and hard over whether attention to "discourse" diverts analysis from the political economy in which people live. I will not rehearse their arguments but simply register my agreement with Ian Hacking that the labeling of human kinds is not a passive system of classifying what already is, but a way of producing those subjects who will be so assigned. The battle lines between those committed to an analysis of discourse and those who see themselves more concerned with the analysis of grounded political and economic relations of power become less relevant and less sharply drawn when the making and imposition of political rationalities is treated as part of the gritty "political" in political economy.

The status of "discourse" was a site of disagreement between myself and some readers but a more important argument of the essay was not contested in part because it was ignored. I argued that scholars have failed to appreciate the power of essentialist thinking. Racial essences are not made up of a fixed and finite set of features but rather an interchanging and malleable range of them. To say that racism "is easy to think" is not necessarily because essences are easy to fix or easy to see. The crucial point is that racial systems combine elements of fixity and fluidity in ways that make them both resilient and impervious to empirical, experiential counterclaims. I would still hold that how people imagine race to be secured should be the subject of sustained analysis.

But why does it matter if we incorrectly caricature racisms in the past as long as we deal squarely with subverting those racisms that persist today? Because the ways in which we rewrite that past matters very much. Originary histories are not just about origins, *tout court*. Histories of racial origins, like those of nationalist origin, make claims on property entitlements, citizenship rights, access to medicine, education, and welfare. Anyone arguing that originary histories are beside the contemporary political point is not reading the daily press. To suggest that liberalism is the "source" of racism is not only an argument about the past but about what subversive strategies are possible within liberalism today. Histories arguing that racism reached its florescence as a scientific doctrine are not innocuous; misconstruals of the sorts of knowledge on which racisms rely condone spurious solutions in the present and the future. "Good guy" scholars disproving the correspondence between race and intelligence, between physical type and cognitive endowment, advocated by *The Bell Curve* "bad guys," are still operating on the latter's epistemic turf. They are still subscribing to a notion that if really good science can relegate race to its proper status as nonbiological and nonscientific, then it will become a nonvalid social category.

But imagining that "race" can be retired from the popular or academic lexicon was as utopian in the past as it is today. To say that race is constructed is not to say that it is not real. The notion that by a scholarly sleight of hand we can erase racism from analytic discourse would be to miss the tactical political practices in which racial discourse is mobilized – as a technology of the state at one moment and against the state at another. Race is not a salient biological category but it is a potent political one.

A final point I would still want to make: the need to continue rethinking the very units of analysis on which histories of racisms have relied. It is not only that social scientists have accepted one particular national reconstruction of "race" – that is prevalent in the US. In assuming that the language of class has dictated the language of race, scholars have rarely questioned how often an imperial language of race may have provided a template for a metropolitan language of class and worked the other way around. A research strategy that unbrackets colonial and metropolitan social policies – and therefore their historiographies – can pose a new set of questions that situate the racial formations of the US and South African histories not as cases *in extremis*, but rather as formations forged in partially shared racial logics of much wider breadth. Race has emerged not only as a key to the making of a nineteenth-century US working-class labor movement and to the making of a European bourgeoisie. Racialized rhetorics underwrite the exclusionary politics of the far right across Europe and the US on the cusp of the twenty-first century. Racial discourse shapes the rules and not just the particular strategies of the political game. The point is not to find yet another site of origin but to understand the broad and contradictory investments that have tied and continue to tie distinctions of human quality to distinctions of human kind.

25

Reflections on "Modernity, Race, and Morality" (D. T. Goldberg)

David Theo Goldberg

I grew up with racism – in the kitchen, in the negotiations of what the family would eat each day, the sandwiches I would take to school, the polishing of my father's shoes, the making of the household's beds, the maid's requests for time off and the garden "boy's" plate of left-over lunch in the back yard. And yet awakening each morning to greet Robben Island across seven tautly stretched miles of sparkling Atlantic served as a daily reminder of the heavy costs of lives seemingly lost, a society long turned against itself, a state more concerned with its own "lore and order" than the social wellbeing of all its inhabitants, if not those it would claim as its citizens. Through those years of struggle against apartheid on picket lines and around parliament, through the mists of tear gas and protest slogans and closing down the college campus, through the heated discussions of neo-Marxist historiography, "autonomy in the last analysis" and Althusserian "overdetermination," somehow the history of racist (re)production, ever present, evaporated. A history to which I would return, as if to face the repressed.

A year in Europe on the way to graduate school in New York only posed the question more pressingly in my mind. Passing across New York's Central Park and through Times Square almost daily on the way to teach or be taught, Reagan's brand of "new racism" reeled all about too. There it lay, not quite invisibly, in the conditions producing both homelessness and homeboys, dramatically differentiated employment rates across race and hypersegregation, in the rap on rap and its early absence from MTV. These were the years too of a heady postmodernism, of storming the bastions of philosophical essentialisms, of an emergent skepticism and transdisciplinarity. Race as an irreducible object of analysis seemed here just to be taking hold, breaking from its super-structural reduction to class concerns, offering a recognizable language of expression and set of self-determining conditions. Orientalism and societies structured in dominance; racial formations emerging and empires striking and writing in return. Race mattered, as Cornel West would later write. But it was a language of race that seemed in this headiness to matter more than racism. A dissertation beckoned to be written.

And so I did, on the "philosophical foundations of racism." Now that turned heads. "Philosophical foundations?" Racism never had any, philosophical liberals insisted, shocked at the irreverence of the sugges-tion, the insurgent colleagues who had been struggling to break down the color bar of the American Philosophical Association for at least a decade invisible from behind the veil of philosophers' supposedly color-blind gaze. Almost a decade later still, approaching the mid-1990s – years turned wiser by a wealth of material on histories of racial dis-course, antiracism, whiteness studies, critical race theory, race and nation, multiculturalism, and the altogether timely rereading of Fanon – I could radically rewrite my dissertation as *Racist Culture*, safe in the knowledge of fellow travelers and co-conspiring colleagues. Race, at last, seemed to be taken seriously. But no comprehensive philosophical archeology of these new arguments seemed to exist. There were frag-ments to be sure, genealogies of racism, studies of white representations on blacks in the western canon and corpus, on race and the difference in writing it makes, on intersectionalities and anti-essentialisms. To give those arguments philosophical resonance, to examine its quieter, less obvious philosophical architecture, that's what I set out to do. And to throw down a gauntlet to the discipline of philosophy, to challenge its parochialism, its self-possessed denial, its blindness to its own traumatic implication in the history of racist reproductions, its sweeping of its own stench behind that veil of ignorance. In a sense, to break with and from those disciplinary chains.

I set out, then, to connect the philosophical dots in the map of racial theorizing and histories of racisms. To link the lines of racial mean-ings and racist rationalities, racial worlds and ways of knowing with repeated modes of racist exclusion, the history of theoretical ethics and colonial studies, shifting configurations of racial space and political theory. If race was a morally irrelevant category and this was the basis of racism's immorality, as liberal philosophical commitments would have it, how could it be that social, economic and political exclusions predicated on racial belonging seemed so readily rationalized, as much contemporarily as historically? If race really is a category that makes no rational sense, why does it enter so readily into the everyday calculations of rational people and politicians? My concern was to show how deeply race entered the rationalities of modernity that a political morality could not simply wish it away by ignoring it. And to insist that although racist exclusions could be rational in their calculability, they were nevertheless politically pernicious and inherently immoral.

My conceptual framework rested upon rejecting reified notions of race and racism as static and unchanging, fixing on biological assumptions about group identity in the first instance and irrational claims about inherent inferiority in the second. I sought to show the fluidity of racial meanings, their embeddedness in readily accepted philosophical conceptions like rationalism and empiricism, utilitarianism and Kantian deontology. And to demonstrate the conceptual and political connectedness of these shifting racial meanings to transforming projects of racial exclusion. In conclusion it struck me that the only framework that could sustain such a dramatically historicizing (rather than historicist) and anti-essentializing critique was a form of self-reflexive and self-critical philosophical pragmatism in the mold of Richard Rorty.

Critical responses were principally twofold, and related. The first was a predictable defensiveness on the part of philosophical liberals. This assumed an insistence on the irrationality of race, on our human commonality, and the rejection of differentiating definitions among groups as necessarily racist. These critics seemed to miss the point, that even universalist conceptions of humanity are open to exclusions by assuming, more or less invisibly, local – western or civilized or European or American – criteria as the basis for the grounds of universalist principles. It suggested also the second, more virulent set of attacks. Somehow I was vilified, most notably by Kenan Malik, as among the most objectionable anti-universalist postmodernists. Odd, this identification, as I was not remotely interested in (pro)claiming the postmodern banner. Concerned with a critique of essentialisms I indeed was, with showing the ways in which local commitments reified into the exclusions of universalist ones, in which knowledge was ordered in altogether partial ways and deathly political projects organized in their name. The rejection of universalist defenses of moral values or standards does not entail a nihilism, as I was accused, a rejection of all moral standards or values, a defense of racial division or apartheid, a defenselessness against terrorism or balkanization. Quite the contrary, it entailed that such critical commitments assume a more subtle and nuanced expression, that a critical political morality and moral politics in the end can only rest upon philosophically pragmatic grounds.

In retrospect, finally, it has struck me that I had much too little to say in *Racist Culture* about two centrally important considerations. The first concerns a more explicit analysis of the entanglements of race and gender, of the intertwined histories of patriarchy and white supremacy. The second has to do with the role of the state in these entanglements, a question much too readily clouded by the culturalist turn in social theorizing the past two decades. It is to these connected issues that my work has now turned.

26

Reflections on "Of Mimicry and Man: The Ambivalence of Colonial Discourse" (H. Bhabha)

Kim Benita Furumoto

Homi Bhabha's provocative body of work poses questions concerning how to undertake the delicate balance between a theorizing of race that maintains the visibility of the structure of power relations with the centering of the agency of the subject. How does one negotiate the "edges" of agency, where the (post)colonial, racial subject's resistances encounter the constraints not only of material relations of power but also of the power of the discursive conditions that can construct (or even erase) subjectivity? Bhabha's critique of binary oppositions raises related questions regarding how to challenge the notion of conceptual fixity and to recognize the openings within racist discourse while also interrogating the power of the binary as a system of representation. How does this representational system's power to "fix" render binaries "real" in the same way that race is "real"?

In discussing colonial governmentality, Bhabha has remarked that racist stereotypical discourse "coexists" with certain forms of social and economic organization in the "same apparatus of colonial power." Probing this coexistence sheds light on how certain interactions of political-economic and discursive elements are conducive to mimicry. Focusing on the theoretical gap between material conditions and discursive representation will help to elucidate the integral role of colonialism and other racially inscribed systems in capitalist development. Additionally, the related question of how contemporary globalization and postcolonial conditions are plagued by the vestiges of colonialism suggests the possibility of a "temporal interstice," of a conception of the role of history and time that lies between historical continuity and day-to-day experience.

Reflecting upon Bhabha's work reminds us that examining the interconnectedness of race and racism with other aspects of the social fabric involves navigating various theoretical and representational inbetweens. Homi Bhabha thus adapts a Derridean, post-structuralist approach to addressing race theorizing. He focuses particularly on the literary text in his examination of race and (post)colonialism. This shift to the literary metaphor and his turn to a discursive reading of these questions provide a theoretical strategy that complicates the reductionism of many of the prior accounts attempting to explain race. Deterministic or functionalist theoretical frameworks and social science methodologies often erase race as an object of analysis in its own right, in part because they are tied to modes of expression that silence language capable of excavating race and the malignant character of racism.

Bhabha's theorizing, which is marked by the surfacing of language that is conducive to an expansive reading of racism and the colonial relation, contributes to a conception of racism not merely as an ideology but as a discursive regime that is both constitutive and reflective of social and economic orderings. Racism features material effects as well as more intangible dimensions, including elements involving the psychoanalytical terrain, which Bhabha addresses provocatively through his "against the grain" readings of Fanon. Thus I have found Bhabha's work especially suited to addressing those aspects of race and racism that defy concrete formulations and elude empirical verification.

Homi Bhabha's theorizing has been useful as a consequence in my current work on federal Indian law in the United States, the body of law that US institutions have established to "govern" affairs concerning American Indians. The essay, "Of Mimicry and Man," accordingly prompted two theoretical frames: to read this body of law, during its formative period in the nineteenth century, as a colonial discourse, while methodologically reading legal text as literary text. In analyzing US law in general, it is particularly useful to deemphasize intentionality in unraveling the meanings of legal texts. Legislative intentionality is at best unknowable, at worst open to manipulation and contestation. What has made legal restriction of racism so nebulous, then, is precisely that in many instances laws require a certain "racist intentionality" to be legally cognizable, a requirement almost impossible to satisfy absent the protagonist's admission of intent.

Bhabha's concept of mimicry opens up lines of analysis otherwise closed to more traditional legal investigation. It is especially useful in interpreting the assimilation policies that pervaded federal Indian law, particularly during the late 1800s. In his discussions of mimicry, Bhabha has invoked Lacan's comparison to the "technique of camouflage practiced in human warfare" – the mimic does not blend completely into the background, but rather becomes mottled against it. Colonial mimicry, Bhabha has explained, is the desire for a reformed "other," one that is "almost the same, but not quite." Ironically, to maintain its effectiveness as a strategy of colonial power, mimicry must reproduce its difference. Thus mimicry appears in the discourse that accompanied policies such as mandatory boarding schools, Christian missionary work, and allotment acts which fragmented tribal land bases into private parcels.

The desire to produce a modified other who is "almost the same but not quite," "almost the same but not white" is suggested in the US Supreme Court's 1876 description of the Pueblo Indians as an industrious, Christianized, and "virtuous" people who are "Indians only in feature, complexion, and a few of their habits." Likewise, discussing the Indian nations that governmental officials often referred to as the "Five Civilized Tribes," Commissioner of Indian Affairs Nathaniel Taylor reported in 1868 that they had "emerged from a state of pagan barbarism and are to-day clothed in the garments of civilization," adding that "their average intelligence is very nearly up to the standard of like communities of whites." Such paraphrases of "almost the same but not quite/not white" suggest a reading of assimilation policies as a process of "partial reform." In assimilation discourse – in which, ironically, the assertion of cultural (white) supremacy depends on the difference it purportedly seeks to eradicate – the ambivalence in the strategy of mimicry lies in the distance between colonial officials' emphatic pronouncements of their endeavors to "civilize" Indians, and their anxious reiterations of the difference, the otherness, of Indians.

The recognition of ambivalence informs a complexified reading of law as a "conflictual economy" rather than a monolithic voice. Contradictory strains appear in the legal legitimations of the expropriation of Indian land, which figured as a crucial element of colonial discourse. In

Johnson v. M'Intosh (1823), the first decision of the "Marshall trilogy" (a set of US Supreme Court cases decided by Chief Justice John Marshall that laid the doctrinal foundation of federal Indian law), the Court ruled that Europeans had validly acquired absolute title to Indian land in virtue of "discovering" it, based on "the original fundamental principle, that discovery gave exclusive title to those who made it." Marshall articulates the reasoning underlying this discovery doctrine with extensive racist dicta that include invocations of "the superior genius of Europe" and descriptions of Indians as "fierce savages whose occupation was war."

Yet alongside these assertions, Marshall admits that the principle of the "conversion" of discovery into conquest (and title) is an "extravagant pretension," but posits that if a country is acquired under it, "it becomes the law of the land." He equivocates similarly with regard to the stripping of tribal land title. Though this principle "may be opposed to natural right, and to the usages of civilized nation," he reasons that if it is "indispensable" to the system that is the basis for the country's settlement "it may, perhaps, be supported by reason, and certainly cannot be rejected by Courts of justice."

Marshall's self-doubting deliberations on the rule of discovery conflict with his stereotypical characterizations of Indians, and contradict the decision's authoritative declaration of the discovery doctrine as the law of the land. Like the split that Bhabha identifies in John Locke's double use of the word "slave," ambivalence lingers in the divide between the Chief Justice's articulations of the discovery doctrine as a legitimate basis of title and as a justification for an illegitimate rights violation and theft. Evidencing the indeterminacy of law, ambivalence haunts the legal validation of the appropriation of Indian land, and of the site for the continued development of the colonial relation. Ambivalence relates to other critical shifts Bhabha brings to race theorizing, including his critique of binaries and of the notion of "fixity" in the construction of otherness, and his rejection of an essentialized notion of identity. His work also accounts for the agency of the (post)colonial subject.

While Bhabha recognizes the effectiveness of mimicry as a strategy of colonial power and knowledge, he also emphasizes the possibility that in the slippages mimicry produces, in the openings that attend ambivalence, there also lies the potential for the subversion of colonial discourse (via strategies that are perhaps reminiscent of Gramsci's notion of the war of position). Mimicry, he has suggested, can be both a mode of appropriation and resistance. His highlighting of subaltern agency reminds us that the relations in colonialism and postcolonialism are dynamic, and that the "marginalized" subject is not merely a receptor of domination. Bhabha's work provides insight even as I contend with my reservations about the discursive slide, as I attempt in my present work to develop a theoretical framework that accounts for the discursive and the political-economic. The story of Indian law and colonialism in the US is missing pieces without a discussion of, for example, the implications of the discovery doctrine's recognition of land as a commodity. Viewing the "interstitial in-between" and the problematization of binaries in Bhabha's work in terms of theoretical positionings has led me to consider the possibility of occupying an interstitial space between the approaches of political economy and cultural studies.

Recalling that ambivalence cautions against illusory closures, I am reminded that my thinking about Bhabha's theorizing (and race theorizing in general) is always a work in progress. For Homi Bhabha's writings also remind us that the process of theoretical (and political) work entails living with tension and incompletion.

Knowledge and Representation

27

Reflections on "A Genealogy of Modern Racism" (C. West)

Howard McGary

In his first book, *Prophesy Deliverance! An Afro-American Revolutionary Christianity* (1982), Cornel West correctly claims that until very recently black people were not considered to be human beings in the modern West. The idea of black inferiority is an important premise of numerous justifications of the denial of opportunities and rights to black people. Black inferiority and white supremacy are a part of the fabric of many institutions in the modern West. Scholars from a number of disciplines and political perspectives have tried to explain the source of the idea of white supremacy. West offers his own contributions to this inquiry in chapter 2 of *Prophesy Deliverance!* entitled "A Genealogy of Modern Racism." He does not focus on the traditional explanations of the source of white supremacy: the economic explanation that it is simply a result of the objective demands of a given mode of production; the historical account which claims that it was in the political interest of the slaveholding class to advance this idea; and the psychological explanation that contends that such an idea served the emotional needs of the dominant white group. He acknowledges the value of these explanations, but he chooses to explore a different and neglected one.

According to West, the language that is used to describe what we take to be beautiful, important, reasonable, and valuable is infused with the idea of white supremacy. This is a valuable insight because a great deal of the discussion of white supremacy has focused on the intentions and motives of those who are thought to be behaving and thinking in white racist ways. If West is correct, the source of white supremacy is not necessarily located in malevolent intentions and motives.

West labels his strategy for explaining an important source of white supremacy a "genealogy." Reminiscent of the work of Friedrich Nietzsche and Michel Foucault, West is concerned with when the idea of white supremacy first emerged in our discourse in the modern West. Towards this end, he proposes a series of questions. These questions raise issues about how our understanding of what constitutes knowledge and value is shaped by the concepts, metaphors, and norms that are embodied in modern discourse. For West, we cannot fully understand modern racism without understanding the structure of this discourse. This idea is taken up and examined in remarkable detail in David Theo Goldberg's book, *Racist Culture* (1993).

West goes on to point out that power not only results from the intentional actions of well-positioned agents, but also from the structure of language and its usage. He argues that modern discourse is a fusion of Descartes's idea of the disembodied, skeptical, value-free subject, Greek metaphors that emphasize the dangers of excess and defect, and classical ideals of beauty and form. This discourse, along with the need to justify practices of domination, helped to unleash modern racism.

Modern discourse was an important part of the development of classificatory schemes that were used in the development of the category of race in natural history. And once race as a concept was classified as a natural kind, this set the stage for using it to mark moral and social distinctions between persons. However, in the latter part of the nineteenth century, race understood as a natural kind was roundly criticized by W. E. B. Du Bois in his classic paper, "The Conservation of Races" (1897). A number of scholars, following West's lead, have revealed the drawbacks of this way of understanding the concept of race. Some have even argued that it is a meaningless concept (Appiah, 1992). Others have claimed that it only is meaningful if it is seen as a social construction (Mills, 1998; Outlaw, 1996). West's paper is an important ancestor of these metaphysical discussions concerning the concept of race.

Another important insight in this chapter is West's point about how the structure of discourse in the modern West limits theoretical challenges to the idea of white supremacy. In other words, modern western discourse precludes certain alternatives to established ideals of beauty, conceptions of knowledge, and standards of value. For example, in regards to traditional western standards of beauty, straight hair and white skin are the measures of beauty in women. The Black Consciousness Movement of the 1960s and 1970s was a direct challenge to this ideal of beauty. The wearing of Afro hair styles and the celebration rather than the bleaching of black skin served to point out that there were other worthy ideals of beauty. Of course, similar challenges and correctives were offered to other theories that were said to describe universal reality.

Finally, West challenges the idea that modern racism is an aberration; something that is believed and practiced by irrational and uneducated people. In order to support his contention, he reveals how major figures in the American, French, German, and Scottish Enlightenments expressed white supremacy. Of course, as a socialist and religious humanist, West does not claim that we should commit the *ad hominem* fallacy of rejecting a position because of the race of the person who articulates it. Nor does he believe that the theories of Immanuel Kant, David Hume, Thomas Jefferson, and other Enlightenment figures are useless. West's point here is that white supremacy has been a central part of modern discourse in the West and that any efforts to eliminate it must be aware of this fact. Recent theorists like Charles Mills (1997) and Howard McGary (1999) have built upon this insight. As we can see, "A Genealogy of Modern Racism," published two decades ago, has clearly influenced current research on racism in important ways.

References

Appiah, Kwame Anthony (1992). *In My Father's House: Africa in the Philosophy of Culture*. New York: Oxford University Press.

Du Bois, W. E. B. (1897). "The Conservation of Races." American Negro Academy Occasional Papers, no. 2 (1897), reprinted in Howard Brotz (ed.), *African-American Social and Political Thought 1850–1920* (New Brunswick, NJ: Transaction Publishers, 1992), pp. 483–92.

Goldberg, David Theo (ed.) (1990). *Anatomy of Racism*. Minneapolis, MN: University of Minnesota Press.

——(1993). *Racist Culture: Philosophy and the Politics of Meaning*. Oxford: Blackwell.

——(1997). *Racial Subjects: Writing on Race in America*. New York: Routledge.

McGary, Howard (1999). *Race and Social Justice*. Oxford: Blackwell.

Mills, Charles W. (1997). *The Racial Contract*. Ithaca, NY: Cornell University Press.

——(1998). *Blackness Visible: Essays on Philosophy and Race*. Ithaca, NY: Cornell University Press.

Outlaw, Lucius (1996). *On Race and Philosophy*. New York: Routledge.

West, Cornel (1982). *Prophesy Deliverance! An Afro-American Revolutionary Christianity*. Philadelphia: Westminster Press.

28

Reflections on "Imaginative Geography and Its Representations: Orientalizing the Oriental" (E. Said)

Saree Makdisi

The publication of Edward Said's *Orientalism* dramatically altered the nature of literary and sociocultural scholarship. On the one hand, it drew together and amplified the arguments of what had been until then a variety of disparate critiques of the hegemonic culture of "the West" (including the works of feminist, Marxist, post-structuralist, and anti-colonial writers). On the other hand, it also made people all the more aware of the highly contingent nature of such categories as "the West" and "the East" (or the "Orient") in the first place – and of the ways in which such categories must be actively produced by scholars, artists, poets, and historians, rather than being taken for granted as natural or inevitable essences.

In demonstrating the extent to which scholars and writers, far from being merely innocent and detached "observers," are actually complicit in the production of worldly reality, the book pays particular attention to the relationship between Orientalist art, writing and scholarship and the invention of the Orient, not only in the classical Orientalism of the eighteenth and nineteenth centuries, but in the practice of late twentieth-century Orientalism as well. According to Said, Orientalism today is no longer primarily the provenance of learned scholars (such as Sir William Jones, the greatest British Orientalist of the eighteenth century), but rather of media hacks and think-tank "experts," or writers such as Bernard Lewis, Daniel Pipes, and Fouad Ajami, whose work is as intimately bound up with the foreign policy apparatus of a neocolonial United States as Jones's work was with the East India Company administration in colonial Bengal.

Lord Byron famously referred to the Orient as "the greenest isle of my imagination," a claim which allows us to address one of the main points made in Orientalism. Said argues that the Orient is the product of what he calls the "imaginative geography" of Orientalists like Byron and Jones. Drawing on the work of Michel Foucault, Gaston Bachelard, and other theorists, Said distinguishes this "imaginative geography" from what he calls "positive geography." He argues that we can think of imaginative geography as something that goes beyond, or gets added to, positive knowledge, by which he means concrete knowledge of actual realities. Thus, for example, imaginative geography provides "the lenses through which the Orient is experienced," and it allows Said to distinguish "the East itself" from "the East made known," or in other words the "actual Orient," to which positive knowledge pertains, from the fictive Orient generated through imaginative geography.

This is obviously a problematic distinction – for how are we to separate the "positive" from the "imaginative"? By what criteria are we to decide where the one ends and the other begins? How do we distinguish the "representations" from the "realities"? Said chooses not to resolve this dilemma: "We need not decide here," he writes, "whether this kind of imaginative knowledge infuses history and geography or whether in some way it overrides them. Let us just say for the time being that it is there as something more than what appears to be merely positive knowledge." This is one of the most difficult moments in Said's argument, but it is also one of the most important, since much of the force of Orientalism emerges from this point. And it is no surprise that much of the criticism directed at Said's book is focused on just this crucial issue.

Some critics have picked up where Said left off, elaborating his arguments, amplifying and adding detail to strokes he sometimes (and often of necessity) painted with a very broad brush. Said, for example, often makes both the Orient and Orientalism itself too monolithic – as though there could be no way for a westerner to view the East other than through the one set of lenses provided by Orientalism; as though, in other words, there has been only one western way of seeing the East, and as though that way has not changed over the past four thousand years (thus Said sometimes moves too quickly between, and hence collapses together, say, Aeschylus and Jones, Herodotus and Goethe, Napoleon and Henry Kissinger, "Monk" Lewis and Bernard Lewis). Scholars following in the wake of Said have deepened many of his claims, replacing some of his broad strokes with fine detail, and allowing us to see a variety of Orientalisms which have over the decades produced a number of different and sometimes conflicting Orients, as well as allowing us to see some of the ways in which the production of the "Orient" was variously modified, accepted, challenged, or altered by Orientals themselves. Indeed, most of what is today recognized in the American and European academy as the fields of colonial and postcolonial studies initially emerged directly from engagements with and elaborations of Said's influential book, though over the past two decades these fields have taken on identities of their own as scholars have diverged from the set of initial studies provoked by Orientalism.

A great many critics, however, have been all too willing to take for granted Said's highly provisional distinction between "positive" and "imaginative" knowledge, but they ask how we can get access to the concrete realities whose true nature is obscured by the imaginative categories through which we approach them. If the representations of Orientalism mask the realities, how, they ask, can we acquire genuine knowledge of the Other – how can we get at the "real" Orient, if not to dominate it, then at least to learn about its cultures and peoples? Hence, one criticism that is often leveled at Said is that although he does an admirable job of demonstrating the ways in which Orientalism has historically mythicized the Orient – a job he has continued ever since the book in his confrontation with Zionist mythography, and in his systematic criticism of the work of such "authorities" as Daniel Pipes and Thomas Friedman – he does not provide a set of tools with which to analyze and interpret the underlying reality in a more "objective" way.

However, such critics are for the most part either unable or unwilling to grasp the enormous potential offered by the ambiguity that Said leaves open: a potential that Said himself has put to use in much of his other work. For by not cleanly resolving the ambiguous distinction between "positive" and "imaginative" knowledge, or in other words reality and representation, the most radical and powerful edge of Said's argument is preserved. To say that the Orient does not exist as such is not to say that the complex realities gathered under the designation of "the Orient" do not exist, but rather that there is ultimately no way to achieve pure or genuinely "positive" knowledge of them, which is precisely the sort of knowledge that the proponents of Orientalism have claimed to produce all along.

In other words, Said's approach pushes us to see the extent to which all knowledge is situated in – and participates in the making of – the worldly realities that we inhabit. Such a proposition makes it much more difficult, or even impossible, to locate a single "objective" standpoint from which to accumulate knowledge. And hence this approach contests and undermines the authority of coercive systems of knowledge like Orientalism – whose very claims to validity depend on the privileging of one particular standpoint, i.e., the West – by bringing to the surface a previously repressed, silenced, or ignored plurality of voices and perspectives. Reality should be seen no longer as a level field that can be known and dominated from one particular standpoint, but rather as an uneven and heterogeneous terrain, in which the project to locate a common ground takes on momentous political importance. Reality can now be seen not as an inert given that we inherit from the past without being able to question it, but rather as a common or shared possession in which all participate. In making this claim, Said reaffirms the point made earlier by Marx and Vico: human beings make their own history. The reality that we inhabit and the futures that we contemplate should no longer be seen as the provenance of licensed experts and certified authorities to whom all knowledge and decision-making should be left – but rather as something in whose making all can take part.

29

Reflections on "Black Matters" (T. Morrison)

Suzette Spencer

When Toni Morrison first published her essay collection, *Playing in the Dark*, featuring this important essay, "Black Matters," I was an undergraduate student. At that time Morrison's collection of elegantly incisive essays both intrigued and inspired me because it unmasked a symbolic vocabulary of race comprised of racialized and racist codes that saturate Euro-American narratives. But Morrison's "Black Matters," which she then described as an "attractive," "critical geography," is not a routine exercise in deconstruction – unrelenting, sanguinary, self-serving. This essay serves as a remarkable illustration of how to orchestrate an excavatory reading; how to probe and connect elusive currents that lay embedded in our nation's literatures, whether these currents register issues of gender, class, race, ethnicity, or nationality. The probing technique of analysis Morrison employs to demonstrate symbolic manifestations of the Africanist presence in Euro-American writing has been extremely useful to my own reinterpretation of Claude McKay's *Home to Harlem*, a reading which posits that McKay simultaneously reveals and represses a homoerotic presence in his book by relying on carefully coded structural and symbolic subtextual interventions.

Of paramount importance to me today, especially because my literary work is premised on the histories and experiences of African Diaspora Maroon groups, is Morrison's assertion that the Africanist population within the United States "has always had a curiously intimate and unhingingly separate existence within the dominant one." Such an existence relates to what I define in my work as two apposite facets of African maroonage in the western hemisphere: an *involuntary state of maroonage* and a *voluntary state of maroonage*. The involuntary state of maroonage is a condition in which subjects are forcibly located both inside and outside of a larger, circumscribing episteme and are both citizens and outcasts, or, more precisely, resident exiles stranded within the oppressive location without recourse to physical escape and without access to the rights and privileges attendant to that location. The voluntary state of maroonage is characterized by concerted physical defection from the oppressive location as exemplified in the histories of the new world Maroon societies. As Morrison's oxymoronic statement implies, however, neither state of maroonage – neither the voluntary nor the involuntary – is severed entirely from the other. Given shape-shifting threats from hegemonic apparatuses, there is always the possibility that the voluntary state of maroonage might become an involuntary state of maroonage, or vice versa.

Morrison typifies the paradoxical core of the involuntary state of maroonage when she indicates that Nancy, Willa Cather's slave girl character, "is at once a fugitive within the [Colbert] household"; she is "in a fugitive state *even before her escape*" (Morrison's emphasis). The implication here, of course, is that while Nancy is a corporeal captive, she is also to some extent, however limited, a spiritual and interior fugitive. Significantly, this emphasis Morrison places on Nancy's fugitivity "before her escape" foregrounds the consequences of the involuntary state of maroonage for enslaved black women who were in many instances considered sexual property and consequently were required to feign an outward appearance of numb acquiescence to their sexual exploitation – in worse cases feign enjoyment – irrespective of interior contest. My point here is not to suggest that enslaved black women were not outwardly resistant to sexual abuse, or, for that matter, to any form of exploitation during enslavement. Rather, I want to suggest that Morrison's sound critique of Cather's conceptual limitations in character and plot construction is a springboard for thinking more acutely about enslaved women's fugitivity and about the complex mental and physical maneuvers it must have required for enslaved black women such as Nancy to maintain fugitive consciousness inside of racial and psychosexual relations of domination.

How might such re-presentations really take shape meaningfully in narratives? What devices do writers deploy to convey the complexity of characters' existence in such untenable spaces? These are challenges addressed in black women's slave narratives and more recently in twentieth-century neoslave narratives such as Barbara Chase Riboud's controversial *Sally Hemings* which places the black slave woman character Sally Hemings in what is presented by Chase Riboud as a vexed and ambivalent but nonetheless passionate love affair with Thomas Jefferson, Hemings's master/owner and president. Shirley Anne Williams's *Dessa Rose* and Morrison's own *Beloved* also take up these challenges by underscoring the ontological significance of black enslaved women's self-ownership gained either through physical flight or through the institution of an alternative logic of "common sense," which in Sethe's case meant murder. Most significantly, these are the challenges that Cather might have undertaken more successfully but, as Morrison shows, did not, given Cather's profound overreliance on what Morrison describes here as "the wholly available and serviceable lives of Africanist others."

Ultimately, there is no question that the Africanist presence in the United States is a racially driven presence which has been used parasitically as both foil and surrogate. . . . The subject of the dream, Morrison tells us, is the dreamer. Incredulous, if demeaning, fabrications of blackness in literatures such as Cather's are but self-projections inflected through a racially conceived Africanist presence and devised to assist the subject in exploring aspects of the self both feared and loved, aspects of the self the subject wants to both engage and disavow. Yet, an Africanist presence that can inspire both dread and desire; signal encroaching threat yet facile ingenuousness; symbolize moral depravity yet spiritual sentience is a most consequential and immensely overworked presence. It is a burdened and burdening presence that remains a paradox in our nation's social and cultural history precisely because its metaphorical value has been so dynamic and overreferenced. It is a presence that, in its dynamism, embodies both facets of African Diasporic maroonage.

Reference

Spencer, Suzette (1998). "Swerving at a Different Angle and Flying in the Face of Tradition: Excavating the Homoerotic Subtext in *Home to Harlem*." *CLA Journal*, v. XLII, no. 2 (December).

30

Reflections on "Defining Black Feminist Thought" (P. H. Collins)

Patricia Hill Collins

I wrote *Black Feminist Thought* in order to contribute to an ongoing, collective effort to empower African-American women. I knew that when an individual Black woman's consciousness concerning how she understands her everyday life undergoes change, she can become more empowered. Such consciousness may stimulate her to embark on a path of personal freedom, even if it exists initially primarily in her own mind. If she is lucky enough to meet others who are undergoing similar journeys, she and they can change the world around them in important ways. If ideas, knowledge, and consciousness can have such an impact on individual Black women, what effect might they have on Black women as a group? I suspected that African-American women had created a collective knowledge that served a similar purpose in fostering Black women's empowerment. *Black Feminist Thought* aimed to document the existence of such knowledge and sketch out its contours.

My commitment to examining how knowledge can foster African-American women's empowerment remains intact. What has changed since I wrote *Black Feminist Thought* is my understanding of the meaning of empowerment and of the processes needed for it to happen. I now recognize that empowerment for African-American women will never occur in a context characterized by oppression and social injustice. A group can gain power in such situations by dominating others, but this is not the type of empowerment that I found within Black women's thinking. Reading Black women's intellectual work, I have come to see how it is possible to be both centered in one's own experiences and engaged in coalitions with others. In its centering on Black women, Black feminist thought embraces a form of identity politics. But the type of identity politics that I envisioned in *Black Feminist Thought* rejects the turning-inward, closed ranks essentialism that characterizes rigid special interest groups. Instead, centering on Black women in order to push for empowerment recognizes that coalitions with other similar groups are essential. In this sense, Black feminist thought works on behalf of Black women, but does so in conjunction with other similar social justice projects. My deepening understanding of empowerment has stimulated more complex arguments concerning Black feminist thought's purpose, namely, fostering both Black women's empowerment and conditions of social justice. Both of these themes permeate the excerpt "Defining Black Feminist Thought," but neither is as fully developed in this excerpt as they are now. Definitions are useful, but can easily be incorporated into western binary thinking in ways that limit their effectiveness. I have come to reject the binary thinking that frames so many western definitions, including my earlier ones, of Black feminist thought. Rather than drawing a firm line around Black feminist thought that aims to classify entities as either being Black feminist or not, I now aim for more fluidity without sacrificing logical rigor.

Most recently, I have shifted my earlier efforts from that of "defining" Black feminist thought to that of identifying its distinguishing features. Black feminist thought's distinguishing features need not be unique and may share much with other bodies of knowledge. Rather, it is the convergence of these distinguishing features that gives US Black feminist thought its distinctive contours. Via this shift, I aim to provide the common ground that is so sorely needed both among African-American women and between African-American women and all others whose collective knowledge or thought also aims to foster social justice.

Systems and Experiences

31

Reflections on "Race, Articulation, and Societies Structured in Dominance" (S. Hall)

Stuart Hall

It is certainly the case that later contributions of mine – "New Ethnicities," "Cultural Identity and Diaspora," "Gramsci and Race" – have attracted more attention and debate than "Race, Articulation, and Societies Structured in Dominance": perhaps – but only partly – because they are written in a less abstract and theoretical style than "Race, Articulation . . ."'s (sometimes forbidding!) cadences. The former essays in any case are more in line with how the debate about race, racism, and difference has developed in the context of post-colonial theorizing. However, I agree that "Race, Articulation . . ." continues to have some interest, if for no other reason than because it is so manifestly a transitional text, a "text of the break," as the Althussereans would have described it. It stands poised between different conceptual paradigms. It was conscious of introducing "race" into a theoretical field from which it had been signally absent and of making a break with the conventional way in which race and racism had been analyzed. But it was certainly not fully aware of all the theoretical implications of the path it chose to tread.

The essay clearly reveals its roots in the Althusserean re-reading of Marx, above all in the "Contradiction and Overdetermination" essay by Althusser in *For Marx* and *Reading Capital*, both of which had had a significant effect on the Center for Cultural Studies in Birmingham. These theoretical perspectives had already been influential for the Center's work on race, especially *Policing the Crisis* (1978). This positioning has to be understood both positively and negatively. Positively, it embraced the antireductionist reading of Marx, in which the classic formulation, "determination in the last instance by the economic base," was abandoned in favor of a nonreductive structuralist theory of the three instances of determination – economy, politics, ideology-culture – working as an "articulated hierarchy." Each of these instances or practices were constitutive, and had to be given their own specificity or "relative autonomy"; all, working together (articulated), were required to provide the conditions of existence of any conjuncture or event. Negatively, it was counterposed to one of the most sophisticated classical Marxist analyses of race in South Africa (that offered by Harold Wolpe) and (perhaps surprisingly) took a hospitable attitude to some aspects of the "Weberian" reading offered by John Rex (without fully embracing a "Weberian" perspective).

"Articulation" (a nonreductionist way of formulating how an overdetermination of factors could produce a historical conjuncture) was borrowed and elaborated from *Reading Capital*. However, I gave it greater conceptual weight and purchase than I believe the Althussereans had intended. At first it appears in the essay in terms of the articulation of different modes of production and forms of labor (forced and "free"). Here I wanted consciously to draw a distinction between "western" Marxist analyses, which assumed that the mode of capitalist production would eventually absorb all other modes, and a different approach, more suitable in my view to non-European, colonial, and imperial situations, where it was precisely the articulation of different modes (e.g., slavery or forms of indenture, or in South Africa, migrant contract labor, with capitalism) that enabled the social formation to "work." I have elaborated elsewhere on this key difference, as I see it, between the classic Marxist account of the trajectory of capitalism in Europe, arising "from the womb of feudalism," and capitalism's "exceptional" pathway, elsewhere where it depended on violence, conquest, and colonization (e.g., in "When was the 'Post-colonial?'").

In later sections of the essay, "articulation" is given much greater room as a general approach to the whole problem of how *different*, relatively autonomous practices, each with its own "conditions of existence," can nevertheless combine "in articulation" to define (determine?) a particular historical "moment" or conjuncture. As is clear from the essay, I came to interpret Gramsci's analysis of conjunctures or "structure–superstructure relations," in *The Prison Notebooks*, as itself really a theory of articulation in this sense. Generally, I regard theoretical concepts as conceptual tools. What "articulation" as a tool enabled me to do was to think the "unity" of a social formation as an "overdetermination" (in fact, to think all "unities" – like the nation, class, ideology – as either overdetermined or "lacking," but never fully self-present to themselves). Also, to think all unitary phenomena (like "identity") in terms of, and without subsuming, "difference" (whereas the tendency in classical Marxism is to overcome or sublate "difference" by drawing everything into an expressive totality). You will see, here, not only the effects of the structuralist critique of Hegelianism, but also anticipations of post-structuralism – e.g., Derrida and the post-Saussurean emphasis on "the play of *différance*," Foucault on "the discursive," Laclau and Butler on "the constitutive outside" and the openness of every "structure" to contingency.

The attempt to apply these ideas to "race" helps to locate the essay in a second conceptual space: the political moment defined by the emergent social movements, in which class, as the "master category," was obliged to take its place alongside other "primordial" social divisions, like race, ethnicity, gender, and sexuality. These had been treated as subordinate or dependent variables in classic Marxist analysis – subeconomic or superstructural. This was impossible, theoretically, after the rise of the antiracist, gender, and sexual liberation movements of the 1970s. My essay attempted to square up to this profound theoretical decentering by giving race its "relatively autonomous" place in a social formation; but also by addressing its articulation with classes in the economic or mode-of-production sense. In that sense, the essay can be taken as "post-Marxist" in its thrust. Rather than holding that an analysis was correct only if it obeyed the classic Marxist protocols, "Race, Articulation . . ." took the position that only if radically emended in these ways could some Marxist concepts (not Marxism as a closed theoretical universe) be rescued for critical work.

The essay is "transitional" in a deeper sense. Alongside the Althusserean model, at least three other theoretical elements were at play. First, there was the view that, as one moved from an analysis of "the structure" based on the articulation of instances in a social formation, to the analysis of a specific historical conjuncture, so one was required to put "more and more determinations" into the equation. Here, one can find the traces in my own thinking, not only of Gramsci's

Prison Notebooks, but of the move from *Capital* to *The Eighteenth Brumaire* in Marx's own work (which I had written about in "The Political and the Economic in Marx" (1977)), and the general specification of "greater and greater determinations" which is at the center of Marx's most advanced theoretical text, *The 1857 Introduction to the Grundrisse*, on which I had commented in a long exegetical essay, "Marx's Notes on Method" (1973) (partly stimulated by a sort of argument with Althusser).

Second, there was the critique of the formalism and closed character of structuralism's very notion of "structure" as, in the end, reproducing all the problems of an Hegelian expressive totality, which it had been designed to surpass. This marks the point of emergence of post-structuralism's critique of structuralism – a development which, like all the subsequent "posts," stands on the back of a profound and irreversible "break," while subjecting the closed, rigid notion of "deep structure" which the break produced to the more discursive or open semiotic movement. We can mark this more broadly in terms of Barthes's movement from *Mythologies* to *The Pleasure of the Text*; or the relation of Foucault's "discursive" or Derrida's "dissemination" or Lacan's "language" to Saussure and Lévi-Strauss. Althusser's "structuralism" is an attempt to "read" the deep structure of social formations as Saussure promised to read the hidden rules and combinations that generated language. The movement towards "the infinite slippage of meaning," "the floating of the signifier," the "disseminated play" of language, of rearticulation and disarticulation (Bakhtin) provided ways of resisting the tendency to formalist or "Spinozean" closure and of allowing "difference" back into the system. The essay is therefore itself already operating, consciously, "beyond structuralism."

Thirdly, "Race, Articulation . . ." does try to address the question of how race can be included in an analysis of this kind. The discursive approach is only lightly sketched in at the end, but the emphasis on "historical specificity" and on racisms, not "racism," and on the discursive "work" of ideology points to the direction which my work on race and racial discourse in the 1980s was to take.

It is true that the movement from the economy to the social, political, and ideological does give the essay a certain "sociological" flavor. But the use of this term in the essay owes more to its context ("Sociological Theories of Race and Colonialism"). For me, at the time, and more so since, I would locate the shift in terms of "the cultural turn." This phrase is too complex to go into at length here. But, essentially, the point to remember is that this does *not* imply that race is purely ideological or cultural, whatever that might mean. The cultural or discursive "turn" proposes that *all* practices (including the economic) have to be reconceptualized as "working *like* a language." *Not* that everything *is* language, but that no social practice works "outside of meaning" and in *that* sense, every social practice is "within discourse" – i.e., it depends on meaning for its effectivity. (Laclau on why building a wall is "a discursive practice" is, to my mind, definitive on this much-misunderstood question. Cf. my "The Centrality of Culture" essay, 1997.) Race, in that sense, is a discursive system, which has "real" social, economic, and political conditions of existence and "real" material and symbolic effects.

Implicit in this essay were a number of new directions, which parallel later developments in critical race theory, including the concerns with race, nation, and culture. I have no idea how actually influential the essay was for these developments. I am certain that much of the conceptual infrastructure, which I have tried to indicate here, was not immediately available to readers at the time – partly because (as is so often the case with "writing") it was simply carried in the bloodstream of the text. It no doubt also, partly, reflected the fact that many of its wider implications were concealed, at the time, from "the author" himself (!) who, when a text is completed, acquires the status of simply one more "reader."

References

Althusser, Louis (1977). *For Marx*. London: New Left Books.
——(1979). *Reading Capital*. London: New Left Books.
Barthes, Roland (1972). *Mythologies*. London: Paladin.
——(1990). *The Pleasure of the Text*. Oxford: Blackwell.
Gramsci, Antonio (1971). *The Prison Notebooks: Selections*. New York: International Publishers.
Hall, Stuart (1973). "Marx's Notes on Method: A 'Reading' of the '1857 Introduction.'" *Working Papers in Cultural Studies*, 6 (Birmingham: University of Birmingham), pp. 132–71.
——(1977). "The 'Political' and the 'Economic' in Marxist Theory of

Classes." In A. Hunt (ed.), *Class and Class Structure*. London: Lawrence and Wishart.

——, Critcher, Chas, Jefferson, Tony, Clarke, John, and Roberts, Brian (1978). *Policing the Crisis: Mugging, the State, and Law and Order*. London: Holmes and Meier.

——(1986). "Gramsci's Relevance for the Study of Race and Ethnicity." *Journal of Communications Inquiry*, 10 (Summer), pp. 5–27.

——(1996). "When was 'the Post-colonial?' Thinking at the Limit." In Iain Chambers and Lydia Curti (eds.), *The Post-colonial Question: Common Skies, Divided Horizons* (London: Routledge), pp. 242–60.

Marx, Karl (1973a). *The Eighteenth Brumaire of Louis Bonaparte*. In *Surveys from Exile* (London: Pelican), pp. 143–249.

——(1973b). *Grundrisse: Foundations of the Critique of Political Economy. 1857 Introduction*. New York: Viking Press.

——(1977). *Capital: A Critique of Political Economy*. New York: Vintage.

UNESCO (1980). *Sociological Theories: Race and Colonialism*. Paris: UNESCO.

32

Reflections on "Racial Formation" (M. Omi and H. Winant)

Michael Omi and Howard Winant

Still Racy After All These Years

Our concept of racial formation emerged out of a particularly heady and tumultuous period of racial politics. By the close of the 1970s, neoconservative perspectives on race and social policy were ascendant and the fragile gains of the black movement for equality and justice were threatened. A number of dramatic Supreme Court cases, notably *Regents of University of California v. Bakke* (1978), fueled white perceptions of "reverse discrimination," and signaled a concerted backlash to the reforms of the previous period. Forces on the left defensively responded to this political turn. We ourselves were active in the mobilization to challenge the *Bakke* case, though we increasingly found that prevailing left wisdom and practices left much to be desired.

Our thinking about race began as an engagement with the dominant modes of left theorizing on the subject. We were critical of several moves. First, there was the left's tendency to treat race as a mere manifestation of class. Race was seen as epiphenomenal to class, class relations, and the broader evolution of class struggle. Racial awareness was often understood as a form of "false consciousness," a strategy propagated by the ruling class to divide the working class and prevent the emergence of a unified working-class praxis. That was one current on the left. In another left analysis, racism was seen as emanating from the white working class itself. From this standpoint, the crucial task was to confront and purge this virulent set of ideas and practices in order to pave the way for socialist (i.e., class-based) politics.

Our second disagreement with the left centered on the concept of class itself. Class was often treated as an objective location determined by the prevailing mode of production. Class was not regarded as something in constant formation, determined by a complex configuration of ideological and structural factors over historical time. Such a static and fixed notion of class provided little room for understanding how race (and gender) could shape class categories, consciousness, and organization.

Our third criticism of the left centered on the absence of race in theories of the state. From the mid-1970s through the early 1980s, creative scholarship proliferated regarding the capitalist state. The "structuralism/instrumentalism" debate raged, the role of state managers was highlighted, and the overall capitalist character of the modern state was being reexamined. What was striking about this burgeoning literature, from our perspective, was the absence of any discussion on race. There simply was no sustained treatment of how the state was implicated in the broader patterns of racialized relations in society as a whole.

The reduction of race to class, the persistence of static conceptions of class itself, and the glaring absence of a concept of the racial state, all contributed to our disagreement with then-prevailing left politics and strategic orientations. Mobilizations against neoconservative initiatives were doomed to fail, it seemed to us, unless a fundamental rethinking of the class-based paradigm was undertaken. We wanted the US left to recognize that class did not only determine race, but was itself shaped by race. By placing race at the center of our analysis, we initially sought to rethink the articulation between race and class.

Our sources of intellectual and political inspiration were many and varied. The new social movements of the 1960s and 1970s highlighted forms of oppression that were not reducible to class, and led to an explosion of social identities that were not framed in terms of class exploitation. The political vocabulary of class proved to be a limited one as volatile issues of race, gender, and sexuality, among others, came to the fore.

We borrowed liberally from a number of thinkers. The work of Antonio Gramsci was central to our rethinking of Marxism, and provided us with core concepts – such as hegemony – by which to under-

stand the nature of racialized power. Neo-Marxists such as Adam Przeworski and Ernesto Laclau challenged the economic determinism inherent in orthodox Marxism. Przeworski's approach to class formation,
emphasizing the highly contingent political dimensions of class conflict,
was instrumental to development of our notion of racial formation.
Laclau   demonstrated   how   populism   and   nationalism   could
be articulated from a variety of political positions, and did not simply
possess a set class "belonging." Through these scholars, we came to
appreciate post-structuralist ideas about discourse and the importance
of political struggles over meaning. Thus we adopted the concept of
rearticulation, and used it to analyze the ongoing contestation over
racial meanings.

We did not proceed with our study of race entirely in a vacuum. To
be sure, we were inspired by and drew upon the work of a small number
of contemporary critical scholars of race. The work of Bob Blauner and
Troy Duster, both based in Berkeley, proved to be extremely influential
in the development of our thinking. Blauner's conceptual distinction
between "colonized and immigrant minorities" shaped our critique of
ethnicity-based theories of race. While we disagreed with his "internal
colonialism" analysis of racism in the US, Blauner's paradigm forced us
to specify and conceptually clarify our own understanding of race
and racism. Troy Duster's insightful work led us to Herbert Blumer's
symbolic interactionist account of group prejudice (and of racialized
experience in general). A crucial insight we took from symbolic interactionism was its emphasis on individual and group agency; its emphasis on our continuing capacity to reinterpret the meaning of
relationships and identities in social interaction. In addition to these
scholars, we drew upon the pioneering work of W. E. B. DuBois, Oliver
C. Cox, and the Chicago School. We were also informed by the academic
struggles taking place in, around, and about "ethnic studies" programs
– particularly those programs committed to establishing firm and coherent linkages between the academy and communities of color.

The concept of "racial formation" first appeared in a two-part article
entitled "By the Rivers of Babylon: Race in the United States," which was
published in *Socialist Review* in 1983/4. A generally positive reception,
and the desire to collaborate further and deepen our ideas, led to the first
edition of *Racial Formation in the United States*, which appeared in 1986.
Much to our disappointment, several years passed before our ideas were
seriously taken up by other social scientists, even in our own field of sociology. Somewhat to our surprise, our earliest "fans" were from other dis-

ciplines: notably history, literary studies, and law. Our approach surfaced during the emergence of "cultural studies" in Britain and the United States, and was taken up by scholars exploring the importance of discursive practices in the formation of various social identities. Historians utilized our approach to examine the transformation of racial categories over time and the consolidation of a hegemonic racial order. In the field of law, critical race theorists employed the concept of racial formation to interrogate the fluidity and ambiguity of concepts of race in legal discourse and practice. We, in turn, learned much from the insights of these colleagues and friends, and from the ways they have extended and creatively engaged the core themes of our work.

Over the years, we have been criticized for many things – some justifiably; others not. We have been faulted, for example, for not providing a clear definition of racism. In the second edition of the book, we explicitly tackle this issue. We have been accused of being "racial determinists," and of being insufficiently attentive to the intersectionality of different axes of stratification and difference. Of course, our initial intention was to reformulate racial theory, not to provide a broad and overarching social theory. We were attempting to critique existing paradigms of race – rooted in notions of ethnicity, class, and nation – and to place the concept of race definitively at the center of our analysis. That said, we are quite taken with the emergent literature that attempts to demonstrate the multiple and simultaneous ways that race, gender, and class interact and mutually constitute each other. We believe that a concept of racial formation can aid in this project; it is certainly not framed in opposition to it.

We have also been accused of being "political determinists": the criticism here is that our analysis tends to focus too narrowly on the dynamic relationship between the state and challenging political movements. A frequent charge is that we are inattentive to the economic dimensions of racism. We are prepared to defend this position, this commitment to the "primacy of the political." While there can be no question that such economic matters as inequality and stratification, competition for scarce resources, and the seeming permanence of discrimination continue to shape the experience of people of all colors, we continue to believe that the way these social structures and practices are politically organized, ideologically articulated, and culturally represented crucially determines their efficacy. The economic dimensions of racism are themselves deeply shaped by political processes. The brutal effectiveness of the neoconservative assault against affirmative action and other racial justice measures dramatically illustrates this.

On balance, we believe that the concept of racial formation has proved remarkably durable over the past fifteen years. While race may be a meaningless biological category, it continues to be an enduring social one. In a period in which "colorblindness" is touted as the ultimate antiracist gesture, it remains vital to interrogate the shifting meaning of race, and to assert that race remains a central dimension of both cultural identity and social structure in the United States. Our current work – Omi's on antiracist organizations and practices in the US, and Winant's on the comparative historical sociology of race – seeks to deepen and expand the racial formation perspective further, and to explicate its meaning for the broader movement for racial justice. *A luta continua!*

33

Reflections on "Everyday Racism" (Ph. Essed)

Philomena Essed

Everyday lives and experiences have always fascinated me. I have read many autobiographies – a substantial proportion authored by African-American men and women. Their stories struck a chord, encouraged me to rethink race and culture in terms of the colonial history of my and other families who migrated to the Netherlands. The muffled heritage of Dutch colonialism, the deafening silences of Indonesians, Surinamese, and other migrants who had come to stay, provoked me. I was what Patricia Hill Collins has called an outsider within, an insider without a sense of belonging. In this essay I try to capture in a nutshell the inter-twining of experience, social positioning, and motivation as a scholar.

My engagement with race critical studies has been influenced pro-foundly by my experiences as a student of anthropology, rooted differ-ently in two countries. Born but not raised in the Netherlands, I had lived long enough in Suriname, the country of my parents, not to feel awkward about the European spectacles, the only pair my professors had to offer, in picturing North–South relations. Immigrants from the colonies were simply invisible in Dutch social sciences of the early 1980s. A friend introduced me to one of the few race critical teachers at that time, Teun van Dijk, with whom I registered for a data-collecting workshop on discourse and ethnic minorities.

Equipped with a tape recorder I marched into the field and turned tables. Rather than merging myself into a so-called third world community somewhere far away across the oceans, as traditional anthropology would have it, I wanted to study Holland through the eyes of the colonized, people who had crossed these oceans. How did they feel about the Dutch, about living in the Netherlands, about Dutch opinions of immigrants, about being seen as foreigners? Du Bois's notion of "double consciousness" I came to understand later.

Curiosity, ambition to discover, to understand hidden dimensions of society have nourished many years of engagement with comparative studies of racism in the Netherlands and the US. My focus on day-to-day experiences was something new. Most available (international) studies of racial discrimination were comprehensive about the macro context of housing, education, the labor market, and other structural dimensions, but what these injustices meant for people in their daily lives was still largely concealed. The concept of everyday racism qualifies how ordinary situations become racist situations. The study and analysis of these situations can be disturbing to comfortable worlds of racial privilege.

The article included in this volume is from my book *Understanding Everyday Racism: An Interdisciplinary Theory* (1991). Preceding *Understanding Everyday Racism* I had published, in Dutch, the book *Everyday Racism: Women in Two Cultures* (1984; English translation, 1990). Both *Everyday Racism*, a book that is easy to read and written for a broad audience, and *Understanding Everyday Racism*, a more theoretical and conceptually driven study, are empirically based in in-depth interviews with Surinamese Dutch women and African-American women. Exposure to hundreds of stories about everyday racism has been demanding. While realizing more and more the magnitude of the problem I also recognized in the lives opening up to me the pain and anger of friends and family. Some women recalled events as if from my own memoirs. To safeguard the reflective space I needed for patient and accurate analyses I needed to disconnect my own feelings as much as possible from my writing. I am not sure whether this has been the most effective solution, but a certain degree of detachment has served at least as self-protection. Publishing about racism in the Netherlands was and still is a risky undertaking. Most people stiffen at the sound of the word racism. It is often stubbornly denied, at times giving rise to malicious vindictiveness against individuals who question Dutch common sense for attributing moral superiority above the rest of the world, especially when it comes to race relations.

My work on everyday racism has stirred people nationwide. I have received positive acknowledgment from women of all colors and from ethnic minority groups in general – the latter mostly informal, many tolerating discrimination in silence. A moving response that has been unequaled in encouraging me was a phone call from a woman of Indonesian background. The myth about Indonesians, who mostly migrated to the Netherlands in the early 1950s, is that they have assimilated smoothly into Dutch society. This is what she said to me: "I am 80 years old and I am grateful that I could live to see someone finally speak out. They deny it. But they do discriminate." Simple and precise, her words expressed why I would resist even in the face of the retaliation that would follow. Over the years opinion-makers from the left, mostly men, have engaged repeatedly in attacks of a very personal nature. The largely emotional response to my studies on everyday racism has overshadowed almost completely, in the Netherlands, the normal response to academic publications: critical engagement at a conceptual, analytical, and theoretical level.

Responses abroad, notably from colleagues in other European countries, the US, Canada, Australia, and South Africa, have been different, generally speaking very positive – qualifying my work, among other things, as "a benchmark," "liberatory," "empirically solid." This international embrace took me by surprise – I was new in the field; English, the language of my writing, was not my own; and I came from a small country – Holland – many did not even realize is ethnically diverse.

I have been confronted with fears and sensitivities, either leading to or resulting from misreadings of my work. *Understanding Everyday Racism* makes visible black women's knowledge and understanding of racism, where that knowledge comes from, and how it is used in everyday life in order to identify even hidden and subtle forms of racism. That does not mean, as some have claimed, that you have to be black to recognize racism. Why would we write and teach about racism if not foremost to share and transmit insights everybody, irrespective of color, can apply in order to identify and challenge racism in everyday life? Some whites have felt offended because they did not see themselves exempted as positive examples. There are people who misread from my work that identifying societies as racist is tantamount to saying that every white person is a racist.

In *Understanding Everyday Racism* I am clear about the fact that my concern is processes of exclusion, racist practices, and not individuals as such. Only the most radical advocates of racism fit a description like "racist human being." To call someone "a racist" on the basis of (some) racism manifest in their behavior is to reduce a multidimensional identity to racial strands only. Depending on time, place, location, and interests at stake, people engage in racist as well as in antidiscriminatory discourses and practices. I could have been more explicit than I have, however, in pointing out that antiblack racism is also transmitted through black people, people of color in general, not by whites only.

The work I am currently doing on gender, ethnicity, and leadership flows naturally from my earlier research. After years of research on racism, I have committed myself to identifying how agency in and through leadership can work to create justice and a sense of social responsibility. A keen interest has stayed with me for life experiences, multiple identities, for details of daily life, the ability of critical minds to question what seems normal, the insights people gain from oppositional dispositions, and how they use this knowledge in setting a different example.

34

Reflections on "Cultural Pluralism and the Subversion of the 'Taken-for-Granted' World" (M. Markus)

Maria R. Markus

It is perhaps a truism to say that ideas do not develop in a vacuum. They are always located in a context, with various components: historical, social, economic, academic/disciplinary, and even personal. The weight of these various components differs from one case to another, but they are always present. Yet, it also has to be said that as each particular context can give rise to a variety of not just different but often contradictory ideas, the ideas themselves cannot be reduced to the context. If it were so, there would be no point today in reading Plato, Marx, or Weber.

The most contentious is perhaps the personal, biographical context of theoretical propositions. With growing emphasis on the experiential aspect of knowledge, there is a widespread belief that a crucial question in understanding any proposition is to know "who is speaking." Without denying the importance of the experience and the biographical specificities of knowledge, including theoretical knowledge, I am convinced that what is said is even more important than who says it. The two have not only different validity claims, they also have different validity duration. This conviction not only has an epistemological basis but also a personal one. Over many years of teaching social theory (both classical and modern), I found it very easy to interest students in the author but this often diminished their attention to the text.

I am saying all this mainly because in my particular case personal biography comes much too close to the bone for the accompanying essay not to be read as coming from, and perhaps being limited by, my personal experience. I am sure that my background does influence my interests and my thinking, but it influences them not in such a direct way as it may seem in the case of this particular work. It is not because I am a "hybrid" that I am promoting hybridity. But perhaps because I am a hybrid, I know that it is possible to be one.

Many authors who argue on similar lines are accused of elitism because it is alleged that their own autonomy in constructing their identities is grounded in the privileges of their social position, which they then generalized as a model to follow. In my essay, I do acknowledge the connection between personal and group autonomy, on the one hand, and access to various social resources, on the other. I recognize the fact that the possibility to construct one's own identity autonomously is not distributed equally across social structure. I am also convinced that the strength of various identifications changes with the changing concrete situation. I never identified myself more strongly with my Polish background than in the high and low periods of the Solidarity movement. For I was born in Poland in a very patriotic Catholic family. My early childhood was framed by the German occupation of Poland, my youth by the communist regime. I lived, for less or more prolonged periods of time (lasting from half a year to over twenty years), in five different countries. For five years I was a student in Moscow and I became a sociologist in Hungary. My husband is a Hungarian Jew and my two children were born in two different countries. I still identify myself as a Pole but I am also a conscious hybrid.

I could then hardly deny that my background influenced my scholarly interest. My first publication on a related topic, under the not too original title of *Pride and Prejudice*, goes back to the 1960s. In that I attempted to argue that the notion of "pride" has nothing to do with one's ethnic origin as there is no greater merit in being a Pole than a German, or vice versa. In the same period I also conducted an empirical investigation of racial, religious, and ethnic prejudices in Hungary.

The present essay, however, is not a continuation of these studies in any direct way. It emerged from a rather different series of questions and in a different historical context (not to speak of the geographic one – I am at present an Australian resident and citizen). Generally speaking, the issues I have been preoccupied with for some time now are the new forms of democratic participation and the possibilities and conditions of active involvement of the citizenry in the processes of social change. I have approached this question in a number of ways and from a number of angles: I have written on civil society, the new social movements, and the process of the *politicization* of needs. All this led me in the direction of considering the possibilities of reconciling various group and individual identities in a way that allows for the maintenance of one's cultural specificity without it acting as a divisive factor within the political community of the nation as a whole.

The theoretical distinction between *political* and *cultural* nationalism has a long history, dating back at least to the beginning of the twentieth century. In fact, these two forms never existed as pure types and there has always been a mixture leaning towards one or another. It is only recently, however, in the context, yet again, of an increasing movement of people between countries and consequently an increasing heterogeneity of virtually all societies, that the practical distinction between the two emerged as a conscious project with normative content. It has been a response to the growing discomfort with the theoretical and practical tensions between the liberal ideals of equal treatment for all and the increased pressure of various groups for recognition and acceptance of differences. This has been theorized as the distinction between cultural and political identities with a different logic concerning their place on the axis of universality versus particularity. Nevertheless, a simple separation of the two proved to be not just difficult but perhaps even impossible for a number of reasons, not least because each of· them contributes in different ways to the outcome of the process of social integration.

The content of "multiculturalism," which is the political response to this problem, is not unambiguous and in practice covers a number of different projects and actual social processes, or even policies. It is, however, often mistakenly understood as a new mode of homogenization, which is supposed to include the elements from various components of a given society blending them into a "common culture" for all. This is hardly a possible or even desirable project.

The focus of my analysis is not so much upon the "blurring" of the cultural boundaries but upon the unfolding possibilities for social integration within a culturally diversified society, which recognizes itself as such and which, at the same time, subscribes to at least basic democratic principles. The concept of hybridization of cultures, while widely used today, is ambiguous. I attempt to explore this ambiguity by connecting hybridization with the concept of cultural reflexivity. I thus distinguish between *spontaneous hybridization*, which can be found above all on the level of everyday practices, where it is mainly a spontaneous outcome of the changing conditions of everyday life, on the one hand, and a conscious self-reflective process of cultural creativity, on the other. While spontaneous hybridization could thus be considered as a sort of "natural" effect, resulting simply from living together, it does not necessarily lead either to the blurring of boundaries or even to a greater understanding and recognition of other cultures. Instead, it often leads to closures that are intended to defend a "purity" of the self-understanding of the particular group. *Reflexive hybridization*, however, has the potential of opening both the majority and minority cultures to genuine plurality, a creative interaction that does not attempt to abolish all differences.

So, while the process of hybridization is ongoing independently of its recognition, misrecognition, or lack of recognition by the social actors themselves, its effects differ depending upon the level of reflexivity of the process. The more conscious and reflexive it is, the more likely is its openness to dialogue and thus the more plausible becomes the establishment of a connection between the two forms of collective identities: the cultural and the political, which do not coincide but which are sufficiently open to coexist.

The emphasis of the argument is placed not just on the different possible strategies, followed by various groups and individuals in the process of the construction and reconstruction of their identities. It also addresses the connection between these strategies and the accessibility of various social resources by the groups and/or individuals in question.

If I am pressed to locate my work within a wide range of theoretical orientations, I would have to define it as broadly situated within the tradition of a critical theory of society without the aspirations of sociological intervention, as promoted for example by Alain Touraine. My reservations in this respect are not oriented to his attempt to create an environment for a reflective confrontation of various ideas (to contribute to the constitution of such an environment would be my aspiration too), but to the way he envisages its accomplishment and to the role he assigns sociologists in this process. I feel strong affinity with Stuart

Hall's ideas, especially as related to my understanding of hybridity and his conception of *open* and *closed* forms of ethnicity. But I am also influenced – as will be clear from my discussion – by Jürgen Habermas's propositions. So my approach is theoretically quite eclectic. More importantly, however, I attempt to find out what tendencies are already at work and in what direction they point. It is always up to the social actors themselves to decide, through the democratic processes available to them, which consequences they are prepared to accept and which ones they ultimately intend to reject.

Elites and Politics

35

Reflections on "The Problems with Racism" (M. Barker)

Martin Barker

In the 1960s I became (and have remained) a supporter of the British International Socialists, now Socialist Workers Party. Anyone who has belonged to a political organization will confirm, if they are honest, that there are moments when an issue arises which causes unease. One, for me, was the moment in 1968 when Enoch Powell made three speeches on immigration, predicting "rivers of blood" – and tripped off a light-ning flash of media and popular support for his views. I still recall the dismay caused by this, but also that within days London dockers and others went on strike in support of Powell. The International Socialists issued a leaflet which all members gave out: it was headed "The Urgent Challenge of Fascism." As we argued with people about Powell, that headline felt out of kilter: there was a problem of fascism – but that didn't explain Powell. It wasn't until some ten years later, as I re-read Powell's speeches with students, that I felt able to come to terms with my doubts. *The New Racism* (henceforth TNR) was my response.

I won't rehearse its propositions here, except to say that I identified a tendency, within political discourses and within biological theories, to argue for a "pseudo-biological culturalism" (henceforth P-BC): seeing cultural responses (including hostility to "others") as somehow fixed within our inherited nature. I can't fully rehearse the debates that seem to have followed the book – and I suspect many have gone on, without my even knowing. The book has had a strange career, being adopted by people with whom I would sharply disagree, and being misunderstood by others whom I would have liked to use its ideas. Broadly, I reckon it is fair to conclude that most people accept that I identified an important phenomenon, but the jury is locked in over its exact nature, scale, and significance. Among the main criticisms are some I would now just accept.

It has been said that TNR (1) exaggerates the unity and coherence of New Right thinking. A number of sociological and political analysts have objected that my account exaggerates the importance of "race" to the new Conservative Right, and that there are real tensions between, for instance, their populist authoritarianism on matters such as "race" and their general *laissez-faire* free-marketeering (Nugent and King, 1977; Levitas, 1986; Hayes, 1994). If I am honest, this criticism has a good deal of force.

(2) TNR draws on too narrow a range of sources and thus misses out other contemporary forms such as, for instance, National Front ideology or the patterns of working-class racism. This criticism was voiced by Robert Miles (1987), and more recently by Andrew Brown (1999). The implication in both cases was that, had I cast my net wider, I would have found a much less tidy set of ideas. Brown's case goes further, and is more detailed, that in fact "new racist" ideas are to be found significantly earlier than I suggested. He also demonstrates very effectively that "new" (cultural) racist ideas remained mixed with "old" (superiorist) views more than I acknowledge, particularly in the use of arguments about birthrates.

The essence of Brown's criticism is that I misread the timing, and thus the significance, of the shift. I think this may be right.

(3) TNR is wrong to see "new racism" as a specifically Conservative phenomenon, since there is an equally important "liberal" version. This criticism, put most effectively by Mark Duffield (1984), convincingly shows this, and points to the important political implications. A second version of this criticism has arisen from a number of political analysts who have closely researched how the Conservative Party operated during the 1960–70s, looking at the role and impact of fringe individuals and groups in the emergence of Thatcherism. Essentially, their argument has been that Powell was more marginal than I allow, evidenced by his departure into the political wilderness. The other groups who continued his campaigns were more jockeying for influence than articulating an alternative ideology. Some of this detailed research is

very useful, but at times it veers disturbingly close to a virtual defense of some "essential English conservatism," as when Paul Rich (1986, p. 67) writes:

> The central ideological challenge the Conservative Party thus faces in the next decade, if it remains in government, is its capacity to adapt towards a more pluralist social make up. This means incorporating many essential liberal arguments, based on the rights of groups, as well as individual expression in a common society. . . . Given . . . the degree of opportunism of mainstream Conservative discourse, . . . this should not necessarily prove an impossible task.

Maybe, but it is not a task in which I wish to play the slightest part.

Some apparent welcomes given to TNR worry me. First, Paul Gordon and Francesca Klug (1987) made extensive use of my ideas in their book. They did a valuable job cataloguing the "new right" (from libertarians to authoritarians), recording some of their more vicious interventions, and connecting these to the role of a poodle press – especially the *Daily Mail* – on "race" topics.

But on reflection their use of my thesis is troublesome. They interpret it as a from of disguise. The book calls itself an exposé of the "hidden agenda of the new right on race." "The new right can be summed up as a political tendency which draws on old ideas and presents them in a new context" (Gordon and Klug, 1987, p. 12). This theorizes "new racism" as essentially a covert reintroduction of old racism. It is the same beast, under a different coat of paint. This is a very common way of (mis)understanding my argument. Thus Alex Callinicos (1992, pp. 16–17) writes:

> The idea that humankind is divided into races with different biological constitutions is no longer scientifically respectable. It is, moreover, positively disreputable morally and politically because of the use the Nazis made of it. The Holocaust made biological racism in its 19th century form stink – hence the shift from biology to culture, and from race to ethnicity.

There is some similarity here with the work of Frank Reeves (1983). In the course of studying the rhetorical strategies in race-talk, Reeves dubbed Powellite racial discourse a "discoursive deracialization" which amounts to a "sanitary coding." "Sanitary" racism is essentially tactical, allowing the benefits of siding with "popular feelings" without having to declare overt racism.

There are several problems with this. First, it still has recourse to some notion of a real, primordial racism: sanitary coding is a form of "weak racism," but, in general, "racism" entails more than this: namely, that "a moral evaluation is being made that the differences between the races are of superior to inferior" (Reeves, 1983, p. 241). Second, it sees racism as a thing apart, a special case which may incidentally have connections with other ideological claims, but is driven by its own intrinsic logic. It assumes that "racism" is to be accounted for in its own terms. My argument was different, that "new racism" was a component within a broader ideology, of a new project of nationhood. This is the aspect of Robert Miles's critique with which I am most in sympathy. He has argued powerfully that "race" is a category that can be explained only once we acknowledge its nonreality. In this sense, it can be argued to be like the category "witchcraft" as deployed against women in the Middle Ages (Miles, 1982).

Oddly, one place where TNR found a home was as a footnote to a wider tendency within my own field of cultural studies, exemplified in the work of Stuart Hall and others. In *Policing the Crisis*, Hall et al. developed a neo-Gramscian account of a "crisis in legitimation" sweeping Britain in the 1970s, in which "race" provided the key to the construction of an "authoritarian populism." Elements of my argument were co-opted to this cause, most explicitly by Errol Lawrence (1982), in the course of a sweeping essay on the history of racism. The key issue turns on our understandings of the concept of "common sense." Lawrence, having reviewed various "images" of blacks, youth, family, and Asian women, declares – apparently by fiat – that these images

> do not of course exist in anything like so coherent fashion in "reality." Common sense is unsystematised, inconsistent and contradictory. Although sections of the media do take up these themes, rework them, and re-present them to "the public," this is a selective and "patchy" process and serves more to "revamp" and "update" common sense than to organise it. (Lawrence, 1982, p. 79)

This is a theoretical declaration precluding empirical tests. What, meantime, did the New Right think about the coherence or otherwise of their own thinking? They were furiously debating it. A wholesale struggle to articulate a fully worked-out coherent philosophy was under way (Barker, 1983, 1987). Organs such as the *Salisbury Review*, *Conservative Papers*, and an unprecedented stream of pamphlets, speeches, and books were seeking to develop a completed account – and in course of that were precisely debating what would for Conservatives count as "coherence." But the disagreement between Hall, Lawrence, and myself goes much deeper than this, and takes us into the heartlands of the theory of ideology.

In this context, it is worth pausing on something often noted but rarely discussed: Enoch Powell's style. Tom Nairn, among others, notes his sonorous, almost patrician style of speaking and writing, of which this is a fair specimen:

> It is nowise given to us to perceive, as the hindsight of history will perceive, the truly significant changes and movement of our own time, those changes and movements – of thought, of spirit and of character – which bring about the rise and fall, the salvation and destruction of nations. Yet we must act and speak as though that vision was already vouchsafed to us, conscious that the confirmation or refutation of what we do and say lies beyond our span. (Powell, 1981)

The issue I would raise now is: to whom does this speak? What social group might assemble itself around such a manner of talking? Since I wrote *The New Racism*, an important body of work has emerged offering an array of tools for examining the social and ideological organization of talk. "Discourse analysis" has had much that is interesting to say about race-discourse (Potter and Wetherell, 1987; Essed, 1991).

A number of critics, notably Robert Miles (1987, p. 34), have criticized TNR for not saying much about "old" racism. A first and important correction came from those who protested that the "new" racism was not so very new.

There remained many elements of crude old racism within the "new": metaphors of disease, fears of miscegenation, assertions of inferiority (Brown, 1999). And the appeal to "culture" as grounds for incompatibility is not so new, either. The anthropologist Adam Kuper (1999) has reminded us of this in his study of the word "culture."

I simply grant these points, but give two protests in my defense. First, I was always primarily interested in the way in which advocates of TNR claimed novelty. They were so quick to distinguish themselves from "old-fashioned" racism. Here, for a small example, is a speaker, Eric Bird, in a crucial Conservative Party conference debate on immigration in 1979:

> Mr Chairman, in supporting this motion, I have to declare an interest. I am an Englishman. I am proud of being an Englishman. [Roar of applause] . . . But let me make it quite clear. In being proud of being an Englishman, I am saying that I am proud of our traditions. That does not make me a racialist. [Applause] It does not make me colour-prejudiced. . . . These are not racialist arguments, they are commonsense arguments.

But at back of this was, therefore, a query: if modern-day racists can claim this difference with such ease, was our account of earlier forms of racism adequate? I only skated over this in the book, in two chapters on David Hume and William MacDougall. This is a task still needing our energies. We need to remind ourselves whence the term "racism" came. A modern term, it owes much of its meaning to the post-World War II drive to come to terms with the specifics of Nazism. In the twenty years after 1945, in many respects led by a series of widely distributed pamphlets from UNESCO, "racism" was accounted for as a combination of irrational hatreds justified by a false biological theory that allocated people to distinct and graded "races." Racism became a combination of bad science plus demagoguery. This UNESCO version of "racism" did a job in that period, but it distracted attention from the political and ideological functioning of racism.

One of the ignored features of racist thinking is its excessiveness. That is to say, ideas about "race" can be said to do far more than is necessary if their role was simply to express dislike or hatred, or to provide the rationale for discrimination. Consider some of the things which racial theorists do as part of their racial theorizing:

- they produce theories whose implications then cause problems for their own putative motives for theorizing (for instance, investigators of inherited intelligence – whose theories are quite properly understood as belonging to the racial superiority tradition – have found that white Europeans are not necessarily highest in their own scales, this going to certain "Oriental" groups);

- they result in overall images or proposals whose implications are depressing or defeatist for the very people whom they are apparently designed to represent (for instance, the frequent claims that "inferior" peoples were virtually certain to outbreed the "superior");
- they require people to participate in debates whose implications are not necessarily "helpful" to the very causes they espouse (for instance, the great debate in America in the early nineteenth century between monogenesis and polygenesis was rendered deeply confused by the awkward cross-cut of beliefs between religion and scientific theory. Logically, it should have suited the slave-owners to argue for polygenesis, because that could be used to prove slaves to be "Other" and therefore properly suited to the condition of slavery. Unfortunately, their adherence to a fundamentalist Christian tradition made this very difficult for many slave-owners. In other words, even though there clearly are relationships between racial ideas and conditions of domination, oppression, and exploitation, these cannot be reduced to simply rationalizing expediency. In reviewing the history of racial ideas, therefore, we cannot "pick out" the "bits" which are most appalling to our ears, or which establish continuities that suit us).

In a footnote to an essay on recent thinking about racism, John Solomos (1986, n. 11) notes that a number of writers have commented on

> the relative absence of historical awareness and specificity from much of the Marxist debate on racism. . . . What is surprising, however, is that despite this awareness few attempts have been made to redress the balance and develop historically based analyses of racist ideologies and practices.

This seems to me to be a truth whose importance is hard to overstate – despite the fact that there has in recent years been quite an "industry" of writing histories of racist ideas. I want to illustrate some of the reasons why, with just one example. In his critique of Anderson, Nairn, and TNR, at one point Miles uses the example of Comte de Gobineau to contest Anderson's claim that "race" and "nation" are necessarily separate tendencies. Gobineau is certainly a significant figure in the history of racism. But Hannah Arendt has argued with considerable force that

Gobineau's ideas do not readily comport with classic "racism" if by that is meant a set of ideas which can serve either to warrant relations of economic domination over "inferior peoples" or to support imperial or colonial policies by nations. For Gobineau's whole thesis is built around a notion of inevitable decline – a fact which leads Arendt (1958), rightly in my view, to read Gobineau as the spokesperson for the failing French aristocracy, appalled at the death of their pan-European hegemony.

But once again this argument is not just about the meaning of "racism." The element of my account of the "new racism" which I stand by, without reservation, is the theory of ideology that lay behind it: ideology as project. Ignored in virtually all commentaries on the book, it still seems to me one of its most important elements, and is ultimately the ground for making the connection between "new racism" and sociobiology.

Although I did not have the ideas to hand when I wrote the book, my reading of Antonio Gramsci's ideas connects here. When a social group emerges and bids for political leadership, it does so on the basis of a "vision" of what needs to be done. That vision has to do two jobs: it has to allow the real interests of that group to be carried through, but it has to win to itself sufficient other support to bring them to power. But I would add something, derived perhaps from Lucien Goldmann: to the extent that the vision offered emerges as a coherent, intelligible, extensive world-view which can in theory be applied, to that extent we are witnessing a new and powerful social force. The fact that, even at its height, most adherents to P-BC were hesitant and tender about its implications marked less their personal caution than the uncertain cohesion of the social stance the ideology represents, and the strength in the world.

P-BC has, it seems, declined since the mid-1980s, at least in its overtly political forms. Within those areas of biological theorizing that readily stretch out their arms to politics (evolutionary theory, the genome project, paramedical theories of human behavior), it has continued in various ways: in the persistence of sociobiological accounts of behavior and evolutionary "explanations" of mental processes, and within regularly discredited but still persistent claims of "genes-for" various bits of behavior. But certainly with the departure of both Reagan and Thatcher, explicitly racialized politics have been less popular, and the biologists have been more cautious about associating with them. Maybe in its small way the arguments *The New Racism* put forward helped in the attacks on these politics. Does this mean they are gone? That is, in my view, unknowable. If it does not reemerge, as I hope, I will have been wrong in my estimation of the social sources of this ideological project. If it does, as I fear, I believe we will have to explore it as the new form of "barbarism" that Karl Marx saw as the ultimate alternative to socialism.

References

Arendt, Hannah (1958). *The Origins of Totalitarianism*. London: Allen & Unwin.

Barker, M. (1983). "Sociobiologie en ideologie: het onvoltooide traject" ("Sociobiology and Ideology: The Unfinished Trajectory"). *Tijdschrift voor Filosofie*, 12, pp. 54–68.

——(1987). "Mass Media Studies and the Question of Ideology." *Radical Philosophy*, 46 (Summer), pp. 27–33.

Brown, Andrew (1999). *Political Languages of Race and the Politics of Exclusion*. Aldershot: Ashgate Publishing.

Callinicos, Alex (1992). "Race and Class." *International Socialism*, 35 (Summer), pp. 3–39.

Duffield, Mark (1984). "New Racism, New Realism . . . Two Sides of the Same Coin." *Radical Philosophy*, 37, pp. 29–34.

Essed, Philomena (1991). *Understanding Everyday Racism: An Interdisciplinary Theory*. London: Sage.

Gordon, Paul and Klug, Francesca (1987). *New Right, New Racism*. London: Searchlight Publications.

Hayes, Mark (1994). *The New Right in Britain*. London: Pluto Press.

Kuper Adam (1999). *Culture: The Anthropologist's Account*. Cambridge, MA: Harvard University Press.

Lawrence, Errol (1982). "Just Plain Common Sense: The Roots of Racism." In CCCS (eds.), *The Empire Strikes Back: Race and Racism in Britain* (London: Hutchinson), pp. 47–94.

Levitas, Ruth (ed.) (1986). *The Ideology of the New Right*. Cambridge: Polity Press.

Miles, Robert (1982). *Racism and Migrant Labour*. London: Routledge.

——(1987). "Recent Marxist Theories of Nationalism and the Issue of Racialism." *British Journal of Sociology*, 28 (1), pp. 24–43.

Nugent, Neil and King, Roger (eds.) (1977) *The British Right*. London: Saxon House.

Potter, Jonathan and Wetherell, Margaret (1987). *Discourse and Social Psychology: Beyond Attitudes and Behaviour*. London: Sage.

Powell, Enoch (1981). "The Spectre of a Britain that has Lost its Claim to be a Nation." *Guardian*, November 9.

Reeves, Frank (1983). *British Racial Discourse: A Study of British Political Discourse about Race and Race-related Matters.* Cambridge: Cambridge University Press.

Rich, Paul B. (1986). "Conservative Ideology and Race in Modern British Politics." In Zig Layton-Henry (ed.), *Race, Government and Politics in Britain* (Basingstoke: Macmillan), pp. 45–72.

Solomos, John (1986). "Varieties of Marxist Conceptions of 'Race,' Class and the State: A Critical Analysis." In John Rex and David Mason (eds.), *Theories of Race and Ethnic Relations* (Cambridge: Cambridge University Press), pp. 84–109.

36

Reflections on "Denying Racism: Elite Discourse and Racism" (T. A. van Dijk)

Teun A. van Dijk

For many people the Netherlands is the paragon of tolerance and progressive liberalism. In a way, this reputation is not totally undeserved, especially when it comes to freedoms of personal choice, including those of religion and sexual orientation. However, those who know the Netherlands well, and who do not mind looking below the surface of self-serving rhetoric, understand that the more fundamental relations of group power are stacked against women and minorities. This is especially the case among the elites and their institutions, most notably in the upper divisions of the media, the universities, and the corporate boardrooms, where people other than white males are still rare.

Those who have done research to prove just that are not exactly beloved in the Netherlands. On the contrary, they face the kind of institutional marginalization and problematization dissidents usually encounter when they speak out against those in power, even in democracies. Thus, to conclude that the Netherlands is a racist country, and mean it too, is asking for trouble. Such a claim produces so much cognitive and emotional dissonance, especially among the Dutch elite – who see themselves as basically tolerant and progressive in ethnic affairs – that silencing or excluding the dissident is the only obvious option.

There is a large volume of research in the Netherlands *about* ethnic minorities. A research report of some years ago showed that more than 95 percent of that research is carried out by white Dutch researchers, and even close to all such projects are headed by white Dutch scholars. It is not surprising, therefore, that this research focuses more often on problems associated with minorities than on the many forms of everyday racism such minorities experience, especially not as expressed by white elites. There is some research on prejudice and discrimination, but these forms of inequality under no condition may be called "racism," a term which in the Netherlands is reserved only for the racism of the extreme right, and never applies to the mainstream, that is, to people like "us."

Research on racism is seldom funded by the many government or other institutions that finance research on minorities. Rather, they tend to support research that confirms stereotypes (such as deviance, drug abuse, and in general problems of/with minorities). The media only speak about racism in the Netherlands by putting the term between quotes – because in their zeal for objectivity they can only see such a term as an accusation by biased white scholars or activists or by minorities themselves.

It is this context of systematic denial by the elites that formed the backdrop of my paper. Even now I hesitate to account for the facts as they apply to my own work, but not only can they not be denied, they simply constitute some concrete evidence of the political, academic, and media marginalization of critical, antiracist research in the Netherlands. Whereas my first project in the early 1980s on "prejudice" in discourse was still (hesitantly) funded by the Dutch Research Organization (NWO), the projects that followed on the various discourses of racism never seemed to qualify for funding, despite the growing number of internationally published books that came out of them. On the contrary, the more the research was able to prove its case, and the more the fundamental role of the elites became the focus of research (culminating in my last books on the topic, *Racism and the Press*, 1991, and *Elite Discourse and Racism*, 1993), the more marginalization I had to face. My colleagues simply ignored my work and so did most of their students. After all, research on racism could only be "political" and not "scientific." If students came to my classes on racism and discourse they were only a handful, and mostly from abroad. The then editor of the major, reputedly liberal, morning newspaper, *De Volkskrant*, prohibited his journalists from cooperating with my students in (otherwise unrelated) field research on news, in a letter denouncing my "unscientific" accusations of racism leveled against the press. In meetings of the Dutch union of journalists that occasionally dealt with the issue of minority coverage, I was not welcome as a speaker after a first appearance, even when I was the only scholar in the country doing research on the topic. My interventions in various debates were seldom published, and I had to use pseudonyms to be able to voice opinions that otherwise would not be published. I was used to a solo role (in the Netherlands) in my earlier research, but these forms of marginalization and silencing were more than just ignoring unpopular academic stances – they were part of the very problem of elite racism that I had been investigating.

The culmination of this process of marginalization came with the publication of a notorious little booklet, *De Ondergang van Nederland* (*The Fall of the Netherlands*), written by someone using an Arabic name as a pseudonym. That racist pamphlet sketches a bleak vision of the future, when "foreigners," and especially Muslims, come to power. Asked by a minority organization to analyze the book in view of a juridical injunction against it, I came to the provisional conclusion that its style and contents were so much like those of an earlier column of a famous Dutch writer, Gerrit Komrij. I voiced the opinion that the booklet may have been written (perhaps as a practical joke) by that same Komrij. Further analysis, other circumstantial evidence, and finally an interview with the (nearly illiterate foreign) man who was the purported writer of the booklet – which was written in excellent, sometimes literary Dutch – convinced me that the real author(s) had to be the famous Dutch writer and some of his cronies.

When that "accusation" became known, it was front-page news. From that point on, my scholarly reputation (if any of that was left after my book on racism in the press), both outside and partly even among my colleagues within academia, was systematically destroyed by the media, though fortunately only in the Netherlands. The campaign was propagated by the Famous Writer himself, who in column after column in the country's most prestigious newspaper, *NRC-Handelsblad*, participated in the public attack against me, including urging the university authorities to fire me because of incompetence. To accuse a Famous Writer of racism was obviously sacrilegious, and a breach of all norms of (apparently not so tolerant) elites who precisely on the occasion of the racist pamphlet, namely the fatwah of Ayatollah Khomeini against Salman Rushdie, had massively defended freedom of speech against Muslim fundamentalism. The Famous Writer went so far as to drag me into court for slander, but even on appeal lost his case, on the argument that he was obviously able to defend himself publicly, and that nobody believed me anyway. That the same writer had publicly written, under his own name, a column with the same topic and the same aggressive style against minorities was conveniently forgotten by everyone. Even for many of my antiracist friends, I obviously had gone too far. Despite my international reputation as a discourse analyst and expert on discursive racism, there was virtually no one in the Netherlands who took my claim seriously. I was literally standing alone.

Several years later I wrote a book on the whole case. No publisher wanted to put its name on the cover, however. And even today the book can only be read on my Internet homepage (www.hum.uva.nl/teun). History may show whether my analysis was correct – when the person who was hired to be the front as a writer will finally tell a judge who really wrote that pamphlet. But I am afraid that no public prosecutor in the Netherlands will ever see reason to reopen the case.

As such, this case was not that important, but for me it has been a unique example of the way the Dutch, and especially the symbolic elites (politicians, writers, scholars, journalists, etc.), handle analyses of racism, their racism. As shown in this article, the result is systematic negation, and when necessary the marginalization of those scholars who are seen as traitors of their own group.

Less relevant here is an account of the similarly discouraging scholarly context for this critical research on racism in the Netherlands, which took place within the broader framework of what is now generally called "critical discourse analysis." Whereas there is some discourse analysis in the Netherlands, very little of this has a critical, sociopolitical orientation among the more linguistically oriented scholars. And conversely, virtually no Dutch scholars in the social and political sciences seem to be interested in a fundamental discourse approach to social problems, as is the case in so many other countries. I mention this fact because in some cases sociopolitical marginalization of scholars as a result of their critical work may go hand in hand with lack of interest in the whole direction of research. So, for many years I virtually only engaged in scholarly contacts, lectures, or cooperation abroad, especially in Europe and the Americas. The obvious consequence is that in the critical battles at home on a "controversial" topic such as racism there were simply no allies, not a support group which could take a political and academic stand collectively. Which shows again that because racism is a social system of inequality that involves groups, it can be effectively challenged only by well-organized groups.

The bleak picture sketched above is admittedly a rough sketch – to give a first impression, especially to those outside the Netherlands, that all is not well in the State of Holland. Yet, the picture is not just black and white. Typically for Holland there are many grey tones. There are some (white) politicians, scholars, and journalists who have engaged in critical, antiracist activities, and they have had some impact, the more so when their analysis was less radical. Slowly some tenets of this more moderate message have been able to get across. Today, racism may be acknowledged more often, although it is still mostly searched for among the extreme right, and never within the mainstream. International research on racism as well as European political action have sensitized at least some of those who earlier would vehemently reject such analyses as unfounded allegations. Things have been changing, especially in respect of the more palatable positive policy of generalized ethnic and gender "diversity," for instance, in business and the state bureaucracy.

Thus, where racism may now sometimes be recognized as a problem, explicitly "antiracist" research has migrated from marginality to the obsolete. But maybe, maybe indirectly, it may have made some impact on those whose more moderate messages made it. This is a well-known way social change takes place. Therefore, to feed that moderate message, lots of radically critical research will be necessary on racism in the Netherlands and elsewhere in Europe (in Austria the racist right received almost 30 percent of the vote in elections in the fall of 1999). Having to face some of the problems that may ensue when one studies racism should only remind us of the fact that, each day, every day, minorities are confronted with much more serious forms of marginalization, problematization, and exclusion, especially by the elites in power. Now, that is the real problem.

37

Reflections on "Turning the Tables: Antisemitic Discourse in Post-war Austria" (R. Wodak)

Ruth Wodak

I started the research into antisemitism and racism about fifteen years ago when the Waldheim affair erupted. Being Jewish myself, I was very concerned with the antisemitic discourse involved, and also frightened. The scholarly study of this topic thus had many motives: to shed light on the events; but also, to be able to depersonalize these events and to understand them better on a historical basis. Working together in a team, moreover, made it possible to experience huge solidarity and to fight together. Our work is always more than just scholarly: I have lectured before many and diverse audiences, in schools, in front of teachers, in museums, and for laypersons. I want to help people understand the functions of discriminating discourse, and to be able to discover stereotypes and prejudices in their own life. This kind of political work for me is part of critical discourse analysis. It is not only important to do research, it is also important to apply the results. The research on these topics has helped me cope with many unpleasant features of Austrian political culture.

Thus, the Waldheim affair had its positive sides as well: the confrontation with the Nazi past of Austria became unavoidable; the taboo surrounding World War II, the extermination of Jews and Roma and the crimes of the Wehrmacht were deconstructed. Symposia,

These reflections are based on a short editorial in *Discourse and Society* 1/2000.

debates, research projects, exhibitions, theater productions, films, TV documentaries, etc. addressed these topics, and school materials were produced for antiracist and anti-antisemitic education (see Wodak et al., 1994; Mitten, 1999; Manoschek, 1996; Good and Wodak, 1999 for details). Franz Vranitzky, chancellor of Austria and head of the Social Democratic Party (SPÖ) until 1996, delivered a pathbreaking speech in the Austrian parliament in 1991 in which he explicitly acknowledged the terrible role of many Austrians during the Nazi period. He repeated this acknowledgment in a speech to the Knesseth (Parliament) in Israel in 1992. Thus, the victim role Austrians had endorsed for so long was finally put to rest. During the same time, however, other events shook the country: a series of letter bombs against progressive politicians and journalists frightened groups who helped immigrants (during 1995/1996). Even the Social Democratic mayor of Vienna, Helmut Zilk, was hit by one of these bombs and severely injured. Four Roma men were murdered by a bomb in February 1995, in Oberwart, Burgenland. The group that declared itself responsible was the Bajuwarische Befreiungsarmee (BBA, the Bavarian Freedom Army), a group with explicit neo-Nazi slogans and ideology. The whole government showed up at their funeral, and the president of Austria, Thomas Klestil, spoke out against discrimination and the injury to human rights. Other prominent politicians from the SPÖ, the then chancellor Franz Vranitzky and president of the parliament Heinz Fischer, followed suit. In 1998, Franz Fuchs was imprisoned for these acts, though to date it is not clear if he was the only person in the BBA or whether there was a group whose other members have not been found.

On October 3, 1999 Austria succeeded in gaining huge international attention again: the "Freedom Party" (FPÖ, a party similar to Le Pen's party in France) won 27.2 percent of the national vote, after conducting an election campaign with blatant and explicit racist slogans against foreigners. The SPÖ lost up to 6 percent, while the Conservative Party, ÖVP, was able to hold onto its electorate (26 percent). The only progressive party that succeeded in winning votes was the Green Party, which gained 2 percent (now totaling 7 percent). The Liberal Party, the most radical in opposing the racist propaganda of the FPÖ during the election campaign, was practically wiped out (2–3 percent). In a first analysis of the election, it became clear that mostly workers and small employees had left the Social Democrats and had joined the Freedom Party. The FPÖ could now be called the Workers Party. But the ÖVP has also lost some of its traditional electorate to the FPÖ. By posing Thomas Prinzhorn, a very rich industrialist, as the main candidate, the FPÖ signaled economic competence and was attractive also to more educated social classes.

During the campaign, the Social Democratic Party as well as the People's Party (together forming a coalition government until October 1999) seemed paralyzed. On October 1, thousands of people gathered on St Stephan's Square and applauded FPÖ's leader Jörg Haider as he delivered his last speech before the elections, welcoming "our Viennese citizens," whom he promised to "protect against foreigners and against unemployment." The slogans "*Stop der Überfremdung*" ("Stop overforeignization"; see below) and "*Stop dem Asylmiszbrauch*" ("Stop the misuse of asylum") were accompanied by loud cheers and some whistles from those who dared to make a disturbance. Police were stationed all around the square, the atmosphere was tense, but most of the bystanders had wide smiles on their faces. Moreover, the headline of the *Neue Kronenzeitung* (the newspaper most widely read in relation to population size) was already celebrating Haider's march into the chancellery four days before the election.

Who is Haider, and what kind of party is the FPÖ? Does this rise of populism and racism manifest broader social changes in Europe or is it a uniquely Austrian phenomenon? After World War II, in 1949, liberals with a strong German National orientation and without any classical liberal tradition founded the VDU (*Verein der Unabhängigen*), which became an electoral home of many former Austrian Nazis. The FPÖ, founded in 1956, was the successor party to the VDU; it retained an explicit attachment to a "German cultural community." The FPÖ itself has thus never been a liberal party, though it has had leaders who have tried to steer the party on a liberal course. In 1986, Haider was elected leader of the party and unseated the then liberal leader, Norbert Steger. Since 1986, the FPÖ's party policy and politics have become anti-foreigner, anti-immigration, anti-European Union, and widely populist. In 1992 and 1993, the FPÖ attempted a petition characterized as "Austria First," which called for political discrimination against foreigners. But the petition was voted down in parliament. Nevertheless, many proposals suggested in the petition were implemented by the governing parties in the following years. In the fall of 1997, the FPÖ presented a new party program, which, in its calculated ambivalence, emphasizes Christian values and succeeded in integrating new voters. Presently, the FPÖ is the largest right-wing party in western Europe (Mitten, 1994; Bailer-Galanda and Neugebauer, 1997). It is this party which more than any other Austrian party persuasively sets the xenophobic antiforeigner tone in Austria. The electoral success achieved with populist slogans is even more surprising if one knows that Austria, nowadays, is one of the richest countries in the world, has one of the lowest inflation rates in western Europe and also one of the lowest rates of unemployment. Comparisons with the Weimar Republic or with Austria between the two World Wars – which are often used by the FPÖ propaganda – are thus completely wrong.

What, then, is responsible for the success of Haider and his party (a classical *Führerpartei*)? I would like to attempt some explanations that illustrate that there are Austrian peculiarities on many levels. But there are also more global (economic and ideological) phenomena. Since 1945, Austria, a very small neutral state with a population of 8 million, has had difficulties in establishing its new identity *vis-à-vis* Germany and in trying to come to terms with its Nazi past (Wodak et al., 1999). The effort to establish a strong identity and positive ingroup, however, is often connected with the construction of negative outgroups. After the fall of the Iron Curtain in 1989, Austria lost its function of being a bridge between the East and the West; and new compensatory functions have not been found yet. Joining the European Union (EU) in 1995 did not solve the problem, either; on the contrary, the tensions between national states and supranational entities have noticeably increased (Matouschek, Wodak, and Januschek, 1995).

Viewed from a historical perspective, racist and ethnic prejudices are strongly rooted in the Austrian tradition. Ethnic groups were often used as scapegoats for economic and social problems. Before World War II, Jews were discriminated against, and antisemitism was a "normal" feature of Austrian political culture (Mitten, 1992; Wodak and Reisigl, 2001). Nowadays, racism against foreigners has become "quasi-normal." When the first immigrants from the former eastern bloc entered Austria in 1989/1990, racist slogans were used by all political parties except for the Green Party (Wodak and Reisigl, 2001), but not as explicitly as they were used by the FPÖ in slogans in the most recent election campaign. The main poster of the FPÖ during the election campaign said *"Stop der Überfremdung"* ("Stop overforeignization"), a term coined by the Nazis and used by Gœbbels in 1933. The opposition to the FPÖ discourse was small: parts of the Catholic and Protestant Churches, the Jewish *Kultusgemeinde*, the Green, Liberal, and Communist Parties, and some intellectuals. The two big parties feared losing voters if they voiced counterslogans, and they condemned the racist propaganda only a week before the election. Moreover, the personality of Haider (and his suntanned telegenic appearance) is a significant factor for the popularity of the FPÖ. Haider is certainly a charismatic politician who is very persuasive and rhetorically suggestive in using the media (Reisigl and Wodak, 2001). He constructs his new image as a statesman in a clever way, for example, by participating in summer courses at Harvard University the past three years in a row.

On a broader European level, the fear of the eastward expansion of the EU is politically mobilized by the FPÖ to evoke fears of unemployment and of being colonized by Islamic culture. The globalization rhetoric of EU policy-making, with its main focus on flexibility and competitiveness as means against unemployment, causes many fears (Weiss and Wodak, 2000; Muntigl, Weiss, and Wodak, 2000). People are afraid of losing their traditional securities in the Austrian welfare state, which have been implemented over the past twenty-five years of Socialist and big coalition government. Change seems inevitable, but the coalition parties have not succeeded in proposing adequate measures; moreover, they seemed caught in the Austrian model of social partnership which has made any significant changes very difficult. The FPÖ, on the other hand, is promising to protect jobs and accuses the coalition parties of giving in to international pressure. They proclaim the necessity of a turn (*Wende*; back as it were) in Austrian politics. The trade unions, therefore, participate in the antiforeigner discourse, and traditional Socialist voters like workers join the FPÖ. Note, however, that the percentage of foreigners of all sorts in Austria is a meager 10 percent of the population. Of course, the populist argumentation provides no constructive programs, but responds to the fears and offers only simplistic answers (Eatwell, 1998).

The search for a new identity and the (discursive) construction of scapegoats are not only Austrian issues but European ones. The competition of the European economy with the USA and Japan has resulted in competitiveness rhetoric (neoliberal concepts) that is taking over eco-

nomic debates (Krugman, 1998). It is the phenomenon of globalization
– as one of the main factors – which is at the core of the anxiety in the
face of the future and which reinforces nationalism and chauvinism as
well as xenophobia. Thus, Austria is unique in many ways, but, on the
other hand, it is a case study for European problems.

References

Bailer-Galanda, Brigitte and Neugebauer, Wolfgang (1997). *Haider und die "Frei-heitlichen" in Österreich*. Berlin: Elefanten Press.

Eatwell, Roger (1998). "The Dynamics of Right-wing Electoral Breakthrough." *Patterns of Prejudice*, 32 (3), pp. 3–31.

Good, David and Wodak, Ruth (1999). *From World War to Waldheim*. New York: Berghahn Books.

Krugman, Paul (1998). *Pop Internationalism*. Cambridge, MA: MIT Press.

Manoschek, Walter (1996). *Die Wehrmacht im Rassenkrieg. Der Vernichtungskrieg hinter der Front*. Vienna: Picus.

Matouschek, Bernd, Wodak, Ruth, and Januschek, F. (1995). *Notwendige Mass-nahmen gegen Fremde? Genese und Formen von rassistischen Diskursen der Dif-ferenz*. Vienna: Passagen Verlag.

Mitten, Richard (1992). *The Politics of Antisemitic Prejudice: The Waldheim Phe-nomenon in Austria*. Boulder, CO: Westview.

——(1994). "Jörg Haider, the Anti-immigrant Petition and Immigration Policy in Austria." *Patterns of Prejudice*, 28 (2), pp. 27–47.

——(1999). "Jews and Other Victims: The 'Jewish Question' and Discourses of Victimhood In Post-war Austria." Paper delivered to the *Dynamics of Anti-semitism in the Second Half of the Twentieth Century* Conference, SICSA, Jerusalem, June.

Muntigl, Peter, Weiss, Gilbert, and Wodak, Ruth (2000). *European Union Dis-courses on Un/employment. An Interdisciplinary Approach to Employment Policy-making and Organizational Change*. Amsterdam: Benjamins.

Reisigl, Martin and Wodak, Ruth (2001). "Austria First. A Discourse-Historical Analysis of the Austrian Anti-foreigner Petition in 1992 and 1993." In Martin Reisigl and Ruth Wodak (eds.), *The Semiotics of Racism*. Vienna: Passagen Verlag.

Weiss, Gilbert and Wodak, Ruth (2000). *Debating Europe. Globalisation Rhetorics in European Union Committees*. In Irene Bellier and Tom Wilson (eds.), *European Identity*. New York: Berg.

Wodak, Ruth, De Cillia, Rudolf, Reisigl, Martin, and Liebhart, Karin (1999). *The Discursive Construction of National Identity*. Edinburgh: Edinburgh University Press.

——Menz, Florian, Mitten, Richard, and Stern, Frank (1994). *Die Sprachen der Vergangenheiten: Öffentliches Gedenken in österreichischen und deutschen Medien.* Frankfurt am Main: Suhrkamp.

——and Reisigl, Martin (2000). *Discourse and Discrimination.* London: Routledge.

38

Reflections on "Whiteness and Ethnicity in the History of 'White Ethnics' in the United States" (D. Roediger)

David Roediger

Although written in the early 1990s, "Whiteness and Ethnicity" is very much a product of the 1980s. For better and worse, it was written in response to the problem of the "Reagan Democrat," the working-class, usually male, ex-supporter of the Democratic Party and of the New Deal whose switch into the Republican electoral column helped to ensure that the conservative leadership of Ronald Reagan and George Bush could count on a substantial share of the labor vote in the US. In *The Wages Of Whiteness* and a series of subsequent essays, I explored the role of white identity in structuring both working-class conservatism and the tepid liberalisms incapable of providing alternatives to that conservatism.

Three elements ran through the analysis, none as innovations, but in a particular mixture which was new. White identity was seen – as per W. E. B. Du Bois's observation that the idea of "personal whiteness," possessed by its owners, lacked not only a biological basis but also long historical roots – as a problem the historical production and reproduction of which urgently required explanation. What, in particular, made workers, of all people, often identify as white? Second, I argued that the experiences of becoming white and of being proletarianized unfolded dialectically in the US. The history of the US, the only settler colonialist nation to experience bourgeois revolution and industrial takeoff while millions were enslaved within its borders, imbricated ideas about property, independence, and whiteness in peculiar ways. Third, the struggle to claim white privilege by those who lacked class privilege was seen in my work as bound up with material gains, to be sure, but also with the acceptance of misery, with what James Baldwin described as the loss of soul among those workers identified as white.

Investigation of the experiences of Irish and later of southern and eastern European immigrants to the US forwarded all of these lines of thought. Probing the categorization of those unproblematically thought of as "white ethnics" in the present revealed the utter instability of racial lines. Such immigrants were neither white nor ethnic on arrival but in "in-between" positions that left them open to the frequent charge that they were racially inferior and less-than-white. The dynamic processes through which such immigrants learned, and taught, each other how race was figured and valued argued for a distinctive, if not wholly exceptional, history of racial formation in the US. Moreover, in learning to want to be, and how to be, white, these immigrants lost much in terms of contact with land, pre-industrial values, and cultures of home. Trapped in what Baldwin called the whiteness "factory," they suffered terrible occupational diseases as they were both proletarianized and whitened.

At the time when the article reprinted here appeared, little else written within the field of social history had addressed the question of how immigrants from Europe came to know and to act upon a United Statesian sense of whiteness. Since then, a growing literature, led by Noel Ignatiev's *How The Irish Became White*, Karen Brodkin's *How Jews Became White Folks*, and Matthew Jacobson's *Whiteness Of A Different Color*, has appeared. My own subsequent work (with James Barrett as co-author), published in *Journal of American Ethnic History* as "In-between Peoples: Race, Nationality and the 'New Immigrant' Working Class" (Spring, 1997), won the article prize from the Immigration and Ethnic History Society in 1999. But far more than the "influence" of my early article is at play in the recent emergence of whiteness as an area of concern for scholars of immigration history. Growing appreciation of work by writers of color, who investigated immigration, nationality, and, whiteness from outside of the field of immigration history, is also at play, with the ideas of Americo Paredes, Toni Morrison, William Attaway, and, above all, Baldwin looming especially large. Contributing too to this new attention to the history of white identity and immigration are urgent questions regarding how today's immigrants are being categorized, learning race, and experiencing racism.

By far the most penetrating criticisms of the article have come from scholars who underscore its overemphasis on a US origin for whiteness and for racism. Rudy Vecoli, Catherine Eagan, and others have shown, as has the contemporary record of racism in Europe, that empire-building, anti-Semitism, antigypsy, antitraveler, and anti-Sicilian mobilizations and antiblack racism at home offered European immigrants (including migrants from Ireland) experience in race-thinking and in claiming white identity before migration. Too stark also is the way in which the article set up whiteness and commitment to a specific ethnic identity as simply in opposition to each other, indeed almost as a zero-sum game. While commitment to white identity generally crowded out ethnic consciousness, in some cases, including that of Jewish Americans, a more secure sense that one would not be victimized as less-than-white permitted greater public expression of ethnicity.

The reactions to the article that have been most distressing are those, sometimes registered by white students, that applaud it for all of the wrong reasons, mistakenly seeing it as endorsing the ideas that everyone was once oppressed and that people of color should simply "get over" race, as white immigrants supposedly did. Such a reaction indexes the formidable task we have in trying to show that what Baldwin called the "lie" of whiteness had pernicious consequences for the whole of US society while refusing to lose sight of the ways in which white identity conferred and confers real benefits to those taken under its wing.

39

Reflections on "Affirmative Action and the Politics of Race" (M. Marable)

Johanna Fernandez

In the 1990s, when erstwhile proponents of civil rights legislation were receding before a mounting conservative initiative, long-time activist and Professor of History at Columbia University, Manning Marable, explained why support for affirmative action had eroded by that time.

The ideological assault on affirmative action reached a crescendo pitch during the 1992 and 1996 US presidential and congressional elections. Absent a clear and public defense of the policy by a broad section of the American left, conservative politicians seeking hegemony made affirmative action a wedge issue arguing that the program discriminated against whites. In so doing, the right succeeded in overturning a quarter-century of policies that aimed to limit institutional discrimination against historical minorities and women.

In this essay, Marable engages the American left in a conversation on affirmative action. He attributes the failure of the liberal defense of affirmative action to a lack of consensus on how to achieve racial equality. Marable argues that the allegiance to the concept of colorblind policy hampered their defense of affirmative action within a system that produces racism. Moreover, this race-neutral position often placed liberals inside the camp of racial reactionaries. Marable concludes that the persistence of racism is the reason why the race-conscious policy should be supported. He also proposes that affirmative action should be critiqued, because it aimed merely to increase the representation of historically oppressed minorities and women within American institutions rather than transform the institutions of authority and privilege which produce discrimination.

By documenting statistically and starkly the persistence and impact of racism, Marable's intervention in the public discourse was critical. This documentation proved a strong defense for a concrete, proactive, race-conscious policy. The necessity to assert that racism still existed in the aftermath of the Rodney King assault is testament to the rightward shift in US politics.

In the 1990s, affirmative action was but one of a medley of explicitly racialized policy concerns that emerged as the social problem of the day. A bipartisan consensus was struck and, according to Washington, welfare, crime, and immigration were the other major issues which, if fixed, would ensure America's greatness. However, seen within the context of the recession of 1991, these highly charged policy debates provided a distorted explanation for why millions were experiencing economic uncertainty. Blacks, poor women, and Mexican immigrants were to blame. The controversy raised by these issues also deflected working-class people's attention away from the larger portrait of US politics.

The theoretical and political shortcoming of Marable's essay is clearer today than at the time he was writing. Although he argues that affirmative action was too conservative a policy, that emphasis seems out of place when read within the political context in which he was writing. Marable's insistence that the policy needs to be critiqued "from the left" cedes ground to the right that attacked and destroyed it. The implication here is that a more progressive policy would have been less susceptible to right-wing denunciations. But affirmative action was not dismantled because it did not go far enough. The assault on affirmative action was part and parcel of an attack on the victories of the movements of the 1960s and 1970s specifically and on working-class standards in general.

Following the US's defeat in Vietnam and the ensuing recession of 1973–5, American capitalism fell into a long-term decline and economic crisis. The crisis' material impact on capital was alleviated at the expense of working people, through labor cost reductions, otherwise known as "the employers' offensive" (i.e., layoffs and productivity increases in the workplace, alongside wage reductions or stagnant wages). The federal government also played a key role in mitigating the impact of the crisis. Federally sponsored tax cuts to corporations were subsidized, in large part, through mass reductions in social spending. In the 1990s, the hot button issues of welfare and affirmative action did more than scapegoat minorities and the poor as the sources of America's growing problems. By painting blacks as the main beneficiaries of social programs which had allegedly outlived their social necessity through the use of thinly veiled racism, the groundwork was set, ideologically, for the continued elimination – now on the state level – of social services once regarded as indispensable government-sponsored reforms.

Within this milieu affirmative action must be defended unconditionally. However, the conservatism of the policy which progressives like Marable and Cornel West have critiqued could be better assessed in the context of the struggle within which it was won. Affirmative action, as civil rights legislation, is a product of the grassroots, reform movement that pressured the government to concede it. If the policy does not go far enough it is because it mirrors the aspirations of the middle-class leaders of the civil rights movement who sought to destroy the barriers to their advancement within the system, not to transform it.

The reforms of the civil rights movement may have had a more profound impact on American society had the force historically concerned with transformative change, the American left, not been decimated and ejected from American institutions during the government-led McCarthyite witch-hunts of the 1940s and 1950s. It was not until a revolutionary left, in the form of the Black Panther Party, was reconstituted with the expressed purpose of exerting deeper pressure on US capitalism that reforms such as affirmative action were extended.

Whereas President Nixon manipulated the legislation to consolidate behind him a more conservative and pro-capitalist constituency of blacks, as Marable rightly suggests, even the most conservative government of the 1970s was forced, under mass pressure from blacks and a working class that was much more class conscious than five years prior, to extend social programs like affirmative action and welfare.

Marable exhorts progressives to rely, in the fight for racial equality, more on mobilization than on electoralism, the courts, and the legislative process. In light of the erosion of civil rights over the 1990s, this is an important historical lesson for the next generation of activists.

Dominance and Struggles

40

Reflections on the "Preface" to Dominance Without Hegemony (R. Guha)

Kelli M. Kobor

With the publication of *A Rule of Property for Bengal* in 1963, Ranajit Guha staked a claim to being one of his generation's foremost historians of South Asia. However, it was his role in establishing the Subaltern Studies group during the 1980s that brought his work to the attention of an international and interdisciplinary group of scholars. *Dominance Without Hegemony* represents a distillation of Guha's historiographical thinking, a manifesto of sorts for the Subalternists and their intellectual allies.

The Subaltern School has been in the forefront of a growing movement whose aim is to expose the western biases inherent in the purportedly universalist – that is, rational, objective – discourse of scholarship in the humanities and social sciences. Above all, Subaltern scholars object to the centrality of the nation-state in traditional historiography, claiming that the experience of colonization, and subsequently of independence, has been grossly overestimated as a factor in determining the consciousness of most nonwesterners. They argue that for a small, highly westernized elite, nationalist and anticolonial sentiment was truly normative for a time; yet for the vast majority of Asians, Africans, and Latin Americans (for that matter, of Europeans and North Americans as well), this has never been true. For these "subaltern" classes, matters of local importance almost invariably took precedence over the national or international concerns of the tiny, cosmopolitan elite.

Among the most valuable contributions of the Subalternists to contemporary scholarship is the recovery – through oral histories and indigenous language sources – of alternate motivations behind various "mass" movements of modern history. What earlier historians, viewing events through an elite/nationalist lens, had identified as expressions of popular nationalism, appear on closer inspection to have been more closely related to political or religious conflicts on a local or regional level.

While Subalternists like Guha have thus broadened our understanding of nonwestern subjectivities, critics argue that they have not yet proven their case for the existence of two "distinct but interacting" spheres – the subaltern and the elite – operating within colonial and postcolonial society. Indeed, critiques of the Subaltern School tend to focus on this foundational argument of the group, that the nonelite classes occupied an "autonomous" space in which they constructed their own political and cultural meanings, quite separate from those held by their social superiors.

Nowhere are presuppositions about the existence of an "autonomous" subaltern space more problematic than in a discussion of race and racism in modern South Asia. This may account for the relative silence of Subalternists in relation to this politically sensitive subject. What is the history of race and race-consciousness in South Asia? Although explorations of the subject are at a very early stage, several key points may be made. First, while divisions based on ethnic, religious, and linguistic differences were recognized in South Asia and elsewhere long before contact with the West, these distinctions were transformed and hardened during the nineteenth and twentieth centuries under the influence of western "scientific" racial theories. Second, it appears that such ideas about race, once introduced to South Asia, spread rapidly and unpredictably across the subcontinent, seeping into the consciousness of all classes, regardless of "subaltern" or "elite" status. Let us take, as an example, the idea – prevalent throughout South Asia – that the population of the subcontinent derives primarily from the Aryan and Dravidian races. Aryans are said to be descended from a band of Indo-European-speaking nomads who entered South Asia via the northwest roughly 1,500 to 2,000 years ago. They have been credited or blamed with introducing to South Asian society Vedic Hinduism, notions of caste, and a distinctive (fairer, more "European") physiognomy, at least among the upper-caste Hindu elite. Dravidians, on the other hand, are often identified as the aboriginal inhabitants of South Asia, and are associated with goddess worship, as well as the civilizations and languages of southern India.

This racial paradigm represents a powerful alternative to the Subalternists' essentially class-based model of Indian society. As such it is regarded by Guha and his associates as a holdover of elite historiography, an ideological construct of the colonial and postcolonial state that has little resonance with the subaltern classes. Much remains to be done before this position can be either accepted or refuted, but the work of Guha and his fellow Subalternists will have to be considered by future researchers working in this area.

41

Reflections on "Cartographies of Struggle: Third World Women and the Politics of Feminism" (C. T. Mohanty)

Sue Kim

Arising out of anticolonial and feminist struggles in the 1960s and 1970s, US women's studies, ethnic studies, and postcolonial studies underwent increasing institutionalization in the 1980s and 1990s. This process of "decolonization" of the university occurred concurrently with the increasing spread, naturalization, and even celebration of capitalist globalization. In this context, "Third World" became increasingly delinked from its previous incarnation as an oppositional identification by formerly colonized peoples and political minorities within the metropole, and increasingly utilized as a vehicle for marking underdevelopment within narrow capitalist narratives. Thus, as Chandra Mohanty discusses in a related article, "Under Western Eyes: Feminist Scholarship and Colonialist Discourses," even oppositional scholarship in the West reinscribed and perpetuated systemic neocolonial relations by reproducing the homogeneous, victimized "Third World woman" through ahistorical, *a priori* social indicators defined by disciplinary strictures and political ideologies (e.g., "free white liberal democracy").

Mohanty's essay included here, "Cartographies of Struggle: Third World Women and the Politics of Feminism," asks if and how a non-colonizing international feminist solidarity is possible. Given that "feminism" had come to be identified with First-Worldist/Eurocentric, bourgeois, individualist, and racist "feminists," how could feminist thought be transformed to include both the specificity of women in different cultural contexts and the oppressive structures which inform and inflect those local contexts?

The essay intervenes by articulating the ways in which Third World women inhabit the intersection of various and mutually reinforcing oppressive structures, and by distinguishing this position from a Third World feminist political identity which recognizes and opposes these intersecting systems. Third World women are a heterogeneous group by race, class, nationality, sexuality, history, ideology, and religion, and with ideological differences in their understandings of the social. "Third World feminism" functions as a unifying term, indicating a feminist politics grounded in the particular political commonalities that Third World women share within and against a myriad of simultaneous, interconnected, internal and external oppressive systems, including global capital, neo-imperialism, and the state. The term can provide a "common context" for women as a category of identification for activists, counteracting isolation, dispersal, and fragmentation. The distinction between politics and structural positions includes a critique of identity politics, thereby seeking to provide a more historical and systemic political analysis of the commonalities of Third World women.

Mohanty's intervention has been influential within studies of race and gender because it insists upon attention to the historicity and intersectionality of social and political determinants as well as to agency and subjectivity. The essay insists upon the necessity of attending to the ways in which gender, race, class, and sexuality have been articulated and manipulated by colonialism, the liberal capitalist state, and multinational capitalism; the agency of women as expressed in the intersection of feminist, anticolonial, and labor struggles, as well as in various forms of communal subject formation; and the politics of knowledge production. In its linking together of "Third World" and "feminist," it seeks to recover the full political potential of anticolonial, cultural nationalist, and feminist struggles by integrating their premises.

The full interventional impact of Mohanty's essay may have been muted by its unproblematic reliance on post-structuralist notions of power, political struggle, and subject formation (e.g., Foucault, Anderson) as well as by its strong critique of western feminism. These tendencies have enabled scholars to draw on the essay's critique of bourgeois liberal humanism, locating resistance in the "gaps, fissures, and silences of hegemonic narratives," at the expense of global systemic analyses and critique. Thus, for example, Maria Mies's critique of capitalist-patriarchy as a historical and global system is less often referenced than the "imagined community" or the "multiple consciousness" of Third World women. Furthermore, while one of the central aims of the essay was to reclaim feminism, it has also been appropriated as an argument for cultural relativism and for the epistemological and political authority of Third World feminists. These deformations of the essay's intent arise in part out of its undertheorizing of the relation between the social location and politics of Third World women.

Today, the basic methodological and political arguments of the essay are still relevant. The ways in which knowledge production is situated within larger political and economic structures must be interrogated. Power must be understood as fluid and changing, as evidenced in variously configured local contexts, oppositional struggles, and modes of subject formation, *as well as* systemic and global, e.g., capitalism and neo-imperialism. Attention to the particular contexts of variously located Third World women leads to a fuller understanding of the dynamic capabilities of power and women's agency, and comparative and systemic analyses of these same contexts yield invaluable insight into the larger structures all politically committed scholars must recognize in order to resist.

42

Reflections on "The End of Antiracism" (P. Gilroy)

Vikki Bell

In "The End of Antiracism" Paul Gilroy vents his frustration with debates that were taking place in Britain in the 1980s concerning how best to plan and implement policies that would promote an antiracist society. Focused on education and social work as the principle arenas for change, these debates were expressed most vociferously at the level of local government. It was a period in which "multiculturalism" was a fashionable term, meant to describe both the aim of these antiracist policies – to create and maintain a multicultural Britain – and the means of attaining that end through the promotion of knowledge of and respect for the different cultural traditions existing in Britain. Gilroy's intervention questioned the framing of these debates by interrogating the way "race" and racism were conceptualized within them. He argued that the battles that were being fought around these antiracist policies had become cast in terms, and across lines, that were unhelpful and even conservative.

Gilroy was concerned that the political nature of racism was being diluted into a focus on cultural traditions, so that the history of the creation and divisive use of something called "race" was absent from the debates that were conducted as if all that would be required to be rid of racism was knowledge of other cultures. Such a stance ignored the fact that knowledge does not automatically result in respect, and that the politics of racism need an analysis that does more than see racism as the result of ignorance. Moreover, it ignores the fact that cultures are not hermetically sealed groups which one can observe and learn about, but are fluid and interdependent. Multiculturalism frequently proceeded as if Britain were like a mosaic, with several different independent traditions yet forming a whole. Gilroy's argument was that this model neither reflected the reality of contemporary Britain nor did it challenge certain racist ways of understanding Britain's demographic history.

These are both arguments that Gilroy has felt it necessary to continue making in the decade since the publication of "The End of Antiracism." At the end of the 1980s, the reification of notions of cultural traditions effected the circulation of images that expressed, for example, an idealized representation of "the black family" in Britain as a unit unto itself, the only source of protection for black children in a racist society in which black people were victims. While this was a response to racist perspectives that saw black families as pathological and dysfunctional, it had some disturbing consequences. It meant that within adoption services, "same-race" policies – in the name of antiracism – resulted in an unquestioned policy of maintaining "races," while those families deemed "unsuitable" for adoption placements reflected the make-up of several "naturally constituted" families in Britain. In the 1990s, Gilroy was still making the point that something crucial is misunderstood wherever "cultures" are understood as static traditions that are passed on in unchanged forms. Modern British culture itself has long been constituted through its relationship and intermixture with black people, both within and beyond its shores, and with various – philosophical, musical, cultural – traditions. Indeed, Gilroy's book, *The Black Atlantic* (1993), was premised on the perspective that cultural processes need to be understood as both mobile and creative. More recently, Gilroy has repeated his argument against easy essentialisms, and against all forms of ethnic absolutism, concerned as he is to argue that true solidarities are formed through harder negotiating work than that supposed by those who rely on simplistic models of shared ethnicities.

This perspective is not equivalent to one that regards "the black community" as fictional and all appeals to it as mere rhetoric. Responding to repeated wrongs have made black communities in Britain a public grouping with moral and political integrity. Writing in 1999, Gilroy points out how black communities in Britain have been willing for years to engage with the wider democratic society, refusing to turn inwards, in the pursuit of a more just democracy. Gilroy's concern is that the important political work that needs to be done to address social exclusion and economic marginalization, overrepresentation in prisons, as well as imbalances in educational careers and in criminal justice, must be central to the question of "race" in contemporary Britain: these are political issues over which the term "multiculturalism" has a weak hold.

Illuminating the political nature of racism remains integral to Gilroy's interventions, as he develops his argument made here that antiracism is necessary to any truly democratic commitment. Injustices that run through British society at the level of its most revered institutions cannot be tackled by remaining focused on the level of equal opportunities. That is, racism is not to be sidelined as an issue to be dealt with by tinkering at policies, or promoting a multiculturalism that celebrates difference while keeping it safely within specified traditions or "communities." The political nature of racism is not about the knowledge and protection of cultures but about protecting the democratic structure of society at large. Thus it needs to be tackled at a more profound level, with a more nuanced view of the history of what Gilroy has termed "race-thinking" in Britain.

One of the main problems of writing "The End of Antiracism" was of course that Gilroy ran the risk of his critique being cast back into the lines of the debate itself: how could he take a stand that was both sympathetic to the intent of the antiracist campaigns and be critical of them? Some responded to his position as if a critique of antiracism meant one was siding with the racist nationalists who wished Britain to remain "British." Criticizing one's own "side" was seen to undermine the solidarity of the antiracist movement; the reception of his arguments in the USA was sometimes wary because he was regarded as undermining the necessary "togetherness" of those subjected to racism. This attempt to reflect continually upon the concepts that are becoming taken for granted as "progressive" is one that Gilroy has continued in his work. He has continued to challenge those who fall too readily into the comfort of repeating a particular line, such that they risk becoming moralistic, unthinking reactions; and this means challenging them from wherever they emanate.

The development of antiracism in Britain into the 1990s might alter the focus of such an intervention today. The debate around the relationship of class and "race" would probably be less of a focus, since that debate has taken a different tack. Political leaders of all major parties now embrace cultural difference in "Cool Britannia," while "class-thinking" is downplayed as irrelevant in a New Labour Britain where governmental rhetoric speaks in terms of opportunity for all rather than in terms of socialist utopias. But many of the arguments in "The End of Antiracism" remain relevant, sadly, and particularly the need to be able to respond to new forms of racism, those that may not use terms of "race" but that trade in images and language that are implicitly racialized. This has been an argument that Gilroy has developed in his most recent work (2000) which continues to emphasize the importance of attending to the development of new modes of racism, especially in the changing technologies that affect ways of viewing and understanding the body and the biological. Antiracism requires one to be able to respond to these developments, which is able to see in them the possibilities they hold for reaching beyond "race-thinking" while one must remain vigilant and vocal about racisms' wounding operations.

References

Gilroy, P. (1993). *The Black Atlantic: Modernity and Double Consciousness*. London: Verso.

—— (1999). "Joined-up Politics and Post-colonial Melancholia." ICA Lecture: London.

—— (2000). *Between Camps: Race and Culture Beyond the Color Line*. London: Penguin. (Published in the US under the title *Against Race*. Cambridge: Harvard University Press.)

43

Reflections on "A Bill of Rights for Racially Mixed People" (M. P. P. Root)

Maria P. P. Root

Of all the research and theory I have written on women's mental health, Asian American mental health, and multiracial identity, my "Bill of Rights for Racially Mixed People," which I first penned in 1993, has had the most impact on the greatest number of people. Initially comprised of fourteen statements, I subsequently distilled it into twelve affirmations. These affirmations may be subgrouped into three sections of four statements each that correspond to *Resistance*, *Revolution*, and *Change*. I did not pen these statements with a conscious awareness that they neatly reflected a foundation for social movements or the transcendence of oppression. However, that both of these principles were present in my former work in trauma, addiction, and mental health, particularly in communities of color, made their way into this work. Change through social movements requires an awakening to and resistance of political ideology that restrains people. Fighting oppression particularly around racial ideology requires a transcendence of rules in order to nurture notions of fluidity in one's identity and boundaries imposed between people. It requires acceptance and love of self and others in the midst of acknowledging difference which is more threatening than sameness. Real change requires resisting a tendency to foreclose conversations and interactions before one truly understands the nature of the difference.

Whereas my "Bill of Rights for Racially Mixed People" has had the least exposure to the academic community, the way in which I laid it out has much foundation in theoretical work on social movements, identity, oppression, social constructionism, and spirituality. In contrast, it has been widely read by a lay community of individuals in search of affirmation of their experience in the United States of America. Despite outwardly appearing to conform to acceptable attitudes about race, many people have harbored very different private feelings. The "Bill of Rights for Racially Mixed People" articulates the private thoughts of thousands of people in this country across several generations and reflects the reality of what a multitude of young people within and after what has been coined "Generation X" live (Gaskins, 1999).

Undoubtedly, the passage of civil rights legislation in the third quarter of the twentieth century, for example, the repeal of antimiscegenation law alongside equal education, fair housing, equal employment, and women's rights legislation have all contributed to the racial mixing of the US population (Root, 2001). Greater mobility of youth and greater means for independence for young women (through employment opportunities and birth control), the lessening of both financial ties to and authority of parents also contribute to miscegenation in a way that coterminously has provoked more fear amongst white supremacists (Ferber, 1998; Macdonald, 1978). This latter, extreme response is a reaction to people enacting the eleventh and twelfth rights: "I have the right to have loyalties and identify with more than one group of people"; and "I have the right to freely choose whom I befriend and love" (Root, 1996, p. 7).

With the baby boom generation – identified sometimes as the peace and love generation – began the significant increase in interracial unions as the antimiscegenation laws were repealed in the late 1960s. Reaching late adolescence and early adulthood amidst US involvement in Vietnam, a significant proportion of this cohort questioned much of what had been assumed status quo around race. This was a generation fully exposed to the struggles of transformation and promise offered by the multitude of civil rights legislations. Many children born to this baby boomer generation know that race is a social construction and thus flaunt centuries of rules around race.

This cohort of multiracial young adults, themselves a multiracial or biracial baby boom, are not as isolated as the generation of multiracial people before them. This decrease in isolation allows many young people to resist longstanding formulations of race and to engage in a revolution started by previous generations. Their engagement in resistance and revolution is not naive. The US saw the conflict over ideologies temporarily explode when a young adult of African American and Thai ethnic heritage, Tiger Woods, proudly declared and identified as both African American and Asian American after having won the Master's golf championship. His confident declaration met with major resistance by some of the African American community. While his contemporaries of mixed race often understood that he had enacted all of the rights of *Resistance* and was quite rational, those race-rule enforcers of previous generations still did not understand that he was an embodiment of a contemporary shift in the performance of race and enactment of multiple identities. Previous generations of citizens of all colors have become good colonized subjects trying to pass on the rules and punish those after them who do not embrace the rules. It is often misunderstood that a declaration such as Tiger Woods's affirmation of self and his family was not about shame or "passing" but pride and empowerment. This was the *Revolution* inherent in his seemingly naive stance.

This ability to embrace multiple heritages seems to stem from the fact that many of the contemporary generations of children and young adults feel loved by both parents despite the commonality of divorce. They are affirmed as a legitimate rather than tragic or simply exotic group in advertising campaigns for jeans, sports equipment, and music. They are beneficiaries of a civil rights movement that worked to a degree. Many young people live among many peers who believe races are equally competent and gifted. Lastly, civil rights legislation has afforded some protections and minimized some penalties that accrued to previous generations that were not perceived as white or were construed as mixed. It is easier to embrace multiple heritages at this point in history. At least there are audible public voices on many sides of any conflict of such a declaration.

The "Bill of Rights for Racially Mixed People" summarizes what I heard from people of mixed African, Asian, Indian, European heritages, particularly in the last decade of the twentieth century. It reflects the private thoughts of older generations of multiracial people and the public thoughts of a young generation. It reflects the individualism rampant within American culture, I admit. However, taken as a whole, it is a "Bill" that has the potential to empower one person at a time in a way that may bring about some collective change in the way conversations about race take place in the United States; there are no longer only two sides.

The "Bill" also has the power to heal. Many young people whether conceived of love or lust have been wounded by our country's history of racial rules and hatred (Funderburg, 1994). Affirmation in writing that they, we, and I have a right to exist – and neither justify our existence nor decipher it – makes a difference. Recognition of the complexity of experiences that accompany the multiracial experience in the United States of America in the early twenty-first century allows persons to reduce their isolation and confirm their reality. These affirmations normalize the multiracial experience.

References

Ferber, Abby L. (1998). *White Man Falling: Race, Gender, and White Supremacy.* Lanham, MD: Rowman & Littlefield.

Funderburg, Lise (1994). *Black, White, Other: Biracial Americans Talk about Race and Identity.* New York: William Morrow and Co.

Gaskins, Pearl F. (1999). *What are You? Voices of Mixed-race Young People.* New York: Henry Holt.

Macdonald, Andrew (1978). *The Turner Diaries.* New York: Barricade Books.

Root, Maria P. P. (1996). *The Multiracial Experience: Racial Borders as the New Frontier.* Thousand Oaks, CA: Sage Publications.

——(2001). *Love's Revolution: Interracial Marriage.* Philadelphia, PA: Temple University Press.

Reflections on "Education and Liberation: Black Women's Perspective" (A. Y. Davis)

Angela Y. Davis

When I sat down to write these reflections I realized how reluctant I was to look back at my old work. In 1977, as I was conducting research for *Women, Race and Class*, from which the accompanying essay is taken, I taught an introductory course in women's studies for the first time at San Francisco State University. In my research, I was interrogating historiographical practices with respect to the major nineteenth-century social movements – women's rights and abolitionism. I was particularly concerned with the erasures of black women's agency at the intersection of these two movements. Although I surmised that my efforts to interrupt the then dominant tellings of women's history would be viewed as controversial – especially in a women's studies program that attracted mainly white students and one in which I was the only woman of color on the faculty – I was nonetheless taken by surprise by my students' mid-semester evaluations of my performance. They overwhelmingly criticized me for raising too many questions regarding race and class, and consequently for not maintaining a sufficient focus on gender. Moreover, they felt that the insertion of black women into the history of the women's rights movement that required us to examine critically the practices of white figures they had grown to respect – Elizabeth Cady Stanton and Susan B. Anthony, for example – militated against the kind of exciting, celebratory women's history they expected from this class. As painful as it was then to try to defend an approach to women's studies that refused to normalize whiteness, I realized that my students' deeply emotional responses meant that the work I had undertaken might have more than a trivial impact. This classroom experience also directed my attention to the potential effect of my work beyond activist circles, where fierce debates regarding black women's place in organizational and family structures had initially motivated me.

I was one of the many activists and scholars drawn into the debates occasioned by the 1965 publication of a government report, *The Negro Family*, authored by Daniel Patrick Moynihan and popularly known as the Moynihan Report. This report crystallized patterns in the social sciences, as well as in the dominant popular discourse, of presenting the putatively matriarchal structure of black families as a major explanatory paradigm for the social problems in black communities. What I found most striking about this report was the way its ideological framework called for a certain relationship to the black past. The matriarchal family structure Moynihan and his researchers identified as the underlying explanation for joblessness, illiteracy, and other problems associated with poverty was directly extrapolated from a particular historical interpretation of slavery. It was the way these ideas were interpellated into the masculinist project of the black movement of the 1960s and 1970s that led me to undertake the work of this essay and the book in which it was originally published.

As is evident from the notes, my sources consisted of popular and scholarly writings by historians widely taught in emergent black studies and women's studies programs. I was not interested in uncovering new historical "facts" but rather in alternative readings of existing literature. Would the available literature – largely by male authors – support arguments regarding black women's major contributions to the literacy project, for example, which defined in fundamental ways black resistance to slavery, as well as the effort to build a potentially revolutionary post-slavery society? To what extent did the post-slavery school-building project encourage cross-racial coalition building and transform the lives of both black and white working-class people in the post-Civil War South?

The essay on education was significantly informed by two contemporary developments. First, the successful literacy campaign that largely defined the Cuban revolution led me to give greater weight to the nineteenth-century literacy work by black and white women and to ask, with Du Bois and Douglass, for example, more wide-ranging questions regarding the relationship between education and liberation. Second, in light of the Supreme Court decision in the case of Alan Bakke, which initiated a protracted process of dismantling affirmative action programs in educational institutions, I wanted to accentuate the historical conjunction of struggles for education and freedom. By suggesting a rethinking of our relationship to the past, I hoped to encourage a more critical sense of the present as history.

This essay was published in 1981, the same year as Cherríe Moraga and Gloria Anzaldúa's *This Bridge Called My Back: Writings by Radical Women of Color*. This was also the year when the annual conference of the National Women's Studies Association was the site of turbulent debates regarding the place of race and, by extension, class, in feminist analyses and the role women of color would play in shaping the future of women's studies. More than two decades later these questions may sound obsolete. Certainly, others have developed far more sophisticated analyses of the issues with which we were engaging twenty years ago. Scholars and activists alike tend to invoke categories like "intersectionality" as evidence that we now understand the complicated terrain on which race, class, and gender interact. My sense, however, in thinking back to the motivations for writing such a book, is that we sometimes overestimate the match between our theoretical expertise, our more grounded analyses, and our everyday politics. Looking back at my work of almost twenty years ago, I find that I am surprised by the absence of some of the language we have come to expect but also encouraged by the sense of how available alternative interpretations are when we allow ourselves to think beyond the conventional frames of knowledge production.

Index